Architecting Web Services

WILLIAM L. OELLERMANN, JR.

Apress™

Architecting Web Services
Copyright ©2001 by William L. Oellermann, Jr.

ISBN (pbk): 1-893115-58-5

Printed and bound in the United States of America 12345678910

Editorial Directors: Dan Appleman, Gary Cornell, Karen Watterson, Jason Gilmore
Technical Reviewers: Thomas Lewis, David McKinstry, Roger Guess III
Managing Editor: Grace Wong
Marketing Manager: Stephanie Rodriguez
Developmental Editor and Project Manager: Kari Brooks
Copy Editors: Tom Gillen, Beverly McGuire
Page Composition: Impressions Book and Journal Services, Inc.
Artist: Tony Jonick
Indexer: Rebecca Plunkett
Cover Design: Tom Debolski

Distributed to the book trade in the United States by Springer-Verlag New York, Inc., 175 Fifth Avenue, New York, NY, 10010
and outside the United States by Springer-Verlag GmbH & Co. KG, Tiergartenstr. 17, 69112 Heidelberg, Germany

In the United States, phone 1-800-SPRINGER; orders@springer-ny.com; http://www.springer-ny.com
Outside the United States, contact orders@springer.de; http://www.springer.de; fax +49 6221 345229

For information on translations, please contact Apress directly at 901 Grayson Street, Suite 204, Berkeley, CA, 94710
Phone: 510-549-5938; Fax: 510-549-5939; info@apress.com; http://www.apress.com

This book is dedicated to my wife, Mary, whose love, support, and encouragement were critical in making this book a reality.

Contents at a Glance

Contents

v

Acknowledgments

I WOULD LIKE TO THANK the great efforts of my primary technical editors, Thomas Lewis and David McKinstry. Not only did they help to catch the mistakes, but they also contributed ideas and opinions that helped to make the book what it is.

Thanks also to Jim Allsopp, who helped me to think through and capture my first ideas and concepts on Web services.

Finally, thanks to Kari Brooks and the entire editorial team at Apress for their help and patience in getting this first-time writer through the process.

Introduction

THE INDUSTRY'S NEED FOR Web services first dawned on me in November of 1999. My realization of their potential has been growing ever since.

At the time I was a consultant struggling with the issues around B2B adoption. I was trying to figure out why, despite the obvious value of B2B automation on paper, only a very few organizations were actually using it. Having grown up with the Web professionally, I related it directly to the massive rush that occurred once companies felt the need to build Web sites. Why wasn't the same rush occurring in B2B?

I identified two main barriers to B2B adoption, one political and the other technical. The political barrier is that B2B takes two sides working together, which always bogs things down. This is made even more complicated by the technical information that has to be communicated between organizations.

The technical barrier is that building these programmatic links between organizations is neither standardized nor easy to implement. Whereas Web pages are easy to build, B2B partnerships are not. HTML is one of the easiest technologies for non-technical people to pick up. Countless people have become IT professionals by first dabbling in HTML and then expanding into other technologies. While anyone can view a Web page, a business transaction is a concept that has to be envisioned. That makes it difficult for business professionals to understand and technical professionals to consistently implement meaningful Web services.

Since becoming aware of Web services and their value, I have been very focused on this area. I have had the privilege of speaking with many organizations on this topic, giving several technical presentations and even designing and deploying a few Web services. I have collected quite a bit of information on the topic and wanted to share my experiences and opinions with the industry to help contribute to the understanding and appreciation for Web services. This book is a culmination of those efforts.

Why Architecting Web Services?

Several vendors are planning and releasing tools and services for their approach to Web services. While each has benefits and shortcomings, there is one area that applies to all of these implementations: architecture. I don't believe that people can rush out and build successful Web services without thinking about the architecture for this new development paradigm.

This book addresses these architecture-level issues, or at least the ones I have identified up to this point. This paradigm borrows a lot of its behavior from Web sites and a lot of its behavior from application development. Web services is a blend of these two areas, and people need to have a good understanding of which concepts can and should be applied from each to build meaningful Web services.

Who This Book is Written For

This book was written for software architects, Web designers, and application developers. Whether you have started playing with the tools available for building Web services or are still looking for time to catch up with XML, this book will provide you with a good foundation to start designing and building Web services.

I have included both Java and Visual Basic examples in this book for the sake of reaching architects and developers from various backgrounds. Web services do not discriminate between platforms, tools, or environments, and neither does this book.

The Supporting Web Site

Because of the subject matter, I can take a unique approach in supporting this book with a Web site. Many technical books are accompanied by a Web site that contains downloadable source code. While this book does as well, I have taken this approach one step further.

The supporting Web site for this book also hosts live, functioning Web services that you can consume today with either the sample clients provided or through custom clients you develop yourself. Even if you don't have the time to develop the examples yourself, the site will allow you to step through the applications demonstrated in the book that utilize those same Web services. Both options will allow you to truly test the concepts presented in this book in a realistic, distributed environment. This book's Web site is located at http://www.architectingwebservices.com.

Following the Examples

This book provides both Java and Visual Basic/ASP examples. The Java examples utilize the IBM development platform, including the following:

- WebSphere Application Server 3.5

- IBM HTTP Server

- Visual Age for Java for Windows Professional 3.5

- Windows 2000 Advanced Server

For the Visual Basic examples, I used the Microsoft development platform, including the following:

- IIS 5.0

- Visual Studio 6.0 Enterprise Edition

- SQL Server 2000 Enterprise Edition

- Windows 2000 Advanced Server

- Windows 2000 Certificate Server

If you do not have the necessary software to follow the examples in this book, you can still see the Web services and sample consumers at work on the supporting Web site at `http://www.architectingwebservices.com`. My hope is that you can transfer the ideas and lessons presented here to another development environment with which you might be more familiar.

About the Author

WILLIAM L. OELLERMANN, JR. is a software architect with over nine years of experience in the IT industry in corporate and consulting capacities. He has worked extensively with XML- and Web-based applications in enterprise settings ranging from integration to e-Commerce at Fortune 500 companies such as American Greetings, Citigroup, Ericsson, and Zale Corporation. Having grown up professionally with the Internet and earning a B.S. in Computer Science from the University of Texas at Dallas, William has a balanced background that makes him well-suited to recognize the value of software engineering while embracing the potential of the Web. This background and his passion for problem-solving and delivering solutions to address real issues compelled him to make the Web services paradigm his primary focus.

To provide feedback or ask questions concerning the material in this book, you can write the author at williamo@architectingwebservices.com.

CHAPTER 1

What Are Web Services?

IMAGINE YOU ARE WRAPPING up a business trip in a strange city and running late getting to the airport. You eventually realize that you will not be able to make your flight. The helpful person who told you to take the expressway didn't realize it was under construction. Besides the bumper-to-bumper traffic, the exit you needed to take was detoured, and you weren't able to get over in time to make the turn.

You're thinking you can just continue on, show up at the airport, and take the next available flight. Of course, that may be in an hour or not until the next morning. How great would it be to know that the next flight you can catch is actually in the morning and you can better use your energy getting a room instead of continuing to fight the traffic? A room? It could take several phone calls and conversations before you find a nonsmoking room with a king-size bed and a data line like you need. How about directions to the hotel that bypass the construction traffic? You also need to adjust your calendar to cancel or reschedule your early morning appointments the next day.

And wouldn't you like to know where you could find a drive-through Starbucks on the way to the airport in the morning?

Imagine being able to do all these things with one or two simple requests from inside your vehicle. Web services can make this possible. *Web services* are processes that can be accessed by other systems over the Internet. Of course, this doesn't just happen magically on its own. Solid designs and implementations are necessary for effective Web services. This book is intended to assist you in making this scenario, and many others like it, a reality.

We start in this chapter by introducing the concept of Web services and how they differ from what we have been doing. For this, we need to look back at how we got here and the obstacles we have encountered. Next, we analyze what it means to share information and processes between users and systems, followed by a look at the evolution of the Web services solution. Finally, we look at some scenarios to help us distinguish this solution from others that may seem similar. These topics lay a conceptual foundation for the remaining chapters, which cover everything you need to know to design and build your own Web services right now.

Background

We are in a very exciting time of technical innovation and development. While the Internet is responsible for much of this innovative state, we have just started to tap into the potential of this paradigm of extensive connectivity. Every day there seems to be a new buzzword, and only people who spend every spare moment studying and reading have any hope of distinguishing the overhyped from the underappreciated.

One of the latest hot topics has been *XML*, for *eXtensible Markup Language*. XML is a standard for defining data in a very simple and flexible format. XML's simplicity and flexibility give it value and merit, but focusing on the technology alone does not help any business solve its problems or aid in its objectives. XML is an enabler of solutions, but is not itself a solution. Being an *enabler* means it is a part of the solution, perhaps unique in what it provides, perhaps not. XML is an enabler because, rightly or wrongly, almost everyone agrees that it is good. A few powerful voices have spoken out, and the rest of the software industry has literally been forced to follow, whether or not they have validated the proclamation. The outcome has been massive support for XML and everyone agreeing that it is a good thing where interconnectivity is concerned!

XML is also an enabler because it provides an essential piece of functionality for many applications. It describes data, which is the root of any worthwhile application, and any method for working with that data has merit. XML has additional value in this area because it makes certain aspects of working with data easy. Easy is usually a good thing also!

Into what kind of solutions does XML fit? Several possible answers exist, including Web services. First let us take a look at how we got to where we are. What have been our limitations, and why are we just now talking about Web services?

> The term *Web* refers to the Internet as a conceptual entity that utilizes the standards defined for its usage. This reference is more logical than physical since Web applications can be utilized on internal networks as well as the Internet itself.

While Web applications were initially very quick and simple to develop, they were also almost all presentation with no real substance. As our use of the Internet has matured, technology has advanced the depth and richness of what we can do on the Web. Most efforts have been focused on expanding the capabilities of what we can do on an application level. Applications are designed for end users, who have specific needs and requirements. We have pushed the boundaries of Web application capabilities to the point where we almost expect them to be accessed programmatically. The Web applications and tools we have today were built on technologies and protocols intended for human consumption, not system consumption. These are fundamentally different concepts.

> An *application* is a program designed for an end user. Therefore, a *Web application* is an application designed for use over Web-based protocols.

Content is by far the most flexible component of a Web application. Most Web developers take advantage of this flexible content and utilize it for more than it was intended. This includes trying to turn Web applications into programmatic services. Often when developers believe they are trying to share content, they are actually trying to share processes. Traditional Web developers must change this approach if they are to effectively utilize Web services.

Meanwhile, application developers approach this same challenge on a more traditional level. They have come up with component architectures to promote the reuse of business logic, but the same architectures don't apply in a massively distributed and disparate environment like the Web. Some compelling selling points of Web-based applications are their speed and ease of development, at least in a single, heterogeneous infrastructure. This does not necessarily carry over once you try to interoperate between disparate systems. For the business trip scenario at the beginning of this chapter, building the interface to access the airport and hotel information is relatively simple, assuming all of that information is in one location. Most likely, though, the hotel owns only its own information, the airline its own, and so on. It is the integration of this information, and more specifically, the process exposing it, that is problematic on the Web or anywhere else today.

Clearly, the partnerships necessary today to bring real value to businesses and applications collaborating over the Internet require much greater interoperability. Since the Internet first emerged to the public as a new medium, most advances have focused on making back-end systems and clients more robust. While this allows for much more productive and feature-rich applications, at this point the innovations of yesterday cannot meet today's needs regardless of effort or determination. The next generation of applications being conceived today (like our trip scenario) is simply not practical, if not impossible, without changing the way we think about Web applications.

Sharing Information

Textbook Web applications are typically developed with an *n*-tier architecture. This architecture separates the presentation, business, and data components into distinct tiers, or layers (see Figure 1-1). The presentation layer contains the user interface (UI), built with HyperText Markup Language (HTML), various scripting languages, and/or client-side components. The business layer (also referred to as the business logic or logic layer) consists of server-side components or objects, which contain all the business rules and application-specific algorithms. The data layer contains at least the database and possibly the data access logic.

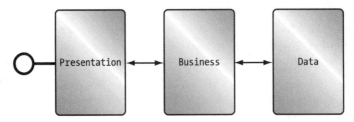

Figure 1-1. N-tier architecture model

The most common layer shared on any Web application is the presentation layer. Whenever one site links to another, both sites share the presentation experience by routing users from one application to another. This was the first example of integration on the Internet and has become commonplace in terms of technology and availability, as evidenced by the millions of Web sites that exist.

Web sites, fundamentally, are about sharing information with people. This information may be generated statically or dynamically, but either way it is information for people. For several years now, we've been developing various methods for displaying this information. These methods have allowed the truly artistic to build very appealing sites and the rest of us to make sites that are truly annoying if not unusable!

Programmatically, presentation-focused efforts have not increased the value of the information being shared in any way. While HTML presents information in a way that is very readable, it takes the human mind to understand the context of what is being displayed. If someone is looking for information on adobe construction, that person can quickly discern by the content of a page whether it is about clay houses or the company that makes the imaging software named PhotoShop. How would a computer make such a distinction?

While this may seem to be an issue of a different sort, it still identifies a fundamental obstacle to sharing on the Internet. One of the most popular instances of sharing is for business-to-business (B2B) partnerships. In this instance you are exposing certain information you have, not to the public, but to a business partner that needs to see it in a consistent format. This could take the form of a custom Web page on your site, but it probably means sharing information with another computer or computers. This is because your partner will not want, and may not even be able, to manually review and discern your information every time it changes.

In a best-case scenario, we could write a program to request information from the Web server and scrape the returned page in a very manual and unsophisticated manner. To assist the reader, the server could possibly expose a simple, unformatted page to help streamline the string parsing that has to occur. This might be a page of duplicate information though, and you can easily slip into building custom solutions to meet your requirements. You also get into a dangerous area of limitations, since even an extra space might throw off a partner's ability to "read" your information.

In our scenario, the first thing we wanted to know was whether we should continue going to the airport or make plans to spend the night in a hotel. Today, most airlines allow you to look up flights on their Web site and check schedule and gate information. To integrate the information from their site into hypothetical application, we could develop a scheduled program designed to call the appropriate Web pages with the required information. This program would be simulating a HyperText Transfer Protocol (HTTP) browser on the airline's site and parsing the required information from the resulting Web page. Because you are using an interface developed for their Web site, there might be several different calls to the site to get the information you want. For example, the airline might have one page that shows the gate and schedule information, but another page that shows availability. Our decision whether to continue going to the airport depends on both, which means that two different routines are necessary.

If you extend this same process out to the hotels, traffic information, and Starbucks, you will have a lot of routines looking up information. Hopefully none of the sites you are researching change their designs, or you will have to make code modifications to your routines. Otherwise, you might get information on an available flight leaving tomorrow at "b>07" instead of "0748." Of course, this is an undependable process on which to build an application, but some applications do use this approach today (but hopefully not to this extreme!). Either way, this scenario illustrates the limitations of using the presentation layer to share information with complex integration applications.

One alternative approach is for companies to directly link their own applications to those of their partners. This approach has limitations in practice, though, such as the unwillingness of most organizations to send users away from their site. If the airline's application sends a user to the hotel site directly for room availability information, the airline is losing all access and reference to that user. Additionally, any sharing of information happens instantly through the linking itself and has very limited capabilities. The airline might tell the hotel automatically what day the user is looking for availability, but after the user leaves, the airline and hotel have no way of communicating about that user. This solution requires much less logic, but companies are at the mercy of their partners and have relatively little to show for it.

Another option is to share the ownership of the presentation layer in an application. Since both partners are bringing one or more application functions, those partners would need to own that function's presentation, because an application's presentation is inherently tied to the application's logic and data in current Web methodologies. Replicating content is far easier than replicating data and logic, so the one with "the back end process" usually wins.

What if a hotel and airline collaborate to build an application for our traffic scenario? If the airline site hosts our application, it has to host some content from the hotel owner that initiates the hotel's process. From that point, the hotel owns the resulting pages of the application until it actively returns users to the airline's site. Figure 1-2 shows how such an application might flow. The airline's application exposes a link called "Find a Hotel" on its site. Clicking this sends the user directly to the hotel's site to access the room availability application. This results in a total handoff of the user to the hotel site, possibly never to return.

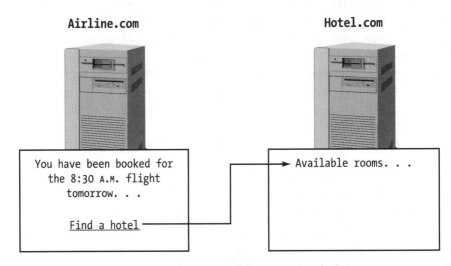

Figure 1-2. Application partnership through presentation links

The physical sharing of the presentation layers by different organizations is very high maintenance, as some content from one partner is located on one server and therefore has one owner. The owner of that system must handle a partner's updates, and thus the partner is at the mercy of the owner and the owner's priorities and timelines. Not many companies like, or even accept, being in that situation.

Yet another approach is to encapsulate a partner's content into your presentation via frames or a client-side script. While this provides more control, you can still potentially lose the viewer. Also, there is no true integration, since the content brought to the collaboration step (the actual linking process) is static HTML ready for viewing. In this instance, the airline may send a frameset definition that references an application from the airline's own site as well as an application from the hotel's site. Figure 1-3 shows a diagram of the integration process in a frameset application. In this implementation, the airline has a link connecting the user to the hotel's site, so the user still physically goes to the hotel's site. The difference is that the airline maintains a presence to the user and has some level of control. However, whatever the hotel does in its frame is unknown to the airline. This could not only affect the functionality of the application, but also the user's view of that functionality.

A *frameset* is a tag in HTML that allows the client to reference separate presentation pages in a single browser window.

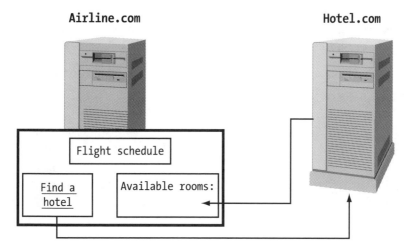

Figure 1-3. Application partnership through a frameset

Here, the exchange of information between the airline and hotel applications is limited, since the browser actually makes independent requests to each. The airline has no knowledge of whether the client even reached the hotel's application. Also, the options for modifying the presentation by one partner are limited to a defined area without directly impacting the other partner's content, and vice versa. Any modifications that do not fit into this defined box impact either its own presentation or the presentation of the applications around it.

All of these approaches should show you why an application's presentation layer leaves limited options for integration. This never improves because it is the top layer and is presented directly to the user. When you integrate presentation layers, you usually push this integration to the browser, and this always has limited success because you have effectively "released" control of the application from the back end systems. Any sharing of this layer by a group of systems can only be superficial since the browser only makes independent requests of one system at a time, receiving a distinct response.

> **CAUTION** *It would be a mistake to believe that there are HTML and script methods that allow for partners to share more than just presentation data. Frames and client-side includes simply package independent requests and responses that do not interact. These methods are simply techniques of "faking it" that may meet certain requirements but are not true enablers for application integration.*

Another approach to making the Internet more interoperable is needed. We need to evolve from the idea of sharing information on the presentation layer and focus on sharing processes earlier in the application's execution.

Sharing Processes

What the presentation layer is to sharing content, the business layer is to sharing processes. This is a fundamental distinction that you must recognize to appreciate what can be accomplished through Web services. When you look at a distributed architecture as a sharing of application processes, the distinction of shared information can become less clear. That is partly because processes can facilitate the sharing of information. The business layer can share information through the presentation layer because it can control the content dynamically. For this reason, shared processes can appear as shared information to an outside observer. This is similar to the distinction of a dynamic Web page and a static Web page to an unknowing viewer. Can they tell the difference between pages where logic is or isn't involved?

Information shared over the Web actually consists of nothing more than references to content provided by other sites. This is all the presentation layer can support, because no logic is available. Without logic, this information can only provide a very limited set of functionality restricted to the existing content. It would likely be independent of who you are, where you are located, what day it is, or any other variable components. Any functionality it could provide would be predetermined and incapable of responding dynamically.

Through the sharing of processes, we can share information that has more meaning because logic that can deliver customized data is involved. Data can be specific to the caller, the environment, or any other criteria. This sharing is accomplished through a request-response mechanism, a concept familiar to most developers. This mechanism allows for variable information to be sent to, and received from, the recipient. This recipient would be a process. This process may be part of an existing application, or it may have been built specifically for the Web service. This distinction typically has no bearing on the use of the process in either situation.

Exposing Processes Through Interfaces

Whereas applications are exposed through a user interface, processes are exposed through a programmatic interface. This interface is designed specifically for other systems, rather than people, to interact with. Processes are essentially defined to the outside world through their interface.

NOTE *The term interface can frequently be used to reference both user interfaces and programmatic interfaces. It is necessary to distinguish its usage unless it is obviously referring to a process (programmatic interface) or an application (user interface).*

The programmatic interface defines how external entities (applications, objects, and so on) can interact with the process. This communication is implemented through payloads sent to the process via a request and returned from the process via a response. When defining the processes' interface, there are three different categories that they can fall into. These categories define what the process is trying to accomplish and can be most easily described through their interface structure.

The first process category is a light request and heavy response (see Figure 1-4). This process is designed to provide a fairly generic response to the caller because the request is very basic, containing no information for the process to consider in providing its response. This can be appropriate when you are providing the same information regardless of who the caller is.

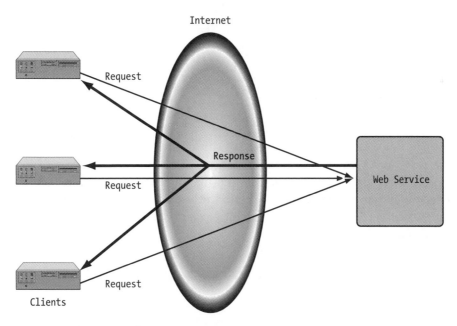

Figure 1-4. Light request/heavy response process

A sharing of processes is usually associated with the submission of data or the retrieval of information based on some data you provide. This information could be who you are, what company you are with, or just some base data that needs to be analyzed. Although this is a process, it can be defined as shared information based on specific information you are sending. This process would be executed through a heavy request and a heavy response (see Figure 1-5).

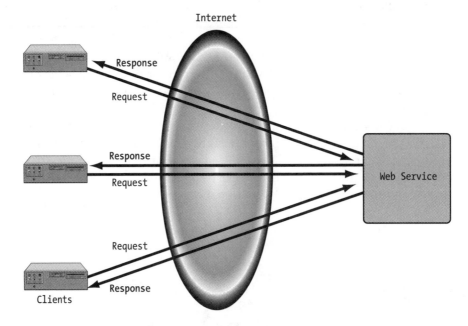

Figure 1-5. Heavy request/heavy response process

The final scenario is a heavy request with a light response (see Figure 1-6). In this case you are only sharing information "upstream." An example would be a process in which you are submitting information to the service owner and getting a simple acknowledgement back that the information was received. Perhaps the service will spend some time with it and get back to you later via email or even another shared process.

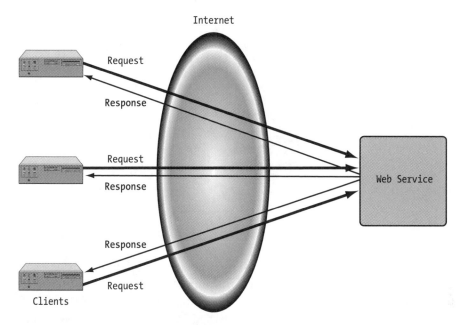

Figure 1-6. Heavy request/light response process

The difference between shared information and shared processes should be fairly clear now. It might be easier to think of the distinction as a methodology instead of a technology. Deploying a shared process means exposing functionality that is much more powerful than simply exposing information. While you can think of shared processes as shared information, and can use one to accomplish the other, you limit the effectiveness of your Web services if you don't understand the distinction.

Sharing Processes Locally

The idea of sharing processes is nothing new to the world of computers—at least sharing processes in a contiguous environment. COM (Component Object Model) and CORBA (Common Object Request Broker Architecture) have been around for a while and allow us to reuse objects in a single system (see Figure 1-7). These methods are proprietary in nature, as they are designed to take advantage of specific features and services in the operating system. Although these technologies are declared standards, unfortunately there is not unanimous support behind them in the industry, and they are also ill prepared to handle the demands of integrating disparate systems.

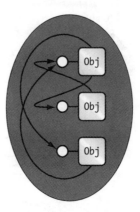

Figure 1-7. Shared objects in a single system

The idea of reusable objects across distributed environments (that is, across distinct systems) is a more recent accomplishment brought about by the next generation of connectivity, such as DCOM (Distributed COM), IIOP (Internet Inter-ORB Protocol), and RMI (Remote Method Invocation). They allow us to escape beyond the confines of the local system (see Figure 1-8), but they require that the external system we communicate with use the specific protocol and object architecture our system has implemented. That limits the reach and extensibility of these methods tremendously. However, this advancement in object reuse is an important building block in the development of Web services.

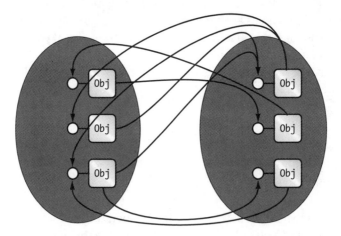

Figure 1-8. Shared objects across systems in a closed environment

We need a way to share these objects over the Internet (see Figure 1-9), and these implementations only work well in a closed environment. That means that as long as you are in a controlled, restricted environment (network), they work great. If you expose processes using these same methods on the Internet, there are some roadblocks.

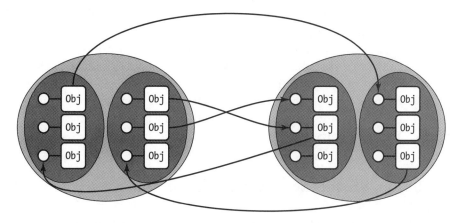

Figure 1-9. Shared objects between distinct environments

Addressing Enterprise Application Integration

This is brings us to a concept that has been a hot topic lately: enterprise application integration (EAI). Sharing applications between distinct systems can involve many challenges, and crossing organizational boundaries amplifies them. Bridges and gateways are often developed to fill the gaps, but these solutions are often cumbersome and configured to work only on a case-by-case basis. These solutions usually involve middleware technologies that are inherently ill prepared to handle this challenge.

First, these distributed technologies have platform and version dependencies. While some might not require a specific platform, you are generally restricted to a set of platforms and/or client software to comply with the service. You also have far less flexibility in updating or enhancing the components of the application independently because of interface or version dependencies.

Second, all of these architectures carry certain security issues that prevent them from working well on the Internet. Although Transmission Control Protocol/Internet Protocol (TCP/IP), the standard communication mechanism for the Internet, can be used as a transport for these architectures, information technology (IT) departments are not likely to open up the necessary ports on their firewall to allow them to cross organizational boundaries. Also, these methods require a tightly administered environment to work well, and this requires extensive cooperation between partners.

Finally, another limitation of these methods is performance. These are all Remote Procedure Call (RPC) mechanisms that depend on some level of session state. In fact, DCOM uses several packet transmissions to maintain a connection. This is very state-full behavior, and the Internet is a stateless infrastructure. The one limitation of the Internet is bandwidth, and streamlining required network communication is one way of limiting this impact.

You can see why, if we want to share applications across the Internet, these existing middleware solutions do not work. They may play a role in the back end of an application, but they clearly cannot play a role in the communication path between the service and its consumers. To meet these challenges, a new implementation, and in reality, a new paradigm, for building Web applications has emerged. This paradigm is called Web services.

Evolution of the Web Service Solution

Depending on whom you ask, you could get any number of answers to the question "What is the definition of a Web service?" This question may someday be as effective as "What platform is best for the enterprise?" in starting a war of words between software developers and system providers. We should all recognize that the success of Web services corresponds directly with the extent of the ability in the industry to agree on what Web services are and how they are implemented. If we all have differences at defining them, it will inevitably be fairly difficult to build and consume them across various implementations.

Although Web services will evolve over time, at some point we will reach the first "final" solution that will build critical mass.

> *Critical mass* is a term used to reference an arbitrary point in time when the use of a solution or product starts to pay off by producing a return on investments and/or is self-propagating.

It may still take a year or more for us the reach this solution, and it is best to take incremental steps of progress, learning and gathering support along the way. The development life cycle for Web services will take four such steps.

This process is shown as a pyramid (see Figure 1-10) for a very important reason. As we take each step and build on it, it will become harder and more painful to go back and make changes. That is why each step should be taken carefully even though we are all excited about getting to the top!

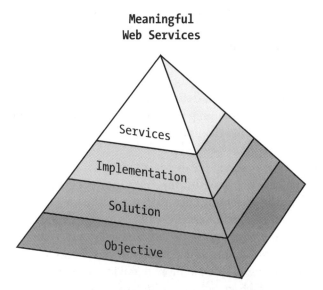

Figure 1-10. Web service development life cycle

Even as every Web service solution steps through this process, the industry is going through this same process on a macro scale. The question is how long the industries will be in step and how far they will get. Every step that the development community can take together through this process will lead to a more meaningful solution of Web services. At some point vendors will start to differentiate their offerings to compete for our attention, but the higher up this pyramid the industry is, the better off the providers, consumers, and users of Web services will be.

Determining the Objective

The first step is to agree on the purpose of Web services and focus industry efforts toward the same objective. Unfortunately, various marketing efforts and press statements have cluttered even this seemingly simple step. If someone wants to achieve something other than this objective, fine, but do everyone a favor and call it something other than Web services! Furthermore, this objective should be broad enough to accommodate changes in the designs and technologies between the first and nth implementations. With these goals in mind, this is what serves as a mission statement, or objective, for Web services that most unbiased experts should agree with:

> *The purpose of a Web service is to programmatically expose a process over a network through an open, standardized communication mechanism and format.*

Parts of this objective should seem obvious when you consider that a service is a programmatically exposed function and we are intending to use these services over the Web. Unfortunately, this statement is so broad that it could apply to a number of things that exist that were not intended or ever thought to be Web services. Many solutions providing programmatic access to objects or components across systems could fit this definition. This purpose attempts to divorce the solution itself from the emerging technologies that have enabled this approach for the sake of longevity and flexibility until the industry agrees on a standard implementation.

Examining this statement in greater detail reveals some core ideas that are important to touch on. First, exposing an application programmatically is very different from exposing a user interface. A UI is not intended for other systems. For instance, a traditional client-server application exposes a screen that allows a user to access the functionality contained in its logic. A Web service has to be accessed by another application, which then provides access to the functionality to an end user. We look at this idea in more detail in the next chapter.

Next, the fact that a Web service is accessed over a network is critical because we are talking about integration. Integration is needed between systems, and the network is our path between those systems. Finally, an open, standardized communication mechanism and format are what will allow wide-scale integration. If everyone implements the same core formats and protocols, organizations should be able to cooperate and integrate regardless of their past and future vendor and technology choices.

Defining the Solution

It is important to realize that Web services are a solution, not a technology. The technology, although critical, is merely the facilitator and not the objective. Recall that our stated objective actually references no technology because it is not part of the requirements. Just like XML is an enabler, all the technologies that we can use to provide Web services are simply enablers facilitating the solution.

The next step in the establishment of Web services as an accepted standard is choosing the technology. The industry agrees on the basic building blocks on which to build Web services. The obvious choices here are TCP/IP and XML. Keep in mind that this step has more flexibility than our previous mission statement. At some point, Web services may utilize Ipv6 (the next version of IP, or Internet Protocol), which would mean a change to one of the building blocks, or at least the addition of a building block. These choices obviously grandfather in other technologies that they are built on (ASCII, physical networks, and so on). At this point, the following definition of a Web service solution is most appropriate:

> A Web service *is any process that can be integrated into external systems through valid XML documents over Internet protocols.*

While still seemingly simplistic, this definition best describes the concept and minimum requirements necessary to solve the problem at hand: how to share processes between distinct systems over the Internet. Still key to this technical solution is its independence from any specific platforms or development tools to maintain the ability to integrate with *any* external system, regardless of its internal dependencies. This aspect is vital to gaining support across vendors for a consistent Web service solution. If this is maintained, Web services should become as accepted and ubiquitous as Web sites are today. The vast growth and proliferation of Web sites early in the Internet's development can be directly attributed to the open standards of HTML and HTTP, and the success of Web services will depend on the existence of nonproprietary implementations.

The core technologies defined here are the ones that the industry has accepted up to now. The inclusion of IP is necessary because it is the network layer for communication via the Internet. XML is the current industry standard for defining data, so XML is used to define the payload of a Web service. These standards may change over time, but today the use of both components is crucial to the value of Web services. Even with the technology advances coming, the definition at this step probably has the most meaning and should allow everyone to have a common understanding of Web services.

A payload is the data transferred between processes during execution.

Optimizing the Implementation

This step is where we are today. We have defined the core technologies that will be used to provide and consume Web services, but we are still working on the specifics around their usage. These specifics include how the XML is utilized, which Internet Protocol is used, and how Web services are discovered. The best practices for Web services also must be defined, but that is difficult without many production implementations to reference. With new standards, such as SOAP (Simple Object Access Protocol) and XML offshoots, becoming defined and established, vendors are trying to build momentum around their implementations through actual usage in real scenarios. We will look at many of these standards in Chapter 9.

Identifying the Services

The final step is defining service offerings around Web services. How do we handle issues like security, authorization, and payment? How do we define the quality of service for Web services, and what is acceptable? Dialog and thoughts around these areas are ongoing, but until we complete the third step, no one can be certain what Web services are actually going to be like. Until then, all we can do is speculate. This topic is discussed further in Chapter 9.

Discerning Web Services

Every technology that has been mentioned for providing Web services is non-proprietary, which means that there is no platform, tool, or language that cannot communicate with Web services (see Figure 1-11). This feature allows the service to be consumed just as today's standard Web pages and applications are. This feature provides the same advantage as providing a Web site today, reaching a broad audience utilizing various infrastructures.

We have also been looking at available technologies. Nothing is required that is only in beta or isn't production ready. It is important to realize that the basic elements of Web services exist today, so nothing is preventing you from deploying and consuming them today. Of course, it will be easier as tools are developed to make the building of Web services easier. Also, as a builder of Web services today, you would likely be considered an early adopter, which carries the usual tradeoffs. It is very much like the situation that existed when the first Web sites came online. You could build Web sites using existing text editors, but it became much easier as HTML editors were developed and became available. Furthermore, you will likely spend time resolving some of the issues discovered as you are breaking ground in this new area.

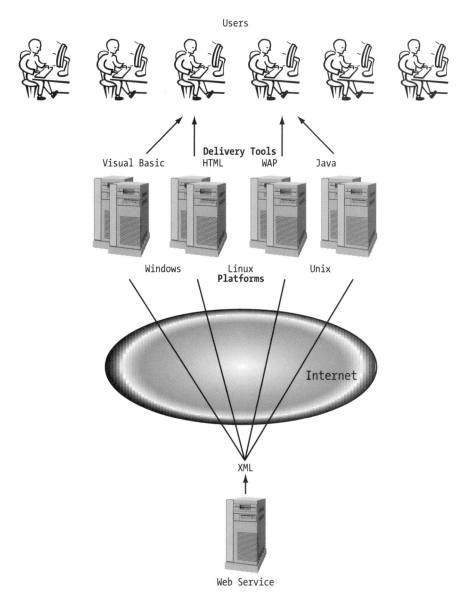

Figure 1-11. Web service integration model

To reinforce the notion that Web services can be built with today's technologies, this book uses only current, production-tested languages and services in its sample applications. This should help convince you that Web services are actually more of an implementation than a technology advance. This is a new way of thinking about how you build your applications.

In reference to the earlier discussion about the presentation layer, a Web service can allow for a single owner of an application's presentation while utilizing a partner's process. You can think of this process as functionality utilized in an application just as you could with any other business object. In relation to Web sites, instead of an HTML link to another document, the Web server links to a Web service and embeds its functionality into the document it delivers to the client (see Figure 1-12). Since this "linking" happens on the business layer, it is transparent to the user and cannot be readily identified through the resulting HTML code.

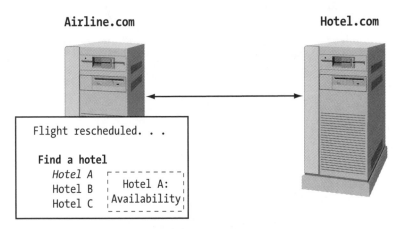

Figure 1-12. Application partnership through Web services

Notice that in Figure 1-12, the "Find a hotel" action is not a link. Instead of linking to the hotel's Web site through the browser, clicking this calls a function in the airline's application to access the hotel's Web service. The results of this function are then displayed through the airline's own presentations.

Depending on the implementation, a Web service can appear very similar to a Web application. So how do we better differentiate between the two? Are they mutually exclusive, or is one a subset of the other? This question can be answered simply: Web applications are designed for browsers; Web services are designed for applications. That means that Web applications are standalone applications, and Web services require a "call" by an application. Because they are always referenced by another application, Web services do not come with an interface for end users.

> **NOTE** *The applications consuming Web services may or may not be Web-based applications. Often this book refers to a Web application as the consumer due to its specific challenges, but it would be short sighted to think that standard desktop applications or device-driven applications could not also utilize Web services.*

While it may seem pretty black and white, this differentiation starts to get a little grayer when you consider that some browsers can support XML natively. Thus, the service could be "called" by a browser directly, and the browser could display the response. However, this wouldn't be a shared process and defeats the whole objective we are trying to accomplish.

To better discern Web services from other applications, it might be helpful to consider a few different application scenarios and determine whether it is a Web service or a Web application. For this exercise, we take a look at a static Web page, an FTP file transfer, and an HTML form submission.

> **NOTE** *Please keep in mind that this is not an attempt to determine whether previous application models are "worthy" of being considered Web services. This is simply an attempt to provide a frame of reference to this new approach by analyzing current models with which you may already be familiar.*

The Static Web Page

A Web page is probably a good scenario to analyze first, since most developers are familiar with Web pages, and they could be considered the ancestors of Web services. First, we need to look at the technology behind Web sites. Pages are requested and sent over HTTP, which runs on the TCP/IP transport layer. However, the document returned is in HTML format, another markup language that is much less stringent and more forgiving than XML. That would disqualify a Web page as a Web service. However, if the HTML in a Web page were built such that the page is a well-formed XML document, it could technically be qualified as a Web service. This would mean that all tags are closed, all tags are nested in order, and no HTML-specific codes (such as the nonbreaking space) are included. With all these restrictions, many Web pages in production would not pass XML validation (as they were likely not required to). Regardless, it wouldn't be true to the meaning of Web services, since XML-valid HTML still describes only the presentation of data and not the data itself. And what would be the value in qualifying Web pages as Web services? Web page delivery is well understood, and Web services should be differentiated from their predecessor. So, in summary, although a Web page could meet the basic requirements, we assume the common Web page exposed today is not a Web service.

FTP File Transfer

In this example, we look at a File Transfer Protocol (FTP) transfer process. Many processes in production today depend on this service, so it's another good scenario for comparing Web services with what we know and use today. Like Web pages, an FTP transfer uses a protocol that utilizes the TCP/IP layer so the communication method meets the criteria of a Web service. The second piece of the qualification is the XML data document. Most FTP processes use either a comma-delimited or a fixed-width format, which would not comply with the requirements. However, if you use XML to define the data being transferred, the application could qualify as a Web service.

Note that this FTP process would obviously not provide the functionality necessary for an interactive application, as FTP only confirms the sending of data and provides no opportunity for a custom response by the server. However, any thought that a Web service must provide a request/response behavior would be inaccurate. Of course, to have any real value, this process would likely only define half the actual service, since there would need to be an application on the server responding to the document deposited. The transfer of XML documents via Simple Mail Transfer Protocol (SMTP) into a mailbox would be very similar.

HTTP Form Submission

Finally, let's look at an HTTP form submission. We will assume, for the sake of discussion, that the response HTML document involved is defined in well-formed XML, also known as XHTML. Obviously, just like in the previous Web page scenario, HTTP and the document involved meet the criteria for a Web service. However, we need to take a closer look at the actual form submission process. To comply with the guidelines, this data should be submitted through an XML document or through a TCP/IP-compliant process. In case you are not familiar with the form submission process, the data from an HTML form can be submitted in two ways: GET and POST. GET actually takes the data in the form and concatenates it to the URL (Uniform Resource Locator) of the receiving process. POST treats the data slightly differently by including it in the request's HTTP header. Both of these methods are HTTP compliant and thus meet the criteria for a Web service.

Without any other logic, the browser would not be able to do anything beyond displaying the returned XML document. We will look later in Chapter 8 at how we might be able to take advantage of this process in an application by using additional components for handling this data and presenting it to the user in some useful manner.

Summary

In this chapter, we've established a basic understanding of what Web services are, what they aren't, and why they are needed. Now let's take a closer look at the architecture of Web services and the applications that can use them.

CHAPTER 2

Web Services Architecture

SINCE WEB SERVICES ARE such a shift in how we approach distributed development, understanding how to model such systems is an important step in understanding how to properly design, develop, and apply Web services. Because these services can be shared across the Internet, the numbers of ways in which they can be modeled make identifying all the possibilities a challenge. For every Web services model one could conceive, extending it one level further through another partnership could lead to yet another model.

The challenge in laying out our architecture is in being able to accommodate all of the scenarios in which they may be used. Our architecture should provide a consistent method for designing Web services independent of the number of participants, the participants' level of involvement, and the technologies and platforms chosen. Let's start by identifying some of the main application scenarios for utilizing Web services.

Web Services Partnership Scenarios

Think of an application utilizing Web services as a chain of links, with each link representing a function in the application (see Figure 2-1). Any links between different partners would represent processes shared via Web services. The connection between those links would then represent the communication between a service and its consumer. That means that a Web service can also be a consumer of another Web service. The first link in any such chain is the only one not eligible to be a Web service. It represents the user interface for the entire application. The partner owning the first link is the "originator" of the application and is responsible for the entire user experience and thus owns the application.

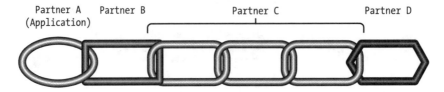

Figure 2-1. The partners in a Web services-based application

Just like a chain depends on each link, the entire application depends on each of its contributing links. This dependency is something that can be shielded from the end user to some extent, but inherently, whatever functionality the link is providing is absent if the link is inoperable. This is no different from any other application that is unable to access functionality from one of its logic or data components.

Figure 2-1 shows four participants in the partnership "chain." Let's say the chain represents the mobile application accessed in our hypothetical traffic scenario from Chapter 1. Partner A is the mobile application owner (perhaps the cellular service provider), partner B is the airline, partner C the hotel, and partner D a third-party vendor providing a calendaring service. In this particular partnership scenario, the application partner knows it is exposing some set of functionality, but does not necessarily know whether it is coming all from one vendor or from multiple vendors.

If each link represents a step (a term that here loosely indicates value), some partners contribute more to the overall application than others. Partners A, B, and D all contribute one link, but partner C contributes three links. Even though they provide more functionality, that doesn't necessarily mean that partner C has the dominant position in the business relationship, since partners A and B are necessary for partner C to be accessed by a user. Partner C may have chosen to focus only on the logic of the functionality and forgo the investment in designing a presentation for end users. However, that means in another application partner C might be directly utilized by the application owner (see Figure 2-2).

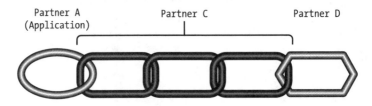

Figure 2-2. The shifting of partners in a Web services-based application

Here you can see that partner C is connected directly to partner A. Perhaps the mobile application wanted to provide just a hotel reservation system, and so the airline's functionality wasn't needed for this application. In another application scenario, partner A might have realized that partner B wasn't providing any value and was only acting as a reseller of partner C's service. Bypassing partner B might not only save costs for the application, but also provide better performance, since a hop is eliminated.

> A *hop* represents a system on the network as the data is transferred between the caller and the caller's destination. A smaller number of hops implies faster throughput given a consistent transfer rate between hops.

When partner C originates the application (see Figure 2-3), partner C must provide functionality over and above what it provided for the other applications. This is because partner C is now responsible for presenting the application to the end user. Previously, partner C was concerned only with providing the functionality for its piece of the process, not delivering the entire application. This scenario is like the hotel company providing the mobile application for the user stuck in traffic. The merits of doing this are obviously up for debate, but the idea is that the option exists.

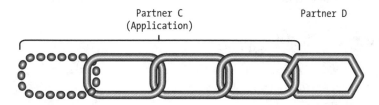

Figure 2-3. Partner C as the application owner

One more high-level scenario that needs mentioning is the owner/broker model. In this kind of partnership, the originator connects to each partner in the process directly and essentially brokers the services into a single application (see Figure 2-4).

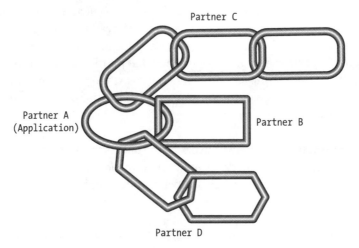

Figure 2-4. Partners in a brokered Web services application

In this scenario, the mobile application provider may be expanding its reservation application to utilize several major hotel chains and their reservation systems. There is less dependency between the partners, since there is no stacking of functionality. This arrangement is appropriate, since each partner is a competitor with the others and would have no incentive to support the others. However, the owner is still just as dependent on each partner for its functionality.

> **NOTE** *This may seem to be the ideal scenario for a Web service, but it may not be possible. You may have some partners that only provide partial service, but are partnering with others to provide a more robust service. In other instances, there may be core functionality that a partner needs, and the partner may be using a Web service partner for that service. A good example of this would be a financial authorization process. A broker may be using a shipping partner, and that shipping partner may use another service to authorize a credit card or account.*

Of course, some hybridization of these models is also possible (see Figure 2-5). Some partners further down the application chain may act as brokers, and some partners may have entire application chains behind their service offering. It doesn't really matter to the partners, since the end result is the same regardless of the model.

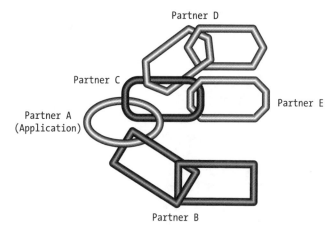

Figure 2-5. Partners in a hybrid Web services application

This idea is very similar to other complex partnerships that exist between businesses today. For example, take a hardware vendor that manufactures computers. While the hardware vendor may assemble the system, the vendor doesn't make every item in it. The vendor has a partner that provides the video card, for instance. If you take this example one level further, the video card manufacturer probably does not make every item on its cards. It may have a partner that provides the memory for its components. You could probably take this example even one level further by identifying the suppliers the memory manufacturer uses to build the memory chips. If you extend this out to every component in a computer, you can see just how many partnerships are involved in the end product.

As you can see, Web service applications can get very complex, depending on how many partners integrate their services. Hopefully, though, you are starting to realize that you could expose Web services to a large pool of users, as well as mix and match services from other providers to build a variety of applications. To aid in this reusability, there are certain rules that have to be followed so that developers on any platform can easily integrate your Web service into their application. Once you have this established, you can then scale this out by integrating additional services just like you would any other type of native object. We will look at specific application scenarios later that will further illustrate this concept.

> *Scale* refers to the ability for an application or process to grow its capacity to meet demand. To scale an application out simply means to increase its load capacity.

Because a Web service is a little different from the applications we are accustomed to, our architecture analysis begins by looking at the communication architecture: that is, the architecture that defines the communication, or transport mechanism, between Web services and their consumers. It is important to understand how consumers communicate with Web services before looking closely at the internal workings, because this communication is what really differentiates Web services from other exposed processes. Once you understand how the externals work, you will have a much better appreciation for the issues that have to be addressed internally.

Then we will look directly at the individual layers of a Web service application, independent of the communication mechanism. This helps to provide a big picture view of the process of using Web services and a breakdown of the *n*-tier view.

Communication Architecture

In the communication architecture, we define the service and consumer interfaces as well as the transport mechanism between these interfaces. In a macro view, you can think of the communication architecture as the protocol that the logical architecture can utilize. It defines the mechanism for two partners to communicate via a Web service—the intersection of two links in our chain analogy, as shown in Figure 2-6. This level is independent of where components reside, how many layers of participants are involved, and all the details of any specific implementation.

> The term *logical* refers to the conceptual view of a system versus the physical view. A logical view of an *n*-tier application would have a distinct separation between the presentation, business, and data layers even if they are physically contained on a single server.

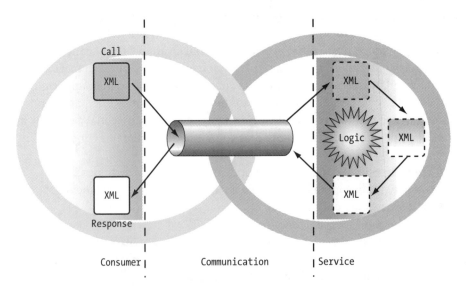

Figure 2-6. The communication architecture for a Web services call

The process is broken into three main components: the consumer, the communication, and the service. The consumer defines the entity utilizing the Web service, the communication defines how the consumer is interacting with the service, and the service defines the provider of the Web service. Each of these components is crucial for Web service execution. Furthermore, each of these three components must be implemented properly to qualify it as a Web service.

Remember that our definition of a Web service is any process that can be integrated into external systems through valid XML documents over Internet Protocols.

While this definition does not mention many specifics beyond the transport, it does demand enough structure to limit our options and focus industry efforts for building Web services. To confirm this, let's look again at our communication architecture, broken up into subcomponents with some of the technologies at our disposal for implementation (see Table 2-1).

Table 2-1. Web Services Communication Technology Options

CONSUMER		TRANSPORT		SERVICE	
REQUESTOR	*PARSER*	*PROTOCOL*	*PAYLOAD*	*LISTENER*	*RESPONDER*
Any logical process or entity that can initiate TCP/IP or UDP requests	DOM	TCP/IP	XML	ASP/JSP/ Java Servlets	Any logical process or entity
	SAX	UDP		Any component that can receive TCP/IP or UDP requests	

While you could certainly justify a different arbitrary breakdown, this one works out nicely with each component containing two subcomponents representing the key functionality of each. Each subcomponent's column lists some options for implementing that functionality. Note that all of the technologies listed are readily available today through multiple tools on multiple platforms. Quite a few areas have unrestricted technology options available for implementation. While a number of tools are available to build this functionality, there will be more "out-of-the-box" choices in the future to help deploy Web services more quickly with more robust services. When we discuss the details of actual implementations, we'll confirm that Web services can be built and consumed with current technologies alone.

Now that we've gotten a high-level view, let's look at each of the components of this architecture in more detail.

The Transport Layer

We'll start by examining the transport mechanism because it is at the heart of making Web services possible. This mechanism facilitates the service interaction by getting the request to the Web service and returning the response to the consumer. Without this step, we would have a service of little value. The importance of standardizing the communication aspects of Web services can't be overstated. In fact, the industry advances in this area are what have produced the environment in which Web services can be conceived and utilized. Without consistent communication methods, every implementation with a new partner might require an entire infrastructure and set of services. This is counterproductive to the goal of interoperability, and specifically, interoperability over the Internet. Fortunately, that requirement of working via the Internet helps establish our baseline requirements, and all of our communication structure falls into place from there.

The transport can be broken up into two components: protocol and payload. The protocol defines how we actually communicate between the Web service and its clients. The payload is the data being transferred, and later we will look at how it is formatted and how we can work with it.

Transport Protocol

This discussion of the protocol for Web services refers to the Open Systems Interconnection (OSI) reference model, an industry-standard model developed by the International Organization for Standardization (ISO) for identifying the layers of a network application. The OSI reference model has seven layers:

- Application

- Presentation

- Session

- Transport

- Network

- Data link

- Physical

Just as they are listed, you can think of these layers as being stacked from the physical layer up to the application layer. Not all layers are required for a functional network application, but if they exist, they can interact with each other. The communication for a Web service application simply specifies two layers in the OSI reference model: network and transport. However, the option selected in the transport layer inherently limits your options in the application layer as well.

The network layer for all Web services is the Internet Protocol (IP), the established standard for all communication over the Internet. By specifying IP, we are limiting our options in the transport layer to TCP (Transmission Control Protocol) and UDP. The only real differences between these two protocols are their reliability and performance. TCP is connection oriented, and UDP is connectionless. This means that TCP tries to ensure delivery at a cost to overall performance, while UDP focuses on the highest possible performance. While it might seem that TCP is the obvious choice for applications, UDP is much more effective for high-bandwidth applications in which the quality doesn't have to be perfect, such as voice. Still, TCP is much more widely used and has many more commercial applications established for working with it and developing on it (hence the common industry reference to TCP/IP when discussing the network of the Internet).

CAUTION   *While UDP does not guarantee delivery, many people expect it to have the same reliability as TCP/IP. Unfortunately this expectation can be deceiving, since applications built on UDP have a noticeable performance improvement. Do not be tempted into developing on UDP without understanding the repercussions and taking the time to build in extra error handling at the application level in case something goes wrong and your application doesn't work!*

Both TCP and UDP are stateless, high-efficiency, routable transport mechanisms that can be very effective when used correctly. Like many things, if you don't depend on them for more than what they are, they will work just fine. However, you can get more enhanced services through the application layer.

Your options in the application layer for Web services are predefined in the sense that they must be fully compliant with TCP/IP or UDP. These are often called the Internet application protocols and include, but are not limited to, HyperText Transfer Protocol (HTTP), secure HTTP (HTTPS), File Transfer Protocol (FTP), and Simple Mail Transfer Protocol (SMTP). All these applications represent port numbers over the IP layer. Port numbers then translate to a socket on the system that allows a client and server to establish a connection. Table 2-2 shows some of these port numbers.

Table 2-2. Some TCP/IP Application Ports

APPLICATION	PORT
FTP	21
SMTP	25
HTTP	80
HTTPS (Secure Sockets Layer, SSL)	443

The applications listed are for TCP/IP, because UDP applications are typically not named and instead are just represented by their port number. For example, we would call an FTP application "a Port 21 application." This would probably change if UDP became as widely used commercially as TCP/IP. Your choice of the transport and application layers comes down to your application requirements. There are options that allow you to perform a multitude of services: simulate remote procedure calls; have a high-performance media service; or send secure, encrypted data to a server. We will take a hands-on look at some of these choices later.

> **NOTE** *Another alternative protocol for the Internet is Internet Control Message Protocol (ICMP), which is not discussed here because its use is reserved for TCP/IP to communicate connection errors to the system.*

Transport Payload

The data transferred during the communication of two systems is referred to as the *payload*. This is how we can send data to a Web service and receive responses. Again, the establishment of standards in this area was critical to enabling a consistent method for defining the data both syntactically and semantically. This means that we not only have a standard format to intelligently parse the data, but we know how to identify specific pieces to interpret or transform it. This allows us to work meaningfully with the data. Let's take a closer look at the enablers of our data component: format and definition.

Format—Speaking the Same Language

The importance of speaking the same language (that is, agreeing to a syntax) is critical to any kind of communication, including Web services. The easier it is to use the language, the quicker and more extensive adoption will be. The lack of a consistent language means that partners would spend more time translating.

If an English-speaking tourist travels to China, how long does it take that tourist to use a translation book to order a glass of water from a non-English-speaking waiter? The tourist has to look up the correct words and then try and pronounce the words correctly and use them in the correct context. While this may seem extreme for a computer application, it still shows how potentially costly and ineffective translating can be. It doesn't matter how fast you are at translating; it is far less productive than speaking the same language.

XML has provided the means for two or more systems to speak the same language. This flexible language describes data syntactically in an industry-accepted standard. While simple in concept, its importance and significance to Web services, and application integration in general, cannot be overstated. We will use XML in our Web services to format our payloads between the consumer and the service. By using a standard like XML, Web services can and will be able to take advantage of tools built for working with XML. Nearly every language, development environment, and service takes, or will take, advantage of XML in some way, and that translates very well to working with Web services.

Definition—Communicating the Same Meaning

Although we have a means for describing our payload, we also need a way of defining it. The semantics of our data will enable everyone "speaking our language" to understand our vocabulary. This means that others will not only be able to read our data, but also have the ability to know what the data is and work with it.

This issue is even evident in the same language. People in both the United States and England speak the same language, but does that mean they share the same understandings? In England, there is a mechanism for taking people vertically up a building's floors called a "lift." In the United States, *lift* is usually used as a verb and means to pick something up. Now, when someone from the United States hears *lift* for the very first time, does that person have any hope of understanding what the speaker means if the speaker is from England? Because they share enough commonality due to the fact they speak the same language, the person from England can either explain the concept in more common words, as I did earlier, or say the word *elevator*. The case is similar in data transfers when everyone talks the same language. It is always possible to "map" a new term to a previously understood term or terms. While our mind remembers to treat the words or phrases as synonyms in the future, an application has to make a record of the relationship in some data store for future reference.

> **NOTE** *It may seem like this idea of mapping words or phrases is the same as translating languages, but they are different processes. You cannot map two words or phrases if they are not synonymous in the language. Before and after the mapping, the context is the same, the usage is consistent, and the meaning doesn't change.*

A standard in this area also enables us to have a more efficient means for communicating the details of our Web services to partners and consumers. Fortunately, we again have some mechanisms in place to make this easy: the Document Type Definitions (DTDs) and XML Schema Definitions (XSDs). A service owner would provide one or the other to communicate the definition of any payload involved in calls and responses. We will talk about these two standards in much greater detail in Chapter 3.

The Web Service

The service contains all the components that make up the actual Web service interface. These components reside on the service owner's infrastructure and can be implemented in a variety of ways. The decisions of platform, technology, tools, and services supporting the service are at the owner's discretion. Furthermore, these decisions can be changed without impacting any existing consumers because the change takes advantage of the Internet's stateless nature. What does it mean to be stateless?

State is the act of remembering what is going on between the interactions of systems, or "calls." That may sound oversimplified, but that is pretty much it. Whenever you have an application or process that manages state, it monitors its users to know if they are logged on, if they are in the middle of doing something, what they might have done yesterday, and so on. The Internet is inherently a stateless environment. That means that every time you make a request to a Web site, the application inherently has no idea if you have ever been there before. Of course there are Web applications on which you can create accounts and that remember what you are doing, because information is being maintained by those sites on the application layer.

> **CAUTION** *Many HTTP servers come with standard and custom services for maintaining state, but there is usually a performance and/or scalability tradeoff. No method is foolproof, so be aware of the implications and risks for each and only use them when necessary.*

Any Web application maintaining any state is using some method to identify users (cookies, HTTP data, and so on) and then storing information about their activities (usually in a database) as their state. This state can then be referenced by the application during later requests by that user. This is how Web-based applications circumvent the stateless environment through which they are communicating. The browser certainly helps in the effort by managing cookies and keeping information in its cache. Any application that does this, though, has to gracefully handle any truncated processes, because the user at any moment can get disconnected or abandon a session, and the application will never be notified.

A *session* is an instance of a single user working with an application in a defined time period.

> **NOTE** *This is why all sessions on Web servers have a timeout property. Without it, the application would always be assuming the user is still connected and would continue maintaining old information.*

Two vital components are required for an application to function as a Web service: a listener and a responder. While these two components can be physically one entity, or distributed among numerous entities (see Figure 2-7), the functionality they provide is what is important for this discussion.

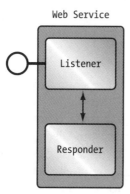

Figure 2-7. A functional view of a Web service

Listener: Waiting for the Call

The listener of a Web service is responsible for handling a Web services call from a consumer. The availability of this listener determines the availability of a Web service because it is essentially the interface. The process of handling a Web services call involves two steps.

The first step is capturing the incoming call. This capturing can manifest itself in many ways with a wide range of complexity. Possibilities for implementation range from having a script document hosted on a Web site to exposing an FTP directory.

The second step is the delivery of the payload package to the actual service logic. Although the listener could contain the actual logic of the Web service, this is not necessarily the best design. Separating the logic and the listener allows all listeners to be aggregated into one location or function, thus reducing the deployment time for each additional Web service. It also provides an extra layer on top of your logic, making it a more secure design.

You can think of this relationship between the listener and the service logic as being much the same as how a post office relates to the mailboxes on the street. The listener serves as the distribution center for the neighborhood (in our case, the service provider), and a process delivers the call to the actual address (in our case, the service).

Again, this functionality can be implemented through a wide range of technologies, but the key is that it is a persistent implementation. If you provide a Web service for your partners and customers, the expectation is that your service is as reliable as your Web site, if not more so. Thus, it is important that your actual implementation is persistent and efficient, and that all starts with your listener. We will look at some approaches for making your implementation persistent and efficient in actual code in Chapters 6 and 7.

Responder: Answering the Call

The responder of a Web service is responsible for providing a response to be returned to the calling consumer. It only provides a response because the listener owns the connection to the client. The response cannot be returned through another process because of the nature of the communication process. The consumer makes the request of the service and either waits for a response or expects no response from that service. Although only a UDP-based Web service could be truly asynchronous, you could simulate an asynchronous call via TCP/IP by providing a simple acknowledgement of the client call and releasing the connection. (This is essentially what happens inherently with SMTP.) You could then later send a response to the request at your convenience, not tying up your listener or the client (see Figure 2-8 for an example). This essentially turns a consumer into a service provider, since it requires a persistent listener on the consumer's side. This is a viable design, but these two steps should be considered two distinct Web services, since they are both acting as a client and a server.

> *Synchronous* refers to the inline execution of a process or set of processes. No other processing can occur in an application during a synchronous call. *Asynchronous* refers to the execution of a process that does not restrict the application from other activity.

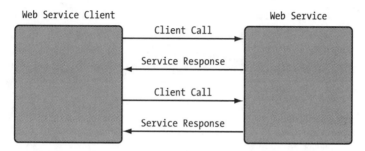

Figure 2-8. Asynchronous or delayed response Web service

This dual Web services solution places much higher demands on your consumer. The challenge of this approach is that you are turning a client-server relationship into a server-client relationship, which means that you are establishing a client-server connection to the client that originally called you. Typically, the client that called you would actually be a server, so it should be capable of supporting the relationship. But does it have an active listener waiting for this response, which is essentially a request? Does the consumer have the logic to handle and process this delayed response? You need to consider these challenges to determine if this is a practical implementation for your Web service.

> **NOTE** *There is a misnomer about synchronous versus asynchronous calls that I will clarify for our discussion. There are very few asynchronous calls over the network. Client applications usually receive at least some notification that a packet has been delivered somewhere. What are thought to be asynchronous calls are actually asynchronous processes. This is accomplished by tying two synchronous calls together. The first one acts as a channel for the send process, the second as a channel for the significant response process. Again, we can relate this to mail delivery. If you were to send off for a rebate, is that synchronous or asynchronous? The sending of the rebate is synchronous because once you fill it out and place it in a mailbox, you know that it will be delivered. However, the entire process is asynchronous because you have no guarantee of getting the rebate.*

The response may or may not depend on the data payload submitted by the client. For instance, a Web service could simply respond with a confirmation that the call was received, or it may process the data and provide a custom response. When the response is simply a confirmation of receipt, the responder may be included in the listener component. But the more your response increases in complexity, the more beneficial it will be to separate these components. In fact, for enterprise-level Web services, you will likely have a responder that is logically separated from all of your Web service application logic to get the most reuse of that functionality.

Since the data in a response has to be encapsulated in a valid XML document, this component might have to build the response or at least transform it from another format. Then again, it could simply pass XML data straight through it. This starts to lead us to implementation designs, which we will discuss later.

Just like the listener, the responder platform and technology choices are independent of the consumer's. However, you may be tied to decisions made in this area for your listener. Assuming that performance is important for the service, you should stick with one set of technologies internally, since you have that luxury when there is single ownership.

The Web Service Consumer

Just as the name implies, the consumer is responsible for using the Web service and for initiating the interaction with the service, not vice versa. Every application or process that uses a Web service is considered a consumer. That means that for a chain of linked partners (as we saw in Figure 2-1), every partner except the last one (partner D) was a consumer. We will see in "Logical Architecture," later in this chapter, how this stacking of consumers can make our Web services extensible.

> **NOTE** *In this book the word consumer refers to the direct caller of the Web service. This might also be called the client since this could be classified as a client-server architecture. However, neither of these names is used in this book to describe the end user. The end user is the person or persons possibly using the service through an application and is likely to be a customer, or at least a client of the actual consumer.*

With our definition of a consumer, we have recognized another fundamental aspect of Web services: namely, that Web services are built exclusively for programmatic access by other applications. Table 2-1, earlier in this chapter, reinforces this by leaving out any mention of a presentation tier. There is no need for a presentation tier internal to our Web services architecture because the consumer calling it has complete control of the end user experience. Even though the presentation layer itself has no place in the Web service architecture, a Web service can provide presentation information, as we will see in Chapter 5.

The consumer of a Web service probably has the widest range of possibilities of all the components when it comes to functionality. The consumer may be responsible for the presentation to the end user brokering multiple Web services, or simply passing through a Web services call. This becomes more obvious when you realize that even different consumers of the same Web service may want to use a Web service in entirely different ways. One consumer may pass information straight through to a client, and another may want use the Web service behind the scenes, completely masking its existence. We will look at some of these possibilities in more detail when we start looking at code in the sample applications. Right now we will only concern ourselves with the functionality that is necessary to make the call to the Web service and "handle" its response.

With today's toolsets and services, that means developing a custom application, or at least expanding the functionality of an existing application. Keep in mind that the great thing about consumers in this architecture is that they are truly independent of the Web service. That means that the options of how to design it, what technology is chosen, and even which platform to use are entirely open and unaffected by those same choices made by the Web service owners. The consumer is completely independent and could be completely unknown to the service, so the details of its implementation and execution are of no consequence to it.

The consumer will consist, by nature, of two different logical, if not physical, parts: the caller and the parser (see Figure 2-9). I stress the logical separation of these two functions, because, just like the service's functional components, they are independent of each other.

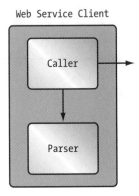

Figure 2-9. A functional view of a Web service client

Caller: Making the Request

The caller component is responsible for initiating the entire process of instantiating a Web service. It is responsible for building the payload for, and making the actual call to, the Web service. The nice thing about the caller is that it can be very generic in nature, so you can get a lot of reuse from a caller component. It can be so generic because of the communication structure we have defined. Regardless of what the consumer wants to do with a Web service, the communication with it is fairly consistent.

As we discussed with the service component, the call to the Web service is actually synchronous. Regardless, all the complexity of the caller lies in the intricacies and nuances of network communication. The steps involved are executed in the following order:

1. Build the payload.

2. Send the payload to the service.

3. Wait for the response from the service.

4. Pass the response to the parser.

More steps could be added to this process, but these are the minimal steps necessary to facilitate the Web service interaction by the consumer. We will look at this in more detail in Chapter 8 when we discuss consuming Web services.

Parser: Handling the Response

Since Web services respond to the consumer in an XML document format, most consumers have the ability to parse XML. This will almost always be necessary, but there are scenarios in which XML could be passed straight through, as we will see in the presentation models in Chapter 5. This functionality is so basic to Web service consumption that it is best isolated and accessed as a reusable object or component. This will keep you from having to incorporate that logic directly in each of your consumer implementations. While this could be done through custom logic, some standards have been defined to keep developers from having to design their own algorithms for parsing XML.

> **NOTE** *Although there is technically a difference between the two, I will treat the words object and component the same for the purpose of this discussion and will use them interchangeably.*

One of those standards is the Document Object Model (DOM). This model allows the loading of an XML document into a tree structure, referencing each of the elements as nodes. This is a good method for parsing XML when you want to work with an entire document. An alternative to the DOM is the Simple API for XML (SAX) standard, which allows for easy access to a single node in an XML document. We will look at both of these access technologies in much more detail in Chapter 4.

Just like the Web service itself, the technology and platform choices made for the consumer are independent of any other entity. You will not be diminishing your capabilities to access true Web services by any choices you make.

> **CAUTION** *I have mentioned several times how the technology choices made at each level have no impact on the other components in a Web service application. While these choices will not prevent you from using any Web service, there may be advances or more robust services in some vendor implementations of XML or Web services that may make the deployment and consumption of Web services easier. The issue to be aware of is a vendor's customization of Web services that actually makes the communication, service, or consumer proprietary. This may be a tradeoff you are willing to make, but you need to be aware of the decision you are making.*

The parser component of a Web service consumer can have the most variation on a per implementation basis because the utilization of a Web service has unlimited possibilities. This becomes more obvious when you realize that even different consumers of the same Web service may want to use it in entirely different ways. One consumer may pass information straight through to a client, and another may want to use the Web service behind the scenes, completely masking its existence. We will look at some of these possibilities in more detail when we start looking at code in the sample applications.

Now that we have a good understanding of how clients communicate with Web services, let's take a look at the actual makeup of a Web service.

Logical Architecture

The logical architecture identifies the functions to be performed by a system without consideration for physical systems or objects. In this case, we will look at the functional components of a Web service from the call on up. We will group these functions into layers to help us relate to current architectures in Web-based applications. This will also help us to later identify ownership and responsibilities in the Web service call. In general, a logical architecture is not intended to be strictly adhered to during implementation. However, it should be useful as a platform for discussion and analysis. Through this exercise, we will look at every component at its lowest possible level. Many implementations may leave out or group components for good reason, but we break them down to recognize the distinction of functionality.

> **NOTE** *Layers and tiers are terms that I will use interchangeably. They both represent a logical grouping of services that may or may not also be physically grouped.*

In the functions themselves we will look at a couple of different aspects. First, we will look at the possible tasks that need to be accomplished at that level. This will help us to identify solutions and opportunities later in our design discussion. Second, we will identify the data that must be passed between the layers based on the functionality. This will help us develop a better understanding of the distribution of responsibility and again help us to identify opportunities during the design of our Web services. We will not look at the process for making a Web service call, because this subject was covered by our earlier look at the communication architecture. In this analysis we will just identify when the interaction between layers could or should be handled through a Web services call.

You can think of this exercise as similar to storyboarding an application. Just like that process, this architecture serves as a focus for discussion and ensures that we look at the same issues during design and implementation. Specifically, we look at where functionality goes and where it might interact with other functionality, but we do not concern ourselves with the implementation details or how it actually works.

> *Storyboarding* is the process of walking through the process or flow of an application and designing a graphical view of the interface that exposes all of the required functionality.

Web Applications

To establish a frame of reference, it is probably worthwhile to review the logical architecture for existing Web applications that are not Web services. This architecture has proven to be very robust. It has managed to grow with the evolving technology because it is a logical architecture. Various changes in tools, implementation, user base, and even physical distribution have not been able to break this model. In fact, when we look at the logical architecture for Web services, we notice that it is merely an extension to this very architecture. So understanding this model will, in essence, be the starting point for understanding the Web services model. It will also help us to distinguish the differences between Web applications and Web services in our designs.

> **CAUTION**   *It is common for less-experienced developers to confuse the logical architecture with the physical architecture in these discussions. The physical architecture is different because it designates objects with the appropriate functionality. The two n-tier models do not always match up, and, in fact, the two are more likely to not match in implementations. For example, data access is a responsibility of the data layer in the logical architecture, but it may make more sense for certain business layer objects to access the data model directly.*

This architecture contains three layers: data, business, and presentation. Each of these layers performs important functionality to achieve the end product of a distributed, Web-based application. As you see in Figure 2-10, the business layer serves as the go-between between the presentation and data layers, and clients can only connect to the presentation layer.

> **NOTE**   *The business layer is often called the logic or logical layer. The presentation layer is also sometimes called the interface layer. However, this usage will cause more confusion as integration with other applications and organizations becomes more prevalent.*

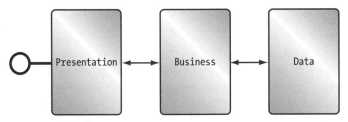

Figure 2-10. Logical architecture of an n-tier Web application

Although it may not be obvious, the presentation layer is responsible for initiating all processes in the application. More precisely, the client calling the presentation layer initiates the process. This means that nothing actually happens independently of client interaction in a true *n*-tier application. Any processes running automatically on the server fall outside of this model.

Also, all interaction in the tiers is synchronous because the initial call is synchronous. If the presentation layer does not get a response from the business layer, the client tier eventually times out, and all hope for fulfilling that request is gone.

Now that we have the high-level view, let's take a quick look at each layer.

> **NOTE** *Notice that there is no inclusion of the client in this architecture, only the acknowledgement of an available interface. This is because no integration or shared ownership is possible in a traditional Web application. The application is designed as an independent entity, and that is one of the existing models that Web services is attempting to break.*

Data Layer

The data layer in any application contains the data source(s) and its components. The data source can take many forms, but the most common form is usually a relational database with tables, stored procedures, and triggers. The tier also contains the data access logic. This is the functionality for managing the connection(s) to the data source and making the actual queries.

This seems fairly simple, but whenever you start putting extended logic in stored procedures, the clarity of this layer starts to blur. By *extended logic* I mean logic that goes beyond the expected functions of data filtering or extraction of normalized data. For instance, if you have a stored procedure that extracts different data based on a parameter, runs some calculations, and includes some formatting, is it now part of the business layer? Is it in the object that knows which stored procedure to call or the stored procedure that has the intelligence built-in to look up a customer and all of its properties and activities? Although the benefit of doing this is debatable, we consider stored procedures fundamentally as part of the data tier, since ultimately stored procedures are really just tools for extracting the data.

The purpose of our data access objects is to isolate the data source from the business logic. This allows the application to not be "married" to the database implementation. While this certainly doesn't make changes in your database solution easy, it could make it possible to change the database without rewriting the entire application.

Business Layer

The business layer contains the application logic, a series of programmatic algorithms that make the necessary decisions to produce the appropriate output. Tasks in this layer can range from complex math calculations to simple data filtering. Because these tasks are so varied, always make sure you choose an appropriate solution for the functionality needed. These solutions can vary from a script in a packaged application server to custom code using just a programming language. Depending on the functionality, performance, and scalability required, there are generally several solutions available.

Since this layer often contains many business rules, you will likely want to be able to reuse the manifestation of this logic (that is, components or objects). The first step to accomplishing this is implementing a solution that is reusable in your current infrastructure. That is the idea of where compatible technologies and objects start to play a significant role.

To make the most of this strategy, you then want to break your logic down into the appropriate chunks. This means breaking your processes down as small as reasonably possible. These can then be aggregated into the necessary transactions and functions to execute your services and applications. The idea is to isolate low-level functions that are likely to be reused in completely different processes. I call this the lowest-common-denominator approach. If you consider applications as numbers and you need to produce the numbers 9, 12, 27, and 48, you can build functions that give you exactly 9, 12, 27, and 48, respectively. However, you will get more reuse in the future if you break these applications into smaller parts. In this case, you can build functions to produce just a 2 and a 3 and assemble them appropriately, since $3 \times 3 = 9$, $3 \times 2 \times 2 = 12$, $3 \times 3 \times 3 = 27$, and $3 \times 2 \times 2 \times 2 \times 2 = 48$. This also allows you to build other applications in the future, such as 6, 8, and so on. But if you never need a 2, or a 6 or 8 for that matter, you may not want to break it down that far. If you could create a function that produced a 4 more efficiently, wouldn't it make sense to do so? Probably. Since the lowest common denominators are 4 and 3, that is likely the best solution.

A *transaction* is a unit of work that should either succeed or fail as a whole.

The client does not access the business layer directly. That is the responsibility of the presentation layer. To accommodate this, the business layer needs some type of hook(s) into it that can be accessed externally. This is often done through the interface of the objects in the business layer.

Presentation Layer

The presentation layer is responsible for the presentation of the application to the end user. This actually involves two functions, the display of information and the collection of information. Any logic necessary to complete these functions is considered part of the presentation layer, not the business layer. This logic includes validation, transformations, layout, format, and style.

Validation is the process of ensuring that the end user enters appropriate and acceptable data. The presentation layer has to ensure that the data collected is acceptable because the data typing for the data is much stricter in the business and data tiers. For example, if a user enters an alpha character for a number, the database raises an error because it obviously isn't allowed. Although you could gracefully handle the error and return it to the user, why waste the cycles traveling back through the tiers? If you catch the error up front, you can impact fewer layers and have the user resolve the error much more quickly. In fact, as a rule, you want to handle as many of these issues as close to the user as possible to avoid taxing the entire system.

Transformation is very similar to validation in that the data may be corrected intelligently without involving the user at all. A common example of this is stripping out certain characters from input data. If a user enters "888-555-1212", the presentation layer may strip out the "-" characters to keep the information as a pure numeric data type for more efficient storage.

Dictating the layout involves the placement of information and controls in the user interface. It takes a good UI to make a successful, intuitive client, and it all starts with the layout. It means knowing when to collect the information through an open text field or a predefined dropdown list. It also means knowing when enough is enough when it comes to collecting information in the individual steps of a process.

Formatting is the process of ensuring that data is presented in the appropriate manner. When you work with real numbers and want to dictate the specific digits displayed behind the decimal, you can often do this through formatting. Another example of this is the treatment of numbers as currency. By using a format routine, the presentation layer can take a number like "3214" and turn it into "$3,214".

Finally, styling is the process of adding window dressing to the information displayed in the presentation layer. Common examples of this would be font treatments and colors. There are a number of ways this can be accomplished, and we will touch on some of these later in our sample Web services.

To complete its objective, the presentation layer has to communicate with the business layer to pass and receive data. That means the designs and technologies chosen at each layer must be compatible with those of the other layers. The advances in technology to enable this integration between the presentation and business layers have enabled Web-based applications to become effective enterprise application solutions.

Web Services

Before we discuss the logical architecture for Web services, let us get a better understanding of why Web services don't have the same architecture as Web applications. While we discussed the difference between shared information and shared processes as well as the difference between Web applications and Web services, we need to understand how this distinction impacts the architecture.

Web services do not have a presentation layer. While Web services can contribute to the information defining the presentation, it does not, and in fact could not, dictate the actual presentation delivery to the end user. This goes back to the whole notion of shared ownership for the entire application. That means that proprietary technology and inconsistent implementations could be huge barriers to integration for either the service owner or, even more likely, the consumer. We have already established the communication architecture, which helps with masking the proprietary technologies involved. Now our logical architecture will provide a consistent breakdown that will identify the responsibilities in the tiers and who the owners of those tiers could and should be.

Although we are looking at the architecture for a Web service, it is an incomplete view of the entire application. Because a consumer is responsible for activating the application, it is important to look at both to (1) get a full understanding of Web services usage and (2) relate it to the architecture of existing Web applications, with which we are familiar. Trying to design a Web service without considering its consumers would be like designing a motor without considering the vehicle in which it is going. What will be the demands on the motor? Is it going to be used to carry heavy loads or just move as quickly as possible? Is it a small or large vehicle? Won't we build far better motors knowing the answers to these questions? Although it isn't quite that extreme, because we have established a baseline for all of our "motors" to work with vehicles via our communication architecture, we really need to analyze the Web service and its consumers so we better understand the big picture. So, let's take a look at the overall logical architecture for both (see Figure 2-11).

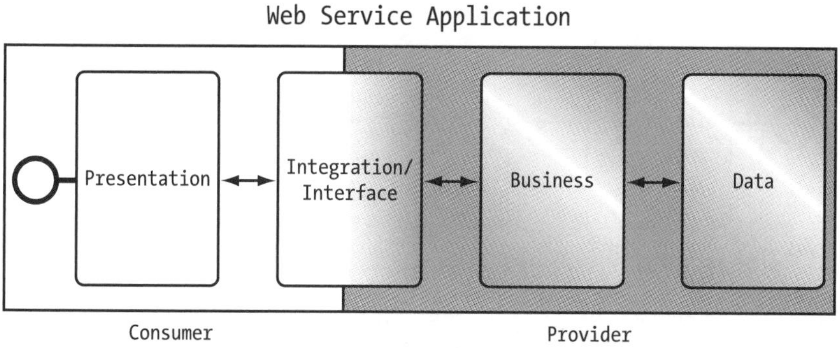

Web Service Application

Figure 2-11. Web service and consumer logical architecture

In the logical architecture for Web services, we will continue to have the same layers of data, business, and presentation. However, we added a fourth layer, the integration/interface layer, between the presentation and business layers. In a Web service, the presentation layer resides on the consumer's infrastructure, and the business layer resides on the service owner's infrastructure. The integration/interface layer crosses the organizational boundaries and allows for the shared ownership of Web services. This layer bridges the provider and consumer by executing the communication architecture outlined earlier for Web services.

The Service

First, we will look in detail at the service itself. Even though it depends on a consumer to be accessed by an end user, it is a freestanding entity. If a Web service is built and available but not being accessed, is it still a Web service? Is a car still a car when nobody is driving it? Of course!

In the Web service logical architecture (see Figure 2-12), you see that we still have three tiers, but instead of the presentation tier exposing the application, we have the interface tier. Since the presentation layer is shared, the data and business logic exposed play a more significant role. If you take into account that the interface tier is simply a connection to the service, it becomes obvious that the real value differentiating different Web services is contained in those two layers. Let's take a closer look.

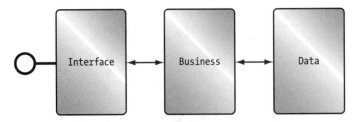

Figure 2-12. Web service logical architecture

Data Layer

Unlike with other enterprise applications, it might be inappropriate to label the data layer as the foundation. Depending on the functionality, the service may be passed every piece of data it needs from the consumer. For instance, if the service is a calculator, the functionality may be contained entirely in logic. However, it could be argued that the more valuable services still have some local set of data they are either referencing or depending on to provide their functionality. After all, any logic might be reverse engineered, and the value of the service could be compromised. If the service provider owns or has access to proprietary data, it is harder to replace.

The real impact on the data layer in a Web service application is the fact that, at some point, the data exposed is defined in XML. This doesn't require data to originate as XML, but that is an option. Multiple transformations of data from one type to another ultimately affect performance of the service. For instance, if you are building your Web service in COM objects and use ActiveX Data Objects (ADO) to extract data into a recordset, encapsulate the necessary data into a property bag to marshal across business objects, and then expose the results in XML, you've gone through three very significant data transformations. There are decisions you can make to avoid this, and we will look at these later.

> *Marshalling* is the process of transferring data between processes. Marshalling objects is more intensive than marshalling strings because the objects have to do more encoding and rebuilding.

Business Layer

The business layer defines the processes behind the service and contains all application-specific logic. This layer is likely to be the least affected by the fact the application is exposed as a Web service. In fact, you should closely scrutinize any changes you might make internally to an existing application's business layer to make it a Web service. This could easily add overhead to an application that is used through channels other than Web services.

When creating a Web service from scratch (meaning not only the Web service, but also the functionality it is exposing), there are decisions that can be made to support a Web service architecture going forward to optimize both performance and extensibility. These decisions revolve around standardizing the approaches to handling data and maintaining security. Again, since all information is collected and exposed as XML, it would be beneficial to keep consistency in your interfaces and transformations. Also, determining a security scheme to account for public programmatic access to your logic may keep you from having to reconfigure, or even worse redesign, your business layer later when limitations are encountered.

The business layer is also the tier of the Web service that could be a consumer of other Web services. This makes sense when you consider that the business layer is responsible for the logic and accessing various local data sources and/or objects. Web services could be utilized just like other objects, and this is the layer at which that integration occurs (see Figure 2-13).

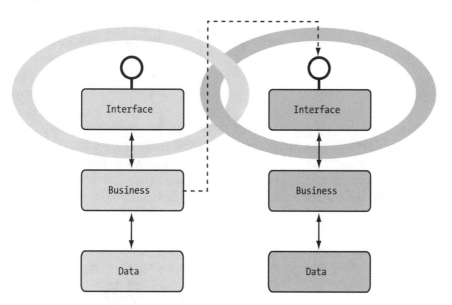

Figure 2-13. Web service integration with another Web service

> **NOTE** *Don't interpret the preceding figure too literally without considering the components that are required in the business layer consuming the Web service. If the business layer is accessing a Web service, it must have the Web service consumer logical architecture, which we will discuss shortly, contained in it.*

This same model holds true for traditional applications. Regardless of whether the application is a Web service, a Web site, or even a fat-client application, an *n*-tier application references Web services from its business layer.

> A *fat client* is commonly referred to as a client application that contains custom logic or processes to facilitate user-interaction with an application.

Interface Layer

This is where we get into the very interesting aspects of Web services. The interface layer is where partnerships are established. For this reason, this layer exposes the service's functionality to its consumers. Don't confuse this with the end user interface, since this interface is designed for programmatic access only. This layer works with the consumer's integration logic to provide the complete tier for our communication architecture.

The interface layer contains the functionality required to expose our Web service. We have to receive the call from the consumer, pass it to our application logic, receive the response from our logic, and return the appropriate information back to the consumer. In the communication architecture, we encapsulated this functionality in a listener and a responder. The listener handles the inbound processes, and the responder the outbound. Both of these components reside in the interface layer.

Although the Web service is not responsible for the presentation layer, it may need to provide information to the owner of the presentation to expose processes directly to the end user. This may involve the filtering and transformation of information or may involve entirely separate processes for extracting data specific to this function. Regardless, any functionality specific to this information is encapsulated in the interface layer.

This would be considered a value-added service to the Web service itself, just as providing a user manual on how to change the oil to the car manufacturer buying our motor would be considered value added. Can you build a motor without providing this information? Probably. The car manufacturer is certainly familiar enough with the process itself they could write the instructions for changing the oil. However, providing the manual makes using the motor easier, and more car manufacturers would be inclined to use your motor because of this value-added service. It also ensures that the car manufacturer is telling the user exactly how you want the oil to be changed. It helps ensure that users aren't abusing your motor (thus making users happier with your product) because they are getting the information straight from the source. Will the car manufacturer use the information? Probably, because of the savings in time and money of reusing our work. Will the manufacturer pass it on directly to the car owner or compile all information about the vehicle into one all-encompassing manual? That depends, but the point is that it is at the car manufacturer's discretion. This same concept can be applied to Web services and the services you provide around it.

Other services may benefit the Web service provider more than its consumers. We will talk about these and other value-added services you can provide later. The main thing to remember for now is that these services are part of the interface layer of your Web service. No matter how complex and robust the functionality, it is all embodied in the interface layer of your logical architecture.

Consumers

In our analysis of the communication architecture, we started to look at the consumer responsibilities and functionality. In this view, we will look a little closer and relate its functionality back again to traditional Web applications. We will start with a high-level view of the entire consumer entity and its layers (see Figure 2-14). In this diagram, we are reinforcing the fact that the consumer owns the presentation layer and its portion of the integration layer.

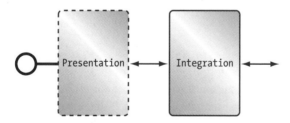

Figure 2-14. Web Service consumer logical architecture

Notice that the presentation layer is actually displayed differently. This is because this layer is optional in the sense that there may be no presentation layer to the application or the consumer of the service may not be the partner ultimately responsible for it.

Although it may be disturbing to think that the consumer may not have a presentation layer, there are many examples where this may be the case. For instance, you could have an automated back end process utilizing Web services to transfer data. Also, if the consumer is a Web service itself, it would pass its information on to another consumer, and it may or may not own the presentation layer. This gets back to the idea of stacking multiple Web services to provide a complete application (see Figure 2-15).

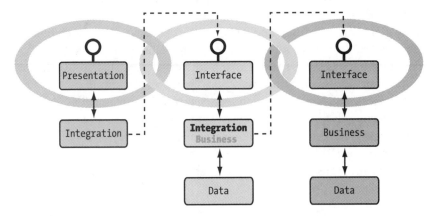

Figure 2-15. Logical architecture of an application with stacked Web services

Remember that the business layer of the first Web service also doubles as the integration/application layer for the second Web service, since it is acting as a consumer of it. Through the rest of the discussion in this chapter, we will work with a simple partnership of one consumer and one Web service. Thus, the consumer will own the presentation layer. Later, we will build logical diagrams of more complex applications based on these same rules.

Integration Layer

In our Web service, the integration/inferface layer was responsible for its interface. In the consumer, the integration portion of that layer is responsible for calling the Web service. Together, these two components allow for the integration of the external process into the local processes. Since the consumer calls the service from its business logic and integrates the two, the distinction of a consumer's integration layer is purely logical, not physical.

As we discussed earlier in "Communication Architecture," the consumer is responsible for packaging up the input data, making the call to the Web service, receiving the response, and parsing out its returned data. These functions were split into the caller and the parser, with the caller responsible for the outbound processes and the parser for the inbound. The additional function not explicitly stated is the communication with the presentation tier. Similar to the relationship in a traditional *n*-tier application between the business and presentation tiers, the consumer's presentation tier would call the integration tier for its functionality, or it could be retrieved through the business layer. Either way, the presentation layer is returned the information necessary to display to the end user. The complexity in this relationship is largely determined by how much of this information came from the Web service versus the application itself. In other words, to what extent must the presentation data be intergrated? The answer to this question can be as easy as "none" and as complex as "a lot!" With more integration comes more logic, but also more functionality and more reuse. As you can suspect, with less integration come fewer benefits. However, if you are interested in Web services, you probably want to maximize your integration potential with your partners.

In our earlier oil change manual scenario, how hard would it have been for the car manufacturer to utilize our oil change documentation? It depends on how integrated the company wanted to make it. The company could have passed it directly on to the end user, as a separate document, but it wouldn't have any of the car manufacturer's branding or information on it. They could have made several copies and manually inserted them into the manual, but it would have looked out of place. If the company had it rekeyed into a word processor, it could have merged it into the existing manual and made it fit much better, but any changes would cause a lot of rework. Certainly there are different levels of effort involved, along with different benefits. By exposing it through a Web service, we can provide a current electronic copy of the manual every time the company requests it. If all of the car manufacturer's partners cooperate on using the same process, how easy would it be to create manuals for the car with every component up to date? Very!

> **NOTE** *In case you didn't notice, we just referenced a scenario encountering the same issues that we saw in Chapter 1 when integrating Web applications through redirection, frames, and duplicate content versus Web services!*

Once a consumer has the logic for working with a Web service, it should have the logic for working with a whole host of Web services. In fact, in the integration layer, calls may be made to multiple Web services. This is the concept of brokering Web services that we saw in Figure 2-4. This may complicate the integration layer a little, but it is primarily the same functionality so will likely benefit from reusable objects. The additional complexity comes from the integration of the resulting information into the business logic.

This is where the definition of data plays an important role. It will be up to the integration layer to parse the data returned to the consumer so that it can work with it or pass it on. This may mean simply putting the information into an XML-compatible data model like the DOM or transforming it into a more system-specific structure like an ADO recordset (if you are working in a COM environment).

> **TIP** *Be aware that when you start to transform data between various formats, your performance is going to suffer. This is not to say transformations should never be used, because they will be necessary. You are just much better off establishing a consistent model format for your data in each tier instead of catering to the model or format preferred by each language or methodology utilized in the system.*

When the application has to work with the data, the consumer has to have a very clear understanding of what the data is and what it means. Referencing one of the industry standards for defining XML datasets will help the consumer accomplish this. However, it is up to the Web service owner to provide a definition and comply with it. If all partners are working with the same definitions, life will be much better for the consumers. Otherwise, the consumers will have to work the data into an acceptable format.

In this case, a complex design will likely be necessary for consistent integration. For instance, what would be easier for the car manufacturer to automate: assembling 100 .txt files or assembling 35 .doc, 30 .txt, 15 .rtf, 5 .sdw, and 15 .ps files from all of its partners into a manual? Sure, either one can be done, but isn't the former going to happen more often, a lot sooner, more easily, and at a lower cost?

Fortunately, if information is going to be passed directly to the end user, there is usually a lower level of understanding about the information required by the business layer. In fact, the integration layer might not even have to share the same physical tier as the business layer. That is because the presentation layer may call it separately from any other logic calls. This means that integrating Web services may not modify your existing business objects, but simply add to them. And minimizing the impact on existing code is always a good thing!

Even in these instances, the integration layer will still have some logic. Some filtering, transforming, or modifying may occur. The integration layer will at least have to parse the data so that the presentation layer can work with it. What do I mean by work with it? Let's find out.

Presentation Layer

The presentation layer can be the most complex layer in an application that consumes Web services. Additionally, this is the layer that can have the most variation from application to application. This is because all of the partnerships and collaboration of services have to come together at this point. They can be as simple as a single consumer calling a single service or as complex as a consumer brokering multiple application chains with multiple partners.

Our logical architecture will be able to support any of these models, so we have a fairly robust architecture on our hands. This will help us to break down the complexity into sublayers so that we can be certain we have accommodated nearly every conceivable scenario.

It could also be argued that this layer should be the most thought out, because it carries the most significance on a business level. It is the presenter of the application to the end user and is also probably one of the reasons the end user is there in the first place. In this competitive industry, there aren't too many poorly designed applications or Web sites with massive success these days.

> **NOTE** *Of course we remember from our earlier analogy that a chain is only as strong as its weakest link. However, many organizations emphasize the presentation more than the back-end processes, since they are more visible, and often perception is reality.*

While I am presenting the logical architecture for a Web service consumer, this same breakdown of the presentation layer could also apply to traditional *n*-tier applications. It is a little more relevant here, since this architecture forces more structure on the design due to its complexity. Web applications are known for being very forgiving to less-structured designs because their demands have been relatively light. This is similar to the forgiving nature of HTML versus XML. You can get away with more inaccuracies in HTML because it isn't considered mission critical, and often "close enough" is fine. Web services require a bit more discipline to be implemented correctly, and this architecture should help achieve that.

One of the biggest reasons for this stricter adherence is the shared nature of the presentation for applications utilizing Web services. As I mentioned before, Web services can contribute to the presentation layer. While this is not a requirement of Web services in general, it is a feature that consumers need to support architecturally. Supporting this means that the integration of the presentation information needs to happen systematically in a way that is effective and repeatable. Keep in mind that we are not talking about actual implementations, but rather the architecture defining the structure for our designs (see Figure 2-16).

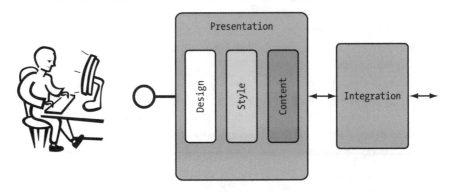

Figure 2-16. Web service consumer presentation logical sublayers

> **NOTE** *Something worth mentioning at this point is that the focus of the presentation layer's abilities center on Web-based clients. Inherent functionality is exposed through HTML on a browser that allows for incredible flexibility in the presentation layer. (For example, it is a simple process to reference .GIF images on external systems over the Internet.) To compensate for these limitations in applications with custom clients that are not Web based, additional functionality would have to be added to your client. Of course you could make your life easier and build your interface for a Web browser!*

Content Layer

The name of this layer tends to give away its jurisdiction. While it is easy enough to say that the content layer is responsible for all the content of the application's presentation, it is really not quite that simple when you take a closer look. That content may be local, or it may be external to the application's environment. Rather than dismissing it as the directory containing all the HTML and graphic files for the content, you need to think of it as a reference to all of the content for the presentation. This puts the content layer in more of a logical state than a physical one.

Just as with current Web sites, it is simple for the local application to reference external as well as internal content. That content may take the form of HTML code, client-side scripts, images, and other supported file formats. However, the content layer may be very dynamic, since the application layer can also pass information that may reference external content. This content could be either embedded or defined in the data or simply referenced by the data. For example, the hotel service in our traffic scenario may have passed our reservation system the necessary data to define a drop-down box that allows users to select a bed size. This would allow the hotel to directly define a piece of information critical to its room availability Web service. The hotel may also reference an image on its own Web site for the purpose of cobranding the reservation application.

> *Cobranding* is the practice of partnering to share the exposure from a public marketing vehicle, in this case a public Web application, by giving exposure to the two or more organizations involved. A good example of this in everyday life is the packaging of toys from a movie inside children's meals at fast food restaurants. This effort gains publicity for both the restaurant and the movie.

CAUTION *It is worth re-emphasizing that the reservation system will have the ultimate choice of whether to utilize this information. The hotel cannot enforce, through technology, any requirements it may make of its consumers to use or not use the data it returns when accessed. We will look later at how the hotel can better protect its processes.*

Another example of service-driven content would be content derived logically by the integration layer based on what was received from the Web service call. An excellent example of this is error handling. If the Web service cannot be reached, the consumer's integration layer should handle the failure and provide some kind of data to the presentation layer to keep the end user from getting stuck in a dead end.

Regardless of the method, all of these processes result in data consisting of the content layer. We could consider our content layer a toolbox of information for building the application's presentation. By being able to work with a simple content layer, the rest of the presentation layer will have no concept of service-fed versus local content. It can treat all content as a group and thus reduce the complexity of the remaining functionality.

The content required of the application beyond the Web service functionality would also be contained in this layer. This is often referred to as base-level content for the application, since it is used independently of the Web service. This content may still be dynamically referenced and utilized by the business layer, but the integration layer will generally have no impact on this content.

Style Layer

The style layer is responsible for the formatting and treatment of all content on the site. This layer is entirely owned by the local application, since its objective is to maintain a consistent look throughout the application, regardless of whether the functionality is provided by a Web service or the local business layer. While it is possible for a Web service to define some styling, it is generally counterproductive, since the consumer will probably want to control it.

This styling can take many different forms, including cascading style sheets (CSSs), eXtensible Style Sheet Language (XSL), and a number of programming languages. Through these methods, the style layer can define how to present everything from currency to HTML form controls to plain text. This is done by either asking the client to map content to a style, as with CSS, or by transforming the content to another format prior to pushing it to the client.

> **CAUTION** *Although XSL can be used to have the browser map content to a style, this is limited to newer versions of browsers and, more importantly, is more limiting to XSL's capabilities than manipulating the content server side.*

Although the style layer defines these functions, even in the case of server-side manipulations, it is not actually responsible for making the changes or transforming the content. This would require the style layer to contain the logic of which pieces of content it should be associated with. That is actually a more involved process, since it is often affected by other content outside of its control. For that, you need functionality that is aware of everything being presented to the user, not just one piece of content. This is the responsibility of the design layer.

Design Layer

The design layer is responsible for building an application's presentation from all the tools provided through the content and style layers. This is the layer with all the control over what content goes where and how much space it consumes, what content is styled, and what content is discarded. The design layer is ultimately responsible for the look and feel of the site.

While much of this functionality can be provided statically through programmatic logic, modifying dynamic content will probably be required, depending on the application's processes. This may be as simple as referencing random images for a look of "freshness" or as sophisticated as transforming raw data into its final format for presentation to the user. While we will look at how to implement this functionality in our sample applications later, suffice it to say here that we demand much more of our presentation layer than we have in traditional *n*-tier applications.

Although this layer can contain quite a bit of sophistication, the ideal design layer implementations will offload as much logic as possible to the integration layer so that it can focus on just the presentation aspects. For instance, if the design layer is getting back 100 data points and filtering for just one to be shown, try to push that responsibility back to the integration or business layer.

The reason for streamlining this layer is twofold. First, any kind of purist will want to limit the amount of logic creeping into the presentation layer, just as you would in an *n*-tier application. Second, if you are following the practice of splitting your presentation and business layers onto separate systems, your presentation system could quickly become a bottleneck from the additional responsibilities it has taken on in dynamically building the presentation. While you can always add more systems to one tier of the system, you want to avoid getting into great disparities of system counts between the tiers. Adding logic to this layer would only compound that issue.

Now that we have discussed all the levels in the presentation layer, let us look at how they might fit together visually. In the sample layout model presented in Figure 2-17, you see a single view with many content elements from different sources. In that layout may be modules of straight content or styled content, depending on the design and the content in question. No distinction is made to where the content originated because it doesn't matter to the presentation layer. In our design scenarios, we will get much more in depth on content sourcing and how that is handled. The focus of this illustration is to present each of these sublayers and where their responsibilities lie.

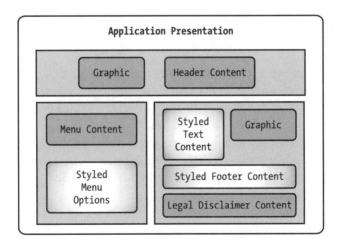

Figure 2-17. Visual segmentation of presentation sublayers

Summary

It is important to have a solid understanding of how to architect Web services before you start building them. This means having a clear picture of how the logical and communication architectures work together to provide the functionality necessary for Web services (see Figure 2-18). Unlike some architecture models, this is not simply an architecture of convenience, but rather an architecture of necessity. Any process exposed as a Web service must have an interface layer that allows consumers to interact with it. Likewise, any application that consumes Web services must have an integration layer. Together, these layers fulfill the communication architecture.

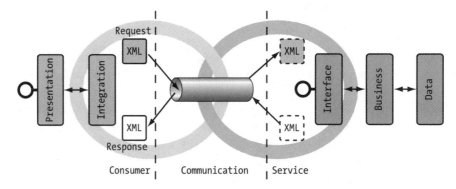

Figure 2-18. Combined logical and communication architecture for a Web services call

In our illustrations and examples, we have focused on applications in which different owners provide the service and consumer. Does this architecture change if its owner is the only consumer of the service? Since this is a logical architecture, the answer is no. The same functions and processes have to be provided regardless of the identities of the consumer and end user. However, in implementation, some things might be done differently if the service and consumer had the same owner. We will look at this scenario in our sample applications in Chapter 8.

The next question might be whether it makes sense for an organization to expose their services as a Web service. This must be answered on a case-by-case basis. For example, in our computer manufacturing process, it might make sense for the video card manufacturer to sell its product directly to consumers. It would require some work on packaging and probably enhancing the company's customer service, but it could certainly be feasible. However, under very few scenarios does it make a lot of sense for a smaller organization to expose a process as a Web service if it will be the only organization using it. That would be like the video card manufacturer using resources on the packaging for its video cards and then purchasing every card made. In fact, if the company cannot get enough external consumers to purchase its video cards, a benefit will likely not be realized because the market reuse won't be there to justify the design and development effort. Likewise, whatever application architecture is being utilized in an organization will continue to serve as the best solution in many instances.

In the next chapter we will take a brief look into some of the newer technologies needed to implement Web services. An understanding of these will be key to knowing when and how to use them in our implementations.

CHAPTER 3

XML Technical Primer

EVEN IF YOU DEVELOP applications daily, it can be quite a challenge to keep up with the constant changes in the technical industry. Between the programming languages, the tools you use to program, the methodologies, the best practices of those methodologies, new architectures, and design techniques, you are fortunate if you can maintain the mastery of your current areas, much less learn about the new entrants into these areas.

Since Web services will certainly touch developers who have been too busy developing more traditional applications over the last few years, I am going to summarize some of the newer technologies to enable you to follow the sample applications we will be designing later in the book. This is not a book about XML (eXtensible Markup Language) or schemas, so the intent is not to give you a complete understanding of each of these technologies, but rather to provide enough information to enable you to follow along through the remaining material in this book. If you are interested in gaining a deeper level of understanding in these technologies, quite a few books are available to assist you (and it seems that number grows on a weekly basis). If you consider yourself proficient in these technologies, you should be able to quickly review the high points I have listed and move on.

I will break this review into two chapters. This chapter will deal with building XML, both in building data documents and in giving them definitions. In the next chapter, we will look specifically at working with XML through methodologies and tools. Aside from getting a fundamental understanding of how to use XML, we will look at different approaches to accomplishing given tasks. This will be an important step in determining how to design our Web service applications.

Building XML

XML is considered the building block for Web services. It provides a standard format that can cross all boundaries, enabling us to share information with literally anyone. However, this empowerment comes with a cost. XML is not the most efficient mechanism for transferring or working with data. To use XML as efficiently as possible, we need a good understanding of what XML is, when to use it, and how to use it.

The Background on Markup Languages

XML is a markup language for defining structured data. Markup languages are sometimes referred to as *metalanguages*. These languages are standardized mechanisms for describing text. These mechanisms are designed to communicate information from the writer to the reader through a series of predetermined notations. For instance, if you print out this page and put a line through some words that don't belong (~~like this~~), most readers will understand that you think those words should be removed. You can almost think of markup languages as programmatic shorthand applied to a document.

> **NOTE** *The word* markup *refers to the process of using some annotation to communicate handling instructions to a processor. This technique was originally used to communicate instructions to typesetters regarding the treatment of content for publishing.*

Any markup language is considered a member of the family of languages that has been derived from SGML (Standard Generalized Markup Language). SGML is an international standard (ISO 8879:1986) for a markup language established in 1986 and is considered to be the father of computer-based markup languages.

> **NOTE** *Unfortunately, the detailed history of SGML seems to be up for debate and a contentious issue for many of the people who were involved. What can be said is that various efforts of multiple individuals dating back to the 1960s led to the development and standardization of SGML.*

HTML (HyperText Markup Language) and XML are the most popular markup languages. There are also many other markup languages, including offshoots of HTML and XML that are starting to blur in distinction from their counterparts. Theoretically, the various markup languages of this family have rules that make them somewhat unique, but they are all markup languages.

The common bond between these languages is the standardized notation used to describe the actual data. There is nothing inherently powerful or special about these tags except that everyone has agreed to recognize these demarcations as tags and distinguish them from the data they are treating. A tag itself is simply some metadata enclosed in greater-than and less-than signs, as shown here:

```
<tag>
```

Data that defines other data is often referred to as *metadata*.

Depending on the implementation, the metadata in this tag will be communicating some information concerning the handling of the data it is related to. The specification for a group of implementations would define the encoding for a markup language. Specifications are typically drafted and maintained through a standards body. The World Wide Web Consortium (W3C) is the standards organization that maintains the HTML and XML specifications. For more information on W3C's organization and processes for drafting and revising specifications, visit its Web site at http://www.w3.org.

Every language has syntax to define what is considered valid and invalid code. The specification for a markup language defines its syntax and/or usage. The latest version of the entire specification for XML is on the W3C site at http://www.w3.org/TR/REC-xml.

XML and markup languages in general have a much less complicated syntax than actual programming languages like C++, Java, or even Visual Basic. The simplicity is both a byproduct and a goal. It is a byproduct because the requirements of XML are much less than those of a programming tool because we are defining data, not building applications. In fact, it is necessary to have a clear distinction between programming languages and markup languages. One allows you to develop an application, and the other can only be used to create the interface or instruction set for an application. In fact, markup language code doesn't even have the ability to interpret or validate itself. All it really does is communicate state to the application on a very simplistic level.

Take, for instance, the following HTML code:

```
<table border="0">
    <tr>
        <td>City</td>
        <td>State</td>
    </tr>
</table>
```

As any programmer will attest, tables are one of the more complex structures in HTML. However, even with this set of tags, the HTML isn't actually creating the table; the browser reading the code is. The HTML is laying out instructions for the browser concerning how many cells are in the table, some aspects of what it should look like, and what the cells' content is. If you were to remove the first `</td>` tag, what would happen? The HTML would be invalid, but the code has no way of validating itself. Browsers have become very intelligent and forgiving over the years because it is up to them to either handle this issue or ignore it. A browser won't get any help resolving an error from the HTML code itself.

At a glance, HTML and XML look very similar. If you weren't an experienced developer in one or the other, you might not be able to distinguish the difference. For instance, if you saw the following line of code, would you be able to determine if it was HTML or XML?

```
<H1>Fundamental Web Services</H1>
```

Of course, if you were an HTML developer, you might recognize this as the Header 1 tag and assume it is HTML. However, this could also be a valid XML tag if the appropriate definitions were given. Given the rest of the document, you could likely determine which language it is because you would have more data to either qualify or disqualify the code as HTML or XML. Let's go ahead and look at the details of XML so we can make a distinction.

The Purpose of XML

The first thing we need to understand about XML is why it was created. After all, we have been using HTML a long time, and it has obviously been accepted worldwide. Why complicate things?

HTML was created for one reason: to present and link academic documents over a network. We have obviously taken HTML a long way, but we couldn't take the next step within the confines of that original design. HTML was designed as a markup language for people. Tags are available for defining fonts and tables and colors and images and links, but they are all tags for instructing the browser how to display data. There are no tags to define actual data contained in the document.

Once Web pages became commonplace, organizations wanted to accomplish more. They wanted to take the information they were sharing between people over the Internet and share it between systems. This has proven to be a challenge using existing technologies. Too often applications have been written to read HTML delivered over the Web and to extract the data they wanted. And we thought building client-server applications meant the end of screen scraping!

> *Screen scraping* is the practice of programmatically reading in a screen of data meant for human eyes and parsing through it to identify and extract the pertinent data.

The following code is a sample of how HTML might present some data to a user:

```
<b><i>Last Name: </i></b>Smith
```

By quickly scanning this code, you know that it will display the last name of some person named Smith. Would a computer be able to read this code and know that Smith is the last name of some person? Certainly you could design an algorithm to process this one instance, but would it also work for the following example?

```
<b><i>Last Name:</i></b>Van Allen
```

If the preceding algorithm parsed through the HTML code to look for `Last Name`, continued past the tags `</i>` and `</b>`, and read Smith, would it have stopped at the first space it read? If so, you would get a last name of Van from this line of code. Assuming your algorithm dealt with that scenario, would it have handled this?

```
<b><i>Last Name:</b></i>Van Allen
```

You can imagine the additional issues that would come from adding font treatments, table elements, or rearranging the page layout. The point is that HTML was designed as a very flexible language that could easily change the presentation of a document—for people, not computers.

For programmatic access to information, we needed more structure. An application doesn't care about the treatment of information; it just wants to be able to work with the data. To do so, the application has to have the ability to interpret the data. The current set of HTML tags does not provide that functionality.

Additionally, the forgivingness of HTML (the tag structure necessary for validity in HTML is very loose) made it convenient for a whole industry of developers to learn a new language, but that approach is counterproductive to the use of markup languages by applications. If a piece of information is supposed to be annotated by a beginning tag and an ending tag, then it must be that way to work. Guessing at the intention programmatically is not only difficult, but also risky.

Along came XML to help with this problem. It was designed to address these issues by describing the data itself and not the presentation of the data. This approach obviously gives much more consideration to presenting information to a computer system than to a human user.

> **NOTE**   *When you realize the distinction between the intended use of XML and HTML, you realize just how inaccurate it is to think that XML will replace HTML.*

Now that we understand why XML was developed and for what it was intended, let's roll up our sleeves and get into it!

XML Structures

When writing in a metalanguage, first you need to consider the components involved. All XML code is defined through documents, elements, and attributes. For an XML data set to be well-formed, it must use these components in the correct manner. Otherwise, any XML parser will reject it.

> *Well-formed XML* is XML that complies with the syntax rules of the XML specification. Well-formed XML is often confused with valid XML, but the two are very different things. *Valid XML* refers to XML that complies with any declared definition(s).

Elements

A data point in XML is called an *element*. Elements are the basic building blocks for XML. They are used to define every piece of data. The following code is an example of an element called "city":

```
<city>Dallas</city>
```

Tags

You'll notice that the element is annotated with two tags. The metadata in each tag is often called the *element name*. However, as we will see later, this may be misleading if additional information is provided in the tag.

A distinction is also made between the two tags surrounding the element data. The *start tag* is the XML code preceding the data, and the *end tag* is the segment of XML code following the data. Together, these tags define an element of XML. At a minimum, the difference between the end tag and the start tag is the / sign preceding the metadata in the end tag. This is standard notation. Additionally, any attributes that are defined for the element will be declared only in the start tag, not in the end tag. We will look at attributes in the next section.

TIP   *As we go through some XML in this book, you may want to modify and test some of the code on your own. Several XML parsers are available, but the easiest option may be to use Internet Explorer (version 5.0 or higher) to run quick tests. (See Figure 3-1.) Internet Explorer includes the Microsoft XML parser, which has been regularly updated to keep pace with the changes made by revisions to the specification. It provides a quick view of any XML file with a collapsible/expandable view, but unfortunately the current version can check only how well-formed code is, not its validity. You can update your browser to support validation if you install the MSXML 4.0 parser.*

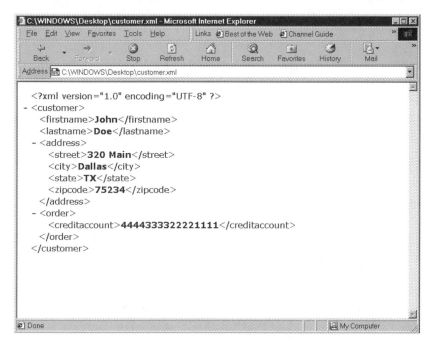

Figure 3-1. Internet Explorer view of an XML document

Empty Elements

In the "Dallas" example, the element contains some data. However, it can also be acceptable for an element to be defined, but contain no data. Such an element, as seen below, is called an *empty element*.

```
<city></city>
```

For reasons we will discuss later, it is often better to have an empty element than simply to remove the element or leave it out. Even if there is no data, the element must have both start and end tags. Without them, it would not be well-formed XML. For example, the following code would produce an error when run through an XML parser:

```
<location>
    <city>
</location>
```

However, there is an acceptable shorthand method for defining elements that are present but empty. This is done by adding a / to the end of what would normally be the start tag. Here is an example of how this shorthand would look:

```
<city/>
```

Nesting

Any procedural or functional language depends on nesting for its code structure, and metalanguages possibly even more so than other languages. An understanding of proper nesting is crucial to writing syntactically proper XML code. If tags are not nested properly, a parsing application will have no way of understanding the relationships between the various elements in your data. This is one area in which HTML parsers are very forgiving, so you will want to make sure that you don't continue any bad habits you may have from working with HTML code.

Nesting is the idea of grouping start and end tags in the appropriate sequence. Here is an example of nesting using just two elements:

```
<element>
    <nested_element>
    </nested_element>
</element>
```

Notice how the nested element's start tag comes after the element's start tag. That means the nested element's end tag must come before the element's end tag.

This makes the nested element entirely contained within the element. The idea is to avoid the intersecting of elements. Here is an example of an intersection:

```
<element>
    <nested_element>
    </element>
</nested_element>
```

In this example the element is closed before the nested element is closed. This would cause an error in an XML parser, but would be overlooked by most HTML parsers. Because start tags can be combined and used in various ways, the key is keeping track of the end tags. Make sure that each end tag only follows its start tag mate or a nested element's end tag.

> **TIP** *It is a good idea to use indentation to keep track of your nested pairs when writing your XML even though it makes the writing go more slowly. If you back out of an element's indention only when the end tag closes the element, it will help you catch errors. Some editors may do this for you, although not without some inconsistency.*

Element Relationships

Elements that are nested within other elements are referred to as *children* or *child nodes*. Not surprisingly, the elements that contain other elements are referred to as *parent nodes*.

Elements do not have to be nested inside other elements. Elements that reside at the same level are often called *peers* or *siblings*. Here is an example of two nested element siblings:

```
<element>
    <nested_element/>
    <nested_element/>
</element>
```

Notice that the nested elements have the same name. This is allowed and acceptable. In fact, this is an example of the extensible nature of the XML specification, which gives you a lot of flexibility. With multiple instances of the same element allowed, it is almost the equivalent data structure to a dynamically allocated array used in some programming languages. We will see later how there are additional mechanisms to disallow our XML data from using this feature in error.

Attributes

A structure is available to provide more information about an element. Attributes are declared and valuated in the start tag of an element. The value is declared within a pair of double quotes, as shown here:

```
<element attribute="value"/>
```

The attribute value has to be defined even if it is empty, as shown here:

```
<element attribute=""/>
```

> **TIP**   *Single quotes can also be used to define the values of attributes but are merely translated into double quotes by most parsers. This can be helpful if you are building XML strings with programming languages in which double quotes have significance. Whenever feasible, you are better off sticking with just double quotes to ensure compliance with applications and maintaining consistency throughout your code.*

Attributes allow you to define information without using extra elements and thus take less space. An attribute requires less space to declare and define because there are no start and end tags. However, some people think that attributes do not provide any advantages because they are more difficult to parse and work with. We will look at some of these arguments when we start working with XML data in the next chapter, but remember that you can choose whether to define your data through attributes or elements. Let's look at some examples.

Data defined through XML elements only:

```
<customer>
    <firstname>John</firstname>
    <lastname>Smith</lastname>
    <birthday>071671</birthday>
    <favorite_sport>hockey</favorite_sport>
</customer>
```

The same data defined through XML attributes:

```
<customer firstname="John" lastname="Smith" birthday="071671"
  favorite_sport="hockey"/>
```

If you look closely at both sets of code, you will notice that they both expose the same data set. However, the strict element approach takes 140 characters, while the attribute approach takes only 87 characters. That is a difference of about 38 percent. Depending on your priorities and situation, this may be pertinent to your application. I recommend reserving judgment until we try working with the XML built with each of these approaches.

> **TIP**   *Referencing the metadata within a tag as the name of the element is complicated if you have an attribute of that element defined as "name." For instance, in the tag* `<customer name="John Smith"/>`, *is the name of the element "customer" or "John Smith"? I recommend avoiding such an attribute for this reason along with the fact that ambiguously named attributes have limited value.*

Documents

Up to this point, we have been talking about XML as free-floating code. One aspect of XML that differentiates it from many other data languages is its top-level structure. Any well-formed XML must always have a single root-level element encapsulating the entire data set. This qualifies an XML data set as a document.

> **NOTE**   *Information can be provided prior to the root node in a well-formed XML document. This can largely be regarded as optional header information, which I will discuss in the next section.*

The Document Node

Often the top-level element is called the *document node*. Here is an example of an XML document:

```
<document>
    <element>
        <nested_element>
        </nested_element>
    </element>
    <element attribute="value"/>
</document>
```

The Invalid Document

Looking at just this structure of XML data, it may seem hard to conceive of another structure in which the XML data would not be considered a well-formed document. To reinforce this definition, here is an example of XML data that is not well formed because it is not in a document.

```
<customer>
    <firstname>John</firstname>
    <lastname>Smith</lastname>
</customer>
<order>
    <number>1198054</number>
    <total>157.45</total>
</order>
```

Here we have some XML defining a customer and an order, presumably related to the customer. We are presuming because there is nothing explicitly telling us they are related because no document node is provided. So we see here an example of what is not a document as well as why we have documents. With a root node, a parser can theoretically look at the first node of an XML document and discern what the information contained pertains to. This helps us to make our algorithms a little more efficient so that we can avoid spending time digging into XML and finding nothing of value.

The Well-formed Document

To make the preceding XML a well-formed document, we have a couple of choices. One is to simply add a root-level node, as shown here:

```
<document>
    <customer>
        <firstname>John</firstname>
        <lastname>Smith</lastname>
    </customer>
    <order>
        <number>1198054</number>
        <total>157.45</total>
    </order>
</document>
```

Adding a root-level node made this XML well formed, but it is really the easy way out. If we put a little more thought into it, we can come up with a more usable solution. For instance, since the order belongs to the customer, we could just make the customer the root node and relate everything to that entity. This way a parser will know at the first level what information it can find in the document. Here is an example:

```
<customer>
    <firstname>John</firstname>
    <lastname>Smith</lastname>
    <order>
        <number>1198054</number>
        <total>157.45</total>
    </order>
</customer>
```

In this implementation, we have also chosen to nest order information as subelements under the root customer node. Other implementations could have the order number and total listed as distinct elements directly under the customer node, as seen later. While this data set provides the same information, it does so in a subtly different way that may have bigger implications than you realize.

```
<customer>
    <firstname>John</firstname>
    <lastname>Smith</lastname>
    <order_number>1198054</order_number>
    <order_total>157.45</order_total>
</customer>
```

One advantage of the document approach is that we are helping our applications to discern, through the parser, what type of data is contained in the document. This same approach can and should be carried throughout the document as a best practice. Whenever you group information in categories, you limit the amount of "crawling" your applications have to do to work with the data. This concept is very similar to the idea of normalizing a database. XML can, after all, be considered a flat file representation of a data source.

> *Normalization* refers to the practice of designing a data model based on normal forms that eliminate redundant data by defining relationships.

The Structure of Your Data

Just as you can overnormalize a database, you can "overtier" your XML data set. For instance, if we take our customer example, we can break it down as shown here:

```
<customer>
    <name>
        <first>John</first>
        <last>Smith</last>
    </name>
    <order>
        <number>1198054</number>
        <total>157.45</total>
    </order>
</customer>
```

Here we are pulling the first and last name into a subelement called *name*. Hopefully this seems pretty ridiculous for this scenario because it is overkill. To help discern when information should be broken out and contained in a subelement, I try to follow a few rules:

- The data can be grouped into a sensible category.

- The data in the category may possibly change.

- The data is typically accessed as a group and rarely accessed separately.

- The data is optional for some processes needing other information in the document.

- The data never or only occasionally contains just one nonempty node.

If we apply these rules to the data set we have been working with, we can probably agree that the following is the most appropriate structure for our document:

```
<customer>
    <firstname>John</firstname>
    <lastname>Smith</lastname>
    <order>
        <number>1198054</number>
        <total>157.45</total>
    </order>
</customer>
```

The XML Declaration

The XML specification also recommends that you include an XML declaration at the top of a document. This is encouraged, but is not a requirement, since no parser will produce an error from the lack of such a declaration. When you use an XML declaration, it is important to list it before any elements.

This declaration would read as shown here:

```
<?xml version="1.0"?>
```

This is basically the equivalent to the standard HTML header tag, as shown here:

```
<!DOCTYPE HTML PUBLIC "-//W3C//DTD HTML 4.0 Transitional//EN">
```

> **NOTE** *If and when the XML specification is updated and backward compatibility is not maintained, this declaration might play a much more vital role. As such, it can be treated as optional header information.*

The Text Declaration

One piece of additional information that can be specified in the XML declaration is the text declaration. This contains the encoding type of the document. Usually you will use one of the standard character encoding types of UTF-8 and UTF-16, which all parsers must support by default and do not need to be explicitly declared. Other encoding schemes you can specify include ISO-10646-UCS-2,

ISO-10646-UCS-4, and ISO-8859-2. Any encoding type specified by the Internet Assigned Numbers Authority (IANA) is recommended. Only one type per document can be specified without error and would look like this:

```
<?xml version="1.0" encoding="EUC-JP"?>
```

Encoding is the process of defining data on a binary level.

Syntax Rules

Now that we have an idea of how to structure our XML documents and the data in them, let's take a look at some of the syntax rules.

Character Conventions

First, we need to cover the character conventions supported by XML. The most common issue with new XML developers is the use of spaces in tag names. Spaces are not legal characters in XML element names. This can be disturbing unless you realize the reason. Consider the following two lines of code:

```
...<first name/>...
...<first name=""/>...
```

When XML parsers encounter a space after the element name, they think you are declaring an attribute. Of course you have to define the value even if it is null, and the parser has no way to discern how the data should be interpreted.

Lowercase Code

Notice that in all of these examples I use lowercase letters. XML is case sensitive, and I prefer to avoid problems in that area by just using lowercase letters when possible. For more advanced or complex names, I prefer to concatenate them with uppercase characters or use the underscore character for readability. The important thing, obviously, is to standardize on an approach in your environment to keep down the number of errors.

Special Characters and the CDATA Tag

As usual, there are some special characters that we need to be aware of. These are special characters because of the meaning they have for XML in defining entities and values. These characters need to be replaced by numeric references.

Table 3-1 identifies these special characters and the numeric equivalents that can be used in their stead.

Table 3-1. XML Special Characters

CHARACTER	NAME	NUMERIC REFERENCE
<	less than	&#60;
>	greater than	&#62;
"	double quote	&#32;
&	ampersand	&#38;
'	apostrophe	&#39;

Another way to contain the special characters in a nonfunctional mode is by using the CDATA tag. This tag tells the parser to treat the entire content as character data and not markup. By using brackets, the CDATA tag encapsulates the tags as such, as shown here:

```
<![CDATA[<city>San Jose</city>]]>
```

This tag should not be confused with the element tag because it cannot be nested.

Comments

Comments should also be a part of any language's syntax, and XML is no different. Fortunately the XML syntax is the same as HTML's, so if you are familiar with that, you don't have to learn anything new! Comments are handled through a single tag along with some additional annotations. Here is a sample:

```
<!-- This is a comment -->
```

Special HTML Tags

Special HTML tags are usually not valid in XML. For example, the nonbreaking space special character in HTML is " ", which produces an error in an XML validator. There are some special tags for XML that allow you to accomplish many of the same things. We will look at some of those a little later.

> **NOTE** *This issue may seem rather moot since XML wasn't intended for presentation delivery. However, this becomes an issue once you get into a situation where your HTML needs to be XML compliant.*

While we now understand how to build XML data sets, we need to establish definitions for our documents. This is important not only for maintaining consistency in our own usage, but also for communicating data to our partners. If we communicate a standard definition for each document, others will be able to parse and understand what our data means. This is a critical component to the implementation of another's Web service.

Defining XML

Because XML is a markup language, there is no internal mechanism for establishing the definition of a document. That fact caused the development and acceptance of other standards to fill this role. These standards work within the native abilities of XML to establish relationships with documents and define what a valid document is.

Because of XML's flexibility, standardizing a method for defining documents is quite an undertaking. XML is not a functional language, so you can't make passes through the code looking for key commands or definitions. In programming languages, you have a limited number of functional commands to be aware of. Variable names are also usually declared in the code with specific commands like "set" or "declare." In XML, any word can be an element name, an attribute name, or a value. Elements can be stacked any number of ways in multiple occurrences with multiple meanings. What number of approaches could you take to define the following code?

```
<name name="name">
    <name/>
    <name>
        <name name="name"/>
        name
    </name>
</name>
```

Of course you are thinking, "Who wants to do this?" The point is that this is legal code, and any means for defining an XML document would have to support it. Fortunately there are mechanisms like Document Type Definitions (DTDs), namespaces, and XML Schemas that help us to define our data.

The Document Type Definition

DTD was the first standard established to allow us to define XML data. In fact, DTD preceded XML a little because it was originally developed to work with SGML data. Of course, this transitioned to XML easily since it is an implementation of the SGML specification. DTDs allow us to specify data in great detail, defining required and optional elements, required and optional attributes, the relationships between our elements, and so forth.

While they do accomplish these objectives, DTDs have proven a little more difficult to work with in practice, mainly because DTDs use a unique language of their own. This issue is further compounded by the fact that DTD tags have a much more complex syntax than XML itself. That means yet another language to learn to define the documents we are creating in XML (the language we are concerned with)!

DTDs also cannot define data in enough detail for some implementations. For instance, DTDs have no way of defining the length of an element. While this may not be of concern for internal XML users, you will likely want partners less familiar with the service to know what the limits are of values being sent and received. Some applications would also benefit from knowing the data types of the elements involved. This could help consumers know whether they are working with numbers or strings.

> **NOTE** *A specification has been submitted to the W3C for defining data types in DTDs. The latest version of this specification, called Datatypes for DTDs (DT4DTD) 1.0, can be found at* http://www.w3.org/TR/dt4dtd. *However, this does not address the other challenges of working with DTDs.*

Despite this shortcoming, since DTDs were first and have been around so long, they have been widely implemented in applications and tools as the default standard for defining XML documents. Therefore, even though there are alternatives, we might have to support DTDs so that we don't exclude any potential consumers of our Web services.

Syntax

I will briefly cover some of the key concepts of the DTD syntax to help you understand the level of effort for building DTDs as well as allow you to build DTDs for some of your more basic documents.

Declaration Tags

While DTD does not use XML, it does utilize the markup language structure and does use tags for declaring components. These tags are used to identify entities, elements, attributes, and notations. Each tag is listed with its corresponding XML component in Table 3-2.

Table 3-2. DTD Declaration Tags

COMPONENT	TAG
Attributes	`<!ATTLIST . . .>`
Document	`<!DOCTYPE . . . [. . .]>`
Elements	`<!ELEMENT . . .>`
Entities	`<!ENTITY . . .>`
Notations	`<!NOTATION . . .>`

You can see that the tags themselves are fairly straightforward. However, the full implementation of these tags is less so.

The first tag you need to become familiar with is the document tag. In a sense this is the document type declaration itself, as all other components fall within the brackets in the document tag. The name you give the `doctype` tag is that of the root element, and you can have only one `doctype` per DTD, for obvious reasons. A sample DTD might look like the following:

```
<!DOCTYPE customer []>
```

Entities

Entities define XML-compliant data that can be referenced throughout an XML document that references the DTD. Often a separate DTD is used to define environment information, similar to the concept of include files. Entity values can only be established in the DTDs and cannot be changed in the XML, so it is more appropriate to think of them as constants instead of variables. If the data is referenced in the XML, the entity declaration looks like this:

```
<!ENTITY    fileroot    "c:\temp">
```

When the entity is referenced in the DTD itself, the entity declaration looks like this:

```
<!ENTITY    % fileroot    "c:\temp">
```

To then reference this entity in the DTD, use the following code:

```
%fileroot;
```

Entities will not support non-XML-compliant data. To define or reference this kind of information, use the notation tag, as shown here:

```
<!NOTATION. . .>
```

Elements

When you define elements, you start with the element type declaration. This involves defining the name and content model for that type. At a minimum, you must define the name of the element for it to be a valid declaration. Do this by following the ELEMENT keyword with the name of the element, as shown here:

```
<!ELEMENT customer>
```

This does more than simply declare the existence of the element. However, declaring a content model after the element name provides more information. The content model provides a high-level definition of the acceptable usage of a subelement in an element. The options are defined in Table 3-3.

Table 3-3. Element Content Models

DECLARATION	MEANING	SAMPLE
ANY	Any use	`<!ELEMENT customer ANY>`
EMPTY	No subelements	`<!ELEMENT customer EMPTY>`
(#PCDATA)	Character data only	`<!ELEMENT customer (#PCDATA)>`
(#PCDATA,. . .)	Mixed content can be used	`<!ELEMENT customer (#PCDATA, address) >`
(<values>,. . .)	Defined subelements used	`<!ELEMENT customer (address, order) >`

EMPTY declares the absolute exclusion of any child elements. ANY is entirely open and is assumed when no content model is provided, as in our customer element definition earlier. PCDATA stands for parsed character data and basically communicates that the data in the element can contain text. Without this listing, an element could contain child elements and attributes but have no actual value itself. With this control, we can restrict our elements to have just data or to have data and elements. However, when you incorporate the #PCDATA control in your elements, you lose some ability to use other control mechanisms. One such mechanism is the evaluation controls. These are listed in Table 3-4.

Table 3-4. Evaluation Controls

CONTROL	MEANING	SAMPLE
,	sequence	address, order
|	OR	address|order
( )	grouping	(address|order), address

In evaluating the content of an element, a comma is used to define a sequence, whereas multiple child elements may be defined. A vertical bar defines the logical OR selection, which means an option between two or more values exists. The parentheses are simply a means for grouping various values for more complex content definitions.

Another method for defining a content sequence is using the content occurrence characters listed in Table 3-5. These characters allow you to define the frequency of child elements in an element's content.

Table 3-5. Occurrence Characters

CHARACTER	MEANING	SAMPLE
*	0 or more instances	address*
+	1 or more instances	address+
?	0 or 1 instances	address?

Building a DTD

To bring all of this together, let's look at a list of possible business rules. To define a customer in an XML document, our code will define a customer element that supports the following rules:

- One first name

- One last name

- Multiple addresses, but at least one

- Up to three street entries per address

- Multiple orders with no minimum

- A credit or checking account for each order

To make sure we have a good understanding of the requirements, it is often helpful to create an XML document or two that might serve as baseline samples to help us build our definition file. Here is a sample customer document:

```
<customer>
      <firstname>John</firstname>
      <lastname>Doe</lastname>
      <address>
            <street>320 Main</street>
            <city>Dallas</city>
            <state>TX</state>
            <zipcode>75234</zipcode>
      </address>
      <order>
            <creditaccount>4444333322221111</creditaccount>
      </order>
</customer>
```

Now let's take a look at the DTD that defines this XML in the following code:

```
<!ELEMENT customer (firstname?, lastname?, address+, order*)>
<!ELEMENT firstname (#PCDATA) >
<!ELEMENT lastname (#PCDATA) >
<!ELEMENT address (street+, city, state, zipcode) >
<!ELEMENT order (creditaccount | checkingaccount) >
<!ELEMENT street (#PCDATA) >
<!ELEMENT city (#PCDATA) >
<!ELEMENT state (#PCDATA) >
<!ELEMENT zipcode (#PCDATA) >
<!ELEMENT creditaccount (#PCDATA) >
<!ELEMENT checkingaccount (#PCDATA) >
```

Notice how we had some limitations in how tightly we could match our requirements. First, we have no way of requiring one and only one instance of a child element as we might want to for the first name and last name elements. Also, we have no mechanism for limiting the number of street entries in our address element to three. These are some of the types of issues that were identified early on and the industry tried to resolve through the XSD standard.

Attributes

Now that we know how to define the elements and their children in a DTD, we will look at defining the attributes of an element. With a first glance at the tag for attributes, you might come to the correct conclusion that the ATTLIST tag contains the list of all attributes instead of singling them out. However, elements and attributes are not tied together through any hierarchical system the way the XML itself would link them. Instead, it relates the two based on the tag name of the element. For instance, if the element name is "customer," then the attribute is identified by the same name, as shown here:

```
<!ELEMENT customer>
<!ATTLIST customer
    firstname
    lastname
>
```

While this may seem unintuitive, it does give you the flexibility of separating the element definition from its defined attributes. Such an organization would, however, make it a little more difficult for human interpretation, as this example shows:

```
<!ELEMENT customer>
<!ELEMENT order>
<!ATTLIST customer
    firstname
    lastname
>
<!ATTLIST order
    number
    status
>
```

Just as we had a way to define the existence of child elements in elements, we have the same control of the attribute definition. We can use the same controls for defining values in each attribute, but instead of the occurrence characters, the keywords in Table 3-6 define the instance restrictions.

Table 3-6. Attribute Declarations

DECLARATION	MEANING
CDATA	Attribute value can be any character data.
#FIXED "value"	Required attribute; value specified in quotes.
#IMPLIED	Optional attribute.
#REQUIRED	Attribute value must be specified.
"value"	Attribute default value specified in quotes.

If we go back to our customer business requirements, we can take a different approach to our definition by maximizing our use of these attribute declarations. If we transition some of our data from elements to attributes, our DTD is shown in the following code:

```
<!ELEMENT customer (address+, order*)>
<!ATTLIST customer
     firstname     CDATA      #REQUIRED
     lastname      CDATA      #REQUIRED
>
<!ELEMENT address (street+) >
<!ATTLIST address
     city     CDATA     #REQUIRED
     state    CDATA     #REQUIRED
     zipcode     CDATA     #REQUIRED
>
<!ELEMENT street (#PCDATA)>
<!ELEMENT order (creditaccount | checkingaccount) >
<!ELEMENT creditaccount (#PCDATA) >
<!ELEMENT checkingaccount (#PCDATA) >
```

This code shows how the XML document produced from this definition might differ from our earlier definition:

```
<customer firstname="John" lastname="Doe">
     <address city="Dallas" state="TX" zipcode="75234">
          <street>320 Main</street>
     </address>
     <order>
          <creditaccount>4444333322221111</creditaccount>
     </order>
</customer>
```

Notice how we split the address element content into child elements and attributes. The street data could not be transitioned to attribute data because we had to support multiple instances, which attributes cannot do. Although we have a tighter definition with city, state, and zip code now required, there are two reasons why this is not be a good implementation. First, we are taking one logical set of data and requiring an application that likely needs both to use two different parsing processes to extract the information. For reasons we will explore later, parsing attributes and parsing elements are two very different tasks, and you want to optimize your applications by utilizing one or the other (probably elements). Second, we are changing our data structure to comply with our data definition mechanism. This is akin to redesigning a database schema to fit inside a diagram view. If possible, we should make our definitions work for us, not the other way around.

To finish our coverage of the syntax of DTDs, let's look at a few very important rules that may not have been obvious during our examples:

- Do not reuse the same element name more than once.

- Make sure your document name matches the name of your root element.

- Do not list child elements more than once in an element's declaration.

- Do not list child elements whose definitions cannot be referenced.

Now that we know how to build DTDs, let's take a quick look at how we can use them to define and validate our XML data.

Implementation

An XML document can either contain the DTD or point to a DTD that contains its definition. This allows you to either reuse your definitions very easily and maintain efficient code or encapsulate all data and its definition in one file for simpler transport. Obviously you want to externalize your definition whenever possible so that you don't transmit extraneous information.

If you list the code directly, place the DTD code after the XML declaration tag, as shown here:

```
<?xml version="1.0" encoding="UTF-8"?>
```

To reference an external DTD, identify the path to the DTD through the document declaration, as shown here:

```
<?xml version="1.0" encoding="UTF-8"?>
<!DOCTYPE customer SYSTEM "http://www.apress.com/customer.dtd">
```

Additionally, you can reference external DTDs from within the DTD itself. This can be helpful for reusing the definitions of elements in other DTDs. We can do this by loading an external DTD into an entity declaration and then exposing it directly in the document type declaration, as shown here:

```
<?xml version="1.0" encoding="UTF-8"?>
<!ENTITY % order.dtd SYSTEM "http://www.apress.com/order.dtd">

    <!ELEMENT customer (firstname?, lastname?, address+, order*)>
    <!ELEMENT firstname (#PCDATA) >
    <!ELEMENT lastname (#PCDATA) >
    <!ELEMENT address (street+, city, state, zipcode) >
%order.dtd;
. . .
```

At this point you should be comfortable with writing your own DTDs. However, even with this quick look we have run into a few barriers with this approach, and you will probably encounter more if you work further with DTDs. Fortunately, we have a new standard in development that can help us with some of these issues.

Namespaces

With the extensibility and flexibility of XML come a few potential data integrity issues that have to be addressed. One of these is definition for our data, which is addressed by DTDs or XML Schemas (which we will look at later in this chapter). Another integrity issue is the coexistence of matching tag names. This is where namespaces can be helpful. *Namespaces* are a mechanism for qualifying elements and attributes as part of an entity structure.

Understanding the Element Conflict Issue

You can think of namespaces as a categorization or grouping of tags that differentiates them from other tags utilizing the same names. Let's consider the potential problems of having common tags used in different ways for different elements. For example, how does one differentiate between element and attribute names that are reused in different contexts?

Consider this example:

```
<movie>
    <title>Forrest Gump</title>
    <actor>
        <character>Forrest Gump</character>
            <name>Tom Hanks</name>
    </actor>
    <director>
        <name>Robert Zemeckis</name>
    </director>
</movie>
```

In parsing this data, how do you differentiate between the names of the actor and the director? If you know the complete path, you can make sure you are getting the name of the actor instead of the director, but without a definition file (which will sometimes be the case), a program may not be able to differentiate the two. This problem becomes even more obvious when sharing XML across organizational boundaries that implement XML in different ways.

Perhaps another organization uses the following document to describe the same information:

```
<movie title="Raiders of the Lost Ark">
    <actor character ="Indiana Jones" name="Harrison Ford"/>
    <director name="Steven Spielberg"/>
</movie>
```

XML definitions can help clarify the data to others, but clearly something more is needed to distinguish the usage of common element and attribute names with different meanings. Fortunately, the W3C has defined a specification called namespaces that addresses this area.

Declaring Namespaces

The qualification namespaces provide is really just a formal declaration of a set of element and attribute names. The actual element name changes only slightly by the addition of a prefix. For instance, the `<movie>` tag might become `<organizationa:movie>`. You can think of the effect of declaring a namespace as similar to naming a place or person. To identify somebody as a girl is very general, but identifying that person as Lauren is more specific. Certainly there can be many Laurens in the world, but you are using a proper noun to identify her. So, in a sense, you can equate regular elements as nouns and namespace elements as proper nouns.

Do not confuse individually declared namespaces with standards. Although namespaces can be used to define standards (such as XHTML and XSLT), namespaces are a tool that can be used at anyone's discretion to help address the problem of uniquely identifying XML data. That means you could standardize your organization on using namespaces for every piece of XML that is created. However, this is probably overkill, since you can use just your XML definition files for defining XML structures. While namespaces don't require definition files (either DTDs or XML Schemas), you also don't need to use namespaces to define your data. Namespaces are a formal declaration of your XML definition, but there is actually no inherent relationship between the two other than the declarations in your XML document.

Each namespace should be declared as a Uniform Resource Identifier (URI) reference in the element of an XML document where you want to utilize it. This URI address actually points to nothing. It is simply using the URI as a global reference point that does nothing but assist you with the declaration of the namespace.

> *URN* (Uniform Resource Name), *URI* (Uniform Resource Identifier), and *URL* (Uniform Resource Locator) are often used interchangeably and mean essentially the same thing: an address referencing information on a server accessible via the Internet or your intranet. There are subtle differences in their formal definitions that should specify what kind of information they can reference, but most uses do not make this distinction.

The following is an example of declaring the namespace for our first movie data set:

```
<movie xmlns:organizationa = "http://organizationa.com/schema">
```

In this example, xmlns is the attribute containing the URI value, and organizationa is the prefix value assigned to that namespace. The movie element is not actually identified as a component of the namespace. To accomplish this, you have to prefix the movie tag name itself, as shown here:

```
<organizationa:movie xmlns:organizationa = "http://organizationa.com/schema">
```

CAUTION *Sample URNs, URIs, and URLs often point to a directory instead of a specific page in the directory. The implication is either that the destination has no real meaning (as is the case with namespaces) or that any request of that directory on the server will return a default page that provides the necessary information. The idea is that you can be more flexible in your definition files (for example, switching from a DTD to an XML Schema). This is not something a server does by default, so you or your Web server's administrator must set this up.*

Referencing Namespaces

This example should make it obvious that we have established a relationship between the namespace reference and the prefix "organizationa." Every subelement that has a declared prefix utilizes its corresponding namespace. However, this explicit declaration is not necessary when only one namespace is utilized because it is implied. For instance, the following two XML data sets work exactly the same way.

This is an explicit namespace reference:

```
<organizationa:movie xmlns:organizationa="http://organizationa.com/schema">
    <organizationa:title>Forrest Gump</organizationa:title>
    <organizationa:actor>
        <organizationa:character>Forrest Gump</organizationa:character>
        <organizationa:name>Tom Hanks</organizationa:name>
    </organizationa:actor>
</organizationa:movie>
```

This is an implicit namespace reference:

```
<organizationa:movie xmlns:organizationa = "http://organizationa.com/schema">
    <title>Forrest Gump</title>
    <actor>
        <character>Forrest Gump</character>
        <name>Tom Hanks</name>
    </actor>
</organizationa:movie>
```

If you choose, or are forced, to use an explicit naming implementation, you may want to put more thought into the prefix you choose for your namespace reference. The prefix organizationa is quite long; org-a would probably suffice.

> **TIP**   *Although some purists believe that no attempt to minimize tag names should be made because it contradicts the spirit of XML, I believe there should be some restraint. For instance, I would maintain some descriptive identity, but not take up excessive space with unnecessary text. More text means more data to send over the wire and more cycles for the parsers and writers working with the data. One character won't make much difference, but five characters actually add up to at least 15 characters (or 15 bytes) once you declare them and use them for one element (start and end tags).*

Referencing Multiple Namespaces

You might have noticed that I left out the director element from the last two code examples. This is because the name element was utilized as a subelement of the director element. Since our namespace had already declared the name element as a subelement of the actor element, we needed a second namespace for the director. Since we are working with a single structure here that will often, if not always, contain actor and director elements, this may be a case in which we should redesign our XML to make it easier to use one namespace. For this scenario, we will do away with the name element under the director element. This leaves us with the following data set:

```
<org-a:movie xmlns:org-a = "http://organizationa.com/schema">
     <title>Forrest Gump</title>
     <actor>
          <character>Forrest Gump</character>
          <name>Tom Hanks</name>
     </actor>
     <director>Robert Zemeckis</director>
</org-a:movie>
```

> **TIP**   *This is an excellent example of a design decision that you may be faced with in the real world when working with XML. While you certainly don't want to compromise the integrity of your data model, you want to make it as easy as possible to build XML that is valid and logical. In this case, the overhead of using two namespaces for one data structure (which you own) is probably not worth the tradeoff of maintaining multiple uses of the name element.*

While this one namespace is a good solution for our movie data structure, some data structures will still need to reference more than one namespace when we start working with multiple forms of the same data. This will require not only two or more namespaces, but also explicit declaration of which namespace each element utilizes. Let's see what the utilization of multiple namespaces looks like by combining our current movie data model with the earlier attribute-centric movie data model. To maintain a well-formed XML structure, let's declare this information as a listing of available videos at a store (thus using videos as our root element). This definition is shown in the following code:

```
<videos>
    <org-a:movie xmlns:org-a="http://organizationa.com/schema">
        <title>Forrest Gump</title>
        <actor>
            <character>Forrest Gump</character>
            <name>Tom Hanks</name>
        </actor>
        <director>Robert Zemeckis</director>
    </org-a:movie>
    <org-b:movie xmlns:org-b = http://organizationb.com/schema
    title="Forrest Gump">
        <actor character ="Forrest Gump" name="Tom Hanks"/>
        <director name="Robert Zemeckis"/>
    </org-b:movie>
</videos>
```

This is really the easy way to use two namespaces in one document. It could be argued that both namespaces should really be declared at the root element and referenced as needed in each element. This is somewhat analogous to declaring global variables versus declaring local variables, but without the same repercussions. This code shows what it looks like:

```
<videos xmlns:org-a = "http://organizationa.com/schema"
  xmlns:org-b ="http://organizationb.com/schema">
    <org-a:movie>
        <org-a:title>Forrest Gump</org-a:title>
        <org-a:actor>
            <org-a:character>Forrest Gump</org-a:character>
            <org-a:name>Tom Hanks</org-a:name>
        </org-a:actor>
        <org-a:director>Robert Zemeckis</org-a:director>
    </org-a:movie>
    <org-b:movie title="Raiders of the Lost Ark">
        <org-b:actor character ="Indiana Jones" name="Harrison Ford"/>
        <org-b:director name="Steven Spielberg"/>
    </org-b:movie>
</videos>
```

> **TIP** *You will want to minimize the number of times you reference a namespace in a given XML document. Accomplishing this may require defining your namespaces at a higher element level than absolutely necessary and then explicitly declaring your namespaces at each element, which requires a bit more effort. The reason you want to minimize the number of namespace declarations is that the parser has to handle the URI every time, and that really should be avoided when unnecessary.*

You can also exempt certain elements from namespaces that have been declared. Remember that all child elements implicitly assume a parent's defined namespace. You may sometimes want to "break out" of that with a child element. You can do this by simply defining a null namespace for that element like this:

```
<movie xmlns=""/>
```

> **CAUTION** *Some XML experts have stated that unprefixed elements do not belong to any namespace declared at any level, but section 5.2, "Namespace Defaulting," of the namespace specification clearly states that child elements implicitly reference their parent's namespace when no namespace has been declared.*

You can also reference namespaces at just the attribute level. You might want to do this to maintain a consistent data type or validation across different elements and schemas. In this example, we are using a namespace to help us define a list of monetary attributes:

```
<price finance:currency="US">3.95</price>
```

Unlike some topics we have discussed, I have probably covered the majority of the specification for namespaces and have certainly covered all of the material relevant to our topic of Web services. Still, if you wish to cover every aspect, I encourage you to visit the W3C site or check out one of the many XML books available that cover namespaces.

The XML Schema

The XML Schema Definition Language (XML Schema, XSD) is the "new kid on the block" for defining XML documents. This is an attempt to modernize the DTD concept and adapt it for the specific needs of XML. With support for tighter validation and strong data typing, it does fill in some of the gaps of DTDs.

One of the biggest improvements in XSD over DTD is the definition language. XML Schemas are created using XML! That means you don't have to learn another syntax just to define your XML data.

At this point, XSD is merely a recommendation to the W3C, so it is likely to go through a few more changes before being finalized. You can find the current version of the specification and its status at the W3C site:
`http://www.w3.org/XML/Schema`.

> **CAUTION** *My discussion of the XML Schema specification is based on the W3C Candidate Recommendation dated October 24, 2000. Any changes to the specification made since this recommendation will not be reflected, so take care in transferring any of this code or information directly to production applications.*

While there are many tools that already support the existing recommendations of XML Schemas, DTDs are also still widely used and supported. Unfortunately, the development and adoption of standards take some time. While most people would have a hard time arguing that XSDs are not better than DTDs for defining XML, these issues have caused hesitation for cautious vendors.

> **CAUTION** *Do not confuse XML Schemas with XDR (XML-Data Reduced) Schemas. XDR was a Microsoft-led attempt to define a new XML Schema language before the W3C started work on it. XDR has been replaced by XML Schema industry-wide and is now supported only by Microsoft parsers.*

I see XSDs as being the practical standard going forward for defining our XML documents. However, many implementations may need to support both for the sake of not excluding legacy XML applications. Instead of focusing on the details, I will cover just the main constructs and minimal requirements for defining schemas for Web services interfaces.

> **NOTE** *Who would have thought we would be discussing "legacy XML applications" at this point?! While some have been critical of the standards process, this really reflects the speed at which new standards can and have been developed and enhanced.*

The XML Schema specification is quite involved and defines a multitude of entities and scenarios. I will not cover the specification in all its details (that is quite easily a book in and of itself), but will merely cover the highlights that will allow you to build the basic schemas necessary for providing Web services and following the samples later in the book.

Schemas

Schemas are actually a collection of entities called *schema components*. There are 12 of these components in total, falling into three main categories as shown in Table 3-7.

Table 3-7. XML Schema Components

CATEGORY	COMPONENT
Primary	Simple type definitions
	Complex type definitions
	Attribute declarations
	Element declarations
Secondary	Attribute group definitions
	Identity-constraint definitions
	Model group definitions
	Notation declarations
Helper	Annotations
	Model groups
	Particles
	Wildcards

We will focus on only a subset of these components, namely, the simple type, complex type, and attribute group definitions and the attribute and element declarations. As a byproduct of this discussion we will also touch on a few other components. There are several mechanisms allowing declarations and definitions that you can utilize in defining your XML documents.

The same high-level concepts of documents and content models from DTDs apply to XML Schemas. That means that much of your knowledge about DTDs should translate easily. For instance, we have a set of base tags that defines every entity in our definition as shown in Table 3-8.

Table 3-8. XML Schema Declaration Tags

COMPONENT	TAG
Document	<schema>
Elements	<simpletype> or <complextype>
Attributes	<attributetype>
Data type	<datatype>

Every definition starts with a schema tag. Every component of the XML document resides in the schema tag. So a valid skeleton schema document looks like the following:

```
<schema>
</schema>
```

> **NOTE** *I will leave out references to the schema namespace until I address that in the next section.*

The schema element is simply a container for the actual definition. If it bothers you that the schema doesn't have a name, keep in mind that the schema is always the root node, and so the filename of the document is actually the name of the schema.

To populate this schema then involves adding a series of elements associated with data types. Unfortunately, this is where the simplicity stops. Schemas are very complex structures that have many rules to go with their flexibility. Like any journey, it is good to begin with a view of the destination. To let you know where we are going and what it will look like, I will give you a snapshot of a complete schema in Listing 3-1. If you are like me, you will want to jump right into it and dissect the syntax and code. However, I recommend not spending too much time looking into this code, since it is likely to confuse you if you do not have a good understanding of the building blocks, which I will attempt to provide in the remaining sections of this chapter.

Listing 3-1. Sample XML Schema

```
<?xml version="1.0" encoding="UTF-8"?>
<xsd:schema xmlns:xsd=http://www.w3.org/2000/10/XMLSchema
elementFormDefault="qualified">
    <xsd:element name="parent">
        <xsd:simpleType>
            <xsd:restriction base="child"/>
        </xsd:simpleType>
    </xsd:element>
    <xsd:element name="child">
        <xsd:complexType>
            <xsd:attribute name="name" type="xsd:string"/>
            <xsd:attribute name="value">
                <xsd:simpleType>
                    <xsd:restriction base="xsd:string">
                        <xsd:enumeration value="yes"/>
                        <xsd:enumeration value="no"/>
                    </xsd:restriction>
                </xsd:simpleType>
            </xsd:attribute>
        </xsd:complexType>
    </xsd:element>
</xsd:schema>
```

At first glance, this schema can look rather intimidating, but the syntax can be broken down into sections, one piece at a time. The first step to learning how to build schemas is gaining an understanding of their data types. We will start there and work our way back up through schema structures to this level of complex schema.

> **TIP** *It will be much easier to work with developing schemas if you select a good tool. Some, like the current version of XML Spy (www.xmlspy.com), will even do much of the work for you by taking an XML document and generating a schema. Since there are multiple ways to define the same XML document, any automated program will make some assumptions, so you may have to modify the resulting schema to match your needs.*

Data Types

The fundamental distinction between XML Schemas and DTDs manifests itself through data types. Schemas are built on this fundamental structure, whereas DTD is only now trying to integrate data typing into its definition of an XML document. The XML Schema specification itself has been defined in two sections, one for data types and the other for structures. The structures section defines the language itself, and the data types section covers the valid mechanisms for defining data types in schemas.

> *Data typing* is the process of defining the lexical and value space of data elements to closely match their intended use.

The root of this distinction between DTDs and XSDs is actually the intent of each standard. DTDs were designed to define documents. Of course any valid XML data set is actually a document, but they can be very different in their approaches. As I pointed out in the "Attributes" section earlier, you can represent the same data through two very different designs by utilizing attributes versus elements and subelements. Choosing the attributes approach creates a more document-oriented XML base, whereas utilizing elements begets a more data-oriented XML base. Attributes are harder and more costly to access and validate, so when this is necessary, pushing those values to elements makes the data more accessible and results in a "tighter" document. XML Schemas were designed as a tool for developers taking this approach.

> **CAUTION** *Although XML Schemas allow you to specify more of your XML data in greater detail, it comes at the cost of efficiency. Schemas can take up to four times the code of DTDs to define the same documents. Remember, DTDs were designed solely for document definition, whereas schemas utilize XML, so it has to be much more self-describing. The tradeoff will become much less as more tools for building schemas become available.*

There are two steps to declaring elements in a schema. The first step is to declare the data type(s) for that element. That is what we are discussing in this section. Once that is done, you must declare the element(s) utilizing that data type. We will discuss that in the following section.

Data types come in two different varieties: primitive and derived. *Primitive data types* are also referred to as the *base types* since they are not based on any other data type. *Derived data types* can be thought of as compound data types based on primitive or other derived data types. The idea of compound or derived data types should not be confused with complex type elements, which we will discuss in the next section.

Primitive Data Types

Table 3-9 shows a list of the available primitive data types in the schema specification. With these, you can both define data fields and generate new data types based on these base types. The only data types that are probably new to you and specific to schemas are recurringDuration and timeDuration. Other defined data types are used for namespaces but fall outside the scope of this book.

Table 3-9. XML Schema Primitive Data Types

NAME	DESCRIPTION	PATTERN
binary*	a base 2 number	0|1 . . .
Boolean	a true or false value	true|false
decimal	a base 10 number with a specification below 1	d.d. . .
double	a 64-bit representation of a float	+|– d. . .
float	a 32-bit, base 10 number that can be positive or negative	+|– d. . .
recurringDuration	a period of time that is recurring	yy-mm-ddThh:mm:ss.sss
string	a finite sequence of characters	
timeDuration	some duration of time	PyymmddThhmmss
uriReference	a network or system resource reference	

Note: Capital letters in the patterns represent required constants.

*The binary data type is not valid directly in schemas. According to the specification, such usage should cause an error in the schema. This data type is intended only as a base type for other derived data types.

Another data type available through schemas is the generated data type timeInstant. This is a single instance of time based on recurringDuration that specifies the century. Its pattern looks like ccyy-mm-ddThh:mm:ss.sss. Additionally, the time zone can be added by a Z to the right followed by a plus or minus sign and the hh:mm pattern representing the difference between the time zone and the local time.

These data types can be qualified in two ways: ordered and unordered. *Ordered data types* are those with values that fall in a specific sequence. For example, numbers increment from one value to another, say, 1 to 999. *Unordered data types* are not so restricted and are fairly independent. Instead of thinking of the different data types as either ordered or unordered, think of the ways in which they could be defined. For instance, a `timeDuration` certainly has a sequence, but it may also have defined, enumerated values.

Each of these two aspects has its own corresponding attributes. These attributes are used to either extend or restrict the data types used to declare the elements in your data. These are listed for you in Table 3-10. Understanding these attributes should help you grasp the difference between ordered and unordered data.

Table 3-10. XML Schema Ordered and Unordered Attributes

ORDERED	UNORDERED
duration	encoding
maxExclusive	enumeration
maxInclusive	length
minExclusive	maxLength
minInclusive	minLength
period	pattern
precision	whitespace
scale	

Ordered Attributes

Notice the commonalities between the ordered attributes in Table 3-10. Each attribute relates to some kind of range. It could be either a value range or a sequence range, but it definitely leads to a restriction of values. These attributes obviously are very appropriate to numbers, times, calendar dates, and even artificial sequences. Let's look at a few of the more common ordered attributes in more detail.

When you define ordered data types, the exclusive and inclusive sets are invaluable for defining ranges. I'm not quite sure why both implementations were incorporated into every numeric data type, but for floats and doubles, the restrictions can allow you to specify the range on a more granular level. For example, the exclusive range of the set (0.0,10.0) allows values only up to 9.9999. . ., but the inclusive range includes 10.0000. . . exactly. Since precision is arbitrary for floats and doubles, this may be your only avenue for defining the value exactly. I recommend using decimal numbers, when possible, to avoid this situation, since it offers precision through the scale attribute.

UPDATE *The W3C Proposed Recommendation of March 30, 2001, changed the* scale *attribute to the* fractionDigits *attribute and the* precision *attribute to the* totalDigits *attribute. They have the same meanings, just different names. Depending on the tool you are using, it may recognize both or just one or the other.*

I recommend that you standardize on one method to maintain consistency in both your data and your parsing applications. The tools you use to build your XML may standardize this for you, but sometimes you may want or need to define schemas manually. Also, if you have not standardized on XML tools, they may take different approaches, which will then be implemented across your organization. In general, I prefer to use inclusive ranges, since that is the typical syntax in most programming languages. Basically, the use of the exclusive set means the values defined are outside the range of your element, as shown here:

```
<simpleType name="exclusiverange">
    <restriction base="integer">
        <minExclusive>0</minExclusive>
        <maxExclusive>101</maxExclusive>
    </restriction>
</simpleType>
```

while use of the inclusive set means the values are in the range of your element, as shown here:

```
<simpleType name="inclusiverange">
    <restriction base="integer">
        <minInclusive>1</minInclusive>
        <maxInclusive>100</maxInclusive>
    </restriction>
</simpleType>
```

The previous two code segments define the same range, 1 to 100.

The precision attribute is used to declare the number of digits used to define a number. The scale is then used to declare the number of specific digits, or those digits to the right of the decimal, to define the number. The logical conclusion is that the scale value is always smaller than or equal to the precision value. The following is the realNumber element that utilizes the precision and scale attributes:

```
<simpleType name="realNumber">
    <restriction base="real">
        <precision>9</precision>
        <scale>2</scale>
    </restriction>
</simpleType>
```

Unordered Attributes

The unordered attributes contain many of the properties a developer would look for in limiting the possible values for very open data types. These attributes obviously have to be much broader in their application and are generally used in combination to formulate a meaningful data type for a document.

When you define the length for a data type, you actually have a couple of options. How you handle length affects how you program your applications to handle unordered data, so make these decisions carefully. First, you can define length like this:

```
<simpleType name="firstName">
    <restriction base="string">
        <length>20</length>
    </restriction>
</simpleType>
```

The necessary design decision here is "How do you handle this?" To better phrase this question, look at this alternative schema for firstName:

```
<simpleType name="firstName">
    <restriction base="string">
        <maxLength>20</maxLength>
    </restriction>
</simpleType>
```

Depending on how your logic is developed, there may be no difference between these two definitions. There may, however, be some size implications when using length, since that attribute defines a fixed size, which the existing data may not utilize completely. The duplication of logic necessary to handle both is unnecessary, so I recommend not implementing both in the same document. Fortunately, the specification prevents the same data type from utilizing length and either the `maxLength` or `minLength` attribute. Unfortunately, when working with XML data from outside your control, you may have to accommodate both meanings for similar nodes in different documents.

The reason for this discrepancy usually has to do with the source of the data and its intended use. If this `firstName` data element came from a database and is intended for recreating a database, `length` would likely be used. However, if the `firstName` data element is defined only as an interface element, a `minLength` as well as a `maxLength` property may be specified to ensure that the data can be validated against the business requirements. The best way to handle this is to stick primarily with the `minLength` and `maxLength` attributes when necessary and avoid the `length` attribute due to its ambiguity.

`Whitespace` is an attribute that is especially important on a data level for handling bulk text. This attribute has three predefined values that allow you to dictate the amount of normalization performed on the text: preserve, replace, and collapse. The *preserve* value means that no normalization should be performed on the string, so it does not change. The *replace* value means that all special layout characters (for example, tab, carriage return) are replaced with spaces. That means that this data:

```
<data>
Jere  Left Wing
Mike  Center
Brett Right Wing
<data>
```

is interpreted as this:

```
<data>Jere Left Wing Mike Center Brett Right Wing<data>
```

Finally, the *collapse* value communicates that all sequences of spaces should be compressed to single spaces (as browsers do with HTML).

Enumeration is one of the more important attributes you will use when defining your data. This is the mechanism for declaring the acceptable values for the field. For instance, to define a field called "sports," you could use the following schema:

```
<simpleType name="sports" base="string">
    <enumeration>Baseball</enumeration>
    <enumeration>Basketball</enumeration>
    <enumeration>Football</enumeration>
    <enumeration>Hockey</enumeration>
    <enumeration>Soccer</enumeration>
</simpleType>
```

The only valid values for the sports node would be Baseball, Basketball, Football, Hockey, and Soccer. (My apologies to the tennis players out there!) There is no mechanism for dictating order or preference through this attribute, so the application of this constraint may not be exactly as you intended.

> **CAUTION** *Remember that an application has to actually enforce the specification by interpreting and performing the functions based on these attributes. A tremendous amount of work is necessary to utilize the rules in the specification, especially for those applications generating XML data. Some of this is done in some of the XML parsers available, but much of it must fall to your applications generating and utilizing the data.*

Derived Data Types

Now that we know how to define and restrict our primitive data types, we can start to create our own. These would be called *derived data types*. These constructed data types are built by "inheriting" the simple types and further defining the different properties.

Many derived data types are also available directly from the specification. These are all based on primitive types or on another derived type. The derived data types provided by the specification are often referred to as "built-in." Some of the more common types are listed in Table 3-11, but you will need to refer to the specification for the current complete list.

Table 3-11. XML Schema Derived Data Types

NAME	DESCRIPTION	DERIVED FROM
CDATA	represents whitespace normalized strings	string
date	a specific day	timePeriod
integer	any whole number	decimal
language	language of the text	token
long	an integer between 2^64 & –2^64	integer
time	the time of a specific day	recurringDuration
timeInstant	single instance of time	recurringDuration
token	a nonsequenced string	CDATA

Simple Types

To create these derived data types, we have to utilize simple types. A *simple type* is an element that allows us to extend our base data types to generate derived data types. This is done by declaring a base type and restricting the available attributes. Simple types cannot extend data types, so only the existing attributes can be defined; no new attributes may be added to the base type. Let's walk through a few examples.

To define the long data type, we first have to define the integer data type by basing a simple type off a decimal and defining the scale as 0, as shown here:

```
<simpleType name="integer">
    <restriction base="decimal">
        <scale>0</scale>
    </restriction>
</simpleType>
```

Next, we will base another simple type called long and define the range to accommodate the appropriate values, as shown here:

```
<simpleType name="long">
    <restriction base="integer">
        <minInclusive>-9223372036854775808</minInclusive>
        <maxInclusive>9223372036854775807</maxInclusive>
    </restriction>
</simpleType>
```

Let's look at another example that isn't number based, but time based. Time stamping can be an important part to creating an audit trail during integration processes, so let's derive the built-in `timeInstant` data type.

> **UPDATE**   *The W3C Proposed Recommendation of March 30, 2001, changed the derived* `timeInstant` *attribute to* `dateTime` *base type. Since it is now a base type, the concept of deriving it is no longer appropriate. Additionally, the* `recurringDuration` *type was changed to the* `time` *data type, and the* `timeDuration` *to the* `duration` *data type. They have the same meanings, just different names and definitions. Depending on the tool you are using, it may recognize both specifications or just one of them.*

First, we will base it on the `recurringDuration` base type, which represents a repeating period of time. Obviously for an instance of time we don't need it recurring, so we will want to constrain the period attribute. Also, the period of time will need to be restricted to a single instance. To accomplish this, we will set the value for both the period and the duration to 0. However, both values are declared as `timeDuration` values and so must comply with the `timeDuration` lexical format. This means adding a "P" to the beginning (for period) and selecting one of the components of `timeDuration` (this can be Year, Month, Day, etc.). This will produce the following schema code:

```
<simpleType name="timeInstant">
    <restriction base="recurringDuration">
        <duration>P0Y</duration>
        <period>P0Y</period>
    </restriction>
</simpleType>
```

> A *lexical* format defines the possible representations for a given data type. For example, 64 and 2^6 are two lexical representations of the same value.

If you look at these derived data types, you may start to wonder what the difference is between these and the data types we were declaring earlier (firstName, sports). The answer is that there is really no difference. This only has value to the person declaring the type and how it will be used. This might do nothing more than add some context to an existing data type. With this realization, we can now consider every data type defined in our XML Schema on equal terms. This understanding is important to have as you define your data documents so that you can define the data elements you need and keep an eye toward reusability.

Keep in mind that we are only declaring data types, not actual elements that can be used in our XML data. What we have been doing is akin to declaring all of the types for variables in your code, but not the actual application variables. In the next section, we will start to tie elements to these data types so that they have meaning and relevance in our data.

Complex Types

We have already used the simple type element to generate derived data types. In the most basic terms, simple types define elements that have no child elements. They occur in an XML document only as the lowest node on their branch. Primitive or derived data types can define simple type elements. Complex type are elements much more robust than simple types because they can group multiple data types and incorporate attributes in their definitions. Complex types are necessary containers because elements cannot be defined as the children of other elements directly in schemas. Whenever you want to establish a parent-child relationship between elements, use the complex type syntactically to accomplish that. Figure 3-2 should help you visualize the relationship between the simple type and complex type elements and the primitive and derived data types that define them.

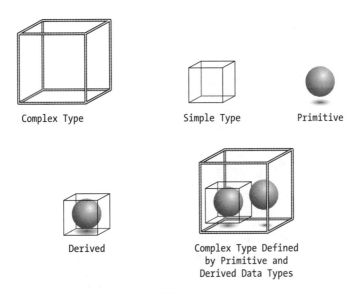

Figure 3-2. Schema data type relationships

As we saw earlier, we can already restrict other data types by creating simple types based on them and utilizing attribute constraints. Complex types can be used to restrict other complex data types in much the same way. However, the true power of complex data types comes from the ability to extend these data types by combining multiple types together. The complex type also allows you to tie attributes to elements. This is very similar to the programmatic concept of classes. Because of the number of permutations possible in this scenario, understanding the structure syntax for the complex type is very important.

First, let's take a look at the attributes available for defining the properties of our complex type elements. They are described briefly in Table 3-12.

Table 3-12. Complex Type Attributes

NAME	DESCRIPTION
id	namespace ID
final	permission to modify this type (#all|extension|restriction)
mixed	referring to the content model (true|false)
name	name of the type

> **UPDATE** *The attributes of the complex type have gone through many changes since the XML Schema draft was first submitted. Many older publications on XML and schemas based on specifications previous to the October 2000 recommendation refer to a content attribute that no longer exists. The March 2001 recommendation replaced the mixed attribute with the content type attribute.*

The final attribute declares what others can do with this type. This was developed with an eye toward the future, when there might be mechanisms that could support this function. Compliance today would be strictly voluntary.

The mixed attribute helps to define the content model of the type. A content model defines what kind of content exists. Declaring this can help an application to efficiently parse a type to know what is valid and invalid with some efficiency. There are basically four types of content models in XML Schemas: empty, text only, element only, and mixed. Figure 3-3 illustrates the difference between these content models. With the mixed attribute set to false, the application knows it should encounter only one of the other content types. If the property is not explicitly stated, it is assumed to be false.

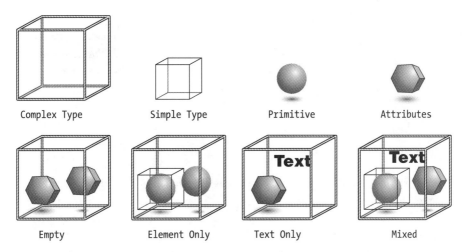

Figure 3-3. Complex type content models

Unfortunately, this system is not the simplest of designs to work with on a human level. The mixed property only marginally helps, because the content is also defined by the subelements declared in the type. The mixed property more or less sets the stage for what the application can expect, but your choice of elements and child elements really dictates the content model.

Before getting into the content model any further, you should learn about the child elements available in the complex type entity. They are described briefly in Table 3-13. We will discuss these throughout the rest of this section.

Table 3-13. Complex Type Child Elements

NAME	DESCRIPTION
all	a list of required elements
annotation	any comments
attributeGroup	a collection of attributes declared externally
choice	a list of elements from which one may be selected
complexContent	a complex type entity
sequence	a list of ordered elements
simpleContent	a simple type entity

Simple and Complex Content

To better understand these content models, we really need to first understand the simple and complex content elements. These are relative newcomers to the XML Schema specification, but are very important for working with complex type elements.

Think of the simple content and complex content elements as containers for the modification of existing types. A complex type can have either a simple content or a complex content, not both. Simple content simply defines elements of actual value. For instance, a complex type that extends the decimal type with a currency attribute utilizes a simple content container like this:

```
<complexType name="money">
    <simpleContent>
        <extension base="decimal">
            <attribute name="currency" type="string" />
        </extension>
    </simpleContent>
</complexType>
```

We see here a new element called extension. Whenever we use the simple and complex types, we are either extending or restricting an existing type or group of types. In fact, those are the only two child elements available to the simpleContent and complexContent elements (aside from annotation). However, the context of the two elements is very different when used in the simple and complex content containers. In fact, the specification would have been justified in creating separate elements under the simpleContent and complexContent entities just to minimize any confusion.

Both the extension and restriction entities support the base property, which declares which type is being manipulated. Under the simple content container, the restriction element supports a range of child elements. These elements comprise the set of attributes listed in Table 3-10 as well as simpleType. The goal is to provide all of the functionality necessary to detail the data validation required for a single element. The restriction and extension elements fully support all the attribute entities as well (attribute, attributeGroup, anyAttribute).

In the `complexContent` container, the restriction and extension elements can support entirely new model groups. I will discuss model groups in the next section, but suffice it for now to say that a model group can support a collection of elements. That means that a complex content element can support not only element information, but also an entirely new branch of elements and attributes. However, you may not always want to do this, and that is where content models come into play.

A complex type has four content models: empty, element only, text only, and mixed. Each of these models automatically supports attributes as well. Table 3-14 provides XML code examples of what each of these models looks like in implementation.

Table 3-14. Content Model Samples

MODEL	CODE
Empty	`<customer/>`
Element only	`<customer>`
	`<firstName>John</firstName>`
	`. . .`
	`</customer>`
Text only	`<customer>John Doe</customer>`
Mixed	`<customer>12345`
	`<firstName>John</firstName>`
	`. . .`
	`</customer>`

If you want to include only attributes in your complex type, then you are using the empty content model, and you need the complex content element. In this scenario, we will transition the money type from a simple content entity (which we just saw) to a complex content, as shown here:

```
<complexType name="money">
    <complexContent>
        <extension base= "anyType">
            <attribute name="value" type="decimal"/>
            <attribute name="currency" type="string"/>
        </extension>
    </complexContent>
</complexType>
```

As you can see, the only differences in the two code bases are the `complex-Content` and `simpleContent` tags. So does it matter which method you use? Only if you ever want to change the definition of your money type. The complex content model is much more extensible in that making it a nonempty type is very simple. In the case of the simple content example, it has to be transferred to a complex content model to support growth going forward. If you don't believe you will ever need this extensibility, then stick with the simple content type.

To generate an element only type, we definitely need to use the complex content element. Remember, the simple content element can support only a single element, so a series of elements falls outside its scope. Let's take the same money type and turn it into an element only type, as shown here:

```
<complexType name="money">
    <complexContent>

        . . .

            <element name="value" type="decimal" />
            <element name="currency" type="string" />

        . . .

    </complexContent>
</complexType>
```

I have masked out some additional tags to avoid confusion. We will be discussing them shortly. Also, keep in mind that we have not discussed the element entity yet, so don't worry if you don't understand the entire code segment. The main idea here is that more than one element can exist through the complex content container. Here is a shorthand version of this same definition that works because the content type is defaulted to complex content for a complex type:

```
<complexType name="money">

    . . .

        <element name="value" type="decimal"/>
        <element name="currency" type="string" />

    . . .
</complexType>
```

Finally, any combination of elements and text data in an element requires the mixed property value to be set to true. Thus this code represents a complex type in which the content model is mixed:

```
<element name="storeSales">
    <complexType>
        <complexContent mixed="true">
            <restriction base="string">
```

```
                    . . .
                        <element name="value" type="decimal"/>
                        <element name="currency" type="string"/>
                    . . .
                </restriction>
            </complexContent>
        </complexType>
    </element>
```

This code, when used in a schema document, defines an element called storeSales that has a string value and contains two child elements. Here is an example of mixed content in XML code:

```
<storeSales>
    MyStore
    <value>8450</value>
    <currency>US Dollars</currency>
</storeSales>
```

Table 3-15 shows the four content models with the appropriate syntax and any shorthand versions. This is meant to be a quick reference for you once you start building complex types in your schemas.

Table 3-15. Content Model Syntax

MODEL	SYNTAX	SHORTHAND
Empty	<complexType mixed="false"> <complexContent/> </complexType>	<complexType/>

Text only	<complexType mixed="false">
	  <simpleContent>
	   . . .
	  </simpleContent>
	</complexType>
		<complexType>
		  <simpleContent>
		   . . .
		  </simpleContent>
		</complexType>

Element only	<complexType mixed="false">
	  <element/>
	</complexType>
		<complexType>
		  <element/>
		</complexType>

Table 3-15. Content Model Syntax (continued)

MODEL	SYNTAX	SHORTHAND
Mixed	<complexType mixed="true">	<complexType>
	<complexContent>	<complexContent>
	. . .	. . .
	</complexContent>	</complexContent>
	</complexType>	</complexType>

Model Groups

Model groups are used to define groups of elements in a very customized manner. While they are somewhat related to groups by their nature, they are actually independent. All three models must be used exclusively of each other. That means that model groups are (for the most part) hierarchical and cannot be peers under any type. Also, while each supports the same attributes of `minOccurs` and `maxOccurs`, the range is restricted between 0 and 1 for each.

`all`

The `all` entity is used to declare a list of required elements that can be listed in any order. This group is slightly different in that it can only be used to define elements, no groups or sequences, as shown here:

```
<complexType name= "customer">
    <all>
        <element name="custID" type="integer"/>
        <element name="fName" type="string"/>
        <element name="lName" type="string"/>
    </all>
</complexType>
```

To get around the limitation of not being able to list all choices in an entity (something that you will likely want to do), you can choose a more verbose schema involving another layer of entities by embedding another complex type in an artificial element. Let's modify the preceding customer example by adding the choice of a home, work, or cellular telephone number, as shown here:

```
<complexType name= "customer">
    <all>
        <element name="custID" type="integer"/>
        <element name="fName" type="string"/>
        <element name="lName" type="string"/>
        <element name="contactNumber">
            <complexType mixed="true">
                <choice>
                    <element name="home" type="string"/>
                    <element name="work" type="string"/>
                    <element name="cellular" type="string"/>
                </choice>
            </complexType>
        </element>
    </all>
</complexType>
```

sequence

The sequence element lets you dictate the order of a list of entities. Like the choice element we will look at next, its child elements can comprise elements, groups, choices, and other sequences, so a wide variety of permutations are available. Sequences are very necessary to writing complex schemas because the all element cannot contain a choice element. However, I do not advise using unnecessary sequences. Among XML's positive qualities are its open nature and structure and its defining sequences. We have these sets of defined tags that have relationships, but dictating the order of tags among peers decreases the extensibility of the language. Some might argue that less work would go into writing applications if XML data were sequenced, but I believe there will always be exceptions to account for that will require the same flexibility from our applications. In other words, as soon as you write an application that depends on sequenced data, an alternative data set will come up from a new scenario that requires changes to the application. I think it is far better to design for the worst-case scenario so you aren't surprised later.

Regardless, the mechanism is necessary, so here is a sample:

```
<complexType name="customer">
    <sequence>
        <element name="custID" type="integer"/>
        <element name="fName" type="string"/>
        <element name="lName" type="string"/>
    </sequence>
</complexType>
```

This then makes the following XML data invalid:

```
<customer>
    <custID>123456</custID>
    <lName>Smith</lName>
    <fName>John</fName>
</customer>
```

choice

As its name implies, the choice element is used to allow the selection of one instance from all possible child elements. Its child elements can comprise elements, groups, sequences, and even other choices so the compound nature can provide various declarations, as shown here:

```
<complexType name="order">
    <sequence>
        <element name="shipMethod" type="shipOption"/>
        <choice>
            <element ref="workAddress" type="address"/>
            <element name="homeAddress" type="address"/>
        </choice>
    </sequence>
</complexType>
```

With some of these examples, we have in fact ventured past data types into some of the structures behind schemas. The two components obviously go hand in hand to build our schemas. So now that we've covered the highlights of data types, let's jump to structures so that we can start bringing closure to this definition language.

Using Data Types

The major topics we have discussed until now have focused on data types. They provide everything we need to define anything we might need for our XML data. However, we now have to utilize these data types by grouping them, extending and restricting them, and associating them with the elements for our documents. To do this, we need to round out our understanding of the various entities available.

Schema Namespace

We have already touched on the schema element, since it is the root node of any schema. A schema should be treated like the container for our definitions, and this container can only accept certain entities directly. These entities are simpleType, complexType, element, attribute, attributeGroup, group, notation, and annotation.

The significant aspect of the schema element is the namespace it represents. Any application that actually validates schemas will need the reference to this model through the namespace referenced when the schema element is declared.

> **NOTE**   *I purposely left out all references to the schema namespace in the data type section so that we could focus on the actual topics at hand. From this point forward, all samples will correctly reference the schema namespace so that our code is compliant with the specification.*

When the schema element is declared, a simple reference to the namespace makes your schema compliant. Thus, instead of just this declaration of the schema:

```
<schema>
</schema>
```

our declaration should now look like this:

```
<xsd:schema xmlns:xsd="http://www.w3.org/2000/10/XMLSchema">
</xsd:schema>
```

When utilizing the namespace throughout a schema, our schemas will look more like this:

```
<xsd:schema xmlns:xsd="http://www.w3.org/2000/10/XMLSchema">
    <xsd:element name="letterBody">
        <xsd:complexType name= "customer">
            <xsd:all>
                <xsd:element name="custID" type="xsd:integer"/>
                <xsd:element name="fName" type="xsd:string"/>
                <xsd:element name="lName" type="xsd:string"/>
                <xsd:element name="contactNumber">
                    <xsd:complexType mixed="true">
                        <xsd:choice>
                            <xsd:element name="home" type="xsd:string"/>
                            <xsd:element name="work" type="xsd:string"/>
                            <xsd:element name="cellular" type="xsd:string"/>
                        </xsd:choice>
                    </xsd:complexType>
                </xsd:element>
            </xsd:all>
        </xsd:complexType>
    </xsd:element>
</xsd:schema>
```

Notice that even our base types reflect the namespace. This is because all of our primitive and derived data types are actually defined by the XML Schema namespace we discussed previously.

Element Declarations

Elements are the entities behind every node in our XML documents. It can be somewhat confusing when referring to the element entity because of its omnipresent use in XML Schemas. In this instance I am referring to the elements we are defining in our XML data sets.

For example, to define the movie-listing document we saw earlier, we must define the movie, actor, and director elements. As mentioned earlier, XML elements can build upon each other, and we need to think of these elements as extensions of existing elements, be they numeric, string, or some other type. We need to focus on the elements we need to define and not get bogged down in the semantics of element definition.

Table 3-16. Element Attributes

NAME	DESCRIPTION
default	the default value, if any, for the element
fixed	the fixed value, if any, for the element
id	the namespace reference
maxOccurs	the maximum number of times this element can occur in this element
minOccurs	the minimum number of times this element can occur in this element
name	the name of the element
nullable	whether the element is nullable (true|false)
type	the base type of the element

Elements come with many properties we can use to declare our data types. (See Table 3-16.) The most significant attribute of the element is type. Elements are always based on some type, and this is how we associate the two. In some earlier samples we used elements to build our complex types. Here is another look at our money type:

```
<xsd:complexType name="money">
    <xsd:sequence>
        <xsd:element name="value" type="xsd:decimal"/>
        <xsd:element name="currency" type="xsd:string"/>
    </xsd:sequence>
</xsd:complexType>
```

> **NOTE** *The schema container and namespace declaration are implied in any code samples referencing the* xsd *namespace.*

Money contains two elements named value and currency. Each one has a type with value typed as decimal and currency typed as string. These are both derived data types that the elements are using for their data type. This is similar to declaring variables in a programming language. What we see here is a declarative typing through the type attribute of the element entity. Another method for declaring element data types is in-line casting. Enclosing a simple or complex type between an element's start and end tags does this. These two methods should be used exclusively of each other in one element. Such an implementation for our value element looks like this:

```
<xsd:element name="value">
    <xsd:simpleType>
        <xsd:restriction base="xsd:decimal"/>
    </xsd:simpleType>
</xsd:element>
```

There are different scenarios in which each would be appropriate, so this isn't a "one size fits all" situation.

The `minOccurs` and `maxOccurs` attributes would also have frequent use in a "tight" schema definition of our data. Through these properties, we can explicitly declare the existence and frequency of our elements. This ability can be invaluable for declaring a sequence of elements or simply making an element required in a structure. For the first scenario, let's declare a structure for an NHL hockey team. (See the `hockeyTeam` element schema that follows.) According to the rules, a team must dress two goaltenders and 18 players. These players can be of any position, but any coach will tell you to have a minimum of five defensemen and 10 forwards. That leaves the maximum number of defensemen at eight and forwards 13, as shown here:

```
<xsd:simpleType name="player">
    <xsd:restriction base="xsd:string"/>
</xsd:simpleType>
<xsd:complexType name="hockeyTeam">
    <xsd:sequence>
        <xsd:element name="goalies" type="player" minOccurs="2" maxOccurs="2"/>
        <xsd:element name="forwards" type="player" minOccurs="10"
maxOccurs="13"/>
        <xsd:element name="defenseman" type="player" minOccurs="5"
maxOccurs="8"/>
    </xsd:sequence>
</xsd:complexType>
```

What we just did as a quick exercise was define a player type and then declare elements using the player data type. The string represents the name of the player. Of course, this schema doesn't address the overall number of players. Using this definition, we could mistakenly field a team of only 15 skaters or find the loophole in the application and dress 21 skaters. The only problem there is fitting them all on the bench!

How do we address this problem? Well, we have to redesign our definition at a lower level to keep this from happening. Instead of defining a type of player and declaring the elements as positions, why don't we define goalies and skaters based on players? That would look like this:

```
<xsd:simpleType name="player">
    <xsd:restriction base="xsd:string"/>
</xsd:simpleType>
<xsd:simpleType name="goalie">
    <xsd:restriction base="player"/>
</xsd:simpleType>
<xsd:complexType name="skater">
    <xsd:choice>
        <xsd:element name="forward" type="player"/>
        <xsd:element name="defenseman" type="player"/>
    </xsd:choice>
</xsd:complexType>
<xsd:complexType name="hockeyTeam">
    <xsd:sequence>
        <xsd:element name="dressedGoalies" type="goalie" minOccurs="2"
          maxOccurs="2"/>
        <xsd:element name="dressedSkaters" type="skater" minOccurs="18"
          maxOccurs="18"/>
    </xsd:sequence>
</xsd:complexType>
```

Of course the tradeoff with this implementation is that I could make a mistake and have 18 forwards or 18 defensemen. While this is bad, it at least isn't illegal. Given the two options, this schema definitely is better and is a good example of the kinds of decisions we have to make when trying to design schemas for our business data.

We have now covered enough material to start making complete schemas. The most basic schemas simply define a single element based on a primitive data type. The following code is an example:

```
<xsd:schema xmlns:xsd="http://www.w3.org/2000/10/XMLSchema">
    <xsd:element name="name" type="xsd:string"/>
</xsd:schema>
```

Most of the code samples in this section are valid schemas with a schema container like this. However, to have much richer and well defined, reusable definitions, we will likely build much more involved schemas. These will inevitably involve the simple and complex types we saw earlier, as well as groups and attribute groups.

Group Declarations

Groups are used to define collections of entities as a whole unit locally and easily reference them elsewhere in your schema. This is different from defining complex types because they are much less robust. The only child elements available to a group element are the all, choice, and sequence elements discussed previously.

The group is referenced through the name attribute of the group declaration. Groups then use the ref attribute to reference the group declaration in a document. As an example, let's revisit the order schema used earlier. This time we will modify the order element from our choice model group example by declaring a group for our home and work addresses and selecting the choice from the group, as shown here:

```
<xsd:complexType name= "order">
    <xsd:sequence>
        . . .
        <xsd:element name="shipMethod" type= "shipOption"/>
        <xsd:group ref="addressOption"/>
    </xsd:sequence>
</xsd:complexType>
<xsd:group name="addressOption">
    <xsd:choice>
        <xsd:element name="homeAddress" type="address"/>
        <xsd:element name="workAddress" type="address"/>
    </xsd:choice>
</xsd:group>
```

You can see how this would be handy if we were going to work with these address elements frequently. This grouping not only makes it easier to work with the elements as a whole, but also conserves space in the schema. Additionally, this addressOption element is more maintainable since a change only needs to be added to one schema and persists throughout the referencing schemas.

Attribute Group Declarations

Attribute groups behave much the same way that groups do. With them, you can group a list of attributes together and reference them anywhere in the schema. For our scenario, let's look again at the shipOption element from our order type. We will flush out some of the details of our shipping options, as shown here:

```
<xsd:attributeGroup name="shippingProperties">
    <xsd:attribute name="priority">
        <xsd:simpleType>
            <xsd:restriction base="xsd:string">
                <xsd:enumeration value="overnight"/>
                <xsd:enumeration value="2-day"/>
                <xsd:enumeration value="ground"/>
            </xsd:restriction>
        </xsd:simpleType>
    </xsd:attribute>
    <xsd:attribute name="cost" type="money"/>
</xsd:attributeGroup>
<xsd:element name="shipMethod">
    <xsd:complexType>
        <xsd:sequence>
            <xsd:element name="deliveryMethod" type="shipOption"/>
        </xsd:sequence>
        <xsd:attributeGroup ref="shippingProperties"/>
    </xsd:complexType>
</xsd:element>
```

Perhaps even more so than with the group element, you can tell that aggregating frequently used attributes together can really lead to more efficient reuse of your schema data. In this example, we also utilized the restriction element as opposed to the extension element to show its use in attributes. You might have to modify your schema's structure slightly to accommodate an attribute-heavy structure.

Implementation

Now that we have looked at the syntax of building schemas, how do we use them? There are basically two aspects of using schemas. The first one, the usage of schemas by your XML data, is obvious. The second, the reuse of schemas, is probably less obvious, but nearly as important. After all, if we can't reuse schemas or their components, that dramatically affects the effort we invest and our usage of them.

Using Schemas

Now that we know how to build schemas, how do we actually use them? We want to be able to reference a schema from within an XML document. The SchemaLocation property, which has two different forms, makes this possible. The first form, named SchemaLocation, is used to identify schemas where a target namespace has been identified. For those who do not use namespaces, the noNamespaceSchemaLocation form is available. This difference is merely to point out to an application the namespace state of the data in the document.

A simple reference to a schema for our customer node looks like this:

```
<customer xmlns:xsi="http://www.w3.org/2000/10/XMLSchema-instance"
  xsi:SchemaLocation="C:\test.xsd">
```

In the latter case, in which no namespace is declared, the call looks much the same, as shown here:

```
<customer xmlns:xsi="http://www.w3.org/2000/10/XMLSchema-instance"
  xsi:noNamespaceSchemaLocation="C:\test.xsd">
```

Reusing Schemas

When we have invested time and effort in defining data types and structures, we would like to be able to reuse them in multiple schemas. Without this reusability, we certainly could question the effort we put into designing our structures and schemas.

To include schemas that share the same target namespace as the local schema, we simply declare an include element and identify the location of the schema through the schemaLocation attribute, as shown here:

```
<xsd:include schemaLocation="http://myDomain.com/schemas/customer.xsd"/>
```

Of course this begs the question how to handle schemas that do not share the local targetNamespace. For such schemas you need to use the import entity. The syntax is virtually identical to that for the include tag, as shown here:

```
<xsd:import schemaLocation="http://myDomain.com/schemas/customer.xsd"/>
```

To take this one step further and modify the schemas when we reference them, we simply exchange the include element for the redefine element, as shown here:

```
<xsd:redefine schemaLocation="http://myDomain.com/schemas/customer.xsd">
```

With this simple change, we now have the ability to either extend or further enhance all of the data types and structures included in the schema. The syntax for these modifications is the same as that for modifying structures defined locally. So if we extend our customer structure defined externally, we use the `redefine` element, as shown here:

```
<xsd:schema xmlns:xsd="http://www.w3.org/2000/10/XMLSchema">
    <xsd:redefine schemaLocation="http://myDomain.com/schemas/customer.xsd">
        <xsd:complexType name="customer">
            <xsd:complexContent>
                <xsd:extension base="customer">
                    <xsd:sequence>
                        <xsd:element name="email" type="xsd:string"/>
                    </xsd:sequence>
                </xsd:extension>
            </xsd:complexContent>
        </xsd:complexType>
    </xsd:redefine>
</xsd:schema>
```

It should seem evident that there are a number of ways to define the same elements. We have talked about some of the tradeoffs and benefits, but those were on the element level. The prospect of instead designing schemas for an entire organization could seem quite overwhelming. Some of the decisions you make early on will dictate how the process is defined. Before making those decisions, it's a good idea to develop a schema strategy.

Schema Strategy

It might seem like overkill, but it makes a lot of sense to outline a strategy for your organization to implement and develop schemas. If all employees use their own methods during design and implementation, your organization will probably be unable to benefit from schema reuse. By taking just a little time to document a schema structure for your organization, you could benefit from reuse for years to come.

A schema strategy should address the following components:

- Selecting development tools

- Identifying your XML repositories

- Defining the design rules

- Establishing a schema hierarchy

- Utilizing namespaces

First you should standardize on the tools your developers will use when creating schemas (and other XML documents, for that matter). Even compliant tools can produce very subtle differences or nuances in the code that may keep it from working as well with other tools. Standardizing on a tool should help you to avoid any such issues.

The next step is to identify a repository for your schemas. There are several options here, but the main thing is that developers can access existing schemas for maintenance and quickly reference other existing schemas during development.

This decision depends on what form you will keep your data in and your performance and scalability requirements. For example, you could keep your schema data in physical files and organize them through a file structure, but your scalability and performance will then be somewhat limited. Conversely, you could have all of your data maintained in a relational database and extract the data as XML. This would help your scalability, but hurt the overall performance.

After establishing the infrastructure, you should lay down some ground rules for schema design in your organization. This involves defining some best practices and coding standards. You could spend forever doing this, but I recommend just hitting some high points and making sure that the first schemas in the organization go through a review process to surface more specific issues.

The next step is to design a schema hierarchy. This means deciding how schemas will align with documents, how these documents will relate to each other, and the data structures within them. In a small organization, you can get away with being rather ad hoc about this. However, larger organizations will suffer greatly if a standard hierarchy map is not created before schemas are assembled.

Schemas should break down rather neatly into at least a three-layer document structure. Base-level documents should contain all data types, including all derived and simple types. The next level of documents could then define all structures using these data types. Finally, the top-level schema documents could actually define your XML documents using the structures. This structure (see Figure 3-4) will provide many benefits if implemented correctly. First, it allows direct application access to only the highest layer, thereby protecting the integrity of your structures and data types. Second, when a data type or structure is needed, the existing repository can be quickly searched for building blocks to assemble it, and once it is done, it is easily found by others. Finally, this structure also allows for easier organization of your namespaces by grouping schemas together naturally.

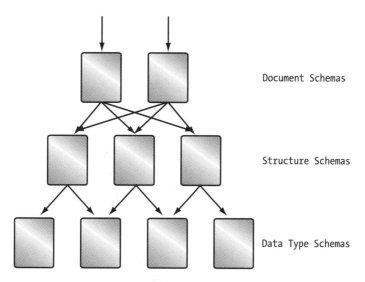

Figure 3-4. Three-tier schema hierarchy design

Let's walk through a hierarchical design using our movie sample. In this document, we had a movie element that contained title, actor, and director elements. The actor then had character and name child elements, and the director a name element. Let's go ahead and enhance that by including the genre(s) and the year of its release, as shown here:

```
<movie>
    <title>Forrest Gump</title>
    <year>1994</year>
    <actor>
        <character>Forrest Gump</character>
        <name>Tom Hanks</name>
    </actor>
    <director>
        <name>Robert Zemeckis</name>
    </director>
    <genre>Drama</genre>
    <genre>Comedy</genre>
</movie>
```

The first thing to do is identify all of the data types we will need. Looking at this scenario, it looks like we will need title, year, character, name, and genre data types. Those all go into our level-one document, as shown here:

```
<xsd:schema xmlns:xsd="http://www.w3.org/2000/10/XMLSchema">
    <xsd:element name="character" type="xsd:string"/>
    <xsd:element name="name" type="xsd:string"/>
    <xsd:element name="title" type="xsd:string"/>
    <xsd:element name="year" type="xsd:short"/>
    <xsd:element name="genre">
        <xsd:simpleType>
            <xsd:restriction base="xsd:string">
                <xsd:enumeration value="Comedy"/>
                <xsd:enumeration value="Drama"/>
                <xsd:enumeration value="Adventure"/>
                <xsd:enumeration value="Documentary"/>
            </xsd:restriction>
        </xsd:simpleType>
    </xsd:element>
</xsd:schema>
```

With our elements defined, we now need to make our structures. The data
type identification is fairly straightforward. However, identifying structures is
a different matter, so this is likely where your difficult design decisions will be
made. The element that could be in question for this particular design is movie. If
it is the document's root element, then we should declare it in our level-three
schema, correct? The best way to resolve this issue is to ask the following question: Will someone else ever reuse this element? If the answer is yes, then
I encourage you to leave it in your level-two schema. In this scenario, it makes
our level-three schema rather insignificant, so I'm going to arbitrarily state that
our root node will not be <movie>, but rather <movieCollection>. This gives us the
flexibility to include multiple movies if necessary and allows us to treat the movie
element as a structure with a clear conscience! Here is the code:

```
<xsd:schema xmlns:xsd="http://www.w3.org/2000/10/XMLSchema">
    <xsd:include schemaLocation="C:\movietypes.xsd"/>
    <xsd:complexType name="actorType">
        <xsd:sequence>
            <xsd:element ref="character"/>
            <xsd:element ref="name"/>
        </xsd:sequence>
    </xsd:complexType>
    <xsd:complexType name="directorType">
        <xsd:sequence>
            <xsd:element ref="name"/>
        </xsd:sequence>
```

```
        </xsd:complexType>
        <xsd:complexType name="movieType">
            <xsd:sequence>
                <xsd:element ref="title"/>
                <xsd:element ref="year"/>
                <xsd:element name="actor" type="actorType"/>
                <xsd:element name="director" type="directorType"/>
                <xsd:element ref="genre" maxOccurs="unbounded"/>
            </xsd:sequence>
        </xsd:complexType>
</xsd:schema>
```

Finally, we get to our level-three schema, which should simply aggregate structures and/or data types together to form the definition for our document. In our case, we will simply be utilizing the movie structure, as shown here:

```
<xsd:schema xmlns:xsd="http://www.w3.org/2000/10/XMLSchema">
    <xsd:include schemaLocation="C:\moviestructures.xsd"/>
    <xsd:element name="movieCollection">
        <xsd:complexType>
            <xsd:sequence>
                <xsd:element name="movie" type="movieType"
                    maxOccurs="unbounded"/>
            </xsd:sequence>
        </xsd:complexType>
    </xsd:element>
</xsd:schema>
```

So there is our three-tier schema definition for our movie collection document. You will probably encounter situations in which you cannot strictly adhere to a schema strategy model, but the more you can do that, the more consistent and efficient your schemas will be.

That brings us to the final strategy topic, which concerns the use of namespaces by large organizations. Namespaces were designed to easily identify and protect XML data. Many organizations allow their departments to create their own systems and services. Your organization needs a plan concerning how namespaces are created and propagated if it is to be as effective as possible at utilizing XML. The larger a consensus you can have on individual namespaces, the more cooperative the areas of your organization will be in developing solutions.

Summary

We have taken a look at the XML Schema specification and how to define our XML documents. There are many ways to declare the same data set, so make your design decisions carefully. Ultimately, you are going to work with your data, so you need to keep efficiency in mind, not just validity. While the development of compression techniques for XML is coming, efficient utilization of XML will always be of benefit. This not only will help with the network load, but also will help to streamline our application by requiring the lowest possible overhead.

We also looked at the various methods for defining XML documents. Keep in mind that, while you have many options for defining XML documents, you really only have control over how you use them in your organization. So, although you may standardize on XML Schemas, you will still have to support DTDs if you want to interact with many external partners. Make sure that you also use namespaces smartly and do not overuse them. The decisions you make will affect your implementations.

With what we have learned so far, we can build and define our data, but we really haven't done anything with it. It is now time to start working with our XML data programmatically.

CHAPTER 4

Using XML

EVEN THOUGH WE'VE LOOKED at how to build XML documents, we haven't done anything with them. Building XML documents in an editor is one thing. Building them dynamically or accessing them programmatically is something else entirely. We have to now take our knowledge of XML and transport it into our applications. Fortunately, we don't have to do it all on our own. There are some tools and standards available that get us about half the way there.

The other half we will have to design and develop, but we're not ready to get into that just yet. In this chapter, we will just get familiar with the existing techniques and standards for working with XML. This is the next step in understanding XML enough to use it in meaningful way: through creating and consuming Web services.

Working with XML

There are several approaches to working with XML. Some developers might take the brute force approach of "It's just ASCII text. I'll parse it myself." No matter how confident you might be, taking on that task is much more than you are bargaining for! If that wasn't obvious as you read Chapter 3, you might want to look through it one more time.

> *ASCII* is an acronym for *American Standard Code for Information Interchange.* This is a 255-character decimal-based system for defining character data. The establishment of this standard was critical to getting computers to communicate with each other. Without every system agreeing on how a character is defined, standards based on character patterns, like XML, would be pointless.

As nice as it would be, I'm afraid this is not a "one size fits all" opportunity or decision. Certainly you will want to avoid some techniques, like building your own programmatic interface into an XML document. Not only can the logic to access XML data be very complex, but others have also already done the work for you. Why reinvent the wheel?

The industry has established two different standards to make it easier to work with XML: the Document Object Model (DOM) and the Simple API for XML (SAX). The DOM has been developed through the W3C, and participants in the XML-DEV mailing list (hosted by OASIS) developed the SAX specification.

These standards in and of themselves would provide little assistance other than direction if not for the vendors that have developed objects and libraries supporting these standards. That is because the DOM and SAX are both merely methodologies for accessing XML data. They are not parsers, but approaches on how to contain and thus interact with the data once it is parsed. Fortunately, the vendors have taken the effort to provide parsers that utilize these standards. That translates into free logic that you can use, which makes your job much easier.

DOM

The Document Object Model is an application programming interface (API) designed as a platform-independent approach to working with HTML and XML. The type of work the DOM formally facilitates is often misunderstood. You would not use the DOM to actually create XML code. Rather, it is an API for accessing and manipulating existing code. This manipulation can result in a new document, but it consists of, or is a copy of, XML code that previously existed. The actual creation of XML code is something the working group chose to leave out, because the construction of elements may have no relationship to the DOM itself. The specification has left it to the implementations themselves to develop their own creation factory and bundle it with the DOM specification. We will discuss these creation techniques later when we start building and consuming Web services in Chapter 6.

The history of the DOM is rather interesting in that it originates from work with JavaScript and Java. While working to find a way to make the languages more usable across various browsers, the working group at the W3C ended up being influenced by HTML and XML authors to broaden the original vision. The resulting efforts of that group became the first DOM specification (now known as Level 1). A revision to the DOM specification, DOM Level 2, was completed in November 2000.

To achieve platform and implementation independence, the DOM defines a logical container to the data. This container takes the shape of a hierarchical tree structure. This logical model is both a familiar concept to developers and a sound model that maintains the hierarchical nature of elements in an XML document. Figure 4-1 shows what the DOM tree structure of the following code might look like:

```
<customer>
    <firstname>John</firstname>
    <lastname>Smith</lastname>
    <birthday>071671</birthday>
    <address>
      <street>41 Mason</street>
      <city>Somerville</city>
      <state>MA</state>
```

```
        <zip>02144</zip>
    </address>
</customer>
```

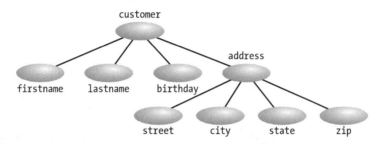

Figure 4-1. A graphical view of the DOM representation of XML

Understanding this data structure is critical to working with the DOM. I will refer to this model constantly when we start looking at the code for traversing data, identifying specific nodes, modifying data, or anything that has to do with the XML data.

> **NOTE** *The DOM tree structure should not be misinterpreted to be a binary tree. A binary tree is similar, but allows only up to two child nodes off of any node of the tree, whereas the DOM tree allows an unlimited number of child nodes.*

A *node* refers to one element in the tree structure. The nodes in Figure 4-1 are represented as circles. A *parent node* is a node that has other nodes extending from it. These nodes are considered *child nodes* because of their dependency on the parent. A parent may have many children, but a child may have only one parent. In Figure 4-1, the street element is a child node of the address element in the DOM structure.

The DOM is merely a logical representation, and it places no demand on the physical data structures behind the applications and tools that may support it. That means the actual data of a DOM application may live in any form, but it must be accessible via the interfaces defined by the specification. This allows us to care nothing about a DOM implementation beyond its performance and reliability (assuming of course that it conforms with the standards it has defined).

Also, the DOM has no support for generating XML constructs in any other object model. This means the DOM will never actually generate an XML document; it will merely support the data it is given and the interfaces it supports.

The tools that implement the DOM will of course have their own mechanisms for generating nodes and then turn to the DOM standard for integrating it into a document.

Finally, the DOM does not in any way compete with any of the other object models for middleware such as COM (Component Object Model) or CORBA (Common Object Request Broker Architecture.) The "object" referred to in DOM simply refers to logical data, not physical software like with the other models.

My objective is to provide you with a sufficient understanding of the DOM to simply use the API, not implement it. If that is your objective, I suggest you look at books dedicated to the DOM as well as digging into the specification itself. If you do look up the specification directly on the W3C, you should be aware of the variations between versions.

Any reference to the core specification refers to the base DOM standard, which must be implemented for correct compliance. Other specifications are also considered part of the DOM (views, events, html, and others), but they are not required for compliance. These other specifications extend upon DOM, usually in specific markup languages or scenarios, and so do not always apply. Here we will be concerned with only the core specification.

NOTE *My look at the DOM standard is based on the Level 2 Recommendation submitted by the W3C in November 2000. The parsers we will later use support this version.*

The DOM is usually implemented through the parsers provided by software vendors (like MSXML by Microsoft and XML4J by IBM). These implementations of the DOM actually extend far beyond the core specification to provide additional functionality such as network communication and file-level access to documents. Usually, vendors have their own specific purposes in mind for the DOM and are simply making it more robust. It is actually misleading to call these tools in their entirety a DOM, but rather the DOM is one component of the entire parser. We will talk about the DOM specifically in this section, but we will get into the specifics of different implementations when we start building Web services in Chapters 6 and 7.

The DOM will be the main interface into our XML data, so understanding the specifics of its components will be important for following the examples later in the book. These components are all mapped to interfaces, not classes. This means we aren't concerned with the logic making it happen and can simply rely on routines that manipulate the data as we want. Since the DOM is intended to be a language-independent API, no pretenses are made concerning the actual implementation. The DOM simply defines how an implementation will look to an external application and this interaction occurs through interfaces.

Node Interfaces

The DOM model is defined by a series of interfaces exposed through a document structure. Think of these interfaces as a set of instructions on how to access and manipulate the data in an XML document. Two different sets of logical interfaces are actually defined. The primary set is the object-oriented approach. In this approach, a series of interfaces is inherited from base interfaces, which makes it quite extensible. However, a performance cost is associated with this approach because casts or query interface calls (in their respective environments) are required for their use. That is why a second set of interfaces was established that is node-centric. In this simplified approach, the DOM treats everything as a node, and so everything is done through that interface. We will look at the DOM through this approach, since it provides all the functionality we need for our Web services and every aspect maps to the original object-oriented interface.

> **CAUTION** *The W3C considers this simplified interface to be extra functionality and so should not be assumed complete in its scope or completeness. That said, this node-based interface is simpler to use and can be used to accomplish most tasks you need in working with XML and especially when just parsing XML. Both of these approaches are part of the DOM core implementation, so any DOM-compliant parser exposes both.*

In this "everything is a node" approach, all the interfaces are implemented through the actual node interface. In the node are a series of types, attributes, and methods that allow you to access and manipulate the DOM. Since this is the key interface into the DOM using this approach, let's take a look at the IDL, or interface definition, for the node in Listing 4-1.

Listing 4-1. DOM node IDL

```
interface Node {
// NodeType
const unsigned short    ELEMENT_NODE                = 1;
const unsigned short    ATTRIBUTE_NODE              = 2;
const unsigned short    TEXT_NODE             = 3;
const unsigned short    CDATA_SECTION_NODE        = 4;
const unsigned short    ENTITY_REFERENCE_NODE     = 5;
const unsigned short    ENTITY_NODE          = 6;
const unsigned short    PROCESSING_INSTRUCTION_NODE  = 7;
const unsigned short    COMMENT_NODE            = 8;
const unsigned short    DOCUMENT_NODE          = 9;
const unsigned short    DOCUMENT_TYPE_NODE        = 10;
const unsigned short    DOCUMENT_FRAGMENT_NODE      = 11;
```

```
const unsigned short   NOTATION_NODE          = 12;

readonly attribute DOMString     nodeName;
     attribute DOMString      nodeValue;
                    // raises(DOMException) on setting
                    // raises(DOMException) on retrieval

readonly attribute unsigned short  nodeType;
readonly attribute Node          parentNode;
readonly attribute NodeList        childNodes;
readonly attribute Node          firstChild;
readonly attribute Node          lastChild;
readonly attribute Node          previousSibling;
readonly attribute Node          nextSibling;
readonly attribute NamedNodeMap    attributes;
// Modified in DOM Level 2:
readonly attribute Document        ownerDocument;
Node          insertBefore(in Node newChild,
                  in Node refChild)
                    raises(DOMException);
Node          replaceChild(in Node newChild,
                  in Node oldChild)
                    raises(DOMException);
Node          removeChild(in Node oldChild)
                    raises(DOMException);
Node          appendChild(in Node newChild)
                    raises(DOMException);
boolean       hasChildNodes();
Node          cloneNode(in boolean deep);
// Modified in DOM Level 2:
void          normalize();
// Introduced in DOM Level 2:
boolean       isSupported(in DOMString feature,
                  in DOMString version);
// Introduced in DOM Level 2:
readonly attribute DOMString     namespaceURI;
// Introduced in DOM Level 2:
     attribute DOMString     prefix;
                    // raises(DOMException) on setting
// Introduced in DOM Level 2:
readonly attribute DOMString     localName;
// Introduced in DOM Level 2:
boolean       hasAttributes();
};
```

Types

You can think of the DOM as a series of interrelated containers that hold your data. These containers may be physically present in the document, like an element, or they may be logical representations of your data, like a text node. (I'll explain each of these shortly.) Regardless of its nature, in this node-based interface to the DOM, each container is treated as a node, and each node has a type that defines and declares what it represents.

We are going to look at all the various node types, or types, that exist in the DOM. When you are working with the DOM, it is important for you to understand these relationships so that you can know what data you are referencing or modifying. There can be a subtle difference between changing the name of an element and changing the text value in it. This look at types will help you to understand that difference.

The headings at the top of each definition are the names of each available node type. Node types are actually defined by integers from 1 through 200, and these constants declare the types currently in use in the specification. More types will probably be added in future revisions, but these are all the valid types available in the DOM Level 2 recommendation.

These types provide the interface for how to view and declare the various nodes in our model. If you are that interested in working with the object-oriented interface, each of these node types actually represents the original interface itself. For example, the Document_Node type is actually a Document interface. Thus, anything you can do with the Document you can do with the Document_Node interface.

Where appropriate, I have added some code samples to help relate these types to actual XML data. These nodes all have strictly defined relationships in the document and with each other that mimic their ancestors. Diagrams for each type illustrate the relationships they have with each other. This can be a quick reference when you start trying to work with a piece of data and have trouble locating it in the DOM tree.

> **NOTE** *If you are having difficulty remembering what each of these types is, please refer back to the section in Chapter 3 on XML structures.*

```
Document_Node
```

The document node is the root of any DOM. The DOM can work only with valid
XML data, which means that a root element must always be present. That would
then be the document node. As the root, the document node obviously has no
legal parent nodes. In this example, `grills` is the document node.

```
<grills>
    <manufacturer>Vermont Castings
        <model>VC-200</model>
        <model>VC-400</model>
    </manufacturer>
    <manufacturer>Fire Magic
        <model>Regal II</model>
    </manufacturer>
</grills>
```

There can be only one `Document_Node` in a valid XML document. The relationships between the `Document_Node` entity and others are shown in Figure 4-2.

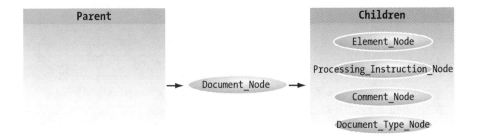

Figure 4-2. `Document_Node` *relationships*

```
Document_Fragment_Node
```

A document fragment is a subset of a valid XML document. This portion is still
considered a valid document, if isolated, because it has a root node. You reference this root node when actually loading the document fragment. For example,
take the following XML document:

```
<calendar>
    <event>
        <concert>
            <artist>U2</artist>
            <city>Boston</city>
            <hall>FleetCenter</hall>
```

```
      </concert>
      <date>060501</date>
   </event>
</calendar>
```

Once you are working with this document, you may want to work with just the concert element, which is a valid subset. This method is often used to work with a portion of a document, perhaps to move, transform, or remove it. The Document_Fragment_Node relationships are shown in Figure 4-3.

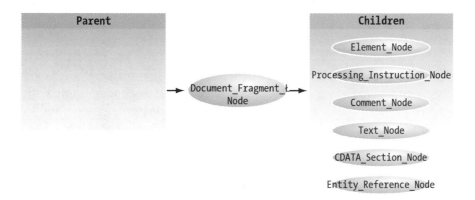

Figure 4-3. Document_Fragment_Node *relationships*

Document_Type_Node

The document type is an element that is actually an attribute of the document node. It is intended as an interface to the entities defined in the document. It is not editable and is generally used only for identifying DTD (Document Type Definition) references. Unfortunately, this uneditable aspect of the document type keeps you from being able to programmatically add a reference to an existing document. Chapter 6 explains why this is such a shortcoming. The following document contains an external DTD reference that defines itself for parsers:

```
<?xml version="1.0" encoding="UTF-8"?>
<!DOCTYPE myData SYSTEM
   "http://www.fundamentalwebservices.com/interface/grills.dtd">
<grills>
     . . .
</grills>
```

Here you see the document type node defined by the !DOCTYPE tag. Notice how the node actually precedes the root node of the document itself. However, in the DOM, it is in a child node of the document node. The reason for this "abnormal" structure in the text representation is likely to facilitate easy reference for when the document is parsed and validated (using the referenced DTD). Figure 4-4 shows the relationships for Document_Type_Node.

Figure 4-4. Document_Type_Node *relationships*

Entity_Node

As you might expect, the entity node defines entities. These entities may be parsed or unparsed, and the entity node, along with all descendents, is handled as read only in the DOM. The entity node is more of a logical container, and so pinpointing an entity node in code is not as meaningful as in other types. The relationships for the Entity_Node are shown in Figure 4-5.

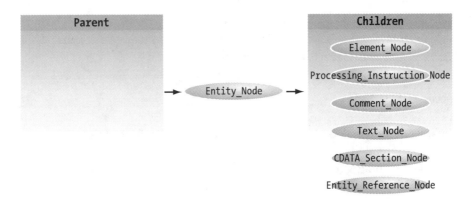

Figure 4-5. Entity_Node *relationships*

Entity_Reference_Node

Entity reference nodes reference entities external to the XML document currently loaded. Processors may retrieve these entities during load, which means that no entity references will exist. Like the document reference node, these nodes are not editable in the DOM. Figure 4-6 illustrates the legal relationships for this type.

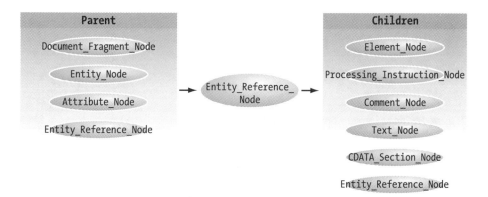

Figure 4-6. Entity_Reference_Node *relationships*

Element_Node

The element node will obviously be the most frequently used node. Every element outside of the root node is in an Element_Node. This concept may be easier to understand by looking at all the relationships the element node has with other types. (See Figure 4-7.)

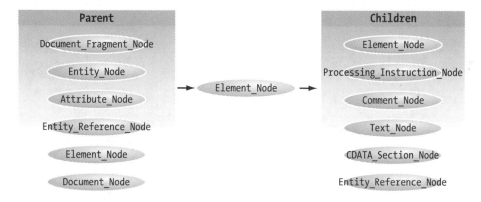

Figure 4-7. Element_Node *relationships*

Attribute_Node

Every attribute of an element is exposed through an attribute node. Notice in Figure 4-8 that the attribute has no parent nodes. This might seem confusing if you don't recognize that your document tree is a logical model only. Even though attributes relate to an element, they are not treated as child nodes of the elements because there would then be no distinction between an element's attributes and its child elements. You will see the need for this distinction when you start looking at the methods of the DOM.

Figure 4-8. `Attribute_Node` *relationships*

`Processing_Instruction_Node`

This node serves as a container for instructions meant specifically for the processor. Unlike other, seemingly similar nodes, this one potentially holds meaningful information to the parser and is not simply passing it along to the DOM. The following code is an example of a processing instruction node:

```
<?AcmeParser Filter(123)?>
```

The first word in a processing instruction is referred to as the target, which is the parsing application at which the instruction is directed. It should then know how to handle the information passed to it. From Figure 4-9, you can see that this node can be the child of several types, but can have no children.

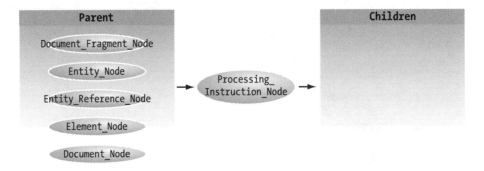

Figure 4-9. `Processing_Instruction_Node` *relationships*

`Comment_Node`

This node contains comments included in the XML document currently loaded. Unlike other nodes distinguished by start and end tags, comments in the XML document would merely be in "<!--" and "-->" delimiters. Like the processing instruction, the comment node can have no children. (See Figure 4-10.)

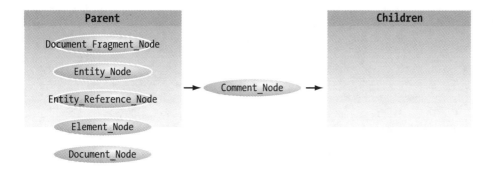

Figure 4-10. Comment_Node *relationships*

Text_Node

The text node contains the textual data value of an element or attribute node. This data cannot contain any markup data. Although it is possible to create multiple text nodes in an element, all text is normalized by rule into one node whenever the data is loaded into the DOM. The only reason to create multiple instances of the text node is as a temporary tactic for management of the data in an element inside the DOM (containing lines of text in separate nodes, for instance). The relationships for a text node are shown in Figure 4-11.

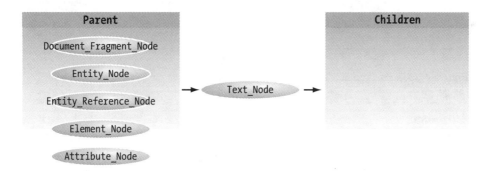

Figure 4-11. Text_Node *relationships*

CDATA_Section_Node

Like other CDATA sections, this node is used to escape blocks of text that may be misconstrued as actual code in a markup document. The legal relationships for a CDATA section node are shown in Figure 4-12.

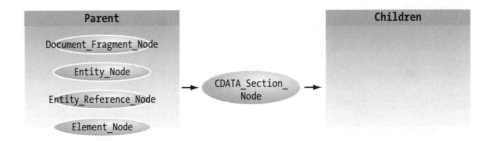

Figure 4-12. `CDATA_Section_Node` *relationships*

`Notation_Node`

This node is used for containing notations in a DTD. Just like comments with the XML data itself, it only has use to a human viewer. The following code is an example of a notation:

```
<!NOTATION gif SYSTEM "viewgif.exe">
```

Unlike other nodes, the notation node has no legal relationships with other nodes. (See Figure 4-13.)

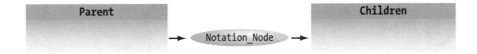

Figure 4-13. `Notation_Node` *relationships*

Attributes

Every node type has three attributes called `nodeName`, `nodeValue`, and `attributes`. However, they are used differently and sometimes ignored based on the type in question. For instance, the element and attribute nodes use `nodeName` to define tag content in XML, but text, comment, and document nodes essentially ignore it. The `nodeValue` attribute applies only to the attribute, CDATA section, comment, processing instruction, and text types.

The `attributes` attribute can be a little confusing. First, it is actually an attribute that declares attributes for the node. Second, `attributes` applies only to element node types. This attributes property will contain all the information that allows us to navigate the DOM tree of our data. This is quite a large collection of data that applies only to elements. Thus, the specification is seeking to minimize the overhead impact on other types that would never utilize this information. Defining the relationships among elements through their own properties has made navigating and manipulating the DOM tree much easier. For example, if you want to know what the parent of the current node is, you can reference that property instead of traversing up the tree and then identifying the node.

> **CAUTION** *Don't confuse the attributes, or properties, of elements in the DOM with the attributes that the elements may have defined in the XML document. These attribute properties exist only with the DOM structure and are not related to any attributes that may be defined by the data writer.*

This attributes property contains an interface to something called a `NamedNodeMap`, which is part of the DOM specification used to define a collection of nodes. In this case, it contains information specific to the current element type. Let's take a look at each of the attribute values in the element node type.

`childNodes`

This is a listing of all the child elements of the current element. These child elements are exposed through a `NodeList`. The `NodeList` is simply another interface that abstracts an ordered list of nodes; similar to how a structured array could contain the nodes. They are accessible through a 0-based index system. Thus, the second child of the current node would be found through the following pseudocode:

```
currentnode.childNodes(1)
```

> **NOTE** *I am using pseudocode in this section in the hope of communicating basic concepts to developers of various languages. You will need to transcribe this logic to your own language and DOM or SAX implementation, because the syntax and even object and method names can vary.*

Earlier I talked about how attributes are not treated logically as child elements of the element to which they relate. If it wasn't clear, this is why that is the case. If you retrieve a list of child nodes that are composed of both attributes and elements, you would then have to qualify each node as an element or attribute. Figure 4-14 should help you to see how these two scenarios would differ in efficiency.

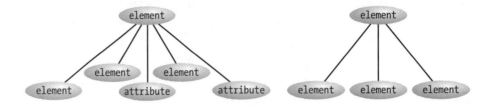

Figure 4-14. Elements versus elements and attributes as child nodes

firstChild

This property returns with the first child element of the current element. Because elements are sequenced in the DOM according to the order in which they were loaded, it would not be appropriate to assume that the firstChild is always the same element in different instances of the same schema. This is usually used more as an immediate, quick reference to the current DOM only.

lastChild

This property returns the last child element of the current element. Like the firstChild attribute, it is unwise to build a dependence upon this property outside of tightly controlled XML documents, even of the same schema.

localName

This property returns the local part of the qualified name for the current node. Any types other than attributes and elements will return a null value.

namespaceURI

This property contains the namespace reference for the current node. This value will be null if not declared in the XML document and that is acceptable.

nextSibling

This property directs you to the next node at the current level. If no additional nodes are present, it returns null. The sequence of nodes is determined by the childNodes property upon loading of the DOM. Just like the firstChild and lastChild nodes, this property depends upon the sequence of elements as they were loaded into the DOM.

ownerDocument

This is a read-only property that associates the current node with the document object of the current DOM. This associates the node with the root node of the entire document.

parentNode

This property returns the parent element of the current node. Only one parent can exist per node, so, given a single instance of a node, this is pretty much foolproof and should not vary from load to load of the same document structure.

> **NOTE** *By a single instance of a node, I am referring to the same node definition in the same location. Certainly the same node can exist in more than one area. City can be a node in a mailing address element and billing address element, as seen in the following code. These would be different instances of the same element.*

```
<shippingData>
     <mailingAddress>
          . . .
          <city></city>   <!--Instance 1-->
     </mailingAddress>
     <billingAddress>
          . . .
          <city></city>   <!--Instance 2-->
     </billingAddress>
</shippingData>
```

prefix

This attribute contains the namespace prefix of the current node. It returns null if it is unspecified. Changing this value is sometimes allowed, but this does have consequences on other properties of certain types. We will not be doing this, but be sure to look into it further if you ever attempt it.

previousSibling

This returns the previous node in the list. The behavior is the same as that of nextSibling, and if no previous nodes are present, it returns null.

Methods

Now that we have covered all the properties of the node interface, it is time to start working with the DOM. Although some tasks can be accomplished by referencing attributes (as we just saw), their capabilities are limited. After all, if you try to work with the property of a node that doesn't exist, you are going to run into problems. The additional functionality needed to have more robust control of your XML data will be attained through the methods exposed by the interface.

appendChild

This method adds a child node to the current node. If a node of the same name already exists, it is removed, and then the new node is added. Therefore, if you append a child node, make changes to its properties, and append it again, your work is lost! Because you are appending, it is simply adding the node to the end of the node list, making it the last child node in any sequence. The pseudocode for appending a child node looks like this:

```
{sourceNode}.appendChild ({newChildNode})
```

As you can see by the code, you are passing in a node as a parameter, which means that you aren't actually creating a node, but are simply taking a node and appending it to the current node. This allows for the migration of an existing node from one area to another in, or even across, DOMs. Remember, this node can also represent a collection of nodes if it is a document fragment type.

cloneNode

This takes a node and makes an existing copy of it. This is just like using the copy routine in an application. The duplicate node does not exist in the current tree and does not have a parent. However, it copies any attributes and copies child nodes if you specify it through the parameter. In the case of child nodes, the resulting node ends up as a document fragment type, as shown here:

```
{clonedNode}={originalNode}.cloneNode([boolean])
```

hasAttributes

This method tells you whether the current node has any attributes. There are no parameters, and it simply returns a true or false. This is a great method added in the Level 2 specification that will help you to avoid the errors that occur if you simply go looking for attributes that are not there. Usage of the `hasAttribute` method is shown here:

```
[boolean]={currentNode}.hasAttributes
```

hasChildNodes

Similar to `hasAttributes`, this is a great mechanism for finding out if the current node has any child nodes without having to traverse the tree. The syntax for this method can be seen here:

```
[boolean]={currentNode}.hasChildNodes
```

insertBefore

This method allows you to add a node previous to the specific node listed. While you may not care about the exact order, this is a convenient method for adding a node to a level without having to use the `appendChild` method. Navigating the DOM is tedious and costly, so being able to manipulate data in one command is a good thing.

Again, this method does not create a node for you, so you pass in the node to insert as well as the node before which you wish to insert it. If the referenced node does not exist, this method simply adds the node to the end of the list of current nodes. Shown next is the usage for `insertBefore`:

```
{insertedNode}=node}.insertBefore({nodeToInsert},{existingNode})
```

isSupported

You use the `isSupported` feature to discover whether an implementation has implemented a specific feature. This is not something you are likely to use in your code (unless you are working with various parsers), but you could use it ahead of time to verify an implementation or troubleshoot unexpected results from the processor. This method returns a simple true or false and takes two parameters, specifying the feature in question and the version of support you are looking for. The syntax for `isSupported` is shown here:

```
[boolean]=node.isSupported({feature},{version})
```

`normalize`

This method collects all text nodes in the element and its subtree into a single child node. This helps to not only aggregate adjacent text nodes, but also eliminate empty ones. The syntax is very simple, as seen here:

`{currentNode}.normalize`

`removeChild`

The `removeChild` method allows you to completely remove a child node from the current node. The return on this call is actually the node you deleted, so this is more of a cut function than a straight deletion. The following code shows the syntax for `removeChild`.

`{removedNode}={parentNode}.removeChild({nodeToRemove})`

`replaceChild`

When you want to swap one node for another in the DOM tree, use this method. Just like the `removeChild` call, this method returns the original node, so no deletion of nodes actually occurs during this process. The syntax for `replaceChild` is given here:

`{oldChild}=node.replaceChild({newChild},{oldChild})`

`DOMException`

`DOMException` is not a method call, but, as you might suspect, is an exception that is raised by the DOM. This happens most frequently when you attempt a method call with invalid parameters or upon inappropriate nodes. Most DOM implementations you work with take advantage of the defined constants for `DOMException`, so I will not go over them here. (Codes are self-explanatory.)

Usage

Now that I have covered all the details of the DOM structure, let's see its usage in actual code. For the sake of accommodating various backgrounds and DOM implementations, I will continue to use pseudocode in these examples. Don't worry; we'll be looking at actual code when we build and consume Web services in Chapter 6 through 8!

Let's start with a scenario in which you add a few nodes to a DOM. The tree is loaded with the following XML data:

```
<sampleRequest>
    <date>2001-07-01</date>
    <customer>ACME
      <contact>John Smith</contact>
      <phone>6175552323</phone>
    </customer>
    <part>
      <partNumber>B89451</partNumber>
      <quantity>1</quantity>
      <dateRequired>2001-07-14</dateRequired>
    </part>
</sampleRequest>
```

You want to add the appropriate data to an approval section so that this request for a sample product can be fulfilled. Based on the business requirements, you know that the following schema defines the approval element:

```
<xsd:element name="approval">
    <xsd:complexType>
      <xsd:all>
          <xsd:element ref="firstName"/>
          <xsd:element ref="lastName"/>
          <xsd:element ref="position"/>
          <xsd:element ref="loanPeriod"/>
          <xsd:element ref="datePromised"/>
      </xsd:all>
    </xsd:complexType>
</xsd:element>
<xsd:element name="datePromised" type="xsd:timeInstant"/>
<xsd:element name="firstName" type="xsd:string"/>
<xsd:element name="lastName" type="xsd:string"/>
<xsd:element name="loanPeriod" type="xsd:timeDuration"/>
<xsd:element name="position">
    <xsd:simpleType>
      <xsd:restriction base="xsd:string">
          <xsd:enumeration value="District Manager"/>
          <xsd:enumeration value="Regional Manager"/>
          <xsd:enumeration value="Chief Financial Officer"/>
      </xsd:restriction>
    </xsd:simpleType>
</xsd:element>
```

You can see from this schema that the `approval` element has five child elements that are all required, and one has a defined set of valid values. There are actually a few different scenarios you could deal with in this situation. One is where this additional data is provided to you in a separate XML document. This makes the process fairly simple. The other case, which is much more likely, is one in which you have the data in some other format. It could be from a database, a user interface, or application-defined constants. In this scenario, we have to get the data into XML.

Remember that the DOM does not facilitate the creation of XML. You can move nodes, change the value of nodes, and delete nodes; you just cannot create them. Most implementations expose a method for creating nodes, but those are customizations of the DOM specification. When appropriate, you can eliminate the wholesale generation of XML code by designing your application to utilize templates. This would be a valueless document that merely has the structure defined. In this sample request scenario, the template might look like this:

```xml
<?xml version="1.0" encoding="UTF-8"?>
<approval>
    <firstName/>
    <lastName/>
    <position/>
    <loanPeriod/>
    <datePromised/>
</approval>
```

This provides all the structure that you need to contain all the data you need to incorporate your approval data. This is also an easy way to adhere to a specific schema. When you take this approach, it is best to declare everything in your template and delete the optional nodes that you won't use for that particular document.

The only other method for getting this data into an XML format involves actually building the code in your applications, and that is both tedious and less efficient. I will walk through the process for handling this scenario and solution, because receiving the data in XML would be elementary in comparison.

You could add your template to the final XML document and then modify it, or you could modify an instance of the template and then add it to your document. I choose the later because the memory consumption is less if you efficiently load and unload your documents.

This example contains two defined data sources. The first, `sampleRequestDoc`, references the sample request itself, and `approvalSegment` is the reference to the template. First make a copy of the template, as shown here:

```
templateNode=approvalSegment.childnodes(1).cloneNode(True)
```

Notice that, in the cloning, we are grabbing the second child node of the template. This is because the first node is a processor instruction node containing the XML header, as shown here:

```
<?xml version="1.0" encoding="UTF-8"?>
```

You'll want to define your node reference of the template at this level for two reasons. First, doing it here keeps you from having to step into the DOM an additional level every time you manipulate the data. For example, this method allows you to reference the position element with the code:

```
approvalSegment.childNodes(2).nodeTypedValue
```

Referencing the document at a higher level would require the following:

```
approvalSegment.childNodes(1).childNodes(2).nodeTypedValue
```

Second, referencing a document at the document level limits the level of access you have to the data. For instance, you cannot append a child to the approvalSegment node even if you drill down to the element level, because the initial reference is to a document node.

Next, you need to set the appropriate values for your approvalSegment, as shown here:

```
templateNode.childNodes(0).nodeValue = "Bill"
templateNode.childNodes(1).nodeValue = "Boxx"
templateNode.childNodes(2).nodeValue = "District Manager"
templateNode.childNodes(3).nodeValue = "P1M"
templateNode.childNodes(4).nodeValue = "1999-05-31T13:20:00.000-05:00"
```

> **CAUTION** *The* nodeValue *property is a read-only property for an element node type in the DOM. However, every modern implementation I have seen has supported this through some means. For instance, the Microsoft parser uses the method* nodeTypeValue *to differentiate it from the* nodeValue *method in the DOM. You could not change any element values at all if the implementation held strictly to the specification.*

Finally, we will append it to the existing sample request document, as shown here:

```
docRoot =sampleRequestDoc.childnodes(1)
docRoot.appendChild templateNode
```

Again, we are building a reference to the sample request at the second child node because the appendChild method is not valid on a document node type. Based on these changes, the completed XML document should now look like this:

```xml
<?xml version="1.0"?>
<sampleRequest>
    <date>2001-07-01</date>
    <customer>ACME
      <contact>John Smith</contact>
      <phone>6175552323</phone>
    </customer>
    <part>
      <partNumber>B89451</partNumber>
      <quantity>1</quantity>
      <dateRequired>2001-07-14</dateRequired>
    </part>
    <approval>
      <firstName>Bill</firstName>
      <lastName>Boxx</lastName>
      <position>District Manager</position>
      <loanPeriod>P1M</loanPeriod>
      <datePromised>1999-05-31T13:20:00.000-05:00</datePromised>
    </approval>
</sampleRequest>
```

Depending on the DOM implementation you are using, you may have some additional information referencing schemas and namespaces. This listing should be the lowest common denominator among all implementations.

As you can see, your access is a little restricted through the DOM. It is very much an all-or-nothing approach because you load entire documents into memory to work with them. Once you parse the document, you can certainly clone just the element or document segment you want to work with, but the loading of the document must occur first. There are several scenarios in which this would be a very inefficient use of your resources. A method for specific access to just one element, or an occurrence of an element, would be much more effective. This was the thinking behind the development of SAX.

SAX

Like the DOM, SAX allows you to access XML data in a document. However, the implementation is very different, and that difference can be either a benefit or a hindrance depending on what you are trying to accomplish.

SAX was created by a collection of developers who recognized the need for another API when working with XML data. These developers collaborated through the XML-DEV mailing list coordinated by David Megginson. (Anyone can join this mailing list, and the list archives are maintained at the site `http://www.lists.ic.ac.uk/hypermail/xml-dev/`.) Work on the initial specification proposal started in December 1997 and took only one month to complete. SAX 1.0 was actually established by the community in another five months. The culture and common interests of the development community allowed the discussion group to avoid much of the bureaucracy that occurs in large, formalized organizations. You can find the specification, as well as implementations, at Megginson's site: `http://www.megginson.com/SAX`.

The SAX specification is developed with Java in mind (the original spec was even named SAX-J) and is actually designed to work on top of existing Java parsers. This is different from the DOM, because parsers are typically built on top of it. Without a technology-agnostic approach to the specification, changes to the original design or intent have to be made to accommodate other languages. This results in implementations varying far more from vendor to vendor than DOM implementations. For the most part, vendors have tried to stay true to the original vision. Compromises have been made only to circumvent technical obstacles.

NOTE   *My discussion of SAX is based on the SAX2 specification released in May 2000. The parsers we will be working with later support this version.*

I've talked quite a bit about XML data in terms of a tree structure when discussing the DOM. The SAX model is different in that it is event driven. This means that SAX reports events to the parser based on what it finds while reading the document. The largest impact of this model is that the entire document is not directly loaded into memory. (See Figure 4-15.) For this reason, SAX is considered a lightweight parser of XML. This actually affords the developer the opportunity to load it into memory through a different model. Accomplishing this specific task using the DOM would be a two-step process, because it imposes its own model. So the main distinctions of SAX over the DOM are the ability to parse documents larger than available system memory and more efficient loading of XML into a custom model. This may or may not translate into a benefit depending on what you are trying to do.

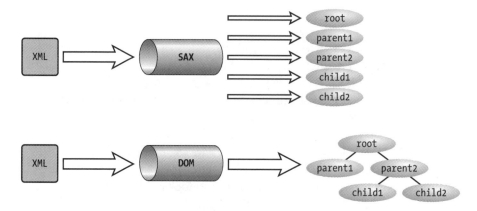

Figure 4-15. Graphical representation of the DOM and SAX APIs

Because SAX does less, it actually gives you less. The main limitation is the synchronous processing nature of parsers utilizing SAX. You are reading one node at a time once. When an XML document is loaded into the DOM, you can potentially have several processes referencing the data simultaneously. There is no dynamic referencing of an element in the document because you don't have it in memory and potentially never do. This also means that using SAX to reference the last node requires reading the entire document synchronously. The law of averages says that, in a given task of looking for one specific node, you should have to parse only half the document. Sometimes it will be the last node, but sometimes it should also be the first node.

The other limitation comes from the lack of a defined model. Obviously, if you aren't loading it, you have no defined data structure for containing the data. Inexperienced programmers could very well access nodes and load their values into variables without any relationships, making for very messy algorithms.

So you can see why different scenarios will require either the DOM or SAX for efficient access of your XML data. This means there is room for both the DOM and SAX to exist in a parser implementation.

Now that I have covered the background of SAX and why it is needed, let's take a look at the specifics.

Events

The basis for the SAX API is event handling. To SAX, every element triggers an event of some kind. The start of an element triggers one event, an attribute another, a text value another, the end of an element another, and so on. Table 4-1 lists each of the events supported in SAX along with a brief description.

Table 4-1. SAX Events

EVENT	DESCRIPTION
startDocument	Notification of the beginning of a document
endDocument	Notification of the completion of a document
startElement	Notification of the beginning of an element
endElement	Notification of the completion of an element
characters	Notification of character data
ignorableWhitespace	Notification of whitespace in an element
processingInstruction	Notification of processing instructions
setDocumentLocator	Notification of the origin for document events
skippedEntity	Notification of a skipped entity
startPrefixMapping	Notification of the beginning of scope on a namespace mapping
endPrefixMapping	Notification of the end of scope on a namespace mapping

When reading a document, SAX views the XML as a series of events. As an example, look at the following XML data:

```
<hotelAvailability>
    <date>2001-08-05</date>
    <hotel>
      <chain>Milton</chain>
      <distance>5</distance>
      <bedSize>King</bedSize>
      <cost>120</cost>
      <nonsmoking>Yes</nonsmoking>
    </hotel>
</hotelAvailability>
```

If we parse this using SAX, our events would trigger the following calls in order (indentions are only for readability):

```
startDocument
startElement ("hotelAvailability ")
    startElement ("date")
      characters ("2001-08-05")
    endElement ("date")
    startElement ("hotel")
      startElement ("chain")
```

```
            characters("Milton")
        endElement ("chain")
        startElement ("distance")
            characters ("5")
        endElement ("distance")
        startElement ("bedSize")
            characters ("king")
        endElement ("bedSize")
        startElement ("cost")
            characters ("120")
        endElement ("cost")
        startElement ("nonsmoking")
            characters ("Yes")
        endElement ("nonsmoking")
    endElement ("hotel")
endElement ("hotelAvailability")
endDocument
```

Of course, while you are parsing this information, you can choose to capture it in some model, but that is not part of the SAX specification. It is simply notifying you of the appropriate information as it parses.

The way you capture these events is by utilizing an event handler. This is basically a routine that is called by a given event. SAX exposes these events through the contentHandler interface. Put another way, the events in Table 4-1 are actually methods of the contentHandler interface.

> **NOTE** *The* contentHandler *interface replaced* documentHandler *with the release of SAX2. Although* documentHandler *is still supported for backward compatibility,* contentHandler *must be used if you want to support namespaces.*

To expose this interface, you must first implement the XMLReader interface. It is responsible for actually initiating a parse and registering the event handlers. As I mentioned earlier, SAX is designed as a synchronous process. XMLReader can utilize only one process thread, because an event handler must return before continuing to parse a document. In other words, a separate thread cannot continue parsing a document while an event handler is working.

Table 4-2 shows the methods of the XMLReader interface. Parse is obviously the most important method. The others can be helpful for querying features or utilizing other applications.

Table 4-2. XMLReader *Methods*

METHOD	DESCRIPTION
parse	Parses an XML document
getContentHandler	Returns the content handler
setContentHandler	Registers a content handler
getDTDHandler	Returns the DTD handler
setDTDHandler	Registers a DTD event handler
getEntityResolver	Returns the entity resolver
setEntityResolver	Registers an entity resolver
getErrorHandler	Returns the error handler
setErrorHandler	Registers an error handler
getFeature	Returns the value of a feature
setFeature	Sets the state of a feature
getProperty	Returns the value of a property
setProperty	Sets the value of a property

Usage

Like with any event-based system, you have to implement routines that "catch" the event as it occurs. If you are used to working with only procedure-based or function-based applications, this may be a bit of an adjustment. It isn't difficult; it's just another way of thinking about an application process.

The difference can probably be best explained through a football analogy in which the two teams line up on either side of the football: offense and defense. The offense is the proactive side, determining which play it runs based on the situation. The defense may try to anticipate, but ultimately reacts to what the offense does. For instance, if the offense runs the ball, everyone converges on the running back. If the quarterback drops back for a pass, some people chase after him, but others drop back, trying to break up the pass.

Writing a procedural application is like playing offense: you dictate the flow of the logic, being very proactive. Writing an event-based application is like playing defense: you anticipate things the application will do and write routines for what the application will do should those things actually occur. Like in football, the key is being prepared by knowing what to do for any given scenario.

Fortunately, the API has defined all the events that can occur, so, if you follow the specification, you shouldn't be surprised. The key for developers is to know what conditions of those events to look out for. If you look for a certain element, or a certain sequence of elements, you need to program those conditions into your event handlers. Let's walk through a scenario.

Say you have an application that needs to filter XML documents for hotel rooms that match some criteria. (Although there may be a more efficient means of doing this, let's say for the sake of argument that this is all you have to work with.) You collect several documents that have hotel rooms in the right city and in your price range, but you want to go one step further by qualifying rooms that are nonsmoking and have a king-sized bed. You will work with the same document structure you saw earlier in the hotel availability sample.

The first thing you need to do is load your XMLReader and start parsing. Look at this in pseudocode:

```
hotelHandler=XMLReader
hotelHandler.contentHandler = myContentHandler
hotelHandler.errorHandler = myErrorHandler
hotelHandler.parse "c:\hotelDoc.xml"
```

Notice that we defined the error handler as well as the content handler. Although we can technically get away with not implementing the error handler, I recommend always implementing it if you have any hope for a reliable application.

The content handler is responsible for capturing all the legal events that occur during the parse. In this case, we are looking for two specific elements: bedSize and nonsmoking. Let's first look at generic event handlers for startElement and characters, as shown here:

```
event startElement(namespaceURI, localName, QName, Attributes)
```

This event passes along four pieces of information, three related to the name of the element and a fourth containing all the attributes. Without namespaces, only the local name is passed. With namespaces, both the URI and the local name are available. The QName, or qualified name (namespace prefix:local name) for an element, is available when namespace prefixes are used. The attributes are always available when present.

The problem with this scenario is that we are looking for the values of these elements and not just the tags themselves. This actually requires two events in SAX. That means we have to work with the characters event, as shown here:

```
event characters(string)
```

This is a very straightforward event collecting the value of the element. The actual form of the data being passed to the event may be an array of characters, depending on the language utilized, but I will treat it as a string for simplicity's sake.

Because these two events are entirely separate and unrelated, you have to coordinate the succession of events that produces a bedSize element with a specific value and a nonsmoking event with a specific value.

One way to accomplish this is to declare a global working variable for capturing your element name when the startElement event fires. This way the characters event can be aware of the activity in the startElement event. Remember that SAX parsing is synchronous, so you don't have to worry about multiple processes touching your variable and corrupting it.

Go ahead and add the logic to filter your hotel data. Declare your global variable as currElement. You also have two declared variables that you used to capture the smoking and bed preference from the end user: smokingSelection and bedSelection, as shown here:

```
event startElement(namespaceURI, localName, QName, Attributes)
    currElement=localName
end event
event characters(string)
    if currElement="bedSize" then
      if string = bedSelection then
        . . .
    else if currElement = "nonsmoking" then
      if string = smokingSelection then
        . . .
end event
```

By collecting the state of the startElement event, you can intelligently interpret the data in your elements, thus filtering your data. I'm sure you've noticed that I conveniently left out the logic to select the hotel once your condition was met. Because no data model is present in SAX, you have to build some mechanism for actually storing the data, in this case just the data you select. This may take the form of an array, a tree, or even a physical document. This is for you to decide, and it falls outside the scope of this book. I recommend getting a book on SAX2 for more ideas on this particular topic.

SAX Versus DOM

Both of these methods for accessing XML data can be effective in the right scenario. They can both ultimately accomplish the same tasks, but they go about them quite differently. This does not mean that one method is more accurate than the other. It is purely an issue of performance. Given a single task, one will probably accomplish it more quickly and efficiently than the other.

Although the quicker approach is often going to be better, the additional aspect of efficiency makes this tradeoff less clear. This metric depends on the resources available in your system and their efficiency, so making a blanket judgment can be quite difficult.

There are always exceptions, but SAX is generally better at referencing specific nodes out of a document or when you need to reference the nodes of a document only once. If you need to do more than that, you will likely benefit from loading the document into memory via the DOM.

Unfortunately, the decision of whether to use SAX or the DOM for an application may be out of your hands. If you use an existing parser to work with your XML data, you use whatever methods are being used behind the scenes. Don't assume that just because you are loading the XML into a DOM that it isn't using SAX to accomplish that task. The same goes for using SAX and thinking that it must not be using a DOM structure behind the scenes. If performance is that important an issue, it will serve you well to research the parsers you select. If the performance of your parsing is not an issue, then you may never have to concern yourself with the tradeoffs.

In general, Java parsers utilize SAX for parsing data, regardless of whether they are storing the data in a DOM structure. Microsoft's MSXML parser let's you choose the parsing method, but only the developers know how it actually works behind the covers. Typically, if you use Visual Basic, you utilize the DOM interface. This is simply because object-oriented languages are much more suited to support event-driven applications (hence, the wide support for SAX by the Java community). Although SAX and DOM can be used to do almost anything with your XML data, some things are better done with a slightly different approach. When you are working with the same data over and over and doing the exact same thing with it, writing an application may not be the most efficient approach. Instead of working with your data at a low level, why not just tweak the data through some high-level manipulations?

Manipulating XML

As your usage of XML continues to evolve, more and more tools will become available to make working with it easier. Many people think developers may someday not work with XML directly, even those of us who enjoy getting our hands dirty! While that day may be a while off, vendors are already making strides at making the usage of XML more efficient. When XML was first introduced, developers had to use compilers and parsers to do anything with XML. Not only is this overkill for a simple scenario (like changing one value of one node in a document), but it also requires a high level of technical expertise.

One community to jump on the XML bandwagon was Web developers, who work with technologies like HTML, CSS (Cascading Style Sheets), and scripts. XML helped them to work with data, but it required a lot of learning on their part to even touch it programmatically. Of course, XML is very similar to HTML, but it defines data, not presentation. This community needed a way to get that data into a presentable form. Some of the initial efforts to bridge this gap took the form of the XSL specification.

XSLT

XSLT (eXtensible Stylesheet Language Transformations) has a somewhat confusing definition. It is actually one of the three specifications that make up the XSL standard. XSL was originally submitted to the W3C in 1997, and XSLT was broken out into its own specification in April 1999. XSLT is now recognized as the language of XSL for transforming XML documents into other XML documents. You can think of XSLT as the language that makes up the content of documents known as XSL stylesheets. The processors that support the XSLT language are considered to be XSL processors.

The second component of XSL is called XSL Formatting Objects and specifies formatting semantics related to presentation-specific functionality. XSL Formatting Objects fall outside the scope of this discussion. The third component of the standard is XPath, which is a non-XML syntax for locating portions of an XML document. You will use XPath in your XSLT when identifying nodes in your XML document.

XSLT became a recommendation of the W3C in November 1999. You can find the entire specification at `http://www.w3.org/TR/xslt.html`. Several fine books cover this standard in depth (for example, *XSLT* by Michael Kay), so I will provide an overview, focusing on the topics that have significance to working with Web services.

Conceptually, XSLT should really be thought of as a scripting language, similar to JavaScript or VBScript. However, it is physically more similar to Cold Fusion because it is a tag-based sequence of rules. Like these languages, XSLT is never actually compiled into a binary. Rather it is a set of rules that are interpreted in real time when applied to an XML document.

> **NOTE** *Some processors are starting to do precompiling of XSL stylesheets, but this is outside the capabilities of XSLT itself.*

An XSL processor is the engine that takes the XML data source(s), loads the XSL document, maps the XML to it, and produces a resulting XML document. (See Figure 4-16.) This process is usually referred to as a transformation, but it can also be referred to as mapping or overlaying. This result is then displayed, saved, or delivered without any reference or relationship to the original XML or XSL.

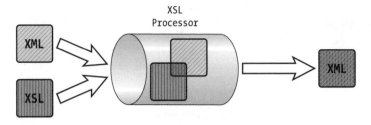

Figure 4-16. XSL mapping of XML

XSLT does not replace the DOM or SAX API. In fact, implementations likely utilize these APIs behind the scenes in their XSL processors. The DOM is especially valuable because XSL borrows its model of XML as a tree. Because XML can be sourced in many ways, XSLT references DOMs through a logical model. This keeps applications from having to send the XML through a document state.

Because XSLT is a rules-based language, the language has two key components: elements and expressions. By identifying the elements in a document and recognizing their expressions, you can extract, modify, and enhance the source into another document.

Elements

Like XML itself, elements are the building blocks of XSLT. These elements are used to identify, describe, qualify, and act upon the data in your source. More than 35 elements are defined in XSLT, but I will not cover them all here. I will discuss only those elements you are most likely to need in working with Web services. These include the following:

- stylesheet

- template

- apply-templates

- element

- attribute

- value-of

- text

- comment

- param

- variable

- for-each

- if

- choose, when, and otherwise

- copy

- copy-of

- sort

For a more complete listing, you can look on the W3C site or in one of the available books dedicated to XSLT.

stylesheet

The fundamental element for all stylesheets is the stylesheet element. This is the root that declares the namespace and establishes the fact that this document is a stylesheet. For organizational purposes, XSL Stylesheets should either be kept separate from non-XSLT XML data documents or they should have a very distinct naming convention. The syntax with the current namespace is as follows:

```
<xsl:stylesheet version="1.0" xmlns:xsl="http://www.w3.org/1999/XSL/Transform" >
</xsl:stylesheet>
```

> **NOTE** *Some stylesheets declare the* transform *element as the root. The* transform *element is synonymous with* stylesheet *and is permissible as a substitute according to the specification. Also, all code examples in this section assume the presence of this* stylesheet *node as the root.*

template

The template element is used to map XSLT code with the appropriate data in an XML document. It does this by acting as a container and defining the appropriate rules. Therefore, the content in the template body is executed whenever the rule applies. At first this might appear to be redundant with the stylesheet element, but a single stylesheet can have many templates, so it is not just a one-to-one relationship.

```
<xsl:template match="/" name="rootTemplate" priority="1">
    . . .
</xsl:template>
```

The rule itself is defined by the match attribute, which identifies a valid path in the XML document, against which it runs. A value of "/" refers to the root node of the document and always leads in precedence to other templates. In the case of multiple rules, the priority attribute determines which one runs, not an order of precedence. The rule with the highest priority value is executed. The others are applied to a document only if this "master" template references them.

The name attribute is optional, but you will want to use it if you ever hope to reference it through the apply-templates element.

apply-templates

This element allows you to apply a defined template. This is very useful whenever you use a template multiple times. Rather than actually listing the template every time it is used, you can define it and reference it. The following templates define the formatting for the name of a customer and reuse it:

```
<xsl:template match="customerData">
    . . .
    <xsl:apply-templates select="customer"/>
    . . .
</xsl:template>

<xsl:template match="customer">
    <xsl:value-of select="name/family"/>
    <xsl:text>,</xsl:text>
    <xsl:value-of select="name/given"/>
</xsl:template>
```

element

Unlike the DOM and SAX, the creation of elements is defined as a part of the XSLT standard. The element element is the mechanism for doing so. The nice thing about the implementation of the element tag is that it allows for the naming of the element to be automated and not just hard coded. The content of this element can also be treated as a template for the value, attributes, and children of the element. The following code:

```
<xsl:element name="bedSize">King</xsl:element>
```

produces this output:

```
<bedSize>King</bedSize>
```

attribute

The attribute element is used to generate new attributes for elements in the resulting document. Attributes can be defined for new elements or existing elements. There actually is no distinction between the two, since even existing elements are recreated in the new document. The following code creates an attribute named "condition" and assigns it a value of "new":

```
<xsl:attribute name="condition">new</xsl:attribute>
```

> **TIP** *I have noticed that XSLT processors behave more consistently when the attribute element is applied before any values in elements. Theoretically, the order should not matter.*

value-of

To reference the value of an element in your source document, you can use the value-of element. This allows you to select the value of any element at the current level (a combination of the template element and this one) and reproduce it. The specific element whose value you reference is given in the select attribute. This is always a closed tag, meaning it has no end tag, because its contents have no meaning to the XSL processor. In the following code, we are selecting any nodes with a value of "bedSize":

```
<xsl:value-of select="bedSize"/>
```

text

The text element can be used to wrap around plain text in XSL. Usually this information can be exposed directly, but there are cases in which you will want to exempt it from the tag-based structure and syntax of XSLT. This can help especially with protecting the stylesheet from special characters that might be in the text data. The following code will produce a simple text node with the value of "Size":

```
<xsl:text>Size</xsl:text>
```

This could be utilized to rewrite the earlier sample for the attribute tag to produce the exact same result, as shown here:

```
<xsl:attribute name="condition"><xsl:text>new</xsl:text></xsl:attribute>
```

comment

To add comments to your transformed document, use the comment tag. The contents of the tag are the actual comments, and there are no attributes for this element as you can see in the following example below:

```
<xsl:comment>This data is provided courtesy of company XYZ.</xsl:comment>
```

This generates the following standard comment line in XML:

```
<!--This data is provided courtesy of company XYZ.-->
```

param

The param element is one of two elements available for binding values to variables. This element is unique in that the assigned value acts as only a default value and can be influenced by external references (through the with-param element). Hence, the param element is similar to a public property in the programming paradigm. The param element can be either declared at the top of the document and referenced globally or declared at the top of a template and referenced locally. The name attribute is required. The following code shows the proper usage for the param element:

```
<xsl:param name="sport">Hockey</xsl:param>
```

A param element can be referenced, in the scope in which it is defined, through the value-of element. This is done by declaring the name of the parameter with a '$' prefix, as shown here:

```
<xsl:value-of select="$sport"/>
```

variable

The `variable` is the other element available for binding values to variables. The `variable` is different in that it is private and can be modified only in the scope in which it is defined. The `variable` is also different from `param` in that it can be declared at any point in a template, not exclusively as the immediate child. The scope of `variable` works the same way as `param`, and its usage is the same, as shown here:

```
<xsl:variable name="sport">Hockey</xsl:variable>
```

This example shows the `variable` with a content template. An alternative implementation utilizes the `select` attribute to declare the value, making the variable a closed tag, as shown here:

```
<xsl:variable name="sport" select="'Hockey'"/>
```

Take care that you properly delineate string values, because the double quotes alone will treat the value not as a string, but as a `node` reference. This subtle difference (seen in the following example) produces not an error, but very likely an empty value if no `Hockey` node is defined:

```
<xsl:variable name="sport" select="Hockey"/>
```

for-each

The `for-each` element allows you to loop through a series of elements that match a specific condition. For example, if you have a series of orders and want to run a certain template on every order to check for some specific condition, the `for-each` element facilitates that.

The `for-each` element has only one attribute, `select`. This is where the condition is defined for this template. The content between the start and end tags of the `for-each` element constitutes the template for the condition. The following is an example of the start and end tags for a `for-each` element:

```
<xsl:for-each select="hotelAvailability/hotel">
    . . .
</xsl:for-each>
```

if

The `if` element is used whenever a condition needs to be tested in your XSLT. Like other programmatic `if` conditions, this is an all-or-nothing test in which the action is either taken (in this case, referencing the template) or ignored. The `if` element can be a child of itself and can be run in succession. There is no `else` condition available, so if you want to determine a series of exclusive conditions, you may prefer using the `choose` element. The following code demonstrates the syntax for the start and end tag of the `if` element:

```
<xsl:if test="nonsmoking='Yes'">
    . . .
</xsl:if>
```

choose, when, *and* otherwise

The `choose` element allows you to choose from a number of possible alternatives. It is always followed by one or more `when` elements and an optional `otherwise` element. When you declare a `choose`, you build a series of conditional tests that allow you to select the appropriate action for each condition. These tests are administered through the `when` elements. The `otherwise` element serves as a catch-all if none of the tests is passed. This logic is very similar to that of a `case` or `switch` statement or a series of `if-thens`, only more efficient.

The `choose` element has no attributes and can contain only `when` and `otherwise` child elements. The following code shows the basic syntax of the `choose` element:

```
<xsl:choose>
    . . .
</xsl:choose>
```

Like the `if` element, the `when` statements have only a test attribute, which declares the expression. Each `when` statement is evaluated in order, and the resulting outcome is always a Boolean answer (true or false). The following example defines a condition in which the value of the `bedSize` element equals the string 'King':

```
<xsl:when test="bedSize='King'">
    . . .
</xsl:when>
```

The `otherwise` element, like `choose` itself, has no attributes. Only one `otherwise` element can exist as a child of a `choose` element, and its content is referenced only when all `when` tests have failed. Because no condition needs to be defined, the `otherwise` syntax is very basic, as seen here:

```
<xsl:otherwise>
    . . .
</xsl:otherwise>
```

Let's look at a complete choose statement that takes a different action based on the evaluation. It will evaluate the price of the room and offer appropriate comments, as seen here:

```
<xsl:choose>
    <xsl:when test="cost&lt; 20">
      <xsl:comment>Too cheap! Move on!</xsl:comment>
    </xsl:when>
    <xsl:when test='cost&lt; 100'>
      <xsl:comment>Could be a bargain!</xsl:comment>
    </xsl:when>
    <xsl:otherwise>
      <xsl:comment>Too much! Move on!</xsl:comment>
    </xsl:otherwise>
</xsl:choose>
```

> **NOTE** < *is the code representation of the < special character in XML documents.*

It is important to note that this routine acts just as a case or switch statement. If the price of the hotel room is $19, only the first when condition is triggered. If you do not want an exclusive selection, use either the if element or multiple choose statements.

copy

The copy element allows you to make a copy of the existing node at your exact location in the XML document. This means you end up making the element a child node of the current node. This statement allows you to copy only the node itself, not its attributes or children. However, you can reference an attribute set through the copy element's properties. For a recursive copy, use the copy-of element.

One use of this function might be when you want to work through a group of nodes and push them down a level. This is accomplished by using a for-each statement, building the node you want at that level, and making the original node a child. Consider the following document for hotel availability:

```
<hotelAvailability>
    <date>2001-08-05</date>
    <hotel>
      <chain>Milton</chain>
```

```
            <distance>5</distance>
            <bedSize>King</bedSize>
            <cost>79.99</cost>
            <nonsmoking>Yes</nonsmoking>
        </hotel>
        <hotel>
            <chain>Harriot</chain>
            <distance>10</distance>
            <bedSize>Queen</bedSize>
            <cost>59.99</cost>
            <nonsmoking>Yes</nonsmoking>
        </hotel>
</hotelAvailability>
```

You can transform the document so that it provides pricing information by chain like this:

```
<hotelPricing>
    <date>2001-08-05</date>
    <chain>Milton
        <cost>79.99</cost>
    </chain>
    <chain>Harriot
        <cost>59.99</cost>
    </chain>
</hotelPricing>
```

This is how you can apply the copy element to get there:

```
. . .
<xsl:template match="/" name="rootTemplate">
    <hotelAvailability>
        <date>
            <xsl:value-of select="/hotelAvailability/date"/>
        </date>
        <xsl:for-each select="hotelAvailability/hotel/chain">
            <xsl:copy>
                <xsl:value-of select="."/>
                <cost>
                    <xsl:value-of select="../cost"/>
                </cost>
            </xsl:copy>
        </xsl:for-each>
    </hotelAvailability>
</xsl:template>
. . .
```

You may not recognize some expressions in this selection of relative nodes. We will look at these and other expressions in the next section.

copy-of

copy-of is just like the copy element, but with a larger scope. This means that all of the element's children are captured with it, which can make a huge difference in the output between the two elements. For example, the following XML code is extracted if we use the copy-of instead of the copy element in our hotel pricing scenario:

```
<hotelPricing>
    <date>2001-08-05</date>
    <chain>Milton</chain>
    <chain>Harriot</chain>
</hotelPricing>
```

Notice that the cost element is not present. This is because copy-of is a closed tag, so you cannot make references in each node to do anything to the document segment copied over. Because this limits what we can do in our XSLT, let's see how that would look:

```
. . .
<xsl:template match="/" name="rootTemplate">
    <hotelAvailability>
        <date>
            <xsl:value-of select="/hotelAvailability/date"/>
        </date>
        <xsl:for-each select="hotelAvailability/hotel/chain">
            <xsl:copy-of select="."/>
        </xsl:for-each>
    </hotelAvailability>
</xsl:template>
. . .
```

In this scenario, the data document has to use another transformation to add the cost data from the chain nodes. You might be wondering why you would ever use the copy-of instead of the copy element. In this example, the chain did not have any attributes or child nodes. If it has, say, an attribute called `standing`, then the output of a `copy-of` reflects that, as shown here:

```
<hotelPricing>
    <date>2001-08-05</date>
    <chain standing="good">Milton</chain>
    <chain standing="great">Harriot</chain>
</hotelPricing>
```

Under the same scenario, the previous copy output would not have changed with the addition of this attribute. The same results apply if `chain` has one or more child nodes.

sort

The `sort` element is a very powerful filter that can order the construction of elements based on one or more keys. It can be used in only a `for-each` or `apply-templates` element, because a sort needs a defined set, or group, of elements. In fact, the `sort` element is a closed tag, which might be a bit misleading. Rather than thinking of `sort` as a collection (as you might in other languages), you should think of it as a property of either the `for-each` or `apply-templates` element.

The attributes of the `sort` element are `select`, `order`, `lang`, `case-order`, and `data-type`. Select obviously allows you to select the node on which you want to sort. Order reflects your requirement to list the values in descending or ascending order. Lang can be used to define the language of this particular sort key. Case-order refers to whether uppercase or lowercase values have priority in the sort. The default value can vary between implementations. The `data-type` property refers to the type of the key being sorted. The valid values are text (the default), number, and QName (qualified name.)

The ability to sort on multiple keys is built into the element. Every successive sort child node reflects a subcategory on which to sort. Consider the following set of hotel data:

```
<hotel>
    <chain>Milton</chain>
    <cost>79.99</cost>
    . . .
</hotel>
<hotel>
    <chain>Harriot</chain>
    <cost>59.99</cost>
    . . .
```

```
</hotel>
<hotel>
   <chain>Pyatt</chain>
   <cost>69.99</cost>
   . . .
</hotel>
<hotel>
   <chain>Heabody</chain>
   <cost>89.99</cost>
   . . .
</hotel>
```

If you simply want to rank these entries by chain in alphabetical order, you can use the following template:

```
<xsl:template match="/" name="rootTemplate">
   <xsl:for-each select="hotelAvailability/hotel">
     <xsl:sort select="chain"/>
     <chain><xsl:value-of select="chain"/></chain>
   </xsl:for-each>
</xsl:template>
```

To take this one step further, you can sort based on price, then chain name. That template looks more like this:

```
<xsl:template match="/" name="rootTemplate">
   <xsl:for-each select="hotelAvailability/hotel">
     <xsl:sort select="price" data-type="number" order="ascending"/>
     <xsl:sort select="chain" data-type="text"/>
     <chain><xsl:value-of select="chain"/></chain>
     <price><xsl:value-of select="cost"/></price>
   </xsl:for-each>
</xsl:template>
```

This takes advantage of a few of the attributes of the sort element to be more explicit in the sort definition. Numbers and text can sort differently, so you want to make sure that your data is treated appropriately. As you might expect, this template produces the following XML:

```
<hotel>
   <chain>Harriot</chain>
   <price>59.99</price>
</hotel>
<hotel>
```

```
    <chain>Pyatt</chain>
    <price>69.99</price>
</hotel>
<hotel>
    <chain>Milton</chain>
    <price>79.99</price>
</hotel>
<hotel>
    <chain>Heabody</chain>
    <price>89.99</price>
</hotel>
```

Expressions

Expressions are used in the XSLT language to reference data. This data can take the form of simple equations, like 2 + 2, or the form of a path reference. The key is an expression can be resolved as only one value for a given situation (document). For a mathematical expression, the laws of mathematics dictate the value. Other expressions may not be as firmly rooted in natural laws, but they are just as absolute in a given set of data.

The most common kind of expression in XSLT is to identify a specific node in an XML data set. Expressions are also used to define conditions for processing routines and to generate text for result sets. This is where mathematical routines can sometimes be useful. Any element that supports the select, match, or test attribute (that is, value-of, apply-templates, for-each, and so on) identifies a certain node, or group of common nodes, to work with. Remember that XSLT treats XML as a node-based tree, just like the DOM, so using paths to specify an element follows that structure. The expressions used in XSLT are actually paths that are defined in the XPath specification. This is part of the reason XPath is a component of the XSL standard.

We will use several expression types that cover a range of techniques and approaches. There is almost always more than one way to reference a node, so I recommend that you find a method, or set of methods, that you are comfortable with and reuse those for consistency. We will look at only some of the most frequently used or needed expressions in this section. For a more thorough discussion of the valid expressions in XSLT, I recommend getting a book dedicated to XSL/XPath or digging through the specification for XPath itself at http://www.w3.org/TR/xpath.html.

Paths

Whenever you identify a path in a data set, understanding the context of that path is critical to success. Context simply refers to the current frame of reference, in this case your current location in a data set. If you give directions based on your current location to someone starting from a different location, your directions will not get that person to the correct destination. Even worse, you may tell the person to turn left on a road where only a right turn is possible. Hopefully, the person will at least have built-in error handling that prevents a crash!

There are some methods for identifying a location globally. This is done by simply starting at the root level of the document. This is great for providing a foolproof method for locating a node, but it is not always appropriate. Perhaps the node you want is specifically related to the current node. Any scenario in which you want only one specific node out of several unordered instances requires relative pathing.

> *Relative pathing* refers to locating a node based on your current location. *Global pathing* or *absolute pathing* refers to locating a node from the root level.

CAUTION *The pathing expressions are somewhat similar to the pathing syntax for HTML. However, there are discrepancies, so don't assume that, if it works for HTML, it works for XSLT.*

When I talk about the current location or the current node, I am talking about a logical location, not a physical one. XSLT does not actually walk a model like the DOM, but rather references it through a series of rules. To "be in a location" actually refers to being in the scope of a certain rule. The hotel example had the following XSLT:

```
<xsl:template match="/" name="rootTemplate">
   <xsl:for-each select="hotelAvailability/hotel">
     <xsl:sort select="chain"/>

     . . .
   </xsl:for-each>
   . . .
```

The first line establishes the template scope at the root level. Anything we reference at this point references the entire document. The for-each rule goes down to the hotel level in hotelAvailability. The context is now at the hotel level, and anything we reference is related to the hotel node(s). The third line defines a sort, but it doesn't change the location. It is just a rule telling how to treat the data at the current level. However, as soon as we close the for-each tag, we are back up to the root level of the document.

Now that you have an understanding of locations, let's look at some of the expressions that allow us to navigate the data.

/

The slash (/) is the character for starting at the root. This is how all global pathing references start because it allows you to back out of your current context. All other paths look at the child elements of only your current element. It is important to realize that this does not actually define a node. Rather, this is treated as a virtual node that is always the parent of your document root. This allows you to treat the root as a container for the entire document. Following that approach, this example takes you to the explicit path of the date node in the hotelPricing document:

```
/hotelPricing/date
```

Without a virtual container, this path would just be /date. That could get confusing if you ever wanted to work with the root node directly. Furthermore, if you remove the slash in front of hotelPricing, it returns the appropriate node only if you are already at the root of the document.

{node}/{node}

The use of the slash between nodes simply communicates a parent-child relationship. This is how we can traverse the children of our data document. The slash can also be used to traverse up the tree through parent relationships when combined with the appropriate syntax.

{node}//{node}

The use of a double slash describes an ancestor-child relationship. That means an instance of one node preceding another, regardless of the levels between them. This would be a superset of the parent-child relationships. The expression hotelAvailability//date applied to the following code results in both instances of the date node:

```
<hotelAvailability>
    <date/>
    <hotel>
      <date/>
    </hotel>
</hotelAvailability>
```

If no node is listed previous to the double slash, this identifies any descendants of the current node.

{node}

This expression selects any matching children of the current node.

.

The period (.) simply selects the current node. There is no difference between the expression `./{node}` and the expression`{node}`.

..

A double period (..) allows you to reference the parent node. This can be used recursively by using the slash in between consecutive pairs of periods: `../../date`.

@{attribute}

This syntax allows you to reference a named attribute. This can be combined with other expressions to reference the attributes of other elements outside your current context. For example, you can use `/@measurement` to retrieve the measurement attribute from all the elements in a document.

*

Like in many other languages, the asterisk (*) represents a wildcard value. This is helpful whenever you want an entire group of entities with various names or if you don't know the specific name. To retrieve all the attributes of the current element, you can use @*. This wildcard can be used in paths as well as node names.

[{#}]

This notation is used to specify a certain number of elements in a document. This is useful only in a document in which data is specifically ordered or when you are writing a routine to traverse a document like you might an array. The expression `/hotelAvailability/hotel[2]` selects the second hotel node in your document. You have to be careful with this approach, however, because, if there is no second hotel, you get an error just like for any other invalid reference.

{node}[{node}]

Used in this syntax, the brackets utilize the node as a child qualifier of the previous node. In other words, you are looking only for those nodes that have one or more children of another node. If you want to consider only hotels that have a distance listed, you can alter the `for-each` element to select `hotelAvailability/hotel[distance]`.

{node}[{node} or {attribute} equality]

This usage of the brackets allows you to further qualify nodes based on `node` or `attribute` values. This can be very helpful in filtering data before even getting to the `value-of` level of the actual nodes. To look at only those hotels within ten miles of your destination, you can take the previous example and enhance it: `hotelAvailability/hotel[distance<10]`.

Axis Notation

All of the path expressions discussed so far have actually been the shorthand representation. If you have worked with HTML reference paths, you are probably familiar with the shorthand syntax, but most of these paths can also be expressed through the axis notation. This is a more explicit notation that can be helpful when dealing with a bit more complicated path, or if you want to expand the current context without changing your location. Because axis notations are so explicit, their expression is fairly straightforward. All of these commands precede a double colon (::) and the listing of a node or group of nodes like `parent::{node}`. These commands are listed in Table 4-3 along with a brief description.

Table 4-3. Axis Names

NAME	DESCRIPTION
`ancestor::`	Any ancestor node
`ancestor-or-self::`	Any ancestor or current node
`attribute::`	Any attribute
`child::`	Any direct child
`descendants::`	Any descendant children
`descendant-or-self::`	Any descendant children or self
`following::`	Any descendants of the document coming after the current node
`following-sibling::`	Any direct siblings coming after the current node
`namespace::`	Any matching namespace-declared nodes
`parent::`	The parent node
`preceding::`	Like following, but only those previous to the current node
`preceding-sibling::`	Like following-sibling, but only those previous to the current node
`self::`	References current node

Usage

Now that you can build a template for your XML data, how exactly do you execute the transformation? Well, like most things we have been discussing, there is more than one option. However, we are really interested in only one of them for our applications. The method that won't apply to us is the internal reference to a template. Just like XML documents can reference their schemas or namespaces, it can also reference a stylesheet for itself. This is done through a single line of code that must be listed directly after the XML header tag, as seen below:

```
<?xml-stylesheet type="text/xsl" href="myhotels.xsl"?>
```

> **TIP** *This is a great way to test your stylesheets through your browser. You may have trouble getting this to work if you view the XML and XSL through local files. These documents need to be served over an HTTP server so that the browser recognizes the stylesheet as XSL. Without this step, you will not get any errors, just a blank screen. You can view the source in your browser to confirm that you are actually getting the XML.*

However, we are much more concerned with the ability to apply external stylesheets. The whole idea of Web services is to expose processes through XML. The provider cannot make any assumption as to what a consumer will do with that data, so providers are woefully unprepared to provide a presentation-oriented response to a request. After all, the consumer may not even be presenting the data to a user, so the provider can't make that assumption.

The Web service provider should also not rely upon the consumer to do any necessary data-level transformations. The data that users provide in the response should be suitable "as is" for the consumer to work with and manipulate as necessary.

This method is really appropriate only for the direct exposure of XML data to the browser (or other client). We will instead use stylesheets to take their data and turn it into either something usable by our applications or presentable to our users. That means referencing an external stylesheet, perhaps even dynamically. Doing this requires a programmatic transformation that provides both the data and the stylesheet to the XSL processor, resulting in an XML string or object.

The syntax for this can vary from processor to processor and obviously language to language. For the Microsoft XML processor, using Visual Basic to transform an XML document into an XML string with an XSL document looks like this:

```
strHotels = sourceDOM.transformNode(myTemplateDOM)
```

You would use this method only if you were done with the XML at this point and simply wanted to pass along a string to a consumer of your service or application. If you had to perform more work on the data, you would want to keep it in an object form instead of loading this string into the DOM again (which is too costly). The key is to identify what you need to do with the result set. The syntax for maintaining the result in a DOM looks a little different:

```
sourceDOM.transformNodeToObject myTemplateDOM, myResultDOM
```

As you can see from these two examples, the process of transforming documents is relatively simple. Obviously, some things have to be done prior to making either of these calls, but I will leave the details to you for now. We will be diving into the entire process in code later, as well as discussing best practices. The intent of this chapter is to give you a basic understanding of how we can manipulate and work with XML and how to take advantage of these technologies.

When you start using XSL in your applications, you need to keep a couple of things in mind. First and foremost, any transformation results in an XML document. There is the misperception that XSL can be used to transform XML into HTML, and that is technically not correct. You can generate HTML tags, but the resulting document is a valid XML document, which HTML does not always comply with.

The main differentiator is a much stricter compliance with the hierarchy of the tag system. HTML is very forgiving in that the code `<b><i>Hello</b></i>` is perfectly valid. However, this will never pass an XML processor. Any HTML produced by XSL has to take the form `<b><i>Hello</i></b>`. While this isn't a technical challenge, it might be an adjustment challenge to HTML developers. There are also special characters in HTML that are no longer valid, like the non-breaking space, for which XML-compliant alternatives will have to be found. My suggestion is to start adhering to the XHTML specification produced by the W3C: `http://www.w3.org/TR/2000/REC-xhtml-basic-20001219/`. It was formalized in December 2000 as an XML-compliant version of HTML. Your target browser(s) may not support the entire specification, so make sure you take the time to test. This shouldn't be as much of a problem in the future, though, and referencing it now should at least help you to make the adjustment from HTML to XML-compliance.

The other consideration you need to make is positioning your XSL to eliminate "catastrophic" errors, those that cause the XSL processor to completely stop the current activity. This is a bad situation to be in because you are at the mercy of the XSL processor's error handler, which may not be very cooperative!

These errors usually occur by referencing nodes that do not exist. Whenever a node's existence is in doubt, make sure you take the time to check. This is typically done through the DOM (`childNodes`) or SAX APIs before applying an XSL to the data. XSL processors don't generally have the ability to "touch" nodes without referencing them, so testing in the template itself is problematic.

Summary

We have looked at a few of the available technologies for working with and manipulating XML data: DOM, SAX, and XSL. When working with entire documents, remember that the DOM is most effective. If you want to work with only a small section of a document, through a search or query, or want to develop your own logical model, the SAX API will likely be a better choice. Whenever you want to map XML data from one schema to another or want to format your data for presentation, turn to XSL. You will find yourself frequently using a combination of these technologies in a single application.

It is easy to blur these technologies together because most vendors package implementations together into a single control or library. As developers, it is important that we distinguish between these approaches, because a poor choice can be the difference between a Web service application that is fast and scalable and one that is slow and bulky.

These technologies will be the building blocks of our applications for both providing and consuming Web services. The same is true of any application that works extensively with XML. Without some knowledge of these technologies, taking advantage of Web services would be difficult, if not impossible. With that said, let's start applying this knowledge to Web services!

CHAPTER 5

Web Services Models

SOME PEOPLE CONSIDER an application model to be the application architecture. I prefer to draw a distinction between the two. I treat architecture as a set of rules established for an entire system or solution. We looked at the architecture for Web services in Chapter 2, which laid out a foundation for us. However, we aren't far enough along to jump into application design yet. We first need to model the solution. This pre-design component is what I will refer to as our *model*.

A Web services model can almost be designed independently of the actual service and consideration for languages, tools, and platforms. I stress *almost,* because inevitably at least some of these decisions will be predetermined. When this is the case, it will be too convenient to extend your model into the application design (similar to having the next piece of a puzzle ready to connect). This is not a bad thing from my perspective, but I'm not a purist when it comes to these areas. The best classification of our model may be as a transition state from the architecture to the design.

This concept is not too different from the approach of space planning for a large building or facility. An architect will specify a façade and the overall look and feel but not necessarily the space within the building. Then, a planner with expertise specific to the building's purpose will come in and allocate the space to different functions and purposes. If the building were an indoor arena, there would need to be special consideration for the space necessary to house a hockey rink, a basketball court, and extra seating. In an office building, extra care might be given to the conference rooms. The model developed by the planner reflects these needs appropriately and, working in cooperation with the architecture, allows for a successful building. This model then leads to a design that specifies in greater detail what goes where and how exactly it comes together. This same concept applies to Web services.

Just like different buildings, different Web service providers adopt different models. Potentially, different Web services can support different models, but the provider benefits from maximum consistency to reduce development and deployment time through reuse of a single model. Regardless, any variance between services doesn't preclude their sharing the same infrastructure, because the architecture is consistent.

Web services models will vary because they will have different requirements. Who is the target consumer? What function does this service provide? Is this service likely to be bundled or directly consumed? Do you need to assist with the presentation of your service? Is your service dynamic or static? Many of these questions relate directly to a provider's strategy around its use of Web services. These are all questions whose answers affect, and in fact help define, the model for your Web services.

It is important to note that these questions are not technical. Rather, they are focused on the business requirements for the Web service. As with other business applications, technology is simply the tool for meeting these requirements. Fortunately, no matter what answers you have to these questions, the Web service architecture should be able to deliver a solution.

> **NOTE**   *I realize that at this point I risk losing my technical audience with all this emphasis on business requirements! Don't worry; the technology is still crucial for building Web services and will continue to be the focus of this book. However, the demands placed on Web services dictate that a good business case is made for creating and hosting one. A Web service can take many technical directions, and it is imperative that the directions selected align with the business drivers.*

The answers to your questions may not be the answers you want, because some will be answered by your consumers. A well-conceived model can actually go a long way to help influence this result, though. For example, if you prefer that consumers present your Web service to the end user, provide some presentation information to make the implementation easy. Your service should have defined goals and priorities, and your model should reflect them. You can build a Web service without defining its model, but just like a building without a thoughtful floor plan, a Web service without a model is not maximizing its potential and is likely to fail in meeting the owner's needs.

Three different models are appropriate to define for Web services today: presentation, interface, and security. Even though I refer to them individually as models, the combination of the three could actually be treated as the model for your Web services. In some situations, you might even have multiple instances of these three parts in your Web service model. For example, you might support more than one security model to accommodate different needs. We'll examine this topic in much more detail in each of these three areas.

It is important to not confuse these models with tiers in application development. You don't necessarily need all three components, and they certainly don't communicate with each other, as tiers do. In fact, there is no direct relationship between these models. There will be some overlap in the implementation of their goals, and some pieces of one model may depend on another, but these models are simply areas of focus to aid you in addressing the important issues of designing Web services. Defining an appropriate model goes a long way toward building a successful Web service.

Remember that the consumers of a Web service play a role in its model. As a developer, you will likely play both roles in various situations. As a provider, you will have predetermined goals for your Web services. As a consumer, you may impose your own expectations, and thus new requirements, upon a service. It is then up to the service provider whether or not those requirements are met. Ultimately, a consumer can only utilize what is there and may choose to use a subset of the total offerings. However, consumers can implement a Web service that falls short in some area(s), add services or functionality to it, and expose it as a new Web service.

Presentation Model

As I mentioned earlier, there is no presentation layer in a Web service. However, this does not mean that our service can't offer to play a role in its own presentation. A service can play an active role by offering assistance with styling, validation, and even content. It can also serve a passive role by not offering any additional data. The presentation model defines the services available for its presentation. These services typically take the form of content or instructions.

Even though the consumer dictates a service's participation in the presentation layer, any assistance in this area is usually welcome. If a consumer is given an option between two Web services, with all other criteria being equal, the one offering the most value to their services usually distinguishes itself. Presentation services are one of the most obvious means for adding value to your Web services.

A provider's offering assistance in the presentation also means that a consumer is less likely to freelance while utilizing your service. It leaves less room for a consumer to implement your services poorly or incorrectly. Because you are the creator and owner of the service, you should know the potential issues or pitfalls in the process or function you are providing, and this is one way of passing that expertise on to your consumers.

Designing the presentation model for your Web services is a two-step process. The first step is to determine the exposure level of the service itself. When I use the term *exposure*, I am referring to the exposure to the end user. Will the service ever have direct interaction with an end user or simply be a process for back end system use? This determination then leads to the next step, defining the presentation services.

An application has to have a user interface provided by at least one of the systems involved, either the consumer or the service itself. Usually, it will fall upon the consumer, but the service can provide value to the consumer in this area. Your presentation model will help you determine what the appropriate offerings might be from the service side and whether they are worthwhile.

You may often want to support different exposure levels for your Web service. You can either design a single complex presentation model or split the functionality between separate models. The difference in the presentation model is merely semantics, because either way you are providing the same service options. This decision does, however, affect your interface model, which we discuss in the next section.

The presentation model might be the hardest one to bring closure to because of the open-slate nature of the Web and the presentation of Web-based applications. Your presentation model will consist of a series of storyboards and document maps that illustrate your presentation services. Just like the presentation itself, the presentation model is basically complete once you are satisfied with the decisions you have made.

Exposure Level

The first step to defining your presentation model is identifying the exposure level for your service. This is almost like doing a feasibility study on how your service should and/or could be used by consumers. A Web service is always called directly by a system, not a user. That system may consume the service in the background, with no knowledge by the user, or the system may expose the service through an application's presentation layer. The service is consumed in exactly the same way in either case, but what the consumer does with the service is very different.

The presentation of a Web service to a user is the responsibility of the consumer, but there may be some appropriate information that the service could provide or reference through its response to assist the application. The use of that information is always optional, but, if the value is provided, some consumer will probably utilize it to reduce development and deployment time.

The exposure-level spectrum has two extreme sides: masked and isolated. The blending of these two extremes generates the most powerful model, the embedded service. Often, a Web service has the potential to fill various roles in different applications. The exception might be if you provide a service that is always part of a larger automated process. Even then, you might be surprised by the possibilities a consumer finds for your service independently.

Masked Web Services

Web services that are used for background processes or offline system processes are basically masked, or hidden, from any user. Such a service is integrated seamlessly, and the application presents no direct output of the service. Such Web services fill the same role as any other business object in an application. (See Figure 5-1.)

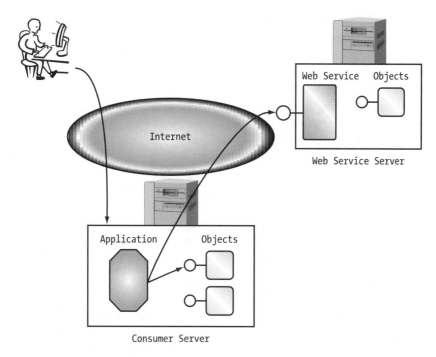

Figure 5-1. Masked Web service usage in an application

Experienced developers will recognize this model as something that is currently used to implement applications without Web services. Any of the established remote invocation methods could achieve this same result. However, Web services can facilitate a more open implementation to this application model because of its use of open standards. Services can be exposed over the Internet through Java RMI, but they would be accessible only to Java clients. This is an issue if you want to allow applications outside of Java to interact with your service. The need for exposing a remote service as a Web service will stem from your intended target consumer base.

The presentation model for a masked Web service is obviously simple, because its service and response require no presentation content. Thus, the masked service is the quickest model to define. Although such a model does not fully exploit the capabilities of Web services, it can be very effective in achieving an integration solution.

A status Web service is a good example of a masked service. If an application wants to check the status of an order, the inventory of an item, or the status of some request, a masked Web service is very appropriate. In this case, a user may not even be involved if the application is an automated routine to periodically "ping" the status. The application is merely consuming a service, and the expectations of it are very straightforward: be available and accurate.

As consumers of Web services, this service type may not be very appealing to us. If we want to implement a masked Web service as a component of an end user application, we are on our own for defining the presentation of the service, if it is necessary. The service is providing us with raw data. Obviously the more data that is exposed, the greater the effort the consumer generally has to put into its presentation, especially if it needs structure (tables or spacing).

When exposing a lot of data through a masked Web service, the service provider may want to reassess their chosen model if the provider can foresee the need to expose it directly to a user. The provider's objectives should be not only to identify the intent with the service but also to foresee what consumers might do with it. Then a model, or models, can be built that will most effectively accommodate those needs. You can provide separate services that address each need or one service that meets both. These approaches are discussed in more detail in the interface model description. The key in this section is to recognize the fundamental difference between a masked Web service and other Web services models, and that sometimes implementing more than one model is necessary.

Another feature of the masked service is that it usually does not have to incorporate any workflow or processes across multiple calls. Because these services are usually part of an automated process, they usually involve only a single request and response, and not a series of requests. This again makes masked services some of the quicker and easier Web services to develop and implement.

Isolated Web Services

The presentation model for an isolated Web services is the antithesis of the model for masked Web services. This model exposes data directly to the user by being passed through the consumer. This can manifest itself via input fields, a result set, or both. This data requires some formatting and/or styling to align with the rest of the application if the consumer wants to maintain a consistent look and feel.

The difference between the isolated model and others lies in the handling of the service itself. Whereas other service models are incorporated in an application's process, an isolated Web service is given a virtual space in which to interact with the user directly. Although all information passes through the consumer's application server, with an isolated model the consumer takes a more hands-off approach to the actual process and functionality. You can think of this concept as piping a protocol directly to the user through the consumer's application. (See Figure 5-2.)

Figure 5-2. Interaction with a user by an isolated Web service

For a consumer, implementing Web services in an isolated model is not something to be taken lightly because such an implementation directly exposes content provided by a third party. Such a partnership requires some trust as well as a tight design to help insulate the application from any problems the service might have. For instance, if the Web service is unavailable, what will the repercussions in the application be? What will the result be if the Web service starts returning invalid responses? You need to keep the outcome of such situations from being catastrophic, but you also need to be careful when selecting service providers with which to establish such a partnership.

NOTE   *This is not meant to scare you away from implementing isolated services; they can be very effective for consuming Web services. Isolated services just require a solid business partnership and should not be done haphazardly.*

Web developers may recognize that isolated services function much the same as content in a frameset reference. Instead of embedding the data directly, Web services give the consumer the opportunity to have some level of control over the entire presentation. In this virtual frame of the Web service, the consumer can apply some formatting or, more importantly, handle any error conditions.

CAUTION   *In evaluating whether you are working with a masked or an isolated model, remember to consider each call individually. If you are considering a sequence of calls, it is an easy trap to start contemplating the requests that are made based on information provided by another Web service call. Each service call can have only one model, and the type of response provided is determined through that model.*

This leads us to another decision that must be made once the isolated presentation model is designated. Will the consumer build the interface for collecting the data from the end user, or will the provider add this as a value-added service? If the provider adds this functionality to its Web service, a single transaction then takes two requests, not one. (See Figure 5-3.) One call retrieves the data defining the user input interface, and a second submits this information to the provider (the original service). This is a less efficient solution due to the extra call, but it automatically updates if a change is made to the service.

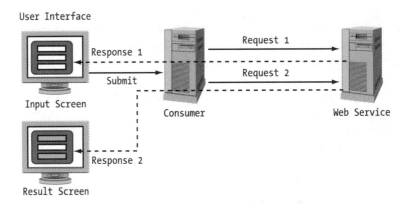

Figure 5-3. An input interface provided by an isolated Web service

If the consumer takes ownership of the collection of input data from the user, it is not automatically updated if the provider makes changes to the service. This creates more maintenance work for the consumer, but is less effort for the provider. (See Figure 5-4.)

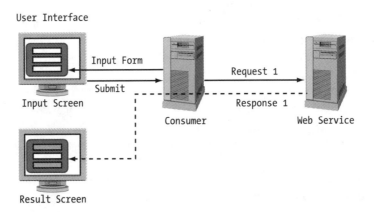

Figure 5-4. An input interface provided by the consumer

Because Web services are such a new concept, consumers might initially feel very comfortable implementing isolated services as their first step in Web service applications. However, once they implement them and become more comfortable, they are likely to want more input and control of the process. They might start peeling back some of the service's offerings and implementing them to more closely match their exact needs. For consumers to achieve the results they want, the presentation model will have to change. Your responses will have to act much more as enablers for presenting data to a user, so that consumers can effectively embed them within their applications.

Embedded Web Services

Once the solution matures, most Web services will likely fall in the category of embedded services. This model takes full advantage of the capabilities available through the Web services architecture to provide an integrated application comprising many independent components. The shared ownership of an application interface is a fairly new and radical concept, so we will spend some time discussing this model.

> **NOTE**   *Don't trivialize this shared UI concept by equating it to an HTML frameset UI. In a frameset application, multiple content providers own sections of the interface in physically independent sections of the screen. This is only slightly more effective than having multiple browsers open and connected to different applications. In this shared UI, the consumer builds the interface out of content they have and what the provider is passing or referencing through their Web service response.*

When you provide or consume Web services with an embedded presentation model, you must decide among several available options. This stems from the different levels of integration available through a Web service. These should be thought of not as clear, distinct levels, but as a blending of different ownership areas that result in the application's processes and interface. Fortunately, these ownership areas can often be directly tied to pieces of the presentation layer. The embedded presentation model should identify which roles the service provides.

For instance, if your Web service requires information from the end user, you can provide the code to produce the HTML form or enough property information for the consumer to build a valid form in the application. Either option is technically feasible, so it comes down to an issue of what you think a consumer of your service will want and what will provide the most value. You can provide all of these services and allow consumers to make their own selection, but there may not be justification for the work involved to do so.

Let's walk through a sample Web service and address the appropriate options available to the provider. We will refer back to our hotel availability scenario and take the perspective of the hotel owner developing a Web service in the reservation system. Our target audience will be online travel sites that provide access to airlines, hotels, and rental cars.

As the hotel owner, we want to provide a list of the available rooms that match a set of criteria. Our goals are to (1) have a quick turnaround of the information, (2) produce an accurate match to the criteria provided, and (3) stand out in a listing that includes competitors. We know that the travel site works with several hotels, so they will probably not want our participation in defining the input interface for the end user. That means we will have to work with the criteria they have provided through their form. Of course, by offering to accept additional criteria through our Web service, we could possibly entice the consumer to extend their input interface to take fuller advantage of our service.

Otherwise, our main focus would likely be the presentation of our resulting information. We could provide some link references or font treatment to our data. We might even be able to include some small graphics. Getting the travel site to respect the information we provide may take some consideration in our business agreement, but we could provide it nonetheless. The key consideration is not to overwhelm the consumer with extraneous data that will never be utilized or, even worse, that interferes with the presentation of our data.

> **CAUTION**   *Making a content-related decision is much safer when you are providing a service for the first time. Making changes after deployment can be harmful where the presentation model is concerned. We will take a closer look at maintaining some measure of backward compatibility in Chapter 6.*

So the service's presentation model could include font treatment, graphic references, and link references. Including this information may result in a presentation of hotel information on the travel site that looks like Figure 5-5. Notice how the Milton Hotel stands out from the other hotels.

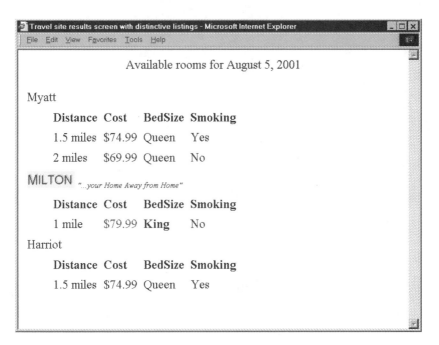

Figure 5-5. Travel site results screen with a distinctive listing

Keep in mind that the consumer application may choose to enforce the treatment of all hotels as equals, in which case the results will look no different from before the integration of our presentation services. (See Figure 5-6.)

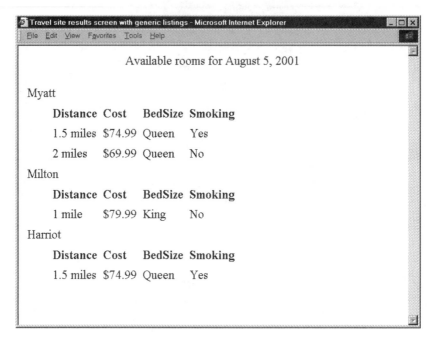

Figure 5-6. Travel site results screen with generic listings

This may seem fairly straightforward, but this example takes into account only one consumer type. Let's take a look at the same Web service in a different scenario. Say we have established an exclusive agreement with a specific airline that will embed our hotel availability service on its Web site when users make an airline reservation. To facilitate this partnership, we want to make it as easy as possible for the airline to use our service. To this end, we want to provide the necessary constructs for collecting and validating the hotel search criteria. Because we also have an exclusive presence in the application, we won't care about standing out and probably want to blend in with the look of the entire site. Our agreement may also be such that all activity takes place through the airline's site, so links may not be appropriate. This service's presentation model would then consist of input form data and validation code.

These two scenarios will inevitably cause someone to ask whether these offerings are two Web services or one. The interface model described in the next section addresses this very important issue. The other question we might ask is what content to provide once we know what presentation model our Web service will have.

Presentation Services

Defining the presentation services of a Web service is where the meat of the presentation model resides. Our determination of the service's exposure level helped us to identify the appropriate environments for our Web service. Now the presentation services themselves will define what offerings we will provide to assist the consumer during implementation.

> **NOTE** *Sometimes I will refer to the support services of a Web service. This might seem confusing at first, but it refers to the additional functionality that a Web service provider makes available to its consumers. The Web service itself is simply the core functionality to access an application with no extra consideration for the consumer's implementation process.*

Presentation services are appropriate only for embedded or isolated models, because masked services don't interact with users. Between those two, the extent of these offerings can vary quite a bit. An isolated service basically provides a lot of data to simulate the application on the server (not too different from any other Web-based interface). It would be overkill for an embedded service to provide that much information, so instead it provides more instruction-oriented services to the consumer.

These two approaches, data and instructions, are the two mechanisms for providing services on the presentation layer. The distinction between these two can sometimes blur, especially when client-side scripts are involved. The easiest way to draw this line is between the target audiences. Instructions are meant explicitly for the consuming application, whereas data is meant for the end user (or the user's browser). Although data is more useful on a passthrough basis, instructions require more implementation time and knowledge on the consumer's part. As I mentioned earlier, the direct approach is initially more appealing, but ultimately the instruction set should be more popular with consumers because it is less of an all-or-nothing approach.

We can provide services in the presentation layer in three different areas: content, style, and validation. Each of these areas may or may not be provided, depending on your objectives. If provided, each of these can be exposed through either a data or instruction delivery. The end result could look the exact same for both delivery methods, but the paths for getting there would be very different. The data-centric method is more appropriate for isolated services, whereas the instruction-centric method is usually necessary for an embedded service. Figure 5-7 should help you visualize the relationship between the different content areas and these two mechanisms for delivery. We will refer back to this relationship as we discuss various presentation services.

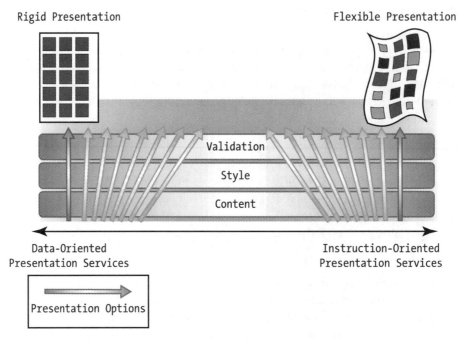

Figure 5-7. Presentation service options

When identifying the services you will provide, you need to consider not only what but also how. Do you provide them as raw data or as instructions to be utilized by the consumer? Because the latter option provides more flexibility, you are less likely to provide content, style, or validation through both data and instructions. Once consumers make the move to accommodate an instruction-oriented delivery, they will want to take advantage of that and get away from blindly accepting presentation data from the service.

It is also logical to make the decision of either providing or not providing information in each area in total. For instance, if you are going to provide some validation, why not provide total validation, at least on a request-by-request basis?

Content-Oriented Services

The distinction between content and style can sometimes be hard to make. This is meant to be more of a logical grouping than physical, because any presentation data can arguably be classified as content. My reference to *content* is meant to identify the data consisting of the user interface itself. This can take the form of HTML, text, graphics, or links. This is all the data that is intended to be used to build or enhance the actual end user experience specific to the Web service's functionality.

Because a Web service responds to a single request, we have only one stream of XML to work with to provide presentation services. Furthermore, there are currently no adopted mechanisms to include binary data in XML, so it is not possible to directly include any image data. Fortunately, because the nature of Web services requires Internet access (or at least access to some network), we can use linking mechanisms to reference external content when necessary. We will address this issue as it applies specifically to each area.

Data-Oriented Services

Passing content through raw data is a simple extension to creating HTML presentations. The most important factor is that all data must be XML compliant. This is especially important for the content portion of your presentation support services, because you will often pass HTML code in your Web services response.

One limitation of providing content through raw data via Web services is the lack of support for binary data. This means that actual images and other non-ASCII data cannot be passed back to the consumer. One workaround is to provide separate data to your partners via templates or content. Templates are a good approach to getting consumers up and running quickly, but providing actual content can be dangerous. Although this approach may suit your needs initially, providing content manually will probably turn into the same maintenance nightmare that sharing content for Web applications is today.

A better solution is to reference graphics and other binary data on your systems. Although this approach makes the application depend more on the availability and performance of external systems, Web services in general create that dependency. This approach will make for a cleaner implementation that is more dynamic and easier to maintain, true to the vision for Web services.

Let's take a look at a scenario for providing content through your presentation services. In reference to our hotel scenario, let's say we have an exclusive agreement with a car rental company to offer room availability searches on its site. This might be a good fit for an isolated model of our Web service that would require us to provide our services through a data-oriented approach.

Assume for now that the car rental company is going to collect the necessary information to check the room availability via our Web service. We then need to provide a clean output of our data so the company can "drop" it into its application page. Our basic response without any presentation services would look something like this:

```
<hotelAvailability xmlns:xsi="http://www.w3.org/2000/10/XMLSchema-instance" >
    <date>2001-08-05</date>
    <hotel>
        <address>
            <street>1500 Campbell Road</street>
            <city>Richarson</city>
        </address>
        <rating>3</rating>
        <distance measurement="miles">1</distance>
        <bedSize>King</bedSize>
        <cost>79.99</cost>
        <nonsmoking>Yes</nonsmoking>
    </hotel>
    <hotel>
        <address>
            <street>1730 Plano Parkway</street>
            <city>Plano</city>
        </address>
        <rating>3</rating>
        <distance measurement="miles">1.5</distance>
        <bedSize>Queen</bedSize>
        <cost>69.99</cost>
        <nonsmoking>Yes</nonsmoking>
    </hotel>
</hotelAvailability>
```

Although this data represents everything we need for the Web service response, the consumer cannot use it as is. Because this information is presented directly to the user, we should provide all the information's formatting. By doing this we, the provider, control how the information looks. It is then up to the consumer to make the information look like it belongs in their application.

There are actually several different approaches to adding content to data. One approach is to simply include the stylesheet as a reference at the top of the XML document. The second approach is to embed the content directly in the XML document. In either case, you use the same stylesheet for formatting the data. The only difference is where the transformation is applied: by the provider before the response is sent, or by the consumer after the response is received. Either way works, but the former places fewer demands on the consumer and is more efficient overall because it likely reduces the overall handling of the data throughout the Web services process. This isn't ideal because the usability of the data in the payload decreases, but the data-oriented approach by nature is not ideal.

Our stylesheet will be designed to loop through all the results and provide some structure for the result set, as shown here:

```
<xsl:stylesheet version="1.0" xmlns:xsl="http://www.w3.org/1999/XSL/Transform">
    <xsl:template match="/" name="rootTemplate">
    <hotelAvailability>
        <date>Available hotels for <xsl:value-of select=
          "/hotelAvailability/date"/></date>
        <p/>
        <table border="1"><tr>
            <td>Rating</td>
            <td>Distance</td>
            <td>Cost</td>
            <td>BedSize</td>
            <td>City</td></tr>
            <xsl:for-each select="hotelAvailability/hotel">
                <tr>
                    <td>
                        <xsl:if test="rating>3"><img src="http://
                          www.architectingwebservices.com/images/
                          star.gif" alt=""/></xsl:if>
                        <xsl:if test="rating>2"><img src="http://
                          www.architectingwebservices.com/images/
                          star.gif" alt=""/></xsl:if>
                        <xsl:if test="rating>1"><img src="http://
                          www.architectingwebservices.com/images/
                          star.gif" alt=""/></xsl:if>
                        <img src="star.gif" alt=""/>
                    </td>
                    <td><xsl:value-of select="distance"/></td>
                    <td><xsl:value-of select="cost"/></td>
                    <td><xsl:value-of select="bedSize"/></td>
                    <td><xsl:value-of select="address/city"/></td>
                </tr>
            </xsl:for-each>
        </table>
    </hotelAvailability>
    </xsl:template>
</xsl:stylesheet>
```

Applying this template to our data produces the following XML-compliant output incorporating content in our response:

```
<hotelAvailability>
    <date>Available hotels for 2001-08-05</date><p/>
    <table border="1">
        <tr>
            <td>Rating</td>
            <td>Distance</td>
            <td>Cost</td>
            <td>BedSize</td>
            <td>City</td>
        </tr>
        <tr>
            <td>
                <img src="http://www.architectingwebservices.com/images/
                  star.gif" alt="" />
                <img src="http://www.architectingwebservices.com/images/
                  star.gif" alt="" />
                <img src="http://www.architectingwebservices.com/images/
                  star.gif" alt="" />
                <img src="http://www.architectingwebservices.com/images/
                  star.gif" alt="" />
            </td>
            <td>1</td>
            <td>79.99</td>
            <td>King</td>
            <td>Richarson</td>
        </tr>
        <tr>
            <td>
                <img src="http://www.architectingwebservices.com/images/
                  star.gif" alt="" />
                <img src="http://www.architectingwebservices.com/images/
                  star.gif" alt="" />
                <img src="http://www.architectingwebservices.com/images/
                  star.gif" alt="" />
            </td>
            <td>2</td>
            <td>69.99</td>
            <td>Queen</td>
            <td>Plano</td>
        </tr>
    </table>
</hotelAvailability>
```

When placed in a Web page by the consumer, the presentation is very simple, but it is completely functional and provides a basic look that allows the consumer to use the output as is. (See Figure 5-8.)

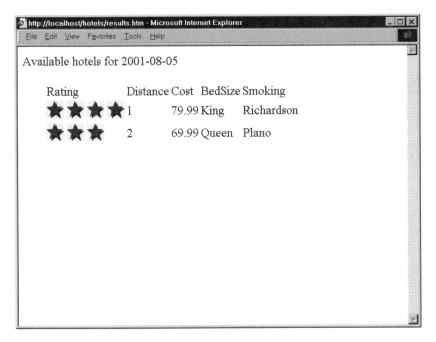

Figure 5-8. Output of Web service result with content

Of course, this could look a little more appealing! After completing the discussion of content, I will look at providing style information, which can help the presentation immensely.

Instruction-Oriented Services

When we need to merely assist the consumer with the presentation of our Web services, an instruction-oriented approach is more appropriate. Through this, we can pass along important knowledge specific to the data, empowering the consumer to handle it appropriately. This allows the consumer to make intelligent decisions about how to present the information, or perhaps even whether to present it. This also gives the consumer a better command of the data, which is what most consumers prefer once they start utilizing Web services.

Let's return to our hotel availability scenario where we are working with a portal site getting information from many hotel chains. This should be an experienced consumer that will want total control over the presentation of the information we give it. The consumer may filter the information to use only pieces of it or may change the representation of the information to suit the consumer's needs, perhaps making the responses of several chains look alike.

We will start with the same basic response of our service and build from that. Let's say we want to provide our logo and a picture of each hotel, a link to more information about each hotel, and the number of room matches we are returning. The pictures and links are obvious efforts to provide visual aids and more detailed information for selecting a hotel. The number of matches is something that simply helps out the consumer so the consumer doesn't have to come up with a counting algorithm. This number is important because the consumer may have to dynamically determine the layout based on the amount of information it receives. Blindly looping through a document can be risky when you are trying to maintain a good user interface.

For the logo, we will simply add an additional field to the data set called logo. This is actually a reference to the image on our site. Each hotel result also includes an image reference as well as a link element. For the number of matches, we will add another child element at the root. With these services, the resulting XML payload would look something like this:

```xml
<hotelAvailability>
    <date>2001-08-05</date>
    <logo>http://www.milton.com/logo.gif</logo>
    <numberMatches>2</numberMatches>
    <hotel>
        <link>http://www.milton.com/richarson/info.htm</link>
        <picture>http://www.milton.com/richarson/image.gif</picture>
        <address>
            <street>1500 Campbell Road</street>
            <city>Richarson</city>
        </address>
        <rating>3</rating>
        <distance measurement="miles">1</distance>
        <bedSize>King</bedSize>
        <cost>79.99</cost>
        <nonsmoking>Yes</nonsmoking>
    </hotel>
    <hotel>
        <link>http://www.milton.com/plano/info.htm</link>
        <picture>http://www.milton.com/plano/info.gif</picture>
        <address>
            <street>1730 Plano Parkway</street>
```

```
            <city>Plano</city>
        </address>
        <rating>3</rating>
        <distance measurement="miles">1.5</distance>
        <bedSize>Queen</bedSize>
        <cost>69.99</cost>
        <nonsmoking>Yes</nonsmoking>
    </hotel>
</hotelAvailability>
```

By providing the content in this manner, we are empowering the consumer to make the choices about what gets used and what does not. Making the most of this avenue will be important as the industry matures in its use of Web services.

> **CAUTION** *Techniques are in development that allow for binary data to be embedded within XML documents. Although this functionality may have practical uses, this would not be one of them. Attaching large files in XML that could be referenced externally would not only be presumptuous of the consumer's needs, but also terribly inefficient in this era of Internet connectivity.*

In this case, we provide images, links, and data information. The consumer can use this information in any number of ways that will meet its needs. Figures 5-9 and 5-10 are two completely different presentations, both based on this same payload of data.

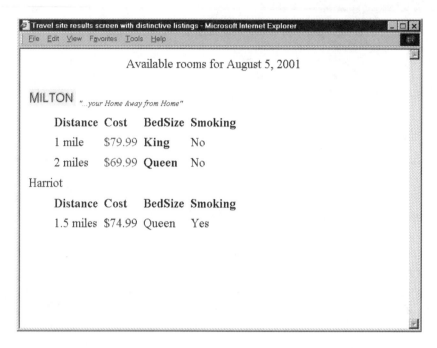

Figure 5-9. Presentation scenario 1

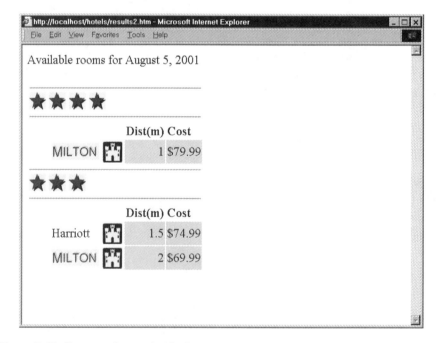

Figure 5-10. Presentation scenario 2

You should have a feel now for the different types of content you can provide for your Web services and how to go about providing them. To really tailor the presentation, though, you need to take advantage of styles. Style can be an underrated aspect of a Web application that distinguishes itself from others by looking professional.

Style

Even with quality content, a presentation may look less than professional without some styling. You could easily consider style as part of the content, but I will treat style and content separately because that is the tendency of the industry. This has really come about through the cascading style sheet (CSS) standard, which gives developers the ability to isolate the two. This way, a designer can tweak certain aspects of Web interfaces en masse without disturbing any of the functionality. This same approach is also useful for developing Web services and their user interfaces.

There can also be some differences in how these two areas are handled because of the nature of style data ownership. If the ownership of content is outside the control of the service provider, the styling of that content is even more so. Because there are mechanisms for affecting the formatting of information externally (CSS and XSL), even prestyled data is not safe from changes because it isn't critical to the service being provided. Keep in mind that these are support services we are discussing, and your primary goal should be delivering an effective Web service. Afterward, you can provide these features, making certain they don't interfere with your original goal. Forcing styles on consumers that may not match their needs could amount to enough interference that they look elsewhere for their Web services.

It is easy to confuse the concepts of style and content if you do not have some design experience. Anything that does not communicate any information on its own falls in the category of style data. This includes colors, font types, backgrounds, and spacing. Images and layouts fall in that gray area that may be hard to discern because their value is a little harder to determine. Images you present may or may not be communicating something. In the hotel availability screen shot (Figure 5-8), the images represent a rating of either three or four stars. It is a visualization of data, so taking it away would affect the information actually communicated to the user. Likewise, the table layout allows for a stacked view of like data. If it were all displayed in a single row, would the information have been communicated correctly? Rather than debate these issues, I will simply make my own qualifications, as you are likely to do on your own. The important issue here is that you determine what you are going to provide to your consumers and how you will go about doing it.

Along those lines, just as you can with content, you can choose to provide actual formatted data or simply aid in the formatting through instructions. Let's look at the difference between the two for this type of information.

Data-Oriented Style

If you are passing straight format and styling data through to the consumer, then you are likely passing the content itself directly. In this case, it is simple enough to add the appropriate information in your payload. To enhance our star-rated availability listing, we could modify the payload by adding font treatments. However, this does take the payload one step further down the road to strictly presentation information, and therefore less and less use on a data level to the consumer. It also makes your service work a little harder to build more data into the payload directly.

A better option for supplying such data is to reference a CSS in your payload. This means that the end user's browser references the style data, bypassing the consumer completely, placing less demand on our service and the application. I'm not going to go into detail about CSS, but a single line added to our payload provides this reference just like any HTML page:

```
<link rel="stylesheet" type="text/css" href="

  http://www.architectingwebservices.com/mystyle.css"/>
```

Some information cannot be communicated through a CSS, and that you must incorporate in your payloads. Just as we included image links in our example, we have to do the same thing with any objects we want to include. Any effects generated via a client-side script also fall outside the capabilities of CSS and must be included in the payload or referenced through other mechanisms. I did not discuss that in the content section, but will in the validation section because client-side script plays such a significant role there.

Instruction-Oriented Style

Instructions for styling a Web service presentation may or may not make sense depending on what you are trying to achieve. This is because the complexity around implementing the instructions is greater than that to actually change inline styling. For instance, if you provide instructions to consumers on what font a particular section of text should be, the consumer has to parse that information and implement a method for applying it. If the text comes predefined, the consumer just has to implement a method for applying the font it chooses.

However, there are some cases in which this is a good approach. If the style information would take up a lot of bandwidth (which is the case with many script-driven browser events), and not many consumers are likely to utilize it, it would be both an inconvenience and a drain on your resources as the provider. By providing instructions instead of applying the actual format to your payload, you have a more flexible offering for a wider range of uses.

This may sound similar to using CSS, but it actually abstracts it one step further. Including an actual stylesheet link means that you pass presentation content directly through your payload. Turning this reference into an instruction means providing the reference as a separate element in your payload. In our hotel availability scenario, we were originally passing raw data in the payload. By adding a stylesheet element, consumers can decide whether to reference it without being too encumbered if they choose not to. Below is an example of how you might present a stylesheet link in a Web services response:

```
. . .
<hotelAvailability>
    <date>2001-08-05</date>
    <stylesheet>http://www.architectingwebservices.com/mystyle.css
      </stylesheet>
    <hotel>
. . .
```

If you were the consumer of this Web service, you could then build the CSS-valid reference to the stylesheet by writing the following XSLT code:

```
<link rel="stylesheet" type="text/css">
    <xsl:attribute name="href">
        <xsl:value-of select="/hotelAvailability/stylesheet"/>
    </xsl:attribute>
</link>
```

And just like that you have provided and consumed style information through an instruction mechanism. Now that we have covered both content and style information, let's look at how to provide the appropriate data for validation.

Validation

Whenever you think of validation in an application, you probably think in terms of data inputs. In Web applications, you probably think more specifically about user inputs. This is exactly the kind of validation we are talking about here. It has a slightly different meaning here, though, because we are specifically concerned with the user data that will be passed on to a Web service. If we have a Web application that takes in user information for placing an order, we will want to collect an entire set of data, including payment, address, and contact information. If we have a Web service that validates address information, we are concerned with only a subset of the data. This is the section where the Web service may assist with the validation.

This situation is unique from any other discussed previously because we are providing assistance before the actual consumption of our Web service. We are validating the user inputs for collecting the appropriate data to use our service correctly. This actually extends the scope of our service and is basically a service in and of itself. Implementing this turns any Web service request into two service requests. We will look in the next section at the affect this has on the interface of our Web service.

Expanding on our scenario a little more, let's say we collect all user data through a single screen (see Figure 5-11). I will simplify the example by saying our Web service validates only U.S. addresses, so it will accept the following inputs:

- Address line 1

- Address line 2

- Address line 3

- City

- State

- ZIP code

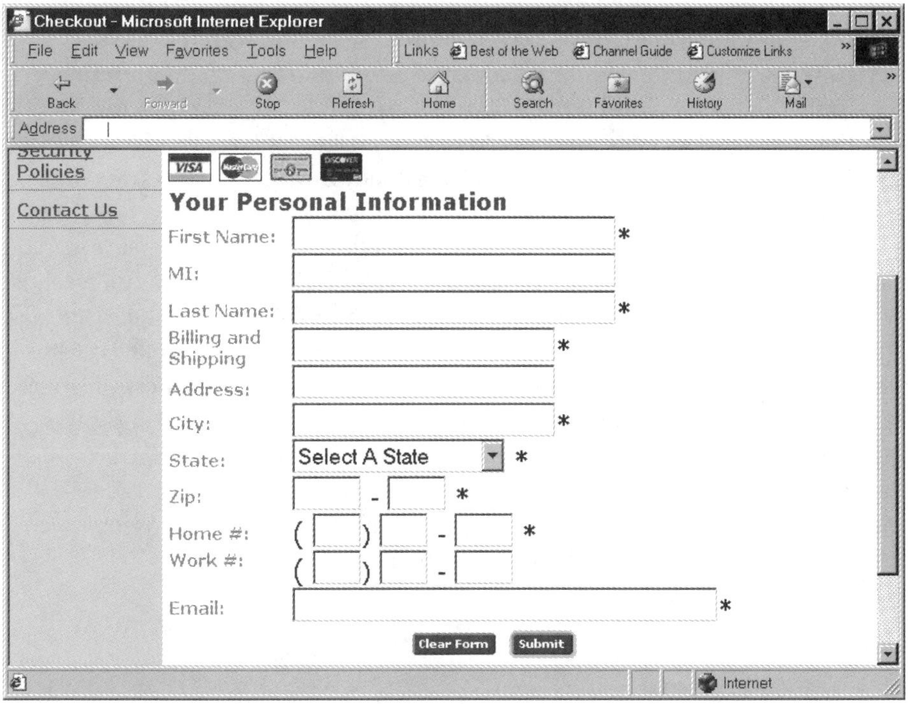

Figure 5-11. Purchase order screen

The service responds with simply a true or false result. Our focus, however, is on the inputs for the service. The XML document sent to the service needs to take the following form:

```
<validationRequest>
    <address1/>
    <address2/>
    <address3/>
    <city/>
    <state/>
    <zipCode/>
</validationRequest>
```

How long can the address and city lines be? Does the state field accept the entire name or standard two-character abbreviations? Does the ZIP code accept +four codes or just the basic five-digit codes? Can I have an address2 element if address1 is blank? Some of these questions can be answered by a schema, but some cannot. A service must provide the details to these answers through another mechanism.

What we are actually concerned with here is the next step after this information is communicated. How do you enforce these rules with the end user? Certainly, the consumer could hardcode the presentation to do this, but that is both inflexible and tedious. If the Web service expands its capacity to support additional data, every consumer would have to make a change to adapt. One solution would be to have the Web service actually provide the necessary data or information to facilitate the enforcing of these rules.

When you provide validation on any Web application, you have three levels you can work with (see Figure 5-12). The first level (1) is in the import forms themselves. With HTML forms, you can limit options through drop-down menus, radio buttons, and check boxes and limit data lengths in text fields. The second level (2) is client-side validation. This adds a little bit of intelligence to the client to perform slightly more sophisticated validation without hitting the application server. Finally, the third level (3) is where logic on an application server can perform very detailed validation. In Web services, this can extrapolate to two levels when you consider that the consumer's application can perform some validation (3a) and the Web service itself (3b) also performs some level of validation.

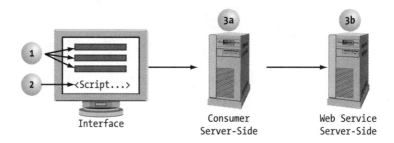

Figure 5-12. Validation levels in a Web service application

Data-Oriented Validation

In a data-oriented approach, a Web service can provide the entire HTML form and client-side script necessary to facilitate and enforce the entire data-entry process. This is the simple way out and asks the consumer to place quite a bit of trust in the Web service provider.

In the case of client-side script, you actually have some choices in how to expose it. Just as with the CSS discussed in the previous section, script documents can be referenced externally or embedded in the payload itself. Also like CSS, referencing scripts externally reduces the burden on the actual service, the consumer application, and the payload between them. Adding the standard external script reference in the presentation's payload achieves this. Just like a

CSS reference, the user's browser references this information (as seen below) directly, bypassing the consumer's application and server.

```
<SCRIPT type="text/javascript"
  src="http://www.architectingwebservices.com/validationscript.scr"/>
```

> **CAUTION** *Take care when developing or utilizing client-side script in this new programming paradigm. The code could get assembled with other scripts, so try to avoid generic function names and global assignments to minimize conflicts.*

As far as the consumer's application goes, a data-oriented approach can't do much to provide assistance, because any data is instruction based and not part of a passthrough system that the data-oriented approach facilitates. Instead, the next level of validation is the Web service itself.

Because the data from this approach is ultimately the user's interface, the end result of any implementation, let's go ahead and look at how to get there through an instruction-oriented approach.

Instruction-Oriented Validation

Instead of passing the data that will be delivered directly to the end result, most consumers want and appreciate a more cooperative methodology to delivering an effective, validating interface to the end user. This is the goal of the instruction-oriented approach. One of the first things to do as a provider is determine the ideal interface for collecting the data that your Web service will need. Remember, you should be the expert behind your service's functionality, and the consumer will be looking to you for guidance in how to expose it. Once you determine the interface, you can then figure out which pieces to validate and how to go about doing so.

Designing the "Ideal" User Interface

The interface for collecting data from an end user is typically presented through an HTML form. In that form, you can limit the options of the user up front. By limiting the range of information the interface collects, you can save some effort in validating certain situations. For instance, if you have a state field, it can simply be an open text field. Because the longest state name is South Carolina, you can limit the maximum length to 14 and set the size to accommodate the layout, as shown here:

```
<INPUT type="text" name="state" maxlength="14" size="10">
```

However, doing this allows the user a lot of room for misspellings, which can be a real problem for your application and may require a second round of data entry for clarification. This will be inefficient for both the user and the system. A better method is to allow only a two-character field for the established state abbreviation, as shown here:

```
<INPUT name="state" maxlength="2" size="2">
```

Even this allows some room for error, though. How many times will people incorrectly use AK for Arkansas? A drop-down list is ideal for further restricting the options, even though it does require a bigger payload for the user. Here we see the HTML for such an approach:

```
<SELECT name="state">
    <OPTION value="" selected></OPTION>
    <OPTION value="AL">Alabama</OPTION>
    . . .
    <OPTION value="WY">Wyoming</OPTION>
</SELECT>
```

With this approach, you can now design the ideal interface for your address verification service. We will make the addresses all match and allow up to 40 characters each. We will allow 30 characters for the city. In our ZIP code, we will support only a five-digit number, so we will define it as such. With these determinations, the entire presentation HTML code looks like this:

```
<INPUT name="address1" maxlength="40" size="20"><br>
<INPUT name="address2" maxlength="40" size="20"><br>
<INPUT name="address3" maxlength="40" size="20"><br>
<INPUT name="city" maxlength="30" size="20"><br>
<SELECT name="state">
    <OPTION value="" selected></OPTION>
    <OPTION value="AL">Alabama</OPTION>
    . . .
    <OPTION value="WY">Wyoming</OPTION>
</SELECT><br>
<INPUT name="zipcode" maxlength="5" size="5">
```

The breaks cause these form elements to align in a column, as you can see in Figure 5-13. Notice that there are no form tags or identification of the fields for the user. We are providing just the basic information necessary to aid with the collection of data. We could provide the appropriate copy for the consumer to use, but we would want to isolate that from this content so the consumer can make that choice.

Figure 5-13. Browser view of address verification form elements

Sharing the Interface with Consumers

Now that we understand the kind of assistance we can provide through the presentation, we need to develop a strategy for communicating this to the consumer. In the data-oriented approach, we would just pass it as is, but we don't want that approach for this more integrated effort. Let's also say, for the sake of argument, that this is a specialized list of state data. If it were simply a list of all 50 states (plus Washington, D.C., of course), the consumer could provide that interface simply enough. Our service may be a tax service that applies to only those states with income taxes, for instance. In this case, the consumer might prefer to defer to our service's ability to provide appropriate custom interface elements.

The effectiveness of our solution will depend largely on how easy it is for the consumer to integrate the information with the rest of the application. For that reason, simply passing back a chunk of XML-compliant HTML for the entire interface is probably not the ideal approach. Doing so would limit the consumer's ability to select the desired pieces or at least require more development and processing to segment it. So, at the very least, we want to break our elements into individual elements that the consumer can work with on a data level. Taking the presentation we designed earlier, the resulting document looks like this:

```
<addressVerification>
    <address1><input name="address1" maxlength="40" size="20"/></address1>
    <address2><input name="address2" maxlength="40" size="20"/></address2>
    <address3><input name="address3" maxlength="40" size="20"/></address3>
    <city><input name="city" maxlength="30" size="20"/></city>
    <state>
        <select name="state">
            <option value="" selected=""></option>
```

```
                    <option value="AL">Alabama</option>
                    . . .
                    <option value="WY">Wyoming</option>
                </select>
            </state>
            <zipCode><input name="zipcode" maxlength="5" size="5"/></zipCode>
        </addressVerification>
```

During the process we had to make our HTML XML-compliant and isolate each element on a data level. You might notice a little redundancy in the fact that our elements are essentially the name attribute of our form fields. We could eliminate this duplicated data, but the consumer application would then have to modify the code before displaying it. The benefit of streamlining the data does not outweigh the processing efficiency in this example, so I chose to leave it as is.

If bandwidth is a real concern of the consumer or service provider, an alternate method can be used for communicating this information through the use of reference links. We can segment the actual HTML code into separate documents, which the consumer can retrieve separately. This keeps the consumer from having to work with unnecessary data and does not prevent the consumer from using other presentation pieces. The following code might be the result of taking this approach:

```
<addressVerification>
        <address>http://www.architectingwebservices.com/interface/
            address.xml</address>
        <address>http://www.architectingwebservices.com/interface/
            address.xml</address>
        <address>http://www.architectingwebservices.com/interface/
            address.xml</address>
        <city>http://www.architectingwebservices.com/interface/
            city.xml</city>
        <state>http://www.architectingwebservices.com/interface/
            state.xml</state>
        <zipCode>http://www.architectingwebservices.com/interface/
            zipCode.xml</zipCode>
</addressVerification>
```

Notice that all three addresses now reference one address file. In fact, all three addresses are now defined the same. The order of multiple address lines often does not matter. In that case, they can be treated the same. If we are talking strictly on a data level, there really is no difference between these fields.

However, for HTML forms, the elements must have unique names to keep the data from being concatenated and thus potentially extending beyond our maximum length of 40. If we are concerned about bandwidth bottlenecks, it might make sense to have the consumer modify the address line by adding the name properties as necessary for the consumer's presentation. This allows both the consumer and the service provider to treat them the same outside of the HTML code.

Adding Client-Side Script

To enforce a higher level of validation on the client, we will need to implement client-side script. This allows us to catch some basic user-entry errors such as invalid alphanumeric values and null fields. Catching this on the client side saves cycles on the server and is the preferred method of validation for any savvy developer.

This is what a client-side script for our address verification interface might look like:

```
<script language="javascript">
    function SubmitAddress()  {
        bValidAddress = true
        if (document.form1.address.value == "")
            alert("Please specify an Address.");
        if (document.form1.city.value == "")
            alert("Please specify a City.");
        if (document.form1.state.value == "")
            alert("Please specify a State.");
        if (document.form1.zipcode.value == "")
            alert("Please specify a Zip Code.");
        ValidateZipType()
        if (bValidAddress)  {
            // TODO:  Submit Data to Application.
        }
    }

    function ValidateZipType()  {
        if (document.form1.zipcode.value < "00100" ||
            document.form1.zipcode.value> "99999")
            alert("Please specify a valid ZipCode.");
    }
</script>
```

Of course, this depends on a few more elements being added correctly to the form's presentation by either the service provider or the consumer. These are the elements that define the form and its name and the function call necessary on submission of the form. This information can be either wrapped around the entire presentation or contained in separate elements. This might be one solution:

```
<formName>form1</formName>
<validationFunction>SubmitAddress()</validationFunction>
```

This can then be integrated into the application's presentation with the following XSL code:

```
<form>
    <xsl:attribute name="name"><xsl:value-of select="formName"/></xsl:attribute>
    . . .
    <input type="submit">
        <xsl:attribute name="onClick">
            <xsl:value-of select="validationScript()"/>
        </xsl:attribute>
    </input>
</form>
```

The body of the form then resides between the form tag and the submit button. Of course, the consumer can certainly name the form, and in fact name it something different and reference that through the script. Editing script can get a bit tricky, however, because you then need to make the script XML compliant to use XSL.

Just as we did in supplying style instructions, we could provide a reference to the actual script through additional nodes. Instead of <stylesheet>, we could use a <script> tag that the consumer can easily process, as shown here:

```
<script>
    <xsl:attribute name="script/type">
        <xsl:value-of select="text/javascript"/>
    </xsl:attribute>
    <xsl:attribute name="script/src">
        <xsl:value-of select="http://www.architectingwebservices.com/
            script.scr"/>
    </xsl:attribute>
</script>
```

We can provide this as all one tag, but this format does several things. First, it keeps the consumer from accidentally passing on the script tag, which could potentially cause errors or problems in the user interface. Second, it keeps the information in a more data-centric format that allows the consumer a little more flexibility in utilizing it. For instance, the consumer may decide to go ahead and reference the script off of the service provider's server and add it inline to the content being delivered to the end user.

Of course, this is all helpful to the process, but validation must still be done by the applications involved. Just as with any enterprise Web application, providing client-side validation is for efficiency's sake to catch the majority of basic errors that can occur. These client-side rules can be turned off or bypassed, however, so you must have server-side validation to protect your application, whether you are the consumer or the Web service provider.

Interface Model

The interface model defines the structure and process of the interaction with your Web services. In this sense, you can think of a Web service as an object. Just as an object's interface may have multiple method calls, a Web service may have multiple calls to consume its functionality. However, because of its open nature, a Web service is abstracted even more than an object is to its caller. Web services consumers may have no idea how many applications are handling their requests and certainly have no idea what platform or tools they were constructed with.

For an object, defining an interface can be a daunting task if you don't have a lot of experience in determining appropriate class structures and datatypes. The abstraction of Web services allow for even more options in designing an interface, which makes the task no less daunting. The level of complexity depends primarily on the functionality and support services you want to provide. You have already seen how providing assistance with the initial presentation to an end user can turn a simple Web services request into a two-step process. That is really just the tip of the iceberg with Web services interfaces.

Because of the complexity, think of your Web services interface as a model, something that cannot effectively be defined through an existing Interface Definition Language (IDL). This model should address two specific areas of the Web services interface: process and payload. Together, these two components will help you to define the workings of your Web services and allow you to expose them to consumers. You will know the interface model for your Web service is complete when the behavior and functionality of your interface are captured in process diagrams and payload definitions.

> *IDL* stands for *Interface Definition Language*. Every object or component protocol has some mechanism for discovering the interface of external entities with which it can communicate. These mechanisms are generally defined through data commonly referred as an IDL. *WSDL* is the *Web Services Definition Language*. It is an existing standard IDL for specifically defining Web services. We will look more closely at WSDL in Chapter 9.

Processes

A Web service can take many shapes. It can expose a very simple process, such as querying a database of information, or it can expose a complex sequence of steps, such as purchasing a car. These are very different functions, but they can both be exposed via Web services. This requires us to have some serious flexibility in how we can design our service's interface, and it also takes some careful thought into how we are going to pull it off, while not scaring off potential consumers!

The interface model's process can take one of two options. It can be a single call (request and response), or it can be a workflow. Obviously, the single call is easier to implement under any condition. It might seem at first that every step through a workflow could just be addressed as a single request and response, but, if you try to design a Web services workflow with that approach, you will quickly realize that you cannot treat the steps as independent islands.

The first issue you will encounter is a need on your part to control the entire process. The obvious example comes up in a transactional process. The classical scenario is the debit/credit process in which one event cannot happen without the successful completion of the other. This is a matter of functional usability that cannot be compromised.

The other issue you will probably encounter is implementation complexity. If a service provider exposes a series of ten independent calls that should be consumed in sequence to make up a process, how much trouble do you think consumers will have during implementation? This not only will frustrate consumers, but also can be harmful to the service provider and its systems. This starts to tread into the security model topic (which is coming up shortly), but you basically want to ensure that a consumer is utilizing every step of your process without bypassing steps or inserting its own steps. (See Figure 5-14.) Such an attempt compromises what control you do have over the process.

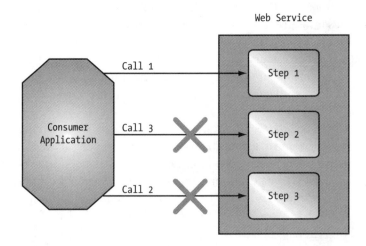

Figure 5-14. Compromising a Web service process

In these cases, you want to expose your Web service as a process, not as individual steps. Doing this requires some careful design work and some additional management on the service provider's part, but it will likely be a great service for you once it is available. It will not only be more efficient to implement, but it should allow for a better experience for any consumer.

Web Services Call

A Web services call is not much different from any other application call. You make a request and get a response. We discussed this communication process quite a bit in Chapter 2. Initially, most Web services will likely follow this model. It is fairly simple to implement and requires little complexity on the consumer's part.

However, because of the nature of Web services, you have quite a bit of flexibility in exposing your service. This requires you to think about the tasks you are trying to accomplish. In Chapter 1, I introduced the idea of heavy and light requests and responses. It is in this section of the interface model where these should be defined.

If you are using an IDL (such as WSDL) to define your interface, this model is already defined for the consumer's technical developers. They will get all the information they need from it. However, on a business level, at least internally, this needs to be determined as part of the business requirements for the Web service. The danger here is trying to do too much in one call. The nature of Web services is to expose functionality, not transfer documents. If you find you are implementing a Web service that is receiving data from a partner and sending back unrelated data in the response, you are not providing a Web service! You are merely taking a batch process and using a different transport mechanism.

I'm not saying this is bad, because it may be a good solution for the need you have. It would just be inappropriate to consider this a Web service just because it transports XML over HTTP. In fact, you might want to consider using a package for data routing and transformations so you don't end up writing custom routines every time you want to transfer some more data.

A Web service's request and response payloads are always going to be related. A consumer is making a request of your service, and you are fulfilling it. That request may be a simple identification of the caller, or it may be a collection of data that needs processing. That fulfillment may be a simple acknowledgment, or it may be a result set of data. Either way, you need to make that determination for your Web services calls before you get caught up in defining the payload itself.

This relationship can be somewhat frustrating, but that is the nature of working with communication protocols over the Web. As long as the consumer wants only one thing, this can be very easy.

Eventually, though, you will want to break out of these single transactions to accomplish something much more robust. This requires a series of interactions that you expose and manage.

Web Services Workflow

I like to refer to a process exposed through a Web service as a *workflow*. Whereas *process* might be misconstrued as just the communication or logic process, *workflow* gives a clear image of what you are trying to accomplish through your service and the nature of it. There is a starting point, there are decision points, and there is a conclusion. There is a sequence involved, and it takes multiple calls to complete the entire process. Many Web applications accomplish this today, but they are in control of the entire experience. Web services offer new challenges to these complex applications because they share the process. The consumer still owns the presentation, but the service actually owns the process itself. These will be some of the most complex Web services that are provided.

The first step to designing a successful workflow model for your Web service is to map out the entire process that is involved. Just like with any business application, mapping out the processes is key to meeting the necessary requirements. A flow diagram is a good method for visually capturing the process. (See Figure 5-15.)

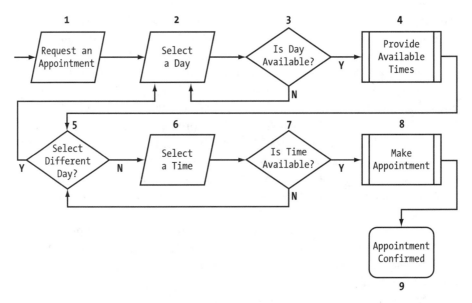

Figure 5-15. A process flow diagram

Once the workflow is defined, exposing it through a Web service is the next step. Let's look at this in more detail by considering an appointment service scenario. This Web service could be applicable to any service industry such as a barber, doctor, or auto mechanic. The use of this kind of functionality is evident when you consider situations in which portal sites or applications want to combine or at least support appointments across multiple vendors of services. Health insurance sites may allow appointments to be made with network doctors; auto manufacturers might facilitate appointments with service departments; and entertainment sites may allow reservations at restaurants, movies, or plays.

Figure 5-15 represents the process flow for an appointment process. We will step through the flow to make sure that what we are trying to accomplish is clear. Keep in mind that this is a generic process that could handle reservations or appointments.

The process is initiated by a request for an appointment (1). The first step to this is selecting the day for the appointment (2). We will run an initial check to make sure the day is valid, because we may not have appointments available on holidays, Sundays, and so on (3). If the day is acceptable, we then look up a list of times that are available and present them (4). The alternative is having the users provide times, hoping they are available. By proactively providing a list, we can reduce the amount of back-and-forth interaction that method could generate.

Based on the list of times, the user either selects one or decides to look at a different day (5). If the user selects a time (6), we run one more confirmation of the time's availability (7). If it is available, we book the opening (8) and send some sort of confirmation (9). If, during the process, another user reserves a time that was presented as available to the user, the user can select a different day (5) or a different time (6).

There are certainly other ways this process could be managed, but I have defined a relatively simple process so that we can easily work through it. Now that it's defined, we have to add the details that are necessary to make it a Web service. This starts with the introduction of the service provider and service consumer. It is always easiest to work with a Web service process in terms of two tiers: the consumer application and the Web service. This allows you to clearly determine which responsibility falls where. With the players identified, we can then identify the interactions necessary over the Internet to make the process functional. Let's step through a direct conversion of this process as a Web service. (See Figure 5-16.)

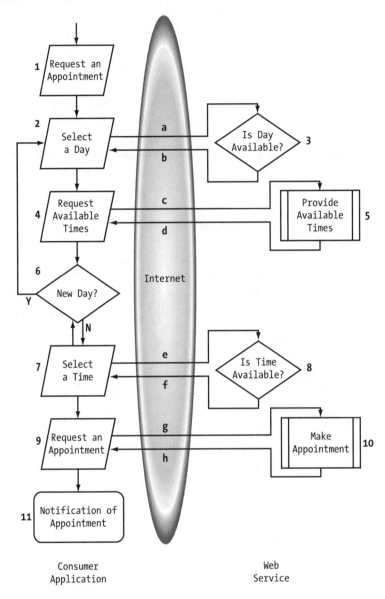

Figure 5-16. Appointment process flow as a Web service

Remember that the process must always begin and end on the consumer side. In this case, the first two steps, starting the process (1) and selecting the day (2), occur on the consumer side. There comes the first call to the service (a) to find out whether the day is available (3). If the response (b) is false, the consumer passes another request with a different day. Once an acceptable day is found, the consumer requests a list of available times for that day (4, c). The service puts the data together (5) and responds to the consumer (d).

At this point, the consumer can determine whether any of the available times are acceptable and either selects a different day (6) or sends the request (e) for one of the times (7). Because another user might have made an appointment between this client's requests, the service provider confirms the availability and reserves the time slot (8). The consumer then decides to actually book the appointment (9) with the Web service (10). The consumer then makes the appropriate notifications of the successful booking (11). The process is then complete.

This diagram (Figure 5-16) is a good visualization of what we are providing through the Web service and what we are expecting of the consumer. It shows, for instance, that we are asking the consumer to provide the mechanism for collecting the initial day of the appointment. This is not a big task, but it does require something of the consumer. At some point, you might decide that you want to provide that functionality as an extension of the main service. (See Figure 5-17.) I would call this a value-added service since it is not crucial to the process, even less so than providing a list of available times is. Available times are based on information that is proprietary to us, making the process more efficient. The consumer could easily provide a functional calendar system to provide days to choose from.

When considering extensions of this nature, you need to be wary of falling into the trap of focusing more on enhancing the services than on the functional service itself. This is similar to buying a smaller house to fit in your budget and meet your needs, and then going crazy with options like marble counters, crystal chandeliers, and extravagant landscaping. Don't lose sight of the actual goal; focus on your Web service, and add only those extensions that will truly add value for the consumer.

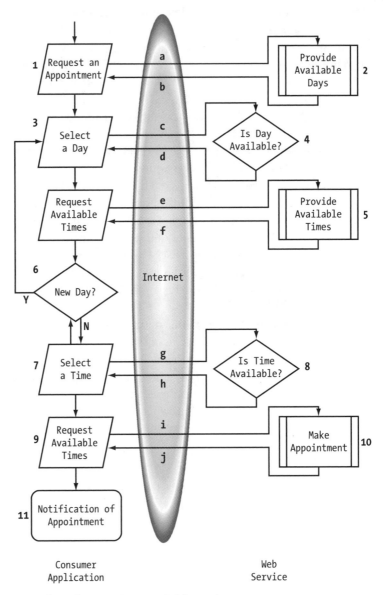

Figure 5-17. Extending the appointment Web service

What Figure 5-17 doesn't tell us is how to manage the process. How do we, as the provider, know whether the consumer is requesting the first step of the process or the last? The additional complexity of a Web services workflow comes from the exposure of the process to both the consuming application and, potentially, an end user. You essentially have two users, not one. A typical Web application design is intended to handle multiple users in independent sessions. With an embedded Web service, you will have two concurrent users that you are accommodating in each session. The application is actually consuming the Web service, but the end user is consuming the process. This places more demands on a Web service in managing the session. This, of course, brings us to state management.

Managing State for Two

A significant technical issue that must be addressed with Web services workflows is the state management. Most Web applications have to deal with this issue today, but Web services that support a workflow add some complexity to state management because they may have to manage two different states: the consumer of the service and the user of the consumer's application. The Web service has to know at what stage during the process a user is and also has to keep track of the consumer so it can enforce security and accommodate any tracking needs. This is especially imperative with fee-based services (which are discussed later).

Because the Web services provider does not establish a physical session with the user, you might think that all we have to do is manage the state with the consumer of our application. This kind of thinking will likely lull you into a trap, because a consumer may have multiple independent sessions occurring simultaneously. This means that you could easily get individual session references mixed up, which essentially breaks all processes in the application.

For this same reason, a consumer cannot implement a workflow Web service and make requests for users anonymously. This doesn't mean that consumers must pass on the user's identity. The provider just needs to be aware of existing users during their processes. Without this mechanism, you could not implement workflow applications consuming Web services.

State is managed in traditional Web applications through cookies, form fields, and query strings. These are all methods for communicating information between an end user and a Web application. State can be managed between the user and the consumer's application, and it can be managed between the consumer and our service. (See Figure 5-18.) Because the service cannot manage state for the end user, the consumer application is going to have to marshal this data for us. Before we get into how this can be done, let's review the methods for managing state between the user and the consumer application.

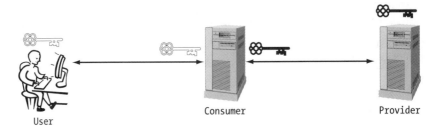

Figure 5-18. State management in a Web service application

When an application receives a request from an end user, information is passed to it in the HTTP header and the requested URL through cookies, HTTP post data, and query strings. Cookies are segments of text data that the server asks the browser to remember for it. Cookies can either be saved to a secluded place on the hard drive (designated by the browser) or just retained in the browser's memory. I will refer to these as *persistent* and *session* cookies, respectively. Obviously, a session cookie lasts only as long as the browser session is open because it is kept only in memory. Both of these cookies are passed to the server through the HTTP header every time the browser makes a request. Cookies are passed only to the site that actually generated them. (This is based on the domain name, so a Web farm of multiple servers can effectively use cookies to manage state between them as well.)

HTTP post data is data that is defined through an HTML form through a post action. This allows HTML to identify and capture data that a user has entered and send it to the server. Most fields are exposed to the user, but sometimes hidden fields are used for passing application data to the browser so the server can recognize it when it is submitted back.

Querystrings are bits of text information that are concatenated onto the end of a URL. This information can be either programmatically provided or automated through HTML forms using the GET action. Multiple pieces of information can be sent through the querystring by delimiting them with an ampersand (&). This is what a properly implemented querystring looks like:

```
http://www.architectingwebservices.com/wservice/purchasecar.htm?id=12345&
   type=fourdoor&color=blue
```

This is a very popular way to manage state because it is fairly efficient and easy to implement, but it does have its drawbacks. Because it is part of the address, you are exposing information to the user that would allow the user to very easily break out of the application's expectations. An educated user can certainly work around cookie or HTTP post state management, but it takes more effort. At the very least, refrain from putting any sensitive data in the querystring, because it is much easier for someone to get to there.

According to our design, we need to maintain a consumer ID and a user ID. To keep track of the process itself, we also need to maintain a state variable.

> **TIP** *We could save the state variable on our side, tied to the user ID, but this makes the application a little more vulnerable to state issues. With the stateless nature of the Web, just because we sent the consumer step 3 doesn't mean it arrived. The consumer might instead be resending step 2. Their view of the user's current state is almost always more accurate than ours (and it's likely the only one that matters), so maintaining state within the process is preferable.*

I will create an element called serviceVariables and place this information in child elements there. That communicates to the consumer what the information is for and perhaps assists the development staff in knowing how to handle it. The following code illustrates this:

```
<serviceVariables>
        <consumerID>987</consumerID>
        <userID>10203</userID>
        <stage>2</stage>
</serviceVariables>
```

Now that we have this in place, what will the consumer do with it? After all, serviceVariables is not a tag standardized to mean anything, right? Although this is true, it also inherently communicates a certain level of purpose that developers might understand without any additional documentation. This is part of the beauty behind XML. The very data itself is capable of communicating information about itself. However, supporting documentation is always helpful to your consumers.

Once the data's purpose is understood, the consumer has two responsibilities. The first is to act as a proxy and simply pass the data on through one of the state mechanisms available to the consumer and their users. This choice is completely outside of our control as the service provider, but, as long as it is done, we really shouldn't concern ourselves with it. Ideally, the consumer should be able to piggyback whatever state mechanisms it uses for the application itself. That requires the least amount of effort to implement. The other thing the consumer should know not to do is actually expose the data to the user. This node should actually act as an envelope for communications between the consumer and Web services provider.

> **CAUTION** *It is important that the consumer respect the values you are passing for state management. Consumers may assume that they can insert their own representation of the user ID for the Web service's user ID. As a provider, you want to make sure that you protect yourself from this threat. We will discuss some of these options in the security model.*

We actually have a little more flexibility with the state management of the consumer of our Web services. Because a direct connection is established between us, we can certainly take advantage of other existing mechanisms such as public keys and certificates. This would remove that responsibility from the interface model and potentially from the application layer altogether. We will discuss these options much more in the security model section later in this chapter.

Another aspect of session management is session length. How long should sessions persist? A typical Web application persists a session over a 20- to 30-minute period of inactivity. Because a Web service can only establish a physical session with the consumer, we have a little more flexibility with this area as the service provider. A Web service can possibly support a shorter period of inactivity. How long will you allow between requests in a process? At some point you have to treat a delay between steps in a process as independent calls. In that case, you might want to start the process over, because continuing with a stale state may cause problems. An indefinite session period can also limit the scalability of the Web service, because sessions will consume the provider's resources while it is active.

To manage our sessions, we need to develop a method for the consumer to pass session data to the provider efficiently. Fortunately, the first step of extracting the data is not difficult, because Web servers typically have an API for accessing this information through objects or components. The trick is in automating as much as possible so the consumer can implement your service as quickly as possible, because, if it takes too long, you are likely to scare the consumer off. At some point, a vendor or two will probably provide this functionality as part of another service or application. In the meantime, we are going to have to provide our own mechanisms if we are going to keep this from being a barrier to implementing our Web services.

The first thing we can do to help is isolate state information from the rest of the application data in the payload of our service. This way, the consumer can recognize the distinction more easily than if it is all grouped together. This may seem like a simple concept, but it is easy to overlook.

Although you don't want to treat a process as an independent Web service, you still should break the process into independent transactions on your side. The key to defining the process workflow is to link these transactions together via the Web services interface. The challenge to implementing the process successfully is the cooperation necessary with the consumer. The consumer initiates every Web services request, so the service can do nothing to force a request. We can work only through the responses to the requests made by the consumer. That is our only opportunity to communicate the necessary information. If we try to tell the consumer how to perform a complicated operation, it will require many requests back and forth! Fortunately, our processes won't be that complicated, but it will sometimes take several steps to accomplish a result. We must get feedback from the client, but, every time we communicate, we are risking a misstep by the consumer or, even worse, a premature end of the process. Although these things are unavoidable, we can develop an interface model that can help the consumer to maintain the process. The key is to provide some sort of mechanism for getting the consumer to make another request for the next step of the process.

Providing Efficient Responses

Our appointment Web service process flow diagram (Figure 5-16) is a great visual aid for what our service is doing and what it provides. As is, it is certainly functional, but it is by no means optimized or efficient. In fact, our diagram also gives us a tangible view of our service, allowing us to identify inefficiencies in it. For example, you might notice right away in our diagram that we show the number of interactions across the Internet. Is there any way to streamline that number? The more interactions our service has, the more involved it is for a consumer to implement and the more potential failure points we have.

Recall that you always have one-way communication occurring because of the nature of Internet protocols. The service cannot initiate communication with the client. One solution to this problem is simply telling the consumer what the next step is through your responses. This can be communicated much the same way as state information is communicated through the header nodes. The consumer can then use this information to request the next step of the process. (See Figure 5-19.)

The problem with this approach is the built-in inefficiencies. You see here that it took four requests to execute a two-step process in which some presentation assistance was provided. We had one call that requested the necessary information for step 1, one call for submitting that information, one call for requesting step 2 information, and finally one more for submitting step 2 information. It works, but doubling the step load in requests leads to a very involved application.

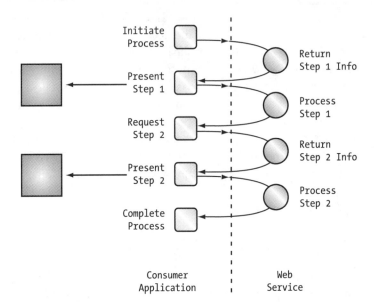

Figure 5-19. A two-step Web service workflow with individual requests

An alternative to this model is doubling up on the information provided through the responses. (See Figure 5-20.) Earlier, we were telling the consumer to request step 2 after completing step 1. Instead, we can include the information for step 2 through the response to step 1. After all, our side of the workflow is complete once the data from step 1 has been submitted. Obviously, this can be done only when you have a defined workflow and know the next step that should be taken.

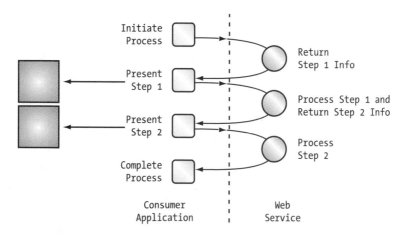

Figure 5-20. A two-step Web service workflow with double-duty responses

This solution gets our two-step process down to three requests, which eliminates 25 percent of the communication. Each additional step also adds only a single request when you continue this approach.

If we apply this approach to our appointment Web service, we can streamline the amount of interaction between the consumer and service provider. In our original interface model, we had a minimum of four requests and responses necessary to consume the service. By being predictive, we can actually make some assumptions and cut this number in half.

The first thing we modify is providing the list of available times when a given day is submitted. Doing this eliminates one of the requests by the client. The other steps we can combine are the time selection and the appointment booking. If clients submit a successful time, we can skip the reservation of the time and simply make the meeting. This is an even easier justification if our Web service allows us to cancel meetings. You can see what our new process diagram looks like in Figure 5-21.

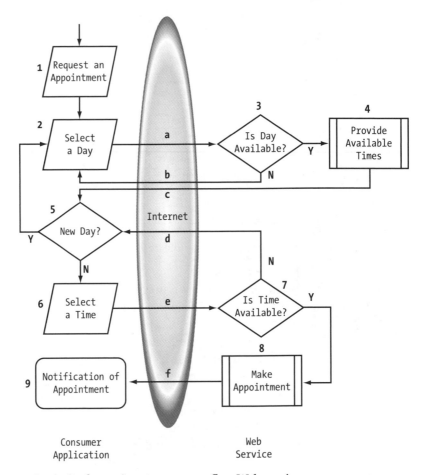

Figure 5-21. Optimized appointment process flow Web service

Let's quickly step through the process. As before, we start the first two steps on the consumer's side (1, 2) and request the availability of the selected day. If the requested day is available, the provider puts together a list of open times (4). If not, we return the process to step 2 on the consumer side. Each of these events has its own response (b and c, respectively). The next step is the consumer determining whether these times are acceptable or if a different day is preferred (5). If a different day is needed, the consumer returns to step 2; otherwise, the consumer selects a time (6). Then comes the second request (e) specifying the time for the appointment. The provider checks to make sure the time is still available (7) and either rejects the request (d) or makes the appointment (8). In the latter case, a response is provided to notify the consumer of the successful appointment booking (9). We have now completed the process.

As you might have noticed, we have eliminated two requests by the client. Instead of

- Request day availability

- Request available times

- Request time availability

- Make appointment

as we had originally, we simply have this:

- Request day availability (a)

- Request time availability (e)

However, also notice that we still have four responses (b, c, d, and f). What we have done is combined the variable responses to work in a two-request interface for the consumer's sake. Two different responses are available for each of the two requests, depending on what the circumstances and outcome are. These two responses are radically different in nature and content. Typically, when we work with interfaces, we are dealing with a determined payload that is consistently defined. Traditional applications achieve this effect by overloading the payload with responses to each situation, and only use the bits necessary at that particular moment.

With XML, you want to make your payloads as efficient as possible. Because of the open nature of Web services, you don't need to take the same approach as in the past. Instead, you can provide different responses based on need to any request you receive from a consumer. In fact, you can also take the opposite approach by supporting different payloads in the Web services request. The concept of dynamic interfaces leads us right into our next topic: payloads.

Payloads

We can't talk about interfaces without discussing payloads. Payloads are even more important to Web services since they contain the entire set of information for your application. There is no method invoked in our application by a payload that contains only parameter data. We also are not passing objects that have properties defined. Our payload is our request, our parameters, and our properties.

Fortunately, our payload is in XML, so we have the ultimate in flexibility. We do need some kind of structure and discipline, though, or we will make our services overly complicated and confusing. So, along with our Web services process, we need to define our payloads, whether they are simple or complex. Payloads are the second component type of the interface model for Web services.

The main distinction we really need to make in our payloads is whether they are static or dynamic. By that, I mean is the payload the same for the Web services call (static), or can it, and should it, change depending on the situation (dynamic)? This is akin to deciding how to handle versioning of a function. Should enhancements in the future be done through a new interface or adding parameters now to accommodate future functionality? There are tradeoffs either way, so we need to look at both carefully.

Static Payloads

Static payloads are easy to define and easy to implement. You do not anticipate changing anything about such a payload in the future: it is what it is, and anything else is a different Web service. You define a schema that defines exactly what format the request should be in and what format the response will be in. These calls are in no way conditional.

> **NOTE** *When I talk about static and dynamic payloads, I am referring to the XML elements, not the data in them. Obviously, the data can and will be different between different calls in different sessions.*

Let's take our original appointment process model and look at some of the payloads. They are static because there was one response option for each request.

Three questions have to be answered before defining our static payload:

- What application data needs to be communicated?

- What session data needs to be maintained?

- What presentation data needs to be included?

Application Data

The application data is probably the easiest to define because it is so straightforward. Before you get to this point, you should have your process diagram completed, and it should answer most of this question for you.

In our case, we have four interactions. The day availability request passes the provider a date, and the response is some form of Boolean. The available times request also passes the date to the service and receives a list of available times. The time selection request passes either a time or some providesr-defined ID representing a time slot and gets a Boolean for that response. The final request for making the appointment includes the date and time for the appointment and the response, a comfirmation of booking.

Let's go ahead and look at the schemas for our first request, the day availablity process. If you refer to Figure 5–18, the request is (a) and the response (b).

This is the schema for the day availability request payload:

```
<xsd:schema xmlns:xsd="http://www.w3.org/2000/10/XMLSchema">
    <xsd:element name="appointmentMaker">
        <xsd:complexType>
            <xsd:sequence>
                <xsd:element name="date" type="xsd:date"/>
            </xsd:sequence>
        </xsd:complexType>
    </xsd:element>
</xsd:schema>
```

This is the schema for the day availability response payload:

```
<xsd:schema xmlns:xsd="http://www.w3.org/2000/10/XMLSchema">
    <xsd:element name="appointmentMaker">
        <xsd:complexType>
            <xsd:sequence>
                <xsd:element name="dateAvailabilityStatus" type="xsd:boolean"/>
            </xsd:sequence>
        </xsd:complexType>
    </xsd:element>
</xsd:schema>
```

> **TIP** *If you are not comfortable reading schemas yet, I recommend getting one of the available XML tools, like XMLSpy, that allows you to load schemas and build compliant XML documents. This allows you to see an actual XML document instance defined by the schema, which may help you to read XML schemas and thus follow these examples.*

Session Data

In determining session data, we first need to ask whether this is part of a process. It is, and so we need some method for determining what stage we are at in the process. Also, because we will be booking something for the user, we need to have some identification for the user. The provider and consumer can handle this in a couple of different ways.

One option is for the provider to assign an ID to the first step of the workflow in the session data. This is effective for state management and is really ideal for the service provider. A consumer may be annoyed at having to pass the data through, but it really should not be a problem. The main drawback for consumers is that they cannot count on it for any use of their own. Because the provider might be using it as just the session ID or part of a long-term ID model, consumers will not know how to utilize it for their own functionality.

A second approach is for consumers to pass an ID to the Web service and count on them to do so consistently. This is a bit riskier because you have to trust the consumers' systems and policies a bit more. It is one thing to ask consumers to pass along state through a process and another to expect them to design and maintain it correctly.

What we will see going forward is a combination of both approaches. The service provider has its own state management, and consumers their own. Obviously, consumers have to support the provider's information through their side of the process, but, for most applications, the consumers need not pass their information to the provider. Because they initiate the connection, they can maintain that state on their own side. Their application makes a request and waits for a response. The exception to this is an asynchronous process in which the response may actually be delivered later through a provider-initiated process.

Both of these approaches are limited in their capabilities as standalone implementations. They are good for guaranteeing a unique user in a session, but this has no long-term benefit because appointments booked by system-assigned numbers are probably not very helpful! At some point, some specific piece of identification is necessary to tie events to an end user beyond the current session.

For our appointment service, we should assign a user ID to allow us to track usage and manage the active session. We will also utilize a consumer session so we can track the consumer's activity as well. For now, let's assume we are not using this for authentication or security purposes. We will get into that topic in the security model section later in this chapter. Let's go ahead and separate this information into a separate section as discussed in the Processes section of our interface model. Here is an example of session data schema code:

```
<xsd:schema xmlns:xsd="http://www.w3.org/2000/10/XMLSchema">
    <xsd:element name="serviceVariables">
        <xsd:complexType>
            <xsd:all>
                <xsd:element name="consumerID" type="xsd:short"/>
                <xsd:element name="stage" type="xsd:short"/>
                <xsd:element name="userID" type="xsd:short"/>
            </xsd:all>
        </xsd:complexType>
    </xsd:element>
</xsd:schema>
```

Session data is included in a header section for every request and response, so you then modify the payload schemas to include this definition, as shown in this code for a day availability request with session data:

```
<xsd:schema xmlns:xsd="http://www.w3.org/2000/10/XMLSchema">
<xsd:import schemaLocation=
   "http://www.architectingwebservices.com/interfaces/sessionHeader.xsd"/>
    <xsd:element name="appointmentMaker">
        <xsd:complexType>
            <xsd:sequence>
                <xsd:element ref="serviceVariables"/>
                <xsd:elementname="dateisAvailable" type="xsd:boolean"/>
            </xsd:sequence>
        </xsd:complexType>
    </xsd:element>
</xsd:schema>
```

The initial request from the client does not necessarily have to incorporate this header, because the service provider usually generates the data. The understanding is that, if the header is missing from the request, it is the initial request to the service for this session.

Presentation Data

Identifying the presentation data you want to incorporate in your payloads may be the most difficult component because it is so subjective. There is no right and wrong, and certainly different cases can be made for different solutions.

The best approach is to make your payloads as lean as possible to accommodate the minimum requirements for utilizing the Web service. That means including presentation by default only when it is either key to the process or likely to be used by 80 percent of consumers. At the very least, other information can always be referenced through links provided through the payload for those who want extra services.

Because we are working with a static payload, we need to make a decision here and stick with it. For our purposes, our Web service does not require any presentation data to function effectively. We will leave it to the consumers on how to format our textual data and lay out our information. However, as part of its strategy, the provider would like to gain some branding awareness for its business. The provider may or may not have actually made this exposure part of its business agreement with consumers, but the provider will at least want to make a logo available via response payloads so that the avenue exists. We will expose presentation data schema for appointment service as a link to the logo on the provider's site, as shown here:

```
<xsd:schema xmlns:xsd="http://www.w3.org/2000/10/XMLSchema">
    <xsd:element name="branding">
        <xsd:complexType>
            <xsd:sequence>
                <xsd:element name="logo" type="xsd:uriReference"/>
            </xsd:sequence>
        </xsd:complexType>
    </xsd:element>
</xsd:schema>
```

> **NOTE** *More extensive usage of presentation data for your Web services is discussed in Chapter 7.*

The following code generates what our response payload might look like if we put all three of these components together for our day availability request:

```
<appointmentMaker xmlns:xsi="http://www.w3.org/2000/10/XMLSchema-instance"
xsi:noNamespaceSchemaLocation="C:\WINDOWS\Desktop\appointmentMaker\static\
response1.xsd">
     <serviceVariables>
          <consumerID>12345</consumerID>
          <userID>5468</userID>
          <stage>1</stage>
     </serviceVariables>
     <branding>
          <logo>http://www.architectingwebservices.com/images/logo.gif</logo>
     </branding>
     <dateAvailabilityStatus>true</dateAvailabilityStatus>
</appointmentMaker>
```

You can see how even this relatively simple function can generate a decent payload size without too many bells and whistles added to it. This is why you need to be careful not to add too much functionality that won't be used by a majority of your consumers.

Because developing static payloads is the easier and quicker solution, most Web services will likely take this approach. This approach can be very effective, but also very limiting and possibly not very efficient. A more flexible and powerful approach is the dynamic payload.

Dynamic Payloads

The idea behind dynamic payloads is to allow the flexibility and expandability of Web services. It is like taking many static payloads and grouping them together. Figure 5-21 showed the results of taking our four-request, four-response system and making it a two-request, four-response system. This is only possible by designing dynamic payloads into the interface model.

Dynamic payloads are also your avenues for personalizing your Web services. By allowing requests and providing responses that are catered for your consumers, you can expose a very efficient process that meets their needs. That said, dynamic payloads are not meant to allow you to customize your services for each and every consumer. Rather, you can develop templates that cover each of the main implementation approaches your consumers might take. Allowing personalization on an individual consumer level would likely be tedious and costly.

Dynamic payloads have three different classifications:

- Dynamic requests

- Dynamic responses

- Conditional responses

A Web service may utilize any, or any combination, of these dynamic payloads to accomplish a certain goal. Each has different benefits and potential drawbacks, so I will look at each in more detail.

Dynamic Requests

The dynamic request is something that ultimately helps take a load off the consumer in working with a Web service. In this approach, the request is treated as a malleable object that can allow the provider and consumer to utilize different services and properties and incorporate them directly into the request. This is similar to the concept of object-oriented inheritance in which a base class can be extended with additional functionality. The alternative to adopting dynamic requests is creating an entirely different request, basically a new interface for every new flavor of that service.

By using dynamic requests, the provider can almost provide a very generic interface that can be suited to any consumer's needs. For instance, a consumer can request that the provider help with tracking of activity by maintaining some header data on a passthrough basis. This can be especially helpful in an asynchronous process, as discussed before.

Of course, every benefit usually has a cost. After all, if dynamic requests were so great, wouldn't everybody use them? The actual cost can be hard to determine, but it is definitely going to be in performance and potentially scalability. The provider will be adding overhead to its Web services because it will be adding some extra handling of the payload at some level. Something has to be done with the data, whether it is just maintained, saved, or acted on. Ignoring it can potentially cost nothing, but then no value is gained from having it at all.

A popular use of dynamic requests will no doubt be for search services. Whether one is searching for a book, a movie, or a CD, an enormous number of criteria can be referenced. A dynamic request potentially allows the search based on any of these criteria, each with its own specific data. Again, the extra effort is placed on the provider, which must take the extra step of determining what the search is for and handling it appropriately. (See Figure 5-22.) However, dynamic requests also allow the ultimate in flexibility by being able to provide new functionality with backward compatibility for consumers of the older functionality.

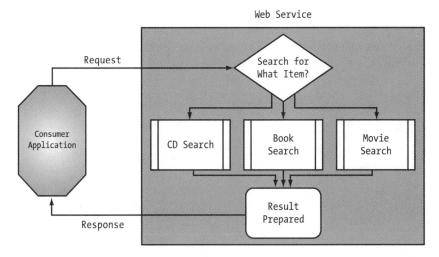

Figure 5-22. Dynamic request handling by the provider

The following code is for two XML documents that are the request payload for your hypothetical search Web service. Here is a search request for a flight from Dallas to Chicago:

```
<searchService>
    <flight>
        <departureCity>Dallas</departureCity>
        <destinationCity>Chicago</destinationCity>
        <departureDate>2001-09-15</departureDate>
        <returnDate>2001-09-17</returnDate>
        <criteria>fare</criteria>
    </flight>
</searchService>
```

Here is a search request for albums on CD by Genesis:

```
<searchService>
    <music>
        <album>
            <artist>Genesis</artist>
            <format>CD</format>
        </album>
    </music>
</searchService>
```

The only commonalities between these two payloads are the Web service invoked and the root node. These can easily be separate static requests with different root nodes invoking different services. The objective here is not to promote the idea that an application can actually service both of these requests. In fact, this shows the ability of a Web service to aggregate several functions available to it through a single interface that can have quite a bit of variation.

Dynamic Responses

A dynamic response can be very helpful in offering multiple versions of your Web services. This allows you to have different offerings around the same functionality without hindering your various customers. Perhaps you would like to provide a lot of presentation data, but you do not want to send it when you know the consumer does not need it. Based on who the consumer is or information provided through the request, the provider can send one of the two following responses to the music request just described. This code gives a simplified response:

```
<searchService>
    <music>
        <criteria type="artist">Genesis</criteria>
        <album>
            <title>Duke</title>
            <releaseYear>1980</releaseYear>
        </album>
        . . .
        <album>
            <title>We Can't Dance</title>
            <releaseYear>1991</releaseYear>
        </album>
    </music>
</searchService>
```

This code provides a formatted response to the music search:

```
<searchService>
    <music><table border="0">
        <tr><td><b><criteria type="artist">Genesis</criteria></b></td></tr>
        <tr><album>
            <td><coverImage><img src="http://domain.com/img/duke.jpg"/>
              </coverImage></td>
            <td><albumTitle>Duke</albumTitle></td>
            <td><releaseYear>1980</releaseYear></td>
        </album></tr>
```

```
        . . .
        <tr><album>
                <td><coverImage><img src="http://domain.com/
                   img/wecantdance.jpg"/></coverImage></td>
                <td><albumTitle>We Can't Dance</albumTitle></td>
                <td><releaseYear>1991</releaseYear></td>
        </album></tr>
    </table></music>
</searchService>
```

> **TIP** *Notice how this response places all formatting outside the individual element tags. For example, the Duke album title element was not presented as* `<albumTitle><td>Duke</td></albumTitle>`. *This is a best practice that allows the consumer to still easily access the raw data. Placing the content tags inside the elements requires the consumer to build logic for stripping HTML tags out to access the data. This is important even when you are adding presentation data to your payloads.*

Although the second response provides a richer response that includes content and formatting, it also makes the response nearly three times larger. Depending on your background and experience, you may look at this difference and think it is either negligible or massive. It is usually neither of those extremes for a given scenario.

This response size difference isn't negligible to the provider if it is supporting large volumes of consumers. There is no exact correlation, but possibly a third fewer requests can be handled by a given system if a more verbose response is provided. Also, the consumer utilizes more resources to handle the data. Obviously, it is not worth decreasing possible customer value to provide verbose data if this data is extraneous.

However, the extra data can save processing time if this data allows the consumer to do less work. It just depends on the situation, and that is why dynamic payloads in general, and dynamic responses specifically, can be very valuable.

With the additional overhead of the verbose response, it might make sense to utilize dynamic responses to not waste the resources for consumers who want only raw data. In fact, it makes a lot of sense to use this model to provide a Web service that you want to support multiple presentation models. In this way, you are not overloading the consumers of the masked service, but are providing the rich content necessary for an isolated service (discussed in the "Presentation Model" section in this chapter). This is where you identify your consumer scenarios and develop your templates. Each of these responses is considered a consumer template. These might be the only ones, or you might identify others. Again, avoid developing too many "one-off" templates, because at some point the differences become somewhat negligible, but the effects on your systems are not.

Another use for dynamic responses is versioning. If you treat your response as a static instance, any enhancements will likely require a new Web service so that you do not break compatibility with your current consumers. Because you are dealing with XML, perhaps adding more data won't be a detriment to your consumers, but you cannot know for certain. If the provider establishes before-hand that there may be different instances of a response (that is, dynamic responses), its consumers will have coded their applications appropriately to simply ignore extra data until they choose to utilize it.

These are all examples of different response payloads based on the same core information and function. There may be even more extreme cases in which the direction your Web service goes may be altered by the request.

Conditional Responses

The difference between a dynamic response and a conditional response can be subtle. The distinction is ultimately made based on the intent. If the consumer can anticipate the exact format of the response, the response is considered static. A conditional response means that there is more than one possible response, not on a data level, but on a structural, or schema level. Instead of just providing a more verbose response, as we did earlier with the music search, we are providing a completely different response.

The purpose of incorporating variable responses into your interface model is to provide a more compressed process via the Web service. As you saw in our appointment service (Figure 5-21), we streamlined the entire process by elimi-nating two of the requests through conditional responses, allowing us to eliminate half of the necessary requests by simply providing a choice between two responses for the remaining two requests. (See Figure 5-23.)

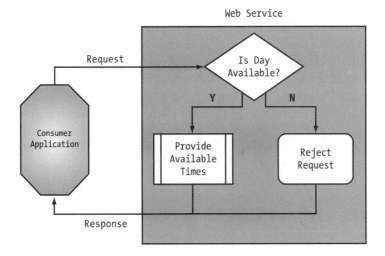

Figure 5-23. Conditional responses for the appointment service

Conditional responses can be very helpful to both the consumer and provider, but these responses definitely expect a bit more from the consumer during implementation. Just as the provider has to do some extra handling in supporting dynamic requests, conditional responses will require the consumer to take an extra step to identify what the response is and to work with the data correctly.

One solution that could take advantage of a conditional response model is a search system that does not want to return a null or infinite result set. Typically, when a null result set is presented, the user must decide how to proceed. Should the user just quit the application or should they modify some of the search criteria, guessing at what might work? On the other hand, in the case of huge result sets, users will probably have to sift through a lot of inappropriate data that they did not screen out through their criteria.

The alternative is to have the provider return a payload to the consumer either requiring further criteria to narrow the result set or recommending changes that could be made to the criteria to find a match. The user can then make a more informed decision on what to do next. Taking this idea one step further, the consumer's application itself can automatically modify the information and resubmit it to the Web service.

Another application of conditional responses that can be most effective is for error handling. When either bad data is submitted or there is some problem with the process, the necessary information has to be returned to the consumer. Without conditional responses, this information would be incorporated into every payload and simply ignored or unused. A Web service provider can have a completely separate error process that is defined for all calls and simply utilized as the response payload when necessary. This also provides a consistent mechanism for your consumers to use to handle errors as necessary. Separate routines to handle each response do not need to be developed and implemented. When designing conditional responses, you have to be careful with how far you take the concept. You aren't going to want to perform every function through a single call and multiple responses, so there is an extreme you should avoid.

Perhaps the best way to work through the appropriate uses is through use case scenarios. Such scenarios involve stepping through an application as an end user. In this case, you act as the consumer and step through each segment of your Web service's process to identify the possibilities. Assume that the first case you walk through is free of errors with no issues encountered. This starts as your baseline process. From there, you then handle the exceptions and alternative paths that might be taken and try to work them into your baseline use case.

Let's walk through this process with the appointment Web service. This process effectively takes us from the original static and isolated process (Figure 5-18) to the streamlined process (Figure 5-21). Without conditional responses, we cannot make this transition.

The first step to defining a conditional response is to walk though the process with an optimistic approach. After initiating the appointment application (see Figure 5-24, step 1), the first thing we do as a consumer is select a day for the appointment (2). Since this is an ideal scenario, we do not have to concern ourselves with a negative response. Because of this, we can immediately provide a list of times that can be selected for the appointment (3). Again, these options are assumed acceptable by default, and we just select one (4). That means we can directly make the appointment request of the service (5). The service doesn't need to worry about checking the appointment time and so can immediately book the appointment (6) and provide a response (7).

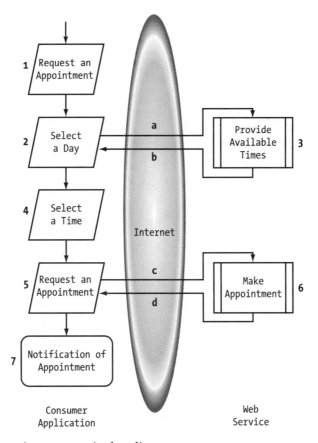

Figure 5-24. Appointment service baseline process

Next, we need to handle the exceptions. Starting with the day selection, we need to check to make sure the day is available for appointments. Because that is an exception to the day selection process, we just modify that one interaction. We will need to insert a step into the service that performs the check and handles the affirmative and negative outcomes. (See Figure 5-25, step 3.) The affirmative is in place because of our baseline, but the negative needs to be added. It should go back to the consumer and allow the selection of another day, basically repeating the current request with different data (b).

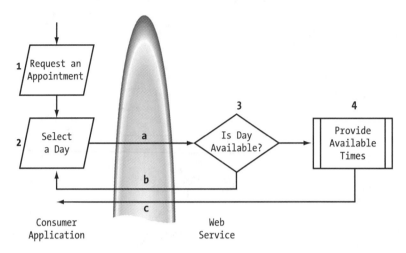

Figure 5-25. Date selection exception handling

The next use case that needs to be incorporated is canceling the current day due to a rejection of the available times provided by the service. In this case, the consumer's application must allow an avenue for also selecting a different day. (See Figure 5-26, step 5.) Otherwise, the user can proceed to select one of the provided times (6).

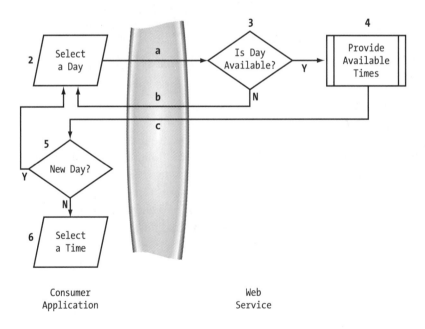

Figure 5-26. Date availability exception handling applications

The final exception that needs to be handled in the process is the time availability. This will catch any times that may have been previously reserved in between the initial time request and the actual booking process. This should prevent the double booking of any appointments.

The next decision point, similar to the day availability check, is an availability check on the time. (See Figure 5-27, step 7.) If it is not available, the response should be sent back to the consumer so that another time, and potentially another day, may be selected (d). Otherwise, the appointment is booked through the mechanism in the baseline process, and an appropriate response is returned.

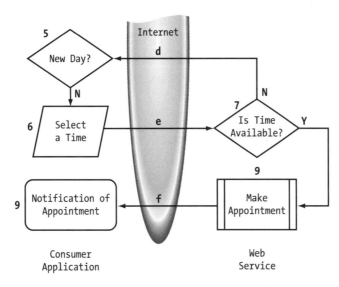

Figure 5-27. Time availability exception handling

Implementing all of these changes produces the streamlined process shown in Figure 5-21. We started with two requests from our baseline and never needed to add more. This may not always be the case, but usually you should need to add few requests to your baseline. We did add two more responses to handle the exceptions that arose, one for an unavailable day and one for an unavailable time. These additions will be much more common.

Of course, the consumer will be asked to do a bit more during the implementation of a Web service with conditional responses. More intelligence will have to be built into an application to handle these responses as they come back. Fortunately, the service will not provide just any response to any request. The responses should be well identified and documented for each request so that the consumer can plan for them appropriately. Overall, consumers will benefit from conditional responses, since it will mean fewer requests for them to implement which results for a more efficient process to be incorporated into their applications.

We have now discussed the presentation and interface models for Web services. The next model, the security model, may be the most important of the three, however, because the success of Web services depends upon its existence and successful implementation.

Security Model

Although Web applications have been relatively quick and easy to implement and deploy, several aspects have historically been neglected due to time constraints and a lack of appreciation for their importance. One might argue that testing is the prime victim of this neglect and make a pretty convincing case. However, I do believe that security has suffered most from the short timeframes and rushed projects that have been expected of this new development paradigm.

A false sense of security (no pun intended) has prevailed over Web developers and caused them to neglect the security requirements for their applications. Some developers are all too eager to defer to infrastructure experts to take care of their applications. Although a lot can be done on the network and system level, nothing will prevent a malicious visitor from attacking an application hole left by developers. Essentially, effective security can never be applied externally to a distributed application and must instead come from within.

Security is essential to building successful Web services and making their use widespread. If providers can't feel safe behind Web services, they won't deploy them. If consumers can't trust Web services, they won't use them. It is really that simple, and it is really that critical.

When it comes to security for Web services, there are four areas of concern: authorization for system access, application authentication, transport integrity, and payload validation. These are all areas of concern that Web developers have when designing and deploying applications, but there are some special concerns in each of these areas specific to Web services. Because Web services expose processes over the Internet and do not just share Web pages, it is critical that these four areas be thoroughly addressed to protect the provider, the consumer, and the end users.

The first two, authorization and authentication, you might be familiar with, because they apply to many current Web applications. However, process execution is a new exposure risk that providers of Web services need to guard against. Because the level of exposure is no longer strictly on the presentation layer, there is a slightly higher potential for vulnerabilities in your system.

System Access

It is easy to blur the lines between access and authentication, so for that reason I am clarifying my use of these terms by prefixing *system* and *application*, respectively. Fundamentally, access is a different concept, but discussions concerning the distinctions between authentication and access can get somewhat convoluted.

Basically, access is an initial qualification that allows a group or category of users to access a system. System accessibility consists of checks that are performed on a system level before you even reach the applications on your system.

This means that you don't know who the user is, but you do know that the user meets the correct criteria. These criteria generally consist of having a valid physical connection on the network and supporting the necessary protocols to establish a connection. (See Figure 5-28.)

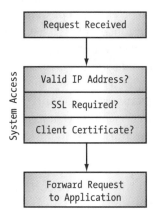

Figure 5-28. Typical system access process for Web servers

For many systems, acceptable credentials consist of connecting to the Internet, supporting HTTP, and supporting basic authentication. Once access is established, this same information can be used to help authenticate a user, but these two processes should not be confused as one.

You would approach the security considerations around system access for a Web service in much the same way you would for a Web application. The difference comes from recognizing who your audience is and what you are exposing to that audience.

The audience for your Web services is the consumer. That means access will always be defined on the consumer level and not the user level. Essentially, users piggyback the connections that the consumer establishes with your service. This is both a blessing and a curse, because you have to establish access for a much smaller group, but have no control over access on a user-by-user basis. To help with the latter concern, you simply must have a well-planned and well-designed authentication model.

What you are exposing to that defined audience is much more than just Web pages. Even sensitive Web applications do not have the level of exposure that Web services bring, because Web applications have an additional layer, the presentation, that can be used to restrict access to your data and processes. With Web services, you allow consumers to execute your logic and access data programmatically. This adds to the risk of your implementation, but there are practices you can put in place to mitigate any potential issues.

A few questions need to be answered to help determine the best access model for your Web service. The first is who your target consumers are. If you develop a service for internal use, it probably makes sense to keep the Web service inside your network, on an intranet, to prevent outside access. In contrast, a Web service meant for public consumption likely belongs in your DMZ or at a hosting provider, just as a Web server would.

DMZ stands for *demilitarized zone* and is really a tongue-in-cheek name for a section of your network that lies between the Internet and an internal, proprietary network. The DMZ is where organizations typically host any systems that are accessible from the Internet. This area is protected by firewalls that make it somewhat secure, but not as secure as the organization's internal network, as we will see in Figure 5-29.

The next question to answer is whether your Web service is meant for public or proprietary consumption. If your Web service is for the public at large, then nothing more really needs to be done. If it is meant to be proprietary, you may want to restrict access further by specifying the IP addresses of consumer systems or by requiring client certificates. Although these mechanisms start to lead us into authentication, their initial use is for allowing access to the system.

The final decision you need to make for your security model is on what physical model you want to host your Web services. Access is determined, to a large extent, by the physical connectivity of the outside world to your services. We have already talked about a DMZ, which involves firewalls and routers. That part has already been determined. However, one more option you have is whether you want consumers to hit your application servers directly or proxy the call to an internal application server. In the direct physical model (Figure 5-29, route 2), the Web service call is received by the application server that runs all processes locally and accesses data contained on the internal network. The alternative physical model (Figure 5-29, route 1) requires establishing a middleware proxy server that can accept the Web service calls and route them to the appropriate application server residing on the internal network.

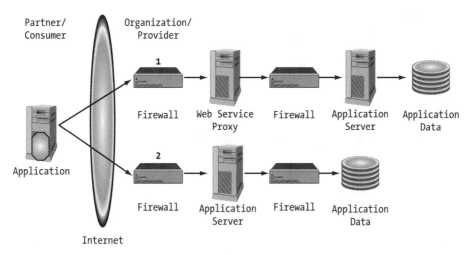

Figure 5-29. Direct versus proxied Web services calls to application servers

The first benefit to the proxy approach is greater isolation of your services from consumers. Having an additional layer will always provide more security, because it adds one more barrier to potential hackers. Some might argue that ports 80 and 443 are safe enough to allow any traffic through, as many firewalls do today. Although you are limited in your capabilities through these ports, there have been plenty of documented cases in which data and program logic have been compromised through them on various platforms. The bottom line is that, if a system routing Web service requests is compromised, there will be far fewer systems and resources that can be exploited, and it will be easier to repair or replace than the actual application server.

The benefits of a proxy configuration also extend beyond security by allowing you to aggregate value-added services at a single location. For instance, you can aggregate authentication services to a single system instead of having to implement those features on your application server. This is of even greater value if you provide many Web services that actually run on multiple application servers. A proxy configuration can act as an infrastructure platform that serves as a conduit for all Web services. (See Figure 5-30.) Such a configuration not only allows you seamless scalability, but also reduces deployment effort for each Web service launched.

Once the decisions around access security have been made, it is time to address authentication security. Some of these decisions are related to the choices made around the access model.

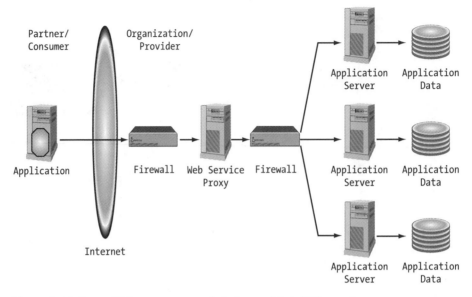

Figure 5-30. Proxy Web server as conduit for multiple Web services

Application Authentication

Authentication for Web services is probably one of the more complex components that has to be addressed in the security model. The reason is that it has
several aspects, and it can be a challenge just to identify them, much less
address them. As with other applications, you need one mechanism for authenticating users and another one for defining the logic that uses that knowledge to
establish rights.

The goal of authentication is to provide the right functionality with the
appropriate data to the right users. This process starts by selecting a method for
authenticating the users of your service. Even this step is not so simple when you
consider the fact that Web services have potentially two users: the consumer and
the end user. Furthermore, because the end user has no direct connection to
a Web service, you are at the mercy of your consumers to facilitate authentication of the user on a meaningful level.

This might make you feel hesitant about your use of Web services, but there
are many cases where that type of business relationship exists. The best example
might be credit card companies and the merchants that execute transactions
against the credit they provide to shoppers. The credit card company has no
guarantee of verification that the actual owner of the card is the one using it.
Instead, the credit card company must rely on the merchants to confirm their
identity through a signature or photo ID. When fraud does take place, agree-

ments are in place concerning how the situation will be handled. The same approach must apply to Web services. The providers have to trust their consumers, but they must have agreements and policies established for when fraudulent uses occur.

The second component of the security model is the authentication logic. This is how you use the knowledge of who is using your application by providing specific functions and/or showing specific information. You have to determine through your security model what these conditions are and how they will be handled. If you look at the functionality specific to each type of user, you can start to understand what you have to accomplish. This part of the model involves selecting the services and mechanisms you will implement to help manage these defined roles and privileges.

Authentication Mechanisms

When determining which authentication method(s) to implement, you have to consider whose identity you are trying to determine and capture. For some Web services, you will only be concerned with the consumer calling your applications. (See Figure 5-31, top scenario.) For other Web services, you will also be concerned with the user connecting through the consumer's application. (See Figure 5-31, bottom scenario.) There will also be Web services that must support both scenarios. Making this determination is the first step to formulating your authentication model.

Figure 5-31. Authentication scenarios

Consumers Authentication

The consumers of your Web services will be establishing direct connections with you over Internet protocols, so a host of established authentication options are available to you. In fact, you may have used some of these options for Web applications that you have previously developed.

The two main criteria for such a solution is that it work over existing Internet protocols and that it be stateless. The first criterion should be obvious to you, but the second one might not be if you haven't analyzed the authentication processes available for Internet applications. Your immediate thought might be that authentication is only needed during the first call. This may be true for some applications, but you cannot depend on this in a Web application.

If an application maintains state with its clients, that state is managed through a logical session, which is an artificial mechanism for streamlining the authentication process. Instead of going through the process of verifying the identity of the client for every interaction, a proprietary method is used to identify the user uniquely and reference the previously associated information. One way of implementing this is through a cookie containing an identification number that is stored in a relational database.

However, sessions can and do die, so Web services and their developers should not depend on the existence of sessions for proper execution. Sessions are merely conveniences that can improve performance by limiting the amount of costly authentication attempts. For any given interaction, authentication may be necessary, regardless of the current state. Therefore, the mechanism must be stateless to be consistently available, regardless of whether it is actually needed.

> **TIP** *Sessions can be great tools for improving performance, so I certainly don't mean to discourage their use. In fact, I very much encourage using them for workflow Web services. When multiple sequential calls are necessary, reducing the amount of overhead can go a long way to helping improve your performance and scalability.*

Many Web sites and applications support anonymous use, and that is an option for Web services. However, service providers are likely to be a little more guarded of their logic and data than they are of their content. As a result, the currently available options might seem limited compared to the demand that is likely to be generated. This is likely to change as Web services become more widely adopted.

Fortunately, the available options can meet your two criteria and so are also suitable for Web services. Some of these are standardized, and some are not. Standardized authentication methods are nice because many of the Web servers you will use to deploy your services will support them. This is very convenient because these Web servers often offer additional services around these authentication methods to reduce the amount of logic necessary to perform and maintain the actual authentication. However, these authentication methods can also be a little more complex for consumers to use because their applications need to integrate this client functionality. This will likely be a new challenge because the client side of these mechanisms is readily available in browsers and therefore taken for granted in applications.

Probably the most popular authentication method for Web applications is the account infrastructure. The user enters a user-specific username and password, and that information is verified against a data store of accounts. This can be very convenient to support when it takes advantage of an existing account infrastructure, like a domain or directory service.

Custom account structures are also common and can be effective. They require a little more time to implement, but they do allow maximum customization to meet the necessary requirements. In this case, an ID is usually generated or referenced on authentication to maintain the session to prevent the need for rekeying of the information.

One of the most powerful options available is a public key infrastructure (PKI). This standardized solution uses client certificates and server certificates to allow both the client and server to confirm the identities of each other as well as communicate securely. Although many developers are probably familiar with server certificates because of their use of SSL for HTTPS, some developers might not be experienced with implementing client certificates. This is a good example of the type of functionality that has been taken for granted in the past. It shouldn't be a major barrier to implementation, just a slight adjustment to timeframe expectations. We will look at the specifics of implementing client certificates in Chapter 6.

User Authentication

Whereas some existing mechanisms are available to help with consumer authentication, nothing is really established to handle user authentication. The methods discussed for authenticating the consumer are usually applied to users in Web applications, but Web services have a very unique relationship with their users. Because there is no direct communication with the user, any authentication method has to circumnavigate the consumer's application. This precludes all of the standardized mechanisms available today.

Instead, we have to take the custom approach. In fact, we have to take the custom account structure approach discussed as an option for authenticating the consumer. The user is identified through some mechanism (usually personal data or an arbitrary ID) and tracked through a unique data element. This data element must be communicated through the payloads between the consumer and provider, with the provider entrusting the consumer with its integrity.

Although this may not seem very secure, it actually can be as secure as necessary. There are not too many scenarios to consider for security concerns. One scenario calls sensitive data to be collected by the consumer application on behalf of the Web service. In the case of a browser-based application, the user shares this data with the consumer, and nothing can prevent the consumer from recording the data before passing it on to the service. However, the consumer is a visible player in the process because they share the ownership of the data with the Web service.

If encryption of this data is necessary to prevent the consumer from "seeing" it, a very different solution is called for. Although this is a possibility, it requires custom clients to accommodate this kind of complexity, since standard HTTP protocols are insufficient. This necessitates some form of peer-to-peer architecture, which establishes a three-way communication link in which the user communicates with the Web service provider and consumer application. (See Figure 5-32.) Any detailed discussion of this type of solution falls outside the scope of this book. Here I will focus on the applications and scenarios in which the user establishes only one connection with the interface application and does not connect directly with Web service providers.

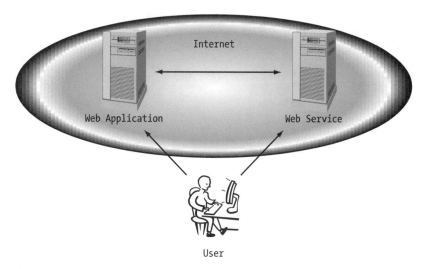

Figure 5-32. Peer-to-peer communication with Web services

This solution is probably not a realistic option in the immediate future unless you are already distributing a client application. Devices might be the early adopters in implementing this type of solution, because they are more proprietary in nature.

> The term *device* refers to wired or wireless equipment that has custom clients, which can be customized to provide certain functionality and features. Although there are many attempts to standardize the communication with these devices, the clients themselves are much more proprietary than the Web browsers that most people are accustomed to.

Another scenario might involve sending information across various services in an application "chain." In this case, the interface owner can encrypt the data for safe passage through the other service providers for the destination service. (See Figure 5-33.) Only scenarios in which one of those providers has additional information to provide the Web service are really of any value. This is because these "middleware" services cannot touch or work with that data. If they are not adding value, they can possibly be removed from that section of the process altogether.

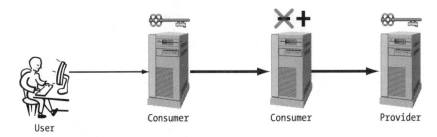

Figure 5-33. Encrypting data between the application provider and the Web service provider

This partner relationship is unique because the Web service provider is establishing a business relationship with its consumer, but yet does not entrust the consumer with the user data collected by the interface owner. In fact, this scenario may seem so ridiculous that you might think it impractical. Consider the following scenario: a travel site establishes a partnership with a credit card company that wants to reduce the amount of risk for its merchants by eliminating them from the payment process. Companies might not want to become some of the latest victims getting burned for compromising the credit card numbers, but obviously they still want to get paid. Even though the reservation goes through the hotel merchant, that merchant needs to see only certain data (the person's identity, travel dates, and so on) and can simply hand off the encrypted credit card data, unencrypted personal data, and the hotel merchant's own information to the service to get paid. The credit card service responds with a confirmation and/or an authorization number for tracking purposes, but at no point does the hotel touch the actual credit card data. This reduces the risk for the merchant and the credit card company.

Once we have determined our methods for authenticating our consumers' and users' identities, we need to use this information to determine how the service should behave. This is where our application's authentication logic takes over.

Authentication Logic

Authentication logic refers to the logic that utilizes the identities of our consumers and users. This logic consists of a series or rules that dictate what can or cannot be done by a user and/or consumer. Many developers think of these rules as permissions, but it is potentially a little more complex than that. Some situations call for some state information to be maintained that is specific to our users and consumers. For this reason, I like to split up these rules into two components: roles and profiles.

Before getting into the specifics of rules, I will discuss the options available for implementing this functionality. At least some of this logic needs to be referenced directly by the Web service. That means it must exist in some object or data source that is compatible with your Web services listener.

One necessary decision is how to encapsulate your authentication logic. It can be another object referenced externally, or it can be a module added internally to your service. Creating an external object allows for maximum reusability, but it also forces the application to depend more on it. This process is basically reduced to a call that says, "This user wants to do such-and-such. Should I let the user do this?" This isn't difficult to implement, but there is also an access question. What if you need to filter data based on the user's identity? You can't answer that question with a simple response. The authentication logic either has to hand the authentication rules over to the object, allowing the object to filter based on the user's identity, or the authentication logic must retrieve the data for you. The first option is somewhat inefficient, and the second probably extends the functionality of the authentication object and expands its scope, thereby compromising the design.

The alternative is to simply have an object that hands the application the necessary information to make its own determinations. For example, once a user is authenticated, the application can ask for a user ID, an access level, and perhaps the roles that the person fills. This is usually a more extensible solution that will best accommodate future needs.

Regardless of how it is designed, this authentication logic allows the Web service to act on the established rules for the service for the identified users. Keep in mind that this logic can become quite complex if the application has very granular access rules that depend upon multiple criteria (like role, geographic location, and access level). It is important that you define the scope of your rules first, and then define the scope and responsibilities of the authentication logic. You then have to be certain you fill in any security gaps between that logic and the Web service.

The rules themselves can be stored through a wide range of solutions, but they will generally be external to the service itself. When establishing the rules for user privileges in your applications, you will benefit from having an isolated location. Some developers tend to embed these rules in the application itself, but this makes maintenance and support very difficult and should be discouraged. This is the equivalent of embedding database query code in an application. At the very least, the definition of who can do what should be kept in an external data store that the application can reference. Even this solution, while very scalable, is not efficient for data that may be accessed frequently.

Many vendors have developed directory service offerings to allow the integration of this information in a central location. This allows developers to avoid duplication of effort for every application developed and deployed. Examples of these solutions include Novell's eDirectory, Microsoft's Active Directory, and the iPlanet Directory Server. You can find a listing of several vendor offerings at `http://www.directoryservice.com`.

Once data is located in a directory, you need to utilize an interface to retrieve information from it. This is the equivalent to using a data connection string to access a database. LDAP (Lightweight Directory Access Protocol) is probably the most popular standard interface for accessing directory data. It provides a very efficient mechanism for retrieving rules by holding them in memory and referencing the supporting database only when necessary.

Other efforts like DSML (Directory Services Markup Language) are also underway to establish XML-based standards for accessing this information. Most directory services support at least a couple of options for accessing the information, so you should not have to address this issue in your security model.

The tradeoff here is that this solution is not as scalable as the database. Splitting the source into two or more physical parts on separate systems or resources can sometimes mitigate this limitation, but it still ultimately falls short of the capacity of an enterprise-level relational database.

Keep in mind that we have potentially two players interacting with our Web services. When this is the case, you should have two different authentication processes designed that cater to the connection you have with each type of user.

As far as sourcing the authentication data, it is important that you keep these users separated at least logically because the consumer and user roles are fundamentally different. That doesn't necessarily mean that they need to be kept in separate physical sources, however. These two participants can be defined through different roles in the same structure, so don't necessarily plan a two-source implementation by default. There will be scenarios that benefit from each approach, with role volumes and scalability requirements having the most impact.

Figure 5-34 shows a logical view of how the authentication logic components may be deployed in a Web services infrastructure. Here you see a distinct separation of the two user models from each other and the application logic.

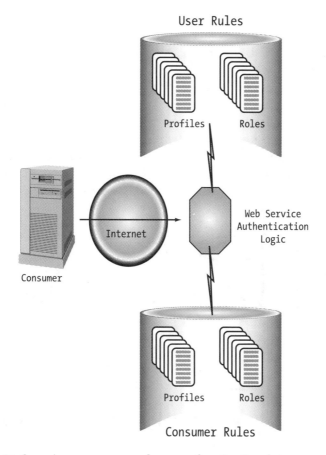

Figure 5-34. Sourcing consumer and user authentication data

Chapters 6 and 7 look more at specific implementations. It is crucial to have a strategy for storing your rules that meets the needs of your service. These decisions can affect your design, because they may have inherent limitations and/or benefits in how you implement your rules and logic.

Roles

When you identify the user types for a given process or application, you are essentially defining roles. An application may have only a single role, or it may have dozens. A user may belong to only one role or several. These are the things that have to be identified before authentication can be effectively implemented. This is where roles are defined.

Does a consumer have access to a specific function of a Web service? Does the user have the right to reference data submitted by others? Can a consumer reference its users' activity on the Web service? Again, these decisions can be more difficult to answer than in traditional Web applications if you are authenticating two users (the consumer and end user), not just one.

Once roles are defined, the authentication logic section of your security model begs you to complete two steps. The first is to identify your method for associating roles with users. Role association is done in one of two ways: either users are assigned to roles, or roles are assigned to each user. For simplicity's sake, you should consider that in one case the user is a container for the role(s), and in the other the role is a container for the users. (See Figure 5-35.) It can make a big difference which approach you take, because you might find limitations in your designs based on this choice.

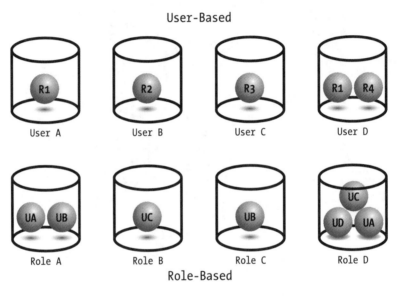

Figure 5-35. Container representation of user-to-role association

In the case of the user-based approach, roles are treated as properties of the users. Conversely, because users are usually treated as objects (because they almost always have their own profile data like first and last name and so on), the roles that users are assigned to will likely take the form of groups. It is easier for an application to incorporate the logic necessary to find a user's role by referencing the user (for example, looking in the user's container). However, this means that a user might be limited to fill only one role, or at least some finite number of roles if the user properties are unable to grow dynamically. A directory or data service that supports array-based properties can overcome this limitation by growing on demand without affecting the structure of your defined user profile. Otherwise, you will need to associate users to roles, which means that the application must "hunt" through each role container looking for the current user. This searching is much less efficient than the previous solution of looking directly within the scope of a single user. For this reason, I prefer implementing directory services that can accommodate variable attributes that can take the user-based approach for assigning roles.

> **NOTE** *The actual efficiency of these methods varies quite a bit depending on the service selected to contain the authentication rules. As a rule, the user-based approach performs better, but the magnitude of that difference varies among services.*

A slight twist to this scenario is when roles are defined on a group level and users are associated with a given group. This situation has the same options available, but the implementation differs slightly, because you are adding an extra layer between the users and their roles. Most directory services allow you to easily reference the group given a user, and from there you can treat the roles as properties of the group or treat roles as containers for the groups.

The second step necessary for completing the authentication logic portion of your security model is identifying your approach to assigning rights. Once your roles are defined, you usually find that a majority of your users have either maximum rights or minimal rights. This leads you to a determination of whether you take the optimistic or pessimistic approach to assigning access rights.

The optimistic approach means that you assume the maximum rights and take away for those users who fall within the exception. The pessimistic approach, conversely, allows the minimum rights and adds as necessary for the exceptions. Each of these can be beneficial from a maintenance standpoint if you are catering to a larger percentage of your user population with a default configuration. However, in the case in which sensitive information can be compromised, it is always best to take the pessimistic approach to mitigate the possibility of human error. Although mistakes are always possible, the optimistic approach tends to overexpose the application, whereas the pessimistic approach underexposes, which is usually safer.

What is important about roles is that they are predetermined for the user by some administrator or superuser. These roles may change, but users certainly don't have the ability to change their own roles automatically. There likely will be information that the user controls. That is where the user profile comes into play.

Profiles

On an individual level, some data or information usually falls within a user's control. This might be personal information, preference information, or both. The idea behind profiles for Web services is very much a personalization of the process, especially when presentation services are provided. One example of utilizing profiles in the CD search service is not showing any polka music because prior feedback collected from the user told us he or she doesn't like polka music. It is easy to confuse this concept with that of roles, but essentially we are catering the service based on user preferences, and not their affiliation with a group.

Profiles can be so broad in their scope that it is very likely that they cross multiple data sources. In the case of low-level state information (like preferences), it may be stored in a cache system for maximum performance. In the case of sensitive personal information, an enterprise-level database should likely be utilized for maximum security.

In the case of Web services, both consumers and users are likely to have profiles. However, the type and use of this information will likely vary between the two. In fact, by nature of the design, the consumers are likely to have more profile data than role information. Even though the profile data is stored under the consumer, it is still most likely to manifest itself through the consumer's use of the service. For instance, in our earlier example of the music search service, we eliminated polka music based on the user's profile. If we have a country music site that wants to be a consumer of our service, they may want to restrict all searches to country music.

Profile data is most suitable to reference from some sort of cache system. The user profile is likely to contain more sensitive information and thus be maintained in a database. (See Figure 5-36.) This is also justified from a performance standpoint because a consumer always has more frequent connections to a service than any given user. After all, many users will be utilizing the service through a single consumer. This means the greater performance gain is had if state information is more readily available for the consumers than for the users. Also, the consumer's portion of the payload is likely to be less sensitive because the consumer will have a previously established relationship and the user may be using the service for the very first time. A new user might have to pass the information necessary to establish identification and perhaps even an account with the Web services provider.

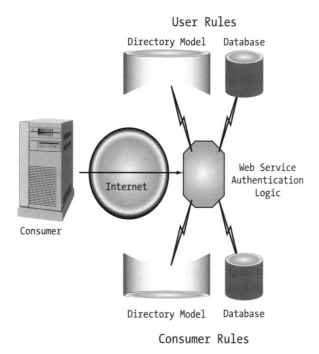

Figure 5-36. Profile storage for the consumer and user

The exception to a heavy cache-based consumer data solution might be in a fee-based Web service. If the provider wants to make certain that it is capturing the activity for a given consumer, or especially any payment data, it will likely store that information in a more robust and secure system. In general, though, the storage ratio for profile information between cache and relational data will probably trend toward 80:20 for the consumer and 20:80 for the user.

Because we now have our players identified and know our options for handling the security issues around that process, we need to turn our attention to the communication between them. We need to make sure that no one can intercept the transmissions between these two participants, thus compromising the data.

Transport Integrity

Like any information sent via the Internet, Web services payloads sometimes require discretion. In many cases, this data is not actually sensitive in nature, but the perception of the Web service by the consumer and/or provider might be better served by implementing a security solution to ensure the integrity of the transport.

By ensuring the security of our transmissions, we are trying to avoid basically two risks. First is the vulnerability of any of our communication over the Internet being intercepted and the data in the payload becoming compromised.

This does not affect the application directly, but it can affect the reputation of the parties involved, especially when they are sharing user information.

The second potential vulnerability during transmission is for someone to not only intercept but to modify the payload before passing it on. This takes quite a bit of ingenuity on the part of a hacker, but it is a possibility. Payload validation (discussed in the next section) can sometimes mitigate this risk. However, something else that can mitigate both of these risks is encryption.

Encryption is the process of encoding a transmission based on some key or code that allows only the involved parties to correctly decode, or interpret, the information. As a Web developer, you use encryption whenever you deploy a site requiring SSL (Secure Sockets Layer). It just so happens that this same technology can also help the client to verify the identity of the provider. Many solutions in this area include authentication necessarily because the identification of the sender and/or receiver needs to be verified as part of the key acceptance process.

> *MD5* is a compression and encryption algorithm that allows data to be securely sent between participants. It uses a private key to generate a 128-bit string, similar to a hash process.

Other solutions that take advantage of this type of methodology include MD5, Smart Cards, and Kerberos. Each of these solutions can be effective when implemented properly. Therein lies the risk, however, because you depend on the consumer of your services to implement its side of the solution correctly. In some cases, this may require your involvement, so you should consider this carefully when a solution is defined.

> *Kerberos* is a network authentication protocol that allows clients and servers to prove their identity securely through encrypted data. Once authentication has occurred, all communication can utilize this same encryption method.

Even when you encrypt the payload and verify the consumer's identity, your application still has a vulnerability exposed through your Web services. If a consumer makes a request of a Web service with an invalid payload, what are the consequences for the provider?

Payload Validation

Payload validation is something that most developers likely take for granted because they are used to working with languages, tools, and/or models that have built-in controls for handling these issues. In the case of Web services, we are exposed to this problem because there are no mechanisms to catch it for us.

The main concern with corrupt payloads is in protecting the provider from wasted cycles and, even worse, downtime. The interface for Web services is not as rigid as it is for RPC models, so getting a service to accept and attempt to process an illegal request is not as difficult.

> *RPC* stands for *remote procedure call.* This is the process of calling external entities to an application to execute a given process. Any object or component call would be an RPC.

Because we are dealing with XML, which is often not strictly data typed, there is no mechanism for immediately rejecting a request based on data type mismatches. If you allow this to go unchecked, you are asking for problems once you start working with the data.

TIP *Because even a Web service request that is rejected wastes precious cycles on your system as a provider, it is always beneficial to offer some client-side validation code as value-added content for your Web services. The consumer may not be motivated enough (or possibly even knowledgeable enough) to provide this valuable functionality on its own. Although you don't want to rely on it for the success of your process, it is always better to catch issues earlier on in the process (before taxing your systems).*

You can take two approaches to handling invalid data: reactive and proactive. The first is to allow the data to go unchecked by the application up front and build extremely graceful error handling to protect the involved service and its processes. This can be very difficult depending on the platform, language, and parser you are developing your Web services on.

The proactive approach means that you are performing extensive payload checking before processing it to ensure that the entire process runs smoothly. Although this provides better protection for the process and user experience, it can also be very demanding of your application resources. We will look at some of the best practices for making the most efficient use of your systems.

When performing payload validation, you will want to inspect two aspects: payload structure and payload data. Each offers its own challenges in securing your Web service offerings.

Payload Structure

The payload structure refers to the actual composition of the payload, not the data in it. Because a Web service's interface consists of an XML document, this basically boils down to the well-formedness of the call. The consumer needs to make sure it sends a well-formed XML document out to the provider, and the provider needs to ensure that it receives a well-formed XML document.

If you use a standard mechanism for parsing XML, like the DOM or SAX, you perform this check whether you want to or not. The trick is to handle this check gracefully so that you can provide some meaningful level of information back to the consumer and/or user. The difficulty with this is that your selected parser, and even the version of the parser you are using, dictates how you should handle an inappropriate call.

Conversely, if you write your own custom routine for parsing the XML, you have to also build the logic for checking well-formedness. This can be quite a bit of effort, so I recommend getting familiar with one of the existing parsers and using it. Although you can possibly get by without performing this check, you are setting a bad precedent and getting away from the concept of sharing your processes by not requiring proper XML data.

It is very important that you get familiar with how your parser handles inconsistencies and problems it discovers with the XML data when it is loaded. Some of the original parsers actually crashed when referencing invalid XML documents. Others either produce an error and stop or produce an error and then continue. It is important to know which approach your parser takes.

Once the application has validated the structure, we need to turn our attention to the data itself.

Payload Data

Validating the data in a payload can be a very intensive process. Again, we are interested in protecting the service itself. Although less harm can come from simply invalid data, it can still potentially kill a process if it is not handled correctly.

As discussed in Chapter 3's section on defining XML, the provider should always have a schema or DTD available to define the interfaces for its Web services. This is key to equipping your consumers with the right information to communicate properly with your Web services. By referencing that information, it is relatively easy to build a payload through either a manual or programmatic process. This definition will also serve you well, as the provider, by helping to programmatically validate the data once it is received.

Depending on your preference, you can also opt to build an XSL stylesheet that can validate the data. This affords you the opportunity to get more specifics on the errors, as well as an avenue for providing detailed messages back to the consumer concerning the error(s).

To use either the schema validation or the XSL approach, you need to use an XML processor. Again, knowing how your selected processor behaves is crucial to providing a reliable application.

Summary

This chapter has discussed the three components that compose a Web services model: presentation, interface, and security. If you carefully identify your objectives in each of these areas, you will be much more successful in your design and deployment of Web services as a provider. Even as a consumer of Web services, you will have a better idea of what to look for in a Web service as well as how to successfully implement Web services in your applications.

The key issues in defining your presentation model are the level of exposure for your Web services and the level of valued-added services you want to provide. The level of exposure may range from masked to isolated or be truly embedded inside your consumer's application(s). The services you provide in the presentation layer might include interface content, style information, or data validation. A combination of these three is usually suitable for any Web services interacting with end users.

Taking either the level of exposure or the level of service to extremes adds to your design and development efforts considerably and may not benefit you if the need doesn't exist. However, if there is a demand for multiple models, it is better to provide them independently so that you do not weigh down the consumers with minimal expectations with extraneous data.

The interface model is defined by the complexity of the processes you expose through your Web services and the amount of efficiency you want to have in the consumer-to-provider communication. A Web service may expose a simple one-call function or an involved workflow. In the case of a workflow, it is important to identify the processes and mechanisms through which you will manage state.

The payload efficiency is determined by the amount of overhead calls involved in the entire process of the Web service. Each step can be treated independently, or steps can lead into one another with inline error handling. Keep in mind that, for every efficiency gained in the process itself, extra effort may be needed by the provider and/or the consumers that implement it.

The main areas of the security model are system access, application authentication, transport integrity, and payload validation. Designing an appropriate solution to handle all four for a given environment should lay a good foundation for many Web services.

System access is the first step to allowing consumers to reference your Web services, and so it is also the first barrier to keeping unwanted users out. Once into the system, the application authentication process determines what users can do in the application. Of course, you want to make sure that you secure the consumer-to-provider communication when necessary, and your transport integrity solution should address that. Finally, you want to be able to trust the data itself as it comes into your Web services listener. Executing processes against invalid data can be potentially damaging, so you need to rely on your payload validation process.

Once you have laid all this out, you are ready to start designing your Web services. Fortunately, your model goes a long way to defining your design, and filling in the gaps will be much easier with the narrowed focus your model provides. You will then be ready to take the next step of developing and deploying Web services.

Building a Web Services Call

WHEN IT COMES TO DESIGNING and building Web services, there are two levels of difficulty: Web services calls and Web services workflows. Every request made to a Web service initiates a Web services call. The response from the provider then completes that interaction. A Web services workflow consists of a series of inter-dependent, if not sequential, Web services calls.

Obviously, before moving on to the workflows, we need to be able to build a Web services call, and that's what this chapter is all about. We will take a couple of existing processes and turn them directly into Web services. Vendors are put-ting much of their effort into defining how to build Web services from scratch, but a lot of existing functionality that's available today could extend their value as Web services. These examples will illustrate exactly how this can be done.

Our first example will take an existing Java class—an amortization calcula-tor—and expose one of its public methods. Then we will take an existing COM object that provides weather updates and expose it. We will then complete the chapter by taking one of these services and adding security and authentication through the use of client certificates.

> **NOTE** *These two examples accommodate very different skill sets and expertise, so my expectation is that most readers will not follow along and build both of these Web services. Some developers are experienced with both environments, but, if you are not, you won't learn them from just this chapter! Although lessons can be learned from reading through both examples, my recommendation is to try to implement only the envi-ronment(s) that you are familiar with.*

Exposing a Java Class

As any Java developer will tell you, Java was designed to be an object-oriented, scalable, and portable language. Although the portability of code is inherently much less of a benefit with Web services (because once the process is exposed from a central location, it no longer needs to be ported across systems), the object-oriented and scalable aspects of Java make its classes very suitable for extending as Web services.

The Web services we end up with will be a very straightforward implementation. We will not add any functionality or try to alter the method in any way. We might even limit its exposure slightly as we find it appropriate or convenient. Object-oriented objects tend to take their interfaces to great extremes, and our Web services will not warrant strict adherence to the native interface.

The requirements for this Web service will be relatively simple: we will build a loan calculator Web service based on IBM's Compound Interest class that ships with IBM's Visual Age for Java v3.5 development tool (`com.ibm.ivj.examples.vc.mortgageamortizer` package). You can download a trial version of this tool at `http://www7.software.ibm.com/vad.nsf/Data/Document2005`.

This class has a number of property values that we can set, providing information about the loan calculations we need (such as the loan amount, interest rate, number of years, and so on). The class then fills in the blanks by calculating those fields that remain. Our ultimate goal is to develop a Web service that exposes this functionality to anonymous consumers.

Building this service involves a few steps. First, we need to design the Web service. This won't be too complex, but some design decisions definitely need to be made up front. After that is complete, we will go ahead and build the Web service implementation. Finally, we will need to deploy and test the service in its target environment.

Designing the Mortgage Calculator Web Service

This will very much be the RAD (rapid application development) approach to building a Web service. There will be no presentation model, the interface model is a simple Web services call, and the security model will essentially be the same as any public Web site (anonymous access).

First, we need to make a few technology decisions. We know we are working with a Java class, which leaves the door wide open on infrastructure options, depending on where this class currently resides. After making these decisions, we then need to define the interface. As I said earlier, we aren't forced to follow the class interface and, in fact, it likely won't make sense to map the object directly to the Web service, so we will need to make a decision on what to support.

Choosing the Technologies

In choosing the technologies we want to build our Web service with, we have to consider a fairly vast range of areas that require a broad understanding of development and infrastructure architecture. It is never a bad idea to consult peers who are more knowledgeable in specific areas when you are uncertain of a technical decision. Backing out of a poor technology decision can be difficult and painful, regardless of your code's portability!

Whenever making technology choices, one area will always have priority over the other between the development and infrastructure architectures. Entire books are probably dedicated to these issues and ideologies, but our prioritization is made easier by the fact that we already have one decision made for us: we are exposing a Java class. This means that we would benefit from addressing our development issues first; otherwise, our infrastructure decisions might limit our options, even on the Java platform.

Development Decisions

The first decision to make is what technology method we want to use for exposing this Java class. We could plan an elaborate architecture with bridges and gateways that would allow us to wrap our class with a COM object, but that wouldn't be making things very easy for ourselves. Besides, we are looking for performance to turn these requests around as quickly as possible, and such an architecture would not help us in that area. Instead, we will make the decision to stick with the Java platform and expose our class through JSP (Java Server Pages) or Java servlet.

> **NOTE** *If you are more familiar with the Microsoft development platform, JSP is very similar to ASP (Active Server Pages), and a Java servlet is similar, architecturally, to an ISAPI extension.*

The next decision we need to make is what method we want to use for exposing our class. As I mentioned, we could use either a JSP or a servlet. Both are written in Java, and JSPs actually compile as a servlet, so the decision may seem somewhat semantic. However, JSP has some inherent limitations that keep it from being quite as robust as a true servlet. If you are serving up a fairly static page with some dynamic data contained within, JSP works great and is a more maintainable solution. However, our Web service will be entirely dynamic and could benefit from the modular nature of servlets by defining private methods. So, for these reasons, we will expose our class through a servlet, although JSP could be used effectively.

We also need to decide which XML parser to use. There are many to choose from, and all of them seem to differ at least slightly in their approach and/or feature set, so this is something we could spend a lot of time researching and agonizing over. Instead, I will select one of the leading vendor's XML parser that works well with Java: IBM XML Parser for Java v.3.1.1 (http://alphaworks.ibm.com/aw.nsf/techmain/F62DB5F8684DCF6A8825671B00682F34).

Typically, when developers have gained some experience with XML, they gravitate to one or two parsers that has worked well for them. As long as it supports the functionality required by the application, those parsers should also work just as well.

> **CAUTION** *This parser has some experimental features (DOM Level 2, SAX Level 2, partial Schema support), but I will stick with the public implementations just so I don't take advantage of something that changes in six months or so.*

Infrastructure Decisions

The next set of decisions to make relates to the infrastructure. The first of these is what platform to run on because the platform lays the groundwork for all other decisions. To maintain consistency across all the samples in this book, I will be hosting the Web service on a Windows 2000 Advanced Server. Despite the perceived Linux/Java union, many developers utilize Java on the Windows platform and swear by the combination. We also have plentiful choices in applications, tools, and services for Java on Windows, so we aren't limiting our implementation options either.

Because we will be developing a Web service, we need to decide what HTTP service to utilize. The easy answer on a Windows 2000 platform would be IIS 5.0, but I will buck that trend and select IBM's HTTP server. Like most HTTP services, it includes the basics and allows for fairly easy administration. Serving up HTTP is not a demanding process, and the operating system actually dictates most of that functionality, regardless of which actual service you utilize. However, this choice will lend itself much easier to my next decision, that of the application server.

Because of the popularity it currently has in the market, I will select IBM's WebSphere Application Server v3.5. You can also get a trial development copy of it from IBM's Web site: `http://www7b.boulder.ibm.com/wsdd/downloads`.

Given the class we are exposing, it should come as no surprise that our development tool is IBM's Visual Age for Java for Windows v3.5. This will complete our development environment, which will provide some synergy within the suite of IBM tools and services. It would be a stretch to say we have set up a completely integrated environment, but they should all "play well" together, and any experienced developer will always want and strive for that.

Designing the Interface

The next component of our design requires some decision-making, but it also gives us our first opportunity to get our hands a little dirty. Designing the interface for the wrapper of an existing object may not sound too exciting, but it does allow us the opportunity to be a little creative.

Analyzing the Existing Class

The first thing we should do is look at the existing class that we are building the Web service to expose. (See Listing 6-1.) The CompoundInterest interface has 23 methods available to us, so we need to see which we would be interested in.

Listing 6-1. CompoundInterest Interface

```
public class CompoundInterest {
    public synchronized void addPropertyChangeListener
        (java.beans.PropertyChangeListener listener)
    public void firePropertyChange
        (String propertyName, Object oldValue, Object newValue)
    public double getAmortizationPeriod()
    public double getEffectiveAnnualRate()
    public double getInterestRate()
    public double getInterestRatePerPayment()
    public double getPaymentAmount()
    public double getPaymentsPerYear()
    public double getPrincipalAmount()
    protected java.beans.PropertyChangeSupport getPropertyChange()
    public double getTimesPerYear()
    public double getTotalInterestCost()
    protected synchronized void recalculate()
    public synchronized void removePropertyChangeListener
        (java.beans.PropertyChangeListener listener)
    public void setAmortizationPeriod(double amortizationPeriod)
    public void setEffectiveAnnualRate(double effectiveAnnualRate)
    public void setInterestRate(double interestRate)
    public void setInterestRatePerPayment(double interestRatePerPayment)
    public void setPaymentAmount(double paymentAmount)
    public void setPaymentsPerYear(double paymentsPerYear)
    public void setPrincipalAmount(double principalAmount)
    public void setTimesPerYear(double timesPerYear)
    public void setTotalInterestCost(double totalInterestCost)
}
```

Only a portion of this interface is useful to us for various reasons. For instance, the recalculate method is necessary only in a stateful environment. Our Web service will instantiate this class, set the available values, and extract all the resulting values. This means that the only methods we need to touch are the gets and sets listed. This whittles down the list of method calls we need to expose as the 18 related to the following nine values:

- Amortization period

- Effective annual rate

- Interest rate

- Interest rate per payment

- Payment amount

- Payments per year

- Principal amount

- Times per year

- Total interest cost

In fact, the only methods we need to expose are the nine sets that relate to each of these data properties. The gets will make up the response data we send back to the consumer.

To maintain this Web service as a stateless entity, handling these nine methods separately (as the class does) is not an option. Nine separate methods would require nine different calls to the service. Maintaining state within a Web service essentially turns it into a Web services workflow, which adds greatly to its complexity. We will look at Web services workflows in Chapter 7.

It would be pointless to make this function a Web services workflow because even though these methods are separate, they are interdependent for our purposes. We are interested in only the final result, and not the state of the values between each value that we set. This means that we need to set all available properties before extracting any results. Fortunately, under these circumstances, setting the interest rate prior to the principal amount is no different from setting the principal amount first and then the interest rate. There is no sequence we need to follow.

Therefore, we can design the Web service to collect all the data from the consumer within a single request and provide the result through a single response. That leads us back to a Web services call, which makes the interaction very clean and minimizes the complexity.

Building Efficient Interfaces

For this scenario, we also have a design decision to make regarding the data we send back to the consumer. If the consumer submits the interest rate, principal amount, and the amortization period, should we respond with just the other six data elements? Although this might seem like an efficient approach, I would argue that it is not worth the tradeoff. Instead, I would recommend responding with all nine data elements in this and other similar situations.

Your Web service interface will not always benefit from the smallest possible data set. Don't get me wrong, size is important, but, in this case, the benefits do not outweigh the negatives. The tradeoff here is three elements, but for what?

First, by responding to the consumer with all data, it can help them to confirm the data they sent in the request. This could help them during development as well as troubleshooting once developed. Also, don't overlook the overhead necessary on our part to discern which data to return and which to not. By sending all nine elements back, it makes our responder logic consistent and much more simple.

Building the Schema

Whether we send all or part of the result data, this type of a call does allow us to have the same definition for the request and the response for our Web service. Because this class allows us to define and retrieve each of these elements, the request and response are virtually mirrors of each other. Other than an error message, there is no need to pass any other data between the consumer and the Web service.

Let's go ahead and define the schema for our interaction. (See Listing 6-2.) Because there is no relevant relationship between each of the nine elements, they will be defined as siblings. However, we need to define a root node to contain these elements to make it a valid XML document. To tie it to the service, I will name it calcInteraction.

Listing 6-2. calcInteraction.xsd

```
<xsd:schema xmlns:xsd="http://www.w3.org/2001/XMLSchema">
    <xsd:element name="calcInteraction">
        <xsd:complexType>
            <xsd:sequence>
                <xsd:element name="amortizationPeriod" type="xsd:decimal"
                    minOccurs="0" maxOccurs="1"/>
                <xsd:element name="effectiveAnnualRate" type="xsd:decimal"
                    minOccurs="0" maxOccurs="1"/>
                <xsd:element name="interestRate" type="xsd:decimal"
                    minOccurs="0" maxOccurs="1"/>
```

```
                          <xsd:element name="interestRatePerPayment" type="xsd:decimal"
                             minOccurs="0" maxOccurs="1"/>
                          <xsd:element name="paymentAmount" type="xsd:decimal"
                             minOccurs="0" maxOccurs="1"/>
                          <xsd:element name="paymentsPerYear" type="xsd:decimal"
                             minOccurs="0" maxOccurs="1"/>
                          <xsd:element name="principalAmount" type="xsd:decimal"
                             minOccurs="0" maxOccurs="1"/>
                          <xsd:element name="timesPerYear" type="xsd:decimal"
                             minOccurs="0" maxOccurs="1"/>
                          <xsd:element name="totalInterestCost" type="xsd:decimal"
                             minOccurs="0" maxOccurs="1"/>
                       </xsd:sequence>
                    </xsd:complexType>
                 </xsd:element>
            </xsd:schema>
```

Besides the naming convention, the most important thing enforced by this schema is the frequency of occurrence for each element. By limiting each element to a maximum occurrence of one, our code can be more trusting of the data coming in. We will see this when we build our responder logic in the next section, "Building the Listener."

Unfortunately, we need to go ahead and define this document in a DTD (see Listing 6-3) as well as a schema. I say unfortunately because, as we saw in Chapter 3, the DTD offers little support for some of the rules we need enforced, like data typing. The reason we need to use a DTD is because the IBM parser does not yet support schemas. (The 3.1.1 version does support a draft revision of the XML Schema recommendation, but the final recommendation of May 2001 is not supported.)

Listing 6-3. calcInteraction.dtd

```
<!ELEMENT amortizationPeriod (#PCDATA)>
<!ELEMENT effectiveAnnualRate (#PCDATA)>
<!ELEMENT interestRate (#PCDATA)>
<!ELEMENT interestRatePerPayment (#PCDATA)>
<!ELEMENT paymentsPerYear (#PCDATA)>
<!ELEMENT paymentAmount (#PCDATA)>
<!ELEMENT principalAmount (#PCDATA)>
<!ELEMENT timesPerYear (#PCDATA)>
<!ELEMENT totalInterestCost (#PCDATA)>
<!ELEMENT calcInteraction (amortizationPeriod?, effectiveAnnualRate?,
   interestRate?, interestRatePerPayment?, paymentAmount?, paymentsPerYear?,
   principalAmount?, timesPerYear?, totalInterestCost?)>
```

This is a good example of reality, however. As I said in Chapter 3, DTDs are not going away anytime soon. It will take a couple of years or more for the newer technology to displace the older one. Until that time, there will be instances in which we need to support (or should support) DTDs.

With our Web service interaction defined by physical definition documents, we are ready to move on to building the Web service.

Building the Web Service

Looking at our implementation effort, we need to keep in mind the two key components that will compose our Web service: the listener and the responder. The listener is responsible for receiving the request from the consumer, and the responder performs the necessary actions to provide the response. Although this might just be a logical separation within our Web service, we can work on each separately to structure our development process.

Developing each of these components separately allows for some efficiencies, especially depending on the complexity of the Web service in question. In Chapter 7, we will see an example of how we can design a Web service to support different versions through multiple listeners and a single responder. Even in the most basic of Web services, however, it allows us to test each separately, which can help speed the development process. Testing the listener requires a client that communicates over HTTP, so why burden the testing of your responder logic with that overhead? Taking on the responder logic and the listener all at once means jumping through a lot of hoops, so I would recommend avoiding that. I'll show you how you can develop each separately and integrate them once they are complete.

Building the Listener

As we stated in our design, we will build our listener as a servlet. A servlet is simply a special class that supports a couple key methods. Visual Age makes this fairly painless by including a wizard that sets it up for you very easily. This wizard walks through several steps to generate a servlet, but I will be breaking this process down in this section so that you have at least a high level understanding of how it works.

> **NOTE** *Although I am using Visual Age for Java as my development tool, you can use any of the available Java IDEs to actually build this Web service. This exercise will not divert into a tutorial on how to use Visual Age, so use whichever tool you are most comfortable with.*

Creating the Servlet

The servlet class, which extends the javax.servlet.http.HttpServlet class, will contain our entire Web service. This class is what will be called by the HTTP service when the consumer makes a request of the appropriate URL. (We will look at this in greater detail in the next section, "Deploying the Web Service.")

Because our Web service is handling requests for the CompoundInterest class, I will call the class CompoundInterestWS. Because we do want it to receive external requests, we will make it public. The resulting class definition is

```
public class CompoundInterestWS extends javax.servlet.http.HttpServlet
```

Although this technically makes the class a servlet, it cannot function as a servlet without implementing one of the two methods that can actually respond to a request: doPost and doGet. These two methods (see Listings 6-4 and 6-5) handle the HTTP POST and GET requests that can be made to the servlet class. Only one of these needs to be overridden for it to be functional, but you can handle both occurrences for the class.

Listing 6-4. Standard doPost *Method in Visual Age*

```
/**
 * Process incoming HTTP POST requests
 *
 * @param request Object that encapsulates the request to the servlet
 * @param response Object that encapsulates the response from the servlet
 */
public void doPost(HttpServletRequest request, HttpServletResponse response)
  throws ServletException, IOException {
    performTask(request, response);
}
```

Listing 6-5. Standard doGet *Method in Visual Age*

```
/**
 * Process incoming HTTP GET requests
 *
 * @param request Object that encapsulates the request to the servlet
 * @param response Object that encapsulates the response from the servlet
 */
public void doGet(HttpServletRequest request, HttpServletResponse response)
  throws ServletException, IOException {
    performTask(request, response);
}
```

> **TIP**   *When you use the Visual Age servlet wizard, the* doGet *and* doPost *methods call the fabricated method* performTask *by default. This is an empty routine that the tool creates to encourage developers to externalize their logic from these two methods. You will likely want to name this method something different. If so, rename it right away because it is easier to make this adjustment before you begin coding.*

The keys to these methods are the HTTPServletRequest and HTTPServletResponse objects. These also come from the javax.servlet.http package and are used to pass the request from the caller to the receiver, as well as the response back.

A few other methods can also be generated as part of your servlet (such as getServletInfo and init), but these are extraneous to this discussion. Instead, let's focus on the changes we need to make to our doGet and doPost methods.

Following Visual Age's lead, let's offload our logic to another method. However, we will call it stagingTask instead of performTask. It will accept the request and response objects as parameters, so our call will look virtually the same. We could call stagingTask from both the doPost and doGet methods, but you may opt to do something a little different.

If you don't want users to easily access your Web service through a browser, you will want to disable the doGet method. The HTTP GET request relies on the query-string to pass data to the provider, and this does a couple of things. A querystring is the portion of a URL that follows a question mark. For instance, in the address http://www.fundamentalwebservices.com/listener.asp?<root></myQuestion> </root>, the querystring is <root></myQuestion></root>.

Accepting data through the querystring allows for someone to manually call the service through the address bar of a browser. If we want to share our calcula-tor with only applications, we don't want to allow this type of request. Although it is easier to test, it is also easier for individuals to use, and to use incorrectly.

This gets to the second issue with the querystring. GET requests are more likely to be invalid requests because the access is so direct. To submit data through the POST action means that some application had to touch it, which means that special characters are already handled, and that there is more likely to be some structure to the data. A querystring could easily contain pure garbage typed into the address bar of a browser, and accepting it means trying to work with it and handling the exceptions. Although this service will be able to handle those scenarios, opening up your service to GET requests will likely mean more wasted cycles for your Web service.

Thus, we will reject any HTTP GET request. However, this doesn't mean we can't be nice about it! If we didn't care, we simply wouldn't implement the doGet method. Instead, I want to override it and respond with a nice error message.

(See Listing 6-6.) We will even contain this message in an XML document because that is the response that the consumer will be expecting.

Listing 6-6. Alternative doGet Method

```
public void doGet(HttpServletRequest request, HttpServletResponse response)
  throws ServletException, IOException {

 //Get method is not accepted by this service
     try
     {
         response.setContentType("text/xml");
         PrintWriter os = response.getWriter();

         os.println("<?xml version='1.0'?>");
         os.println("<calcInteraction><error>You must use the HTTP POST action
         to  Interact with this Web service.</error></calcInteraction>");
     }
     catch(Throwable theException)
     {
         // add code here when necessary to debug unexpected exceptions
         //theException.printStackTrace(System.err);
     }
}
```

To contain the message in the response, I am using the getWriter method of the response object. This allows us to write to the response document just like we would the console. Also note how I am setting the content type to XML so that the browser will handle the data accordingly.

The other thing this does is provide an easy way to unit test our servlet. All we need to do is connect to it through a browser, and we should get back the message we are responding with from the doGet method. We get the doGet response because we are not posting anything to the address. By default, a Web browser uses the HTTP GET to retrieve data from an address unless we are submitting a change to POST.

> **TIP** *To test this servlet in Visual Age, you need to install the WebSphere Test Environment. This is done, somewhat cryptically, by selecting File\Quick Start. In the dialog box that appears, select Features on the left and Add Feature on the right; then select OK. In the next box that appears, select WebSphere Test Environment and select OK. Once this is installed, you can bring it up by selecting Workspace\Tools\WebSphere Test Environment. . . from the menu. It can take a while to start up, but, once it appears, select the Servlet Engine in the left pane and select the Edit Class Path button on the right to add the project(s) you want to test. Once that is done, click on the Start Servlet Engine button to activate the test environment. You can now access any classes contained in the Class Path through the HTTP site. The address will have the following structure:*
> http://<server name>:8080/servlet/<package name>.<class name>.

Parsing the Request

Now that we have our POST and GET handlers built, we need to build our stagingTask method. This is what the doPost handed off the request and response objects to. The listener is responsible for validating the data before handing it off to the responder. It's always better if the responder can trust the data that it is given, so the listener needs to try to ensure that.

By trusting the data, I mean trusting that it is valid and well formed. The listener will not, and should not, contain all the logic to validate the request on a data element level. The responder still needs to be able to handle those issues if present. Ideally, the responder should not have to handle XML errors and should be able to count on the required elements to exist when it tries to reference them.

The first thing we need to do is define our stagingTask method. (See Listing 6-7.) As we saw from the request in doPost, it will accept an HTTPServletRequest and an HTTPServletResponse object.

Listing 6-7. stagingTask *Method*

```
/**
 * Process incoming requests for information
 *
 * @param request Object that encapsulates the request to the servlet
 * @param response Object that encapsulates the response from the servlet
 */
private void stagingTask(HttpServletRequest request, HttpServletResponse response)
{
    return;
}
```

Next, we need to create an instance of our XML parser. We could create one of a few different instances, such as DOMParser, NonValidatingParser, and NonValidatingDOMParser. You usually have a couple of options available given your scenario, so there isn't always a necessarily right or wrong answer.

One of the biggest differences between the features of these parsers is whether they implement the DOM. If you want to work with the data in a DOM tree structure, you should select one of the DOM-based parsers; otherwise, one of the other parsers will meet your needs with a little less overhead. However, the DOM is very useful if you want to work with all the data or with portions of it multiple times. Because we are working with the entire request document and I want to be able to validate it, I will use the TXRevalidatingDOMParser instance, which allows you to revalidate the document at any point. This can be helpful if you are adding or modifying data in a document. Although we won't likely need it for this aspect, we do want to validate the document, so it will work just as well and allow for that possibility.

Now that we have chosen our parser, we need to put it to work. We will start by declaring it and then submitting the request to it. To submit the request, we use the ImportSource object, which allows us to stream the request in through the getReader method. (See Listing 6-8.) Because we have defined the POST as just a single block of information, this is the easiest way to handle the incoming data. If this were a form with several fields of data, we would use a different method for accessing each of the fields independently.

Listing 6-8. Parsing and Capturing the Request Data

```
try
{     //Parsing the request and capturing it in the request document
      RevalidatingDOMParser parser = new RevalidatingDOMParser();
      parser.parse(new InputSource(request.getReader()));
      reqDocument = parser.getDocument();
}
catch(Exception e)
{
      os.println ("<?xml version='1.0'?>");
      os.println("<calcInteraction><error>The data submitted is not valid. Please
         validate it against the DTD or schema provided.</error></calcInteraction>");
}
```

Once the data has been parsed, we will use the getDocument method to store it into a document object. Doing this allows us to continue working with the data beyond the scope of the parser itself and to send it to other methods.

We are also handling the exception. Because this exception would be caused by the validity of the document, we should be able to make a response to the consumer, informing them of what the problem was. Again, anything we can do to help the consumer troubleshoot the implementation of our Web service will be paid back through quicker adoptions and fewer phone calls to our technical staff.

Validating the Data

Now that we know we are working with a valid XML document, we need to ensure that it is well formed. If it is, we know that the data contained within the document has the structure we need for the request to be legal.

Performing this function will be the validate method of our parser. (See Listing 6-9.) Like the loading of the request, we will need to handle the cases in which this step does not succeed. We will again provide an explanatory message to help them troubleshoot whatever problem was encountered.

Listing 6-9. Validating the Request Document

```
//Validate the document
if (parser.validate(reqDocument.getDocumentElement()) != null)
{
     os.println("<?xml version='1.0'?>");
     os.println("<calcInteraction><error>The data submitted is not
        valid. Please validate it against the DTD or schema provided.
        </error></calcInteraction>");
}
else
{    //Calling the getRate method
     resDocument = getRate(reqDocument);

     //Transfer the results from the document to the HTTPServletResponse
}
```

Unfortunately, this is where some of the parser's limitations become a hindrance. The first limitation is that the current parser does not support the XML Schema recommendation. This means that we have to resort to working with DTDs, which means that we may not be able to define the interaction as tightly as we would like. As we saw in Chapter 3, we do not have as much control over defining datatypes and the occurrences of elements as we do with XML Schema. Fortunately, in this situation, every element occurs either once or not at all, so our DTD can support our structure.

The other limitation comes from our inability to specify an external DTD reference. This is because we can neither edit a DOCTYPE element (as the specification dictates for compliance with the standard) nor reference an external DTD within the parser. The first reason can be justified, but the second reason is rather disappointing.

As a result, we have to trust the consumer to reference the correct DTD within their request documents. Although any abuses of this trust could allow potentially invalid data into our Web service, the consequences are dire for only the consumer and their user, and not our service.

However, if we wanted to make the extra effort, we could potentially validate the DTD reference independently before doing anything else, so that we could more gracefully handle the situation. Parsing the attributes of the DOCTYPE element would capture the DTD reference.

To do this, we would need to require that the consumers explicitly reference the DTD on our system. Then we could use the parser to view the path referenced for their DTD and compare it with the path we have defined. Anything that does not match our path would simply be rejected, even if it were a copy of the appropriate DTD in another location. We will not need to go into this effort for this example, and I will not go through the exercise to show the details of implementing it here. I suspect that, if you find yourself going to this extreme to ensure the legitimacy of a request, you will likely need to use a parser that supports schemas or at least allows you to define DTD references externally.

Now that we have all of our validation process defined, we need to integrate it into our stagingTask method as shown in Listing 6-10.

Listing 6-10. Updated stagingTask *Method*

```
private void stagingTask(HttpServletRequest request, HttpServletResponse
    response){
//Objects for the request and response documents
Document reqDocument;
Document resDocument;

try
{     //Staging the response object for the results
      response.setContentType("text/xml");
      PrintWriter os = response.getWriter();
      try
      {     //Parsing the request and capturing it in the request document
            RevalidatingDOMParser parser = new RevalidatingDOMParser();
            parser.parse(new InputSource(request.getReader()));
            reqDocument = parser.getDocument();

            //Validate the document
            if (parser.validate(reqDocument.getDocumentElement()) != null)
            {
                  os.println("<?xml version='1.0'?>");
                  os.println("<calcInteraction><error>The data submitted is not
                    valid. Please validate it against the DTD or schema provided.
                    </error></calcInteraction>");
```

```
            }
            else
            {     //Calling the getRate method
                  resDocument = getRate(reqDocument);

                  //Transfer the results from the document to the HTTPServletResponse
            }
        }
        catch(Exception e)
        {
            os.println("<?xml version='1.0'?>");
            os.println("<calcInteraction><error>The data submitted is not valid.
              Please validate it against the DTD or schema provided.</error>
              </calcInteraction>");
        }
    }
    catch (Exception e)
    {
        //If there is an error here, we aren't able to respond to the caller
        //e.printStackTrace(System.err);
    }
    return;
}
```

Once we have built and tested the listener, we can start working on the responder logic for our mortgage calculator Web service.

Building the Responder

The responder is typically responsible for all the real work in a Web service, and this one is no different. In fact, this is the area in which your Web services will be differentiated from each other. Up until now, we have been working with data in only a very generic sense, capturing it, validating it against the appropriate external definitions, and handing it off. This is when we start performing the tasks that are specific to the Web service.

We have already defined the main method for our service as getRate, and we will be passing it a document object that has been loaded and validated. Getting the data at this stage should keep any consumer-related issues from affecting the execution of our Web service. Another way of looking at it is that we should take responsibility for any issues that might occur at this point in the process.

> **TIP** *This clear, logical, separation of listener and responder is a very purist approach that, if upheld, will help with your Web service implementation and the development of future enhancements. To maintain this approach, any data issues encountered at this point that might have been overlooked should not cause a change in the responder, but in either the definition file or the parsing process.*

Let's start by looking at the skeleton definition of getRate in Listing 6-11. The only thing going on here, besides the method definition, is the declaration of a document object and its return from the call. TXDocument is a class that implements the DOM document object within IBM's parser. This object will contain the response that we eventually build in this routine.

Listing 6-11. Skeleton of the getRate *method*

```
/**
* getRate takes the XML document passed to it, extracts the property data,
* calls the CompoundInterest() method and builds the XML document
* for the response.
*
* @param document contains the XML document sent through the POST method
* from the consumer
*
* Returns the properties from the CompoundInterest() method through an
* XML document
*/
static private Document getRate(Document document) {
    Document response;

    response = new TXDocument();
    return response;
}
```

At this point, we have defined all of our methods for our servlet. You can see how this will all look within Visual Age if you have followed along with the process up to this point. (See Figure 6-1.)

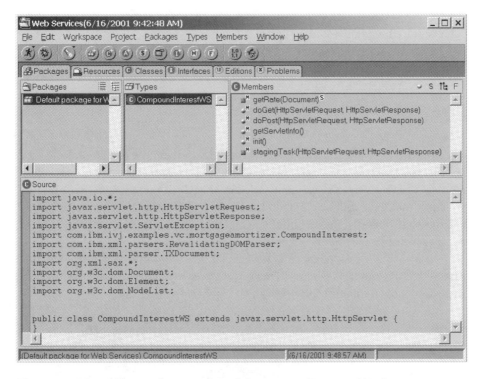

Figure 6-1. Visual Age workspace view of the CompoundInterestWS *class*

Now that we have declared the method, let's look at what we need to accomplish. We need to:

1. Extract the information out of the submitted request document.

2. Set the properties of CompoundInterest.

3. Retrieve the properties of CompoundInterest.

4. Add the data to an XML data structure.

5. Return the document to the calling routine.

Extracting the Data

Because we have a very flat document structure, extracting the data from it will be a fairly simple and direct process. The only potential "gotcha" in the process is that we don't know which properties were provided because many are optional.

We do, however, know that there can be only a maximum of one legal node for each value, which helps to limit some of the uncertainties.

Before we start, we need to set up a couple of variables. The first is the root of the document itself. This will provide a reference point for the document that will allow us to fetch any value we need:

```
Element docRoot = document.getDocumentElement();
```

Now that we have the root node, we could take a couple of different approaches in parsing the data. Because of the unknown existence of most elements, the safest way is to create a node list of each element based on its name. We know that there will be a maximum of one instance for each element, so we will have a list of only one or none. The fact that a node list can support an empty state obviously helps our cause.

Once we have the list, we can check its length to determine if any action is required. If the length is greater than zero, we know we have a value to work with. Let's look at this process for the amortizationPeriod node:

```
NodeList elements = docRoot.getElementsByTagName("amortizationPeriod");
if (elements.getLength() > 0)
{ }
```

We are using the getElementsByTagName to match all the appropriate elements. Notice that, even if the document is not validated, the existence of more than one element matching the name will not create an error. Multiple instances beyond the first will simply never be referenced.

We need to perform this step for each of our parameters, so we will have nine in total (this could be component-ized through a helper function, but I am choosing to handle these explicitly for demonstration purposes.) Now we need to define the actions that we need to perform once we have met these conditions and have some data to work with.

Setting the Properties

Each parameter has a corresponding method within the CompoundInterest class that allows you to set the value. As we identify the data in the request, we need to call these methods to pass this data on.

One decision that usually needs to be made when working with XML documents is whether to store the data in variables or to call the methods using the data stored in our document structure. Using variables versus direct references has advantages and disadvantages that any developer has likely encountered for different applications. In this particular situation, the debatable nature of the decision is somewhat circumvented because of our uncertainty in the document's optional nodes.

> **TIP** *Whenever working with request documents that can be validated only by DTDs, it is always a good idea to store the data in a typed variable before passing it on to other processes to help with type validation. This will keep you from passing inappropriate data to other objects, which may be harder to catch and handle.*

A minimal amount of information needs to be provided for our service to calculate the different properties. We don't know which values are set, but we can assume for various reasons that the primary concerns for a user are the interest rate, the principal, the life of the loan, and the payment amount. However, two other properties are equally important to our class: payments per year and times per year.

The first property deals with the number of payments that will be made each year, which most users will likely assume to be once a month, for a total of 12 payments a year. The second property sets the number of times per year that interest is calculated. Again, in most cases, this number will be 12, as users will also likely assume.

If we left this requirement, we would probably return some uncalculated values because the information was not complete. However, we could predefine some values to help minimize this occurrence. Doing this efficiently requires us to maintain variables for these parameters. To maintain consistency then, we will use variables to store all of our parameters before referencing the `CompoundInterest` class, as seen here:

```
double amortizationPeriod = 30;      //Defaulting to 30 years
double effectiveAnnualRate;
double interestRate;
double interestRatePerPayment;
double paymentAmount;
double paymentsPerYear = 12;         //Defaulting to 12 payments/year
double principalAmount;
double timesPerYear = 12;       //Defaulting to 12 times/year
double totalInterestCost;
```

We are also defaulting the amortization period to 30 years as a benefit to any home loan applications using our service. Keep in mind that we are also returning every value in the response, so all defaulted values will also be provided back to the user so that they know how the calculations were performed.

Now that we have all of our variables defined, let's go ahead and look at setting the value for one of our parameters, `amortizationPeriod`.

```
amortizationPeriod =
   Double.parseDouble(elements.item(0).getFirstChild().getNodeValue());
calculator.setAmortizationPeriod(amortizationPeriod);
```

This process will then be called for each value that is provided to us, so we will need to add it to each of the nine extraction routines we have. Once this is done, we need to turn around and reference each property of `CompoundInterest`.

Retrieving the Properties

The only decision we need to make when retrieving the values from the `CompoundInterest` class is how to store them. We could save them off in the variables that we used to set the same values, which might make sense if we have to do some work with the data (such as perform calculations or filter the data).

Because we want to pass the data back "as is" and the data will end up in an XML structure, it makes sense to go ahead and store these values directly to `Element` objects. Then, we can later add them to the document that is our response. Let's look at this step for the amortization period value:

```
Element elem = response.createElement("amortizationPeriod");
elem.appendChild(response.createTextNode(String.valueOf
   (calculator.getAmortizationPeriod())));
```

Here, we are using a temporary `Element` object called `elem` to create an element named `amortizationPeriod` and then saving the value from the appropriate method of our instance of the `CompoundInterest` class, called calculator. Pay special attention to two things here. First, notice how we are creating a text node consisting of our `amortizationPeriod` value and appending it to the `amortizationPeriod` element. Although in the XML world we are dealing with a single element, in this strict definition of the DOM we are creating two nodes and relating them: the value node as a child of the element node. This can be a difficult concept to grasp if you aren't used to it, and some parsers will mask this from you by allowing you to interface this as a single entity.

Second, notice that, even though we are converting this value to a string, it has no bearing on the actual node data type. One of the paradoxes of working with XML is that, even if data types are declared for your elements, the data is inherently typed as a string. In other words, there is no `integerNode` type, just `textNodes` that contain string values that represent integers. It is the validation process that then checks to see if those strings can be converted to the appropriate types.

Now that we have our data, we need to go about adding it to our response document.

Adding the Data to Our Document

In our response, we will be returning an XML document that will contain all the information from our `CompoundInterest` class. Now that we have the data, we need to build that document. We have already taken the first step by storing the data in element objects. This keeps us from having to touch that data directly.

In our skeleton class, we have defined the document already, so that step has been achieved. What we must do next is define the root element for our document. As we have discussed, every XML document must have a single root node, so we can't just add the elements we have to the document directly. The root node for our document is `calcInteraction`, so let's go ahead and create that:

```
Element root = response.createElement("calcInteraction");
```

Keep in mind that this is a standalone entity. No relationship is established with our response document at this point. You can think of this as the root of our working document for the purpose of building the response. Once we are done, we will "move" this root node over to our actual response document, like this:

```
response.appendChild(root);
```

Before we can do this, however, we need to finish building our working document by adding all of our values. We saw in the previous section where we extracted the data from `CompoundInterest` into an element called `elem`. We also need to "move" the element over to our root with an `appendChild` call, just like we will do for moving the root over to our response document:

```
root.appendChild(elem);
```

Now we have an entire document that contains the result values from the `CompoundInterest` class. This actually completes the `getRate` method, so let's take a look at the entire routine, which puts all of these tasks together. (See Listing 6-12.)

Listing 6-12. The `getRate` Method

```
/**
 * getRate takes the XML document passed to it, extracts the property data,
 * calls the CompoundInterest() method and builds the XML document
 * for the response.
 *
 * @param document contains the XML document sent through the POST method
 * from the consumer
 *
 * Returns the properties from the CompoundInterest() method through an
 * XML document
```

```
*/
static private Document getRate(Document document) {
    NodeList elements;
    Element elem, root;
    Document response;

    //Declaring the variables for the CompoundInterest properties
    double amortizationPeriod = 30;      //Defaulting to 30 years
    double effectiveAnnualRate;
    double interestRate;
    double interestRatePerPayment;
    double paymentAmount;
    double paymentsPerYear = 12;      //Defaulting to 12 payments/year
    double principalAmount;
    double timesPerYear = 12;      //Defaulting to 12 times/year
    double totalInterestCost;

    CompoundInterest calculator = new CompoundInterest();

    //Defaulting the baseline data values
    calculator.setAmortizationPeriod(amortizationPeriod);
    calculator.setPaymentsPerYear(paymentsPerYear);
    calculator.setTimesPerYear(timesPerYear);

    //Referencing the submitted document object
    Element docRoot = document.getDocumentElement();

    //Each property is handled in the same manner:
    //  if a value was provided, the property is set
    elements = docRoot.getElementsByTagName("amortizationPeriod");
    if (elements.getLength() > 0)
    {
        amortizationPeriod =
           Double.parseDouble(elements.item(0).getFirstChild().getNodeValue());
        calculator.setAmortizationPeriod(amortizationPeriod);
    }

    elements = docRoot.getElementsByTagName("effectiveAnnualRate");
    if (elements.getLength() > 0)
    {
        effectiveAnnualRate =
           Double.parseDouble(elements.item(0).getFirstChild().getNodeValue());
        calculator.setEffectiveAnnualRate(effectiveAnnualRate);
    }
```

```
elements = docRoot.getElementsByTagName("interestRate");
if (elements.getLength() > 0)
{
    interestRate =
        Double.parseDouble(elements.item(0).getFirstChild().getNodeValue());
    calculator.setInterestRate(interestRate);
}

elements = docRoot.getElementsByTagName("interestRatePerPayment");
if (elements.getLength() > 0)
{
    interestRatePerPayment =
        Double.parseDouble(elements.item(0).getFirstChild().getNodeValue());
    calculator.setInterestRatePerPayment(interestRatePerPayment);
}

elements = docRoot.getElementsByTagName("paymentAmount");
if (elements.getLength() > 0)
{
    paymentAmount =
        Double.parseDouble(elements.item(0).getFirstChild().getNodeValue());
    calculator.setPaymentAmount(paymentAmount);
}

elements = docRoot.getElementsByTagName("paymentsPerYear");
if (elements.getLength() > 0)
{
    paymentsPerYear =
        Double.parseDouble(elements.item(0).getFirstChild().getNodeValue());
    calculator.setPaymentsPerYear(paymentsPerYear);
}

elements = docRoot.getElementsByTagName("principalAmount");
if (elements.getLength() > 0)
{
    principalAmount =
        Double.parseDouble(elements.item(0).getFirstChild().getNodeValue());
    calculator.setPrincipalAmount(principalAmount);
}

elements = docRoot.getElementsByTagName("timesPerYear");
if (elements.getLength() > 0)
{
```

```
        timesPerYear =
          Double.parseDouble(elements.item(0).getFirstChild().getNodeValue());
        calculator.setTimesPerYear(timesPerYear);
}


elements = docRoot.getElementsByTagName("totalInterestCost");
if (elements.getLength() > 0)
{
        totalInterestCost =
          Double.parseDouble(elements.item(0).getFirstChild().getNodeValue());
        calculator.setTotalInterestCost(totalInterestCost);
}


//Staging the response document
response = new TXDocument();

//Staging the working node: root
root = response.createElement("calcInteraction");

//Extracting all the properties - if call was successful, all properties are
//  available all elements are created and added to our root node
elem = response.createElement("amortizationPeriod");
elem.appendChild(response.createTextNode(String.valueOf
  (calculator.getAmortizationPeriod())));
root.appendChild(elem);


elem = response.createElement("effectiveAnnualRate");
elem.appendChild(response.createTextNode(String.valueOf
  (calculator.getEffectiveAnnualRate())));
root.appendChild(elem);


elem = response.createElement("interestRate");
elem.appendChild(response.createTextNode(String.valueOf
  (calculator.getInterestRate())));
root.appendChild(elem);


elem = response.createElement("interestRatePerPayment");
elem.appendChild(response.createTextNode(String.valueOf
  (calculator.getInterestRatePerPayment())));
root.appendChild(elem);


elem = response.createElement("paymentAmount");
elem.appendChild(response.createTextNode(String.valueOf
  (calculator.getPaymentAmount())));
root.appendChild(elem);
```

```
elem = response.createElement("paymentsPerYear");
elem.appendChild(response.createTextNode(String.valueOf
  (calculator.getPaymentsPerYear())));
root.appendChild(elem);

elem = response.createElement("principalAmount");
elem.appendChild(response.createTextNode(String.valueOf
  (calculator.getPrincipalAmount())));
root.appendChild(elem);

elem = response.createElement("timesPerYear");
elem.appendChild(response.createTextNode(String.valueOf
  (calculator.getTimesPerYear())));
root.appendChild(elem);

elem = response.createElement("totalInterestCost");
elem.appendChild(response.createTextNode(String.valueOf
  (calculator.getTotalInterestCost())));
root.appendChild(elem);

//Appending the root node to the response document
response.appendChild(root);

return response;
}
```

Returning the Document

The only thing we have left to do now is return the XML document to the consumer. Because getRate has returned it to stagingTask, it now needs to transfer the document to the HTTPServletResponse object that was passed by the doPost routine. Using the same PrintWriter object that we used to return the error messages for validation or parsing errors, we can write out our document object. The difference with this response is that we are working with a document, and not text that we can pass through a println command.

To handle the conversion for the document object, we will use its printWithFormat routine. This essentially presents the data in the document object with the format appropriate for an XML document. Prior to actually writing the document, it is a good practice to set the version for your XML header.

```
((TXDocument)resDocument).setVersion("1.0");
((TXDocument)resDocument).printWithFormat(os);
```

Now that we have returned the response document, we have built our Web service. However, because it is still in a code form, we need to deploy the Web service through an HTTP server and test it all the way through.

Deploying the Web Service

The deployment of a Web service will closely follow the deployment of an *n*-tier application. Of course, which platform you deploy the application on will cause the exact process to vary. As we indicated at the beginning of the chapter, this deployment will be based on the Windows 2000 platform, IBM HTTP Server, and IBM WebSphere Application Server.

Exporting the Servlet

If we start at the back and work our way up, the first step is to deploy the CompoundInterestWS servlet. This is done within our Visual Age using the export option. First, we must select the CompoundInterestWS class in our workspace. Then, select File|Export from the menu. (See Figure 6-2.)

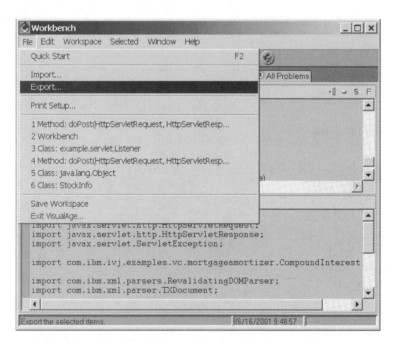

Figure 6-2. Selecting the export function in Visual Age

You are now presented with the export options, from which you should select Directory. (See Figure 6-3.)

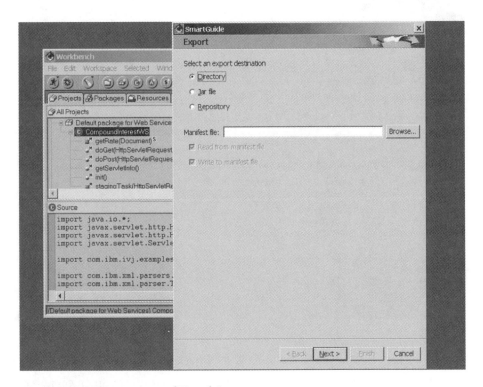

Figure 6-3. Export options of Visual Age

Doing so displays the options screen for executing the export to a directory structure. (See Figure 6-4.) The first value to set (or at least confirm) is the directory to which you want to export the class. Although you can select any directory, the default directory for your WebSphere Application Server is a good choice (if WebSphere is installed locally, that is). However, these files can be moved to wherever your final destination may be, whether local or on another system. This path is where you can locate the file(s) once the export is complete.

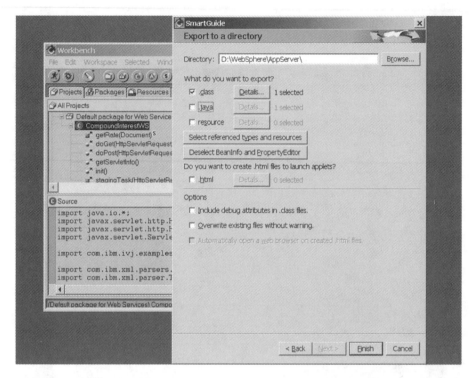

Figure 6-4. Directory export options of Visual Age

The next option is what files to export to your directory. Although you might want to export the other two files for various reasons (which we will not get into here), the only file type required is the class file itself.

If you are deploying to a new system without any Java classes already installed, the next option is very important. This is where we can have Visual Age automatically grab all dependencies for our class. Once you select the "Select referenced types and resources" option, you should end up with a total of 190 files for this servlet. You can select details to view all the files that were collected. (See Figure 6-5.) This is where you can also deselect any classes or references that are already present on the system you are deploying to.

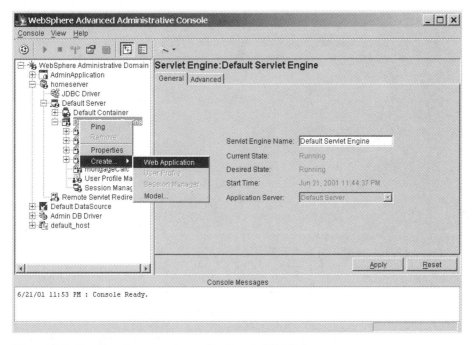

Figure 6-7. Creating a new web application in WebSphere

When you start the new Web application process, you need to define three values: Web application name, virtual host, and Web application Web path. You can also use an optional description field. (See Figure 6-8.) The Web application name will be used by default to help define the Web path. The Web path is probably the most important value to note because this is how you will reference your Web service.

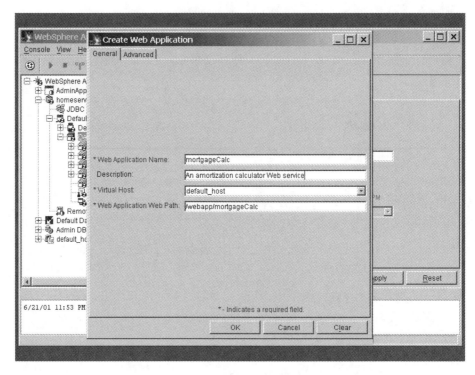

Figure 6-8. The WebSphere new web application dialog box

Selecting the Advanced tab will take you to the dialog box where you can specify the document and class path for your application. Once you have set up your Web application, you need to define the servlet in your application. This is similar to creating a new Web application: you right-click on the application and select Create. . .|Servlet. (See Figure 6-9.)

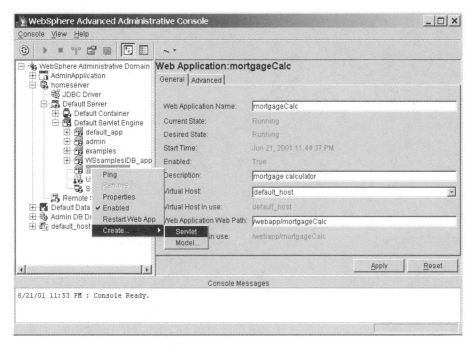

Figure 6-9. Creating a new servlet in WebSphere

Now you're presented with the servlet dialog box, which allows you to specify the name and class name for your servlet. (See Figure 6-10.)

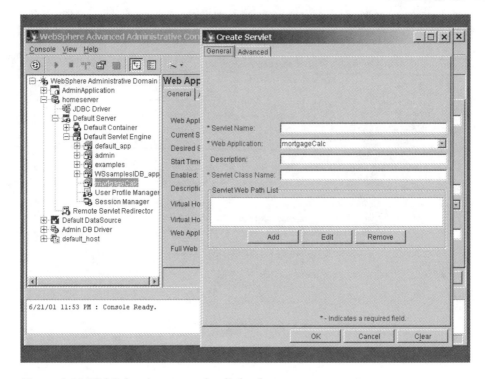

Figure 6-10. WebSphere's new servlet dialog box

You also need to specify the Web path for your servlet. (See Figure 6-11.)
This is the address at which the servlet will be found, and the entire URL will
consist of this path and the name for your class, which we just specified.
WebSphere can support multiple addresses for your servlet, and this capability
can be helpful in situations in which you need to host the same servlet with
different identities.

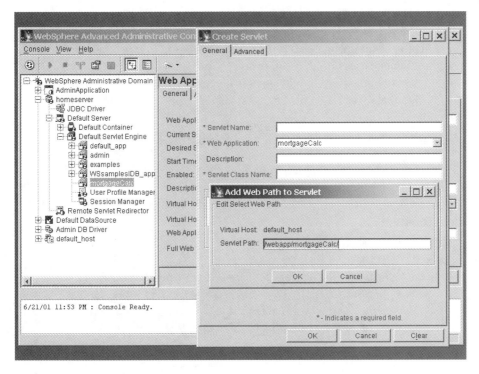

Figure 6-11. Specifying a servlet's web path(s) in WebSphere

You should have a servlet that is ready to receive requests at the path(s) we specified. However, we need to make sure that our HTTP server is ready to receive requests.

Configuring IBM HTTP Server

Because WebSphere handles the servlet directly, no additional configuration is needed for the HTTP server. The only thing that needs to be made certain is that the HTTP server is actually running. Without this service running, no Web services will work!

Testing the Web Service

Now that we have our Web service deployed, we need to test it. Just as in an application, we need to focus on two areas in the testing of our Web services: accuracy and performance. Although testing a Web service carries many similarities to testing a Web application, special considerations need to be made for Web services testing as we will see.

Accuracy Testing

In testing the accuracy of a Web service, we are looking to reproduce the desired result from every situation that can occur. In the case of our mortgage calculator Web service, the questions would specifically be: Is the data correct? Do the appropriate messages get returned if there is an error? Are all errors handled gracefully when possible?

To answer these questions, we must have some type of client to act as a consumer of our Web service. An actual application will do, but it is possible to utilize a simple browser, depending on how the Web service was developed. In our mortgage calculator, we decided to deny consumer requests using an HTTP GET request. Accepting only HTTP POST requests means that we must build a client application.

> **NOTE** *Some of you are no doubt aware that we could generate a POST request from a static HTML page with a Form element. Although this would generate the POST request that the service requires, submitting the data in an XML format would be problematic, if not impossible.*

We will focus on building test clients more in the next two examples, so, for our purposes, we will simply assume its existence. You can download a generic test client from the supporting site for this book at `http://www.architectingwebservices.com/testclient`. This test client takes a request document, submits it to our Web service, and displays the response—which means that we need to come up with some request documents for our Web service. An example of a valid request is shown in Listing 6-13. This should produce an error-free response from the Web service.

Listing 6-13. Sample `calcInteraction` *Request*

```
<?xml version="1.0" encoding="UTF-8"?>
<calcInteraction>
      <amortizationPeriod>30</amortizationPeriod>
      <interestRate>.0725</interestRate>
      <paymentsPerYear>12</paymentsPerYear>
      <principalAmount>150000</principalAmount>
</calcInteraction>
```

When the request is made, the response that should be returned will look like Listing 6-14.

Listing 6-14. `calcInteraction` *Response*

```
<?xml version="1.0"?>
<calcInteraction>
     <amortizationPeriod>30.0</amortizationPeriod>
     <effectiveAnnualRate>0.07495829742132853</effectiveAnnualRate>
     <interestRate>0.0725</interestRate>
     <interestRatePerPayment>0.07228912470025328
     </interestRatePerPayment>
     <paymentAmount>1021.1198323383267</paymentAmount>
     <paymentsPerYear>12.0</paymentsPerYear>
     <principalAmount>150000.0</principalAmount>
     <timesPerYear>12.0</timesPerYear>
     <totalInterestCost>217603.13964179758</totalInterestCost>
</calcInteraction>
```

Sending invalid or incomplete data through the request of our Web service can help us to test the error handling. This can range from sending no data, to sending invalid data types within the elements, to sending unnecessary data.

Performance Testing

Testing the performance of a Web service is a little different from testing other applications because you have to consider the impact on the consumers' implementations. It would be a mistake to assume that the overall performance of your Web services is based on the processing that you are providing. You could build the fastest possible Web service, but, if you are simply pushing off processing duties to the consumer, the overall performance could suffer.

This is the tradeoff we identified in Chapter 5 when we looked at the possibility of transforming the resulting data on the provider's system versus the consumer's system. Because the provider already has the XML document loaded into a DOM, they would take a minimal hit in manipulating the data compared to the consumer, if they never intended or otherwise needed to load it into a DOM structure.

As with any application, the first thing that needs to be realized in performance testing is that an application will always have a bottleneck. So, the objective is not to eliminate all bottlenecks, because that is impossible. We simply want to address the bottlenecks that keep our Web service from performing as quickly and efficiently as we would like. Of course, metrics are necessary to identify where that limit lies. Resources addressing software testing can also be very helpful in your approach to testing Web services.

In our performance testing, we will simulate a large user base accessing the Web service directly and through a consumer. To do this with any accuracy or dependability, we will need a testing tool. There are many to choose from, ranging in a variety of price ranges and functionality, but, if you or your organization does not already own one, I would recommend looking at a free tool provided from Microsoft called Web Application Stress Tool (WAST). You can get more information on WAST, as well as download it, from Microsoft's site at `http://msdn.microsoft.com/library/default.asp?url=/library/en-us/ dnduwon/html/d5wast_2.asp`.

Once we have selected the testing tool(s), we will then need to test the Web service both directly (essentially the responder) and through a consumer application (through the listener). If we use a tool like WAST that can monitor the system's status (for Windows platforms), we should be able to identify the largest delay in both processes. If this bottleneck exists for both, then we know that the Web service itself will require our attention and that our model is likely sound. If the biggest bottleneck occurs within the consumer and it is built fairly efficiently, it may take a design change to address the problem. Hopefully, we can address it through system tuning, logic changes, or both. Regardless of the changes we made, we should afterwards retest both processes. This retesting will confirm how much improvement was made through our changes, and it may identify the next-largest bottleneck.

Once your testing has been completed and the results are to your satisfaction, you will have a working Web service based on a Java class ready to release. We will get into more robust Web service consumers in Chapter 8. Until then, we have some more work to do in designing and building Web services. We will now turn our attention towards taking another type of object and extending it as a Web service—a COM object.

Exposing a COM Object

When exposing an existing COM object as a Web service, we will encounter many of the same issues we did in exposing a Java class. We must determine which aspects we want to expose, what the interface for the Web service will be, and how to hand off the data between the listener and the responder. However, the platform and environment differences will present us with a few new options while eliminating others. The best way to address those is by going through the exercise of actually building a Web service.

> **NOTE** *This section is not just a rehash of the previous exercise using the Microsoft toolset. Even if you have a good understanding of all the concepts presented through that section, you should still read through this example because it addresses a few additional issues that concern the building of XML data and implementing security.*

The component we will be exposing is a weather component developed by SoftShell Solutions called S3Weather 2.0 (`http://www.softshell.net/asp/cp/weather.asp`). This component will accept a ZIP code and provide an assortment of weather information specific to that area. Although the details of how it works aren't important to us for this exercise, it retrieves data from the weather.com Web site.

Unlike the previous Web service, this will be a restricted-use service. We will allow only authorized consumers to access our service, which means that we will have to perform some type of authorization check on consumer requests in order to validate them. Otherwise, the service itself is very straightforward, and the effort will be very similar to the Java class.

As in the previous example, we need to go through a process of designing, building, and testing to implement our Web service. This will ensure that we have an end product that our consumers and ourselves are happy with.

Designing the Weather Web Service

Like our calculator Web service, the weather Web service will be very much a quick and direct exercise in exposing some functionality "as is." Just as we saw in our earlier example, though, this does not mean that the process is devoid of any design decisions. We must address these design concerns before moving on, or else we might end up having to redo work because we did not think through all of our issues.

The first design issue that we need to address before we can start building our Web service concerns the technologies that we will choose for exposing our Web service. The second is the interface we will define to communicate our service's functionality to consumers.

Choosing the Technology

The very nature of working with the Microsoft development platform makes many of our technology choices routine, if not predetermined. Although some people dislike the notion of a close-nit platform, it certainly lends itself to a consistent architecture and design. Nonetheless, some decisions need to be made or at least recognized.

Because we are again working with an existing component, I think it helps to provide a direction as to which decisions take the higher priority: development or infrastructure. Because we must run and maintain the existing COM object, our infrastructure must support that architecture.

Development Decisions

In the current Microsoft development environment, we can approach the interaction with this existing COM object in a few different ways. If we start at the listener and work our way back to the S3Weather component, we have two different approaches: ASP (Active Server Pages) and ISAPI (Internet Server Application Program Interface) extensions.

An ASP poses a quick solution to getting a listener for our Web service constructed very rapidly. However, the performance would not be the best. For optimum performance, we would need to develop an ISAPI extension because performance comes down to the multithreading capabilities of the extension versus ASP. This means that ISAPI extensions must be developed in C++, not Visual Basic. Using an ISAPI extension also places a restriction on what components you can expose as a Web service because it must also support ISAPI's threading model. Assuming both options are still available, the tradeoff here is that a more advanced skill set is necessary for ISAPI development than for ASP development.

> **NOTE** *If you are more familiar with the Java development platform, ASP is the equivalent of JSP and an ISAPI extension would be similar to a Java servlet.*

This does not mean that building an ASP listener for your Web services is not practical. In fact, because this Web service will have a restricted user base, our systems could have plenty of resources available for processing an ASP listener, so that is what I will choose. (Because I also want as many people as possible to follow along in the code and actually test these concepts, an ASP listener also makes sense!)

The next decision we need to make is what kind of middleware to use between our listener and the component. This middleware would essentially consist of the responder, with all the logic for extracting data from the request, making the call to S3Weather, and building the response. We could simply extend our ASP page to incorporate that functionality, or we could build a custom component that could serve as a wrapper to our object.

Because we don't have multiple instances of this service or plan on calling other services with this listener, we will simply extend the functionality within its page. This will make the listener and the responder one physical entity, but we will continue to treat them as separate logical entities to enforce our architecture.

Another option available to us is the language used within our ASP: we could choose either JScript or VBScript. VBScript is by far the more popular choice of ASP developers, so we will continue that trend here.

We will also use the Microsoft XML parser for our Web service. Several versions are available, which can be run side by side, so it is important to note the version you use. I want to take advantage of some of the newer functionality available, so we will utilize the parser available at this writing: version 4 technical preview. This will allow us to perform some validation against the very recent release of the final XML Schema specification. You can find all the available versions of the MSXML parser at `http://msdn.microsoft.com/xml`.

Infrastructure Decisions

As mentioned earlier, many of the infrastructure decisions are predetermined by the fact that we are using Microsoft's development platform. Of course, it all starts with Windows 2000 Advanced Server. We will also utilize IIS 5.0 as the Web server hosting our service. Likewise, any other services that we need will come from the Windows platform. I will mention other services as we walk through the design and identify a need for bringing them into the solution.

Defining the Security Model

Once the technology decisions are made, we need to define each of the three models for our Web service: presentation, interface, and security. This is done before the design because these high-level decisions will likely have an impact on our options and requirements. The first two are easy enough to resolve in this scenario because we will be providing no presentation information and our interface is a direct call. This was also true for our mortgage calculator service. However, unlike that Web service, we will need to define a security model.

Identifying the Pertinent Relationships

The security model for a Web service defines the relationship between the provider and their consumers and users. This means that the requirements for those relationships need to be well understood before a security model can even be discussed. For the purposes of this exercise, we have determined that we do not want an open, publicly available Web service. Thus, we must spend some time defining how we discern between those requests that are valid and those that are not. Given the fact that our user base is entirely dependent on the consumer, the identity of the user will have no significance.

After determining that we have a restricted consumer base for our Web service, the first thing we need to do is identify the criteria for legal consumers. Most applications will maintain qualification criteria based on the client's identity. When a request is made, that identity could be used to look up the status of the consumer or perhaps some financial accounts. Sometimes the identity itself is sufficient. This means that, if the consumer can be identified, they are considered legal and can make a request of the Web service. If there may be instances where consumers could be expired, this approach would likely not be appropriate.

For this scenario, we will want to identify consumers and be able to control their status. This means that some form of validation will need to occur with every request that is received. This validation ensures that the consumers have a current status that allows them to utilize the service. Keep in mind that this kind of functionality will have a performance cost against the service because every check will be an extra step that has to be performed. To help minimize this cost, we should try to utilize an efficient method for identifying the consumer.

Identifying the Consumer

The next issue, then, is how to identify the consumer. We could certainly use a cookie, URL, or HTML form data, but all of these things are not very well protected to ensure data integrity. If we are serious about this process, we need to choose a different method for verifying the identity of a consumer that cannot be compromised by the consumers themselves.

The most feasible solution currently available is certificates. This physical piece of code is supported by Internet standards to validate the identity of different systems and users. We use one component of this security infrastructure on a regular basis through the use of HTTPS. The secure sockets layer (SSL) uses server certificates to allow Web sites to identify themselves to users through their browser. This verification is taken one step further when organizations get their certificates through an independent, third-party organization like Verisign. With this validation, a user can trust that the provider is who they claim to be.

Our need of certificates further extends this usage by requiring that the clients provide proof of their identity to the provider. This is a less common implementation of certificates, but it is very appropriate for this particular case.

The follow-up decision that then needs to be made is what type of certificates to use. The certificates provided by third-party companies cost money, so we might scare consumers away if we require that they acquire them. Another option would be to set up our own CA (certificate authority). We could provide certificates to our consumers as needed free of charge. Of course, we are taking on more responsibility and maintenance of our Web service by doing this, so the decision should not be made lightly.

We will take this approach and host our own CA and service new consumers as they are brought on board. To support this, we will take advantage of Certificate Server, which is available with Windows 2000 Advanced Server. This will be a crucial component in the deployment of our Web service.

Designing the Interface

Now that we have defined the security model, we can move on to designing our interface. We now understand the effect our security model will have on our interface and logic (which is essentially none at all). It could have turned out that we needed to programmatically track the user as they use our service, but that was not the case. Nonetheless, it is much better for us to make that determination ahead of time to maximize our productivity in building our Web services.

> **NOTE** *It is important to realize that designing the interface is different from defining the interface model. Our model is actually predetermined by the fact that this is a static Web services call. The consumer will make a single request of us, and we will provide a single response. We would need to define an interface model if this was a workflow, as we will see in Chapter 8 ("Building a Web Service Workflow"), or a dynamic Web services call.*

The interface of our Web service will communicate with potential consumers what kind of information we are expecting and what information we will return to them. This consists of a couple of different steps because we are exposing an existing component. The first task is to analyze the component we are exposing as a Web service. Without this analysis, we have no idea what kind of information we could possible handle or deliver. We will then build the definition files for our interface which all interested parties can reference for communicating with us.

Analyzing the Existing Component

The existing S3Weather component will provide the outline for what our Web services interface will look like. We will not be adding any functionality to the component, so this will represent a maximum potential for what we can expose. Of course, we can always choose to not expose some functionality, and that determination will come from our analysis of the existing component.

The S3Weather component's class ID is S3Weather.Current. Its interface has only one method call, called GetWeather, which accepts a single string value representing the location. This service will be designed for U.S. use only, so we will use the most common location identifier, the postal ZIP code:

```
GetWeather(Location as String) as Integer
```

This call returns an integer with the value possibilities shown in Table 6-1.

Table 6-1. S3Weather GetWeather *Return Values*

VALUE	DESCRIPTION
0	No error
1	No location entered
2	No content received from weather.com
4	Incorrect information entered (no match for code provided)
64	Internal error (check S3Debug property)

The remaining portions of the public interface comprise a series of properties. Most of the pertinent properties are used only to retrieve the matching data, not to set it. This list of properties can be seen along with their type, access, and a brief description in Table 6-2. For a more complete understanding of this component, please reference the documentation provided on the SoftShell site.

Table 6-2. S3Weather Component Properties

PROPERTY	DATA TYPE	ACCESS	DESCRIPTION
Barometer	String	Read-only	Current barometer information
BlockTracking	Boolean	Write-only	Allows SoftShell to track the component's usage
City	String	Read-Only	The city matching the ZIP code provided
Dewpoint	String	Read-only	Current dew point information
ErrorMessage	String	Read-only	Text message for troubleshooting external errors
FeelsLike	String	Read-only	Current temperature factoring wind, humidity, and so on
Forecast	String	Read-only	Current conditions information
Humidity	String	Read-only	Current humidity information
ImageID	String	Read-only	Image ID for map without the file extension
ImageSmall	String	Read-only	URL for small area map (277×187)
ImageBig	String	Read-only	URL for large area map (720×478)
ImageOldAnimated	String	Read-only	URL for animated icon showing current conditions
ImageOldTrans	String	Read-only	URL for daylight icon showing current conditions
ImageOldNight	String	Read-only	URL for night icon showing current conditions
NewVersion	String	Read-only	Will alert if a newer version exists (when tracking allowed)

Table 6-2. S3Weather Component Properties (continued)

PROPERTY	DATA TYPE	ACCESS	DESCRIPTION
Reported	String	Read-only	The time the conditions were last updated
S3Debug	String	Read-only	Text message for troubleshooting internal errors
State	String	Read-only	The state matching the ZIP code provided
Temperature	String	Read-only	Current temperature information
UserAgent	String	Write-only	User agent used in HTTP request
UVIndex	String	Read-only	Current UV index information
UVWarning	String	Read-only	Current UV warning information
Visibility	String	Read-only	Current visibility information
WeatherAlert	Boolean	Read-only	Returns TRUE when a weather alert for the area is in effect
Wind	String	Read-only	Current wind information

Browsing through these properties, we obviously don't want to expose some to our consumers. We can probably determine right away that all the write-only values will be for our use only.

The next issue to determine is how to handle any errors that might occur. Certainly, we will want to provide a friendly message to the consumer when a failure does occur, but more than likely you will not want to expose the details to the consumer. Thus, we will not expose the S3Debug or ErrorMessage properties.

This leaves us with all the properties associated specifically to the weather information that consumers will be specifically interested in. Most of this is textual data, but five image paths can also be referenced. Two of them, ImageSmall and ImageBig, are maps showing the local weather patterns. The other three graphic paths (ImageOldAnimated, ImageOldTrans, and ImageOldNight) show graphical icons that represent the current weather conditions (for example, a cloud with a lightning bolt, a sun, and so on).

The documentation mentions that these icons might go away at some point. Regardless, a good case could be made for not using these graphics. You could argue that they are superfluous and that they don't provide any real value. At the very least, I would argue that, because such graphics aren't dynamic (like the weather maps are), a provider would be better off having their own icons to reference in conjunction with the conditions that are provided through the other properties. This is likely what the source site is doing, and this would give our Web service a little more control over the presentation data provided to our consumers.

Because we are trying to expose this functionality in a very quick and efficient manner, we will just omit those three graphic references entirely. This then leaves us with the following data elements we will expose through our Web service:

Barometer

City

Dewpoint

FeelsLike

Forecast

Humidity

ImageID

ImageSmall

ImageBig

Reported

State

Temperature

UVIndex

UVWarning

Visibility

WeatherAlert

Wind

This data would then consist of our response to the consumers. If we take into consideration the ZIP code information for our input, we have identified all the data that will be involved in our Web services interaction.

Building the Schema

Now that we know what kind of data our component will work with, we have an idea of what our options are. We still need to identify the elements outside of the component's own that we will want to either collect or expose from the consumer.

Although we have identified all the data we are passing to and receiving from the S3Weather component, we need to identify any other information that needs to be included. We have already mentioned an error message in case of failures. This would obviously be an optional element that is hopefully never used, but it needs to be accounted for nonetheless.

Another option for the response would be the inclusion of the parameter that was passed to us by the consumer. This is a good practice to use, especially when the request data is so minimal, as it is in this case. Including a parameter passed by the consumer effectively makes the request a subset of the response, which helps in streamlining our interaction schema.

However, the one distinction between this Web service interaction and the one for our mortgage calculator is that the data received and the data returned are distinctly different. For our calculator service, all values were treated as both input and output values. For this weather service, we are receiving one piece of information and returning potentially seventeen data elements. With the request and response being so different, it doesn't make sense to define one schema that defines the request and response as the same document.

This does not mean, however, that we necessarily need two different definition schemas. We could still have one schema that defines the entire interaction, but the request and the response could have different definitions within that schema. Let's first look at what the request schema might look at if that were all we had to concern ourselves with, as shown in Listing 6-15.

Listing 6-15. weatherCheck *Request Schema*

```
<xsd:schema xmlns:xsd="http://www.w3.org/2000/10/XMLSchema"
  elementFormDefault="qualified">
    <xsd:element name="weatherCheck">
        <xsd:complexType>
            <xsd:sequence>
                <xsd:element name="zipCode" type="xsd:string"/>
            </xsd:sequence>
        </xsd:complexType>
    </xsd:element>
</xsd:schema>
```

What we have done is create a root node called weatherCheck and placed within it the one node that is necessary for the request. Let's now take a look at the response (see Listing 6-16) as it would stand on its own as a valid document.

Listing 6-16. weatherCheck *Response Schema*

```
<xsd:schema xmlns:xsd="http://www.w3.org/2000/10/XMLSchema"
  elementFormDefault="qualified">
    <xsd:element name="weatherCheck">
        <xsd:complexType>
            <xsd:sequence>
                <xsd:element name="barometer" type="xsd:string"/>
                <xsd:element name="city" type="xsd:string"/>
                <xsd:element name="dewpoint" type="xsd:decimal"/>
                <xsd:element name="errorMessage"
                  type="xsd:string" minOccurs="0"/>
                <xsd:element name="feelsLike" type="xsd:string"/>
                <xsd:element name="forecast" type="xsd:string"/>
                <xsd:element name="humidity" type="xsd:string"/>
                <xsd:element name="imageID" type="xsd:string"/>
                <xsd:element name="imageSmall" type="xsd:uri"/>
                <xsd:element name="imageBig" type="xsd:uri"/>
                <xsd:element name="reportedTime" type="xsd:string"/>
                <xsd:element name="state" type="xsd:string"/>
                <xsd:element name="temperature" type="xsd:decimal"/>
                <xsd:element name="uvIndex" type="xsd:decimal"/>
```

```
            <xsd:element name="uvWarning" type="xsd:string"/>
            <xsd:element name="visibility" type="xsd:string"/>
            <xsd:element name="weatherAlert" type="xsd:boolean"/>
            <xsd:element name="windDescription" type="xsd:string"/>
        </xsd:sequence>
    </xsd:complexType>
  </xsd:element>
</xsd:schema>
```

You see that, although the request has a very similar document structure to that of the response, there is a vast difference between their definitions. If all of the response elements were optional, we could easily turn this into a single document in which the request omits all the optional elements and the response utilizes them. However, if we want a more exact definition of the interaction, we would not want to take that approach.

A better approach in this case would be to take the response-specific data and place it in its own child element, and make that element optional—but all of the response data within it required. That way you have an "all or nothing" definition of the response data. To maintain this new approach, we will also separate the errorMessage element from the rest of the data so that it can be utilized independently. The assumption would be that you would have either an errorMessage or the data from the weather component, but that is not necessarily the case. This definition will allow us the flexibility to handle either situation regardless of the scenario.

If we call the response container node conditions, our interaction schema would look like Listing 6-17.

Listing 6-17. Weather Web service interaction schema
```
<xsd:schema xmlns:xsd="http://www.w3.org/2000/10/XMLSchema"
  elementFormDefault="qualified">
    <xsd:element name="weatherCheck">
        <xsd:complexType>
            <xsd:sequence>
                <xsd:element name="zipCode" type="xsd:string"/>
                <xsd:element name="errorMessage" type="xsd:string"
                  minOccurs="0"/>
                <xsd:element name="conditions" minOccurs="0">
                    <xsd:complexType>
                        <xsd:sequence>
                            <xsd:element name="barometer" type="xsd:
                              string"/>
                            <xsd:element name="city" type="xsd:string"/>
                            <xsd:element name="dewpoint" type="xsd:
                              decimal"/>
```

```
                                     <xsd:element name="feelsLike" type="xsd:
                                        string"/>
                                     <xsd:element name="forecast" type="xsd:
                                        string"/>
                                     <xsd:element name="humidity" type="xsd:
                                        string"/>
                                     <xsd:element name="imageID" type="xsd:string"/>
                                     <xsd:element name="imageSmall" type="xsd:uri"/>
                                     <xsd:element name="imageBig" type="xsd:uri"/>
                                     <xsd:element name="reportedTime" type="xsd:
                                        string"/>
                                     <xsd:element name="state" type="xsd:string"/>
                                     <xsd:element name="temperature" type="xsd:
                                        decimal"/>
                                     <xsd:element name="uvIndex" type="xsd:
                                        decimal"/>
                                     <xsd:element name="uvWarning" type="xsd:
                                        string"/>
                                     <xsd:element name="visibility" type="xsd:
                                        string"/>
                                     <xsd:element name="weatherAlert" type="xsd:
                                        boolean"/>
                                     <xsd:element name="windDescription" type="xsd:
                                        string"/>
                                 </xsd:sequence>
                            </xsd:complexType>
                        </xsd:element>
                    </xsd:sequence>
                </xsd:complexType>
            </xsd:element>
        </xsd:schema>
```

The nice thing about the sequence element is that it assumes by default that the maximum and minimum occurrences of a child element are one. This means that all we have to specify are the exceptions to that condition, which are the conditions and errorMessage elements.

Now that we have designed the interface for our Web service, we have completed the design process, which means that we've come to the build portion of the process.

Building the Web Service

As we saw in the previous example, the two key components to our Web service are the listener and the responder. Even though they will not be physically separate entities, we need to ensure that we have a clear distinction logically, so that we can be confident we are covering each of their responsibilities.

We will also consider each of these components a distinct milestone in the build process. After developing each, we will perform a unit test to make sure that the behavior follows our expectations.

Building the Listener

We will be building our listener as an ASP page hosted by our IIS service. Building ASP pages is simple, assuming that you are familiar with VBScript. (If not, you can pick up one of the many VBScript books available.) Writing an ASP page is not all that different from writing an HTML page, architecturally speaking, and the same development tools can often be used for both. For this example, I will be using Visual Interdev 6.0, a component of Microsoft's Visual Studio IDE. Just like HTML, though, an ASP page can be created using any text editor; you just won't have the assistance you get from a development tool.

Creating the Active Server Page

When you first open Visual Interdev, the New Project dialog box appears. I am not going to go into the details of the tool, so you can create a new project if you wish, but it is not necessary. Once you are ready, create a new ASP file by going to File|New File to display the New File dialog box, which gives you a few different file types to choose from. (See Figure 6-12.) Select the ASP Page and click on Open.

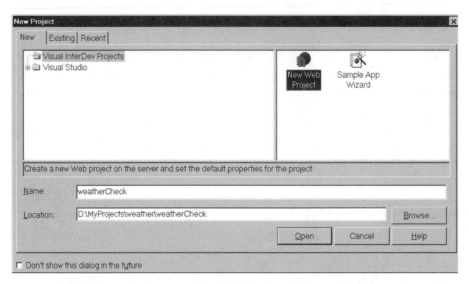

Figure 6-12. Visual Interdev New File dialog box

In creating a new ASP file, Visual Interdev will give you a shell for your page that should look like this:

```
<%@ Language=VBScript %>
<HTML>
<HEAD>
<META NAME="GENERATOR" Content="Microsoft Visual Studio 6.0">
</HEAD>
<BODY>

<P> </P>

</BODY>
</HTML>
```

Because we will not be delivering HTML content through this page, go ahead and delete everything beneath the <%@ Language=VBScript %> tag. This then gives us the starting point we need for our listener.

Parsing the Request

The first task for our listener is to parse the request that comes in from the consumer. We will be using the MSXML 4.0 Technical Preview from Microsoft as our parser, so we will need to create an instance of it and load the request into it:

```
<%
Dim objDOM
set objDOM = server.createobject("msxml2.DOMDocument")
objDOM.async = false
objDOM.load(request)
%>
```

> **CAUTION** *Another ProgID that can be used for the MSXML parser is* microsoft.xmldom, *but this references an older version of the parser if installed in side-by-side mode. If you want to ensure on any system that you are using the latest version of the parser, you should use the* msxml2.DOMDocument *ProgID.*

As you can see, this is a fairly quick and easy process to perform using this parser. You see here that we are setting the async property of our DOM instance to False. This means that we are requiring that the DOM fully load the data before processing any other code. Without this setting, we might get a failure if code referencing the DOM executes before it is finished loading.

Validating the Data

The validation for the requests into this Web service can also be greatly simplified. Because we were potentially receiving a lot of data in our calculator service, we went with document-wide validation using the specified DTD. However, for this service, we are concerned with only a single data element within the request, the ZIP code. Anything else is entirely superficial and will be throwaway data to us.

This means we don't necessarily need to validate the entire request against a schema. Instead, we could try to reference just the node we are concerned with and handle any errors around our failure to do so. That means the request could contain a lot of other data making the request technically illegal, but we can save some processing resources by taking this approach. Keep in mind that, if we were dealing with even a handful of data, this manual validation approach would be much too inefficient to use.

To reference the appropriate node, we will utilize the selectsinglenode method of our DOM and specify the required path for the value. If that process fails, then we know we have an illegal request, and we will end the process right there with an error message and move on. Below is an example of the error handling for an invalid ZIP code value.

```
Dim strRequest
strRequest = objDOM.selectsinglenode("weatherCheck/zipCode").text
If strRequest = "" then
    errorText = "There was a problem with the data in your request. Please
        confirm the request against the XML Schema provided at
        http://www.fundamentalwebservices.com/interfaces/weather/
        weatherCheck.xsd"
    response.Write("Error")
Else
    response.Write("Success!")
End If
```

You'll see that we are setting the text for the error message, but we aren't actually writing it out at this point. That is the responsibility of the responder, so we will look at that process when we look at the responder in the next section. What I have done is add some debug output so that we can tell whether or not we were successfully able to reference the ZIP code data from the request.

Putting all of this together, we will end up with the entire listener for our Web service. (See Listing 6-18.) This file will need to be saved to a directory exposed by the IIS service so that it is accessible via HTTP. We will talk about this step in more detail in the "Deploying the Web Service" section.

Listing 6-18. Base Listener for Weather Web Service

```
<%@ Language=VBScript
On Error Resume Next

dim objDOM
dim strRequest
dim intResult
dim errorText
```

```
'Create and load the DOM object for the request
set objDOM = server.createobject("mxsml2.DOMDocument")
objDOM.async = false
objDOM.load(request)

'Extract the zipCode value from the DOM for the call
strRequest = objDOM.selectsinglenode("weatherCheck/zipCode").text
if strRequest = "" then
    errorText = "There was a problem with the data in your request. Please
      confirm the request against the XML Schema provided at
      http://www.fundamentalwebservices.com/interfaces/weather/
      weatherCheck.xsd"
    response.Write("Error")
else
    response.Write("Success!")
End If
%>
```

This listener is suitable for receiving requests and confirming whether the request data is valid for your Web service. If you can host it via IIS already and have a test client available, this would be a good time to test the listener by sending it legal and illegal requests. (Again, we will discuss this whole process in more detail, including the building of a test client in the "Deploying the Web Service" section.)

We are now ready to move on to the building of the responder for our Web service. This is where the weather component is called and a response is built for the consumer.

Building the Responder

The responder takes the data from the request, calls any business logic, references any data sources, and builds the response document for the client. This may be an elaborate process or it may be a simple process, depending on the structure of the documents, the technology you are using, and the entities you are working with. In our Java Web service, our effort was redundant, but fairly simple. This service will be similar in scope, but it will require more of an effort to build the response (due to its slightly higher structure complexity) and less of an effort in extracting data from the request.

The first step within the responder is usually the extraction of the necessary data from the request. However, our listener already extracted the data for us through its validation process. The listener has captured this information in a local variable called strRequest, and so we will reference it directly in our call to S3Weather.

Calling the S3Weather Component

In calling our component, the only thing we need to be aware of is the value returned from its call. (See Listing 6-19.) If we are referencing the component correctly and it is properly installed on our system, any errors should be external to it, and it will communicate any such errors to us through this result code.

Listing 6-19. Calling the S3Weather Component

```
dim objS3W
dim intResult

intResult = objS3W.getWeather(strRequest)

'Check results to see if an error was generated from the call
If intResult = 4 then
    errorText = "There was no data found for the code that was entered.
      Please check the code and try again."
    writeError(errorText)
elseif intResult <> 0 then
    errorText = "There was a problem processing your request. Please try your
      request again later."
    writeError(errorText)
else
. . .
```

The else condition from this code snippet triggers the building of the response based on the data available through the component's properties. We also see here the use of a `writeError` subprocedure. This will be used to write out any error that we might encounter during the process. Before we look at that, however, we need to discuss how we are going to generate the XML data returned to the consumer.

Building the Response

Once again, we can take one of a few different approaches in building the response for our Web service. These approaches vary widely from assembling a string from scratch to building a DOM from scratch to using a template to loading an entire data document. All these methods will achieve the exact same result, but the process for providing the actual data is very different, and each can have their own advantages and disadvantages.

The string assembly method is a straightforward approach of taking data and wrapping the appropriate strings around it to make the end result an XML document. If you are familiar with ASP, this approach is very similar to taking data from an ADO (ActiveX Data Objects) recordset and organizing it in an HTML table structure. You go about building the HTML to build the actual table and reference the appropriate data to fill in the cells. Building an XML string from scratch (using dynamic data) is very much the same approach. If we took that approach for this exercise, the building of our response would look much like Listing 6-20.

Listing 6-20. Writing the Response from Scratch

```
Response.ContentType = "text/xml"
response.write "<?xml version=""1.0""?>"
response.write "<weatherCheck>"
response.write "<zipCode>" & strRequest & "</zipCode>"
response.write "<conditions>"
response.write "<barometer>" & objS3W.barometer & "</barometer>"
response.write "<city>" & objS3W.city & "</city>"
response.write "<dewpoint>" & objS3W.dewpoint & "</dewpoint>"
response.write "<feelsLike>" & objS3W.feelslike & "</feelsLike>"
response.write "<forecast>" & objS3W.forecast & "</forecast>"
response.write "<humidity>" & objS3W.humidity & "</humidity>"
response.write "<imageID>" & objS3W.imageid & "</imageID>"
response.write "<imageSmall>" & objS3W.imagesmall & "</imageSmall>"
response.write "<imageBig>" & objS3W.imagebig & "</imageBig>"
response.write "<reportedTime>" & objS3W.reported & "</reportedTime>"
response.write "<state>" & objS3W.state & "</state>"
response.write "<temperature>" & objS3W.temperature & "</temperature>"
response.write "<uvIndex>" & objS3W.uvindex & "</uvIndex>"
response.write "<uvWarning>" & objS3W.uvwarning & "</uvWarning>"
response.write "<visibility>" & objS3W.visibility & "</visibility>"
response.write "<weatherAlert>" & objS3W.weatheralert & "</weatherAlert>"
response.write "<windDescription>" & objS3W.wind & "</windDescription>"
response.write "</conditions>"
response.write "</weatherCheck>"
```

Although this gets the job done, it isn't the cleanest possible approach. It is actually impossible to programmatically verify that you are sending out valid XML. All you are creating is a string, so you have no validation methods available to you. Once you test the output to ensure it is legitimate, you should be fine as long as you don't have any changes, but getting there might be a little time consuming. I would recommend only using this method for building very small documents or document fragments. At the very least, you would want to leave yourself some extra time for testing if you took this approach.

Another approach that is somewhat similar is the building of a DOM from scratch or DOM assembly. This is actually the approach we took in building the calculator Web service; we used a validated structure to create the nodes and populated them with the appropriate data. The benefit to this approach is that we have a legitimate structure that we know can produce only well-formed XML. We could have even gone one step further by validating the data with our DTD, but that could be considered overkill given the circumstances.

The downside is that we are still creating the document structure over and over. It would be most appropriate to use this method when the response document is dynamic in nature. By building the document dynamically, you can account for only the data that needs to be returned.

The next approach we will look at is using a template. This is a great approach when defining the same document structure repeatedly, but with dynamic data elements. This template would serve as a skeleton that simply needs to be loaded into a DOM and the values populated. A template for the response for our weather Web service would look like Listing 6-21.

Listing 6-21. Response Template

```xml
<?xml version="1.0"?>
<weatherCheck>
    <zipCode/>
    <conditions>
        <barometer/>
        <city/>
        <dewpoint/>
        <feelsLike/>
        <forecast/>
        <humidity/>
        <imageID/>
        <imageSmall/>
        <imageBig/>
        <reportedTime/>
        <state/>
        <temperature/>
        <uvIndex/>
        <uvWarning/>
        <visibility/>
        <weatherAlert/>
        <windDescription/>
    </conditions>
</weatherCheck>
```

One of the benefits with this approach is that you don't have to spend the processing time to build each node independently. This saves cycles, which improves the overall performance of the service. The other benefit of this approach is that you can be guaranteed that you have the correct document structure for a valid response document. This just helps to ensure the integrity of your service without needing extra validation.

Like the string assembly method, the exercise of populating the data in the template is fairly simple. In fact, it is even more direct because we don't have to build all the filler information (start tags, end tags, and so on). For our weather service, we just identify the nodes and set their values to the appropriate data from our component's properties. (See Listing 6-22.)

Listing 6-22. Building the Response from a Template

```
objdom.selectsinglenode("weatherCheck/zipCode").text = strRequest
objdom.selectsinglenode("weatherCheck/conditions/barometer").text =
   objS3W.Barometer
objdom.selectsinglenode("weatherCheck/conditions/city").text = objS3W.City
objdom.selectsinglenode("weatherCheck/conditions/dewpoint").text =
   objS3W.Dewpoint
objdom.selectsinglenode("weatherCheck/conditions/feelsLike").text =
   objS3W.FeelsLike
objdom.selectsinglenode("weatherCheck/conditions/forecast").text =
   objS3W.Forecast
objdom.selectsinglenode("weatherCheck/conditions/humidity").text =
   objS3W.Humidity
objdom.selectsinglenode("weatherCheck/conditions/imageID").text =
   objS3W.ImageID
objdom.selectsinglenode("weatherCheck/conditions/imageSmall").text =
   objS3W.ImageSmall
objdom.selectsinglenode("weatherCheck/conditions/imageBig").text =
   objS3W.ImageBig
objdom.selectsinglenode("weatherCheck/conditions/reportedTime").text =
   objS3W.Reported
objdom.selectsinglenode("weatherCheck/conditions/state").text = objS3W.State
objdom.selectsinglenode("weatherCheck/conditions/temperature").text =
   objS3W.Temperature
objdom.selectsinglenode("weatherCheck/conditions/uvIndex").text = objS3W.uvindex
objdom.selectsinglenode("weatherCheck/conditions/uvWarning").text =
   objS3W.uvwarning
objdom.selectsinglenode("weatherCheck/conditions/visibility").text =
   objS3W.Visibility
objdom.selectsinglenode("weatherCheck/conditions/weatherAlert").text =
   objS3W.WeatherAlert
objdom.selectsinglenode("weatherCheck/conditions/windDescription").text =
   objS3W.Wind


response.write objdom.xml
```

After setting all the values for the nodes in the document, we use the xml method to output the result string from the DOM structure. This method would gain even more efficiencies if the template were preloaded in a DOM structure so that the overhead of retrieving the document from an external data source isn't incurred on every request. This also would help to insulate the service from external problems with the data source that may keep the template from being available.

The last approach we will discuss is the direct document load. This is when an entire document is loaded from an external data source, perhaps a file, database, or in memory. This is a very effective method when working with the same document structure and static data. It can also be a very efficient process if the document is stored locally once it is referenced and has maximum reusability.

These four methods we have discussed, along with their high-level benefits and shortcomings, are captured for you in Table 6-3. As you can see, different approaches can be very useful and effective in different scenarios. In some situations, a blending of two or more of these approaches would also be appropriate. We will see examples of this in the next chapter.

Table 6-3. Methods for Building XML

METHOD	BENEFITS	SHORTCOMINGS	APPROPRIATE FOR...
String Assembly	Easy to develop; very dynamic	Slower performance; prone to errors	Individual elements and very small dynamic documents
DOM Assembly	Guaranteed well-formedness; can be validated; very dynamic	Processor-intensive; low reusability	Larger documents of dynamic structure
Template	Very efficient; high reusability; high reliability	Dependency on external data source	Consistent data structures containing dynamic data
Direct Load	Maximum reusability; high dependability	Dependency on external data source	Consistent documents containing static data

For our weather Web service, we will continue down the template approach for building our response. As I mentioned, this method would gain even more benefit if the template were preloaded into a DOM structure to reduce the input/output (I/O) overhead on every request.

This can be done very easily with a feature of the MSXML parser called a *free-threaded document*. This is an instance of the DOM that can support multiple simultaneous accesses, which would be necessary for a shared resource. We will use the `FreeThreadedDOMDocument` class from the parser to accomplish this.

As most ASP developers are aware, the `Application_OnStart` procedure in the global.asa file runs every time that a Web application starts for the first time on a system. It is in this routine that we will place the necessary code to load the template into the free-threaded DOM object and load it into an application variable. (See Listing 6-23.) Because the object is free-threaded and will never need to be written to, only read, it is safe to do this.

Listing 6-23. Global.asa Code for Caching the Response Template

```
Sub Application_OnStart
    Dim objRT
    set objRT = server.createobject("Msxml2.FreeThreadedDOMDocument")
    objRT.async = false
    objRT.load Server.MapPath("reponseTemplate.xml")
    Application("responseTemplate") = objRT
End Sub
```

If we now put the whole ASP page together, incorporating the listener and the responder, we should end up with the code in Listing 6-24.

Listing 6-24. Final ASP Page for Weather Web Service

```
<%@ Language=VBScript
On Error Resume Next

dim objS3W
dim objDOM
dim strRequest
dim intResult
dim errorText

'Create the Weather component
set objS3W = Server.CreateObject("S3Weather.Current")

'Create and load the DOM object for the request
set objDOM = server.createobject("mxsml2.DOMDocument")
objDOM.async = false
objDOM.load(request)

'Extract the zipCode value from the DOM for the call from the application
'variable
strRequest = objDOM.selectsinglenode("weatherCheck/zipCode").text
If strRequest = "" then
```

```
                    errorText = "There was a problem with the data in your request. Please
                       confirm the request against the XML Schema provided at
                       http://www.fundamentalwebservices.com/interfaces/weather/
                       weatherCheck.xsd"
                    writeError(errorText)
              else
                    intResult = objS3W.getWeather(strRequest)

                    'Check results to see if an error was generated from the call
                    If intResult = 4 then
                         errorText = "There was no data found for the code that was entered.
                            Please check the code and try again."
                         writeError(errorText)
                    ElseIf intResult <> 0 then
                         errorText = "There was a problem processing your request. Please try
                            your request again later."
                         writeError(errorText)
                    Else
                         'Load the template for the response DOM
                         set objDOM = Application("responseTemplate")

                         Response.ContentType = "text/xml"

                         if err.number=0 then
                              'Build the response through a DOM instance
                              objdom.selectsinglenode("weatherCheck/zipCode").text = strRequest
                              objdom.selectsinglenode("weatherCheck/conditions/barometer").text =
                                 objS3W.Barometer
                              objdom.selectsinglenode("weatherCheck/conditions/city").text =
                                 objS3W.City
                              objdom.selectsinglenode("weatherCheck/conditions/dewpoint").text =
                                 objS3W.Dewpoint
                              objdom.selectsinglenode("weatherCheck/conditions/feelsLike").text =
                                 objS3W.FeelsLike
                              objdom.selectsinglenode("weatherCheck/conditions/forecast").text =
                                 objS3W.Forecast
                              objdom.selectsinglenode("weatherCheck/conditions/humidity").text =
                                 objS3W.Humidity
                              objdom.selectsinglenode("weatherCheck/conditions/imageID").text =
                                 objS3W.ImageID
                              objdom.selectsinglenode("weatherCheck/conditions/imageSmall")
                                 .text = objS3W.ImageSmall
                              objdom.selectsinglenode("weatherCheck/conditions/imageBig").text =
                                 objS3W.ImageBig
```

```
                objdom.selectsinglenode("weatherCheck/conditions/reportedTime")
                  .text = objS3W.Reported
                objdom.selectsinglenode("weatherCheck/conditions/state").text =
                  objS3W.State
                objdom.selectsinglenode("weatherCheck/conditions/temperature")
                  .text = objS3W.Temperature
                objdom.selectsinglenode("weatherCheck/conditions/uvIndex").text =
                  objS3W.UVIndex
                objdom.selectsinglenode("weatherCheck/conditions/uvWarning")
                  .text = objS3W.UVWarning
                objdom.selectsinglenode("weatherCheck/conditions/visibility")
                  .text = objS3W.Visibility
                objdom.selectsinglenode("weatherCheck/conditions/weatherAlert")
                  .text = objS3W.WeatherAlert
                objdom.selectsinglenode("weatherCheck/conditions/windDescription")
                  .text = objS3W.Wind

                'Extract the string from the DOM to the Response
                Response.write objDOM.xml
            else
                errorText = "The service could not load the response template."
                WriteError(errorText)
            End If
        End If
End If

set objDOM = nothing
set objS3W = nothing

Sub writeError()
        Response.write "<?xml version=""1.0""?>"
        Response.write "<weatherCheck><zipCode>" & strRequest &
          "</zipCode><errorMessage>" & errorText & "</errorMessage></weatherCheck>"
End Sub
%>
```

Deploying the Web Service

Now that we have completed the coding for the Web service, we need to deploy
it. The deployment of this service should be slightly less complex than the calculator Web service just because of the nature of the platform. However, we do

have the additional responsibility of setting up the certificates to support our security model, so there will be approximately the same level of effort involved.

Along with the certificates, we need to establish the site for our service, deploy the S3Weather component, and test the service once it is integrated. This will require a test client, which we will build for just that purpose.

Deploying the S3Weather Component

For our Web service to work at all, we must, of course, have the component we are exposing available on the system. This component must be installed on the server using the regsvr32.exe utility that comes with the Windows 2000 operating system.

To use this utility, you must first copy the DLL file wherever you want it to be hosted from on your physical drive. Then, you can either use the Run dialog or open a Command Prompt window to type in the command with the full file path and the name of the DLL file. Following is an example of how the full command might look:

```
regsvr32 c:/windows/system32/s3weather.dll
```

The component also claims to support COM+, so you could deploy it in a package via the COM+ Explorer. This would be the equivalent to WebSphere for our Java class, except it is not a requirement on the Windows 2000 platform for COM objects.

Now that we have taken care of our component one way or another, we are ready to create the site that will host our Web service exposing this component.

Establishing the Site

The first step to deploying the Web service is designating a home for it. With IIS 5.0, this is a very easy step that shouldn't take too much effort. By now, you presumably have been saving your ASP page somewhere. If it isn't in the physical location where you want it to reside, you will want to move it there. It will be helpful to at least have the physical directory created for when we create our new virtual directory (so that it can be specified). We will also need to create the

Web application where it will reside. This will provide our service with its own memory space and insulate it from other activities on the Web server.

To create the Web application, we need to first open the IIS administrator console by going to Start|Programs|Administrative Tools|Internet Services Manager on your Windows 2000 system. If this tool does not exist, you have not installed the IIS service on your system. You will need to go back and add that component through your Windows 2000 setup. Please refer to your system documentation for further details.

Once the Internet Services Manager starts, you should see your server listed in the left-hand pane. (See Figure 6-13.) In the tree underneath it, you will see a listing for the default Web site. Right-click on that item and select New|Virtual Directory.

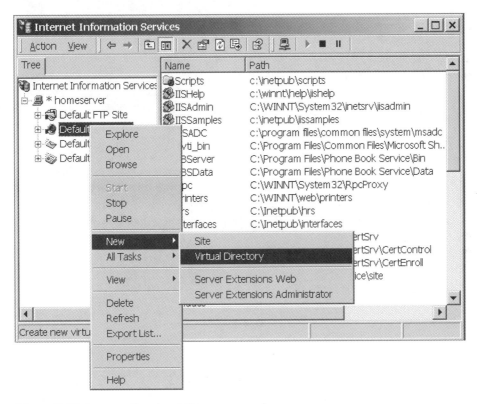

Figure 6-13. Internet Services Manager console

This starts the Virtual Directory Creation wizard. Click on Next on the initial splash screen to proceed to the Virtual Directory Alias screen. (See Figure 6-14.) This is where you enter the alias that you'll use to reference the path containing your Web service.

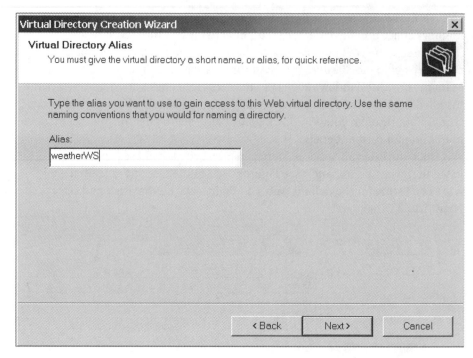

Figure 6-14. Virtual Directory Alias screen

After selecting Next, you come to the Web Site Content Directory screen (Figure 6-15), which is where you specify the physical directory path on your system where the files for your site will be contained. If the directory you want to use is not created yet, you will need to create it before continuing. Otherwise, you can select a different directory and change it later, once the virtual directory is created.

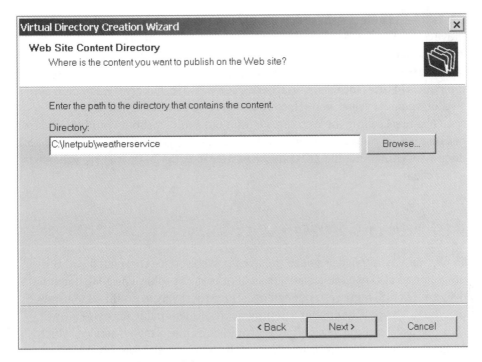

Figure 6-15. Web Site Content Directory screen

After entering the directory and clicking on Next, you come to the Access Permissions screen, which is where you specify the activities that a user can perform within this Web site. If we had used an ISAPI extension for our listener, we would need to add Execute permissions here. Because we are using an ASP script, we can leave this screen with its defaults and click on Next.

Doing so takes us to the final confirmation screen where we can click on Finish to complete the wizard and this process. By default, IIS 5.0 adds new virtual directories to a pool of applications outside of IIS's processes, making it a Web application.

> **NOTE** *For simplicity's sake, I chose to create a virtual directory to host this Web service, but we could have just as easily created a unique Web site, or hosted it directly under the default Web site. Feel free to select any of these options for your own implementations. You can find more information on each of these in your IIS documentation.*

If your ASP file doesn't reside in our application's directory path, you should move it there now. Once that is complete, we should be able to test our new application by opening a browser and entering the address of our local system, the alias we specified, and the name of our ASP file. If you followed along exactly, the path is `http://localhost/weatherWS/default.asp`. Otherwise, the path consists of whatever values you selected, which is perfectly acceptable.

Of course, calling the Web service from our browser should produce an error because we are not submitting a legal request. A legal request consists of an XML document containing the ZIP code we wish to look up. To do this, we will need a test client.

Testing the Web Service

To test our Web service, we need to have the Web service completed and running, but we also need to create a test client that can submit an XML document over an HTTP(S) request to our listener. The easiest way to do this is to throw together a VB application that can provide this functionality for us. (This will also give us a brief preview of how we could consume our Web service, which I will cover in Chapter 8.) Using VB, it will be quicker and easier than other alternatives, and we don't need to concern ourselves with design or performance issues.

This task is actually made even easier by the MSXML parser we used within our Web service. We will be able to utilize functionality within our client to also make the request of our Web service. Let's see how this is done.

First, we need to create a simple VB executable and create a form with a text box and a single button. We will use the text box to display the request results and the button to send the request. We also have to add the MSXML 4.0 reference to our application to utilize the parser.

Behind the button, we will have all the processing to make the request. First, we will reference an external document as the request to be made. We then load this in much the same manner that we loaded the template in our service, but we won't concern ourselves with caching it. Once the document is loaded, we need to create an instance of the `ServerXMLHTTP40` class to serve as our communication link to the Web service. We will specify in its open method that we are making a POST request and the URL we want to send the request to. The `send` method will specify the data to send, which is the XML output of our DOM. Then, we capture the response in a local string variable using the `responseText` method and display it through our text box. All together, the code behind our button procedure should look similar to Listing 6-25.

Listing 6-25. Visual Basic Test Client for weatherWS

```
Private Sub Command1_Click()

Dim objXMLDoc As MSXML2.DOMDocument40
Dim objXMLSend As MSXML2.ServerXMLHTTP40

Dim currNode As String
Dim strServiceURL As String

Set objXMLDoc = New DOMDocument40
Set objXMLSend = New MSXML2.ServerXMLHTTP40

strServiceURL = "http://localhost/weather/default.asp"
objXMLDoc.async = False

Text1.Text = "————-Calling Weather Checker————"
boolTest = objXMLDoc.Load("http://localhost/weather/sampleRequest.xml")

If boolTest Then
     objXMLSend.open "POST", strServiceURL, False
     objXMLSend.send (objXMLDoc.xml)
     currNode = objXMLSend.responseText

     objXMLDoc.loadXML (currNode)
     Text13.Text = Text13.Text & currNode
Else
     Text1.Text = "error in load"
End If
End Sub
```

The sample request that we will want to send should look something
like this:

```
<?xml version="1.0" encoding="UTF-8"?>
<weatherCheck>
     <zipCode>90210</zipCode>
</weatherCheck>
```

Of course, the sample request can be altered to be invalid or to provide different data to thoroughly test your Web service's behavior. Doing so is critical to ensure that your consumers don't have difficulty in using your service. Just as with a Web site that is too slow or generates errors, users get turned off very quickly and are even more hesitant to ever come back, so make sure that, when you are ready to expose your Web service, you are truly ready.

Although we have a fully functional Web service at this point, we have failed to meet one very large requirement that we identified at the beginning of this chapter: we must restrict access to only valid consumers through the use of certificates.

Implementing Certificate Security

Although many Web developers are familiar with server certificates, client certificates are something that most applications have either not required or not exploited. Some of this is due to the unawareness of architects and developers in this area. Server certificates have always been treated as almost a black box and that hasn't helped develop an understanding of its inner workings by even its implementers. An administrator generates a key, sends off for a certificate, installs it when it arrives, and—*presto!*—the server now supports HTTPS. The latest version of Certificate Server by Microsoft may help in this area for at least the designers and administrators of that platform by making client certificates as easy to use and implement as server certificates.

With the Windows 2000 Advanced Server release has come a very slick enhancement of the original Certificate Server that came with Windows NT 4.0. It makes certificate management and deployment much easier. Keep in mind that we will be maintaining our own certificate authority so that consumers can simply come to us for the certificate, and that way we won't require consumers to spend money on the certificates.

To get started, you need to install the certificate authority on the Windows 2000 system that will be responsible for managing certificates. Its presence can be verified by checking Start|Programs|Administrative Tools|Certification Authority. If that management tool is present, then certificate server is installed. This service is a component of the Windows 2000 Advanced Server operating system, so you can go to the Add/Remove Programs utility on your system's control panel to install this feature. Please refer to your system documentation for further details.

Requesting Consumer Certificates

Once the Certification Authority is installed, your Web server will have a new site established at `http://localhost/certsrv`. This is the application that all of your consumers will use to make certificate requests of your certificate authority except they will need to use your domain name in lieu of "localhost." (See Figure 6-16.) It will be helpful if the consumer is actually on the system that he or she will use to connect to our Web service. Certificates can get very picky when they start moving across systems, and it makes this process much easier if it is run from the system with which they intend to access the Web service.

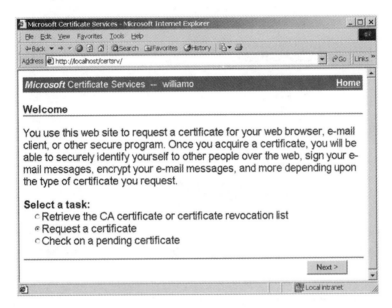

Figure 6-16. Certificate Authority Web site

Your consumers will start by selecting the Request a Certificate option and selecting Next. This brings up the Request Type screen in which the consumer specifies the Web Browser Certificate. (See Figure 6-17.) It is a little misleading calling it a "Web browser Certificate" because it is actually a client certificate that could be used by any client over HTTP/S.

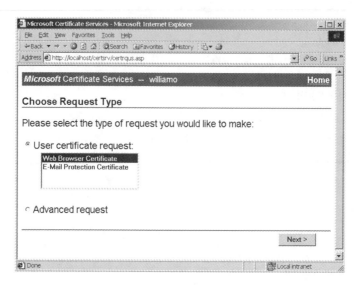

Figure 6-17. Request Certificate Type screen

Selecting Next then displays the Identifying Information screen (Figure 6-18). This is where the consumer will enter all the pertinent data about themselves to aid in establishing their identity.

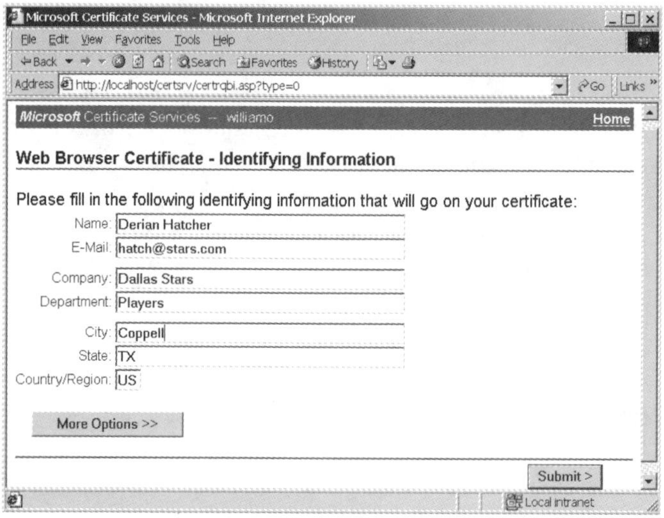

Figure 6-18. Identifying Information screen

Completing this information and submitting it will then bring the consumer to the pending window. (See Figure 6-19.) As the screen indicates, the consumer will need to come back after the authority makes a determination on their request. At this point, they have completed the process of requesting a certificate, and it is now up to the provider to disposition it.

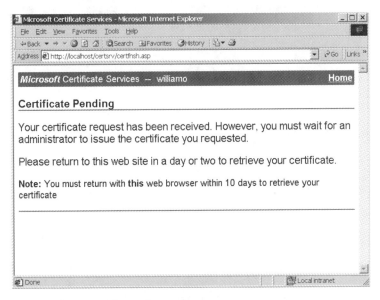

Figure 6-19. Pending Certificate Request screen

Managing Certificate Requests

The Certification Authority has an interface for helping the certificate manager to manage the authority's certificates. This is accessed by clicking on Start|Programs|Administrative Tools|Certification Authority, which opens the console for issuing, denying, and revoking certificates. For now, we are concerned with handling the certificate requests coming in, like the one we just submitted.

To see all of the pending requests, we need to simply click on the Pending Requests folder in the left-hand pane. We should then see in the right-hand pane any requests that have yet to be dispositioned (Figure 6-20). We can scroll horizontally to see all of the information that was entered by the requestor.

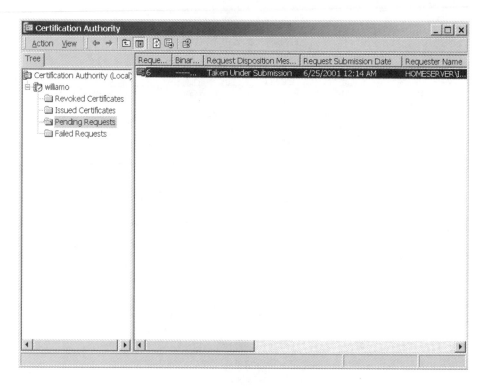

Figure 6-20. Viewing the pending certificate requests

If this were a production senario, we might need to contact the consumer to ensure the authenticity of the request and the person making it. We can then choose to either issue or deny the request by right-clicking on the particular request. (See Figure 6-21.)

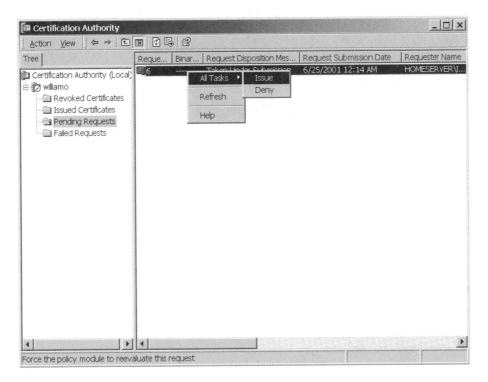

Figure 6-21. Issuing a certificate request

We will choose to issue this certificate, which should send it over to the Issued Certificates folder. (See Figure 6-22.) Once in this state, the only option available to us is to revoke the certificate. This might be done if a partnership expired or if a consumer was found to be negligent in their use of the Web service.

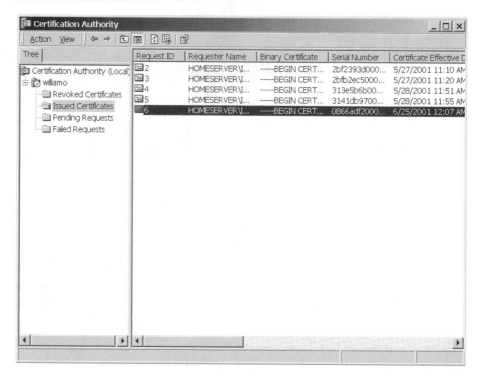

Figure 6-22. Viewing issued certificates

Now that the certificate has been issued, we only have to wait for the consumer to come back to our site to check their status and install the certificate.

Installing Issued Certificates

When we come back to the site as a consumer to check on the status of our certificate request, we are greeted with the same screen as before. This time, however, we will elect to check on a pending certificate. (See Figure 6-23.) This allows us to check the status, if nothing else.

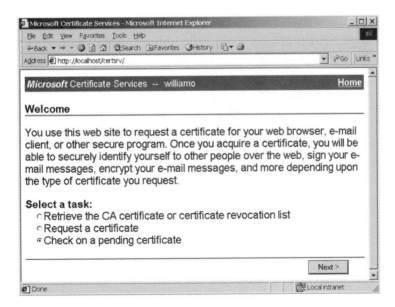

Figure 6-23. Checking on pending certificate requests

After selecting Next, the certificate site presents the list of certificate requests we have made. (See Figure 6-24.) This allows us to specify a specific certificate in case we have made multiple requests. More than likely, we will have made only one, so the default selection will be correct and we will click on Next.

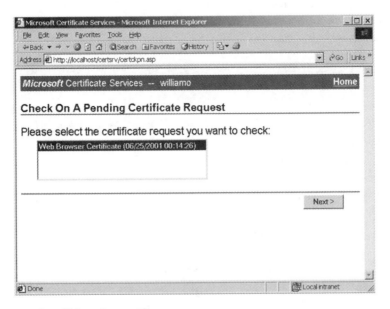

Figure 6-24. Specifying the certificate request

This then displays the status of the certificate request (Figure 6-25). Because we issued the certificate earlier, we see that the certificate has been issued, and we have the option to go ahead and install it on our browser's system.

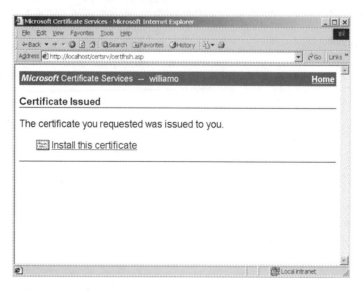

Figure 6-25. Installing the issued certificate

Once the link is clicked on, the process to install the certificate has begun. Once the process has completed, a confirmation screen appears indicating whether it was successful. (See Figure 6-26.) The consumer can now utilize his or her client certificate when connecting to our Web service. This can be done in a number of ways, which we will specify in Chapter 8 ("Consuming Web Services").

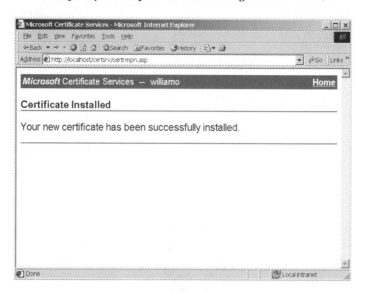

Figure 6-26. Successful certificate installation

Although the consumer is now ready to connect to us, we still haven't set up our Web service to require client certificates. As of right now, it accepts anonymous requests, so we need to configure our Web server to require valid certificates.

Adding Authentication to the Service

Although the consumer now has the client certificate, we aren't enforcing their usage through our Web site. We will have to make a few configuration changes to our site to do that.

To start, we need to go to the properties of the Web site containing our Web service. We can do this within the IIS console by right-clicking on the site and selecting Properties. Once this screen is open, we can select the Directory Security tab to specify our configuration information. (See Figure 6-27.)

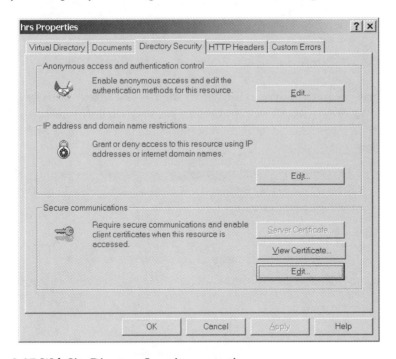

Figure 6-27. Web Site Directory Security properties

Once here, we can select Edit in the Secure Communications section to pull up the Secure Communications property sheet (Figure 6-28). It is here where we can choose to specify a certificate trust list. This is the means by which we define which certificate authorities we will trust.

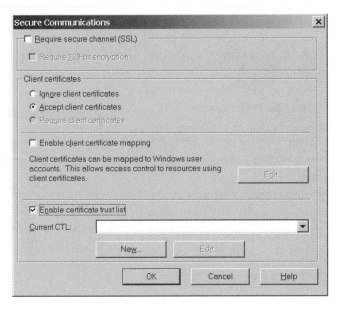

Figure 6-28. Web Site Secure Communications properties

When we select New, we start the Certificate Trust List wizard. (See Figure 6-29.) This shows all of the lists we currently have and allows us to define new ones. There are no lists by default, so we will select Add from Store to specify new certificate authorities to add to our list.

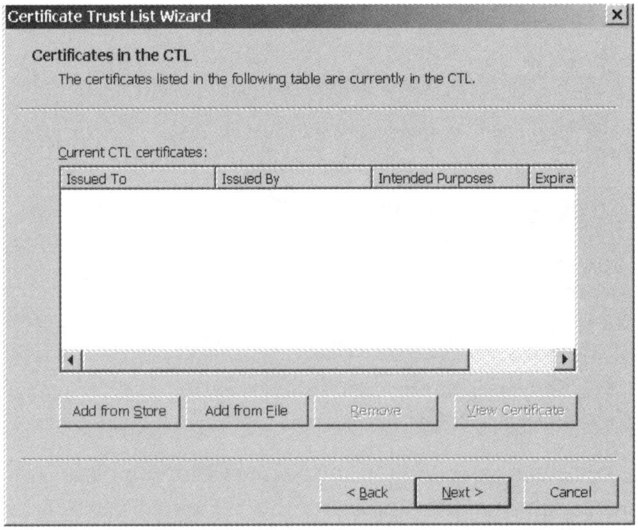

Figure 6-29. Certificate Trust List wizard

This sends us to a screen to specify which certificate authorities we want to trust (Figure 6-30). As an example, we could specify Verisign as a trusted authority, and we would then trust all client certificates granted by it. Because we are acting as our own certificate authority, we will only need to reference our local system as a trusted authority.

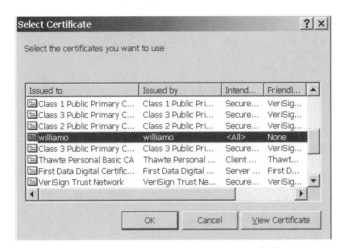

Figure 6-30. Selecting trusted certificate authorities

Once this is completed, we need to enter some information about this list of authorities. (See Figure 6-31.) This simply helps us to recall the common denominator between all entries and the purpose of this aggregation.

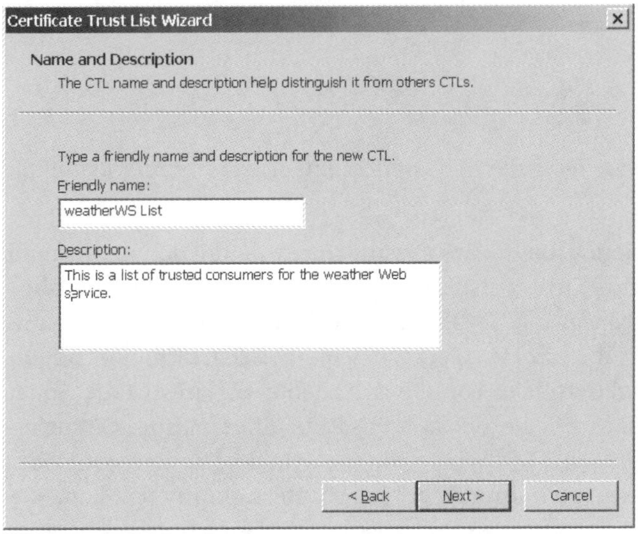

Figure 6-31. Entering certificate trust list information

We then click on Finish on the next screen to complete the process. We have now established our certificate authority as the only trusted authority, but we still aren't set up to require client certificates. We could choose to do it at the Web site level, thereby affecting all applications hosted on the site, but that is probably not acceptable unless this Web service was the only entity hosted by the site.

Instead, we should go to the properties of the Web application we made earlier, weatherWS. Like the site itself, we can get to its properties by right-clicking on the application in the left pane. This displays the properties for just this application. We want to go to the directory security panel, which looks the same as the Web site's in Figure 6-27. We also select Edit here to go to our application's secure communications properties, which looks slightly different from the site's. (See Figure 6-32.)

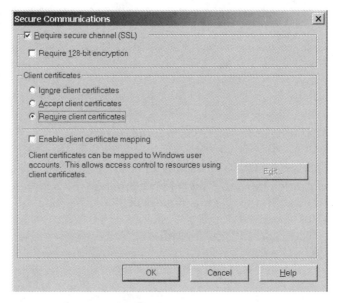

Figure 6-32. Specifying the Web application's secure communictions properties

You will notice that we are missing the extra function on the bottom concerning certificate trust lists. Lists can be maintained only at the site level. However, we can specify at this level that a client certificate is required, as shown in Figure 6-32. You have to select the Requires Secure Channel option before the Requires Client Certificates option is available. This means that you have to install a server certificate. Because this is no different from getting a server certificate for a Web site, I will spare you the details of that process. We could actually issue our own through our certificate authority, so the process could be hastened by using our own rather than waiting for a third-party processor.

Now we are requiring our consumers to use client certificates from our certificate authority to make requests of our weather Web service. We even have a fairly simple interface in place for them to request and install the client certificates, so they should not have too much difficulty. We will look at this process from the consumer's perspective a little more in Chapter 8.

In the meantime, we need to at least test our Web service with our test client. As of right now, it will fail because it is not using a client certificate or even SSL. The first step to remedying that is to change the URL to HTTPS instead of HTTP. We will also need to request a client certificate from our own authority. Once issued and installed using the process we just outlined, we will need to have our client reference it.

Once again, our MSXML parser comes to the rescue! Using a property called `setOption`, we can actually specify an installed certificate in communicating our request over HTTP(S). We need to specify the constant associated with the certificate property as well as the name of the client certificate. The full line would look something like:

```
objXMLSend.setOption SXH_OPTION_SELECT_CLIENT_SSL_CERT, "myCert"
```

With this additional line and the HTTPS reference in the URL, we should be ready to test our Web service, meeting its new requirement. In Chapter 7 ("Building a Web Services Workflow"), we will further extend this functionality by accessing the information from the client certificate programmatically. This will give us the ability to match up session-level data with identities that have the strong integrity of the certificates. It's a powerful combination that will allow us to build very robust and secure Web services.

Future Enhancements

At some point, you will want to make changes or enhancements to your Web service. Before you even start to think about these possibilities, make sure you have a good compatibility plan in place. Once you provide a Web service and consumers start using it, there will be applications depending on your service "as is." This is a critical area to be defined for Web services to be successful in the industry, and every provider will have a responsibility to err on the side of caution.

Summary

We have now designed, developed, and deployed two Web services; one based on a Java class and one based on a COM object. We addressed some issues in working with two different development environments and saw what each had to offer during the process. We got to work with two different parsers, each taking different approaches to accomplish the same objectives.

We looked at different ways we can provide XML data back to our consumers. Those approaches could extend beyond even Web services to help us in working with XML more efficiently in other applications. We also got a pretty good look at implementing security for a Web service. We created a certificate authority and used it to generate client certificates and modified our Web service to require their use by consumers. We have accomplished quite a bit in this chapter, but we have actually just hit the tip of the iceberg in the development of Web services.

In the next chapter, we will need to combine all of these approaches and take on the building of a Web services workflow. Although this will also be working off of an existing service, it is an entire system, not just a single component or class. We will have to address state and session maintenance, and we will be providing some additional functionality to make the Web service a robust offering to consumers. It will basically be more complex and require us to extend our understanding and use of Web services.

Building a Web Services Workflow

A Hotel Reservation System

WE HAVE LOOKED AT how to build a Web services call. Even more value can come from exposing entire processes, or workflows, through Web services. In this chapter we will build on our ability to expose a single call by linking multiple calls together to expose a Web services workflow.

Since Chapter 1, I have been referencing a hotel reservation system as a sample Web service, so our workflow will be based on those examples. We are playing the role of a hotel chain owner who wants to allow external applications to check room availability and book rooms on their existing systems. This service will target both large travel sites as well as isolated niche applications that might want to reserve rooms. A good example of the latter scenario would be an event site that has an exclusive arrangement with the hotel to provide discounted rooms for attendees. The Web service should be generic enough to fit all of these scenarios.

Understanding the Requirements

As with any successful project, we must first determine the requirements. Unidentified requirements tend to surface as issues in a project as it progresses, so in a real world setting it is crucial to be as thorough as possible in gathering the requirements. This will provide direction in your design and will also verify that there is business justification for the project. Fortunately we won't get bogged down in extensive analysis for these examples. I will simply present a list of requirements that meet a fairly realistic scenario and offers up enough challenges that we can encounter, and therefore overcome.

Our primary requirement is to expose an existing room reservation system as a Web service. This legacy system is called the Hotel Reservation System (HRS) and was only ever intended to be a private reservation system for the hotel's reservation agents. HRS has a couple of COM interfaces that expose all of your functionality required, and the service workflow will utilize these interfaces to execute the necessary processes.

> **NOTE**   *To follow along with this chapter, you can download this "legacy system" in the form of a COM object from* http://www.architectingwebservices.com/hrsws/hrs.

The service workflow breaks down into two main components: availability and reservation. The availability service takes an assortment of criteria to find an appropriate hotel and room match for the user. The reservation allows the user to reserve the room type for the dates requested with a valid credit card. The availability service must be utilized prior to reserving a room in the given session. This requirement will keep users from attempting to reserve rooms from one day to the next when they may no longer be available.

For the availability request, we need to collect some criteria to find a proper match. Those criteria should include the following:

- Check-in date*

- Check-out date*

- Number of adults*

- Number of children*

- (City and state) or landmark*

- Coupon code

- Price preference

- Bed size preference

- Smoking preference

- Requested hotel amenities

The criteria denoted by an asterisk represent the information required to perform the hotel search. The requested hotel amenities criteria must allow for future expandability. This means that it must be an open-ended field. Initially, the options will consist of the following amenities:

- Concierge

- Workout facilities

- Pool

- Restaurant

- 24-hour room service

- High-speed Internet access

You will need to provide some additional information about the hotels themselves. These will be mostly marketing-driven verbiage and images such as the following:

- Picture of hotel

- Picture of lobby or meeting rooms

- Picture of pool or workout facilities

- Picture of room A

- Picture of room B

- Paragraph (50 to 100 words) describing hotel

For the bookings service, we need to collect information about the room to be booked as well as the user. The current reservation system provides its own identifiers for available rooms, so you simply need to utilize its information. We then need to include all of the user's pertinent data. We end up with the following data to collect for the booking service:

- Hotel ID*

- Room type*

- Check-in date*

- Check-out date*

- Number of adults*

- Number of children*

- First name*

- Last name*

- Home address*

- Home phone number*

- Credit card number*

- Credit card expiration date*

- Card issuer*

- Name on credit card*

- Coupon code

- Billing address

Again, the required fields are noted with an asterisk. The address information should consist of the usual two address lines, city, state, and Zip code. Also, if the billing address is left null, the home address is assumed as the billing address.

The hotel chain is also considering an incentive plan for their Web service for consumers, based on the reservations that are booked and used through the service. This means that we need to authenticate consumers and track their users' activities when a reservation is made.

For the purposes of this exercise, we will not address availability and scalability expectations. These are typically going to be very important requirements in real life, however, not to be overlooked or ignored.

Selecting the Technologies

For this Web service, we will be referencing an existing COM-based system. To most efficiently interact with this platform, we will build the Web service on a Microsoft Windows 2000 platform. We will also utilize the Microsoft development platform of COM+ for the objects and ASP for the interface middleware. We will also use Microsoft's SQL Server 2000 for maintaining consumer accounts and session data.

> **NOTE** *We will not use the .NET framework or development environment for this Web service. While .NET will hide some of the plumbing details we will cover, this exposure will give you a more complete understanding of how Web services work.*

Modeling the Web Service

As we saw in Chapter 5, the first step we should take in designing our Web service is to define our model. Through this exercise we will examine the presentation, interface, and security models to make certain we have thought through all of our options before we start designing and developing.

The Presentation Model

The first component of our model to define is our presentation. This is where we determine how robust we want to make responses and how much assistance we want to provide for consumers. The first step to accomplishing this is determining our service's exposure level.

Since we are looking at a very user-interactive process, we will probably not use a masked service. Since a user must go through the availability service prior to making a reservation, this is not conducive to a back end process. That leaves us with the possibilities of an isolated service or an embedded service. To make this determination, we really need to identify our target consumers.

I mentioned earlier that we want to reach a broad grouping of consumers: ranging from travel sites to dedicated event sites. We are not targeting a specific travel site, but rather want to provide a service that appeals to all of them. The same goes for the event sites. This presents a bit of a challenge because we will likely be working with the two extremes of consumers in terms of experience and focus. The travel site will be working with several hotels and will probably expect us to match its requirements in terms of search criteria, response data, and any peripheral content. The event site may be very dependent on us, not only because they have fewer resources, but also because we may be the only Web service they are working with. The event coordinators are much more likely to give us control of the process and the entire experience related to the room reservation.

To reach these two targets, we should probably develop two different processes. Don't worry about duplication, because we will reuse much of the process in both. However, we need to think of each individually because of their very different needs.

In the case of the travel sites, the service will almost certainly be embedded in their existing application. They will want to own the entire user experience and maintain control over the process. For the event site consumers we will need to do much more handholding. That might go as far as being an isolated service and thus driving and owning the entire process. Let's say for the sake of argument that we don't want to miss any business opportunities with the events for which we establish discount agreements and will therefore take on that responsibility. That leaves us with one instance of our service capable of being embedded and another that can be isolated in an application.

The next step is to determine the amount of presentation information or assistance we want to provide. Again, we need to identify the type of consumer that we are targeting with our service to come up with an accurate answer.

In the case of the event site, we already determined that you need to provide an isolated service, and that means providing an entire presentation of our result information. Additionally, we need to provide user interface (UI) information for collecting both the search criteria and the user information for making the reservations. The next step, then, is to assemble a storyboard of the entire user experience for our isolated service. (See Figure 7-1.) The keys here are to identify the necessary information to capture and to create an interface that can interact effectively with users. Later we will actually design the interface in detail.

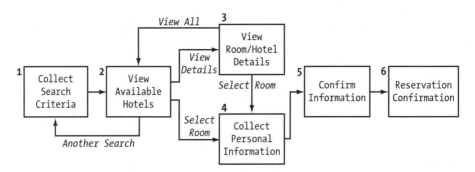

Figure 7-1. Storyboard for the isolated service user interface

> **NOTE**   *Keep in mind that the storyboard design for your services is closely related to your process flow, discussed shortly. The two will impact each other, so don't consider this storyboard complete until you complete your process diagrams, and vice versa.*

For our travel site consumers, the presentation will be fairly light. We will provide some image references to views of our hotels and links to our site and further information, which they can use at their discretion, but for the most part the response will consist of the raw data without a lot of extraneous information. This translates into providing instruction-oriented content. No style data will be provided to the consumers. They are also not likely to need any assistance from us in collecting any of the user inputs, so there is no need to develop a story-board; our process flow will be sufficient.

The Interface Model

In defining the interface for our Web service model, we must look at the process we are exposing and the payloads that define our interaction with consumers. First we need to develop the process flow for our service. Just as we did in Chapter 5, start with the basic flow defined by the business requirements. (See Figure 7-2.)

Identifying the Process Flow

We first need to identify the process flow of the entire system without regard to how we will deploy this functionality. This process flow should define the work-flow independent of whether it is to be developed into an application, a Web service, or another mechanism.

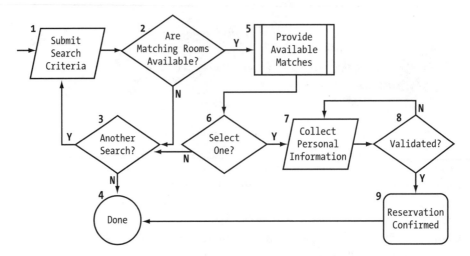

Figure 7-2. Baseline reservation system business process flow

This process flow identifies the various states of the process and how they can be altered based on results or actions. This serves as our baseline, which we can modify to meet our intended output mechanism(s).

In this instance, we want to expose this functionality through a Web service. However, we have two different Web service models to target: isolated and embedded. The specific process flow for these two models will differ because different functionality relies on different owners. Whenever you have a scenario where you provide both an embedded and isolated service, you are better off designing the embedded service process first because it contains the core functionality of the Web service. Since the consumer is assuming responsibility for providing the process UI, less functionality is required of the Web service, and there is a less complex process flow. (See Figure 7-3.) Afterwards, the functionality specific to the isolated service can then be added to the embedded Web service.

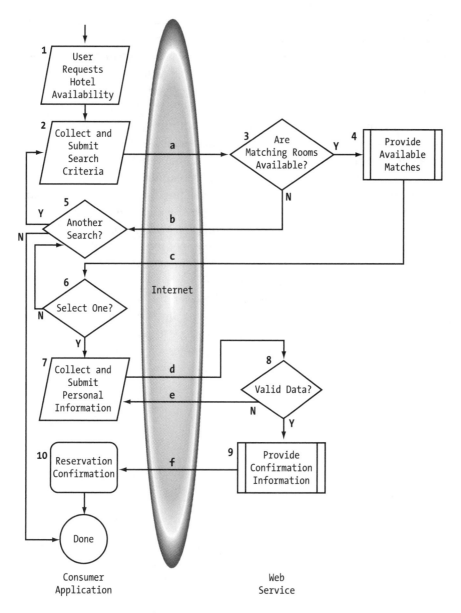

Figure 7-3. Modified process flow for embedded service consumers

Let's walk through this flow to make sure we have the process captured correctly. When the user initiates the process (Figure 7-3, step 1), the consumer collects the search criteria (2) and submits it to the Web service (a). The Web service runs a search based on the criteria (3) to determine if there are any matches. If a match is found, the service assembles the appropriate data on the available rooms (4) and responds to the consumer (c). If a match is not found, the consumer asks the user whether to execute another search (5). This may involve a slight modification or a completely new set of inputs. The distinction does not matter for this process or to the service. If the user finds an available room and wants to reserve it (6), the consumer proceeds to collect the personal information necessary to make the reservation request (7). If the user is not happy with the returned matches, the user again has the option to run another search with different criteria. When the appropriate information has been collected, it is submitted to the service for validation (8). If it cannot be validated, the service makes the appropriate response (e), and the consumer can attempt to collect the information again. If the information is validated, the appropriate confirmation information is assembled by the service (9) and sent back to the consumer (f), which displays it (10) and completes the process.

You should be able to tell from this diagram of the process that we are essentially looking at two requests (a and d) with dynamic responses (b, c and e, f). I will take a closer look at this in the next section when we define our payloads.

There is much more communication between the consumer and provider in the isolated process flow. This is necessary to facilitate the functionality exposed by the provider's service because the provider is assuming more ownership of the entire process. The consumer is taking a hands-off approach to the whole process and is simply giving the provider a space in which to execute its processes. (See Figure 7-4.)

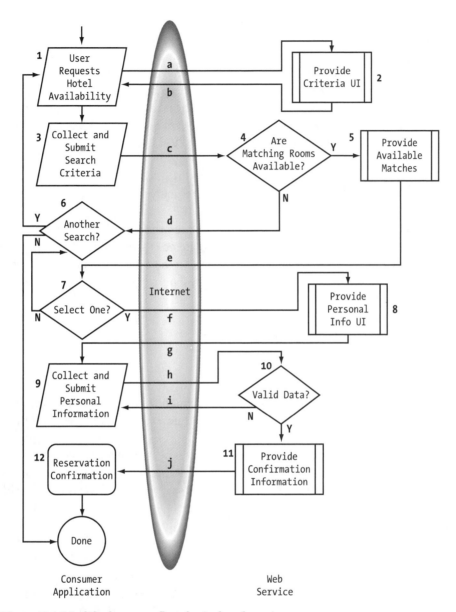

Figure 7-4. Modified process flow for isolated service consumers

The process is still essentially the same. The provider simply provides some extra functionality (or services) around the user experience. In some cases this is manifested through more robust payloads in the responses we have already defined. However, as you can see in Figure 7-4, this also usually requires additional interaction through requests and responses.

For most processes, this approach requires an extra request to establish the initial UI to begin the process. For our hotel availability service, this means defining the hotel search criteria presentation to the end user (2). The other extra functionality necessary for the isolated model of our service is the reservation request UI (8). You can see that each of these is a static request and response, and so the additional development effort required for this functionality is oriented more toward creativity than toward programming. Recognizing this will help you to determine the ROI for such functionality.

> *ROI—return on investment—*is often a key business criterion when determining whether to invest money and resources in a proposed effort.

You'll also notice that, aside from the extra requests to the Web service, the consumer side of the process flow remains unaltered. The functionality we provide does not reduce the number of steps necessary on the consumer's part, but does reduce the amount of effort necessary for each step that interacts with the user.

Reconciling with the Presentation Model

Before defining the payload, it is imperative that you reconcile your process flow with your presentation model. A Web services process is not completely defined until it provides all the functionality demanded of the presentation model. Likewise, the presentation model must match the workflow defined by the process model.

This might strike some traditional developers or managers as being an unnecessary step if all participants fill their roles appropriately. This process will serve as a sanity check for the convergence of these two models. Developers with a UI-centric background and focus often define the presentation model. They should be thinking about the user's interaction with the application consuming the Web service. Conversely, developers that focus on the consumer's interaction with the service define the process model. These are two very different approaches that can result in very different designs. The process of developing and reconciling these inconsistencies is ultimately going to make the Web service a better offering because of the different approaches and mindsets addressing the model.

The inconsistencies themselves can manifest themselves in different ways. Quite often extra functionality can be added to the process through the presentation model definition. This occurs through the splitting of tasks into multiple UI steps or even combining tasks into a single UI screen. Likewise, the process model may expose issues or barriers the presentation model did not foresee or consider. To mitigate these issues, neither model should be considered complete until this reconciliation has occurred.

As it happens, we do have a few extra steps identified in our storyboard that were not captured in our process model. If you refer back to the storyboard in Figure 7-1 you will see that we have one step that allows for viewing of more detailed information on the room and/or hotel selected (3) and another step for confirming the user's information (5). We need to reconcile these differences and modify the models appropriately so that they are in sync.

The detail view step is a good example of how the presentation model exposes something the process model does not. The assumption likely made by the process model is that all availability information is viewed on a single screen. The presentation model took the approach of optimizing the initial view to compactly show all results and allow for a drilldown. A user who is taking a business trip and is merely staying one night may not need to view detailed amenities to make a decision on whether to stay in hotel A or hotel B. In this case, the user only needs to see high-level information such as price and proximity, since the rest of the criteria should be met based on the initial search information. This not only optimizes screen space on the presentation, but also optimizes our payloads to provide less wasted data that the user may not require. Since this streamlines the process for the average user, we should integrate this functionality into our process model. (See Figure 7-5.)

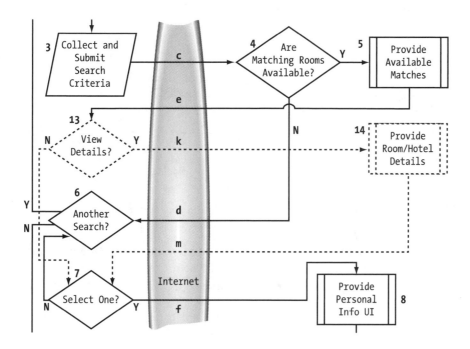

Figure 7-5. Hotel detail view for reservation service

Integrating this step is the same regardless of whether we define the isolated or embedded model, since it requires interaction with the Web service either way. In Figure 7-5, we have modified the isolated service model by adding two entities. The first entity allows the consumer to expose the decision of whether to view the details of a specific room or hotel to the user (13). If the user selects this option, the consumer sends the request to the service (k), and it packages this information together (14) and responds (m). If the user chooses not to view the details, the process continues on to the selection entity.

The second inconsistency between the presentation and process models is the confirmation of user information. This is standard functionality in Web-based applications to give the user the opportunity to change critical information like payment details. The decision that needs to be made here is where to maintain this step. For our embedded model, it makes sense that the consumer would handle this functionality. For the isolated model, this decision is a little more difficult. Going back to the user for a confirmation from a Web service is a very costly operation. There is really no need for going all the way back to the service other than that the consumer doesn't want to handle it.

One solution that works for an isolated model and yet does not require an extra round trip to the server is client-side script. The script can use a simple pop-up window confirming the entered information with the user. For efficiency's sake, we will take this approach. This step for both the embedded and isolated services is identical. (See Figure 7-6.)

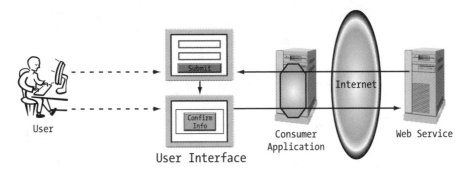

Figure 7-6. Confirmation of personal information for reservation request

With these changes, we now have a presentation model that matches our two process models, isolated and embedded. The next step is to drill down into the communication paths defined in our process model to define the payloads.

Defining the Payloads

The payloads we define for our interaction between the service and its consumers essentially define our interface. Although our two models have similar process flows, their payload definitions are very different. Like the process flow, the isolated service payload builds onto a core of information that is necessary for the embedded service. However, once the necessary presentation information is added, this relationship is virtually unrecognizable.

Since we are dealing with essentially two different services, we need to make a determination of distinction. How will we distinguish between a call for the embedded service versus a call for the isolated service? There are basically two approaches to handling this: differentiate externally or internally to the payload. Making the distinction externally means defining two different URLs for the two services. Internalized distinction means handling the requests for both services through the same location and using the payloads to make the distinction. Both approaches work, so this is simply an aspect of this particular model that we need to determine before we can move forward.

I prefer distinguishing externally for the benefit of eliminating additional checks in the service. We need to parse out data from the request to route our services to our business logic already, but in this case such an approach adds an extra layer of processing. When the distinction is externalized, it is already made for you, and each process can assume the service requested. The drawback to this approach is that you have two listeners, not one. With reuse of most of the overall functionality a strong likelihood, I consider the trade-off worthwhile.

The other decision we have to make is whether to define a unique interface for each model or incorporate them both into a single interface. To make this decision, we really need to understand what is involved with each model. If they are too dissimilar, it probably is not feasible to make a single interface, or at the very least it won't be very efficient. However, we don't want to duplicate designs or logic in an attempt to keep the interfaces independent. We know that the isolated service will build on the embedded service, but we can't be certain how much just yet. To make the best decision for our interface model, we had better model the two interfaces independently and then address this issue afterward. We will do so as part of the interface layer design later in this chapter.

Embedded Service Payload

Before looking at individual payloads, we first need to identify any system information we might need to maintain separately from the main data in every call. As we saw in Chapter 5, we can define header sections in our payloads to contain data that helps us to identify users and maintain state information.

Fundamentally, an embedded service requires less of this kind of functionality simply because the consumer owns more of the process. For our service, the only requirement we need to concern ourselves with is the sequence of availability lookup and reservation request. As I stated in our requirements, we want to catch attempts by a user to reserve a room that had availability determined at a much earlier time. It is not so much that we can't catch this later and handle it, but for the sake of this example I will assume that we want to manage this process to avoid extra overhead on the actual reservation system.

To accomplish this objective, we will develop a simple ID system that references a listing local to the service that provides the time the corresponding availability request was made for each reservation request. If the time was over 30 minutes prior to the reservation request or non-existent, the service responds to the consumer that the current selection is not available and another selection must be made. The consumer could modify the process slightly to more gracefully handle this result by redirecting the consumer to the availability search interface. We will place this ID in a service variable section, as discussed in Chapter 5.

The other determination we need to make is whether we want to manage the current state of the process via state variables. If every request payload is unique, we can simply load the payload and decipher the stage that is inherently obvious. However, the drawback is that not only are you adding process cycles to your Web service listener, but you are also building dependencies on your current payload structure. It is better to generate a system for managing the state whenever modeling Web services with workflow. Again, we will add this state data to our service variable header.

Another piece of information to consider is a consumer ID. We could use this to track the consumer from one step to another. Because of its very nature, we will want the Web service to authenticate the consumer on each call, regardless. This means that any state information we persist in our service variables is only useful on an application level. Depending on what method you are using for authentication, this may or may not be useful and/or necessary. Since we will be authenticating against client certificates, our service can access this information. This is much more reliable than any ID we pass, so we need not bother.

Now that we have defined our header information, we need to look at the specific request and response payloads that define the interactions. For the embedded model of our service, we have three interactions defined:

- Availability request

- Hotel detail view

- Reservation request

Our embedded service has little concern for the presentation of this information, so these payloads essentially provide the appropriate data in a raw format. This allows the consumer to utilize the data in any way necessary to meet requirements.

Availability Request

The availability request consists of the data elements I listed in our requirements. At this point, the design of our payloads simply resolves the structure of the data and identifies which elements are required and which are optional. We will walk through the process of designing our payloads in the section about designing this Web service later in this chapter.

With the availability request payload essentially defined by our requirements, we need to turn our attention to its response payload. This is the data we have to assemble and return to the consumer on receiving this request. For our embedded responses, the payload is fairly direct, without a lot of extraneous information for presentation purposes. If we decide to pass on some extra nonessential information, we will utilize reference links to allow consumers to use it at their discretion while not overloading the payload.

Whenever you expose existing applications or processes as Web services, the response is based on the information returned from those systems. Because these systems were not designed as Web services, you will likely choose to either add more information or to use only a subset of that information. Working with what you get from these systems already gets you going in the right direction to defining your responses.

As identified in our requirements, we are working off of existing COM objects accessing our reservation system. For simplicity's sake, we will have a single object that exposes our functionality. You will need to reference a few different methods to return the correct information to the consumer. We already know the basic parameters from our requirements, so we will look at those specifics later when we start designing our service. Let's at least look now at the call and their returns, shown here:

```
Public Function fetchAvailability(...) As Variant()
Public Function fetchHotel(...) As Variant()
```

The `fetchAvailability` method returns a two-dimensional array that contains the matching hotels based on the criteria submitted. This array consists of the following information, in this order:

- Hotel ID

- Proximity to location

- Room type

- Room rate

Unfortunately, this is only a portion of the data we need to retrieve. We need to reference the other method to get the detailed information on the hotel that users will need to make a decision on the available options.

Like the `fetchAvailability` call, the `fetchHotel` method also returns an array containing the information we are requesting:

- Hotel name

- Hotel manager

- Hotel address

- Hotel city

- Hotel state

- Hotel phone

- Hotel amenities

As we look through the information passed, we can see that there is some information the user will not need to see, such as hotel ID and hotel manager. We could choose to completely leave this information out of the response. However, just because the user or consumer doesn't need the information doesn't necessarily mean that the information is not useful. You might find that utilizing some information "behind the scenes," perhaps through the service variables, can help with tracking or the functionality itself. In this example, the hotel ID might be such a piece of data. While we have not gotten there yet, we will in fact need the hotel ID for our detail view and reservation request. So we can only leave the hotel manager field out of our Web service response. That leaves our response with the following data (in no particular order):

- Hotel ID

- Proximity to location

- Room type

- Room rate

- Hotel name

- Hotel address

- Hotel city

- Hotel state

- Hotel phone

- Hotel amenities

For this service, we include a few additional pieces of information in our response to the user. One is a date element to help with "stamping" the resulting information. This can't actually be relied on as a true timestamp, since it can easily be altered and is specific to the current time zone, but it could be helpful for the presentation of the data and with any auditing or troubleshooting. We also turn around the data used to make the request. This is a nicety that may help the consumer with maintaining state for the current user. This will keep the consumer from needing to track the information that was sent to the service.

Hotel Detail View

Now that we have defined the availability request and response model, we need to turn our attention to the supporting detail view of the hotel information. This is not a function that is available through the reservation system, but rather something that was conceived for this particular service. This will largely consist of content providing additional information about the hotels that match the availability request. This function could be made generic enough to serve other purposes later, so we will take that approach.

As I just mentioned, we will utilize the hotel ID information from the availability request to make this request. In fact, we will allow that to essentially be the request, along with the service variables. The response then consists of the data listed in our requirements. Again, since this is an embedded service, we provide this information in raw XML form, allowing the consumer to determine how to use and structure it.

Reservation Request

Up until now we have been modeling the process leading up to making a hotel reservation. We have reached the point at which we can address the reservation process itself. We have the information outlined for us already, so we just need to determine if we need to make any changes or additions.

The existing COM object has a single call that can make a reservation request, as shown here:

```
Public Function makeReservation(. . .) As Long
```

I mentioned that we would need the hotel ID for this call. This is because the consumer may have more than one hotel match, so there is no way for us to know in that case which was selected without some kind of identification. Along with this, we will also need some of the matching criteria from the availability request. This information is not passed through the consumer, but rather we will maintain it on our side as part of the state managed by the session ID.

Personal and payment information is also required for the user to place the reservation. Since this data is fairly sensitive and critical, there is an opportunity to provide some validation information. However, since we are defining the embedded process, this is not something that can be done seamlessly. The consumer owns the UI, so we are not providing any content for the data entry steps. We can include the validation in the response of the availability request, but that potentially adds a lot of overhead. To avoid this, we can add just a reference (link) to the validation data maintained separately on our Web server.

For this scenario, we will pass on this approach. Our travel site would already be collecting payment data for other vendors, so they are not likely to need any validation code we generate. Of bigger concern would be the consumer's utilization of our reservation request schema. This helps to ensure that you don't have to reject the request due to bad data. We will take a closer look at this issue in more detail when we build our Web service in the implementation section, and consume Web services in Chapter 8.

Since we will not be adding any services, our reservation request ends up being very much a match of our requirements. We simply need to define how we want this information structured in our design, coming up in the design section.

The response from the reservation request essentially consists of the confirmation information. The system provides a confirmation number, but we also provide a phone number for further assistance (which will be the same for all reservations) and a description of any error encountered during processing. We package this into three elements:

- Confirmation number

- Phone number

- Problem text

This completes the presentation model for our embedded Web service. Next, we need to step through this same exercise for our isolated Web service. This will build on the work we have done here by adding many more services and content to provide a complete user experience through the consumer.

Isolated Service Payload

Our isolated hotel reservation Web service provides a more complete UI for the consumer. This UI falls just short of being a complete Web page because consumers can make changes to our service as it passes through their system(s). Our data is still defined via XML, so they can still modify the content to more exactly match their look and feel.

As with the embedded model, we need to make a determination on our state management. Because this service represents the same process, we have the same requirements. They include identifying the current step in the process as well as tracking the session. It also makes sense then that we handle this data the same way, through the service variables. This also buys us some reuse across the two services, so we will take this same approach.

Some of the extra services our isolated service provides simply expand the existing interactions we have defined for our embedded service. However, some need to be exposed through extra steps. If we refer back to the storyboard we generated for our presentation model (Figure 7-1), we come up with the following interactions:

- Availability form

- Availability request

- Hotel detail view

- Reservation form

- Reservation request

Availability Form

The availability form is the request that starts the entire process. The request itself essentially tells us who the consumer is, and we return the necessary information to define the input form for the user to make an availability request. The basic design is based on the availability request itself. The other decisions we have to make are how you should structure it and how much content we should provide.

Since we are assuming a lot of responsibility with an isolated service and the consumer can always modify the data, you should provide as much information as necessary to present a good interface to the user. This approach is even easier to justify, since we are providing a separate embedded service. If this were not the case, we would be adding a lot of overhead to the payload for consumers that would want to design their own UI.

For our availability request UI we will design an HTML form in a table layout, add some font treatments, and include the client-side validation. This provides an interface robust enough that it can be exposed "as is" to the end user. However, when we get to the implementation phase, we will see that the consumer still needs to provide some information so that the form we designed is submitted correctly through the consumer's system.

Availability Request

The availability request is the same as that of the embedded service. The response, however, is different because we provide some formatting. Like with the availability request form, we will put the response data in a table structure and include some font treatment. No data entry is necessary on this UI, so client-side validation is not necessary. However, we need to facilitate two activities from this interface, not just one. One activity is to make a reservation off of one of the matches. The other activity is the viewing of hotel details. Both of these are exposed through either buttons or links. Making this determination is not necessary until we get to design. It is just important that we identify the required functionality for our model so that you can identify the interactions and determine the extent of our presentation services.

Hotel Detail View

The detail view interaction is similar to the availability interaction in that the request does not change from the embedded model, but the response does provide some extra formatting to the existing response. Again, we will use a table structure to define the layout of this data and include some font treatment. The only activities available on this UI are to go back to the results view or make a reservation with the current hotel.

Reservation Form

The reservation form interaction is a new step added for the isolated process. This is only necessary in the isolated process because we are providing the UI and need a way to collect the appropriate information for requesting a reservation. Like the availability request form, we will build an HTML form that aligns to our reservation request interface. We will also provide this form in a table structure with font treatments and the appropriate client-side validation.

Reservation Request

Finally, we have the reservation request. This will follow the same process as the embedded reservation request. We will receive the data identifying the hotel and the room selected, and the response will provide a phone number and either a confirmation number or problem text, depending on whether the reservation was successful.

Looking back over these interactions, we can see that we have a lot of overlap between the embedded and isolated models of our service. The difference in the overlapping functions is actually just the response format. The data doesn't change, simply its presentation. For this service, we should try to aggregate these two processes into one for the sake of efficiency and reusability.

Combining the Two Services

To maximize the reuse of our logic and design we will take both of these services and turn them into one physical service with two interfaces. Taking the least common denominator approach, we will develop one set of logic for both services and simply modify the result as necessary for the service type requested. The two form requests can be left as is because they are not valid for the embedded service. That leaves us with a single process for both requests.

The other three requests (availability, hotel detail view, and reservation) are shared by both services. The requests are the same, but the responses are different. In each case, we need to provide data that is essentially XHTML to be exposed directly to the user. You can accomplish this in several different ways. The worst way is to actually code the logic to provide these two responses. This is needless because we have a tool at our disposal for taking our response data and transforming it into this XHTML: XSL.

We can define an XSL template that formats the data response we provide for our embedded service customers. The only question then is how to apply the template. The options are to apply the template before sending the response to the consumer or to simply reference the template in the response, allowing the consumer to provide it. There are tradeoffs in either scenario.

Applying the template before responding removes some logic on the consumer's side, but also "dumbs down" the response so that it can be very hard for the consumer to ever work with it. The data element tags are replaced by formatting tags; so referencing the data in the response is problematic, if not impossible.

Allowing consumers to apply the template gives them more access to the response on a data level, but also asks them to add some more functionality on their side. This approach would also reduce some of the workload on the Web service provider's system. Given the state of the parsers available today, the transforming of an XML document with an XSL template is becoming very simple, easily accomplished in just a few lines of code in nearly any language. For this reason, we will take the approach of allowing the consumers to apply the template.

This means that the only modification we have to make to the responses is the addition of the XSL template reference. We will add this node in the service variables section for only the isolated service type requests. Otherwise, every response is identical, ensuring the reusability of our application logic.

This completes the interface model for both service versions. We will complete the payload definitions in the design section, coming up later. Before getting to that, we need to define our security model.

The Security Model

The security model is a very important component to address before you get into the design of your Web service. As we saw in Chapter 5, this model consists of system access, application authentication, transport integrity, and payload validation. We need to determine how we will handle each of these areas.

One of the challenges with defining the security model is that it is not likely that your requirements will provide much direction in this area. The business driver is not likely to be aware of or understand these issues, so they are not in a position to address them. That usually means that your requirements may be dictated by your existing IT policies.

> **NOTE** *This may be your biggest challenge to deploying Web services. You may be pushing beyond the existing boundaries of your IT policies because Web services are such a new paradigm. That means that you might have to be the driver to change your IT policies. To do this, you will have to define your secure solution and convince your IT department that it is secure. You may also have to educate your business driver so that they can help to apply the necessary pressure.*

System Access

The infrastructure on which you are hosting your Web service will dictate most of your system access model. If you have an open connection to the Internet, anyone will be able to consume your Web service. If you build your Web service correctly, this will essentially be a harmless situation. However, you are opening yourself up to the possibility of people snooping around, making invalid requests, and/or using up your available bandwidth.

In this scenario, our Web service requires that a partner establish an account with us so that we can track activity and usage (as stated in our requirements). Since we are going to that trouble, we might as well require partners to provide us with the IP address or addresses from which they will be making requests. We can then add rules to our routers to only pass on requests to our Web service system from established IP addresses. Sure, IP addresses can be spoofed, but our objective is to limit the volume of invalid requests, and this rule will help.

The other issue we have to consider, especially if this is our organization's first Web service, is the hosting infrastructure. We have an existing set of COM objects through which we will access our reservation system. We could host the Web service directly on the application server with these COM objects, or we could go through ten systems to access the reservation system. I talked about these tradeoffs in Chapter 5, so I will avoid any further discussion about these options.

This is the hotel chain's first Web service, so we have a clean slate to start with. We will implement a proxy-host infrastructure that puts our Web service system in the DMZ and have it access the application server off the internal network. (See Figure 7-7.) We will put the appropriate measures in place to ensure that there is a secure tunnel between those two systems and that no one can access the application server directly through the Web server. The added benefit of this infrastructure model is that we could support a single or multiple application and Web servers supporting our Web services.

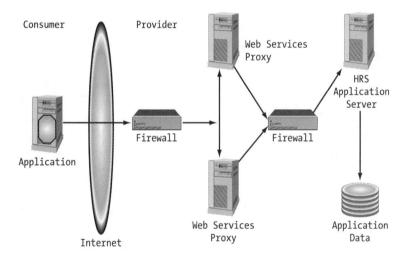

Figure 7-7. Web service proxy-host infrastructure

Application Authentication

Our application authentication model will be responsible for keeping unauthorized requests from getting processed by our service. This means that even a spoofed IP address that slips through our system access rules will not be handled by our service.

We can use any existing HTTP-supported mechanisms for providing authentication. This can include a variety of choices, as discussed in Chapter 5. If you recall, we actually have two authentication scenarios to consider. One covers the consumer and the other the end user. Fortunately, we can get by without authenticating the end user for this Web service because we have only a single transaction utilizing sensitive information: the reservation request. If we were going to store this information and have users come back to reference it for other reservations, this would definitely be an issue.

We do still want to authenticate consumers, however, so that we know they are partners and not unknown consumers. For this Web service, we will utilize certificates to authenticate consumers. This means distributing a file to each consumer, but since we are making them establish accounts, this is a minor addition to the existing process. When your infrastructure is set up correctly, this authentication will happen automatically by exposing your Web service through HTTPS addresses and configuring the site accordingly.

> **CAUTION** *There is a risk to distributing client certificates to some consumers, especially for an isolated service. If they are not technically savvy, you may find yourself having to walk them through the process of setting it up correctly. If you are going to be working with a large volume of consumers, this may not be a realistic option. We looked at this process in the "Implementing Certificate Security" section of Chapter 6.*

Although we are not concerned with the identity of the end user, we do want to identify an end user's session for the sake of processing requests appropriately. Remember that we will process a reservation only after an availability request is made; therefore we need to be able to match up their activities in a session. We can also use this functionality to track activities for audit purposes.

We have already taken one step for tracking activity by including a session ID in our system variables. That ID identifies the session for each request, but not the consumer. You might be inclined to incorporate a consumer ID, but that would expose a potentially serious security hole. This could be manipulated by the end user or the consumer to spoof another consumer, so we should not utilize this method for authentication purposes on a persistent basis. By persistent, I mean having consumers use a single ID for every request by every user.

We could, however, utilize the session IDs, established with the initial request of each session independently. During that request we could authenticate the consumer and tie that identity to the session ID through some data source. This session ID could then be traced back to the consumer once the consumer has been authenticated.

By using this session ID to track the consumer, as well as the session, we could not only meet the needs for the service, but also streamline our back-end processing of that information. Of course, this entire model assumes that the data is secure as it travels between the consumer and the Web services provider.

Transport Integrity

Without integrity, we can't really rely on the data transferred between the consumer and the provider. For some services, this may not be an issue. Since we are dealing with users' credit card information, this is very much an issue in this case.

Fortunately, we chose an authentication method that comes with an encryption service: HTTPS. This protocol utilizes SSL to encrypt the data sent between us and the consumer so that each end point can confirm not only the other party's identity, but also that no other party intercepts or modifies the data we send each other. Of course, that doesn't mean that we should implicitly trust the data itself.

Payload Validation

Unfortunately, we cannot be certain that the consumer is sending us the exact information we are expecting. After all, everyone makes mistakes, but we have to make sure that we do what we can to minimize the impact mistakes have on our systems, and thus on other consumers.

For this assurance, we need a method for validating a payload once it is received. Fortunately, we already have a method for this security via our defined XML Schemas. The definitions of our request payloads provide the template we need to check the requests made by our consumers.

We will utilize a parser that provides the function inherently when we process the payload. In this case, we will utilize the MSXML parser.

> **NOTE** *The MSXML 4.0 parser from Microsoft includes validation against XML Schemas. Previous versions supported only DTD validation of XML documents.*

Designing the Web Service

We have now laid the appropriate groundwork to start the design of our Web service. This effort will build directly off of our Web service model and technology decisions.

I will approach this similarly to the way I approach a traditional *n*-tier application: by looking at each tier individually. Since we are building a Web service off of an existing system, I will start with the business layer and work up to the interface layer and then back down to the data layer. This may seem to be an odd order, but in this scenario, the business layer drives everything from the existing system, and the data layer exists primarily to support the interface and business layers.

Business Layer

The business layer for a brand-new Web service is typically very similar to that of a traditional *n*-tier application. That changes somewhat in this case because we are exposing an existing process. The business layer for our Web service will actually be fairly light, simply providing any functionality not directly exposed by the existing system.

We need to start the design of our business layer by analyzing the current COM objects and their interfaces. We have already had a look at them because our payload models were so dependent on them. However, we did not look at the parameters of the method calls because the information was already available through our requirements. Now that we have entered the design, we need to see the details. Let's start with the fetchAvailability call, shown here:

```
Public Function fetchAvailability( _
    ByVal dtmCheck_In As Date, _
    ByVal dtmCheck_Out As Date, _
    ByVal intAdults As Integer, _
    ByVal intChildren As Integer, _
    ByVal strCity As String, _
    ByVal strState As String, _
    ByVal strLandmark As String, _
    ByVal strCoupon As String, _
    ByVal curPrice As Currency, _
    ByVal strBed As String, _
    ByVal blnSmoking As Boolean, _
    ByVal objAmenities As Variant) As Variant
```

As discussed earlier, we need to traverse the variant array coming back to get the necessary information for our response. The only thing new to note here is that the amenities are defined through a variant object. This variant is used as a ranking of the amenities so that they can be prioritized. This is a little less efficient than another structure (like a dictionary) could be, since the variant has to be predefined and could potentially be empty, but this is the system we have to work with. The maximum size is 6 values, so the overhead isn't terrible.

We discovered earlier that fetchAvailability would not provide all the information we need. Because of this fact we need to utilize a second function called fetchHotel to build the entire availability response, as shown here:

```
Public Function fetchHotel(ByVal Hotel_ID As Integer) As Variant
```

The fetchHotel call returns a variant array that we also need to navigate. Otherwise, the call is fairly straightforward.

Since we have two calls with some arrays to handle, the best approach is probably to develop our own object that takes our request data, makes these two calls, traverses the arrays, builds the response payload, and returns it. Let's call the method `wsFetchAvailability` and define the method similarly to the `fetchAvailability` method, with the exception of returning a string instead of a variant array. The `wsFetchAvailability` function is seen here:

```
Public Function wsFetchAvailability(...) as String
```

We need to put a process flow together so that we have a clear definition of how to execute this process. (See Figure 7-8.) The first step is to take the data we have been provided and call the `hotelAvailability` interface into the HRS system. For each match that we get back, we then need to call the `fetchHotel` interface to get all the specifics about the hotel. Finally, we need to package all this data into the valid format to provide back to the consumer.

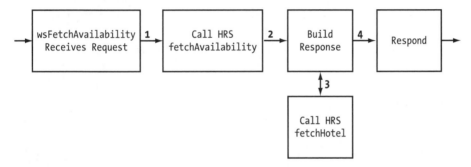

Figure 7-8. The `wsFetchAvailability` *process flow*

We now need to look at the detail view request. This should not be confused with the `fetchHotel` method because it does not involve the reservation system. Instead, this simply involves the retrieval of content hosted on our Web server. The only "logic" needed is to reference the appropriate information when a request is received.

We already defined the request as the hotel ID, so we have a unique identifier to work from. The next design question is how to store and retrieve this data. To refresh your memory, the content potentially consists of the following:

- Picture of hotel

- Picture of lobby or meeting rooms

- Picture of pool or workout facilities

- Picture of Room A

- Picture of Room B

- Paragraph (50 to 100 words) describing hotel

Probably some of this information is already available for a Web site, but assume for this exercise that this is brand new content not referenced anywhere else. Remember that we want to expose this generically, since other systems and processes could utilize it. To accommodate this type of scenario, I suggest that you store the image files in a file structure rather than as binaries in a database. Furthermore, you should reference the image data in the payload instead of embedding it. This way data can be retrieved by the end user directly and does not have to be sent from us to the consumer and then on the user.

To support this approach, we will store the images on a Web server in a defined file structure and then store the path to these images in a database along with the paragraph of text associated with the appropriate hotel IDs. Although this content can be stored on our Web services system, it is best to post it on an existing content-based Web server so that we don't have to extend the access to our Web services box to our consumers' users.

Our logic then has to take the hotel ID and perform a lookup in the database, build the XML payload from the retrieved data, and return it. We can put this into the same object and call the method wsFetchHotelContent, shown here:

```
Public Function wsFetchHotelContent(ByVal Hotel_ID As Integer) As String
```

Now it is time to turn our attention to the reservation request itself. There is a single call exposed in the existing system that will handle this functionality. Let's take a look at it in its entirety, shown in Listing 7-1.

Listing 7-1. Reservation system's makeReservation *method*

```
Public Function makeReservation( _
    ByVal intHotelID As Integer, _
    ByVal intRoomType As Integer, _
    ByVal dtmCheck_In As Date, _
    ByVal dtmCheck_Out As Date, _
    ByVal intAdults As Integer, _
    ByVal intChildren As Integer, _
    ByVal strFName As String, _
    ByVal strMInitial As String, _
    ByVal strLName As String, _
    ByVal strHAddress1 As String, _
    ByVal strHAddress2 As String, _
    ByVal strHCity As String, _
```

```
        ByVal strHState As String, _
        ByVal intHZip As Integer, _
        ByVal strHPhone As String, _
        ByVal intCCNo As String, _
        ByVal strCCIssuer As String, _
        ByVal intCCExpMonth As Integer, _
        ByVal intCCExpYear As Integer, _
        ByVal strBAddress1 As String, _
        ByVal strBAddress2 As String, _
        ByVal strBCity As String, _
        ByVal strBState As String, _
        ByVal intBZip As Integer, _
        ByVal strCoupon As String) As Long
```

> **CAUTION**   *This function code is not valid "as is" in VB 6.0 because there is a 24-count limit on the number of line continuations it will support. You would just need to combine a few of the parameters onto a single line.*

This call returns an integer value that represents the confirmation number for the reservation, if made. If for any reason the reservation is not made, a 0 is returned. The question that obviously presents itself in that case is how to handle the returned 0. The answer depends on which service model we are dealing with. Because of that dependency, we will leave this issue to our interface design.

Because this only has a single value returned and the parameters are all simple data types, we do not need to create a custom wrapper. We just call this functionality directly from our listener.

That of course brings us to the Web services listener. If you remember from Chapter 2, this is the component responsible for receiving the request and routing it appropriately. This is considered part of our interface layer, so let's proceed to that tier.

Interface Layer

The purpose of our interface layer is to define the Web services interface, handle requests from consumers, access the appropriate business logic, and return a response. To receive and handle the requests, this layer is also responsible for enforcing our interface. This layer almost acts as a gatekeeper to our service to ensure that only valid requests are passed along. The interface defines the rules for making a request of our Web services, and this layer is the enforcer.

We have already defined our business logic and covered at a high level how we are going to handle each request. Before really designing those processes any further, we need to define our interfaces. These should match up fairly closely to the calls of the business objects we have defined. If we designed our interfaces prior to designing our business objects, we will probably have to revisit them. This might be unavoidable, but you have the best chance of only going through this process once if you have your business objects designed.

When you think about designing your interface layer, you need to think in terms of designing schemas. If you are exposing your processes as XML, a schema will always be a necessary component of your interface. However, like in traditional object development, before designing the interface, you need to identify the building blocks that make it up. You may be used to inheriting objects to create new objects, or wrapping existing components with new components, but here you need to think of schemas made up of other schemas.

The unique perspective of Web services is that our interface doubles as a data definition. The interface we define is essentially a piece of data that can extend far beyond the existing interface. To maximize our reuse, we then need to think about what data, or subsets of data, may need to go to different destinations in that XML format.

You can relate this same concept to taking lunch orders from coworkers for a local fast food restaurant. Efficient schemas are like the numbered meals that come prepackaged with a sandwich, side item, and drink. Taking orders from 10 people could be as easy as the following:

- Three number 1s with cola

- Two number 1s with diet cola

- One number 3 with cola

- Two number 3s with lemon-lime soda

- Two number 5s with cola

If all the meals of each type are packaged together, determining whose item is whose is very easy. Without this element of packaged meals, the task of ordering lunch is much harder. It could easily turn into this organizational mess:

- Five hamburgers

- Three cheeseburgers

- Two chicken sandwiches

- Four large fries

- Three medium fries

- Three small fries

- Six colas

- Two diet colas

- Two lemon-lime sodas

The distribution of the correct orders is then made worse if everything is put in bags without any order. This is the kind of situation we will be in if we simply identify all the data necessary for our interface and make each element a child of the root. It will be harder to verify that we have all the data captured, harder to read, and more difficult to distribute portions of the data.

So before we jump into the schema designs themselves, let's try to map out the schemas we need to define. If we start out with a map of our schemas, it will help us to look ahead and try to anticipate some of the issues we might encounter and also identify opportunities for reuse. This will also ultimately make it easier for our applications to work with the data.

One Interface or Two?

The first question we need to answer in our interface design is whether to use one interface or two in defining the two "views" of our Web service. The issue is one of redundancy versus encumbrance.

Even though our payload model has been defined to support one set of logic for both services, there are still two Web services that could be exposed by either one or two interfaces. Recall that we also made the decision to utilize two different addresses for our two services. That already provides us with a convenient logical distinction between the two service types. Utilizing two different physical schemas to represent their interfaces takes this separation one step further.

As we saw in our analysis, the embedded model contains three interactions, while the isolated model contains five. Three of the five interactions in the isolated model are redundant with the three embedded interactions. We need to provide some additional content to those three through our XSL templates, but fundamentally they are responding with the same data. If these templates are applied to the payload before responding, the two interactions will be very different. However, we are adding an external reference to an XSL template that can be used to format the data on the consumer's side.

If we take this approach, we can theoretically reuse the three embedded interactions directly for our isolated model. Then we can add the two isolated interactions to the interface to develop a single schema for both service types. We just need to be aware that we need an optional element available in our interface (in the service variables element) to define an XSL template to meet the isolated model's needs. A good place for this is in our service variables!

Service Variables

This application is slightly more complicated than the norm, since we have two interface layers we are actually designing: embedded and isolated. The design of these interfaces picks right up where our model definition left off.

The one constant in both interfaces will be the service variables section. It will be treated as a header for all request and response payloads. This is where our service variables are defined, and both the embedded and isolated models will contain this information.

The service variables consist of information on the current session and state. Additionally, we now add an optional reference to an XSL template that can be used to format our responses for our isolated model. The XSD defining the entire service variables element is shown in Listing 7-2.

Listing 7-2. Service variables schema

```
<xsd:schema xmlns:xsd="http://www.w3.org/2001/XMLSchema">
    <xsd:element name="serviceVariables">
        <xsd:complexType>
            <xsd:sequence>
                <xsd:element name="sessionID" type="xsd:int"/>
                <xsd:element name="stage" type="xsd:short" minOccurs="1"
                    maxOccurs="1"/>
                <xsd:element name="stylesheet" type="xsd:anyURI"
                    minOccurs="0"/>
            </xsd:sequence>
        </xsd:complexType>
    </xsd:element>
</xsd:schema>
```

We could potentially find the stage from a lookup of the sessionID, but keeping the stage separate does two things for us. First, it allows the service to recover gracefully if for any reason the session expires or is not found. Second, it allows us to route the request more efficiently without doing a lookup on the session. This assumes a certain amount of trust with the consumer, but that is acceptable for this scenario, since we are establishing a formal partnership anyway.

Interface Document

I need to point out here that the `stage` element is also redundant for another reason. Each interaction has a request and a response that contains various elements that make up its payload. Rather than define these payloads generically and force all data into a single structure, each interaction has its own document defined. The service provider can simply interpret the payload to determine what stage the consumer is requesting. However, the performance improves greatly if a stage value can be provided and maintained, since checking the existence of elements can be time consuming. If the session variables are maintained on a consistent level (relative to the root document), that value can easily be retrieved, and the entire payload can be processed by the appropriate logic. Otherwise, the logic has to take on a "pecking order" routine of searching for the appropriate element for stage 1, the appropriate element for stage 2, and so on until a match is found. This is very inefficient and burns valuable cycles in turning around a response to the consumer.

For this reason, all interactions also have the same document element (or root node). This means that the service variables are always in the exact same path. For this service, `reservationWS` will be our root node. That makes the path for the stage element `reservationWS/serviceVariables/stage`.

Without this standard root node defined, we can end up with multiple paths to our service variables, which essentially require the same "pecking order" routine we have without the `stage` element.

At this point we should design our interface schema document map. This is essentially our roadmap as we design the schemas for the Web services interface. (See Figure 7-9.) You can think of this as a template for structuring the various documents that will make up our interface.

We just determined that we will have one root document for both services' interface. However, we really have two different interfaces, one for embedded and another for isolated. This is a logical map, so it applies to both. Once we design the interfaces, we will develop a physical map for each.

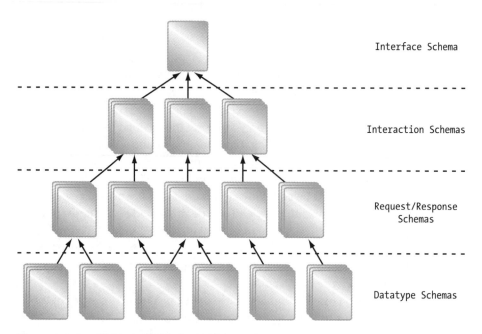

Figure 7-9. Logical interface schema hierarchy map

Beneath the interface schema, we have the interaction schemas. These are the different calls in the interface that the consumer can make. We already identified a total of five interactions that our service will support for both interfaces. These schemas then reference the payloads for the specific requests and responses, which then reference data type schemas that define our reusable elements.

With the global ground rules for our interfaces defined, let's proceed to design the specific interfaces for our embedded and isolated models.

Embedded Service Interactions

At this point, we do not want to identify every single schema we will build, but rather the high-level schemas that will define our interactions with the consumer and other objects. This level of analysis will help us to recognize what data is getting transferred around so that you can determine during design where potential redundancies will lie. If you recall, the embedded interface has three interactions with the consumer: availability request, hotel detail view, and reservation request.

Schema Maps

For the availability request, we need to define a schema for the request from the consumer. (See Figure 7-10.) Once we receive that, we need to make a request of our wsFetchAvailability component. This will be a standard COM method call, and we will pass the data through parameters. It is, however, going to be returning data in an XML string, so we need to define the schema for that. We are then going to add the session data to that document, so let's call that a third schema.

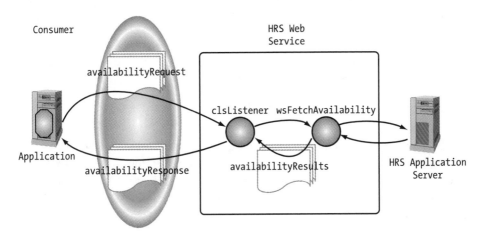

Figure 7-10. Availability request schema map

The detail view request requires an initial schema. (See Figure 7-11.) Again, we will break the data down and call a component. It will provide an XML string back, to which we will again want to add the session data. As with the availability request, we are looking at three main schemas for our interactions.

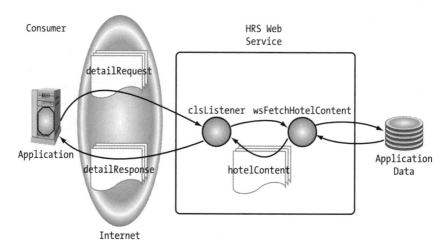

Figure 7-11. Hotel detail view schema map

The reservation process is slightly different than the others, since we are calling a component of the reservation system directly. It does not pass XML back, so we do not need a schema for its response. This leaves us with one schema for the request coming in and another for the response we are sending back. (See Figure 7-12.)

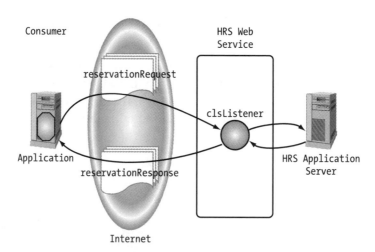

Figure 7-12. Reservation request schema map

With these schemas identified, we can confidently move on and proceed to design the specific schemas for our interface.

Schema Designs

We now know at a high level what steps need to be carried out for each request and pretty much how we are going to accomplish them. The next step is to build out the schemas for each step so that we can validate both the consumer requests coming in and the data we are sending out.

Availability Request

The availability request will consist of the data elements we listed previously in our requirements. At this point, all we need to do is structure the data appropriately and identify which elements are required and which are optional. We also need to determine if there are any data elements that need to be defined through a subschema, which would simply be their own schema.

We should first look over our request data and define any appropriate categories. As we look through the list, defined by the requirements, the groups that jump out are preferences and amenities. Everything else is fairly simple and specific to the availability request process.

The next decision is whether these groups should be defined externally or simply in our schema. The preferences data includes price, bed size, and smoking. As preferences, we would probably get little reuse by defining them externally, since that is specific to looking for a matching room. However, we may need to ask ourselves if these preferences could ever be utilized as properties for other functions. Because this is such a narrow group of data that is neither generic nor complete, we will just define preferences as an internal entity.

The amenities group is a little different. These are all aspects of hotels that might have value in a few different ways. This includes a list of attributes such as concierge, room service, and workout facilities. In this context, we want to know which amenities the user would like to find in matching hotels. This definition of this information could also easily be used to describe a particular hotel. It ends up later that we will need this functionality ourselves, so let's go ahead and define the amenities entity on its own, as shown in Listing 7-3.

Listing 7-3. Amenity element schema

```
<xsd:schema xmlns:xsd="http://www.w3.org/2001/XMLSchema">
    <xsd:simpleType name="amenity">
        <xsd:restriction base="xsd:string">
            <xsd:enumeration value="Concierge"/>
            <xsd:enumeration value="Workout Facilities"/>
            <xsd:enumeration value="Pool"/>
            <xsd:enumeration value="Restaurant"/>
            <xsd:enumeration value="24-hour Room Service"/>
```

```
                    <xsd:enumeration value="High Speed Internet Access"/>
            </xsd:restriction>
        </xsd:simpleType>
</xsd:schema>
```

This is a relatively simple schema, but reusing it will make our applications more efficient as well as make any updating of these properties very simple. Keep in mind during implementation that this can be a growing list so our applications do not break because of new values.

With our only external dependency defined, we can turn our attention to the availability request schema. The one requirement that is a little tricky here is the option of entering a city and state or landmark for the search location. This means that someone should be able to enter either "St. Louis, MO" or "The Arch" and successfully run an availability search. These either/or cases are always among the trickier ones to define.

Defining the "or" scenario is easiest through a choice element. The fact that you are choosing between using a two-element option and a single-element option just adds an extra twist to it. To get around this, I will define city and state as a single element and simply make the city and state elements children of it. This makes the choice between the landmark and citystate nodes. Of course, this choice requires an element to define it. That puts our city and state data deeper in our "tree," but it allows us to enforce the rule through our schema. We might be adding a little overhead in our schema, but the dividends will be worth it when we are working with the data.

So let's go ahead and define all of our availability criteria. These include all of the base elements that make up the availability request and allow for reuse across other schemas, as shown in Listing 7-4.

Listing 7-4. Availability criteria schema

```
<xsd:schema xmlns:xsd="http://www.w3.org/2001/XMLSchema">
    <xsd:include schemaLocation="http://www.architectingwebservices.com/
        interfaces/hrsws/amenities.xsd"/>
    <xsd:include schemaLocation="http://www.architectingwebservices.com/
        interfaces/hrsws/USAddress.xsd"/>
    <xsd:element name="locale">
        <xsd:complexType>
            <xsd:choice>
                <xsd:element ref="cityState"/>
                <xsd:element ref="landmark"/>
            </xsd:choice>
        </xsd:complexType>
    </xsd:element>
    <xsd:element name="bedSize">
        <xsd:simpleType>
```

```xml
                <xsd:restriction base="xsd:string">
                     <xsd:enumeration value="King"/>
                     <xsd:enumeration value="Queen"/>
                     <xsd:enumeration value="Double"/>
                </xsd:restriction>
           </xsd:simpleType>
</xsd:element>
<xsd:element name="cityState">
      <xsd:complexType>
            <xsd:sequence>
                  <xsd:element name="city" type="city"/>
                  <xsd:element name="state" type="state"/>
            </xsd:sequence>
      </xsd:complexType>
</xsd:element>
<xsd:element name="approxPrice" type="xsd:decimal"/>

<xsd:element name="couponCode">
      <xsd:simpleType>
            <xsd:restriction base="xsd:string">
                  <xsd:maxLength value="10"/>
            </xsd:restriction>
      </xsd:simpleType>
</xsd:element>
<xsd:element name="preferences">
      <xsd:complexType>
            <xsd:sequence>
                  <xsd:element ref="bedSize" minOccurs="0"/>
                  <xsd:element name="smoking" type="xsd:boolean" minOccurs="0"/>
                  <xsd:element name="amenity" type="amenity" minOccurs="0"
                     maxOccurs="unbounded"/>
            </xsd:sequence>
      </xsd:complexType>
</xsd:element>
<xsd:element name="landmark">
      <xsd:simpleType>
            <xsd:restriction base="xsd:string">
                  <xsd:maxLength value="50"/>
            </xsd:restriction>
      </xsd:simpleType>
</xsd:element>
<xsd:element name="numberAdults">
      <xsd:simpleType>
            <xsd:restriction base="xsd:short">
```

```
                    <xsd:minInclusive value="1"/>
                    <xsd:maxInclusive value="4"/>
                </xsd:restriction>
            </xsd:simpleType>
        </xsd:element>
        <xsd:element name="numberChildren">
            <xsd:simpleType>
                <xsd:restriction base="xsd:short">
                    <xsd:minInclusive value="0"/>
                    <xsd:maxInclusive value="4"/>
                </xsd:restriction>
            </xsd:simpleType>
        </xsd:element>
</xsd:schema>
```

You might have noticed that I am referencing the USAddress schema, which
we have not yet discussed. What it defines is likely self-evident, but this is
a schema that we will cover later in our reservation request. (See Listing 7-14.)
This is looking a little ahead, but in this instance, we are referencing a state element that has an enumeration defined for every state by abbreviation. Nothing
exciting, but definitely something we don't want to define multiple times!

As I mentioned earlier, we will reference our amenity schema and group the
preference data into its own element for readability. Since the amenities are part
of the user's preferences, we will define them as part of that group, as shown in
Listing 7-5.

Listing 7-5. Availability request schema

```
<xsd:schema xmlns:xsd="http://www.w3.org/2001/XMLSchema">
    <xsd:include schemaLocation="http://www.architectingwebservices.com/
        interfaces/hrsws/availabilityCriteria.xsd"/>
    <xsd:element name="availabilityRequest">
        <xsd:complexType>
            <xsd:sequence>
                <xsd:element name="checkInDate" type="xsd:date"/>
                <xsd:element name="checkOutDate" type="xsd:date"/>
                <xsd:element ref="numberAdults"/>
                <xsd:element ref="numberChildren"/>
                <xsd:element ref="locale" maxOccurs="2"/>
                <xsd:element ref="couponCode" minOccurs="0"/>
                <xsd:element ref="approxPrice"/>
                <xsd:element ref="preferences" minOccurs="0"/>
            </xsd:sequence>
```

```
            </xsd:complexType>
        </xsd:element>
</xsd:schema>
```

We identified earlier that we need the service variables present, even in an initial request. There are a couple different ways to handle this. One is to add the service variables to this schema. We can add them to the `availabilityRequest` sequence and simply make them optional. The other option is to add them to the root document defining our interface. We will take this second approach, which externalizes the handling of the service variables from this level of definition. This makes for a much cleaner design that is easier to modify in the future in case we decide to add more information to our header.

The availability request payload "as is" exposes the functionality as a Web service. We are then adding session data for the sake of managing the entire response. Since the existing interface definition has value through other services, or perhaps even internally, I would hate to modify it directly. Instead, let's take the other approach and define a new schema strictly for this Web service we are creating.

This new schema basically consists of wrapping this data with the root node and including the necessary header data. We do need to think of a new root node name. We don't want to reuse the `availabilityRequest` node here because that is likely to cause confusion between the two schemas. Since it is a Web service, let's have some reference to that in the name, like a prefix of "ws." In other examples we used the node `hotelAvailability`, so take that and add our prefix.

Notice that you are keeping the core availability request and service variable definitions external to this definition. You are simply including their independent schemas to efficiently reuse those definitions without duplication. This is also only the request at this point. We will address the response shortly.

When this request comes in from a consumer, the first thing we need to do is determine if a session already exists. If it does not, we need to create one. This session is defined in our data source and consists of the consumer, the time, the request type, and some of the main information from any availability requests. We will design this more completely when we get to our data layer.

Once this is done, we will want to submit this information to our `wsFetchAvailability` business object. This should return an XML document containing the matching data. We should now define the schema for that matching hotel data, as shown in Listing 7-6.

Listing 7-6. Availability results schema

```
<xsd:schema xmlns:xsd="http://www.w3.org/2001/XMLSchema">
    <xsd:include schemaLocation="http://www.architectingwebservices.com/
        interfaces/hrsws/amenities.xsd"/>
    <xsd:include schemaLocation="http://www.architectingwebservices.com/
```

```
                              interfaces/hrsws/USAddress.xsd"/>
              <xsd:element name="availabilityResults">
                   <xsd:complexType>
                        <xsd:sequence>
                             <xsd:element ref="hotel" maxOccurs="unbounded"/>
                        </xsd:sequence>
                   </xsd:complexType>
              </xsd:element>
              <xsd:element name="hotel">
                   <xsd:complexType>
                        <xsd:sequence>
                             <xsd:element name="hotelName" type="xsd:string"/>
                             <xsd:element name="hotelID" type="xsd:integer"/>
                             <xsd:element name="proximity" type="proximity"/>
                             <xsd:element name="roomType" type="roomType"/>
                             <xsd:element name="roomRate" type="xsd:decimal"/>
                             <xsd:element name="hotelAddress" type="USAddress"/>
                             <xsd:element name="hotelPhone" type="xsd:string"/>
                             <xsd:element name="roomAmenity" type="amenity" minOccurs="0"
                                maxOccurs="unbounded"/>
                        </xsd:sequence>
                   </xsd:complexType>
              </xsd:element>
              <xsd:complexType name="proximity">
                   <xsd:simpleContent>
                        <xsd:extension base="xsd:integer">
                             <xsd:attribute name="measurement" type="xsd:string"
                                use="required"/>
                        </xsd:extension>
                   </xsd:simpleContent>
              </xsd:complexType>
              <xsd:simpleType name="roomType">
                   <xsd:restriction base="xsd:string">
                        <xsd:enumeration value="Value"/>
                        <xsd:enumeration value="Business"/>
                        <xsd:enumeration value="Suite"/>
                        <xsd:enumeration value="Premiere"/>
                   </xsd:restriction>
              </xsd:simpleType>
         </xsd:schema>
```

We now have the raw matching hotel data. However, we still need to package it as an appropriate response to the consumer. We need to add our date stamp for when the request was made. We are also going to add a copy of the request that was made of us for reference by the consumer and/or user. We could modify the availabilityResults schema to incorporate these changes, but this would compromise the data we need to validate from that object. Instead, we will create a new root node for the response payload. You'll create an availabilityResponse node, as shown in Listing 7-7.

Listing 7-7. Availability Response Schema

```
<xsd:schema xmlns:xsd="http://www.w3.org/2001/XMLSchema">
    <xsd:include schemaLocation="http://www.architectingwebservices.com/
     interfaces/hrsws/availabilityRequest.xsd"/>
    <xsd:include schemaLocation="http://www.architectingwebservices.com/
      interfaces/hrsws/availabilityResults.xsd"/>
    <xsd:element name="availabilityResponse">
        <xsd:complexType>
            <xsd:sequence>
                <xsd:element name="searchDate" type="xsd:date"/>
                <xsd:element ref="availabilityRequest"/>
                <xsd:element ref="availabilityResults" minOccurs="0"
                  maxOccurs="unbounded"/>
            </xsd:sequence>
        </xsd:complexType>
    </xsd:element>
</xsd:schema>
```

The condition we have not addressed yet is how to handle empty results from the reservation system. Should we develop a completely different schema for that payload? In this case, that really is not necessary. The main objective in such a situation is to communicate to the consumer that no matches were found. To accomplish this for this service, I would simply modify the existing schema to allow for no hotel nodes, as shown here:

```
<xsd:element ref="hotel" minOccurs="0" maxOccurs="unbounded"/>
```

I would then utilize this option when the search comes back empty and leave the rest of the nodes the same. (See Listing 7-8.) This still provides the same information to the consumer in the rest of the payload and allows consumers to easily run a check to see if any matches were found.

Listing 7-8. Sample null result payload for an availability request

```
<hotelAvailabilityResponse xmlns:xsi=
  "http://www.w3.org/2001/XMLSchema-instance"
  xsi:noNamespaceSchemaLocation="http://www.architectingwebservices.com/
  interfaces/hrsws/availabilityResponse.xsd">
    <searchDate>2001-07-16</searchDate>
    <availabilityRequest>
        <checkInDate>2001-08-01</checkInDate>
        <checkOutDate>2001-08-03</checkOutDate>
        <numberAdults>1</numberAdults>
        <numberChildren>0</numberChildren>
        <locale>
            <cityState>
                <city>Memphis</city>
                <state>TN</state>
            </cityState>
        </locale>
        <approxPrice>50</approxPrice>
    </availabilityRequest>
</hotelAvailabilityResponse>
```

We now have one schema defined for the request and the response data payloads. However, we need to combine these two schemas into a single interaction schema. After all, when you look up the interface on an object or component, you don't have to go to different places to find the call and the response details! Our objective should be to combine these two schemas into one schema that can be referred to for the entire interaction.

The easiest approach is to add one more level of schema and simply reference each of those. I will use a simple choice element to choose between our two definitions for the response and the request and will utilize a parent node called availabilityInteraction, as shown in Listing 7-9.

Listing 7-9. Integrated hotel availability interaction schema

```
<xsd:schema xmlns:xsd="http://www.w3.org/2001/XMLSchema">
    <xsd:include schemaLocation="http://www.architectingwebservices.com/
      interfaces/hrsws/availabilityResponse.xsd"/>
    <xsd:element name="availabilityInteraction">
        <xsd:complexType>
            <xsd:choice>
                <xsd:element name="availabilityRequest"/>
                <xsd:element name="availabilityResponse"/>
            </xsd:choice>
        </xsd:complexType>
    </xsd:element>
</xsd:schema>
```

Notice that even though I am referencing both availabilityRequest and availabilityResponse elements, I have only included a reference to the availabilityResponse schema. This is because availabilityResponse schema references the availabilityRequest, since it can include an image of the request that generated the results. Including the availabilityRequest schema directly in this schema would generate an error, since you would effectively have two definitions for a single element. You can get around this by importing the schema and associating a namespace, but there really is no need. Adding multiple instances of the same schema is not only redundant but also more demanding of the applications that work with the data. The downside is that if we de-reference the request in the response, we have to modify this schema to reference it directly. Since interface changes can be such a dangerous issue, this should be avoided whenever possible.

> **TIP** *As we discussed in Chapter 6, enhancements or changes to Web services should be approached with caution. If a Web services interface needs to be changed after being deployed, the most responsible, efficient solution is to create a new interface, reusing as many structure schemas as possible from the old interface. The old interface could then be maintained at least until all of its consumers have been transitioned over.*

We can take this one step further and say that we need to combine all interactions into a single document to define the interface for the Web service. This is where the reservationWS document node comes into play. We obviously do not have the other interactions defined, but we can at least reference this interaction and see how we will add the service variables, as shown in Listing 7-10.

Listing 7-10. The reservationWS *interface schema*

```
<xsd:schema xmlns:xsd="http://www.w3.org/2001/XMLSchema">
    <xsd:include schemaLocation="http://www.architectingwebservices.com/
        interfaces/hrsws/serviceVariables.xsd"/>
    <xsd:include schemaLocation="http://www.architectingwebservices.com/
        interfaces/hrsws/availabilityInteraction.xsd"/>
    <xsd:element name="reservationWS">
        <xsd:complexType>
            <xsd:sequence>
                <xsd:element ref="serviceVariables"/>
                <xsd:element ref="payload" minOccurs="0"/>
            </xsd:sequence>
        </xsd:complexType>
    </xsd:element>
    <xsd:element name="payload">
```

```
            <xsd:complexType>
                <xsd:choice>
                    <xsd:element ref="availabilityInteraction"/>
                </xsd:choice>
            </xsd:complexType>
        </xsd:element>
</xsd:schema>
```

Hotel Detail View

Now that we have the availability interface defined, we need to define the interface for our detailed view. This is a fairly simple process, but does not have an existing object to work from. We created our own method to provide this functionality, so we will draw mostly from it.

The request itself only consists of the hotel ID, aside from the service variables. Since the data only consists of the one variable, it is not necessary to define it separately and reference it from the interaction schema. Instead we will define it directly in our interaction schema. If we decide to make it more robust, we can always pull it out into its own schema in the future. For now, let's define the request schema internally.

After receiving the detail request, call the `wsFetchHotelContent` method and receive the data it retrieved from our data source. We covered the information earlier, so let's look at the schema for this data, as shown in Listing 7-11.

Listing 7-11. Hotel detail response schema

```
<xsd:schema xmlns:xsd="http://www.w3.org/2001/XMLSchema">
    <xsd:element name="hotelContent">
        <xsd:complexType>
            <xsd:sequence>
                <xsd:element name="mainPicture" type="xsd:anyURI"/>
                <xsd:element name="facilitiesPicture" type="xsd:anyURI"
                  minOccurs="2" maxOccurs="2"/>
                <xsd:element name="roomPicture" type="xsd:anyURI"
                  minOccurs="2" maxOccurs="2"/>
                <xsd:element name="hotelDescription" type="xsd:string"/>
            </xsd:sequence>
        </xsd:complexType>
    </xsd:element>
</xsd:schema>
```

I have made a few modifications here, so we should briefly walk through this schema. Our requirements stated that you needed to provide five pictures and a description of the hotel itself. The main picture is set aside on its own, but I have grouped the other four into two pairs: facilitiesPicture and roomPicture. Since the content of the pictures was so loosely defined, I decided to group them accordingly with a common name to give a little more meaning to them. That way if the picture is of a pool or a meeting room, it doesn't really matter because they are both facilities. This also allows for future growth, since we can easily add more pictures to either of these groups in the schema.

Since we want to avoid separate schemas for each request and response, let's build on the request schema we already have defined. By taking roughly the same approach we did for the availability interaction, the schema defining this interaction takes the form shown in Listing 7-12.

Listing 7-12. Detail interaction schema

```
<xsd:schema xmlns:xsd="http://www.w3.org/2001/XMLSchema">
    <xsd:include schemaLocation="http://www.architectingwebservices.com/
      interfaces/hrsws/hotelContent.xsd"/>
    <xsd:element name="detailInteraction">
        <xsd:complexType>
            <xsd:choice>
                <xsd:element name="hotelID" type="xsd:short"/>
                <xsd:element ref="hotelContent"/>
            </xsd:choice>
        </xsd:complexType>
    </xsd:element>
</xsd:schema>
```

Next, we need to add this interaction to our interface schema. This essentially involves adding a reference to the interaction schema and adding the detailInteraction element as an option in our payload, as shown in Listing 7-13.

Listing 7-13. The reservationWS *interface with availability interaction*

```
<xsd:schema xmlns:xsd="http://www.w3.org/2001/XMLSchema">
    <xsd:include schemaLocation="http://www.architectingwebservices.com/
      interfaces/hrsws/serviceVariables.xsd"/>
    <xsd:include schemaLocation="http://www.architectingwebservices.com/
      interfaces/hrsws/availabilityInteraction.xsd"/>
    <xsd:include schemaLocation="http://www.architectingwebservices.com/
      interfaces/hrsws/detailInteraction.xsd"/>
    <xsd:element name="reservationWS">
        <xsd:complexType>
            <xsd:sequence>
                <xsd:element ref="serviceVariables"/>
                <xsd:element ref="payload" minOccurs="0"/>
            </xsd:sequence>
        </xsd:complexType>
```

```
        </xsd:element>
        <xsd:element name="payload">
            <xsd:complexType>
                <xsd:choice>
                    <xsd:element ref="availabilityInteraction"/>
                    <xsd:element ref="detailInteraction"/>
                </xsd:choice>
            </xsd:complexType>
        </xsd:element>
</xsd:schema>
```

Reservation Request

The next interaction to define is the reservation request. This interface closely matches the makeReservation object from the existing system, with only a few possible exceptions. This service is an excellent example of a heavy request and light response. We are going to perform a process for the consumer and simply respond with a confirmation ID to show that the reservation was made.

The main design issue for this interface is determining how to structure the data. We are receiving a lot of data on the user, and we can define it all in a "flat," single-layer structure, or we can provide some hierarchy. This especially makes sense if the data has a logical grouping. In this case, we are dealing with personal information in the form of addresses, names, and criteria. Since we are potentially dealing with two different addresses that are structured the same, it makes sense to reuse the same definition. We should also make the schema generic enough to be reused for other documents (as we did earlier for our availability criteria). I have chosen to define just U.S. addresses to keep from needlessly overcomplicating the example in Listing 7-14.

Listing 7-14. U.S. address data type schema
```
<xsd:schema xmlns:xsd="http://www.w3.org/2001/XMLSchema">
    <xsd:complexType name="USAddress">
        <xsd:sequence>
            <xsd:element name="address" type="address" maxOccurs="3"/>
            <xsd:element name="city" type="city"/>
            <xsd:element name="state" type="state"/>
            <xsd:element name="zipCode" type="xsd:string"/>
        </xsd:sequence>
    </xsd:complexType>
    <xsd:simpleType name="city">
        <xsd:restriction base="xsd:string">
            <xsd:maxLength value="30"/>
        </xsd:restriction>
```

```
        </xsd:simpleType>
        <xsd:simpleType name="address">
            <xsd:restriction base="xsd:string">
                <xsd:maxLength value="30"/>
            </xsd:restriction>
        </xsd:simpleType>
        <xsd:simpleType name="state">
            <xsd:restriction base="xsd:string">
                <xsd:enumeration value="AL"/>
                ...<!—I will spare listing all 59 US states and properties here —>
                <xsd:enumeration value="WY"/>
            </xsd:restriction>
        </xsd:simpleType>
</xsd:schema>
```

We will save this separately as an independent schema and reference it when necessary. Our request payload will potentially reference this twice for both the home address and billing address. The other obvious opportunity we have for creating a subschema is the credit card data. We have four pieces of data that have little value independently and can potentially be used elsewhere. Let's go ahead and define it separately in Listing 7-15.

Listing 7-15. Credit card data type schema

```
<xsd:schema xmlns:xsd="http://www.w3.org/2001/XMLSchema">
    <xsd:element name="ccData">
        <xsd:complexType>
            <xsd:all>
                <xsd:element name="number" type="ccNumber"/>
                <xsd:element name="issuer" type="ccBanks"/>
                <xsd:element name="expirationDate" type="xsd:date"/>
                <xsd:element name="nameOfOwner" type="xsd:string"/>
            </xsd:all>
        </xsd:complexType>
    </xsd:element>
    <xsd:simpleType name="ccNumber">
        <xsd:restriction type="xsd:string">
            <xsd:length value="16"/>
        </xsd:restriction>
    </xsd:simpleType>
    <xsd:simpleType name="ccBanks">
        <xsd:restriction base="xsd:string">
            <xsd:enumeration value="Visa"/>
            <xsd:enumeration value="Mastercard"/>
            <xsd:enumeration value="American Express"/>
```

```
                          <xsd:enumeration value="Discover"/>
                  </xsd:restriction>
          </xsd:simpleType>
</xsd:schema>
```

The data for the credit card has to be fairly open to accommodate all the different types. We can, however, restrict the issuer to those that we accept and define the valid credit card number length. By separating this, we can reuse it for other schemas that require credit card data, which we can likely expect to have.

With those two entities defined, we can define the schema for the entire payload. What we are left with are the personal information of the user and hotel data specifying the hotel and room type. Since there is a very clean separation between these two types of data, I'm going to separate them into separate nodes. This doesn't necessarily buy us reuse, but does make your code a little more readable, as you can see in Listing 7-16.

Listing 7-16. Reservation request schema

```
<xsd:schema xmlns:xsd="http://www.w3.org/2001/XMLSchema">
    <xsd:include schemaLocation="http://www.architectingwebservices.com/
      interfaces/hrsws/USAddress.xsd"/>
    <xsd:include schemaLocation="http://www.architectingwebservices.com/
      interfaces/hrsws/ccData.xsd"/>
    <xsd:element name="reservationRequest">
        <xsd:complexType>
            <xsd:all>
                    <xsd:element ref="hotelData"/>
                    <xsd:element ref="personalData"/>
            </xsd:all>
        </xsd:complexType>
    </xsd:element>
    <xsd:element name="hotelData">
        <xsd:complexType>
            <xsd:sequence>
                    <xsd:element name="hotelID" type="xsd:short"/>
                    <xsd:element name="roomType" type="xsd:string"/>
            </xsd:sequence>
        </xsd:complexType>
    </xsd:element>
    <xsd:element name="personalData">
        <xsd:complexType>
            <xsd:sequence>
                    <xsd:element name="homeAddress" type="USAddress"/>
                    <xsd:element name="firstName" type="xsd:string"/>
                    <xsd:element name="lastName" type="xsd:string"/>
```

```
                    <xsd:element name="homePhone" type="xsd:string"/>
                    <xsd:element name="billAddress" type="USAddress"
                      minOccurs="0"/>
                    <xsd:element ref="ccData"/>
                </xsd:sequence>
            </xsd:complexType>
        </xsd:element>
</xsd:schema>
```

Notice how I am referencing the USAddress element from our previous schema, but naming it something pertinent to its usage in this schema. Also, the billing address is optional for when it and the home address are the same.

We still have to add the service variables to this payload before it will fit the interface structure we have established for the other two calls of this service. We will wait to do that until we define the response and build our interface schema incorporating both pieces of the interaction.

After receiving this request, we will verify that the session is current. On doing this, we will need to look up data related to the session concerning the original request. Specifically, we will need to retrieve the following information:

- Check-in date

- Check-out date

- Number of adults

- Number of children

- Coupon

Add this information to the data received from the consumer and call the existing makeReservation method utilizing the appropriate parameters. It then responds with either a reservation number or an error number. If it is a reservation number, we simply pass it back to the consumer. If it is an error, we interpret it and send back a meaningful message to the consumer. In these instances, we can send back some of the data we were sent so that information could be verified, as shown in Listing 7-17.

Listing 7-17. Reservation response schema

```
<xsd:schema xmlns:xsd="http://www.w3.org/2001/XMLSchema">
    <xsd:include schemaLocation="http://www.architectingwebservices.com/
      interfaces/hrsws/reservationRequest.xsd"/>
    <xsd:element name="reservationResponse">
        <xsd:complexType>
```

```
            <xsd:sequence>
                <xsd:element ref="reservationRequest" minOccurs="1"
                  maxOccurs="1"/>
                <xsd:element name="confirmationID" type="xsd:integer"/>
                <xsd:element name="error" type="xsd:string" minOccurs="0"/>
            </xsd:sequence>
        </xsd:complexType>
    </xsd:element>
</xsd:schema>
```

As before, we need to now bring this together with the request to define the interaction schema. We will call it `reservationInteraction`. As with the availability interaction schema, only include the response schema, because it references the request schema in it, as shown by Listing 7-18.

Listing 7-18. Reservation interaction schema
```
<xsd:schema xmlns:xsd="http://www.w3.org/2001/XMLSchema">
    <xsd:include schemaLocation="http://www.architectingwebservices.com/
      interfaces/hrsws/reservationResponse.xsd"/>
    <xsd:element name="reservationInteraction">
        <xsd:complexType>
            <xsd:choice>
                <xsd:element name="reservationRequest"/>
                <xsd:element name="reservationResponse"/>
            </xsd:choice>
        </xsd:complexType>
    </xsd:element>
</xsd:schema>
```

Finally, we need to incorporate this interaction into our interface schema. This consists of the same steps we took to incorporate the `detailInteraction` schema, as shown in Listing 7-19.

Listing 7-19. The `reservationWS` *interface schema with reservation interaction*
```
<xsd:schema xmlns:xsd="http://www.w3.org/2001/XMLSchema">
    <xsd:include schemaLocation="http://www.architectingwebservices.com/
      interfaces/hrsws/serviceVariables.xsd"/>
    <xsd:include schemaLocation="http://www.architectingwebservices.com/
      interfaces/hrsws/availabilityInteraction.xsd"/>
    <xsd:include schemaLocation="http://www.architectingwebservices.com/
      interfaces/hrsws/detailInteraction.xsd"/>
    <xsd:include schemaLocation="http://www.architectingwebservices.com/
      interfaces/hrsws/reservationInteraction.xsd"/>
```

```
<xsd:element name="reservationWS">
    <xsd:complexType>
        <xsd:sequence>
            <xsd:element ref="serviceVariables"/>
            <xsd:element ref="payload" minOccurs="0"/>
        </xsd:sequence>
    </xsd:complexType>
</xsd:element>
<xsd:element name="payload">
    <xsd:complexType>
        <xsd:choice>
            <xsd:element ref="availabilityInteraction"/>
            <xsd:element ref="detailInteraction"/>
            <xsd:element ref="reservationInteraction"/>
        </xsd:choice>
    </xsd:complexType>
</xsd:element>
</xsd:schema>
```

As I promised, I have assembled a physical interface schema hierarchy map to help illustrate the relationships between each of our schemas. (See Figure 7-13.) Notice that this falls in line with the earlier logical map we saw in Figure 7-9.

Now that we have designed our interface for the embedded model of our service, it is time to turn our attention to the isolated model.

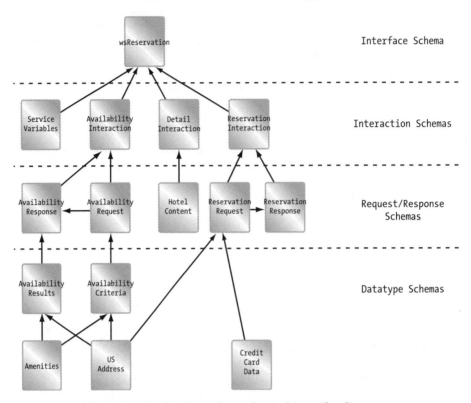

Figure 7-13. Physical embedded interface schema hierarchy diagram

Isolated Service Interactions

The other "flavor" of our Web service is the isolated model. The interface for this model will be much more robust than the embedded model, but it will build on this same interface. The same process will be in place, but we will add an initial request to retrieve the hotel availability form for presentation to the user. Fundamentally, the two existing request payloads will be very similar, if not identical, but the response payloads will contain more presentation-ready data.

As with the embedded model's design, we will base our isolated service on the model we defined earlier in the section about modeling the Web service. It might be obvious to you that the existing logic and functionality still apply to this version of the service so we won't have to generate a lot of new business logic. This works to our advantage during implementation, since we don't have to develop two separate services.

Schema Maps

If you compare the two process models we developed for the embedded and isolated processes (see Figures 7-3 and 7-4), you see that we have a few additional interactions the embedded process does not. Here is the entire list of interactions, with the ones specific to the isolated service denoted by an asterisk:

- Availability form*

- Availability request

- Detail view

- Reservation form*

- Reservation request

The first additional interaction is the request starting the process. Whereas the consumer provides the UI for the hotel availability request in the embedded service, the service provider provides the UI data for the isolated service. The consumer makes this initial request of the service to initiate the process for each new user. The service then responds with the hotel availability form data. We will develop an external XSL template that the consumer can reference to generate a look and feel. This information can then be presented to the user. (See Figure 7-14.) Consumers have the option to forgo our stylesheet for their own, or even apply an additional transformation on top of ours to modify a few elements. I will look at these options in more detail in Chapter 8.

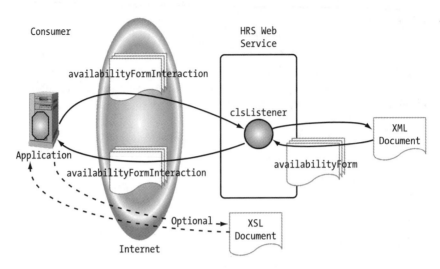

Figure 7-14. Availability form schema map

The next interaction we need to map out is the reservation request interface.
The response to this request will contain a valid input form that collects the
information from the user that the consumer will submit to the service to make
the reservation. Like the previous map, the request is very light, simply asking
for the UI components to provide the form for the end user. (See Figure 7-15.)
Like with the other interactions, we will provide a reference to an external XSL
template that consumers can use at their discretion.

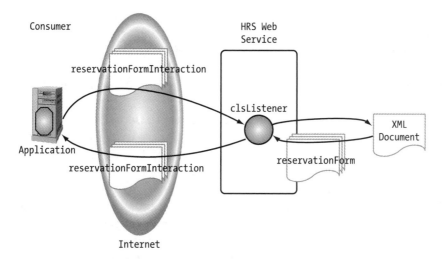

Consumer

reservationFormInteraction

Application

reservationFormInteraction

HRS Web
Service

clsListener

reservationForm

XML
Document

Internet

Figure 7-15. Reservation form schema map

These are the only additional schema maps we need to generate for the isolated service. The other isolated interactions will be exactly the same as the embedded model. (See Figures 7-10, 7-11, and 7-12.) Thus we can proceed on to design the schemas for our interface.

Schema Designs

It is now time to turn our attention back to schema development. We will take what we have just laid out as our roadmap for both steps we are adding to our service and create definition schemas so that we can validate the requests coming in and the responses we are sending out.

Availability Form

The first interface to design is the initial service request. This will consist of a very light request that simply needs to communicate the identity of the consumer and the service the consumer is requesting. The identity will be handled through our authentication process, which we will design when we address the service listener design.

There are several ways to go about declaring the service the consumer is requesting. We can have different URLs for each service, or we can have specific header variables that identify this. When we defined our model earlier, we decided to go ahead and use separate URLs for each of our services, but the same URL for each step of the process. This means that our listeners will automatically know they are requesting the isolated service instead of the embedded model.

This means that your request payload actually becomes nondescript. We can essentially take any request that comes in any unrecognizable form and assume it is an initial request of the service. By unrecognizable, I mean that it does not contain any payload data that has any meaning to us. All consecutive requests will actually contain header data at the very least to communicate the session information.

This might seem like a risky proposition security-wise, but keep in mind that we will use a different mechanism for authentication, so we will be able to determine if this is one of our consumers and not some random visitor. There might be an issue if we were allowing anonymous consumer access to the service, but fortunately we have ruled out that option.

What has to be recognized is that, through this approach, we will be making an ideological decision to support invalid requests, assuming they are meant as the initial service request. This can be dangerous, since we will essentially never generate an error on an invalid request format. For this reason, it is best to still have some method for explicitly requesting even this initial step. This will pay dividends down the road when the consumer is trying to implement your service by providing a more accurate response to a request. If the consumer is requesting a reservation and receives the hotel availability UI, the consumer will have accidentally requested it explicitly, not just provided an invalid request of any type.

So, for our request, let's essentially utilize the header data that provides the session and state data. (See Listing 7-2.) For this initial request, we will require that the state element be set to 0, with the session ID only set if it is an existing session (thus not actually the first request from a user but another hotel availability search).

In terms of our schema hierarchy, we will not need a request defined for this interaction, only a response. Let's go ahead and define that response. Remember that this will be an XML document, but will need to define the UI. The easy option here is to simply provide XML-compliant HTML (or XHTML) as our response. However, this is not going to give us (or the consumer) the most flexibility.

A better option is to provide the data that makes up the interface through an XML data response and create an XSL document that can then structure the document into a form. This approach allows the consumer to utilize our format, but provides the consumer the flexibility to change it when more comfortable with Web services.

In the interface design for our isolated service, we simply need to define the data that makes up the interface. This produces response documents that are very similar to the embedded response, with additional information for validation purposes. Later, in the implementation section, we will concern ourselves with building the XSL document(s) that define the form for the user.

To define the data for our availability form response, we need to refer first to our hotel availability request schema. (See Listing 7-5.) This is the most fundamental definition for the user request, so this is what we must comply with to define a user interface. Through that schema we can define all the elements and their attributes that are pertinent to an HTML interface. (See Table 7-1.)

Table 7-1. Availability Form Elements and Attributes

ELEMENT	DATA TYPE	RANGE/LENGTH	VALUES
checkInDate	date		
checkOutDate	date		
numberAdults	numeric	1–4	
numberChildren	numeric	0–4	
city	text	max=30	
state	text	min=2 max=2	
landmark	text	max=50	
couponCode	text	max=10	
approxPrice	decimal		
bedSize	Text		King
			Queen
			Double
smoking	boolean		True
			False
amenities	string		Concierge
			Workout facilities
			Pool
			Restaurant
			24-hour room service
			High speed Internet access

Some of this information will be of no use to us in creating an HTML interface. For example, the data types for elements with defined values will not be necessary, since we can define a simple drop-down box or checkbox interface that controls the input values.

Remember that while we want to end up with an HTML interface, we need to define this information in XML, which can be transformed into the eventual HTML output. Because this process is so new, it is probably helpful to first generate an HTML page that takes into account each of these elements and their attributes. (See Listing 7-20.) This will help you to identify which data needs to be included in your XML.

Listing 7-20. Basic HTML output for an availability form

```html
<html>
    <body>
    <form action="availability.asp" method="post">
        Check-In Date<br/>
        <select id="check-in-month" name="check-in-month">
            <option value="1">January</option>
            . . .
            <option value="12">December</option>
        </select>
        <select id="check-in-day" name="check-in-day">
            <option value="1">1</option>
            . . .
            <option value="31">31</option>
        </select>
        <select id="check-in-year" name="check-in-year">
            <option value="2001">2001</option>
            <option value="2002">2002</option>
        </select><br/>
        Check-Out Date<br/>
        <select id="check-out-month" name="check-out-month">
            <option value="1">January</option>
            . . .
            <option value="12">December</option>
        </select>
        <select id="check-out-day" name="check-out-day">
            <option value="1">1</option>
            . . .
            <option value="31">31</option>
        </select>
        <select id="check-out-year" name="check-out-year">
            <option value="2001">2001</option>
            <option value="2002">2002</option>
        </select>
        <p/>
        Number of Adults<br/>
        <select id="numAdults" name="numAdults">
            <option selected="" value="1">1</option>
            <option value="2">2</option>
            <option value="3">3</option>
            <option value="4">4</option>
        </select>
        <p/>
        Number of Children</br>
```

```
<select id="numChild" name="numChild">
     <option selected="" value="0">0</option>
     <option value="1">1</option>
     <option value="2">2</option>
     <option value="3">3</option>
     <option value="4">4</option>
</select>
<p/>
City<input type="text" id="city" name="city" maxlength="30" size="30"/>
<p/>
State<input type="text" id="state" name="state" maxlength="2" size="2"/>
<p/>
Landmark
<input type="text" id="landmark" name="landmark" maxlength="30"
  size="30"/>
<p/>
Price Preference<BR/>
$<input type="approxPrice" id="approxPrice" name="approxPrice"
  maxlength="4" size="4"/>
<p/>
Coupon Code<BR/>
<input type="text" id="coupon" name="coupon" maxlength="30" size="20"/>
<p/>
Smoking Preference<br/>
<input type="radio" id="smokePref" name="smokePref"
  value="Yes">Yes</input>
<input type="radio" id="smokePref" name="smokePref" value="No">No
</input>
<p/>
Bed Size<br/>
<select id="bedSize" name="bedSize">
     <option selected="" value="KING">King</option>
     <option value="QUEEN">Queen</option>
     <option value="DOUBLE">Double</option>
</select>
<p/>
Hotel Amenities<br/>
<input type="checkbox" id="amenities" name="amenities" value="concierge">
  Concierge</input >
<input type="checkbox" id="amenities" name="amenities" value="pool">
```

```
            Pool</input >
        <input type="checkbox" id="amenities" name="amenities" value="workout
           facilities">Workout Facilities</input >
        <input type="checkbox" id="amenities" name="amenities"
           value="24-hour room service">24-hour Room Service</input >
        <input type="checkbox" id="amenities" name="amenities" value="restaurant">
           Restaurant</input>
        <input type="checkbox" id="amenities" name="amenities"
           value="high speed internet access">High Speed Internet Access</input >
        <input type="submit" value="Check Availability">
     </form>
     </body>
</html>
```

Viewing this code in a browser, you will see that this is truly a minimalist definition of the elements themselves, taking advantage of the attributes as appropriate. What we have done is made some of the decisions necessary to take a defined element and capture it through an HTML interface. (See Figure 7-16.)

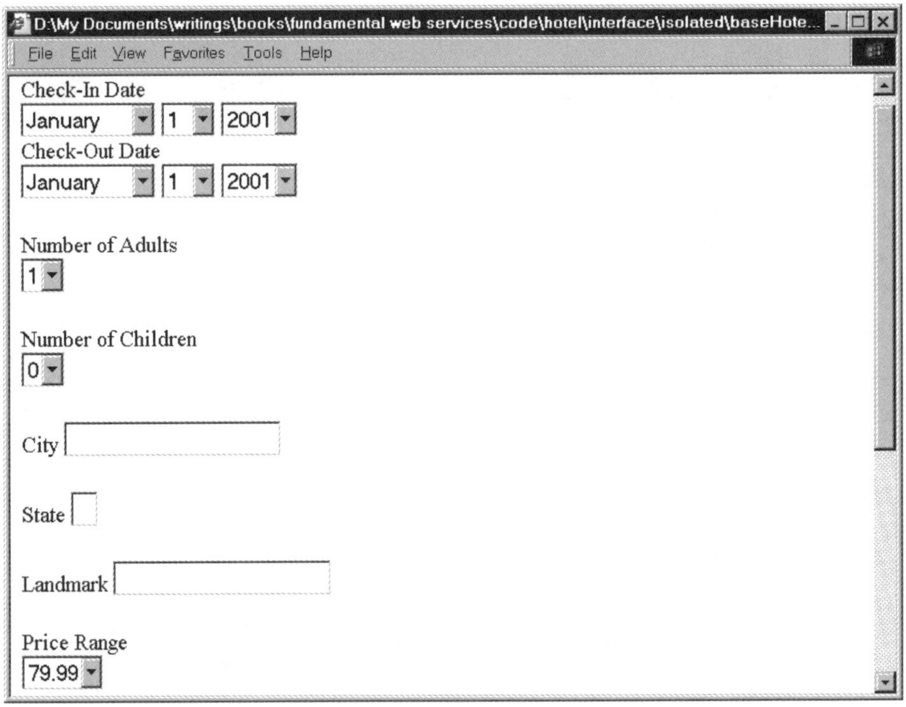

Figure 7-16. Browser view of hotel availability request form

The next step is to determine how we want to present this information in an XML format. If you look closely at our base HTML form document in Listing 7-20, you will see that it is already XML compliant. The question that then comes up is "Why not just send this as your response?" The problem is that although this will pass through all applications as valid XML, it is not accessible data. It is, after all, HTML and so is focused on presentation, not data definition. This is a problem if we want to work with individual elements or the components of those elements.

For instance, if the consumer wants to take the captions and values for these elements and place them in separate cells of a table layout, they will not be able to. We need to break this representation down to be able to work with the individual pieces.

You can think of this effort as combining the XML definition of this data and incorporating the HTML presentation elements that make up its interface. Let's look at the numberAdults element as an example. The XML definition of this data is the following:

```
<xsd:element name="numberAdults">
    <xsd:simpleType>
        <xsd:restriction base="xsd:short">
            <xsd:minInclusive value="1"/>
            <xsd:maxInclusive value="4"/>
        </xsd:restriction>
    </xsd:simpleType>
</xsd:element>
```

The HTML interface defining this element is the following:

```
Number of Adults<br/>
<select id="numAdults" name="numAdults">
    <option selected="" value="1">1</option>
    <option value="2">2</option>
    <option value="3">3</option>
    <option value="4">4</option>
</select>
```

What we need to do is identify the elements that make up this interface and incorporate them into this element's data. Looking at the HTML code, we have a caption and four values to choose from. Incorporating this into a data centric XML document might yield the following results:

```
<numberAdults maxValues="1">
    <name>numberAdults</name>
    <caption>Number of Adults</caption>
    <option value="1" caption="1"/>
    <option value="2" caption="2"/>
    <option value="3" caption="3"/>
    <option value="4" caption="4"/>
</numberAdults>
```

You see that we have defined the element, its name, an appropriate caption, and each acceptable value. We could have gotten away with not defining the name, but doing so does afford us the option of changing it later without affecting any existing implementations. This allows us to programmatically reference it as numberAdults regardless of how we name it in the HTML form.

Even though we have defined our values as options, this does not mean that this data must be exposed through a select box. Because this information is defined on a data level, this element could easily be displayed through radio buttons, or even a series of buttons. That is the flexibility we gain by having a data centric interface definition. I also defined a maxValues attribute for the numberAdults element so that it is understood that multiple values for this element are not legal. This eliminates checkboxes and other multiple selection mechanisms from being valid for this element.

Let's walk through another example of this process with the city field. First let's look at the schema definition for the city element, shown here:

```
<xsd:element name="city">
    <xsd:simpleType>
        <xsd:restriction base="xsd:string">
            <xsd:maxLength value="30"/>
        </xsd:restriction>
    </xsd:simpleType>
</xsd:element>
```

Now let's look at the HTML-defined interface for the city element, shown here:

```
City <input type="text" id="city" name="city" maxlength="30" size="30"/>
```

The size that we define in our HTML is extraneous and should really be defined later by our XSL, so we can drop that value. Otherwise, everything else pretty much carries over to our XML interface definition, as shown here:

```
<city>
     <name>city</name>
     <caption>City</caption>
     <maxLength>30</maxLength>
</city>
```

We will now take this same approach and apply it to each element in our form to design the payload portion of the availability response, as shown in Listing 7-21.

Listing 7-21. XML data payload for hotel availability form

```
<hotelAvailabilityForm>
     <checkInDate>
          <name>checkInDate</name>
          <caption>Check-In Date</caption>
          <checkInMonth maxValues="1">
               <name>checkInMonth</name>
               <option value="1" caption="Jan"/>
               . . .
               <option value="12" caption="Dec"/>
          </checkInMonth>
          <checkInDay maxValues="1">
               <name>checkInDay</name>
               <option value="1" caption="1"/>
               . . .
               <option value="31" caption="31"/>
          </checkInDay>
          <checkInYear maxValues="1">
               <name>checkInYear</name>
               <option value="2001" caption="2001"/>
               <option value="2002" caption="2002"/>
          </checkInYear>
     </checkInDate>
     <checkOutDate>
          <name>checkOutDate</name>
          <caption>Check-Out Date</caption>
          <checkOutMonth maxValues="1">
               <name>checkInMonth</name>
               <option value="1" caption="Jan"/>
               . . .
```

```
                    <option value="12" caption="Dec"/>
            </checkOutMonth>
            <checkOutDay maxValues="1">
                    <name>checkInDay</name>
                    <option value="1" caption="1"/>
                    . . .
                    <option value="31" caption="31"/>
            </checkOutDay>
            <checkOutYear maxValues="1">
                    <name>checkInYear</name>
                    <option value="2001" caption="2001"/>
                    <option value="2002" caption="2002"/>
            </checkOutYear>
    </checkOutDate>
    <numberAdults maxValues="1">
        <name>numberAdults</name>
        <caption>Number of Adults</caption>
        <option selected="TRUE" value="1" caption="1"/>
        <option value="2" caption="2"/>
        <option value="3" caption="3"/>
        <option value="4" caption="4"/>
    </numberAdults>
    <numberChildren maxValues="1">
        <name>numberChildren</name>
        <caption>Number of Children</caption>
        <option selected="TRUE" value="0" caption="0"/>
        <option value="1" caption="1"/>
        <option value="2" caption="2"/>
        <option value="3" caption="3"/>
        <option value="4" caption="4"/>
    </numberChildren>
    <city>
        <name>city</name>
        <caption>City</caption>
        <maxLength>30</maxLength>
    </city>
    <state>
        <name>state</name>
        <caption>State</caption>
        <maxLength>2</maxLength>
        <minLength>2</minLength>
    </state>
    <landmark>
        <name>landmark</name>
```

```
            <caption>Landmark</caption>
            <maxLength>50</maxLength>
        </landmark>
        <approxPrice>
            <name>approxPrice</name>
            <caption>Price Preference</caption>
            <maxLength>4</maxLength>

        </approxPrice>
        <smoking maxValues="1">
            <name>smoking</name>
            <caption>Smoking</caption>
            <option value="TRUE" caption="Yes"/>
            <option value="FALSE" caption="No"/>
        </smoking>
        <couponCode>
            <name>couponCode</name>
            <caption>Coupon Code</caption>
            <maxLength>10</maxLength>
        </couponCode>
        <bedSize maxValues="1">
            <name>bedSize</name>
            <caption>Bed Size</caption>
            <option value="King" caption="King"/>
            <option value="Queen" caption="Queen"/>
            <option value="Double" caption="Double"/>
        </bedSize>
        <hotelAmenities maxValues="*">
            <name>amenity</name>
            <caption>Hotel Amenities</caption>
            <option value="Concierge" caption="Concierge"/>
            <option value="Pool" caption="Pool"/>
            <option value="Workout Facilities" caption="Workout Facilities"/>
            <option value="24-hour Room Service" caption="24-hour Room Service"/>
            <option value="Restaurant" caption="Restaurant"/>
            <option value="High Speed Internet Access" caption="High Speed Internet
                Access"/>
        </hotelAmenities>
    </hotelAvailabilityForm>
```

Unlike our previous responses, here we are defining XML instead of XML Schemas. This is because these responses are static. There is less need to develop a schema because we are not building this response dynamically. Our applications will basically skip the step of building an XML document against a schema and will reference the XML directly to build the response. That is not to say that we should not develop a schema for our response for integrity's sake. It will help us to utilize this data in other schemas, and it will help us if we want to make changes to this request in the future.

> **TIP** *If you ever find yourself needing to generate an XML Schema from an existing XML document, you should seriously consider getting one of the tools that has the ability to generate schemas, such as XML Spy. The end result from any tool will almost never be exactly what you want, since there are numerous ways to define a single XML document, but it will provide you with a significant head start to defining your schema.*

Unfortunately, generating a schema directly off of this document won't help us to define other responses. This schema is very specific to the elements we defined: `couponCode`, `city`, `checkInDate`, etc. Unless we are defining these elements specifically, this schema is of little use. To build a schema that is generic enough to define all such responses would require making the responses themselves more generic. That would compromise their effectiveness, so we will not take on that effort.

We can, however, use the XML we did produce as a template. If you look through our availability form document, you see that we have two main element types, open entry (`city`, `couponCode`) and constrained values (`checkInDate`, `hotelAmenities`). All of our input data will fall into these categories, so we can reuse these structures for each element as appropriate. This not only helps reduce our design effort, but also helps us to remain consistent in the definition of our elements.

We now need to define the interaction schema for this availability form request. We will reference the schema we generated from our XML payload (I will forego listing that schema here because it has limited value to you). We will name this interaction `availabilityFormInteraction`, as shown in Listing 7-22.

Listing 7-22. Availability form interaction

```
<xsd:schema xmlns:xsd="http://www.w3.org/2001/XMLSchema">
    <xsd:include schemaLocation="http://www.architectingwebservices.com/
        interfaces/hrsws/availabilityForm.xsd"/>
    <xsd:element name="availabilityFormInteraction">
        <xsd:complexType>
            <xsd:sequence>
```

```
                    <xsd:element name="availabilityForm" minOccurs="0"/>
              </xsd:sequence>
        </xsd:complexType>
     </xsd:element>
</xsd:schema>
```

Notice that in this interaction we have only the response defined. This will require the availabilityFormInteraction to always be present, but to have a null value when it is a request. Next we need to add this interaction to our interface document, reservationWS, as shown in Listing 7-23.

Listing 7-23. The reservationWS *interface schema with availability form interaction*

```
<xsd:schema xmlns:xsd="http://www.w3.org/2001/XMLSchema">
     <xsd:include schemaLocation="http://www.architectingwebservices.com/
        interfaces/hrsws/serviceVariables.xsd"/>
     <xsd:include schemaLocation="http://www.architectingwebservices.com/
        interfaces/hrsws/availabilityFormInteraction.xsd"/>
     <xsd:include schemaLocation="http://www.architectingwebservices.com/
        interfaces/hrsws/availabilityInteraction.xsd"/>
     <xsd:include schemaLocation="http://www.architectingwebservices.com/
        interfaces/hrsws/detailInteraction.xsd"/>
     <xsd:include schemaLocation="http://www.architectingwebservices.com/
        interfaces/hrsws/reservationInteraction.xsd"/>
     <xsd:element name="reservationWS">
          <xsd:complexType>
               <xsd:sequence>
                    <xsd:element ref="serviceVariables"/>
                    <xsd:element ref="payload" minOccurs="0"/>
               </xsd:sequence>
          </xsd:complexType>
     </xsd:element>
     <xsd:element name="payload">
          <xsd:complexType>
               <xsd:choice>
                    <xsd:element ref="availabilityFormInteraction"/>
                    <xsd:element ref="availabilityInteraction"/>
                    <xsd:element ref="detailInteraction"/>
                    <xsd:element ref="reservationInteraction"/>
               </xsd:choice>
          </xsd:complexType>
     </xsd:element>
</xsd:schema>
```

Reservation Form

The next interaction we need to address is the reservation form. This is very similar to the availability form in that we are using an XML document to define the data for a suitable UI. We are providing a definition for a data entry form that can be transformed with a stylesheet we reference in the interaction, as shown in Listing 7-24.

Listing 7-24. XML data payload for reservation form

```
<reservationForm>
    <firstName>
        <name>firstName</name>
        <caption>First Name</caption>
        <maxLength>20</maxLength>
    </firstName>
    <lastName>
        <name>lastName</name>
        <caption>Last Name</caption>
        <maxLength>30</maxLength>
    </lastName>
    <homePhone>
        <name>homePhone</name>
        <caption>Home Phone Number</caption>
        <maxLength>15</maxLength>
    </homePhone>
    <homeAddress>
        <address>
            <name>address</name>
            <caption>Address</caption>
            <maxLength>30</maxLength>
        </address>
        <address>
            <name>address</name>
            <caption>Address</caption>
            <maxLength>30</maxLength>
        </address>
        <city>
            <name>city</name>
            <caption>City</caption>
            <maxLength>30</maxLength>
        </city>
        <state>
            <name>state</name>
            <caption>State</caption>
```

```
            <maxLength>2</maxLength>
            <minLength>2</minLength>
     </state>
     <zipCode>
            <name>zipCode</name>
            <caption>Zip-Code</caption>
            <maxLength>5</maxLength>
            <minLength>5</minLength>
     </zipCode>
</homeAddress>
<couponCode>
     <name>couponCode</name>
     <caption>Coupon Code</caption>
     <maxLength>10</maxLength>
</couponCode>
<cardNumber>
     <name>cardNumber</name>
     <caption>Credit Card Number</caption>
     <maxLength>16</maxLength>
</cardNumber>
<nameOfOwner>
     <name>nameOfOwner</name>
     <caption>Name on Credit Card</caption>
     <maxLength>50</maxLength>
</nameOfOwner>
<cardIssuer maxValues="1">
     <name>cardIssuer</name>
     <caption>Card Issuer</caption>
     <option value="Visa" caption="Visa"/>
     <option value="Mastercard" caption="Mastercard"/>
     <option value="American Express" caption="American Express"/>
     <option value="Discover" caption="Discover"/>
</cardIssuer>
<ccExpirDate>
     <name>ccExpirDate</name>
     <caption>Credit Card Expiration Date</caption>
     <ccExpirMonth maxValues="1">
            <name>ccExpirMonth</name>
            <option value="1" caption="Jan"/>
            . . .
            <option value="12" caption="Dec"/>
     </ccExpirMonth>
     <ccExpirYear maxValues="1">
            <name>ccExpirYear</name>
```

```
                          <option value="2001" caption="2001"/>
                          . . .
                          <option value="2006" caption="2006"/>
                 </ccExpirYear>
          </ccExpirDate>
          <billingAddress>
                 <address>
                          <name>address</name>
                          <caption>Address</caption>
                          <maxLength>30</maxLength>
                 </address>
                 <address>
                          <name>address</name>
                          <caption>Address</caption>
                          <maxLength>30</maxLength>
                 </address>
                 <city>
                          <name>city</name>
                          <caption>City</caption>
                          <maxLength>30</maxLength>
                 </city>
                 <state>
                          <name>state</name>
                          <caption>State</caption>
                          <maxLength>2</maxLength>
                          <minLength>2</minLength>
                 </state>
                 <zipCode>
                          <name>zipCode</name>
                          <caption>Zip-Code</caption>
                          <maxLength>5</maxLength>
                          <minLength>5</minLength>
                 </zipCode>
          </billingAddress>
</reservationForm>
```

Like with the availability form, we will only require the service variables to be present in the request. However, in this case we will be running some validation of this information because it can never be the first request of a session. We know this because all reservations must be preceded by an availability request.

The schema shown in Listing 7-25 will define our reservation form interaction.

Listing 7-25. Reservation form interaction schema

```
<xsd:schema xmlns:xsd="http://www.w3.org/2001/XMLSchema">
    <xsd:include schemaLocation="http://www.architectingwebservices.com/
       interface/hrsws/reservationForm.xsd"/>
    <xsd:element name="reservationFormInteraction">
        <xsd:complexType>
            <xsd:sequence>
                <xsd:element ref="reservationForm" minOccurs="0"/>
            </xsd:sequence>
        </xsd:complexType>
    </xsd:element>
</xsd:schema>
```

Adding this interaction to our service will follow the same pattern as the other interactions, as shown in Listing 7-26.

Listing 7-26. The reservationWS *interface schema with reservation form interaction*

```
<xsd:schema xmlns:xsd="http://www.w3.org/2001/XMLSchema">
    <xsd:include schemaLocation="http://www.architectingwebservices.com/
       interfaces/hrsws/serviceVariables.xsd"/>
    <xsd:include schemaLocation="http://www.architectingwebservices.com/
       interfaces/hrsws/availabilityFormInteraction.xsd"/>
    <xsd:include schemaLocation="http://www.architectingwebservices.com/
       interfaces/hrsws/availabilityInteraction.xsd"/>
    <xsd:include schemaLocation="http://www.architectingwebservices.com/
       interfaces/hrsws/detailInteraction.xsd"/>
    <xsd:include schemaLocation="http://www.architectingwebservices.com/
       interfaces/hrsws/reservationFormInteraction.xsd"/>
    <xsd:include schemaLocation="http://www.architectingwebservices.com/
       interfaces/hrsws/reservationInteraction.xsd"/>
    <xsd:element name="reservationWS">
        <xsd:complexType>
            <xsd:sequence>
                <xsd:element ref="serviceVariables"/>
                <xsd:element ref="payload" minOccurs="0"/>
            </xsd:sequence>
        </xsd:complexType>
    </xsd:element>
    <xsd:element name="payload">
        <xsd:complexType>
            <xsd:choice>
```

```
                         <xsd:element ref="availabilityFormInteraction"/>
                         <xsd:element ref="availabilityInteraction"/>
                         <xsd:element ref="detailInteraction"/>
                         <xsd:element ref="reservationFormInteraction"/>
                         <xsd:element ref="reservationInteraction"/>
                   </xsd:choice>
             </xsd:complexType>
        </xsd:element>
</xsd:schema>
```

The final interaction we have to define is the reservation confirmation. Recall, that we identified this as an interaction because a UI typically confirms the collection of critical information (in this case personal and financial data). The consumer is typically responsible for this, but we are taking an active role in defining the interface for our isolated model, so we must come up with a solution.

Our goal is to simply confirm the data that was entered, so all of this data moving around seems a bit excessive. Rather than defining another interface, it is better to design a method for keeping the data on the client side until the information is confirmed.

We decided earlier that we would do this through the use of client-side script. We will have a pop-up window simply ask for a confirmation, with an option to edit the data if necessary as we saw in Figure 7-6. This will change the overall workflow by eliminating this interaction. (See Figure 7-17.) This helps improve the service's overall performance and reduces the implementation effort.

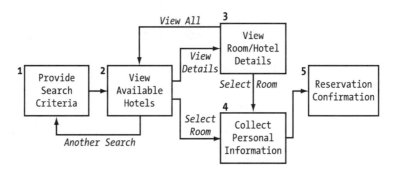

Figure 7-17. Process flow for isolated service without confirmation interaction

This client-side script will be distributed through our style sheets, so we need to keep this functionality in mind when we design the XSL template for our reservation form.

That actually completes the modifications to our service to support the isolated service model. Before moving on to the rest of the interface layer, let's take a look at our updated schema hierarchy diagram in Figure 7-18.

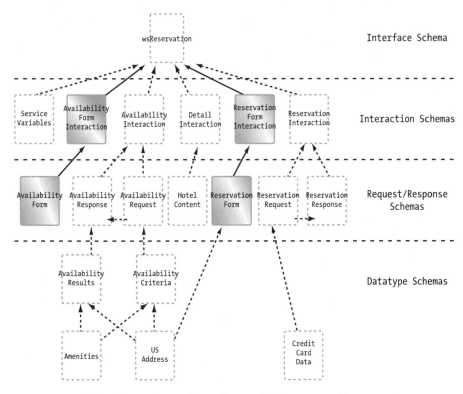

Figure 7-18. Physical interface schema hierarchy diagram with isolated interactions

Service Listener

The service listener is responsible for handling the incoming requests and routing them to the appropriate logic. Its sole responsibility is to take the incoming request and identify the pertinent information in it. I talked about this process at a high level in Chapter 2. Now it is time to look at the design of a listener, and specifically the listener for our reservation service.

Designing the listener involves four aspects:

- Listener technology

- Authentication method

- Validation process

- Data extraction

Listener Technology

We have a few options available for containing the listener itself. Regardless of the method chosen, the underlying requirement is that it resides on an HTTP(S) server. Without this service, a listener will not be able to receive any requests, which is obviously a necessity!

We are building this service on a Microsoft platform, so our HTTP server will be Internet Information Server (IIS). As I stated earlier, we will be establishing two sites for our service, one each for the embedded and isolated models. However, only the listener itself will be duplicated; the rest of the logic and functionality will be reused for both services.

> **NOTE** *This presents us with the conundrum of whether we are providing two Web services or one. Does an interface equate to a Web service, or can a single Web service support more than one interface? A good argument can be made either way, and I probably utilize different approaches when they are convenient for the discussion. It really comes down to whose perspective you are taking: the consumer's or the provider's. Officially, I would have to say that the perspective of the consumer is the one that matters most, so each interface should define a Web service.*

The recipient of the request can be either an ASP (Active Server Pages) page or an ISAPI (Information Server API) extension. For the sake of keeping this example simple, we will use an ASP page containing VBScript code. For a production system that is expected to support a heavy request load, an ISAPI component will provide a better solution.

Even though the listener itself is an ASP page, it does not require that all logic be contained in it. The same is true of an ISAPI-based design. In fact, it is better to make the listener, regardless of form, as light and generic as possible for performance and reuse purposes.

Exposing a light listener is especially pertinent to this Web service because we will have two different sites to host each model of our service. If our listener contains a lot of logic, that will be duplicated under each site, which makes maintenance less efficient. We should design listeners that receive the request, capture which site it came through, and pass it on to the other functionality in the service.

Now that we have determined what the makeup of our listener will be, let's look at the specific tasks we need to accomplish in it.

Authentication Method

Both the authentication method and validation process are components of our security model, but their responsibility falls in the interface layer. For that reason, I have included their design in this layer of our Web service solution.

We determined in our security model that we would be using a certificate system for identifying our consumers. However, identification does not equal authentication, so we will need to check the identified consumer against a data source. This will validate the consumer as a current, legal user of this service.

For this service, we will use a reference table to contain all of our consumer information. The methodology for referencing this information can take one of two approaches. The first is an optimistic approach that does an initial lookup for every new session and maintains the consumer indirectly through the session. This approach puts a lot of trust into the session, since the session is not validated with the consumer's certificate for every request. The other approach is more pessimistic in that it verifies the consumer against every call in a session. The tradeoff here is a higher level of security but slower performance. Even though the performance of such a solution should be acceptable for a moderate amount of Web service traffic, there are caching technologies that could be used to help with this lookup (such as LDAP or the COM+ shared property manager). For the sake of this exercise, we will just reference the database directly.

> **CAUTION** *Choose carefully when considering caching technologies for your Web services. There is always a trade-off of performance for scalability whenever a cache system is utilized and that trade-off will usually be realized very quickly once a threshold is reached.*

Validation Process

Once we have determined that the request comes from an eligible consumer, we need to execute a validation of it. This validation includes not only the structure, but potentially the data itself as well. Specifically, we will be ensuring that any session IDs and stages included in our service variables are valid. This should also be self-contained in some form so that it can be reused. Ideally, it is generic enough to handle any request for validation.

As discussed in Chapter 3, the term *valid XML* is very ambiguous. There are actually different ways of validating XML, and we need to perform each step for the requests coming into our Web service. Furthermore, these steps build on each other in such a way that you cannot perform the second step without verifying the first, and so on. The three steps are the following:

- XML well-formedness

- XML validity

- Data validity

The first step to validating the request is ensuring that a well-formed XML document has been sent in the request. This is a validation not of the content, but simply of the structure of the document and the XML data itself. An illegal XML document could cause catastrophic failure in your application, so you want to catch this as soon as possible. The longer you go without running this check, the more code you will have to produce to handle an error if it occurs. Fortunately, the MSXML parser automatically checks for well-formedness and allows us to handle the error as gracefully as possible.

Once the document's well-formedness has been established, the data in it needs to be validated. This is where our schemas become very valuable. Once the document is loaded into the DOM, we can validate its contents against the appropriate schema. Keep in mind that this validates the data types, data structure, and enumerated data, but not the rest of the data.

Validating the data in the document requires programmatic logic in the application. This is where we verify that the data values in total are valid. An example of an invalid document in this sense is a consumer making a request against another consumer's session. This is something schemas are not capable of handling, and so it falls to our application, and more specifically the data extraction component of our listener.

Data Extraction

There is a necessary blending of activities between the data extraction and validation logic. After all, you have to extract the data to validate it. To keep the two distinct, just think of the validation process as the logical process that incorporates the error handling for the data extraction process.

The data that needs to be extracted varies from call to call because the payloads are different. One of the constants in our Web service is the serviceVariables element. Every call includes this data so that the request session and activity can be quickly identified. For this reason, the data extraction should be separate from the conditional data extraction for maximum efficiency and reusability.

Now that we have identified each of the stages in the service listener, let's put this together in a flow diagram. (See Figure 7-19.) This flow diagram is a significant portion of our listener design because it shows the precedence that must take place in its logic.

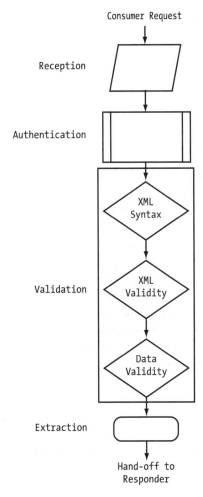

Figure 7-19. Flow diagram for the service listener

Service Responder

Whereas the service listener is focused on taking the request and validating it, the service responder's sole responsibility is to provide the response to be returned to the consumer. For our hotel reservation service, this response has three steps:

- Identify the service type

- Define the workflow

- Build the response

Identify the Service Type

Because we are supporting two different services through our logic, one of the key pieces of information critical to get to the responder is the service type requested. This tells us whether we are responding to a consumer who is using the embedded service or the isolated service. The service type is critical because it affects the payload, what the workflow is, and what information is provided in the response.

As an outcome of the service type, we may need to modify the stage requested by the consumer. Since the isolated service has five stages and the isolated service three, we have to determine how to handle this. We have already designed the process so that the three overlapping requests are identical. However, stage one of the embedded service is actually stage two of the isolated service. We could try to keep these separate and manage them independently, but that would likely create some confusion during development and testing. Instead, we could map the embedded requests to the isolated requests once as they come in. This remains internal to the service, so there should be no confusion to the consumer. This actually helps to maintain the distinct identities of our two services. We just have to make sure that we map it back correctly when we build our response! We will discuss this in more detail during implementation.

Define the Workflow

The workflow for our service manages the information that is utilized to make requests of data sources, components, and other external resources. As we saw in our payload model, we essentially have a single, large workflow defined in our service. This provides all the functionality needed for an isolated service type request. The embedded service type will then use a subset of these.

Most workflow is specific to each request in the service's process, but some of the workflow can be overhead that applies to all requests. This doesn't apply in our case because the functionality is all request type specific. Let's walk through these workflow steps again to determine what they need to accomplish in their workflow. This includes identifying the key logic as well as any external references.

Availability Form

The availability form is the UI provided to the consumer as assistance to collecting the pertinent information. This is a static response that is not consumer or session specific because it collects the information necessary to simply reference our Web service.

Because this is not a dynamic response, we can define a physical document and have the workflow simply respond to the consumer with it as the bulk of the payload. This document can be referenced from the database, a cache, or even a physical file. This determination should be made based on scalability and performance considerations for the anticipated volume of traffic. For convenience's sake, we will keep the document as a physical file for this Web service.

Another topic for consideration was whether this document should be formatted or reference an XSL stylesheet like the dynamic responses. The idea here is that this dynamic transformation would be overhead for a static document. Even though this is a response defining a UI, I would still like to provide the option to the consumers for taking a data-level definition of the interface to make their own changes to it. Several techniques available are to the consumer for caching this resulting transformation to keep performance from being a big issue. We will look at these in Chapter 8.

Availability Request

This request to check the room availability for our hotel chain ultimately needs to get to our existing hotel reservation system (HRS). It is the data store and logical processor that determines whether there are hotels that match the criteria provided by the user and whether these hotels have rooms available.

If you recall, we actually have to make two requests of the HRS system to accomplish our availability request. There is one class that exposes all the necessary methods for us: reservationSystem.clsHRS. One method (fetchAvailability) takes in the criteria and runs the actual availability search against its database. However, this comes back with very raw data, identifying the hotel by ID, along with some price, room type, and proximity data. We have to take the hotel IDs that are returned and look up the hotel-specific data, such as name and location. That request is made through the fetchHotel method call.

Like I mentioned earlier, we will encapsulate this process into our own function, so we will not be referencing these two methods independently from our workflow. This breaks it out of the rest of our responder for the sake of efficiency. We will call this method wsFetchAvailability, and it will return the data in the appropriate XML format to append to our response payload.

Part of our workflow will involve building the request to the HRS system. Since the interface is a DCOM object call and we are getting the data in XML format, we have a little bit of work to do, especially when you consider that we may have multiple instances of a single element that needs to get transformed into a variant array (addresses, amenities).

Hotel Detail View

The hotel content is something of the service's own creation. Fortunately, this is a fairly simple process that we can execute in a number of ways. We can take the same approach as for the availability form request and reference a static XML document, but that is a tad inefficient!

A much better method is to define a data model to contain this data (which we will do in designing the data layer in the next section), create a stored procedure, and write the simple logic to reference it. The method we define for our hotel content retrieval will be named wsFetchHotelContent, and it will return the data in the appropriate XML document structure to append to our response payload.

Reservation Form

We will handle the reservation form in the same way that we handled the availability form. We will reference a physical file that contains the XML data defining our interface and then use the same process as the other responses in adding the stylesheet reference to the serviceVariables element for transformation on the consumer's side.

Reservation Request

This request also needs to be handled by the existing HRS system, but unlike the availability request, a single method call (makeReservation) takes care of the entire process. Also like the availability request, we need to deal with creating variant arrays from duplicate XML data nodes.

One additional catch to the makeReservation method is that it requires our room type value to be an integer. The fetchAvailability method returned the room type as a string (Suite, Value, etc.). Consider it a quirk in the interface of the HRS system. It just means that we need to have our own internal mappings of the integer values with the string values. There are only four possible values, and it isn't expected to change, so that is not a big task.

To take a better look at all of this functionality in the service responder, we should put together a flow diagram based on the physical components we have identified to visualize the solution. (See Figure 7-20.) This will help us to identify any potential bottlenecks or any excessive shuffling of data between logic.

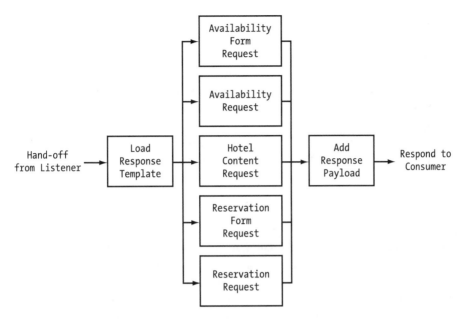

Figure 7-20. Process diagram for the service responder workflow

Build the Response

The final step of the service responder is to build the response to the consumer. Since much of the workflow has built the data to be contained in the payload, the building of the response just needs to append it to the appropriate header data and make any other necessary additions or modifications.

The service variables can typically be referenced from the request itself. After all, the response is still the same session and stage in the process. The one exception to this is when the request is the first of a session. In these cases, no session has been established. We need to create one and set the session element value accordingly.

Another twist in our response build process is the support of two different service models. One service has three steps and the other five. I mentioned earlier that we modified the request coming in appropriately to route the request to the appropriate workflow. Now we simply need to map it back to the consumer's "view" of the service.

The final step in building our response is determining whether to add the reference for the XSL template to the service variables. This check can actually be incorporated into our stage-mapping logic, since the opposite state requires this modification. This way, if the request is embedded, the stage is mapped, and if it is isolated, the XSL reference is added.

This completes the interface layer design. That leaves only the data layer left before we move on to the actual implementation.

Data Layer

Most Web services that expose functionality provided by existing systems have a very small data layer. The only data we need to concern ourselves with maintaining is the information we need to support the Web services process itself. This typically comes down to session data, consumer data, an audit trail, and perhaps content data.

For our reservation Web service we have two main models to design: session and hotel content.

The Session Data Model

The first model to define is the session and consumer relationship. This is how we will maintain the various user sessions with our consumers. This involves two entities, the session and the consumer, which have a one-to-many relationship because each consumer can be supporting multiple users in our service.

Additionally, we need to keep track of the availability requests that come through the system. This contains all the specific information about the trip the user has requested, such as date of arrival and departure, the number of occupants, and other request details. This keeps us from having to overload the room reservation request with every piece of information again. This data can also act as an audit trail for troubleshooting and debugging during testing and implementation.

This information only needs to be persisted on a per session basis, so some type of archival strategy is also called for on this availability request data. Otherwise, one record per session is all that is required and is either created on the first request or updated on subsequent availability requests. Therefore, requests will be tied to the sessions in a one-to-one relationship.

So we have three entities defined in total for our session-consumer model: consumer, session, and availability request. The consumer table will not only act as a reference table for our sessions, but also can be used to validate the consumer requests coming in. For this service, we are using client certificates to identify the consumer. Since we are not identifying the consumer in our service variables, we need to relate these certificates to our consumer data so that we can properly create and maintain our sessions. There are a number of data fields we could cross-reference, but let's save that decision for later. We will just recognize for now that we need a field to cross-reference our consumers with their certificates.

Our session entity will simply reference the consumer to which it belongs and have a key field. Since we know we will want to archive them, let's go ahead and add a date/time stamp as well.

The availability request will be a little larger, since it contains some of the user's search criteria. The search criteria we will capture are the following:

- Check-in date

- Check-out date

- Number of adults

- Number of children

- Coupon code

- Smoking preference

We will also add a search date field so that we can efficiently archive this data as a history of activity on the service. Notice that we left out location, price, bed size, and the hotel amenities from the search criteria. The purpose of storing these criteria is to support a potential reservation request and some of the availability criteria will not be needed. A reservation request will be made through a hotel ID and a room type, which will inherently define that information. For example, a room at a hotel has a given price so we don't need to store it. However, we do need to store the coupon code so we can apply any discounts. Putting all of this together gives us a data model that allows us to keep track of our consumers, users, and their activities. (See Figure 7-21.)

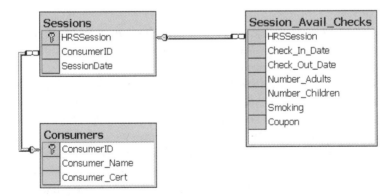

Figure 7-21. Session-consumer data model

The Content Data Model

The next model we need to design is the content model. One of our service requests is the retrieval of hotel-specific content, including descriptions and pictures. The existing system does not contain any content, just data, so it is up to us to develop a separate source to contain and reference in our service. This is an excellent example of how you might need, or want, to augment an existing system to create a robust Web service.

For our data, we have a number of options on how we can model this relationship. Each hotel will have five pictures and one description. Of course, experience might tell us that rarely are such business rules adhered to, especially when dealing with marketing material. Inevitably, some hotels are likely to not have all five pictures, or some will have more.

Therefore, we should design a data model that is very flexible. To gain this flexibility, we simply normalize our data by defining the content, not the hotel, as the entity. This turns every piece of content into a record, with hotels having multiple records. We can then externalize the content names so that we can have common identifiers of each content item. (See Figure 7-22.)

Figure 7-22. Hotel content data model

Since hotels are "defined" by the reservation system, there really is no need to have a separate hotel entity. We are simply defining content based on external hotel IDs, so defining the content is sufficient.

We will also need some individual reference tables for our Web service. These will be used individually to either help map individual elements or serve as lookup tables. One example of this is the `HRS_Errors` table. This table contains a list of the error codes the HRS system could return. We will have a corresponding column that contains the description text we want to present back to the consumer/user. This table is not related to any other data entity, but simply enhances the user experience of the service. I will discuss these tables as I walk you through the implementation of the Web service.

This completes the data layer design for our Web service. The data layer was also the last design component remaining in our overall design, so we are now ready to move on to implementing the Web service!

Implementing the Web Service

Now that we have our requirements, have defined our model, and have completed the design, it is time to pull it all together into a working Web service. The implementation of a Web service with a workflow can seem a little overwhelming at first. Since each request is nearly its own application, the task of managing it can be complex.

To help with this implementation, we are going to take a somewhat different approach. Traditional Web applications tend to break an application into the different tiers and work on them, much like we did in our design process. Instead of this traditional approach, we will go through a request-by-request build of the Web service. Since we have a design to keep us "rooted" in a common approach, it is safe to take on each request independently without as much concern for deviations among them. We will then address each piece of logic, each interface, and each data element as we encounter them.

We will start by developing the base service itself. This is the container for all of our Web service logic and gives us an initial working prototype to start adding our logic to. Then we will add each of the five requests independently, adding data elements, interfaces, and code as needed. Let's get started.

> **NOTE** *If you want to build this Web service, you need to have the HRS system interfaces to base it on. You can write your own according to the specifications I have provided, or you can download the COM object available at* `http://www.architectingwebservices.com/hrsws/hrs`.

Base Service

Since we are going to build the Web service by request functionality, we need to start with the base service. This provides the infrastructure for handling all the requests coming in and the creation of responses sent out. This is analogous to the development of our `reservationWS` schema document. We started out with a schema that contained the `serviceVariables`, and we added the interaction schemas one by one.

The base service will need to accomplish some base functionality that will be required of all interactions. This functionality will consist of the following:

- HRSWS component

- Listener

- HRSWS database

- Session model tables

- Validation logic

Each of these components will provide functionality that is crucial to our service for each and every request. As we build and test this base service, we should also build a test client that will help by sending valid requests to our Web service. This will provide us an efficient means for testing as we implement each of the five interactions.

HRSWS Component

The HRSWS component contains all the compiled functionality for our Web service. It consists of just one class, clsListener. The only public method in this class is the processRequest function. This method will be called by our listener ASP pages (one each for the embedded and isolated URLs). We will start our implementation by defining this function as shown here:

```
Public Function processRequest(ByVal serviceType As Integer, _
    ByVal xmlRequest As String, ByVal consumerName As String) As String
```

We will have three parameters to our processRequest function: the service type, the request document, and the consumer name. Each listener defines the service type, since it is determined through the URL referenced by the consumer. The request document is the XML data payload passed by the consumer. The consumer name is determined through the client certificate provided by the consumer. The processRequest method returns the XML response in a string format that can be exposed directly to the consumer.

The first thing we need in our function is to reference all the necessary objects to work with the XML. This is essentially the Microsoft XML parser, MSXML. For this service we will work with the Version 4.0 Technical Preview. This is the first version of the parser to support the validation of XML via XML Schemas, so the reasoning behind using a prerelease version is justified.

Let's go ahead and take a look at the initial processRequest function (Listing 7-27) and discuss the interesting parts afterward. Since this is a shell for the function, I have added comments where the business logic will need to be added.

NOTE *If you want electronic copies of any code in this book, please go to* http://www.architectingwebservices.com. *All code there will be compilable and fully functional.*

Listing 7-27. The `clsListener` *initial implementation*

```
Public Function processRequest(ByVal serviceType As Integer,
  ByVal xmlRequest As String, ByVal consumerName As String) As String

    '-DOM for the request payload
    Dim objDomRequest As MSXML2.DOMDocument40
    '-DOM for the response payload
    Dim objDomResponse As MSXML2.DOMDocument40
    '-working DOM for building intermediate documents
    Dim objDomWorking As MSXML2.DOMDocument40

    '-Variables
    Dim blnLoad As Boolean
    Dim intSession as Integer
    Dim intStage as Integer

    '-Database access objects
    Dim objConn As ADODB.Connection
    Dim objCommand As ADODB.Command
    Dim objRS As ADODB.Recordset

    '-Create all the XML objects
    Set objDomRequest = New MSXML2.DOMDocument40
    Set objDomResponse = New MSXML2.DOMDocument40
    Set objDomWorking = New MSXML2.DOMDocument40

    objDomRequest.async = False
    objDomResponse.async = False
    objDomWorking.async = False

    Set objConn = New Connection

    '-Set connection properties
    '-connection values defined in global constants for this example
    With objConn
        .ConnectionTimeout = 25
        .Provider = "sqloledb"
```

```
            .Properties("Data Source").Value = ServerName
            .Properties("Initial Catalog").Value = DBName
            .Properties("Integrated Security").Value = "SSPI"
            .Properties("User ID").Value = UserName
            .Properties("password").Value = Password
            .Open
        End With

    Set objCommand = New Command

    '-load the xml
    objDomRequest.loadXML xmlRequest

    '- add validation code here -

    '-extract the session and stage data from the service variables
    intSession = objDomRequest.selectSingleNode("hrs:reservationWS/
        hrs:serviceVariables/sessionID").nodeTypedValue
    intStage = objDomRequest.selectSingleNode("hrs:reservationWS/
        hrs:serviceVariables/stage").Text

    '-Load the base response document template
    blnLoad = objDomResponse.Load("http://www.architectingwebservices.com/
        interfaces/hrsws/responseTemplate.xml")
    if blnLoad then
        objDomResponse.selectSingleNode
            ("hrs:reservationWS/hrs:serviceVariables/sessionID").nodeTypedValue
            = intSession
    Else
        GoTo Data_Error
    End If

    '-Adjust intStage if embedded service requested
    If serviceType = 1 Then
        If intStage = 3 Then intStage = 5
        If intStage = 2 Then intStage = 3
        If intStage = 1 Then intStage = 2
    End If

    '-Case statement to handle each request
    Select Case intStage
    Case 1
        '- add request form responder logic here -
```

```
      Case 2
          '- add availability request responder logic here -
      Case 3
          '- add detail request responder logic here -
      Case 4
          '- add reservation form responder logic here -
      Case 5
          '- add reservation request responder logic here -
      Case Else
      End Select


      '-Adjust intStage back for embedded service request
      If serviceType = 1 Then
          If intStage = 2 Then intStage = 1
          If intStage = 3 Then intStage = 2
          If intStage = 5 Then intStage = 3
      Else
          '-append stylesheet reference to payload
      End If


      '-Set the stage value in the service variables
      objDomResponse.selectSingleNode
        ("hrs:reservationWS/hrs:serviceVariables/stage").nodeTypedValue = intStage


      processRequest = CStr(objDomResponse.xml)


      GoTo End_Proc

End_Proc:
      '-Cleanup
      Set objDomRequest = Nothing
      Set objDomResponse = Nothing
      Set objDomWorking = Nothing
      Set objConn = Nothing


End Function
```

To support all the XML handling, we will define three DOM document objects. These will contain the request, the response, and a working document. The working document will be used to build nodes and temporary documents that will eventually make up our response.

Notice that I set all three document's async property to false. This is necessary if you want to be guaranteed that the data is loaded before continuing in the application. If you immediately start trying to reference this DOM after issuing a `load` or `loadXML` request, you will likely get an error because it hasn't completely loaded the data yet.

After extracting the `session` and `stage` from the service variables, we also load the response document template. Using a template is an efficient way of getting a jump-start on building an XML document. When you have at least a handful of elements that you know are going to exist and simply need to populate their values, a template approach should be considered. The template for our response document looks like this:

```
<hrs:reservationWS xmlns:hrs="urn:reservationWS">
    <hrs:serviceVariables>
        <sessionID/>
        <stage/>
    </hrs:serviceVariables>
    <hrs:payload/>
</hrs:reservationWS>
```

Next, we set the `sessionID` element value that we referenced from the request. Remember that we have not gotten to any validation of the request coming in yet. We will implement that logic shortly.

The next steps involve the stage mapping that takes the three embedded requests and maps them to the isolated requests. Once this is done we can define the decision tree for each of the five stages through a case statement. Afterward we map the stage back for the embedded requests and set the stage on the response document.

Finally we return the response document and perform some cleanup on our objects. We don't have any error handling included yet because that will be part of the validation logic we will add.

The resulting response is a very simple document that essentially consists of our response document template shown earlier with the `sessionID` and `stage` variables set to the values provided in the request. To verify this, we need to develop a listener to send requests to our new class.

Listener

Our listener consists of a couple of ASP pages that essentially collect the request from the consumer, identify the consumer through its client certificate, and make the request of our HRSWS component. I will hold off on the details with the client certificate right now and simply populate that spot with a default value, as shown here:

```
dim objHRSRequest
dim objDOM

set objHRSRequest = Server.CreateObject("HRSWS.clsListener")
set objDOM = Server.Createobject("MSXML2.DOMDocument")

objdom.async = false
objdom.load request
Response.ContentType = "text/xml"
response.write objHRSRequest.processRequest(2,objdom.xml,"consumer")

set objdom = nothing
set objhrsrequest = nothing
```

Normally we could pass the request object directly on, and ASP would do the binary read for us automatically and send the data through the parameter to our class. However, there is a problem with this method when you want to access the request object for other information, such as client certificate data.

The workaround involves loading the request into a DOM and passing in the document manually. We are taking some overhead with this approach, but unfortunately this seems to be the only workaround available when working with XML data sent in binary and utilizing client certificates for authentication.

> **NOTE** *Depending on the information you reference, this behavior is either a bug or a feature of ASP's request object. I have no information on whether a fix or update is planned by Microsoft.*

This ASP page came from the isolated site so the service type parameter is set to 2. The embedded site's ASP page is identical to this one, except that its service type parameter is set to 1.

Test Client

To test this listener and our service, we cannot simply view it in a typical Web browser. This attempt to contact the ASP page will produce an error because no XML data will be sent. To perform a test, we need to create a custom test client. This can be done using almost any language or platform. You can create your own or follow the Visual Basic design I have here. I will not discuss the technical details of a consumer application until the next chapter, when we start consuming Web services. This is a rudimentary, static client that will serve our purposes for testing only.

To build a test client, start by creating a standard Visual Basic EXE inside of Visual Studio and add three text fields and a button to your form to look roughly like the form shown in Figure 7-23.

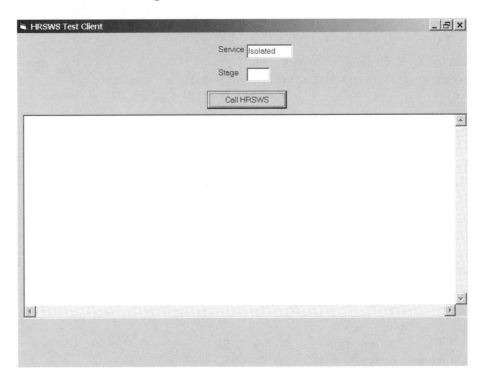

Figure 7-23. Test client form view

> **TIP** *Whenever you want to display XML data in a Visual Basic text box (as we are here in the third text box), set the* multiline *property to true. This allows the data to wrap and indent properly, making it much more readable.*

Next, you need to add a reference to the Microsoft XML, V4.0 library. This is the MSXML4 parser, which we will need in our client to handle the XML data sent and returned from the service, as well as the HTTP communication we need to connect. Then, you need to add the code in Listing 7-28 to define your click procedure.

Listing 7-28. HRSWS test consumer subroutine

```
Private Sub Command1_Click()

    Dim objXMLDoc As MSXML2.DOMDocument40
    Dim objXMLNode As MSXML2.IXMLDOMNode
    Dim objXMLSend As MSXML2.ServerXMLHTTP40

    Dim currNode As String
    Dim strServiceURL As String

    Set objXMLDoc = New DOMDocument40
    Set objXMLSend = New MSXML2.ServerXMLHTTP40

    objXMLDoc.async = False

    If Text2.Text = "Isolated" Then

        Select Case Text1.Text
        Case "1"
            Text3.text "————Calling Availability Form————"
            boolTest = objXMLDoc.Load("http://www.architectingwebservices.com/
                interfaces/hrsws/availabilityFormRequest.xml")
        Case "2"
            Text3.text "————Calling Availability Process————"
            boolTest = objXMLDoc.Load("http://www.architectingwebservices.com/
                interfaces/hrsws/availabilityRequest.xml")
```

```
    Case "3"
        Text3.text "————Calling Detail Process————"
        boolTest = objXMLDoc.Load("http://www.architectingwebservices.com/
          interfaces/hrsws/detailRequest.xml")
    Case "4"
        Text3.text "————Calling Reservation Form————"
        boolTest = objXMLDoc.Load("http://www.architectingwebservices.com/
          interfaces/hrsws/reservationFormRequest.xml")
    Case "5"
        Text3.text "————Calling Reservation Process————"
        boolTest = objXMLDoc.Load("http://www.architectingwebservices.com/
          interfaces/hrsws/reservationRequest.xml")
    End Select

    strServiceURL = "http://www.architectingwebservices.com/hrsws/isolated"


Else
    Select Case Text1.Text
    Case "1"
        Text3.text "————Calling Availability Process————"
        boolTest = objXMLDoc.Load("http://www.architectingwebservices.com/
          interfaces/hrsws/availabilityRequest.xml")
        objXMLDoc.selectSingleNode
          ("hrs:reservationWS/hrs:serviceVariables/stage")
          .nodeTypedValue = "1"
    Case "2"
        Text3.text "————Calling Detail Process————"
        boolTest = objXMLDoc.Load("http://www.architectingwebservices.com/
          interfaces/hrsws/detailRequest.xml")
        objXMLDoc.selectSingleNode("hrs:reservationWS/hrs:serviceVariables/
          stage").nodeTypedValue = "2"
    Case "3"
        Text3.text "————Calling Reservation Process————"
        boolTest = objXMLDoc.Load("http://www.architectingwebservices.com/
          interfaces/hrsws/reservationRequest.xml")
```

```
                objXMLDoc.selectSingleNode("hrs:reservationWS/hrs:serviceVariables/
                    stage").nodeTypedValue = "3"
            End Select

            strServiceURL = "http://www.architectingwebservices.com/hrsws/embedded"
        End If


        If boolTest Then
            objXMLSend.setOption SXH_OPTION_SELECT_CLIENT_SSL_CERT,
                "myCertificate"
'This certificate should match a valid client certificate installed on the server
            objXMLSend.open "POST", strServiceURL, False
            objXMLSend.send (objXMLDoc.xml)
            currNode = objXMLSend.responseText

            Text3.text (currNode)
        Else
            Text3.text "error in load"
        End If

        Set objXMLDoc = nothing
        Set objXMLNode = nothing
        Set objXMLSend = nothing


End Sub
```

In our form we are collecting the stage and the type of service we would like to request. Based on that information, this application references the appropriate request document and submits it to the appropriate listener for the type of service requested. To keep the client simple, I have just created two separate case statements that handle each request accordingly. Every request is handled the exact same way right now by our HRS Web service, so we don't need to get into their details yet.

Now that we have the function for our component defined, a listener that will send it the request, and a means for testing all of these, we can start building out the base service functionality. Like most dynamic applications, this starts with the database behind the process.

TIP *The XML request files as listed here in the code do exist on the book's Web site,* www.architectingwebservices.com. *You can either reference these directly in your copy of this code or copy the files down locally on your system and change the paths accordingly. In fact, if you need help troubleshooting your test client, you can point it to the Web service located on this site. Its URLs are* http://www.architectingwebservices.com/embedded *and* http://www.architectingwebservices.com/isolated. *You can learn more about this instance of the hotel reservation Web service in the next chapter.*

HRSWS Database

It is important to keep in mind that the HRSWS database only contains the data that isn't contained or exposed through the existing HRS system. We are not replicating any data, but either augmenting its functionality or supporting the Web services process itself.

For this service our database will consist of the two models that we defined in our design: the session data model and the content data model. However, for the core service, only the session data model is significant, because it is used by every request made to the Web service.

Session Model

The session data model will contain our customer data along with the sessions and some of their activities. We will use this data to validate the consumer, verify existing sessions and create new sessions, and verify their request precedence. If you recall, the request precedence is important because we have to know that the user makes an availability request prior to making a reservation request.

We have already identified the three tables and their fields in our design, but we have yet to define their data types. Let's go ahead and look at each table's details for our implementation.

The parent table of our entire session model is the consumer table. (See Table 7-2.) Everything is based on it. Without a valid consumer no session can be created and no activity can occur. This table is not meant as a partner contact table, so the data is kept fairly simple. We have a unique identifier, a name for readability, and a certificate field at our disposal. We have yet to determine what value we will actually place in the Consumer_Cert field, but we will implement the entire security model once we build our service.

Table 7-2. Consumers Table Implementation

COLUMN	DATA TYPE	SIZE	NOTES
ConsumerID	int	4	Primary key
Consumer_Name	varchar	50	
Consumer_Cert	varchar	50	

The sessions table (Table 7-3) is the direct child of the consumers table. All sessions will exist in this table during their lifespan. This means that the expiration of a session will require the deletion or archival of this session data accordingly (hence the SessionDate column). The unique identifier is an identity field, which will help us to keep up with our session generation. We also have a ConsumerID maintaining integrity with the Consumers table along with a date field for our archival process.

Table 7-3. Sessions Table Implementation

COLUMN	DATA TYPE	SIZE	NOTES
HRSSession	int	4	identity
ConsumerID	int	4	Foreign Key ->Consumers
SessionDate	datetime	8	default is getdate()

The Session_Avail_Checks table will be used to track availability requests made in a session as well as the data provided in the request. This keeps us from having to pass the availability information back and forth with the consumer while the user makes a reservation. Stored in this table, this data will be combined with the data in the reservation request to provide all the information we need to make the reservation request of the HRS system.

The data we will store from the availability request includes the arrival date, the departure date, the number of adults, the number of children, the smoking preference, and any coupons that we used in quoting the price. Table 7-4 also has an HRSSession column to maintain integrity with the Sessions table.

Table 7-4. Session_Avail_Checks *Table Implementation*

COLUMN	DATA TYPE	SIZE	NOTES
HRSSession	int	4	Foreign key ->Sessions
Check_In_Date	datetime	8	
Check_Out_Date	datetime	8	
Number_Adults	tinyint	1	
Number_Children	tinyint	1	
Smoking	bit		nullable
Coupon	varchar	20	nullable

Now that we have our session data model defined, we need to reference our data. All data access will be done through a stored procedure, so we now need to develop those.

Session Data Access

Our interaction with this data model actually involves two steps. The first is to validate, for each request, whether it is part of an existing session. This simply means that the same user has accessed our service through the same consumer in an established amount of time. For this service, we are setting our session to 30 minutes.

If the session already exists, we simply need to communicate that to our service so that it can validate that fact. If the session does not exist, we need to create a session and then pass its session ID back to our service. To accomplish these two tasks, we will utilize a stored procedure through ADO (ActiveX Data Objects).

Our stored procedure will be called getSessionID (see Listing 7-29.) It will accept as inputs a session ID, a consumer ID, and a found bit (or flag). The session ID serves as an input and an output, since we will pass in any existing session from our service variables and will reference it as the new session ID if necessary. We will know it is necessary because of the found bit. If true, then the session was found, and we can continue processing as requested. If false, then we need to reference the session parameter and make note of the session state of "new" for some processes where it matters.

Listing 7-29. The getSessionID *and* updateSession *stored procedures*

```
CREATE PROCEDURE dbo.getSessionID(@sessionID int output, @consumerID int,
    @found bit output) AS declare @intSession int

select @intSession = HRSSession from Sessions where HRSSession = @sessionID
    and consumerID = @consumerID
```

```
if @intSession is NULL
begin
     insert into sessions(consumerID)Values(@consumerID)
     SELECT @sessionID = @@Identity
     select @found = 0
end
else
begin
     execute updateSession @intSession
     select @sessionID = @intSession
     select @found = 1
end
GO



CREATE PROCEDURE dbo.updateSession(@sessionID int) AS
update sessions set SessionDate = getdate() where hrssession = @sessionID
GO
```

> **NOTE** *The* updateSession *stored procedure is referenced by* getSessionID
> *for updating the date of last activity for the session. This will help with the
> archival of our sessions. Other processes that touch the session could also
> utilize this stored procedure.*

You might question why we need a found parameter if we can simply compare the session ID submitted to the one returned to determine that for
ourselves. The reason is the very rare scenario in which a session ID could be
submitted that would match the next session ID to be created. This is unlikely to
happen, but better safe than sorry!

Finally, we are also passing in the consumer ID as a parameter to simply validate that this consumer is the owner of the session that is referenced. Without
this check, consumers could potentially, and successfully, reference the sessions
of other consumers in error.

Notice that since we are using an identity field to create our unique identifiers, you need to reference the @@Identity value to properly extract it. This
method keeps you from mistakenly grabbing a different session ID that may
have been created at the same time.

> **CAUTION** *From a security perspective, the fact that we are using an identity field makes you inherently vulnerable to hacker attempts by users on other users in the same consumer. For this to be an actual vulnerability, the consumer would have to expose the session ID to users and allow them to change it on their end. In Chapter 8 I will look at how we should handle this kind of implementation to avoid that risk. Also, as the provider, we can feel comfortable in the fact that at no point are users able to see personal data that they themselves did not enter. Thus, a consecutive request to our Web service will not reveal the personal data that was entered to make a reservation.*

processRequest *Validation Logic*

With our database established and ready to utilize, we can start to build out some of the logic in our function. The next thing we need to do is finish the build out of our listener by adding some validation processing and logic. In our design, we identified three main areas for this validation: well-formedness, schema validation, and data validation. Let's validate the requests coming in taking this approach.

Validate XML Well-formedness

XML well-formedness refers to its syntax legality. This pays attention not to the content in the elements, but simply to the true existence of the elements themselves. Fortunately, our MSXML4 parser will accomplish this task for us by default when we load an XML dataset into its DOM object. In fact, you will have a tough time (perhaps impossible) finding a parser that will allow you to load an illegal XML document into the DOM.

To show how this done, I have listed the code following this paragraph. Notice that I start by setting the async property to False. The MXSML parser is a multithreaded library that by default loads XML data asynchronously, meaning it starts the process and continues processing the remaining steps. For most applications, this is inappropriate because programmers have been taught to create objects only at the last possible moment. This means that once we get around to creating an object, we want to start working with it right away. Unfortunately, if you try to access the DOM as it is still loading, you will likely end up with an error message telling you that whatever you are referencing doesn't exist. Setting the async property to False avoids this issue by requiring the routine to wait for the completion of the load before moving on. Here is the code:

```
objDomRequest.async = False
blnLoad = objDomRequest.loadXML(xmlRequest)
If Not blnLoad Then GoTo Data_Error
```

Data_Error is a subroutine that returns a nice message whenever there is an error in the load. It is important to handle your errors very gracefully, and defining different routines for the different errors that can be encountered can help you to do this. Because this is a memory reference, the most likely reason for a failure is that the XML is ill-formed.

The following is a simple routine that provides a user-readable error along with the request package to aid the consumer with troubleshooting the problem:

```
Data_Error:
    processRequest = "<error><level>critical</level><description>Internal XML Data
       Error</description><payload>" & xmlRequest & "</payload></error>"
    GoTo End_Proc
```

Validate XML Against Schemas

The next step in the validation process is to validate the request against the design schema. We have already developed our schemas. This is how we apply them in our service.

The MSXML4 Technical Preview parser allows us for the first time, to validate XML data against XSD Schemas. Previously, the MSXML parser supported only validation against DTDs and XDRs. Just like with the well-formedness check, you must first load the document into the DOM object.

The schema itself is then loaded into a SchemaCache object. This object allows us to add schemas to it as necessary for validation. After creating the cache object itself, we simply need to reference the schemas along with their namespaces. (See Listing 7-30.) Failing to identify the correct namespaces will either cause validation to not happen at all or, even worse, validate the wrong portion of the document.

Listing 7-30. Schema validation with the MSXML4 parser

```
Dim objCache As MSXML2.XMLSchemaCache40
Set objCache = New MSXML2.XMLSchemaCache40
objCache.Add "urn:serviceVariables","http://www.architectingwebservices.com/
   interfaces/hrsws/serviceVariables.xsd"
Set objDomRequest.schemas = objCache
```

```
'-Check for failure to load
If blnLoad Then
      objDomResponse.selectSingleNode
        ("hrs:reservationWS/hrs:serviceVariables/sessionID").nodeTypedValue =
        intSession
Else
      GoTo Data_Error
End If
```

Next we have to set the DOM schema property to the schema cache object. You then have two choices on how to perform the validation itself. You can either set the ValidateOnParse value to True (which validates on loading the data) or call the validate method of the DOM object to manually validate the document in question. The only difference is that in the validation on load, you will not know if it fails due to the legality of the XML syntax or its compliance with the associated schema. For this application we are choosing the latter option, so we are executing the validate method. We are handling the error in the same handler as the other.

Validate Service Variables

Once we have confirmed that the data document can be trusted as legal and valid, we can start referencing its nodes to validate the necessary data. In our initial base functionality, we just need to validate the session data. We saw the stored procedure in the previous section, but now we need to reference it in our code.

We will use the previously established connection, since it is in the same database. We will pass in the sessionID, consumerID, and sessionFound flags. Once they are returned, we will reference the sessionFound and sessionID flags. Adding this code after the request is validated in our processRequest function should produce the desired result. (See Listing 7-31.)

Listing 7-31. Calling getSessionID *stored procedure from the* processRequest *function*

```
Set objCommand = New Command

'-Identify or Create new Session
strSession = objDomRequest.selectSingleNode
  ("hrs:reservationWS/hrs:serviceVariables/sessionID").nodeTypedValue
If strSession = "" Then strSession = "0"
With objCommand
      .ActiveConnection = objConn
      .CommandText = "getSessionID"
      .CommandType = adCmdStoredProc
      .Parameters.Append .CreateParameter("sessionID", adInteger,
        adParamInputOutput, , CInt(strSession))
```

```
   .Parameters.Append .CreateParameter("consumerID", adInteger, adParamInput, ,
     501)
   .Parameters.Append .CreateParameter("sessionFound", adBoolean,
     adParamOutput)
   .Execute
   intSession = .Parameters("sessionID")
   blnNewSession = Not .Parameters("sessionFound")
End With
```

> **NOTE** *If you are not familiar with using the ADO Command object, you may prefer using a Recordset option. If you are not familiar with ADO at all, I recommend that you get an ADO reference book such as ADO Examples and Best Practices by William Vaughn.*

You might notice that we are extracting the session value as a string even though it is an integer data type. The reason for this is that the session could be null if it is the first request. Setting an integer to the null value will give you an error, and rather than handle an error, it is easier to extract it as a string. This is even further justified in this situation because we are validating it through our getSessionID stored procedure, which can handle invalid session IDs. This allows us to set the session to 0 if it is empty and call our procedure just as if we had received a session ID in the request. I did not need to take this same approach with the stage value because the schema defines that value as required.

At the end you see where we are saving the session ID to a local variable and setting a local flag for the session state for efficiency's sake. So, regardless of whether we are in a new or an existing session, we are done with our base session validation. Each interaction stage will also have its own validation, but that process is different for each request and can simply reference the local variables we have assigned.

At this point, if you make a request of the Web service, you will end up getting very much a skeleton form of what the response should be as shown here:

```
<?xml version="1.0"?>
<hrs:reservationWS xmlns:hrs="urn:reservationWS">
    <hrs:serviceVariables>
        <sessionID>1210</sessionID>
        <stage>1</stage>
    </hrs:serviceVariables>
    <hrs:payload/>
</hrs:reservationWS>
```

We basically are getting the valid session ID and the stage of our request. We have yet to add any of the logic to populate our payload according to the request that was made. However, we have laid the groundwork now to add that functionality, so we will start doing so.

Availability Form

The availability form is the first request in our isolated service model. Based on sheer data volume, this will be a light request, heavy response call. Fortunately, this is a fairly simple response to assemble because the response payload is always the same for every request.

The payload refers to the content of the response, not the service variables. The service variables will never be static, since they must be validated and potentially modified or created. Fortunately, our base service takes care of that for every request already, so all we are left with is a simple inclusion of static data in the response skeleton we have already created. What we need to do then is add the responder logic and unit test our response.

processRequest Logic

The logic for our availability form will fall into our group of case statements in the middle of our current processRequest function. We will specifically be dealing with the case in which our intStage value is 1, since that is the stage of our availability form request. The code for our responder logic is shown in Listing 7-32.

Listing 7-32. Availability form responder logic

```
Case 1
     '-Load the availability form
     objDomWorking.Load ("http://www.architectingwebservices.com/
       interfaces/hrsws/availabilityFormResponse.xml")

     '-Load the response into the Response Node
     Set objNodeWorkingList = objDomWorking.selectNodes
       ("hrs:availabilityFormInteraction")
     Set objResponseNode = objNodeWorkingList.Item(0)
     Set objNodeWorkingList = Nothing
```

The first thing we have to do is load the availabilityFormResponse XML document that we defined in the "Isolated Service Interactions" section of our design process. This document is then loaded into our working node list so that we can transfer the document into a node. We have to do this because we cannot take one XML document and append it to another. Instead, we must transfer the document to be embedded into a node element. The difference here is somewhat semantic, since any node can be considered a legal document. The problem is that you can only load a document and can only "move" a node, so this intermediate transfer step is necessary.

Finally, we clean up our working list object, and we are done. The only other necessary step is to add our stylesheet reference, since this is an isolated service request, but we will add that functionality globally after we complete all the individual responses.

Sample Response

The response to a stage 1 request of your isolated service should now look like Listing 7-33.

Listing 7-33. Availability form sample response

```xml
<?xml version="1.0"?>
<hrs:reservationWS xmlns:hrs="urn:reservationWS">
    <hrs:serviceVariables>
        <sessionID>1210</sessionID>
        <stage>1</stage>
    </hrs:serviceVariables>
    <hrs:payload>
        <hrs:hotelAvailabilityForm>
            <checkInDate>
                <name>checkInDate</name>
                <caption>Check-In Date</caption>
                <checkInMonth maxValues="1">
                    <name>checkInMonth</name>
                    <option value="1" caption="Jan"/>
                    . . .
                    <option value="12" caption="Dec"/>
                </checkInMonth>
                <checkInDay maxValues="1">
                    <name>checkInDay</name>
                    <option value="1" caption="1"/>
                    . . .
                    <option value="31" caption="31"/>
                </checkInDay>
                <checkInYear maxValues="1">
                    <name>checkInYear</name>
                    <option value="2001" caption="2001"/>
                    <option value="2002" caption="2002"/>
                </checkInYear>
```

```
            </checkInDate>
            <checkOutDate>
                <name>checkOutDate</name>
                <caption>Check-Out Date</caption>
                <checkOutMonth maxValues="1">
                    <name>checkInMonth</name>
                    <option value="1" caption="Jan"/>
                    . . .
                    <option value="12" caption="Dec"/>
                </checkOutMonth>
                <checkOutDay maxValues="1">
                    <name>checkInDay</name>
                    <option value="1" caption="1"/>
                    . . .
                    <option value="31" caption="31"/>
                </checkOutDay>
                <checkOutYear maxValues="1">
                    <name>checkInYear</name>
                    <option value="2001" caption="2001"/>
                    <option value="2002" caption="2002"/>
                </checkOutYear>
            </checkOutDate>
            <numberAdults maxValues="1">
                <name>numberAdults</name>
                <caption>Number of Adults</caption>
                <option selected="TRUE" value="1" caption="1"/>
                <option value="2" caption="2"/>
                <option value="3" caption="3"/>
                <option value="4" caption="4"/>
            </numberAdults>
            <numberChildren maxValues="1">
                <name>numberChildren</name>
                <caption>Number of Children</caption>
                <option selected="TRUE" value="0" caption="0"/>
                <option value="1" caption="1"/>
                <option value="2" caption="2"/>
                <option value="3" caption="3"/>
                <option value="4" caption="4"/>
            </numberChildren>
            <city>
                <name>city</name>
                <caption>City</caption>
                <maxLength>30</maxLength>
            </city>
```

```
<state>
     <name>state</name>
     <caption>State</caption>
     <maxLength>2</maxLength>
     <minLength>2</minLength>
</state>
<landmark>
     <name>landmark</name>
     <caption>Landmark</caption>
     <maxLength>50</maxLength>
</landmark>
<approxPrice>
     <name>approxPrice</name>
     <caption>Price Preference</caption>
     <maxLength>4</maxLength>

</approxPrice>
<smoking maxValues="1">
     <name>smoking</name>
     <caption>Smoking</caption>
     <option value="TRUE" caption="Yes"/>
     <option value="FALSE" caption="No"/>
</smoking>
<couponCode>
     <name>couponCode</name>
     <caption>Coupon Code</caption>
     <maxLength>10</maxLength>
</couponCode>
<bedSize maxValues="1">
     <name>bedSize</name>
     <caption>Bed Size</caption>
     <option value="King" caption="King"/>
     <option value="Queen" caption="Queen"/>
     <option value="Double" caption="Double"/>
</bedSize>
<hotelAmenities maxValues="*">
     <name>amenity</name>
     <caption>Hotel Amenities</caption>
     <option value="Concierge" caption="Concierge"/>
     <option value="Pool" caption="Pool"/>
     <option value="Workout Facilities" caption="Workout
       Facilities"/>
     <option value="24-hour Room Service" caption="24-hour Room
       Service"/>
```

```
                    <option value="Restaurant" caption="Restaurant"/>
                    <option value="High Speed Internet Access" caption="High
                       Speed Internet Access"/>
                </hotelAmenities>
            </hrs:hotelAvailabilityForm>
        </hrs:payload>
</hrs:reservationWS>
```

The only difference between your response and this one might be the session ID itself for reasons that should be obvious by now. All other requests will still have only the simple response that is provided by our base service.

That is it for the availability form response. This may seem elementary, and it should. Very little logic is required for this response. However, the availability request is much more involved, as we will now find out.

Availability Request

This request is one of the most challenging because it touches several external systems. We will need to interact with the session model in our database and access two interfaces of the HRS system. We will start by developing the logic for working with our session data.

Data Logic

We need to reference our data model to create or update the session data for each availability request made of the system. The only table we need to touch for this purpose is the Session_Avail_Checks table we developed earlier. This table contains the pertinent information for each availability check so that it can be referenced when a reservation is made. This information consists of the following:

- Check-in date

- Check-out date

- Number of adults

- Number of children

- Smoking preference

- Coupon

We now just need to determine whether to perform an insert or an update of this information. This data has a one-to-one relationship with the sessions table, so a matching session must already exist for you to enter a record in this table. At this point in the process, we do not need to concern ourselves with whether the session exists because that has already been resolved by the base service logic. We even have the session ID already available to you.

We also have the session state available to us but it won't help us with this process. That flag tells us if this is a new session, which means that you would need to create the record in the Session_Avail_Checks table, but the fact that it is an existing session does not necessarily mean that a previous availability request has been made. The user may have simply made an availability form request.

This means that we need the database to logically determine whether this data should be inserted or updated in the table. Since we are accessing all of our data through stored procedures, it makes sense to go ahead and embed this there and externalize it to our service logic. Let's go ahead and create the stored procedure and name it setAvailabilityCriteria. We will pass it the session ID as well as the data from our preceding list as shown in Listing 7-34.

Listing 7-34. setAvailabilityCriteria *stored procedure*

```
CREATE PROCEDURE dbo.setAvailabilityCriteria(@sessionID int,
    @checkInDate datetime, @checkOutDate datetime,
    @numberAdults int, @numberChild int, @coupon varchar(10), @smoke bit)
    AS

declare @intSession int

select @intSession = hrssession
from session_avail_checks
where HRSSession = @sessionID

if @intSession is NULL
    insert into session_avail_checks (hrssession,check_in_date,check_out_date,
      number_adults,number_children,coupon,smoking)
    Values(@sessionID,@checkindate,@checkoutdate,
      @numberadults,@numberChild,@coupon,@smoke)
else
    update session_avail_checks set
        hrssession=@sessionID,
        check_in_date=@checkindate,
        check_out_date=@checkoutdate,
        number_adults=@numberadults,
        number_children=@numberChild,
        coupon=@coupon,
        smoking=@smoke
GO
```

This is a relatively simple stored procedure that takes the data and determines whether to execute an insert or update and then does so. You might have noticed that the @smoke parameter, representing users' smoking preference, is defined as a bit here. It was typed as a Boolean in our XML schema, but the two data types are equivalents. Let's go ahead and develop the business logic for our HRS system calls.

wsFetchAvailability Logic

The business logic is typically nonexistent in Web services because they tend to feed off of existing systems and logic. That becomes obvious in dealing with the HRS system for our reservation Web service. Everything between the listener and the HRS system deals with packaging and formatting the data it shuttles between the consumer and our system. I call this section the HRS interface logic because that is what it is.

We determined earlier that we would need two calls to the HRS system to make an availability request and build the appropriate response. To do this we are going to create a single private method that contains all this logic, called wsFetchAvailability. We have already designed its interface, but we need to build out its functionality. The functionality essentially consists of just four steps:

- Call HRS availability routine

- Build results XML document

- Call HRS hotel details routine

- Provide results

We need to assemble the request to the availability routine to get any available matches. The data is passed from the responder just as we need it to make the request, so that step is relatively simple, as shown here:

```
varResult = objHRSavailability.fetchAvailability(dtmCheck_In, dtmCheck_Out,
    intAdults, intChildren, strCity, strState, strLandmark, strCoupon, curPrice,
    strBed, blnSmoking, varAmenities)
```

What we get back is a variant two-dimensional array that contains all the matching hotels returned by the HRS system. This array contains the following data:

- Hotel ID

- Proximity to specified location

- Room type

- Room rate

We need to then take this data and assemble it in an XML format for our response. Since this is the first time we have looked at creating nodes in the DOM, let's take a closer look at this process.

There are actually two steps to creating a node in the DOM. The first is the creation of a node object, which has to be based on an existing document, as seen here:

```
Set objResponseNode = objDomResponse.createElement("hotel")
```

I'm not sure what, if any, relationship there is to the document it was created from because this step does not modify the DOM in any way. To then add this node to the document, we need to utilize the appendChild method of the DOM, specifying the parent for the node we want to add, as shown here:

```
objDomResponse.selectSingleNode("availabilityResults").appendChild
   objResponseNode
```

These two steps actually add an element node named hotel to the availabilityResults node in the root of the objDomResponse document. It is very simple to add a node when you know the path where you want it and that path is valid. Unfortunately this will not always be the case, like when you are building a dynamic dataset.

This situation actually occurs in this function because we do not know how many hotels may be returned from the availability search. The information comes back in an array for this reason. If we have three matching hotels returned from the HRS system, how do we specify the path for adding the hotel details? This dilemma is shown in the following XML data set:

```
<availabilityResults>
    <hotel>
        <hotelID>1234</hotelID>
        . . .
    </hotel>
    <hotel>
        <hotelID>1235</hotelID>
        . . .
    </hotel>
</availabilityResults>
```

If we want to add the room type to the second hotel listing, how do we do that? If we list the path availabilityResults/hotel in any reference in the document, it references the first instance. We can build an involved algorithm in which we keep track of the hotel IDs for each instance and then search for the proper parent based on the value of that child element. Of course, I'd rather not!

The approach I would rather take when building a sequence of like nodes is to implement the logic such that I am always working with the last child of that sequence. That means completing one instance of the hotel element before moving on to the next. Then we can reference the "active" instance with the following code reliably:

```
objDomResponse.selectSingleNode("availabilityResults").lastChild.appendChild
    objResponseNode
```

In keeping with this approach, we are calling the HRS system's fetchHotel routine while we are building the hotel node:

```
varDetails = objHRSavailability.fetchHotel(varResult(x, 0))
```

This routine returns us the following data in a sequenced array:

- Hotel name

- Manager

- Address

- City

- State

- Phone number

We don't care about the manager, so we will ignore that data. The rest we will utilize in our response. Putting all this together, we end up with the function in Listing 7-35.

Listing 7-35. The wsFetchAvailability *method*
```
Private Function wsFetchAvailability( _
    ByVal dtmCheck_In As Date, _
    ByVal dtmCheck_Out As Date, _
    ByVal intAdults As Integer, _
    ByVal intChildren As Integer, _
    ByVal strCity As String, _
```

```
ByVal strState As String, _
ByVal strLandmark As String, _
ByVal strCoupon As String, _
ByVal curPrice As Currency, _
ByVal strBed As String, _
ByVal blnSmoking As Boolean, _
ByVal varAmenities As Variant) As String

    Dim objDomResponse As MSXML2.DOMDocument40
    Dim objResponseNode As MSXML2.IXMLDOMNode
    Dim root As IXMLDOMElement

    Dim objHRSavailability As reservationSystem.clsHRS

    Dim varResult As Variant
    Dim varDetails As Variant
    Dim currElement As Variant

    Dim hotelID As Integer
    Dim x As Integer

    On Error GoTo End_Proc

    Set objDomResponse = New DOMDocument
    objDomResponse.async = False
    Set objHRSavailability = New clsHRS

    objDomResponse.loadXML ("<availabilityResults/>")

    '-call fetchavailability
    varResult = objHRSavailability.fetchAvailability(dtmCheck_In, dtmCheck_Out, _
      intAdults, intChildren, strCity, strState, strLandmark, strCoupon, _
      curPrice,strBed, blnSmoking, varAmenities)

    '-parse through results to get hotelID's
    Dim counter As Integer
    Set root = objDomResponse.documentElement

    '-navigating the resulting array that contains 4x records for x matches
    For x = 0 To UBound(varResult)
```

```
'—create a new hotel node
Set objResponseNode = objDomResponse.createElement("hotel")
objDomResponse.selectSingleNode("availabilityResults").appendChild
  objResponseNode

Set objResponseNode = objDomResponse.createElement("hotelID")
objResponseNode.nodeTypedValue = varResult(x, 0)
objDomResponse.selectSingleNode("availabilityResults").lastChild
  .appendChild objResponseNode

Set objResponseNode = objDomResponse.createElement("proximity")
objResponseNode.nodeTypedValue = varResult(x, 1)
objDomResponse.selectSingleNode("availabilityResults").lastChild
  .appendChild objResponseNode

Set objResponseNode = objDomResponse.createElement("roomType")
objResponseNode.nodeTypedValue = varResult(x, 2)
objDomResponse.selectSingleNode("availabilityResults").lastChild
  .appendChild objResponseNode

Set objResponseNode = objDomResponse.createElement("roomRate")
objResponseNode.nodeTypedValue = varResult(x, 3)
objDomResponse.selectSingleNode("availabilityResults").lastChild
  .appendChild objResponseNode

'—call fetchhotel
varDetails = objHRSavailability.fetchHotel(varResult(x, 0))

'—Navigate hotel details return data
Set objResponseNode = objDomResponse.createElement("hotelName")
objResponseNode.nodeTypedValue = varDetails(0)
objDomResponse.selectSingleNode("availabilityResults").lastChild
  .appendChild objResponseNode

Set objResponseNode = objDomResponse.createElement("hotelPhone")
objResponseNode.nodeTypedValue = varDetails(5)
objDomResponse.selectSingleNode("availabilityResults").lastChild
  .appendChild objResponseNode

Set objResponseNode = objDomResponse.createElement("hotelAddress")
objDomResponse.selectSingleNode("availabilityResults").lastChild
  .appendChild objResponseNode
```

```
                '—Build the hotel address element
                Set objResponseNode = objDomResponse.createElement("address")
                objResponseNode.nodeTypedValue = varDetails(2)
                objDomResponse.selectSingleNode("availabilityResults").lastChild
                  .selectSingleNode("hotelAddress").appendChild objResponseNode

                Set objResponseNode = objDomResponse.createElement("city")
                objResponseNode.nodeTypedValue = varDetails(3)
                objDomResponse.selectSingleNode("availabilityResults").lastChild
                  .selectSingleNode("hotelAddress").appendChild objResponseNode

                Set objResponseNode = objDomResponse.createElement("state")
                objResponseNode.nodeTypedValue = varDetails(4)
                objDomResponse.selectSingleNode("availabilityResults").lastChild
                  .selectSingleNode("hotelAddress").appendChild objResponseNode

        Next

        wsFetchAvailability = objDomResponse.xml

End_Proc:
        Set objDomResponse = Nothing
        Set objResponseNode = Nothing
        Set root = Nothing
        Set objHRSavailability = Nothing

End Function
```

With the wsFetchAvailability method developed, we now need to integrate it into our responder logic.

processRequest *Logic*

Just like with the availability form request, we have a placeholder in the processRequest function for the availability request. In the case statement in which intStage=2 we will add the responder logic for this request.

To call the wsFetchAvailability method, we have to parse out the XML data into local variables. You could theoretically reference the DOM elements directly in the method call, but that gets very unwieldy with 12 elements with one variant array and one optional value.

One way to handle a mixture of optional and required nodes is to borrow a concept from the SAX approach to parsing. In the DOM model, we can traverse the nodes and capture each node value as it is encountered. That keeps you from having to handle errors when attempting to access nonexistent nodes. Also, since we are validating the request through the schema, we don't need to check that the required nodes are present.

I implement this approach by creating a node list out of the request document, as shown here:

```
Set objNodeWorkingList = objDomRequest.selectNodes("hrs:reservationWS/
hrs:payload/hrs:availabilityInteraction/availabilityRequest")
Set objNodeWorking = objNodeWorkingList.Item(0)
```

After creating my list of nodes, I find the number of nodes through the length property and walk one child at a time through a For loop. A Case statement then works well for "capturing" the nodes as they are encountered, as shown here:

```
intLen = objNodeWorking.childNodes.length
For x = 0 To intLen - 1
    Select Case objNodeWorking.childNodes(x).nodeName
    Case "checkInDate"
    . . .
    End Select
Next
```

In most of the cases I am using a simple text reference to save the value to a local variable:

```
strCheckIn = CStr(objNodeWorking.selectSingleNode("checkInDate").Text)
```

The only exceptions to this example are situations in which the child nodes have child nodes of their own. This occurs in two occasions in this request: in the locale and preferences elements. In the case of the locale node, we need to come up with an algorithm for determining which of the city, state, and landmark nodes are present. The business rule is that either the city and state must be present or the landmark must be present. However, both nodes may also be present, so we need to account for that as well. I used a series of If. . .Then statements to perform this check, as you will see in the code.

That takes care of extracting the data to build the parameter list to send to the wsFetchAvailability function. Before making that call, we need to log the request with our database. This is done through the setAvailabilityCriteria stored procedure we created earlier. We will reuse our connection and redefine our command object to call our procedure.

After that is successful, we can then make our call to wsFetchAvailability. Since we are getting back an XML document, we simply need to add the root node for our interaction and return it. It is probably a good idea to validate this document just to make sure your routine did not generate any inconsistencies with your schema. Listing 7-36 shows the responder logic in its entirety.

Listing 7-36. Availability request responder logic

```
Case 2
    '-call availability process
    Set objNodeWorkingList = objDomRequest.selectNodes
      ("hrs:reservationWS/hrs:payload/hrs:availabilityInteraction/
      availabilityRequest")
    Set objNodeWorking = objNodeWorkingList.Item(0)

    intLen = objNodeWorking.childNodes.length
    For x = 0 To intLen - 1
        Select Case objNodeWorking.childNodes(x).nodeName
        Case "checkInDate"
            strCheckIn = CStr(objNodeWorking.selectSingleNode("checkInDate")
                .Text)
        Case "checkOutDate"
            strCheckOut = CStr(objNodeWorking.selectSingleNode
                ("checkOutDate").Text)
        Case "numberAdults"
            strAdults = CStr(objNodeWorking.selectSingleNode("numberAdults")
                .Text)
        Case "numberChildren"
            strChild = CStr(objNodeWorking.selectSingleNode("numberChildren")
                .Text)
        Case "coupon"
            strCoupon = CStr(objNodeWorking.selectSingleNode("coupon")
                .Text)
        Case "approxPrice"
            strPrice = CStr(objNodeWorking.selectSingleNode("approxPrice")
                .Text)
        Case "locale"
            If objNodeWorking.childNodes(x).firstChild.nodeName =
                "cityState" Then
                    strCity = CStr(objNodeWorking.childNodes(x).firstChild
                        .selectSingleNode("city").Text)
                    strState = CStr(objNodeWorking.childNodes(x).firstChild
                        .selectSingleNode("state").Text)
                    If objNodeWorking.childNodes(x).lastChild.nodeName =
                        "landmark" Then
                            strLandmark = CStr(objNodeWorking.childNodes(x).lastChild
                                .selectSingleNode("landmark").Text)
```

```
                    End If
              Else
                  strLandmark = CStr(objNodeWorking.childNodes(x).firstChild
                    .selectSingleNode("landmark").Text)
                  If objNodeWorking.childNodes(x).lastChild.nodeName
                    = "cityState" Then
                      strCity = CStr(objNodeWorking.childNodes(x).lastChild
                        .selectSingleNode("city").Text)
                      strState = CStr(objNodeWorking.childNodes(x).lastChild
                        .selectSingleNode("state").Text)
                  End If
              End If
        Case "preferences"
              intLen2 = objNodeWorking.selectSingleNode("preferences").childNodes
                .length
              z = 0
              For y = 0 To intLen2 - 1
                  Select Case objNodeWorking.selectSingleNode("preferences")
                    .childNodes(y).nodeName
                  Case "bedSize"
                      strBed = CStr(objNodeWorking.selectSingleNode
                        ("preferences").selectSingleNode("bedSize").Text)
                  Case "smoking"
                      strSmoke = CStr(objNodeWorking.selectSingleNode
                        ("preferences").selectSingleNode("smoking").Text)
                  Case "amenity"
                      varAmenities(z) = CStr(objNodeWorking
                        .selectSingleNode("preferences").childNodes(y).Text)
                      z = z + 1
                  End Select
              Next
        Case Else
        End Select
Next

'-Enter selected criteria into database
Set objCommand = New Command
With objCommand
     .ActiveConnection = objConn
     .CommandText = "setAvailabilityCriteria"
     .CommandType = adCmdStoredProc
     .Parameters.Append .CreateParameter("sessionID", adInteger,
       adParamInput, , CInt(strSession))
```

```
        .Parameters.Append .CreateParameter("checkInDate", adDate, adParamInput
          ,,CDate(strCheckIn))
        .Parameters.Append .CreateParameter("checkOutDate", adDate,
          adParamInput, , CDate(strCheckOut))
        .Parameters.Append .CreateParameter("numberAdults", adInteger,
          adParamInput, , CInt(strAdults))
        .Parameters.Append .CreateParameter("numberChildren", adInteger,
          adParamInput, , CInt(strChild))
        .Parameters.Append .CreateParameter("coupon", adChar, adParamInput, 10,
          strCoupon)
        .Parameters.Append .CreateParameter("smoking", adBoolean, adParamInput
          ,,CBool(strSmoke))
        .Execute
End With


'—Call wsFetchAvailability
strPayload = wsFetchAvailability(CDate(strCheckIn), _
  CDate(strCheckOut), _
  CInt(strAdults), _
  CInt(strChild), _
  strCity, _
  strState, _
  strLandmark, _
  strCoupon, _
  CCur(strPrice), _
  strBed, _
  CBool(strSmoke), _
  varAmenities)


'Add root node for availability interaction
strPayload = "<hrs:availabilityInteraction xmlns:hrs=""urn:
  availabilityInteraction"">" & strPayload & "</hrs:availabilityInteraction>"

'—Load the availability results into a DOM and validate
objDomWorking.loadXML (strPayload)
blnLoad = objDomWorking.Validate

If Not blnLoad Then GoTo Data_Error

'—Load the response into the Response Node
```

```
Set objNodeWorkingList = objDomWorking.selectNodes
    ("hrs:availabilityInteraction")
Set objResponseNode = objNodeWorkingList.Item(0)
Set objNodeWorkingList = Nothing
```

Sample Response

With that complete, we should next run a unit test of this interaction by making the request with our test client. Listing 7-37 shows a valid response that we might get.

Listing 7-37. Availability request response

```xml
<?xml version="1.0"?>
<hrs:reservationWS xmlns:hrs="urn:reservationWS">
    <hrs:serviceVariables>
        <sessionID>1086</sessionID>
        <stage>2</stage>
    </hrs:serviceVariables>
    <hrs:payload>
        <hrs:availabilityInteraction xmlns:hrs="urn:availabilityInteraction">
            <availabilityResults>
                <hotel>
                    <hotelID>543</hotelID>
                    <proximity>1.5</proximity>
                    <roomType>Suite</roomType>
                    <roomRate>69.99</roomRate>
                    <hotelName>Plano West</hotelName>
                    <hotelPhone>972-555-1212</hotelPhone>
                    <hotelAddress>
                        <address>555 Main Street</address>
                        <city>Plano</city>
                        <state>TX</state>
                    </hotelAddress>
                </hotel>
                <hotel>
                    <hotelID>12345</hotelID>
                    <proximity>3</proximity>
                    <roomType>Economy</roomType>
                    <roomRate>49.99</roomRate>
                    <hotelName>Plano West</hotelName>
                    <hotelPhone>972-555-1212</hotelPhone>
```

```
                    <hotelAddress>
                        <address>555 Main Street</address>
                        <city>Plano</city>
                        <state>TX</state>
                    </hotelAddress>
                </hotel>
            </availabilityResults>
        </hrs:availabilityInteraction>
    </hrs:payload>
</hrs:reservationWS>
```

If you are following along and creating your own version of this Web service, your results will likely be different, but your structure should still be the same.

Hotel Detail View

This is the interaction for which we have to provide all the logic and data. The form requests we have to support are simply referencing XML documents and embedding them, so this one will be a little more challenging.

In this request, the consumer is requesting more information on one of our hotels. The idea is that this request will follow an availability request, but we are not enforcing such a rule. Theoretically, the consumer could request this information for any reason and we would provide it. This makes the process a little easier on us.

If we refer to the Hotel Detail View section in our design, we'll see that we have to build these three entities to provide this functionality:

- Content data model

- Stored procedure

- wsFetchHotelContent function

Content Data Model

The content data model has already been designed, but we have not specified the field types and details. We need to start there before doing anything else.

The data model consists of two tables: Hotel_Content and Content_Ref_Table. The Content_Ref_Table (Table 7-5) acts as a reference table for the actual content stored in Hotel_Content (Table 7-6), as we saw in the design of the data model.

Table 7-5. `Content_Ref_Table` *Implementation*

COLUMN	DATA TYPE	SIZE	NOTES
ContentRef_Key	tinyint	1	Primary key
Ref_Name	varchar	20	

Table 7-6. `Hotel_Content` *Implementation*

COLUMN	DATA TYPE	SIZE	NOTES
HotelID	int	4	Primary key
ContentRef_Key	tinyint	1	Foreign key -> Content_Ref_Table
Ref_Value	varchar	255	

We have some predefined content that we want to expose immediately, so we should populate the `Content_Ref_Table` with that data. The four content types are shown in Table 7-7.

Table 7-7. Initial Data Values in `Content_Ref_Table`

CONTENT_REF_KEY	REF_NAME
1	mainPicture
2	facilitiesPicture
3	roomPicture
4	hotelDescription

I have already discussed the relationship between these two tables, so let's move on to exposing this data to our service.

Data Logic

We eventually need to expose this data in XML, so typically you might consider using SQL Server 2000's "for XML" functionality. Unfortunately, our database model is set up so that the element name must be built dynamically (the Ref_Name field), and that is something SQL Server still cannot do. Instead, we have to extract the data through the usual recordset object and build the XML manually in our program logic.

Like I said, we are building the XML dynamically by retrieving the element name and values that relate to each other for a given hotel ID. That means that we have an integer input parameter and will return a series of records containing the content. It is fairly straightforward when you look at it in Listing 7-38:

Listing 7-38. The getHotelContent *stored procedure*

```
CREATE PROCEDURE getHotelContent(@hotelID int) AS
select   Ref_Name, Ref_Value
from Hotel_Content join Content_Ref_Table on Hotel_Content.ContentRef_Key =
  Content_Ref_Table.ContentRef_Key
where hotelID = @hotelID
GO
```

We are now ready to move on to the code that will access our data in the content data model.

wsFetchHotelContent *Logic*

This logic was turned into a function because it really represents a unit of work that could easily be utilized by other processes as either an extension to our Web service or possibly even other applications and services.

This function takes a hotel ID number, extracts the content data from our database, and formats it in XML for the response. This function builds the XML manually. This is not something you want to do regularly, but when the data is dynamic and yet clean enough for XML (as ours was designed), then this approach can make sense.

There is nothing very special about this function or logic, so I'll just present it in Listing 7-39 for your review.

Listing 7-39. The wsFetchHotelContent *function*

```
Public Function wsFetchHotelContent(ByVal Hotel_ID As Integer) As String

    Dim objDomResponse As MSXML2.DOMDocument40

    '-Database access objects
    Dim objConn As ADODB.Connection
    Dim objCommand As ADODB.Command
    Dim objRecordset As ADODB.Recordset

    Dim strResponse As String
    Dim strDomain As String
    Dim strPayload as String

    '-If an error is encountered, just return an empty string
```

```
On Error GoTo End_Proc

Set objConn = New Connection

'—Set connection properties.
With objConn
     .ConnectionTimeout = 25
     .Provider = "sqloledb"
     .Properties("Data Source").Value = ServerName
     .Properties("Initial Catalog").Value = DBName
     .Properties("Integrated Security").Value = "SSPI"
     .Properties("User ID").Value = UserName
     .Properties("password").Value = Password
     .Open
End With

Set objCommand = New Command
Set objCommand.ActiveConnection = objConn
objCommand.CommandText = "getHotelContent" & Hotel_ID
Set objRecordset = New Recordset
objRecordset.Open objCommand
objRecordset.MoveFirst

'—Dynamically build the XML response from the recordset returned
strResponse = "<hotelContent>"

strDomain = "http://www.architectingwebservices.com"

Do while Not objRecordset.EOF
    If objRecordset(0) <> "Hotel Description" then
         strPayload = strDomain & objRecordset(1)
    Else
         strPayload = strDomain & objRecordset(1)
    End If
    strResponse = strResponse & "<" & objRecordset(0) & ">" & strPayload &
    "</" & objRecordset(0) & ">"
    objRecordset.MoveNext
Loop

strResponse = strResponse & "</hotelContent>"

wsFetchHotelContent = strResponse
```

```
End_Proc:
    '—cleanup
    objRecordset.Close
    objConn.Close

    Set objDomResponse = Nothing
    Set objConn = Nothing
    Set objCommand = Nothing
    Set objRecordset = Nothing

End Function
```

processRequest *Logic*

Now we need to integrate our function into the responder logic in the
processRequest function. This is less involved simply because we are only passing one piece of information to it, the hotel ID. This eliminates the need for a lot
of parsing. In fact, we can actually reference the element in the request DOM
directly in our function call.

Like the wsFetchHotelContent function itself, we will be adding a parent
node to its response manually to keep it simple. This makes it a valid
detailInteraction document, which is loaded into the objResponseNode object,
as shown in Listing 7-40.

Listing 7-40. Hotel detail responder logic

```
Case 3
    '—call detail process
    strPayload = wsFetchHotelContent(objDomRequest.selectSingleNode
        ("hrs:reservationWS/hrs:payload/detailInteraction/detailRequest/hotelID")
        .nodeTypedValue)

    strPayload = "<hrs:detailInteraction xmlns:hrs=""urn:detailInteraction"">" &
        strPayload & "</hrs:detailInteraction>"

    '—Load the availability results into a DOM
    blnLoad = objDomWorking.loadXML(strPayload)

    If Not blnLoad Then GoTo Data_Error

    '—Load the response into the Response Node
    Set objNodeWorkingList = objDomWorking.selectNodes("hrs:detailInteraction")
    Set objResponseNode = objNodeWorkingList.Item(0)
    Set objNodeWorkingList = Nothing
```

Sample Response

Once the database is populated with information on the hotels, you should be able to make a request through the test client that produces something similar to the document in Listing 7-41.

Listing 7-41. Hotel detail request response

```xml
<?xml version="1.0"?>
<hrs:reservationWS xmlns:hrs="urn:reservationWS">
    <hrs:serviceVariables>
        <sessionID>1218</sessionID>
        <stage>3</stage>
    </hrs:serviceVariables>
    <hrs:payload>
        <hrs:detailInteraction xmlns:hrs="urn:detailInteraction">
            <hotelContent>
                <mainPicture>http://www.architectingwebservices.com/hrsws/
                    images/dfw/dwntwn/front.gif</mainPicture>
                <facilitiesPicture>http://www.architectingwebservices.com/
                    hrsws/images/dfw/dwntwn/banquethall.gif</facilitiesPicture>
                <facilitiesPicture>http://www.architectingwebservices.com/
                    hrsws/images/dfw/dwntwn/pool.gif</facilitiesPicture>
                <roomPicture>http://www.architectingwebservices.com/hrsws/
                    images/dfw/dwntwn/economy.gif</roomPicture>
                <roomPicture>http://www.architectingwebservices.com/hrsws/
                    images/dfw/dwntwn/suite.gif</roomPicture>
                <hotelDescription>Our four-star resort is close to downtown
                    with easy access to all of DFW's major attractions.
                    Recently renovated with all the amenities a business
                    traveler needs to stay productive while on the
                    road.</hotelDescription>
            </hotelContent>
        </hrs:detailInteraction>
    </hrs:payload>
</hrs:reservationWS>
```

This completes the hotel detail step of our hotel reservation Web service. This functionality is a significant example of how it is possible to augment an existing process that wasn't originally designed for use on the Internet. This hopefully gives you confidence that such an approach can be taken when dealing with processes on legacy systems.

The next request we need to build out is the reservation form. This will be the first step for isolated service consumers to submit an actual reservation request.

Reservation Form

The reservation form process is virtually identical to the availability form process. We will be referencing a physical document, loading it into our application, and appending it to our response document.

processRequest Logic

The processRequest function is responsible for loading the physical file containing the reservation form and adding it to our response document (see Listing 7-42.) The only difference is that we are adding a precedence check to see if this is a new session. There is no reason for this step to be the first in a session, because an availability request must be made before a reservation request will even be accepted. We are just catching this error early so that users won't go through the trouble of completing the form only to have it be rejected due to the business rules.

Listing 7-42. Reservation form responder logic

```
Case 4
     '—Check if new session - if so, this request is illegal
     If blnNewSession = True Then GoTo Precedence_Error

     '—Load the reservation form
     objDomWorking.Load ("http://www.architectingwebservices.com/
       interfaces/hrsws/reservationFormResponse.xml")

     '—Load the response into the Response Node
     Set objNodeWorkingList = objDomWorking.selectNodes
       ("hrs:reservationFormInteraction")
     Set objResponseNode = objNodeWorkingList.Item(0)
     Set objNodeWorkingList = Nothing
```

Sample Response

If we look at the response, we'll see that it is very similar to the availability form response. That is only logical, since we have the same header data and are using the same methodology in defining the data elements. (See Listing 7-43.)

Listing 7-43. Reservation form response

```xml
<?xml version="1.0"?>
<hrs:reservationWS xmlns:hrs="urn:reservationWS">
    <hrs:serviceVariables>
        <sessionID>1072</sessionID>
        <stage>4</stage>
    </hrs:serviceVariables>
    <hrs:payload>
        <hrs:reservationFormInteraction xmlns:hrs=
            "urn:reservationFormInteraction">
            <reservationForm>
                <firstName>
                    <name>firstName</name>
                    <caption>First Name</caption>
                    <maxLength>20</maxLength>
                </firstName>
                <lastName>
                    <name>lastName</name>
                    <caption>Last Name</caption>
                    <maxLength>30</maxLength>
                </lastName>
                <homePhone>
                    <name>homePhone</name>
                    <caption>Home Phone Number</caption>
                    <maxLength>15</maxLength>
                </homePhone>
                <homeAddress>
                    <address>
                        <name>address</name>
                        <caption>Address</caption>
                        <maxLength>30</maxLength>
                    </address>
                    <address>
                        <name>address</name>
                        <caption>Address</caption>
                        <maxLength>30</maxLength>
                    </address>
                    <city>
```

```
              <name>city</name>
              <caption>City</caption>
              <maxLength>30</maxLength>
       </city>
       <state>
              <name>state</name>
              <caption>State</caption>
              <maxLength>2</maxLength>
              <minLength>2</minLength>
       </state>
       <zipCode>
              <name>zipCode</name>
              <caption>Zip-Code</caption>
              <maxLength>5</maxLength>
              <minLength>5</minLength>
       </zipCode>
</homeAddress>
<couponCode>
       <name>couponCode</name>
       <caption>Coupon Code</caption>
       <maxLength>10</maxLength>
</couponCode>
<cardNumber>
       <name>cardNumber</name>
       <caption>Credit Card Number</caption>
       <maxLength>16</maxLength>
</cardNumber>
<nameOfOwner>
       <name>nameOfOwner</name>
       <caption>Name on Credit Card</caption>
       <maxLength>50</maxLength>
</nameOfOwner>
<cardIssuer maxValues="1">
       <name>cardIssuer</name>
       <caption>Card Issuer</caption>
       <option value="Visa" caption="Visa"/>
       <option value="Mastercard" caption="Mastercard"/>
       <option value="American Express" caption="American
          Express"/>
       <option value="Discover" caption="Discover"/>
</cardIssuer>
<ccExpirDate>
       <name>ccExpirDate</name>
       <caption>Credit Card Expiration Date</caption>
```

```
                                <ccExpirMonth maxValues="1">
                                    <name>ccExpirMonth</name>
                                    <option value="1" caption="Jan"/>
                                    . . .
                                    <option value="12" caption="Dec"/>
                                </ccExpirMonth>
                                <ccExpirYear maxValues="1">
                                    <name>ccExpirYear</name>
                                    <option value="2001" caption="2001"/>
                                    <option value="2002" caption="2002"/>
                                    <option value="2003" caption="2003"/>
                                    <option value="2004" caption="2004"/>
                                    <option value="2005" caption="2005"/>
                                    <option value="2006" caption="2006"/>
                                </ccExpirYear>
                        </ccExpirDate>
                        <billingAddress>
                            <address>
                                    <name>address</name>
                                    <caption>Address</caption>
                                    <maxLength>30</maxLength>
                            </address>
                            <address>
                                    <name>address</name>
                                    <caption>Address</caption>
                                    <maxLength>30</maxLength>
                            </address>
                            <city>
                                    <name>city</name>
                                    <caption>City</caption>
                                    <maxLength>30</maxLength>
                            </city>
                            <state>
                                    <name>state</name>
                                    <caption>State</caption>
                                    <maxLength>2</maxLength>
                                    <minLength>2</minLength>
                            </state>
                            <zipCode>
                                    <name>zipCode</name>
                                    <caption>Zip-Code</caption>
                                    <maxLength>5</maxLength>
                                    <minLength>5</minLength>
                            </zipCode>
```

```
        </billingAddress>
      </reservationForm>
    </hrs:reservationFormInteraction>
  </hrs:payload>
</hrs:reservationWS>
```

Reservation Request

We have arrived at the final step of this Web service workflow. Everything has been building up to this point, when a reservation request is submitted to the system for a person's travel plans. This step is a little different from all the others because we have to retrieve some data from the database, utilize a little business logic, and interact with the HRS system. The anticipated result will be a confirmation number that should assure the user that the reservation has been made.

Data Elements and Logic

We need to potentially retrieve three groups of data from our data store. The first one is the availability criteria from the last availability request the user submitted. This data will be used to limit the amount of data requested of the user, as well as sent between the service and consumer, in the reservation request process.

To expose the criteria to the application, we will build a simple stored procedure called getAvailabilityCriteria. It accepts a session ID as its lone parameter, and a recordset is returned with the criteria that were saved through the setAvailabilityCriteria stored procedure, as shown in Listing 7-44.

Listing 7-44. The getAvailabilityCriteria *stored procedure*
```
CREATE PROCEDURE dbo.getAvailabilityCriteria(@sessionID int) AS
Select check_in_date,check_out_date,number_adults,number_children,coupon,
   smoking
from session_avail_checks
where hrssession = @sessionID
GO
```

The second piece of data we need is for transcribing room type descriptions to room type codes. As we identified in our design process, the HRS availability interface returns the room type as a string, but the reservation interface requires a code. To handle this appropriately, we need our own index matching the room codes with the room names. There are only four room types available today, but by putting this in the database, we will be able to easily adapt to any changes in the HRS system.

The table will consist of two simple columns, one for the code and one for the name, as seen in Table 7-8.

Table 7-8. HRS_roomTypes *Implementation*

COLUMN	DATA TYPE	SIZE	NOTES
RoomType_code	int	4	Primary key
RoomType_name	varchar	20	

The table will initially be populated with four records, show in Table 7-9.

Table 7-9. Initial Data Values in Content_Ref_Table

ROOMTYPE_CODE	ROOMTYPE_NAME
101	Suite
201	Value
301	Business
401	Premiere

Now all we need is the stored procedure to retrieve this information. For this situation, all we need to do is retrieve a code for the name that we have. However, it is easy to see the possibility for needing to do the opposite sometime later: retrieve a name given a code. For this reason we will make the stored procedure slightly more robust by allowing both values as inputs and outputs. Then we just need the If. . .Then logic to determine which process to run. The key for making this determination is the roomType_code input. If the value is 0, then look up the code for the name, otherwise look up the name for the code as seen in Listing 7-45.

Listing 7-45. The getRoomTypes *stored procedure*

```
CREATE PROCEDURE dbo.getRoomTypes(@roomType_code int output,
  @roomType_name varchar(20) output) AS
if @roomType_code = 0
    Select @roomType_code = roomType_code from HRS_roomTypes
    where roomType_name = @roomType_name
else
    Select @roomType_name = roomType_name from HRS_roomTypes
    where roomType_code = @roomType_code
GO
```

The last data reference is related to reservation failures, so it won't be necessary for every request. These are not system failure errors, but processing errors due to the sudden lack of availability, credit card problems, etc. If there is a problem with the reservation process, a code is returned from the HRS system. We know what the codes stand for, but no description is provided by the HRS interface. To address this issue, we will maintain our own table with codes and a human-readable description available to consumers and/or users.

The table itself is called `HRS_errors` and has a simple layout, shown in Table 7-10.

Table 7-10. `HRS_errors` *Implementation*

COLUMN	DATA TYPE	SIZE	NOTES
Error_key	tinyint	1	Primary key
Error_descrip	varchar	255	

Any confirmation returned with a value below 100 is an error code. Through this table we can provide the descriptions we want for each code. The error codes that will initially populate this table are listed in Table 7-11.

Table 7-11. Initial Data Values in `Content_Ref_Table`

ERROR_KEY	ERROR_DESCRIP
0	"The reservation you requested is unavailable at this time."
1	"The personal information supplied is incomplete. Please check the information and try again."
2	"The credit card provided for this reservation could not be approved at this time. Please try another credit card."
3	"The credit card information is not valid. Please check the information and try again."

To access this error data we have a simple stored procedure that accepts the error code and returns the corresponding description, as shown here:

```
CREATE PROCEDURE dbo.lookupError(@error int,@errorText varchar(255) output)
   AS
select @errorText =  error_descrip from HRS_errors where error_key = @error
GO
```

Now that we have our data elements and logic defined, let's look at implementing all the functionality for our reservation requests in the `processRequest` function.

processRequest *Logic*

Unlike the availability request and hotel detail process, we will not be creating a separate function to contain logic for this request. A lot of data is involved in this request, and there probably wouldn't be much benefit to moving it around between functions.

The first step in processing this request is checking for precedence. This is done with a check of the `blnNewSession` value. If it is set to true, we know that an availability request has not been made. However, this only checks the existence of the session. This does not qualify that an availability request was actually made. We will validate that later when we retrieve the availability criteria.

Prior to that we have a lot of parsing to do. We will take each value in the reservation request document and save it as a local variable. This task is easier than it was in some of our other processes because there are no arrays and very few optional fields. Parsing XML is relatively simple when you specify which nodes you are accessing and can trust that they will be there.

With that, let's go ahead and take a look at our responder code, shown in Listing 7-46, which will provide the response to the reservation request.

Listing 7-46. Reservation interaction responder code

```
Case 5
    '—Check if new session - if so, this request is illegal
    If blnNewSession = True Then GoTo Precedence_Error

    '—parse xml data for HRS reservation call
    Dim objMakeReservation As reservationSystem.clsHRS
    Dim intConfirmNum As Long

    Set objNodeWorkingList = objDomRequest.selectNodes("hrs:reservationWS/
        hrs:payload/hrs:reservationInteraction/hrs:reservationRequest")
    Set objNodeWorking = objNodeWorkingList.Item(0)

    '—Extract hotel data
    strHotelID = objNodeWorking.selectSingleNode
        ("hrs:hotelData/hotelID").nodeTypedValue
    strRoomType = objNodeWorking.selectSingleNode
        ("hrs:hotelData/roomType").nodeTypedValue
```

```
'—Extract personal data
strFirstName = objNodeWorking.selectSingleNode
  ("hrs:personalData/firstName").nodeTypedValue
strLastName = objNodeWorking.selectSingleNode
  ("hrs:personalData/lastName").nodeTypedValue
strHomePhone = objNodeWorking.selectSingleNode
  ("hrs:personalData/homePhone").nodeTypedValue
strHomeAddress1 = objNodeWorking.selectSingleNode
  ("hrs:personalData/homeAddress/address").nodeTypedValue
If objNodeWorking.selectSingleNode("hrs:personalData/homeAddress/address")
  .nextSibling.nodeName = "address" Then
  strHomeAddress2 = bjNodeWorking.selectSingleNode("hrs:personalData/
  homeAddress/address").nextSibling.nodeTypedValue
strHomeCity = objNodeWorking.selectSingleNode
  ("hrs:personalData/homeAddress/city").nodeTypedValue
strHomeState = objNodeWorking.selectSingleNode
  ("hrs:personalData/homeAddress/state").nodeTypedValue
strHomeZip = objNodeWorking.selectSingleNode
  ("hrs:personalData/homeAddress/zipCode").nodeTypedValue
strBillAddress1 = objNodeWorking.selectSingleNode
  ("hrs:personalData/billAddress/address").nodeTypedValue
If objNodeWorking.selectSingleNode("hrs:personalData/billAddress/address")
  .nextSibling.nodeName = "address" Then _
strBillAddress2 = objNodeWorking.selectSingleNode("hrs:personalData/
  billAddress/address").nextSibling.nodeTypedValue
strBillCity = objNodeWorking.selectSingleNode("hrs:personalData/
  billAddress/city").nodeTypedValue
strBillState = objNodeWorking.selectSingleNode("hrs:personalData/
  billAddress/state").nodeTypedValue
strBillZip = objNodeWorking.selectSingleNode("hrs:personalData/
  billAddress/zipCode").nodeTypedValue
strCCnumber = objNodeWorking.selectSingleNode("hrs:personalData/
  hrs:ccData/number").nodeTypedValue
strccexpdate = objNodeWorking.selectSingleNode("hrs:personalData/
  hrs:ccData/expirationDate").nodeTypedValue
strCCName = objNodeWorking.selectSingleNode("hrs:personalData/
  hrs:ccData/nameOfOwner").nodeTypedValue
strccissuer = objNodeWorking.selectSingleNode("hrs:personalData/
  hrs:ccData/issuer").nodeTypedValue
```

```
'—Lookup previous session data in database for criteria information
Set objCommand = New Command
Set objRS = New Recordset

With objCommand
    .ActiveConnection = objConn
    .CommandText = "getAvailabilityCriteria"
    .CommandType = adCmdStoredProc
    .Parameters.Append .CreateParameter("sessionID", adInteger,
      adParamInput, , CInt(strSession))
    Set objRS = .Execute
End With

If Not objRS.EOF Then
    '—Set Criteria values
    strCheckIn = objRS(0)
    strCheckOut = objRS(1)
    strAdults = objRS(2)
    strChild = objRS(3)
    strSmoke = objRS(5)
    If objRS(4) <> Null Then strCoupon = objRS(4)
Else
    GoTo Precedence_Error
End If

'—Convert room type to integer
Set objCommand = New Command

With objCommand
    .ActiveConnection = objConn
    .CommandText = "getRoomTypes"
    .CommandType = adCmdStoredProc
    .Parameters.Append .CreateParameter("intRoomType", adInteger,
      adParamInputOutput, , 0)
    .Parameters.Append .CreateParameter("strRoomType", adChar,
      adParamInputOutput, 20, strRoomType)
    .Execute
    strRoomType = .Parameters("intRoomType").Value
End With
```

```
'—Call HRS interface
Set objMakeReservation = New clsHRS
intConfirmNum = objMakeReservation.makeReservation(CLng(strHotelID), _
  CInt(strRoomType), _
  CDate(strCheckIn), _
  CDate(strCheckOut), _
  CInt(strAdults), _
  CInt(strChild), _
  strFirstName, _
  strLastName, _
  strHomeAddress1, _
  strHomeAddress2, _
  strHomeCity, _
  strHomeState, _
  strHomeZip, _
  strHomePhone, _
  strCCnumber, _
  CInt(strHotelID), _
  CInt(strHotelID), _
  strccissuer, _
  strBillAddress1, _
  strBillAddress2, _
  strBillCity, _
  strBillState, _
  strBillZip, _
  strCoupon, _
  CBool(strSmoke))

strPayload = "<confirmationID>" & CStr(intConfirmNum) & "</confirmationID>"
strPayload = strPayload & "<phoneNumber>800-555-1234</phoneNumber>"
strPayload = "<hrs:reservationResponse>" & strPayload & _
  "</hrs:reservationResponse>"
strPayload = "<hrs:reservationInteraction xmlns:hrs=
  ""urn:reservationInteraction"">" & strPayload & _
  "</hrs:reservationInteraction>"

'—Load the availability results into a DOM
blnLoad = objDomWorking.loadXML(strPayload)

If Not blnLoad Then GoTo Data_Error
```

```
'—Check if confirmation is an error
If intConfirmNum < 100 Then

        '—look up error codes
    Set objCommand = New Command
    With objCommand
        .ActiveConnection = objConn
        .CommandText = "HRSerrorLookUp"
        .CommandType = adCmdStoredProc
        .Parameters.Append .CreateParameter("error", adInteger, adParamInput
            ,, intConfirmNum)
        .Parameters.Append .CreateParameter("errorText", adChar,
            adParamInput, 255, strCoupon)
        .Execute
    End With

    'append description to payload
    Set objNodeWorking = objDomWorking.createElement("description")
    objResponseNode.nodeTypedValue =
        objCommand.Parameters("errorText").Value
    objDomWorking.selectSingleNode("hrs:reservationInteraction").appendChild
        objNodeWorkingList

End If

Set objNodeWorkingList = objDomRequest.selectNodes("hrs:reservationWS/
    hrs:payload/hrs:reservationInteraction/hrs:reservationRequest")
objDomWorking.selectSingleNode("hrs:reservationInteraction").appendChild
    objNodeWorkingList.Item(0)

'—Load the response into the Response Node
Set objNodeWorkingList =
    objDomWorking.selectNodes("hrs:reservationInteraction")
Set objResponseNode = objNodeWorkingList.Item(0)
Set objNodeWorkingList = Nothing
```

Sample Response

In a sample response, we will see just how small a portion of the entire document is made up of the resulting information. Our confirmation ID is slipped in between our service variables and the copy of the reservation request (see Listing 7-47), which we decided to include in our design process.

Listing 7-47. Response from reservation request

```
<?xml version="1.0"?>
<hrs:reservationWS xmlns:hrs="urn:reservationWS">
    <hrs:serviceVariables>
        <sessionID>1086</sessionID>
        <stage>5</stage>
    </hrs:serviceVariables>
    <hrs:payload>
        <hrs:reservationInteraction xmlns:hrs="urn:reservationInteraction">
        <hrs:reservationResponse>
            <confirmationID>678</confirmationID>
            <phoneNumber>800-555-1234</phoneNumber>
        </hrs:reservationResponse>
            <hrs:reservationRequest xmlns:hrs="urn:reservationRequest">
                <hrs:hotelData>
                    <hotelID>1234</hotelID>
                    <roomType>Suite</roomType>
                </hrs:hotelData>
                <hrs:personalData>
                    <homeAddress>
                        <address>301 Main St.</address>
                        <city>Edwardsville</city>
                        <state>IL</state>
                        <zipCode>62025</zipCode>
                    </homeAddress>
                    <firstName>Jamie</firstName>
                    <lastName>Langenbrunner</lastName>
                    <homePhone>618-555-1111</homePhone>
                    <billAddress>
                        <address>301 Main St.</address>
                        <city>Edwardsville</city>
                        <state>IL</state>
                        <zipCode>62025</zipCode>
                    </billAddress>
                    <hrs:ccData>
                        <number>4444333322221111</number>
                        <issuer>Visa</issuer>
                        <expirationDate>2003-05-01</expirationDate>
                        <nameOfOwner>James Langenbrunner</nameOfOwner>
```

```
            </hrs:ccData>
          </hrs:personalData>
        </hrs:reservationRequest>
      </hrs:reservationInteraction>
    </hrs:payload>
</hrs:reservationWS>
```

The only difference between this response and a failed reservation request response is that the confirmation ID would be a number lower than 100 and it would be followed by a description field containing the text from our HRS_errors reference table.

This actually completes all of the request-specific logic necessary for our Web service. This does not mean that we are done, however. We still have two more steps to implement to complete the entire service: the security model and the presentation model for the isolated service.

Security Model

Now that we have built and tested our Web service, it would be appropriate to go back and modify the program to secure it. Some might argue that this should have been set up with the initial base service, but I did not simplify the troubleshooting process. We had already developed our security model, so we wouldn't code ourselves into a corner, but adding it at such an early stage is taking on more effort than necessary.

Since we are using client certificates, you might be wondering why we need to validate the consumer on a data level. Although this method could be used to authenticate consumers, the purpose here is less about authentication and more about session management.

Because the users do not connect directly to our service, we have no reliable means for tracking session activity between the requests of various users via various consumers. We have the service variables, but that is simply XML data and is relatively easy to spoof. We chose not to maintain consumer IDs in the service variables for this very reason. Being able to reference a consumer through the consumer's client certificate gives us a means for "grounding" our sessions. This limits the potential for consumers to spoof the sessions of other consumers. Of course they can still spoof the sessions in their domain, but they control their users' experience regardless. They can abuse their own users regardless of our service, so we have to accept that possibility.

The security for this service is similar to the security we set up for the Web service call of our COM object in Chapter 6. In that example, we set up our service to only accept calls coming from trusted consumers. We will simply extend that functionality to integrate the consumer identity into our Web service workflow. This integration will involve two additional steps: extracting the certificate data and validating the consumer.

> **NOTE** *If you have questions about setting up the site security or client cer-tificates for our Web service, review the section in Chapter 6.*

Extracting the Certificate Data

The first thing we have to do is modify our listener to extract the information provided by the client certificate. This data is actually exposed through the ASP request object in the form of a dictionary object. To reference this data, you simply need to create the dictionary object and set it to the `request.clientcertificate` method, as shown here:

```
set objDic = Server.CreateObject("Scripting.Dictionary")
set objDic = request.clientcertificate()
```

As an experiment, you could walk through the entire dictionary to see all of the data provided by the client certificate. You might be surprised by the amount of data you see by using the following code:

```
For Each key in Request.ClientCertificate
    Response.Write(key & " = " & Request.ClientCertificate(key) & "<BR>")
Next
```

Notice by all the key names that this information is structured in an active directory format. If you are familiar with active directories or LDAP systems, you will likely recognize the naming convention of the data values.

We want to reference one specific piece of information from this dictionary object, the `subjecto`. This name equates to the organization the client carrying this certificate belongs to. We will want to utilize this field over the others because they can be user dependent. We are treating the organization as our consumer, not an individual user. It would be just as easy to utilize any other data element in the certificate, so feel free to reference whatever you need for your own implementations.

Listing 7-48 shows what our listener now looks like with the changes to extract the client certificate data.

Listing 7-48. Web services listener with integrated security

```
<%@ Language=VBScript %>
<%
    dim objHRSRequest
    dim objDOM
```

```
    set objHRSRequest = Server.CreateObject("HRSWS.clsListener")
    set objDic = Server.CreateObject("Scripting.Dictionary")

    set objDOM = server.createobject("MSXML2.DOMDocument")
    objdom.async = false
    objdom.load(request)

    set objdic = request.clientcertificate()

    Response.ContentType = "text/xml"
    response.write objHRSRequest.processRequest(1,objdom.xml,objdic("subjecto"))

    set objdom = nothing
    set objdic = nothing
    set objhrsrequest = nothing
%>
```

Validating the Consumer

Now that we have programmatically captured the consumer's identity, we need to validate it against the consumers in our data model. The specific field we are comparing against is consumer_cert. This name was purposely left generic so that its purpose was clear and could serve as a reference to any certificate data element. After all, we may decide to switch to a user-based system instead of an organization-based one.

Since we already have the consumer data in our database, the first thing we need to add is a stored procedure for accessing the data. We will pass it the consumer name and get back a consumer ID and a Boolean representing a successful or unsuccessful match. This stored procedure, called getConsumerID, is shown in Listing 7-49.

Listing 7-49. The getConsumerID *stored procedure*

```
CREATE PROCEDURE dbo.getConsumerID(@consumerName varchar(30),
  @consumerID int output, @found bit output) AS

select @consumerID = consumerID from consumers where consumer_cert =
  @consumerName

if @consumerID is NULL
    select @found = 0
else
    select @found = 1
GO
```

What I have not addressed here is how to handle the consumers that are not present in this data store. If the consumer has gotten to the point of making this request, it obviously has a client certificate that is accepted by our site. If the assumption is that anyone with a valid client certificate should be in the table, we could easily add the code to automatically add such consumers. However, this is a bit too optimistic an approach for this senario.

I could foresee a situation in which a partnership with a consumer has ended and the consumer's client certificate is still valid. This automation would automatically add the consumer back into the database. Furthermore, if you were to ever expand your Web service offerings to include other services, not all valid clients may be allowed access to all services. This gets back into the Web service site security topics discussed in Chapter 6.

For this implementation, we will take the pessimistic approach and leave the consumer accounts as is. What we might want to do is set up some email notification in the case of a failed consumer certificate match. That would at least notify us as soon as such a situation occurs and allow us to anticipate any calls from consumers! This could be done through the stored procedure and the email services of SQL Server 2000, but I will not lead you down that tangent effort here.

Authentication

Now we need to add the authentication check to our processRequest function. We will use the same connection and command objects we are using for other database calls to call the getConsumerID stored procedure. Based on the setting of the sessionFound parameter, we will either set the consumer ID or produce an error through the consumer_error procedure as seen in Listing 7-50.

Listing 7-50. Responder code for authentication check and error handling

```
Set objCommand = New Command

With objCommand
    .ActiveConnection = objConn
    .CommandText = "getConsumerID"
    .CommandType = adCmdStoredProc
    .Parameters.Append .CreateParameter("consumerName", adChar, adParamInput,
        30, consumerName)
    .Parameters.Append .CreateParameter("consumerID", adInteger, adParamOutput)
    .Parameters.Append .CreateParameter("sessionFound", adBoolean,
        adParamOutput)
    .Execute
    If .Parameters("sessionFound") Then
        intConsumerID = .Parameters("consumerID").Value
    Else
```

```
            GoTo Consumer_Error
        End If
End With
. . .
'near the end of the function. . .
Consumer_Error:
        processRequest="<error><level>critical</level><description>The Web service
        could not validate the consumer making the request.  Please contact the
        provider to establish an account for this service.</description></error>"
        GoTo End_Proc
```

This completes our security model implementation. As you can see, it was fairly easy to add after our implementation was complete and did not encumber us while troubleshooting the functionality. There may be times this approach cannot be taken, but when available, I think you will benefit from it through better productivity.

Presentation Model

The only remaining component of our implementation is the presentation model. In fact, this only applies to our isolated service model, so for all intents and purposes, our embedded service model is already finished!

For our isolated service consumers, we will provide XSL templates that they can use to transform our data-oriented responses into presentable HTML interfaces. To implement this model, there are two things we need to do: develop the XSL documents and add the XSL references to our responses.

Developing the XSL Documents

Our XSL templates will effectively be utilizing XHTML-compliant data (as discussed in Chapter 4). Since this is a key component of a consumer implementation of a Web service, I will not go into the technical details of making the templates. In this chapter, I will instead focus on the approach providers should take whenever they decide to provide templates for their consumers. For information on building XSL templates for Web services, please read on to Chapter 8, where we will build a consumer application for this service. You can also go to http://www.architectingwebservices.com to download and view the templates that are provided for this Web service.

The purpose of an XSL stylesheet exposed by a provider is to act as a template for a suitable interface containing the necessary data from the response. There are two intentions consumers will have when utilizing your templates, and you should keep them in mind.

The first is that the consumer will want to get up and running very quickly. It should work right away "as is" with your responses to provide all the necessary functionality to be acceptable for your Web service. The most effective way to meet this expectation is to define a minimal interface that meets the basic requirements. The focus will not be making it look fancy or "finished," but providing a base that can accommodate a given look and feel. You aren't going to guess how your consumers will want to present the interface, so instead of trying to meet everyone's needs, try to keep it simple and make it flexible.

The key to making the stylesheet flexible is having clearly defined variables that provide easy access to things like colors and aesthetic attributes. For example, the top of the stylesheet could include a section like the following:

```
<xsl:variable name="backgroundColor" select="white"/>
<xsl:variable name="fontColor" select="blue"/>
<xsl:variable name="frameBorder" select="true"/>
```

You can then reference these variables wherever appropriate in your XSL document to apply these attributes. Again, we will look at implementing XSL in much more detail in Chapter 8.

The second intention consumers will have is to learn how your template works so that they can learn enough about XSLT to start modifying the template, if not make their own. This is very desirable because it allows your consumers to be more knowledgeable and self-reliant. A knowledgeable consumer is more likely to provide you good feedback on your Web service so that you can make changes and enhancements to it.

To aid your consumers with this, it is important to provide simple, well-written XSL documents. Overly complicated approaches to building the interface will only intimidate or confuse your consumers, which will set back their attempts to learn the technology.

The other thing you should do is provide very good comments in your template. This is a little bit of a double-edged sword, because the more comments you have, the bigger a drain on resources there will be to transfer the template and work with it. Keep in mind that I said "very good comments," not "a lot of comments." Try to be succinct, but also try to keep any readers informed as to what you are doing at different points in the template.

Once the stylesheets for our hotel reservation Web service have been created, the only thing left to do is add a reference to them in our response.

Adding the XSL Reference

In our design process, we decided to add the stylesheet references for our isolated service consumers in the service variables of our response. The only other decision that needs to be made is how to name the templates.

To keep it simple, we will name the stylesheets according to the interaction responses for which they are built. For instance, the stylesheet for the availability form response will be `availabilityFormInteraction.xsl`. This will allow us to build the reference dynamically off the response, as opposed to keeping another data source for mapping to an independent naming convention. The code for building the node and adding it to the response is shown in Listing 7-51. This code will go in the else case of our `serviceType` check as was commented in our base service.

Listing 7-51. XSL template node creation and response modification

```
Set objNodeWorking = objDomResponse.createElement("stylesheet")

'—Assign path and filename to template
objNodeWorking.nodeTypedValue =
  "http://www.architectingwebservices.com/hrsws/stylesheet/" &
  Right(objDomResponse.selectSingleNode("hrs:reservationWS/hrs:payload")
  .firstChild.nodeName, Len(objDomResponse.selectSingleNode
  ("hrs:reservationWS/hrs:payload").firstChild.nodeName) - 4) & ".xsl"

'—Add the node to the response DOM
objDomResponse.selectSingleNode("hrs:reservationWS/hrs:serviceVariables")
  .appendChild objNodeWorking
```

Testing the Service

That actually completes the building of our hotel reservation Web service. The only thing left to do now is to test both services. In Chapter 6, we discussed two different types of tests that should be run on your Web services: accuracy and performance. While both still apply for Web services workflows, the accuracy tests should have additional emphasis placed on the error handling of the service. There will be times that your Web services have problems processing a request, and you will need to ensure you are handling them as gracefully as possible to accommodate the user and your consumer. The most helpful tests in this area are use cases that generate error scenarios to make sure the various failure point possibilities are accounted for. Your tests should include at least the following scenarios:

- Provide invalid service variables

- Provide invalid payloads (empty and invalid elements and structures)

- Act as a consumer accessing the session of another consumer

- Change the location of your schemas and XML documents

The idea isn't that all of these situations will work (because not all of them could), but that you handle the errors gracefully. Remember that you are working with your consumers to provide the user experience, and you need to do as much as possible to provide good feedback when something goes awry.

Summary

We have completed the building of an entire Web service workflow from the ground up in this chapter. There are many components to it, but as long as you are organized and take everything one step at a time through the planning, designing, building, and testing processes, it can be done without too many problems. Now, we just have to sit back and wait for the consumers to come calling!

CHAPTER 8

Consuming Web Services

UP TO THIS POINT, we have built three different Web services: the mortgage calculator, the weather forecaster, and the hotel reservation system. Although we have built test clients for each, we have not built productive applications to consume them. We will now take the opportunity to switch roles and work with our Web services from this new perspective. Consuming a Web service presents different challenges than does building a service, but you will see that they both rely on the same technologies and our understanding of them.

As you go through this chapter, keep in mind how much effort we are putting into the design and coding of our Web services consumers. We've already seen how building Web services can get pretty involved, and it might be discouraging to think that consumers would have to put just as much effort into consuming them. Fortunately, you should find that the considerations that we give to the model and design of our Web services will pay dividends to our consumers in terms of integration complexity and effort.

One thing that we should definitely be assured of is that we will not dictate the platforms and tools that our consumers use. To demonstrate the ubiquity of Web services, we will consume our Microsoft-based weather service through a Java application and our Java-based mortgage calculator through a Microsoft-based Web application. We will then walk through an implementation of our hotel reservation Web service, incorporating this process into an existing conference registration system.

> **NOTE** *All three Web services are available online on the book's companion site (*http://www.architectingwebservices.com*) so that you can build these consumers and test them against a working Web service.*

Consuming a Web Services Call

Just as with building a Web services call, consuming one takes a similar, stream-lined approach. There isn't nearly the wide-ranging scope of a Web services workflow, so the effort to design and build the consumer is comparatively minor.

In this section, we will implement both of the Web services that we built in Chapter 6—the mortgage calculator and the weather forecaster. If you recall, the mortgage calculator was built on a Java-based development platform, whereas the weather forecaster was built on a COM-based platform. However, we will approach both in a very similar manner because the Web services interface will mask those details from us. What will concern us is the technology that we use to consume the Web services. First up will be a Java application that consumes the weather forecaster service. We will follow that up with an ASP Web application that consumes the mortgage calculator.

Consuming the Weather Forecast Web Service via Java

For our consumer scenario, we will take a very direct approach: building a very simple Java application that exposes the functionality of the Web service. We will continue to use IBM's Visual Age for Java as our development tool, but any Java IDE should suffice here.

For this example, we will build the application's interface using Java Swing, although nothing prevents us from using AWT (Abstract Windows Toolkit), the original interface class for Java. Swing is part of the Java Foundation Classes (JFC) that provides a series of containers and controls for building user inter-faces very quickly. I have chosen to use Swing over the AWT because it is currently the more popular choice and because the Swing support in Visual Age is pretty good. We won't go into the details of Swing here, so, if you are inter-ested in learning more about it, I recommend getting a book dedicated to that technology, such as *Definitive Guide to Swing for Java 2, Second Edition*, by John Zukowski.

As I said earlier, our design and development efforts will be focused on our technology platform, not that of the weather forecaster. We will be working with XML and HTTP only, so its implementation details will truly be abstracted away from our concerns.

Designing the Consumer

When designing the consumer of a Web service, there are two main areas of concern: the integration layer and the presentation layer. (See Figure 8-1.) The integration layer is responsible for interacting with the Web service itself. This includes not only the direct communication piece, but also the building of request documents and the handling of response documents. The presentation layer is then responsible for collecting the information from the user and presenting the data to the user.

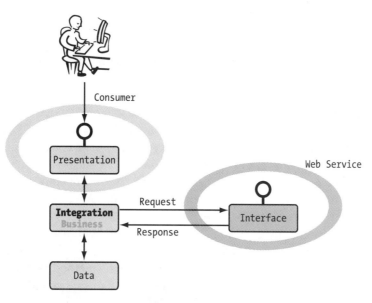

Figure 8-1. The integration and presentation layers in a consumer application

As we discussed in Chapter 2 ("Web Services Architecture"), a consumer of a Web service doesn't necessarily interact with a user. It may simply be facilitating the use of the Web service logic to a system or through its own Web service to another consumer. Because this type of consumer would contain a subset of an application-based consumer, our examples will all take the direct approach and expose the functionality to a user.

Designing the Integration Layer

The integration layer is where all the real work is done on the consumer side of a Web services interaction. It is where data for the request is assembled, the data is communicated over to the Web service, and the response is collected and parsed into some usable form for the presentation layer. Again, it is important to keep in mind that these two layers (presentation and integration) are logical, not physical. There may or may not be a physical distinction in these responsibilities between methods or entities. It is simply important to account for the functionality and to keep future reuse in mind.

As we saw in building the Java-based Web service, Visual Age provides a lot of skeleton code that gives your class a structure. It might be tempting to add your logic directly to this existing code, but this temptation should be resisted. For instance, in our Java Web service, we could have added the responder logic directly to the doPost and doGet methods. Instead, we created a couple of separate private methods that contained this logic.

> *Skeleton* or *stub code* refers to code that is automatically developed by a routine, typically through a developer tool. This code contains little or no logic, but it provides empty containers and helpers (functions, procedures, and such) that are appropriate for the language and environment you are working in.

In this scenario, we have even more of a reason to resist overextending the skeleton code because the skeleton structure may need to change. Whenever you make changes to your interface, it may also require a change to the code (such as if you add or modify the controls on the interface.) If you have Visual Age regenerate the code, it may mean overwriting some of your own hard work. To avoid this, you are better off making your own custom classes so that they are insulated from these modifications.

We can essentially accomplish most of our work within a single method call. This makes sense if you consider that our consumer is essentially acting as a proxy to a single Web service call. We will name the method callWeatherWS. This method will work directly with the controls on the application interface, so there will be no parameters or return values defined for this call.

The next step in designing the integration layer is to determine how we are going to assemble the data for the request and parse the response. We are looking at only one value going out to the Web service, so we will likely build that document programmatically. We could be looking at many nodes coming back, so, in Listing 8-1, let's review the schema definition for the Web service response.

Listing 8-1. The Weather Forecaster Response Schema

```
<xsd:schema xmlns:xsd="http://www.w3.org/2001/XMLSchema"
  elementFormDefault="qualified">
    <xsd:element name="weatherCheck">
        <xsd:complexType>
            <xsd:sequence>
                <xsd:element name="barometer" type="xsd:string"/>
                <xsd:element name="city" type="xsd:string"/>
                <xsd:element name="dewpoint" type="xsd:decimal"/>
                <xsd:element name="errorMessage" type="xsd:string"
                    minOccurs="0"/>
                <xsd:element name="feelsLike" type="xsd:string"/>
                <xsd:element name="forecast" type="xsd:string"/>
                <xsd:element name="humidity" type="xsd:string"/>
                <xsd:element name="imageID" type="xsd:string"/>
```

```
                    <xsd:element name="imageSmall" type="xsd:uri"/>
                    <xsd:element name="imageBig" type="xsd:uri"/>
                    <xsd:element name="reportedTime" type="xsd:string"/>
                    <xsd:element name="state" type="xsd:string"/>
                    <xsd:element name="temperature" type="xsd:decimal"/>
                    <xsd:element name="uvIndex" type="xsd:decimal"/>
                    <xsd:element name="uvWarning" type="xsd:string"/>
                    <xsd:element name="visibility" type="xsd:string"/>
                    <xsd:element name="weatherAlert" type="xsd:boolean"/>
                    <xsd:element name="windDescription" type="xsd:string"/>
                </xsd:sequence>
            </xsd:complexType>
        </xsd:element>
</xsd:schema>
```

We have potentially eighteen fields of data to extract from the response, but it will likely be far less. Because we aren't dealing with a Web application, XSL doesn't make sense as an alternative. Instead, we will manually extract the data through our parser as necessary. Because of the flat structure and the antici- pated volume, this should be a fairly simple process.

The only other determination that we need to make for the integration layer at the design stage is what parser and communication classes will be used to execute the actual communication. Many options are available, but they vary in performance and features, and so we need to make sure that all of our require- ments will be met.

For this application, we will utilize the IBM parser that we used for the mort- gage calculator service. We will also use the DOM class for working with the data. For our communication, we will utilize IBM's WebDAV (Web-based Distributed Authoring and Versioning) implementation. WebDAV is a standardized set of extensions defined by the IETF (Internet Engineering Task Force) for working with files on remote servers over HTTP. It will provide us with the ability to send an HTTP POST request to a URL containing our XML data request document.

We will identify the other classes as they come up, but the following list includes all of the imports for our application:

- `java.awt.*;`

- `javax.swing.*;`

- `java.io.*;`

- `java.net.*;`

- `org.w3c.dom.NodeList;`

- `org.w3c.dom.Element;`

- `org.w3c.dom.Document;`

- `com.ibm.xml.parsers.RevalidatingDOMParser;`

- `com.ibm.webdav.Resource;`

- `org.xml.sax.InputSource;`

Designing the Presentation Layer

Before starting on the design of our interface, we need to first identify what information needs to be collected and presented. We already know that we will have only one field going in the request (the ZIP code). Coming back, we have the eighteen fields that we saw earlier, but we aren't likely to want them all.

Because we are the consumers of this Web service, it is entirely our discretion which data we use and which we cast aside. For this application, we are primarily interested in the base weather information. Although it is technically possible, it isn't practical to use the image links in our Java application, so we can immediately drop those three fields. For simplicity's sake, we will pare down our list of response data to the following: temperature, "feels like" temperature, city, state, reported time, forecast, and wind description. If you are like me, you don't understand what the other information means, and it won't affect what you do or how you dress when you go out! Thus, we've reduced the number of fields from eighteen to seven.

We can now turn our attention towards building the interface for our application. Within Visual Age, it's fairly easy to build the application's presentation using the Visual Composition editor. In this view, various controls and objects can be dropped into the window of your application. We can assign values to these controls (like text labels, colors, and such) through the properties dialog box for each. The result of this view is a Java Bean. When so directed, Visual Age can then produce the skeleton code necessary for adding the logic behind these controls and the events related to them.

Our interface will be a very simplistic window that contains two text boxes, a button, and several text labels. (See Figure 8-2.) The text box is where the ZIP code for the forecast can be entered, and the Get Forecast button will trigger the use of the service. As you can see in the figure, this button is tied to our `callWeatherWS` function. This is exactly how events, such as clicking on a button, can be tied to logic within the application.

Labels on our interface clearly point out where our temperature and relative temperature will be presented. In the text area beneath the "Get Forecast"

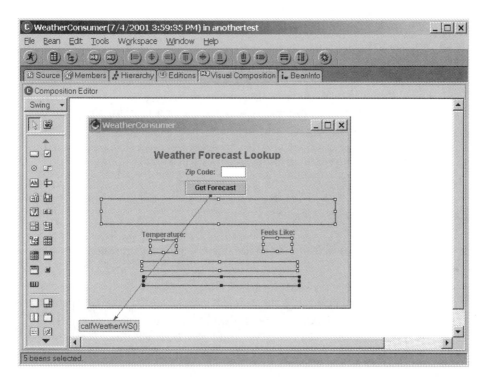

Figure 8-2. Java application consumer interface in the Visual Composition editor

button, we will present the time of the forecast along with the area identified by the ZIP code provided by the user. The forecast and location needed to be contained in a text area control because the volume was too large to contain within a text field or label.

Beneath the temperatures, we have two additional text labels that we will use to present information from the service. The upper text label will provide the forecast itself, and the lower will present the wind information. These could have been text fields, but I used labels instead because they are not editable and the user will not be misled into thinking they are meant to collect input data. As text labels, they will also blend into the background when empty.

So, those are the design decisions for our presentation layer and essentially the entire consumer. We now need to implement the designs we have discussed and run a few tests to confirm our success.

Implementing the Consumer

The consumer application will fall into two elements that we need to build: the interface window and the `callWeatherWS` method. Although this might seem to fall in line with our logical model of the integration and presentation layers, there is interaction between the two, which necessitates crossing that boundary within each element. Specifically, our method will be responsible for presenting the information on the interface and the presentation layer doesn't just include the physical screen, but the logic for formatting and presenting the data on that screen.

Developing the Application Interface

With the conveniences of using Swing and Visual Age as our development tools, our ability to develop a good interface depends on our own creativity and ability to position controls just as we want. The IDE generates everything else we need to have a functioning application. Of course, we do need to construct the interface for our application through the Visual Composition editor as we saw in Figure 8-2. Doing so isn't difficult, but it can be frustrating if you aren't used to GUI tools or are used to other GUI tools that behave differently than this one.

Once the window is assembled and the properties are set how we would like, the only thing to do is tie the button event to our class. This is done by simply right-clicking on the button and selecting "event to code". This feature even allows you to define a new method, so you could use this to define the skeleton structure for `callWeatherWS`. Otherwise, you would select the existing call you want to have 'triggered' when a user clicks on the button, as shown in Figure 8-3.

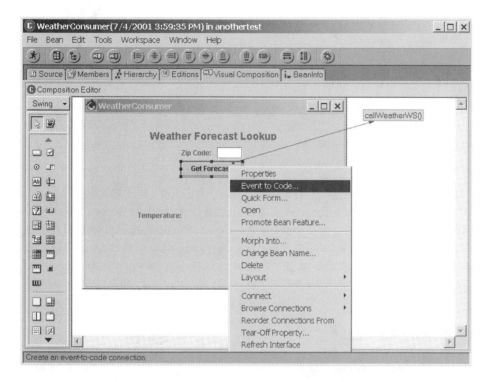

Figure 8-3. Tying the Button Click event to logic in Visual Age

This completes the development of the interface for our application. Now we get to add the code for our application's logic.

Developing the Application Logic

Using the "event to code" feature, we should at least have a skeleton for our `callWeatherWS` method. It should look something like this:

```
/**
 * Comment
*/
public void callWeatherWS(){
    return;
}
```

It isn't much, but it is a start! Earlier, we identified the technologies that we would utilize for our application and now it is time to put them to work. Let's get started by looking at the steps we need to perform.

Whenever Web services are consumed, three essential steps have to be executed in sequence:

1. Build the request.

2. Invoke the Web service.

3. Parse the response.

Even in rare instances in which the request or the response is nondescript, these steps are performed at some level. For instance, if a Web service is simply broadcasting the same information to everyone that makes a request, you may not be sending any XML data, but there is data in the header of your HTTP request, which makes it valid. In most normal cases, each of these steps is critical to the consumer's ability to interact with the Web service. Performing these steps out of sequence when they are necessary is obviously ineffective because each step builds on the completion of the previous one.

Building the Request

For this Web service, our request consists of a single piece of data: the ZIP code. This makes the task very simple and justifies a decision to build the request manually. (Later, we will look at an example for which this is not practical.)

If we review the request schema (Listing 8-2), we can identify the exact structure that we need for our request document.

Listing 8-2. The Weather Forecaster Request Schema

```
<xsd:schema xmlns:xsd="http://www.w3.org/2001/XMLSchema"
  elementFormDefault="qualified">
    <xsd:element name="weatherCheck">
        <xsd:complexType>
            <xsd:sequence>
                <xsd:element name="zipCode" type="xsd:string"/>
            </xsd:sequence>
        </xsd:complexType>
    </xsd:element>
</xsd:schema>
```

We have a root element called weatherCheck and an element called zipCode within it. All we need to do is reference the data in the text field in our Swing interface. Regardless of how you designed your screen, your text field will have a name assigned to it and will have a method for getting the data contained within it called getText (courtesy of Visual Age). Thus, building our request document can be accomplished by a single line that should look something like this:

```
String myData = "<?xml version='1.0'?><weatherCheck><zipCode>"+
  vjzipCode.getText() + "</zipCode></weatherCheck>";
```

Now that we have our request document, we need to send it off to the weather forecaster Web service—which is where our connection comes into play.

Invoking the Web service

Invoking the Web service is very similar to invoking any other object or component in practice. Technically, it is very similar to other remote invocation methods: much more is going on behind the scenes to handle the process. Because we are working with a stateless environment, the connection is established through the request and disconnected once the response is provided.

To invoke the Web service, the first piece of information we need is the address for the Web service. Like a data connection, this could be retrieved from an external source, but we will simply define a local variable for our application.

```
String url = "http://www.architectingwebservices.com/weather";
```

We decided earlier that we would utilize the WebDAV extensions for our connectivity to the Web service. Specifically, its resource class is a powerful tool that suits most of our needs for communicating with a Web service. The resource constructor will take our URL as its parameter. Once built, we need to use its performWith method to send the request document that we built. The result of this is a string containing the response from the Web service. Of course, we need to catch any exceptions that might occur during this process. The most common exceptions during this step will involve connectivity between the Web service and our application.

```
try {
    // get a resource that exists
    Resource resource = new Resource(url);
    String contents = new String(resource.performWith(myData));
}
catch (Exception exc) {
    System.out.println("TestPOST exception: "+exc);
}
```

Now that we have made our request and received a response, it is time to turn it over to our parser. It will be responsible for deciphering the information within that response document.

Parsing the Response

Most of the code will actually involve the parsing of the response from the Web service. We will be working with seven of the eighteen elements returned to us. We saw the response schema earlier in Listing 8-1 (if you would like to review it again).

As the consumer, we might look at this response as being bloated for our purposes, but, in the grand scheme of things, the throwaway data won't affect us on any meaningful level. Although it is feasible for a provider to provide custom responses for each request, the savings would more than likely be offset by a larger request. Remember that our request is only one field of data and that any request incorporating a custom format preference for the response would be bigger. This approach can make sense in some scenarios, but this is not one of them.

We can approach getting the data out of the response document in several ways. Although we decided earlier that we would use the parser from IBM, any parser would work. However, loading it and accessing the data through it might work a little differently. In this case, we need to use the `InputSource` from IBM's SAX implementation, which allows us to read in XML data. However, the `InputSource` requires a byte or character stream, and this XML data is contained in a string. To bridge the gap, we will need to use the `StringReader` class to turn the XML string into the stream we require.

```
try{
     //Parsing the request and capturing it in the request document
     RevalidatingDOMParser parser = new RevalidatingDOMParser();
     parser.parse(new InputSource(new StringReader(contents)));
}
catch (Exception E){
     System.out.println("Parser exception: " + E);
}
```

Now that we have the data in a parser, we will save it to a document object so we can access our data. We will then go one step further and declare an element as the root of that document so that we can easily reference the data. Declaring this root element, as seen here, gives us the starting point we need to reliably and efficiently reference the data programmatically.

```
Document results = parser.getDocument();
Element docRoot = results.getDocumentElement();
```

We are now in a position to reference the data directly through this root element. However, one of the things that we need to consider is whether we can trust the data that was returned to us. We have performed no validation on the response document, and everything we have done up until now has been schema independent. As the consumer, we need to decide how we want to handle the possibility of bad data that could range from illegal XML (which would have already generated an exception) to a single field missing that we don't even intend to use (like imageID). Do we want to "error out" on the entire response for any problem or only when something drastic happens?

A direct reference on a nonexistent node will generate an exception, and the application will abort if it isn't caught. If we want to get the data that is available, we are better off using a method that is less direct, such as the getElementsByTagName method. This method assembles a list of nodes that have a specific tag name, and, if no nodes are found, the list is simply empty. This would allow us to bypass a missing windDescription element and continue to collect the other elements that are present.

After building our node list, we can simply check the length, and, if it is greater than zero, we retrieve the first child and set the appropriate control on our interface to its value. Following is an example of this approach for the temperature element:

```
elements = docRoot.getElementsByTagName("temperature");
if (elements.getLength() > 0)
{
     ivjtemperature.setText(elements.item(0).getFirstChild().getNodeValue());
}
```

This approach can accommodate another scenario: an instance in which a duplicate node is present. We are simply taking the first instance and ignoring any duplicates, and this approach makes our consumer very resilient and capable of handling all but the most severe of errors produced by the Web service. Obviously, it would be nice to assume perfection on the part of the Web service, but, as a consumer, we must take the realistic approach and protect our integrity as much as possible from the worst-case scenario.

> **NOTE**   *Consumers of Web services need to make a decision: Is bad data better than no data when handling payload integrity issues? This is more of an issue with Web services because their scope may be targeted for the masses, which means they are providing more data than the majority of their consumers actually want. The extreme approach would advocate throwing out the entire payload if some of the data is found to be of questionable integrity. The more flexible approach would be concerned with only the integrity of the data needed. Good cases can be made for either approach, but the criticality of this issue varies with the type of the data involved. Whereas a zero tolerance for errors is warranted for financial services, such a restriction might not be necessary for a weather service.*

Something else we might decide to do here is to handle the exception to this instance. If we are making a duplicate call to the weather forecaster, we might want to make sure that we erase any preexisting values in the ivjtemperature text label. This would be accomplished by tagging on the following else case:

```
else
{
    ivjtemperature.setText("");
}
```

Once we have done this for each of our seven elements, our parsing of the response is complete. You can see in these statements exactly how the logical integration and presentation layers are overlapping within the application's logic. We are both parsing the response and presenting it to the user within the exact same command, which is fine, but it is important that you account for those two functions somewhere within your consumer.

Pulling It All Together

Now that we have implemented all of the application's logical components, it is time to bring it all together. We walked through building our callWeatherWS method in pieces, so we should take a look at it in its entirety, including variable declarations. (See Listing 8-3.)

Listing 8-3. The callWeatherWS() *Method*

```
public void callWeatherWS() {

    NodeList elements;
    Element elem;
    Element root;
```

```
String url = "http://www.architectingwebservices.com/weather";
String myData = "<?xml version='1.0'?><weatherCheck><zipCode>"+
  vjzipCode.getText() + "</zipCode></weatherCheck>";

try {
    // get a resource that exists
    Resource resource = new Resource(url);
    String contents = new String(resource.performWith(myData));
    try {
        //Parsing the request and capturing it in the request document
        RevalidatingDOMParser parser = new RevalidatingDOMParser();
        parser.parse(new InputSource(new StringReader(contents)));
        Document results = parser.getDocument();

        //Referencing the response document object
        Element docRoot = results.getDocumentElement();

        elements = docRoot.getElementsByTagName("temperature");
        if (elements.getLength() > 0)
        {
            ivjtemperature.setText(elements.item(0).getFirstChild().
              getNodeValue());
        }
        else
        {
            ivjtemperature.setText("");
        }

        elements = docRoot.getElementsByTagName("feelsLike");
        if (elements.getLength() > 0)
        {
            ivjfeelsLike.setText(elements.item(0).getFirstChild().
              getNodeValue());
        }
        else
        {
            ivjfeelsLike.setText("");
        }

        elements = docRoot.getElementsByTagName("forecast");
        if (elements.getLength() > 0)
        {
            ivjforecast.setText("Forecast calls for " +
```

```
                                elements.item(0).getFirstChild().getNodeValue());
                }
                else
                {
                    ivjforecast.setText("");
                }

                elements = docRoot.getElementsByTagName("windDescription");
                if (elements.getLength() > 0)
                {
                ivjwindDescription.setText("Wind" +
                  elements.item(0).getFirstChild().getNodeValue());
                }
                else
                {
                    ivjwindDescription.setText("");
                }

                ivjSummaryText.setText("Forecast for ");

                elements = docRoot.getElementsByTagName("city");
                if (elements.getLength() > 0)
                {
                    ivjSummaryText.setText(ivjSummaryText.getText() +
                        elements.item(0).getFirstChild().getNodeValue());
                }

                elements = docRoot.getElementsByTagName("state");
                if (elements.getLength() > 0)
                {
                    ivjSummaryText.setText(ivjSummaryText.getText()+ ", " +
                        elements.item(0).getFirstChild().getNodeValue());
                }

                elements = docRoot.getElementsByTagName("reportedTime");
                if (elements.getLength() > 0)
                {
                    ivjSummaryText.setText(ivjSummaryText.getText() + "at" +
                        elements.item(0).getFirstChild().getNodeValue());
                }
            }
        catch (Exception E){
            ivjSummaryText.setText("There was a problem interpretting the
```

```
                results from this location code. Please check your zip code and
                try again.");}
        }
    catch (Exception exc) {
        ivjSummaryText.setText("There was a problem with connecting to the
          Weather Forecaster. Please try again later.");
    }
}
}
```

Testing the Consumer

Now that we have our application completed, we need to test it to make sure that it works as expected. Doing so involves tests in which we expect (or at least hope) that everything goes correctly, as well as those tests in which we expect to see problems, such as a loss of connectivity to the Web service. Fortunately, a Java application is very easy to test, especially within the Visual Age IDE. We simply need to select the "running man" button at the top left of our screen, or right-click on our application and select Run.

If the application runs successfully, it should generate an interface that looks similar to that shown in Figure 8-4. An error should, at worst, cause some or all of the fields to be blank with an error message appearing below the Get Forecast button.

Next, in consuming our mortgage calculator Web service, we will increase the level of complexity.

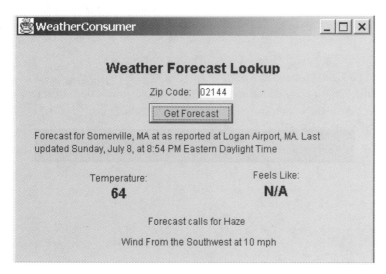

Figure 8-4. A successful run of our weather forecaster consumer application

Consuming the Mortgage Calculator Web Service via ASP

If you recall, our mortgage calculator is a Web service that calculates an amortization plan given a set of data points. This is a Java-based service, but, as we saw with our weather forecaster application, this won't be a factor in our design or implementation.

Unlike our previous example, we will actually integrate this service into an existing application. This presents a few more challenges because we don't have the liberty of just building an application from scratch and focus on exposing the functionality of the Web service. Specifically, we need to spend a little more time up front understanding the current application's process and outline a clear plan for integrating the Web services functionality.

Analyzing the Existing Application

We will be incorporating the mortgage calculator Web service into the Find-A-Home Realtors Web site. Find-A-Home specializes in high-profile home sales, and it has not had much success with moving some of their homes. Additionally, they get a lot of calls from prospective buyers that don't realize the homes are out of their price range. By providing an online payment calculator, Find-A-Home is hoping that it can generate more interest in its listings, as well as screen out unqualified home-seekers.

The Find-A-Home site is hosted on a Windows 2000 server and consists entirely of ASP pages, no COM objects. It is a fairly low-tech customer and needs a low-maintenance solution to which changes can be made very quickly without calling in high-priced talent (which could change, of course, if they could just sell a few of their homes).

The site is very basic, essentially consisting of two tiers: the main page we see in Figure 8-5 and the details page in Figure 8-6. The main page acts as a catalog page, which then connects the user to individual homes with descriptions and pricing. Some information on Find-A-Home Realtors is also featured, but this has no significance to us.

Our challenge is to incorporate the mortgage calculator Web service into the site so that it appears as an integrated feature of Find-A-Home Realtors. Because of the existing application platform, we will be building a Microsoft-based solution. This makes our choice of parser—MSXML—a no-brainer. More specifically, we will use the MSXML 4 Technology Preview to maintain consistency with the rest of the examples in this book.

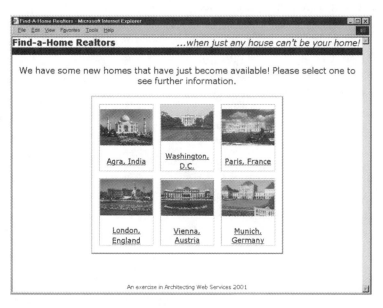

Figure 8-5. The Web site for Find-A-Home Realtors

Designing the Consumer

Because we aren't writing this Web service consumer from scratch, this design process will be a little different from our weather service consumer. In that scenario, we led with the integration layer, which we followed up with the presentation layer design. Because we are integrating this functionality into an existing application, we will benefit from doing the reverse here. This is especially true in this scenario because we are dealing strictly with ASP pages. Our logic will inherently be tied to the pages that actually present the information to the user, so we need to identify the pages that we will be modifying.

Designing the Presentation Layer

The first thing we need to do is determine what information needs to be collected and what data needs to be displayed. We have a large group of data to select from, so let's review the schema for the request again. (See Listing 8-4.) If you recall, this Web service call was simplified by the fact the request and response schemas are exactly the same.

Listing 8-4. The Mortgage Calculator Request/Response Interface Schema

```
<xsd:schema xmlns:xsd="http://www.w3.org/20001/XMLSchema">
     <xsd:element name="calcInteraction">
          <xsd:complexType>
               <xsd:sequence>
                    <xsd:element name="amortizationPeriod" type="xsd:decimal"
                      minOccurs="0"/>
                    <xsd:element name="effectiveAnnualRate" type="xsd:decimal"
                      minOccurs="0"/>
                    <xsd:element name="interestRate" type="xsd:decimal"
                      minOccurs="0"/>
                    <xsd:element name="interestRatePerPayment" type="xsd:decimal"
                      minOccurs="0"/>
                    <xsd:element name="paymentAmount" type="xsd:decimal"
                      minOccurs="0"/>
                    <xsd:element name="paymentsPerYear" type="xsd:decimal"
                      minOccurs="0"/>
                    <xsd:element name="principalAmount" type="xsd:decimal"
                      minOccurs="0"/>
                    <xsd:element name="timesPerYear" type="xsd:decimal"
                      minOccurs="0"/>
                    <xsd:element name="totalInterestCost" type="xsd:decimal"
                      minOccurs="0"/>
               </xsd:sequence>
          </xsd:complexType>
     </xsd:element>
</xsd:schema>
```

Many things can be done with this service, but we only want to calculate payments based on the base loan information: principal, down payment, interest rate, and the loan period. We have three of these four available, with down payment being the odd element. Fortunately, we can handle that on our end by reducing the principal amount before calling the Web service.

Because nothing else seems to be of interest, it looks like we have identified four input parameters and one output parameter, the payment. The next thing we need to do is determine how we want to integrate the calculator into the site.

> **NOTE** *One thing to note here is that we don't have a source for the current interest rate. The plan will be for Find-A-Home to update its site daily with its interest rate. Not only is this a constantly updated figure, but many factors can affect this rate, such as the loan amount, the loan period, and the user's credit rating. Find-A-Home will be using an average rate that can be used for the purposes of the site. Still, we are probably identifying an opportunity for the mortgage calculator provider to expand its service, or even an opportunity for another provider that already has access to that information. This would generate a multipartner scenario like we discussed back in Chapter 2 ("Web Services Architecture").*

The logical placement for this service would be on the details page. (See Figure 8-6.) We don't want it to take away from the main purpose of the page, which is to present the information on the house, so we will set it aside on the left as a sidebar. Placing it here provides easy access to the functionality and yet prevents it from being distracting of the existing content.

Figure 8-6. Find-A-Home Realtors home details view

Next, we need to determine how to handle the results from this call. Our two options are to push to another page or simply handle it within this view. Handling it within the view is the better choice because we don't want to take away from the current purpose of this page. Also, a page with just a price on it without the information on the home is only slightly useful. Taking this approach, we can simply present the calculated payment beneath the price at the bottom of the details page. This solution will also allow the user easy access to the calculator interface for subsequent calculations if they want to tweak variables such as the amount of the down payment or number of payments.

Although it is fairly simple, we should also probably map out this process. (See Figure 8-7.) In the diagram, we see that the page is calling itself to trigger the Web service (Mortgage Calculator). This will help us in communicating the design to others and make sure that we are consistent in our treatment of the application. This is a good exercise to go through because it will have great significance in the design of our next application and probably in many of the Web services consumers you build.

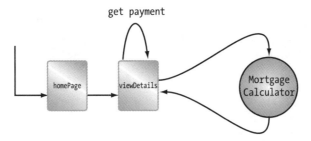

Figure 8-7. The process flow for the Find-A-Home Realtors updated Web site

This completes the design of the presentation layer for the Find-A-Home Realtors Web site. We now need to turn our attention to the design of the integration layer, which will make all of this functionality a reality.

Designing the Integration Layer—ASP vs. COM?

Although the integration layer consumes the most effort in the implementation of our consumer, the design is somewhat dictated by the requirements and existing application structure. The logic will obviously be in ASP, so there are no objects to define like we had for our Java application.

One of the things that should be understood at this point is that the scalability of this application will be limited because of the decision to use ASP instead of COM objects for the logic. Although this is consistently true when both are properly implemented, regardless of the task, it is especially true for applications in which server-to-server communication is occurring. Because of the nature of HTTP and TCP/IP, it will always be most efficient to have that process occurring within their own dedicated thread instead of a shared process space.

Without diving too much into the details, you should realize that any ASP pages contained within a site or virtual directory would run in a shared process. You can isolate virtual directories and sites from each other, but all pages within those directories will share that process.

Conversely, a COM object can run in its own process space. This effectively allows it to act as a client when communicating with the Web service, which is optimal for HTTP communication. Either one will work, but the COM solution would be optimal. For this application, the anticipated volume would be too low to merit a more costly approach and the ASP-based solution should be adequate for their needs. In the next section we will build another consumer that will need scalability, so we will build a more robust solution using COM objects for our application logic.

> **NOTE** *.NET will affect this decision considerably, if for no other reason than ASP. NET pages are compiled code and can be cached to provide a much improved response rate over the previous ASP processor.*

Implementing the Consumer

Now that we have made our design decisions and technology decisions (or those that were available to us), we are ready to proceed with the implementation phase of our Web service consumer. Like the Java application we built, we have two main components to build: the application interface and the application logic. Unlike the Java application, both components are tied closely physically within our ASP page. They should still be implemented separately, perhaps even more so than in the Java example because the skill sets are different for the two. Some very good HTML developers do not do any ASP programming, and some very good ASP developers are lousy at building good application interfaces! Maintaining this approach allows you to have different roles focus on different components, especially within bigger projects.

Developing the Application Interface

For the application's interface, we will need to develop some HTML to define the inputs for the calculator service. Depending on the tool you are using (and perhaps the mode within that tool, for instance, Design versus Source for Visual Interdev), this may involve actual coding or dropping controls on a GUI tool as we did for our Java application. Personally, I still prefer to edit the source directly because any GUI, due to its very nature, has to make assumptions about what you are trying to accomplish, and there hasn't been an algorithm developed yet that can read my mind.

We determined in our design that we want to locate the interface for our service on a sidebar within the details page. This layout can be defined in a number of ways, but I think a table makes the most sense to use here. It will make it look like a part of the page and yet distinguish it enough to give it some recognition.

We need to capture within the table the appropriate data elements. Remember that, for the calculator service, we are concerned with four: principal, down payment, interest rate, and loan period. Of these four, only two can be manipulated by the user: down payment and loan period. The other two are set by Find-A-Home and cannot be edited. It would still be a good idea to have that information present within the table to give the user a complete view of all the data utilized for the calculation.

The down payment should probably be an open text field and the loan period restricted to a choice between the traditional 15- and 30-year finance plans on a home. Of course, we also need to have a submit button for the user to click on once he or she is done entering the data. The HTML code defining the interface we have just specified can be seen in Listing 8-5.

Listing 8-5. The Mortgage Calculator Presentation Code

```
<table border= "1" size="100%" align="left">
    <tr>
        <td align="middle" width="100%" height="100%">
            <font color="black" face="verdana" size="2"><b>Calculate<br>your
              Payment </b><hr>
            <form method="post" action="details_new.asp?
              <%=Request.QueryString%>">
                <p><font size=1>Principal:<br>
                <b><i><%=FormatCurrency(price*1000000)%></i></b>
                <p>Amount Down:<br>
                <input type="text" size="9" maxlength="8" name="downPayment"
                  value="<%=Request("downPayment")%>">
                <p>Interest Rate:<br>
                <input type="hidden" name="rate" value="6.25">
                <i><b>6.25% Fixed</b></i>
                <p>Loan Period:<br>
                <b><i>15</i></b>
                <input type="radio" name="period" value="15" align=baseline
                  <% if Request("period") = "15" then Response.Write
                  ("Checked")%>>
                or <b><i>30</i></b>
                <input type="radio" name="period" value="30" align=absBottom
                  <% if Request("period") = "30" then Response.Write
                  ("Checked")%>>
                <p><input type="submit" name="Submit" value="Submit"></p>
            </form></font>
        </td>
    </tr>
</table>
```

If you noticed, we also added some ASP code to this form to add some intelligence to it. First, we are passing the querystring through our form post to help keep track of what home is currently being viewed. We are also using some code to populate the form values so the user can see what was selected after submission. This is a standard nicety that most HTML interfaces incorporate to reduce the data entry within a Web application.

Now that we have the code defining our interface, we need to incorporate it into the details page on the site. (See Figure 8-8.) The details of how it's integrated aren't important, but, if you do want to see the complete code for the page, you can do so on `http://www.architectingwebservices.com`.

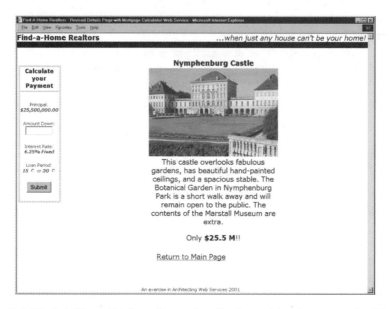

Figure 8-8. Find-A-Home Realtors home details view with mortgage calculator

This nearly completes the application interface for our Web service. We haven't discussed the presentation for the calculated payment, but that will simply be an added line under the price. We will leave that for when we parse the response from the Web service.

Developing the Application Logic

Just as with the Java application, we have three fundamental tasks we need to perform for this Web service call: building the request, establishing the connection, and parsing the response. These tasks must be done in sequence to facilitate the consumption of this Web service correctly.

Building the Request

The request for this application is a little more involved than it was in our Java application. Instead of one field, we have three to incorporate into our document. Fortunately, every field is defined in the Web services interface schema as optional (see Listing 8-4), so we don't need to physically account for the other six elements in our document.

Because we are still dealing with only three data elements, it still makes sense to build the document dynamically. In fact, I would even stick with building the document as a string instead of creating a DOM object as seen below. (I'm actually hedging a little bit here because I know that I won't need the document in a DOM for sending to the Web service. If I did, I would probably change my stance on this because we would end up loading the string in a DOM anyway.)

```
strRequest = "<calcInteraction>"
strRequest = strRequest & "<amortizationPeriod>" & Request("Period") &
  "</amortizationPeriod>"
strRequest = strRequest & "<interestRate>" & Request("rate") & "</interestRate>"
strRequest = strRequest & "<principalAmount>" &
  cstr(price*1000000-Request("downPayment")) & "</principalAmount>"
strRequest = strRequest & "</calcInteraction>"
```

You'll notice that every value is a value from the form we just built, with the exception of price (the local variable already used to display the price of the house on that page). Everything else about this is fairly straightforward.

Establishing the Connection

The MSXML parser is quite enjoyable to work with because it contains not only the functionality to access, manipulate, and format XML data, but also the mechanisms for sending that data to other systems. Unlike the Java application, we need to work with only one library to utilize all of this functionality. Say what you will about the pros and cons of IBM's Java and Microsoft's ASP/COM development platforms, but the Microsoft parser wins this battle, hands down.

To facilitate the connection to the Web service, we first need to define the URL where it can be reached.

```
strServiceURL = "http://www.architectingwebservices.com/mortgageCalc"
```

We then need to use the XMLHTTP class of the MSXML parser to make our HTTP request. Once instantiated, its properties can be set through the open method. For this example, we will want to use the post method and set the URL to our `strServiceURL` string, and, because we don't want to make the call asynchronously, we set that flag to False.

```
set objXMLConnect = Server.createobject("Microsoft.XMLHTTP")
objXMLConnect.open "POST", strServiceURL, False
```

All we have done at this point is opened an object on our side and set its properties; we haven't actually made the request yet. (That's a good thing because we haven't specified our request document yet!) Both of these are done through the send method of our XMLHTTP object.

```
objXMLConnect.send (strRequest)
```

With that, we are actually done with our connection to the Web service. Remember that, because the connection is stateless, no close needs to be executed. We established the connection, made the request, received a response, and closed the connection all with that one send command. The response is contained in the responseText property of our XMLHTTP object, so let's press forward and parse it.

Parsing the Response

The parsing of this particular response couldn't be too much easier because we want to reference only a single element (the payment). We already have the physical response in the property of our XMLHTTP object in a string format, so what we need to do is extract the value that is significant to us.

I prefer to use the DOM structure when accessing data, so we will take that approach here. We could use the SAX reader in the MSXML parser if this were a COM object, but, because we are doing this in ASP with VBScript, an event-driven system would be a little problematic! Here we see the standard code for creating and using the DOM to load our response document:

```
Set objXMLDoc = Server.CreateObject("Microsoft.XMLDOM")
objXMLDoc.async = false
objXMLDoc.loadXML objXMLConnect.responseText
```

Now that we have the data in a DOM structure, access is greatly simplified through the selectSingleNode method:

```
objXMLDoc.selectSingleNode ("paymentCalculator/paymentAmount").text
```

We will format this value using the formatCurrency procedure and place it underneath the home price in our page layout. (See Figure 8-9.) With this accomplished, we have completed the implementation for our Web service consumer. Before moving on to testing the application, let's go ahead and pull all of these code fragments we have seen into a cohesive block.

Figure 8-9. Find-A-Home Realtors home details view with calculated payment

Pulling It All Together

Because the details page is submitting the form to itself, we can contain all of this logic in a single condition within that ASP page. (See Listing 8-6.) The ideal candidate for identifying that condition is the down payment value from our interface form. If it is empty, we don't want to request a calculation because we don't have the necessary data to build a valid request. You might question whether we can build a valid request without having the user select the loan period (either the 15- or 30-year option), but, having built the Web service, we know that, if the service isn't supplied a loan period, it defaults to 30 years.

Listing 8-6. The Mortgage Calculator Consumer Code

```
<%
if request("downPayment") <> "" then
    Dim objXMLDoc 'As XMLDOM
    Dim objXMLConnect 'As XMLHTTP
```

```
set objXMLDoc = Server.CreateObject("MSXML2.DOMDocument")
set objXMLConnect = Server.createobject("MSXML2.XMLHTTP")

Dim strResponse 'As String
Dim strServiceURL 'As String
Dim strRequest

'Build the request Document
strRequest = "<calcInteraction>"
strRequest = strRequest & "<amortizationPeriod>" & Request("Period") &
  "</amortizationPeriod>"
strRequest = strRequest & "<interestRate>" & Request("rate") &
  "</interestRate>"
strRequest = strRequest & "<principalAmount>" &
  cstr(price*1000000-Request("downPayment")) & "</principalAmount>"
strRequest = strRequest & "</calcInteraction>"

'Set the Web service URL
strServiceURL = "http://www.architectingwebservices.com/mortgageCalc"

'Make the request of the Web service
objXMLConnect.open "POST", strServiceURL, False
objXMLConnect.send (strRequest)

'Load the response into a DOM
objXMLDoc.async = false
objXMLDoc.loadXML objXMLConnect.responseText
%>
<tr><td height="10"></td></tr>
<tr>
     <td align="middle">
          <font color="black" face="verdana">Your payment is only<b><i>
          <%=FormatCurrency(objXMLDoc.selectSingleNode
            ("paymentCalculator/paymentAmount").text)%>
          *</i></b>
     </td>
</tr>
<tr><td height="20"></td></tr>
<tr>
     <td align="middle">
          <font color="black" face="verdana" size="1"><i>*This payment is
            subject to taxes and insurance premiums that cannot be calculated
            at this time.</i>
     </td>
```

```
        </tr>
        <%
        Set objXMLDoc = nothing
        Set objXMLConnect = nothing
end if
%>
```

Testing the Consumer

Testing the consumer is similar to testing the Java application in that the two main states to test are connected and disconnected. In a connected state, everything should work just fine. When connectivity is lost, however, no price value is shown when the form is submitted, and no message explaining the problem to the user is communicated either.

A modification we should make to this application is to add the error handling necessary to catch a connection failure and provide a user-friendly message. This essentially means utilizing the infamous `On Error Resume Next` line and doing our own error handling.

To make this change, add the `On Error Resume Next` line right after our condition on the down payment value has been met. Then, right before loading the response into our DOM object, we should add the following code:

```
If err.number <> 0 then %>
<tr><td height="20"></td></tr>
        <tr>
            <td align="middle">
                <font color="black" face="verdana" size="2"><i>There was a problem
                    calculating this payment at this time. Please try again later.</i>
            </td>
        </tr>
<% else
```

Then, immediately before you set the `objXMLDoc` and `objXMLConnect` objects equal to nothing, you want to add an `end if` to complete the conditional loop. After setting those objects, you could go ahead and add the line `On Error GoTo 0` to resume normal error handling as seen in bold case in the following code:

```
<% end if
        Set objXMLDoc = nothing
        Set objXMLConnect = nothing
        On Error GoTo 0
end if %>
```

Now, whenever an error does occur within the application, users at least get a message letting them know that the payment could not be calculated. This can be verified by disconnecting either the Web service provider or consumer from the network.

After running through these tests, our Web service is ready to be rolled out. Hopefully, you've gotten the impression that consuming Web services isn't particularly hard. Although your observation would be accurate, you also haven't consumed a Web services workflow, which will demand a little more effort. That is next!

Consuming a Web Services Workflow

For our final Web services consumer, we are going to encounter a scenario similar to our mortgage calculator consumer, but this time we will be consuming a Web services workflow. We will be adding this Web service to an existing application, but our previous consumers had to support only a single task: one request and one response. A consumer using a Web services workflow will require integration at several points, not just a single call for a single function.

As we saw while building them, a Web services workflow is more complex than a Web services call. Now we will see how this complexity carries over to the consumer. As I alluded to earlier, we would hope that the adoption effort is far less effort for the sake of mass adoption of our Web service. The first thing we need to recognize as a consumer is that adopting a workflow is more effort than a call due to the multiple interactions (either three or five depending on the presentation model we adopt for this specific Web service). This translates into a linear growth of effort from a call to a workflow, which shouldn't be too bad based on the relative ease with which we built the prior consumers.

However, an experienced developer will quickly recognize that a linear effort isn't realistic when complexity is also a factor. The good news is that the extra effort for the consumer is at the beginning, in the design phase. We will have many options to choose from, and it is important to make as many of those decisions as possible before we start the implementation phase. If we can come to our decisions beforehand, doing so will not only lead to a much better process and end product, but it should also help us to achieve linear growth in the implementation phase.

Even though consuming a Web services workflow is more complex, it will still use the same building blocks as the previous exercises. We will thus be required to build upon the concepts used for those consumers and extend them into some new areas. Consuming a Web service such as this demonstrates some of the capabilities and limits of what can be accomplished today with a feature-rich Web services workflow.

Our Scenario

We have a company, AAA Conferences, which sponsors conferences of all types all over the nation. Just like other event companies such as a CMP or DCI that sponsor technical conferences, this company does the same, but on a much broader scope of topics.

AAA Conferences has an existing and fairly robust Web site that allows users to browse its list of conferences and to register for any that they wish to attend. It accepts credit card transactions for the registration, so the company has some good exposure to Web applications as opposed to just Web sites.

The company has recently established a partnership with Milton hotels, a nationwide chain that offers a whole range of rooms in every major city in the United States. Through this partnership, AAA Conferences has been able to broker good discounts for all conference attendees anywhere in the United States.

Currently, prospective attendees need to call in to make a hotel reservation, which makes it difficult for both AAA Conferences and Milton to keep track of who is actually taking advantage of their partnership. In response to AAA Conferences and several other partners, Milton has developed a Web service that exposes their hotel reservation system (HRS) to partners over the Internet. This service is capable of checking room availability and providing additional content on its many hotels (such as images and marketing materials), as well as making reservations.

AAA Conferences wants to integrate this Web service into its site immediately and is looking to us to do it. Company officials want it implemented as quickly as possible because several conferences are scheduled for this very month. However, at the same time, the company doesn't want to compromise the quality of its Web site.

Analyzing the Existing Application

Now that we have our scenario, we need to do some analysis on the current application. (Fortunately, we are familiar with the Web service provided by Milton, so we don't need to spend time analyzing it.) AAA Conferences runs its site on a Microsoft-based platform, and the company officials shy away from putting too much logic in ASP. The company has a good staff, but they are new to Web services and need our assistance in just this implementation. The company's staff will be able to maintain any VB COM/ASP solution we develop.

Because we are integrating the Web service into a Web application, it's probably a good idea to start our analysis by walking through the site. Specifically, we want to explore the current registration process so that we can get some ideas on how we can integrate the service into the site. We will want to go all the way through the process, from selection of the conference to registration, payment, and confirmation.

> **NOTE** *This entire application is actually available online for viewing if you want to walk through it yourself. T he address is* `http://www.architectingwebservices.com/AAA.`

If we start at the company's homepage, we will see a listing of this month's conferences, a couple of highlighted conferences, and a drop-down list of all upcoming conferences. (See Figure 8-10.)

Figure 8-10. AAA Conferences homepage

Clicking on any conference on the home page, or selecting a conference from the drop-down list, takes us to the conference details page (Figure 8-11). Here we can see the location, the date, and description for the event.

Figure 8-11. View conference details page

If we choose to register, we can click on the button on the details page to bring up the registration page. (See Figure 8-12.) Here we enter all of the personal information for our registration.

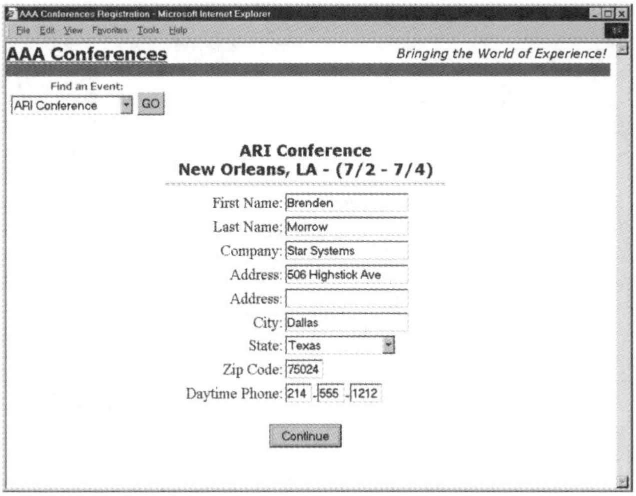

Figure 8-12. Personal registration page

Once we submit this information, we come to the payment page (Figure 8-13). This is a standard online credit card form that accepts all the necessary information to make a transaction for payment of the conference. AAA Conferences does not accept any other form of payment for their registration fees.

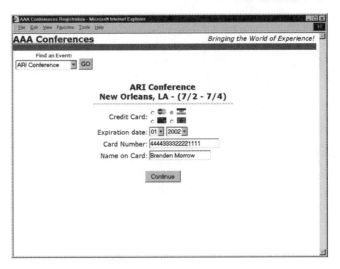

Figure 8-13. Credit card payment page

Submitting the credit card data brings us to the usual confirmation page where the consumer has one last chance to back out of the transaction. (See Figure 8-14.) The confirmation page also features a disclaimer to advise the user that the registration fee is nonrefundable.

Figure 8-14. Registration confirmation page

Accepting the charges then takes you to the obligatory "Thanks for your order" page (Figure 8-15). Rejecting the charge on the previous screen takes you back to the homepage.

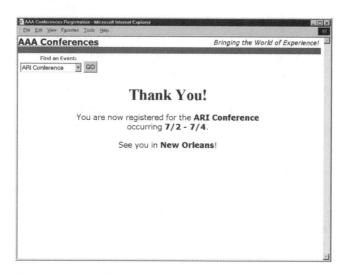

Figure 8-15. Registration confirmed page

We likely did not cover some other areas of the site in this process, but they are of no real concern for this project. Let's go ahead and build a flow diagram of this process. (See Figure 8-16.) Such a diagram will be helpful in examining options for integrating the Web services workflow during our design phase, which is next.

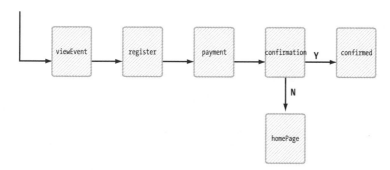

Figure 8-16. AAA Conferences registration process workflow

Designing the Consumer

In looking at these consumers we have been developing, it should become clear that the consumer is much more of a logical entity than it is a physical one. In our first scenario, we built a Java application that was specifically built for consuming the weather Web service. In the second scenario, we had to integrate the consumer into a page of a Web site. In this instance, the consumer will actually be spread out among different interfaces at different points. The AAA Conferences application will actually become the consumer, and we will provide the enhancements necessary to incorporate this functionality.

Because we are working with an existing application, we will start our design on the presentation layer. We will identify how and where we want to incorporate the Web service into the existing interface. We will then address the design of the integration layer to support our presentation layer design.

Designing the Presentation Layer

The design of our presentation layer will take a slightly different approach for this application. We will be concerned with the interfaces, but we first need to back up and look at the process as a whole. We need to take more of a storyboarding approach to developing the presentation layer because we are dealing with so many steps. We actually took this same approach for the Find-A-Home consumer, which was easily identified because it was a single page that integrated a Web services call. Here, we are looking at two processes with multiple steps (workflows), so, before designing the screens, we need to identify what is happening behind them.

To determine a design of this scale, we need to break this process into two steps: identifying the processes and then integrating the processes. If we don't have the exact functionality determined for each process, trying to integrate the two will likely be a very redundant and frustrating process.

Identifying the Two Processes

In our presentation layer design, our main objective is to incorporate the two processes and identify what needs to be added or changed on the AAA site. We have already mapped out the current registration process in Figure 8-16. We also know from our experience with the hotel reservation Web service that we have potentially five functions available to us:

- Availability form

- Availability request

- Hotel detail view

- Reservation form

- Reservation request

These five constitute the maximum amount of functionality that we can count on from the Web service. In fact, along with this functionality comes stylesheets that can define the presentation for the entire process. Because we want to integrate this into an existing process, we will not want to utilize this as an isolated Web service. This means that we can eliminate two of the five steps: the availability and registration forms.

Looking at the remaining three functions, only the hotel detail view may be eliminated. Because this request produces only hotel-specific information that consists of five image references and some marketing text, the information is of questionable value. After all, the main appeal of these hotels is the pricing and the one-stop shopping convenience. Because we want to integrate this Web service quickly, dropping this function is certainly worth considering.

The risk of leaving the function out, however, is whether users are willing to make reservations for a hotel without having much information about it. Although this is a possibility, sacrificing this functionality might make the success of this new hotel reservation process less certain. Let's plan on going ahead and integrating this functionality, and we will determine later how much of the content we actually utilize.

To minimize the workload of the hotel detail view, our application could automatically make the Web services request for every availability match (similar to the hidden Web service model we discussed in Chapter 5). This would eliminate an extra process step and a separate hotel detail screen for the user. Because this isn't a travel site producing several matches per request, we don't need the information quite so streamlined, as provided by the service owner. Depending on the criteria selected by the user, up to three hotels may be returned for a given availability request, which would mean three extra calls to the service. However, because we are programming this logic in a COM object, our performance shouldn't suffer too much from those extra requests.

> **NOTE** *You should be aware that this type of design decision is feasible only because the responses from these requests are exposed on a data level to us. Without the ability to manipulate the data on our side, matching up the data from these two requests would be problematic, if not impossible.*

This leaves us with essentially two exposed steps to integrate from the Web service. The first step is the availability request, which we will supplement with a back end request to the detail view process. The second function will then be the reservation request. If we map the process to these functions and add the necessary interfaces, we will end up with five steps in our Web services consumer: selection of hotel criteria (hotelCriteria), hotel selection (hotelAvailability), reservation request (`registration`), reservation confirmation (`confirmation`), and a reservation confirmed page (`confirmed`). (See Figure 8-17.) Now that we have our Web services process mapped out, let's proceed with integrating the two.

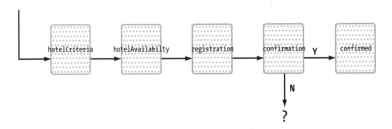

Figure 8-17. Reservation Web service consumer process workflow

Integrating the Two Processes

If we look at our two processes, we have one consisting of six steps and one consisting of five. One of the key objectives in designing a Web application is to minimize the number of clicks necessary to accomplish a given task. To help in this effort, we should try to find the lowest common denominator of these two processes in an attempt to create one straightforward process for the user. We should end up with no more than eleven total steps if we design it properly. This is because, no matter your skill and savvy as a designer, if two processes have absolutely no overlapping functionality or usability, you are essentially stacking one process on top of another. However, you should always try to lower the total number of steps when possible.

In this scenario, we have some clearly overlapping functionality. For instance, the payment, reservation confirmation, and confirmed steps can essentially be merged together. Unfortunately, the merging of steps within these two processes ends there. We have two more steps that we need to integrate from our Web services workflow: availability request and hotel selection.

What we need to do next is identify the entry points for these two steps in the current registration process. This determines where to expose the hotel registration process to the user and how to do it. We don't want to be so subtle that it is glossed over, but we also want to protect the existing process for those users who want to just register for the conference. Our choices for entry essentially fall between the conference selection and payment steps of the registration process.

Because each step is a transaction in the registration process, we can't very easily lead them off to the hotel registration process within one of these steps. Taking this approach, we would either be asking users to enter their personal information or payment information, and at the same time asking them if they want to make a hotel reservation. This doesn't flow very well, and so we will likely need to interrupt the current flow with a new screen that asks them if they also want to reserve a hotel room. (See Figure 8-18.) This approach may not be as integrated as we might like it, but it certainly isn't overly subtle!

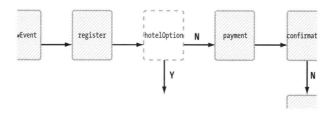

Figure 8-18. Adding the hotel option step to the registration process

Once we establish this intercept point, we can branch our availability request and hotel selection off of it. This could then lead directly back into the payment step of our registration process. The issue here might be that we are moving too quickly through the process for the user. We would essentially move from a list of hotels that are available and go directly on to the payment information.

If we look back to where we integrated the two registration confirmations, we might start to reconsider that decision. After all, one is confirming a single registration fee. It doesn't matter when you actually attend the conference. The hotel confirmation is for specific dates, and the charges are even dependent on those dates. Although we can augment the information presented in that step, we should probably maintain our own confirmation step prior to forwarding the user to the payment step.

If we look at where we are, we will see that we have all of our steps accounted for. We should go ahead and develop our modified registration process diagram (Figure 8-19) so that we have clearly accounted for each step. With some shades and patterns, we can even identify which steps come from which process, which are brand new, and which are modified. This will help us tremendously during the implementation of our presentation layer.

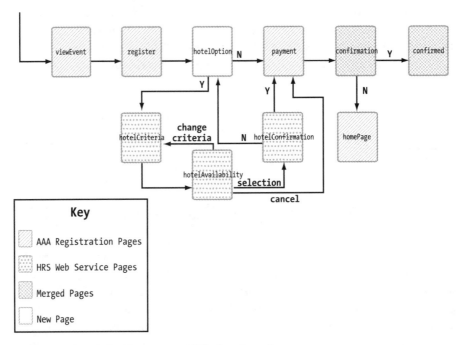

Figure 8-19. AAA Conferences modified registration process

Between the two processes, we need to make very few big decisions on a screen level in the modified process. Either the information already exists in the existing process, or the Web service requires it to process a request. We will leave the other details on the screens to the implementation phase of the project and the Web developers who handle those issues best. This means that we are ready to move on to the integration layer.

Designing the Integration Layer

In this scenario, the integration layer becomes the true middleware tier that it was intended to be in our architecture models from Chapter 2. This layer facilitates the functionality necessary at the steps that involve the Web service, and this process involves defining some logic and some data integration.

If we take a different view of the modified registration process (see Figure 8-20), we can see where the Web service interaction takes place in the process. It is here where the integration layer comes into play. It is also helpful to identify in this view the different data elements that must be collected to build the requests for the Web service.

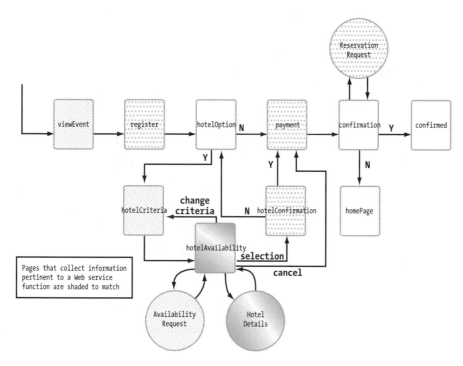

Figure 8-20. Web service interaction within the registration process

Although we already knew we were dealing with three Web service requests at two steps, it is always reassuring to confirm that with the presentation layer design. We see in our flow that the availability request and hotel detail calls are both made at the availability view, and that the reservation request is made at the reservation confirmed step.

The next thing we need to do is design the logical components for making these Web service requests. We have already determined that we will use a COM component for our logic, so we have an interface to define.

Defining the COM Interface

The first design decision to make is how to handle the availability/hotel details request. We could define two different methods and allow the ASP to control that, but this would not benefit as much from the potential COM scalability and performance. We could define one method that handles both Web service requests, but any changes to this process would be more difficult to make.

Although officials at AAA Conferences could change their minds later, it is more likely that they will maintain this consecutive-calls approach because their reasons for doing so today are not likely to change down the road. The company won't become a travel agency overnight, and, if it does, it has bigger issues to deal with than this little COM object. What we will do is allow the call to the object to dictate whether the additional detail information should be requested with the availability matches. This will affect our component's interface, which is appropriate because that is what we need to look at next.

We need to determine what parameters to pass to our component and what information it will return. The return is probably a little easier to handle first: we want the data in a string. A lot of information of arbitrary sizes will be coming back, so we are most likely to want it in some XML/HTML format. We will leave these details for later when we define our data integration points.

The parameter structure for this hotel availability/details request will not be so easy to define. We could take the same approach as the return, defining a single string for the input and pass in XML. This would be somewhat self-defeating, though, because one of the reasons we are using the COM object is to avoid having to work with XML directly in the ASP page. If we defined the parameter as a string, the ASP would then be responsible for converting the form values into XML.

If we look at the data that is necessary to make the availability request (as shown in the following list), we see that it contains a lot of the information we will be collecting in our HTML form:

- Check-in date

- Check-out date

- Number of adults

- Number of children

- City and state

- Coupon code

- Price preference

- Bed size preference

- Smoking preference

- Requested hotel amenities

Because all the data necessary to initiate this step is coming from the form, we could pass the request object to our method and be done with it. However, not all the information needs to be collected by the user. For instance, the city, state, and coupon code are all defined by AAA Conferences for a given event. We could pass these as hidden form values, but this makes them vulnerable to manipulation by the user. Because the agreement applies to the cities in which AAA Conferences is holding events, we should probably be more protective of that information. So, if we add these data elements to the details flag we defined earlier, we will end up with a method that looks something like:

```
Public Function checkAvailability(myRequest As Request, couponCode As String,
    eventCity As String, eventState As String, getDetails As Boolean) As String
```

> **CAUTION** *At some point, you will have to account for the individual form values within the Request object. If you pass it as an object instead of enumerating each form field (as we have done here), you are potentially passing bad data to other components. Although corrupt data could cause an error, catching this kind of an error is only protecting malicious users from themselves because it would involve tampering with our HTML form. Although we could catch this exception, we will not do so in this implementation. You can test this case for yourself at* http://www.architectingwebservices.com/AAA.

Next, we need to define the method for our reservation request process. We could take the same approach as the checkAvailability method and pass it the request object, but remember that the reservation request is made long after the data is collected. That information will need to be persisted somewhere other than the request object. AAA currently uses the session object for long-term state management (of variables only, no objects), so that is what we will use as well.

Unlike the availability request function, the session will contain all of our data, so no other parameters are necessary. We will also receive the return value through a string. Putting this together then gives us the following method:

```
Public Function makeReservation(mySession As Session) As String
```

Now that we have our COM interface defined, it is time to turn our attention to how we will expose this data through the registration process. We will be dealing with more data than in any of the other examples, so this topic needs some special consideration.

Defining the Data Integration Points

Before proceeding on to our implementation, we need to spend a little more time on defining how the data from our Web service requests will integrate with the data from the registration process. Part of this was accomplished through Figure 8-20 and identifying where the data elements required by our Web service will be collected. We know that we can fairly easily capture that data in the appropriate format to make our requests of the Web service. Because these requests are somewhat substantial, we will aid this process by providing templates for each request just as we did for some of the responses in our Web services. With that defined, what we need to focus our attention on now is integrating the data from our Web service into the registration application.

We know that we are receiving the data from the Web service in an XML format. We also know that we are presenting the data to the user via HTML. So far, so good! What we must determine now is how to get the data from the one format to the other. The options we have include element extraction from a DOM, SAX, manual parsing, and XSL stylesheets. As usual, different methods have different benefits, depending on the situation.

What we have are two different points at which the data produced from the Web service must be presented to the user. One is where we present the availability matches based on the criteria submitted. This could potentially be zero or several matches (based on the constraints of the Web service). Because the data volume is so variable, this is a good opportunity to use an XSL stylesheet. The question then is whether to run this transformation within the COM object or within the ASP page.

Besides the performance benefit of running the process inside the object, we also have to consider reusability. More than likely, this data will be contained in a DOM at some point if we are working with it. Because it is necessary for the data to be contained in a DOM to perform the transformation, it makes sense to do it there. Otherwise, we would be loading the XML data into another DOM in the ASP to perform the transformation.

The other curve thrown at us in this scenario is that the response from the `checkAvailability` call will provide data from two different Web service calls: one for the actual availability request and another for the hotel details. At some point, this data needs to be integrated if it is to be returned as a single XML string. Although we will handle this issue in our implementation phase, we need to consider how this will affect the XSL transformation approach. Do we run two transformations separately and then combine them? If so, that would be a lot of effort for what will become a single data set. Or do we run a transformation on one of the data sets that generates the stylesheet for the next transformation, essentially combining the two data sets? Although this is feasible, it is not simple and certainly not maintainable for AAA Conferences. Instead of either of these approaches, let's assume that we will combine the data and run a single transformation that produces the desired final output for our application.

The other data interaction point is the reservation request. This is a little more similar to our calculator service in which we were interested in only a single piece of data from the response. In this situation, the data element we want is the confirmation number, so that is what we will pass directly through the response.

With our data integration points defined, at least at a high level, we have completed enough of the design to confidently move on to the implementation of our Web service consumer. Undoubtedly, there will be more design decisions to come, but they either should be on a micro level relative to these decisions or they will simply not reveal themselves until we start the implementation process.

Implementing the Consumer

This consumer is much larger than the previous consumers, so we will be developing far more. This consumer will manifest itself through four different entity types: ASP pages, a COM object, XML templates, and XSL stylesheets. Together, all four will be able to provide something that previously was not possible: integrating two different processes via the Internet.

ASP Pages

The first thing we will work on is creating the new ASP pages and modifying the necessary existing pages. If we refer back to Figure 8-19, we can see exactly where these changes will need to take place. The best way to approach the ASP pages is to step through the process like we did in our analysis and take it a page at a time. I will spare you from walking through all the code in these pages. Instead, I will present you with a screenshot of their view and highlight only the most interesting code bits.

hotelOption.asp

The first page we need to generate is the hotel options page—the page where the user is first presented with the opportunity to make a hotel reservation using the new functionality on the site. (See Figure 8-21.) This really is a very simple page with no logic, so there isn't any complexity in the code behind it.

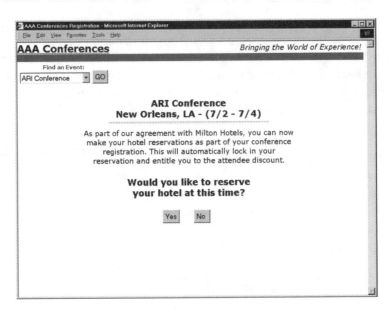

Figure 8-21. Hotel option web page

hotelCriteria.asp

If the user chooses to make a hotel reservation, the hotel criteria page is the next one presented. (See Figure 8-22.) Here, all the user's criteria will be collected and combined with AAA Conference's data to make the availability request of the Web service. The available dates utilize a checkbox input field, which presents the possibility of having a gap between dates. For example, the user could select the checkboxes for Sunday and Wednesday and not Monday or Tuesday. We don't want to allow this kind of gap, so we will add some client-side script to eliminate that possibility.

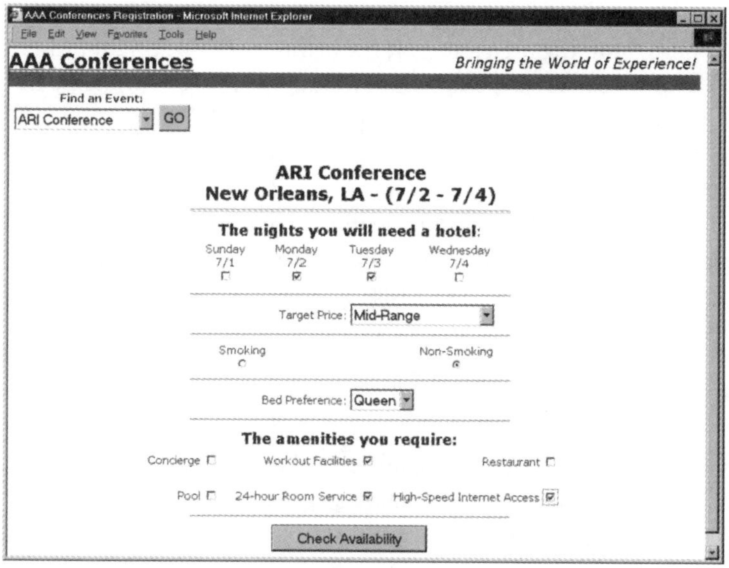

Figure 8-22. Hotel criteria web page

The interesting bit of code in this interface comes through the building of the available nights at the top of the form. What we are doing is taking the start and end dates of the conference and calculating all the valid nights necessary for an accommodating hotel reservation, starting with the night before the first day and ending with the evening of the last day.

```
<%for x = 1 to (datediff("d",startDate,endDate)+2)%>
    <td align="center">;nbsp;
        <FONT face=Verdana size="1">;nbsp;
        <%=weekdayname(datepart("w",Dateadd("d",x-2,startDate)))%> <BR>
        <%=datepart("m",Dateadd("d",x-2,startDate))%>/
          <%=datepart("d",Dateadd("d",x-2,startDate))%><BR>
        <input type="checkbox" name="resDate"
          value="<%=dateadd("d",x-2,startDate)%>">
    </td>
<%next%>
```

One other thing to note here is that, instead of giving users an option to enter their preferred price range, AAA Conferences wanted to instead try a more general approach by listing the criteria of cheapest available, midrange, and best room available. This approach was taken because AAA thought that a price was too dependent upon the area and that these three options might present the user with a more realistic expectation of the rooms that are available for a given range of prices in that area.

This sounds complicated, but its execution is elementary. Behind these values are basic dollar amounts that should generate the desired result. For instance, behind the cheapest available option is a value of $50. Behind the best room available is a value of $500. Although it might be hard to find a room that actually costs that much within the Milton system, it at least communicates that the sky is the limit for this request.

hotelAvailability.asp

Once the criteria are submitted, the hotel availability page presents the results to the user. There may have been no matches, or several, depending on the criteria submitted. This information is laid out in simple rows with the fields identified at the top. (See Figure 8-23.) To the right are the buttons for actually selecting one of these hotels. The options at the bottom are for making another request using different criteria or escaping the process entirely.

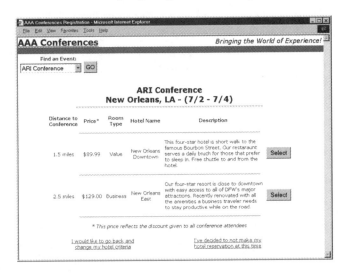

Figure 8-23. Hotel selection web page

This page is actually making the call to our checkAvailability method, so it is worthwhile to show that request here. Notice how the return value is later displayed "as is" within a table cell on the page. This means that the response is properly formatted for presentation directly to the user. We will look at that functionality later in the "COM Object" section.

```
<%
set objWS = Server.Createobject("hotelResWS.WSRequest")
myResponse = objWS.CheckAvailability(Request,"AAA456",city,state,true)
set objWS = nothing
%>
. . .
<TD colspan="2"><%=myResponse%></TD>
. . .
```

hotelConfirmation.asp

This is the additional page that we added when reflecting on our process flow. Here we are confirming just the selection of the hotel and giving one more convenient escape out of their selection. (See Figure 8-24.)

Figure 8-24. Hotel confirmation web page

Although this page doesn't have any code that's too exciting, it is worth recognizing that we are storing some data in session variables here. This information will be referenced later when we make the registration request. Notice that one of these elements is a session ID, that is from the reservation Web service. (Hence, the mSessionID name to identify it as Milton's.) Part of our compliance in consuming this Web service is that we maintain the session ID provided after our initial request to the service for the length of the session. This allows the Web service to maintain state on its side between the availability and reservation requests.

```
session("hotelID") = Request("hotelID")
session("roomType") = Request("roomType")
session("mSessionID") = Request("session")
```

confirmation.asp

This page has only a few minor text changes that present some of the information concerning the hotel component of the registration. (See Figure 8-25.) Everything here is entirely visual, not functional.

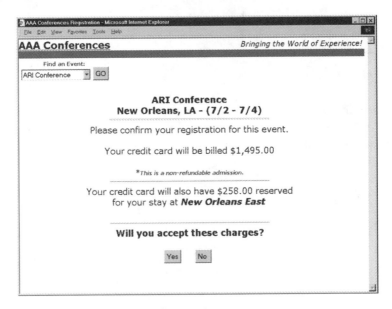

Figure 8-25. Registration confirmation web page

confirmed.asp

This process is completed with the registration confirmed page. We are adding on this page the call to the makeReservation method and providing a confirmation to the user when the reservation is successful. (See Figure 8-26.)

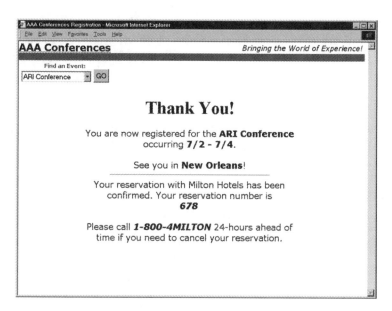

Figure 8-26. Registration confirmed web page

It is worth noting here that we are using the session variable hotelID to know whether to trigger the reservation request. We are setting that only on the hotel confirmation page, and we are deleting it whenever the user exits the process, so it should be safe to use for that purpose.

```
<%
if session("hotelID") <> "" then
    set objWS = Server.Createobject("hotelResWS.WSRequest")
    myResponse = objWS.makeReservation(Session)
    set objWS = nothing
end if
%>
```

If the request encounters an error during the process, the Web service will respond with an error tag within the XML document. Because there is nothing we could do to compensate for an error, we just need to let the user know if the reservation failed to go through and direct him or her to the appropriate phone number. Instead of loading the response into a DOM to make this determination,

I am simply searching for a substring that contains the error tag name, which should be quicker and just as effective. This simple string search can be very effective in situations such as this where you need to check for the presence of a specific element.

```
<% if instr(myResponse,"<Error>") <> 0 then %>
    We are sorry, but there was a problem with your reservation request with
        Milton hotels.<br>Please call <b><i>1-800-4MILTON</i></b> to make your
        reservations for the conference.
<% else %>
    Your reservation with Milton Hotels has been confirmed. Your reservation
        number is<br> <b><i><%=myResponse%></i></b><p>Please call<b><i>1-
        800-4MILTON</i></b> 24-hours ahead of time if you need to cancel your
        reservation.
<% end if %>
```

XML Templates

With our ASP pages completed, it is now time to build our request templates. These documents will help in ensuring that our requests are valid as well as helping in the performance of our XML handling. Any consistent document structure containing dynamic data will benefit from this approach, and these requests are no different.

For the most part, these templates are taken directly from the Web services interface schemas. When appropriate, we have removed optional nodes that will go unused and repopulated the data when it is static.

Availability Request Template

For this template, we have populated the stage and sessionID service variables. Although this may be a secondary request, most of the time it is not, and the logic will benefit from assuming it does not have to manipulate that element unless it has a value on hand.

We have also populated the adult and child values because all reservations will be done on an individual basis. If Milton and AAA Conferences determine that they want to extend their discounts to the families of the conference attendees, a change will need to be made to accommodate this.

We have also defined a preferences node but have left it devoid of any of its children: amenity, bedSize, and smoking. If these properties are provided, the nodes will be created and added to the preferences node. If none are added, the preferences node will be deleted. The thinking here is that the probability of at least one of the children being necessary is high, but we don't know which one it might be. Even though the preference node must have a child node added or removed, this is most likely the most efficient structure for this node.

The optional landmark field has also been removed because all hotels will be searched for by only city and state. If this requirement changed, this template would need to be changed, but, more importantly, the logic in our COM object would have to change, which would be far more significant. You can see the final template for our availability request in Listing 8-7.

Listing 8-7. `availabilityRequestTemplate.xml`

```xml
<?xml version="1.0" encoding="UTF-8"?>
<hrs:reservationWS xmlns:hrs="urn:reservationWS">
    <hrs:serviceVariables>
        <sessionID>0</sessionID>
        <stage>1</stage>
    </hrs:serviceVariables>
    <hrs:payload>
        <hrs:availabilityInteraction>
            <availabilityRequest>
                <checkInDate/>
                <checkOutDate/>
                <numberAdults>1</numberAdults>
                <numberChildren>0</numberChildren>
                <locale>
                    <cityState>
                        <city/>
                        <state/>
                    </cityState>
                </locale>
                <couponCode/>
                <approxPrice/>
                <preferences/>
            </availabilityRequest>
        </hrs:availabilityInteraction>
    </hrs:payload>
</hrs:reservationWS>
```

Detail Request Template

The detail request template (Listing 8-8) is the smallest because all it needs to contain is the ID for the hotel for which content should be retrieved. We have already populated the stage variable because we know this is a stage 2 request.

Listing 8-8. detailRequestTemplate.xml

```xml
<?xml version="1.0" encoding="UTF-8"?>
<hrs:reservationWS xmlns:hrs="urn:reservationWS">
     <hrs:serviceVariables>
          <sessionID/>
          <stage>2</stage>
     </hrs:serviceVariables>
     <hrs:payload>
          <hrs:detailInteraction>
               <detailRequest>
                    <hotelID/>
               </detailRequest>
          </hrs:detailInteraction>
     </hrs:payload>
</hrs:reservationWS>
```

Reservation Request Template

The reservation request template is the one in which we have deviated the most from the service's interface schema. Although we are only populating the stage element as we did in the other templates, we are removing several optional nodes from the schema. First is the second address node under the homeAddress element. More times than not, this data will not be provided by the user, so we will create it when necessary as opposed to deleting it when it is not.

Finally, we also removed the entire billAddress element and its children. It is optional because when it is not present, the home address is used by default. AAA Conferences already requests that the user's address entered in the registration form match the billing address for the credit card that is used for payment. You can see the entire request template in Listing 8-9.

Listing 8-9. reservationRequestTemplate.xml

```xml
<?xml version="1.0" encoding="UTF-8"?>
<hrs:reservationWS xmlns:hrs="urn:reservationWS">
     <hrs:serviceVariables xmlns:hrs="urn:serviceVariables">
          <sessionID/>
          <stage>3</stage>
     </hrs:serviceVariables>
     <hrs:payload>
          <hrs:reservationInteraction xmlns:hrs="urn:reservationInteraction">
               <hrs:reservationRequest xmlns:hrs="urn:reservationRequest">
                    <hrs:hotelData>
                         <hotelID/>
                         <roomType/>
                    </hrs:hotelData>
```

```
                    <hrs:personalData>
                        <homeAddress>
                            <address/>
                            <city/>
                            <state/>
                            <zipCode/>
                        </homeAddress>
                        <firstName/>
                        <lastName/>
                        <homePhone/>
                        <hrs:ccData>
                            <number/>
                            <issuer/>
                            <expirationDate/>
                            <nameOfOwner/>
                        </hrs:ccData>
                    </hrs:personalData>
                </hrs:reservationRequest>
            </hrs:reservationInteraction>
        </hrs:payload>
</hrs:reservationWS>
```

COM Object

Now that we have completed the development of our ASP pages and templates, we have some code to put together in our COM objects to bring this all together. As we defined earlier, we have two public methods: checkAvailability and makeReservation. As with our two previous consumers, we need a way to store the address of the Web service. For this purpose, we have declared a global constant that can be referenced by both functions:

```
Const strServiceURL = "https://www.architectingwebservices.com/
  hrsws/embedded/default.asp"
```

We should also recognize the library references that we will need to make to incorporate the appropriate functionality for this component. As with the other examples, we will be using the Microsoft, XML v4.0 parser (currently the MSXML4 Technical Preview). Because we will be working with the request and session objects, we will also need to reference the Microsoft Active Server Pages Object Library.

The development of these COM objects will be made easier if you have, in fact, developed the ASP pages already. These pages can call the functions in their various stages of development if they are running within the development environment. This can help you to debug whether the component is behaving correctly or if your logic is working correctly.

> **CAUTION** *Although running the component in the Visual Studio IDE is a great way to debug distributed applications, certain combinations of platforms and tool versions have kept this from being successful. Microsoft has an article on this issue (`http://support.microsoft.com/support/kb/articles/Q259/7/25.ASP`), which contains workaround information if you have trouble running in this mode.*

checkAvailability

This method is responsible for making the availability request and making the second request for each matching hotel, retrieving its content. That may not sound like much, but several steps need to be performed both before and after these requests to make this information applicable and usable.

We can actually group these tasks similarly to how we grouped the application logic for our previous consumers. The one exception from that process is that we won't be programmatically parsing the response. We will be using an XSL stylesheet to do that for us. However, we also have an extra task that we need to perform: we need to enhance the response before sending it on for the transformation.

We need to add the appropriate data from the secondary request for the hotel details. However, this process has some added complexity because we need to pass data through that transformation to maintain AAA's existing registration process.

Because the XSL will now be responsible for all of the data on the page, it needs to maintain the current application's state, such as what conference is being registered. This may appear to complicate the process (the effect of which is actually rather slight), but the alternative is to add a step in the ASP by loading the response into a DOM and then performing another transformation that incorporates this state data.

This leaves our list of tasks for this method at (1) build the request, (2) invoke the Web service, and (3) modify the response. This XSL approach works well because the transformation of the data can be treated as further tweaking of the response without pushing responsibility to the ASP.

Building the Request

Building this request will be a little more complex than anything we have encountered yet. We have a few challenges due to the variation and even existence of criteria data. Additionally, we will need to do some massaging of the submitted data due to the format of the submitted data (HTML form fields.) This is the data that we will use for our Web service request, so we need to spend a little effort prepping this data for use within our payload.

The first challenge we will tackle is the reservation dates, and it is a good example of the problems we can encounter in this area. We have a variable number of days for which the user wishes to check for room availability. It could be one night during the conference, or all four or five nights. This information was collected in a series of checkboxes, so we will have a string delimited by commas to parse through.

The easiest way to accomplish this is by splitting the string into an array. We can then use the LBound and UBound functions to reference the first and last days in the array. This process is shown in the following code:

```
myArray = Split(myRequest.Form("resDate"), ",")

dtCheckIn = myArray(LBound(myArray))
dtCheckOut = myArray(UBound(myArray))
```

Now that we have the date of arrival and the date of departure, we need to format them for use as an XML date data type. This takes the form of "yyyy-mm-dd". Unfortunately, there is no VB function that will convert a date to this format automatically, so we will need to build it manually. It looks something like this:

```
strCheckIn = DatePart("yyyy", dtCheckIn) & "-"
If Len(DatePart("m", dtCheckIn)) < 2 Then strCheckIn = strCheckIn & "0"
strCheckIn = strCheckIn & DatePart("m", dtCheckIn) & "-"
If Len(DatePart("d", dtCheckIn)) < 2 Then strCheckIn = strCheckIn & "0"
strCheckIn = strCheckIn & DatePart("d", dtCheckIn)
```

Once this is done for both the check-in and check-out dates, they are ready to use in our request document. The next challenge arises from the amenities element, which is another element that was exposed through an HTML checkbox, meaning that zero or multiple values may be provided. Unlike the date, we don't need to find the minimum and maximum values within the values, so we can simply split this string into an array for now:

```
myArray = Split(myRequest.Form("amenities"), ",")
```

Now that we have all our data in a usable format, we can proceed with building the request document for the availability request service. As we saw before, we have developed a template to aid in building each of our requests. All we need to do is load the template into a DOM, create a reference to it through a node object, and we will be ready to start putting data in it.

```
objXMLDoc.async = False
booltest = objXMLDoc.Load("http://www.architectingwebservices.com/aaa
  /templates/availabilityRequestTemplate.xml")
Set objXMLNode = objXMLDoc.selectSingleNode("hrs:reservationWS/hrs:payload/
  hrs:availabilityInteraction/availabilityRequest")
```

With our template now loaded, we can proceed to set the values of the various nodes. We will start with the variables that don't require any further checking or qualification:

```
objXMLNode.selectSingleNode("checkInDate").nodeTypedValue = strCheckIn
objXMLNode.selectSingleNode("checkOutDate").nodeTypedValue = strCheckOut
objXMLNode.selectSingleNode("locale/cityState/city").nodeTypedValue = eventCity
objXMLNode.selectSingleNode("locale/cityState/state").nodeTypedValue = eventState
objXMLNode.selectSingleNode("approxPrice").nodeTypedValue =
  CInt(myRequest.Form("pricerange"))
objXMLNode.selectSingleNode("couponCode").nodeTypedValue = couponCode
```

> **TIP** *Notice how I used the* CInt *conversion call to format the* pricerange *variable for storing it in the* approxPrice *node. It is always a good idea to type the data correctly when using the* nodeTypedValue *property for setting the node value. The conversion doesn't happen automatically, and it will likely generate an error if it is incorrectly typed.*

We now come to a few tricky little variables that require some special attention. The `session` variable in the service variables may or may not exist, so we need to first check for its existence. If it is present, then we will add it. Otherwise, it will remain the default value defined in our template, zero.

```
If myRequest.Form("session") <> "" Then
  objXMLDoc.selectSingleNode("hrs:reservationWS/hrs:serviceVariables/sessionID").
  nodeTypedValue = CInt(myRequest.Form("session"))
```

We will now need a different approach to handle a couple of similar variables where, if they do exist, we need to create the node, set its value, and then append it in the proper location. Following is the code for handling the smoking element. The `bedSize` element would need to be handled in a similar manner.

```
If myRequest.Form("smoking") <> "" Then
    Set objXMLChild = objXMLDoc.createElement("smoking")
    objXMLChild.nodeTypedValue = CBool(myRequest.Form("smoking"))
    objXMLNode.selectSingleNode("preferences").appendChild objXMLChild
End If
```

Another slightly different scenario exists for populating the amenity value(s). Here we will step through the array, creating and adding an element for each instance within it.

```
For Each amenity In myArray
    Set objXMLChild = objXMLDoc.createElement("amenity")
    objXMLChild.nodeTypedValue = CStr(amenity)
    objXMLNode.selectSingleNode("preferences").appendChild objXMLChild
Next
```

> **CAUTION**   *It is tempting to think that we could make this process more efficient by pulling the* createElement *call out of the loop. Although it is rational to think that this might work, in reality it does not, at least if you are adding elements in the same level within the DOM. In this scenario, each subsequent* appendChild *call overwrites any prior nodes added. You must create a new element for this process to work correctly. If you want to add the same node type to a different location in the DOM, this would be an acceptable approach.*

Finally, we need to remove the preferences node if we did not add any children to it:

```
If objXMLNode.selectSingleNode("preferences").hasChildNodes = False Then
   objXMLNode.removeChild (objXMLNode.selectSingleNode("preferences"))
```

Establishing the Connection

As we saw in the previous consumer, making the Web service request with the MSXML parser's XMLHTTP class is fairly simple and direct. We have added a little more complexity to this particular scenario because the service requires a client certificate. Once our server installs the client certificate (see Chapter 6), we need to simply reference it using the setOption property of our XMLHTTP class. Then we make the request just as we did before:

```
objXMLConnect.setOption SXH_OPTION_SELECT_CLIENT_SSL_CERT, "AAACert"
objXMLConnect.open "POST", strServiceURL, False
objXMLConnect.send (objXMLDoc.xml)
objXMLAvailResponse.loadXML (objXMLConnect.responseText)
```

Modifying the Response

In this scenario, we are modifying the response instead of just parsing it. As we discussed earlier, the XSL will be providing the final response to our caller, but we need to ensure that it has all the necessary data to maintain state for the application through the hotel selection process.

The variables we need to maintain are the conference ID and the arrival and departure dates. We will look here specifically at the code for the conference ID. First, we need to create a node that will represent the conference ID. Next, we set the value to the conference variable in our request object, and, finally, we append the node to our response document. I have selected the serviceVariables element because it is a fairly safe location, and we won't be sending this document back to the Web service:

```
Set objXMLChild = objXMLDoc.createElement("conference")
objXMLChild.nodeTypedValue = CInt(myRequest.Form("conference"))
objXMLAvailResponse.selectSingleNode("hrs:reservationWS/
   hrs:serviceVariables").appendChild objXMLChild
```

Now that we have added these variables, this response is ready to be transformed. But, before we can do that, we need to add the content from the hotel details response. Just like we did for the availability request, we will be loading a template to help us generate a valid request document for the hotel details. Once this template is loaded, we will load a node list with all instances of the hotel ID in our availability response and loop through it, setting the hotel ID for each request. We also maintain a separate node instance that keeps track of which hotel we are working with. Once the request is made, we will create an element called `description` and use this node to locate it within our DOM. You can see the logic for integrating the hotel detail content into the availability function in Listing 8-10.

Listing 8-10. The Hotel Detail View Integration

```
logicSet objXMLNodeList = objXMLAvailResponse.getElementsByTagName("hotelID")
Set objXMLNode = objXMLAvailResponse.selectSingleNode("hrs:reservationWS/
  hrs:payload/hrs:availabilityInteraction/availabilityResults/hotel")
For x = 0 To objXMLNodeList.length - 1
    If x > 0 Then Set objXMLNode = objXMLNode.nextSibling
    objXMLDoc.selectSingleNode("hrs:reservationWS/hrs:payload/
      hrs:detailInteraction/detailRequest/hotelID").nodeTypedValue =
      objXMLNodeList.Item(x).nodeTypedValue
    '—Make the request
    Set objXMLChild = objXMLDoc.createElement("description")
    objXMLChild.Text = objXMLDetResponse.selectSingleNode
      ("hrs:reservationWS/hrs:payload/hrs:detailInteraction/hotelContent/
      hotelDescription").Text
    objXMLNode.appendChild objXMLChild
Next
```

And, finally, we are ready to transform our data to the final output format:

```
checkAvailability = objXMLAvailResponse.transformNode
  (objXSLDoc.documentElement)
```

We will look at the XSLT in the stylesheet we are using later in the "XSL Stylesheet" section. It was more important to define our data structure than it was to have our stylesheet available now, but built on assumptions.

Pulling It All Together

Before moving on, let's go ahead and review the `checkAvailability` method in its entirety. (See Listing 8-11.) We omitted some of the details on purpose so that we could concentrate on the core issues, but we should now review the entire code set to make sure that we understand how this all comes together to provide the correct response.

Listing 8-11. The checkAvailability *Method*

```
Public Function checkAvailability(myRequest As Request, couponCode As String,
    eventCity As String, eventState As String, getDetails As Boolean) As String

Dim objXMLDoc As MSXML2.DOMDocument40
Dim objXMLNode As MSXML2.IXMLDOMNode
Dim objXMLChild As MSXML2.IXMLDOMNode
Dim objXMLConnect As MSXML2.ServerXMLHTTP40
Dim objXMLAvailResponse As MSXML2.DOMDocument40
Dim objXMLDetResponse As MSXML2.DOMDocument40
Dim objXMLNodeList As MSXML2.IXMLDOMNodeList
Dim objXSLDoc As MSXML2.DOMDocument40

Dim dtCheckIn As Date
Dim dtCheckOut As Date
Dim myArray As Variant
Dim arrLen As Integer
Dim price As Integer

Dim strCheckIn As String
Dim strCheckOut As String

Dim booltest As Boolean

Set objXMLDoc = New DOMDocument40
Set objXSLDoc = New DOMDocument40
Set objXMLAvailResponse = New DOMDocument40
Set objXMLConnect = New MSXML2.ServerXMLHTTP40

'Extract arrival and departure dates
arrLen = 0
myArray = Split(myRequest.Form("resDate"), ",")
For Each i In myArray
     arrLen = arrLen + 1
Next

dtCheckIn = myArray(0)
dtCheckOut = myArray(arrLen - 1)

'Format arrival and departure dates for XML date format
strCheckIn = DatePart("yyyy", dtCheckIn) & "-"
If Len(DatePart("m", dtCheckIn)) < 2 Then strCheckIn = strCheckIn & "0"
     strCheckIn = strCheckIn & DatePart("m", dtCheckIn) & "-"
```

```
If Len(DatePart("d", dtCheckIn)) < 2 Then strCheckIn = strCheckIn & "0"
strCheckIn = strCheckIn & DatePart("d", dtCheckIn)

strCheckOut = DatePart("yyyy", dtCheckOut) & "-"
If Len(DatePart("m", dtCheckOut)) < 2 Then strCheckOut = strCheckOut & "0"
strCheckOut = strCheckOut & DatePart("m", dtCheckOut) & "-"
If Len(DatePart("d", dtCheckOut)) < 2 Then strCheckOut = strCheckOut & "0"
strCheckOut = strCheckOut & DatePart("d", dtCheckOut)

'Extract amenities
myArray = Split(myRequest.Form("amenities"), ",")

'Load Template
objXMLDoc.async = False
objXSLDoc.Load ("http://www.architectingwebservices.com/aaa/transforms/
  availabilityResponse.xsl")
booltest = objXMLDoc.Load("http://www.architectingwebservices.com/aaa/
  templates/availabilityRequestTemplate.xml")
Set objXMLNode = objXMLDoc.selectSingleNode("hrs:reservationWS/hrs:payload/
  hrs:availabilityInteraction/availabilityRequest")

'Set the values in the template
objXMLNode.selectSingleNode("checkInDate").nodeTypedValue = strCheckIn
objXMLNode.selectSingleNode("checkOutDate").nodeTypedValue = strCheckOut
objXMLNode.selectSingleNode("locale/cityState/city").nodeTypedValue =
  eventCity
objXMLNode.selectSingleNode("locale/cityState/state").nodeTypedValue =
  eventState
objXMLNode.selectSingleNode("approxPrice").nodeTypedValue =
  CInt(myRequest.Form("pricerange"))
objXMLNode.selectSingleNode("couponCode").nodeTypedValue = couponCode

'Check to see if there is an existing session
If myRequest.Form("session") <> "" Then
 objXMLDoc.selectSingleNode("hrs:reservationWS/
  hrs:serviceVariables/sessionID").nodeTypedValue =
  CInt(myRequest.Form("session"))

'Check to see if smoking should be created
If myRequest.Form("smoking") <> "" Then
     Set objXMLChild = objXMLDoc.createElement("smoking")
     objXMLChild.nodeTypedValue = CBool(myRequest.Form("smoking"))
     objXMLNode.selectSingleNode("preferences").appendChild objXMLChild
 End If
```

```
'Check to see if bedsize should be created
If myRequest.Form("bed") <> "" Then
    Set objXMLChild = objXMLDoc.createElement("bedSize")
    objXMLChild.nodeTypedValue = CStr(myRequest.Form("bed"))
    objXMLNode.selectSingleNode("preferences").appendChild objXMLChild
End If

'create amenity element
For Each amenity In myArray
    Set objXMLChild = objXMLDoc.createElement("amenity")
    objXMLChild.nodeTypedValue = CStr(amenity)
    objXMLNode.selectSingleNode("preferences").appendChild objXMLChild
Next

'If no preferences have been set, then remove the preferences element
If objXMLNode.selectSingleNode("preferences").hasChildNodes = False Then
  objXMLNode.removeChild (objXMLNode.selectSingleNode("preferences"))

'Call Availability Service
objXMLConnect.setOption SXH_OPTION_SELECT_CLIENT_SSL_CERT, "AAACert"
objXMLConnect.open "POST", strServiceURL, False
objXMLConnect.send (objXMLDoc.xml)
objXMLAvailResponse.loadXML (objXMLConnect.responseText)

'variables necessary for AAA conference registration process
Set objXMLChild = objXMLDoc.createElement("conference")
objXMLChild.nodeTypedValue = CInt(myRequest.Form("conference"))
objXMLAvailResponse.selectSingleNode("hrs:reservationWS/
  hrs:serviceVariables").appendChild objXMLChild

Set objXMLChild = objXMLDoc.createElement("checkIn")
objXMLChild.nodeTypedValue = CDate(dtCheckIn)
objXMLAvailResponse.selectSingleNode("hrs:reservationWS/
  hrs:serviceVariables").appendChild objXMLChild

Set objXMLChild = objXMLDoc.createElement("checkOut")
objXMLChild.nodeTypedValue = CDate(dtCheckOut)
objXMLAvailResponse.selectSingleNode("hrs:reservationWS/
  hrs:serviceVariables").appendChild objXMLChild

'Add hotel details if requested
If getDetails Then

    'now that we know we need it, let's create it
```

```
          Set objXMLDetResponse = New DOMDocument40

          'load the detail request template
          booltest = objXMLDoc.Load("http://www.architectingwebservices.com/aaa/
            templates/detailRequestTemplate.xml")
          'set the sessionID for the detail request
          objXMLDoc.selectSingleNode("hrs:reservationWS/hrs:serviceVariables/
            sessionID").nodeTypedValue = objXMLAvailResponse.selectSingleNode
            ("hrs:reservationWS/hrs:serviceVariables/sessionID").nodeTypedValue

          'Get hotel ID's from availability response
          Set objXMLNodeList =
            objXMLAvailResponse.getElementsByTagName("hotelID")
          Set objXMLNode =
            objXMLAvailResponse.selectSingleNode("hrs:reservationWS/hrs:payload/
            hrs:availabilityInteraction/availabilityResults/hotel")

          For x = 0 To objXMLNodeList.length - 1
              If x > 0 Then Set objXMLNode = objXMLNode.nextSibling
              objXMLDoc.selectSingleNode("hrs:reservationWS/hrs:payload/
                hrs:detailInteraction/detailRequest/hotelID").nodeTypedValue =
                objXMLNodeList.Item(x).nodeTypedValue

              'Call Detail Service
              objXMLConnect.setOption SXH_OPTION_SELECT_CLIENT_SSL_CERT,
                "AAACert"
              objXMLConnect.open "POST", strServiceURL, False
              objXMLConnect.send (objXMLDoc.xml)
              objXMLDetResponse.loadXML (objXMLConnect.responseText)

              Set objXMLChild = objXMLDoc.createElement("description")
              objXMLChild.Text = objXMLDetResponse.selectSingleNode
                ("hrs:reservationWS/hrs:payload/hrs:detailInteraction/
                hotelContent/hotelDescription").Text

              objXMLNode.appendChild objXMLChild
        Next
End If

checkAvailability =
    objXMLAvailResponse.transformNode(objXSLDoc.documentElement)

Set objXMLDoc = Nothing
Set objXSLDoc = Nothing
Set objXMLAvailResponse = Nothing
```

```
          Set objXMLConnect = Nothing
          Set objXMLNode = Nothing
          Set objXMLChild = Nothing
End Function
```

makeReservation

The makeReservation method is much simpler than our checkAvailability method simply because it is a single request and is providing only a single piece of information back to us. This will follow the more traditional task list of build the request, establish the connection, and parse the response.

Instead of using a request object as our input parameter, we will be utilizing a session object. Accessing the information within it will be virtually the same, and there are no other parameters outside of the session object to be concerned with.

Building the Request

In building this request, we will load the reservation request template and assign a node to the root of the reservationRequest node as our reference. It is most effective here because nearly all of the nodes we will work with are contained within this node.

```
objXMLDoc.async = False
booltest = objXMLDoc.Load("http://www.architectingwebservices.com/aaa/
  templates/reservationRequestTemplate.xml")
Set objXMLNode = objXMLDoc.selectSingleNode("hrs:reservationWS/hrs:payload/
  hrs:reservationInteraction/hrs:reservationRequest")
```

Setting the node values will be terribly unexciting compared with the checkAvailability method.

```
objXMLNode.selectSingleNode("hrs:hotelData/hotelID").nodeTypedValue =
  CInt(mySession("hotelID"))
```

The only mildly interesting change in this straightforward approach is when a second address line is submitted through the address form. In this case, we need to create the second address node and add it to the homeAddress node because we chose to leave it out of the template for efficiency's sake.

```
If mySession("address2") <> "" Then
    Set objXMLChild = objXMLDoc.createElement("address")
    objXMLChild.nodeTypedValue = mySession("address2")
    objXMLNode.selectSingleNode("hrs:personalData/homeAddress").appendChild
      objXMLChild
End If
```

Establishing the Connection

The connection for the makeReservation method is nearly identical to the checkAvailability method. The only difference is that we are reusing the objXMLDoc object that contained our request to capture our response. In the checkAvailability method, we continued to use that object for other tasks, but it is available for us to reuse in this method:

```
objXMLConnect.setOption SXH_OPTION_SELECT_CLIENT_SSL_CERT, "AAACert"
objXMLConnect.open "POST", strServiceURL, False
objXMLConnect.send (objXMLDoc.xml)
objXMLDoc.loadXML (objXMLConnect.responseText)
```

Parsing the Response

Parsing the response for this method is very short and direct. We are interested in only one piece of data in the response, the confirmation number:

```
makeReservation = objXMLDoc.selectSingleNode("hrs:reservationWS/
  hrs:payload/hrs:reservationInteraction/hrs:reservationResponse/
  confirmationID").nodeTypedValue
```

Pulling It All Together

This completes the implementation of the makeReservation method in our COM object. Because this was the last function within the component to be developed, this also makes the object completed. Let's go ahead and put all the code for the makeReservation function together to see it in its entirety. (See Listing 8-12).

Listing 8-12. The makeReservation *Method*

```
Public Function makeReservation(mySession As Session) As String

Dim objXMLDoc As MSXML2.DOMDocument40
Dim objXMLNode As MSXML2.IXMLDOMNode
Dim objXMLChild As MSXML2.IXMLDOMNode
Dim objXMLConnect As MSXML2.ServerXMLHTTP40

Dim booltest As Boolean

Set objXMLDoc = New DOMDocument40
Set objXMLConnect = New MSXML2.ServerXMLHTTP40

'Loading Template
objXMLDoc.async = False
booltest = objXMLDoc.Load("http://www.architectingwebservices.com/aaa/
  templates/reservationRequestTemplate.xml")
Set objXMLNode = objXMLDoc.selectSingleNode("hrs:reservationWS/hrs:payload/
  hrs:reservationInteraction/hrs:reservationRequest")

'set the sessionID for the reservation request
objXMLDoc.selectSingleNode("hrs:reservationWS/hrs:serviceVariables/
  sessionID").nodeTypedValue = CInt(mySession("mSessionID"))

objXMLNode.selectSingleNode("hrs:hotelData/hotelID").nodeTypedValue =
  CInt(mySession("hotelID"))
objXMLNode.selectSingleNode("hrs:hotelData/roomType").nodeTypedValue =
  mySession("roomType")
objXMLNode.selectSingleNode("hrs:personalData/homeAddress/
  address").nodeTypedValue = mySession("address1")
If mySession("address2") <> "" Then
    Set objXMLChild = objXMLDoc.createElement("address")
    objXMLChild.nodeTypedValue = mySession("address2")
    objXMLNode.selectSingleNode("hrs:personalData/homeAddress").appendChild
      objXMLChild
End If
objXMLNode.selectSingleNode("hrs:personalData/homeAddress/
  city").nodeTypedValue = mySession("city")
objXMLNode.selectSingleNode("hrs:personalData/homeAddress/
  state").nodeTypedValue = mySession("state")
objXMLNode.selectSingleNode("hrs:personalData/homeAddress/
  zipCode").nodeTypedValue = mySession("zipCode")
objXMLNode.selectSingleNode("hrs:personalData/firstName").nodeTypedValue =
```

```
  mySession("firstName")
objXMLNode.selectSingleNode("hrs:personalData/lastName").nodeTypedValue =
  mySession("lastName")
objXMLNode.selectSingleNode("hrs:personalData/homePhone").nodeTypedValue =
  mySession("phone")
objXMLNode.selectSingleNode("hrs:personalData/hrs:ccData/
  number").nodeTypedValue = mySession("ccNumber")
objXMLNode.selectSingleNode("hrs:personalData/hrs:ccData/
  issuer").nodeTypedValue = mySession("ccType")
objXMLNode.selectSingleNode("hrs:personalData/hrs:ccData/
  expirationDate").nodeTypedValue = mySession("ccExpYear") & "-" &
  mySession("ccExpMonth") & "-01"
objXMLNode.selectSingleNode("hrs:personalData/hrs:ccData/
  nameOfOwner").nodeTypedValue = mySession("ccOwner")

'Call reservation Service
objXMLConnect.setOption SXH_OPTION_SELECT_CLIENT_SSL_CERT, "AAACert"
objXMLConnect.open "POST", strServiceURL, False
objXMLConnect.send (objXMLDoc.xml)
objXMLDoc.loadXML (objXMLConnect.responseText)

makeReservation = objXMLDoc.selectSingleNode("hrs:reservationWS/hrs:payload/
  hrs:reservationInteraction/hrs:reservationResponse/
  /confirmationID").nodeTypedValue

Set objXMLDoc = Nothing
Set objXMLConnect = Nothing
Set objXMLNode = Nothing
Set objXMLChild = Nothing

End Function
```

The only thing left to look at in our implementation now is our XSL stylesheet for transforming the checkAvailability response before handing it back to its caller.

XSL Stylesheet

As we saw in Chapter 4 ("Using XML"), the XSLT language is a very simple, tag-based language. It can be very effective in manipulating XML data, but it can also be equally frustrating at times. Inevitably, you will want to do something that is seemingly impossible that could be done quickly with one or two lines of VBScript or Java.

Fortunately, what we want to accomplish is not too sophisticated: our objective is to generate the view that we saw back in Figure 8-22. We want to have our matching hotels aligned in rows, and we need all the necessary information to be contained in a form element that can be passed when the select button is clicked.

When developing stylesheets, you will benefit from limiting the amount of data you pass through the transformation process. We could have easily incorporated the entire hotel selection page within this stylesheet. However, there would be no need for it. Although it might be more convenient in some ways, you can get a stylesheet to work with a base page just as well as if it were all one page. Also, be aware that any data you send through a transformation must be XML compliant, which places additional demands on any data that is not crucial to the transformation process.

> **TIP** *Because most HTML editors do not yet support XHTML, it can be challenging to build XML-compliant HTML pages. The best approach is to build the page in your HTML editor of choice and then "clean it up" in one of the many XML editors available, such as XML Spy. This will ensure that you are building your creative content appropriately for your Web services.*

One of the tasks we are charged with in our XSL transformation is to maintain some process variables through hidden fields. If you take the approach of building these tags directly, as you would with VBScript, you will quickly get frustrated. Instead, you need to recognize the power of the attribute tag. You can use it to build any tag dynamically, like this one:

```
<input type="hidden" name="session">
    <xsl:attribute name="value">
        <xsl:value-of select="//sessionID"/>
    </xsl:attribute>
</input>
```

Another feature of XSLT that we are using is its formatting capabilities. Through them, we actually have greater control than we do with VBScript. With a `roomRate` value of 190, the code

```
<xsl:value-of select="format-number(roomRate,'$#.00')"/>
```

produces an output of $190.00. This level of control allows an incredible number of possibilities in working with data in XSLT.

Our stylesheet (Listing 8-13) will generate a table with one row of headers and build a row for each hotel element that is returned. This output can then be easily placed anywhere on a page, but, as we saw in our `hotelAvailability.asp` page, we already have a designated place for it.

Listing 8-13. The `checkAvailability` *Response Stylesheet*

```
<?xml version="1.0" encoding="UTF-8"?>
<xsl:stylesheet version="1.0" xmlns:xsl="http://www.w3.org/1999/XSL/Transform"
  xmlns:fo="http://www.w3.org/1999/XSL/Format">
<xsl:template match = "/"><!-apply to entire result set ->
    <table width="100%" cellspacing="10">
        <tr><!-list column headers ->
            <td align="center">
                <font face="Verdana" size="1"><b>Distance to
                <br/>Conference</b>
                </font>
            </td>
            <td align="center">
                <font face="Verdana" size="1"><b>Price*</b></font>
            </td>
            <td align="center">
                <font face="Verdana" size="1"><b>Room Type</b></font>
            </td>
            <td align="center">
                <font face="Verdana" size="1"><b>Hotel Name</b></font>
            </td>
            <td align="center">
                <font face="Verdana" size="1"><b>Description</b></font>
            </td>
            <td align="center"></td>
        </tr>
        <tr><td colspan="6"><hr width="75%" size="2"/></td></tr>
        <xsl:for-each select="//hotel">
            <!-list each matching room's specifics ->
            <form action="hotelConfirmation.asp" method="post">
                <input type="hidden" name="roomType">
```

```
                    <xsl:attribute name="value">
                        <xsl:value-of select="roomType"/>
                    </xsl:attribute>
                </input>
                <input type="hidden" name="hotelID">
                    <xsl:attribute name="value">
                        <xsl:value-of select="hotelID"/>
                    </xsl:attribute>
                </input>
                <input type="hidden" name="session">
                    <xsl:attribute name="value">
                        <xsl:value-of select="//sessionID"/>
                    </xsl:attribute>
                </input>
                <input type="hidden" name="conference">
                    <xsl:attribute name="value">
                        <xsl:value-of select="//conference"/>
                    </xsl:attribute>
                </input>
                <input type="hidden" name="checkIn">
                    <xsl:attribute name="value">
                        <xsl:value-of select="//checkIn"/>
                    </xsl:attribute>
                </input>
                <input type="hidden" name="checkOut">
                    <xsl:attribute name="value">
                        <xsl:value-of select="//checkOut"/>
                    </xsl:attribute>
                </input>
                <input type="hidden" name="price">
                    <xsl:attribute name="value">
                        <xsl:value-of select="roomRate"/>
                    </xsl:attribute>
                </input>
                <input type="hidden" name="hotelName">
                    <xsl:attribute name="value">
                        <xsl:value-of select="hotelName"/>
                    </xsl:attribute>
                </input>
                <tr>
                    <td align="center">
                        <font face="Verdana" size="1">
                            <xsl:value-of select="proximity"/> miles
                        </font>
```

```
                        </td>
                        <td align="center">
                            <font face="Verdana" size="1">
                                <xsl:value-of select="format-number(roomRate,
                                    '$#.00')"/>
                            </font>
                        </td>
                        <td align="center">
                            <font face="Verdana" size="1">
                                <xsl:value-of select="roomType"/>
                            </font>
                        </td>
                        <td align="center">
                            <font face="Verdana" size="1">
                                <xsl:value-of select="hotelName"/>
                            </font>
                        </td>
                        <td align="left">
                            <font face="Verdana" size="1">
                                <xsl:value-of select="description"/>
                            </font>
                        </td>
                        <td align="right">
                            <input type="submit" value="Select"/>
                        </td>
                    </tr>
                </form>
                <tr><td colspan="6"><hr width="75%" size="2"/></td></tr>
            </xsl:for-each>
            <!--completed presentation of each matching room -->
            <tr>
                <td colspan="6" align="center">
                    <font face="Verdana" size="1"><i>* This price reflects the
                        discount given to all conference attendees</i>
                    </font>
                </td>
            </tr>
        </table>
    </xsl:template>
</xsl:stylesheet>
```

Testing the Consumer

This actually completes the integration of the hotel reservation Web service into the AAA Conferences Web site. As is typical with more complex applications, they have many more areas where things can go wrong with the application when compared to the previous consumers. As a result, multiple scenarios should be tested, beyond just connectivity. The best way to address these scenarios is to ask the following questions and test them out:

- What happens if connectivity is lost between the user and the AAA Conferences site during a Web service request?

- What happens if connectivity between the application and the Web service is lost?

- Is it possible for a user to spoof another user's session?

- Is it possible for a user to erroneously get another user's data through the application?

- Is it possible for a user to be abandoned within the application due to a failure somewhere?

These are all valid questions that should be answered when testing your implementation of a Web services consumer. When these questions have been answered, it is appropriate to stress test the entire process, as we discussed in Chapter 6. This is where the Web Application Stress Tool can be very helpful because it can simulate user sessions, which you will need for an application that implements Web services workflows. Once you are satisfied with those test results, you can be confident that your application can be safely deployed.

Summary

In this chapter, we completed the design and implementation of three different Web services consumers under different scenarios. Hopefully, you are somewhat surprised by the relative ease we had in integrating these Web services, especially given what they accomplished. We were able to bridge across platforms and technologies, and we did so with fairly simple tools and technologies for experienced developers.

It should be somewhat reassuring to you now that, if you build meaningful Web services, consumers will be capable of using them fairly quickly regardless of their choices of internal platform and technology. Web services workflows obviously take a little more effort than do Web services calls, especially in the design phase, but this should be offset somewhat by the realization of the potential of Web services workflows to expand our current horizons and capabilities in application integration and partner relationships.

Of course, we have only just started down this road. As more standards and technologies are developed, building and consuming Web services will become even easier. Thus, more people will be capable of doing so and adding to the growing volume of services available on the Web. This also means that we need to be careful in discerning the technologies and tools developed around Web services to ensure that we are staying true to the vision. Remember from Chapter 1:

> *The purpose of a Web service is to programmatically expose a process over a network through an open, standardized communication mechanism and format.*

Next, we will take a look at where the industry is heading in this new development paradigm and perhaps determine if we are heading on the right path to enabling meaningful Web services.

CHAPTER 9

The Direction of Web Services

THE EVOLUTION OF WEB SERVICES is not something that can be predicted or projected. Those who have been around this industry for even a few years know the futility in predicting the impact that specific technologies will have tomorrow, much less the evolutionary path those technologies will take.

With Web services still in its infancy, many technologies are still being developed to address the gaps and meet the needs of providers and consumers. The direction of Web services is very dependent upon these technologies. For Web services to succeed, the technologies on which they're built must be ubiquitous, robust, reliable, and accepted.

The two most prominent sources for generating new technology are standards and vendor strategies. Standards are developed by independent organizations comprising some of the most prominent experts in the field; their work gets tremendous respect, and hence, their standards are adopted in many cases. Vendors have incredible influence over the industry through both their products and their clout. Once a vendor gains prominence and acceptance, it can be difficult to convince followers to consider alternative solutions.

Emerging Standards

If we can point to what will be the single biggest factor in the successful adoption of Web services in the industry, it is standardization. For Web services to be successful, the majority of implementations must have a certain commonality to them. Otherwise, we have gained nothing over what we have through the proprietary distributed middleware solutions that have been available for years.

To validate this, we have to look no further than the Internet itself. Standards are how we have achieved our success on the Internet up to this point: TCP/IP, HTTP, HTML, SSL, DNS (Domain Name Services), and so on. If we are successful in defining standards that will be adopted for working with Web services, the closer we are to producing meaningful Web services.

Five years ago, we could have relied on this standardization process to guide us into this new paradigm of Web services, but times have changed. Recapturing the magic that gave us the Internet won't happen exactly as it did then because the standards process has seen a shift in recent years. Previously, a standards body typically consisted of academia and government researchers. With the incredible success of the Internet, companies have recognized the power of these bodies in dictating the future direction of technology. As a result, companies started playing a much more active role in specifying the emerging standards. Even more recently, companies have been developing technology on their own—or in partnership with one or a handful of other companies—and then looking for acceptance by a standards body. Clearly, the process has changed and will probably continue to do so.

Companies also seem to be aligning themselves with different standards bodies and their activities, which has lead to a segmentation of the industry's efforts. The three most prominent organizations with activities in the Web services space are the IETF (Internet Engineering Task Force), W3C (World Wide Web Consortium), and OASIS (Organization for the Advancement of Structured Information Standards). Although these organizations have on occasion cooperated on an activity, they are independent and often act as such.

For these reasons, standards probably need to be more scrutinized now than ever. Hopefully, these efforts in support of standards will still result in good, solid solutions, but many of the standards authors now have a vested interest in the standards they are creating. Tim Berners-Lee did not directly make money off of HTML, and he had no vested financial interest in how he designed the solution; he just wanted to develop a good method for connecting documents over a network.

This is not to say that these companies don't make valuable contributions. In fact, they certainly bring with them some of the best people available and the resources to devise better solutions more quickly because they are paid for their involvement. Hopefully, they will continue to produce great solutions that appropriately address the needs of the industry, but to do so requires the participants in these groups to balance a split allegiance that did not exist in past standards efforts.

In this chapter, we will take a look at the leading standards that exist and, in most cases, are continuing to evolve. These standards cover a wide range of areas that all affect Web services in one way or another, so it will be important to continue to follow their development as Web services mature. This chapter is intended as an overview to help you gain a high-level of understanding of what these technologies offer; it is not a detailed study that will enable you to start using them. In each section, I will list at least one reference where you can find further information on each topic.

XML-RPC (XML-Remote Procedure Call)

Currently defined as a specification and a series of implementations, XML-RPC was originally authored by Dave Winer of Userland in 1998. Dave worked with Don Box of DevelopMentor and Microsoft to develop the very first SOAP (Simple Object Access Protocol) specification, which was shelved by Microsoft. (You can read more about this in the "SOAP" section later in the chapter.) Dave then developed XML-RPC to solve the problem that a Userland application had in communicating with different instances of itself on Windows and Macintosh machines.

Not only was XML-RPC the first public attempt at standardizing the process of communicating over HTTP through XML documents, but it also happens to be one of the few successful standards developed outside of one of the major standards boards. From the outset, the goal of XML-RPC was to specify a standard format for making remote procedure calls using the standard HTTP protocol, keeping it as simple as possible. Along those lines, one of the appeals of XML-RPC is its consistency: the specification has not changed since 1999. It is nice to know that, when you design an application using XML-RPC, it's not likely to get revised before you deploy! At the very least, developers don't have to worry about learning a new version once they get comfortable with the present one.

Technically, each XML-RPC is defined through a single node called `methodCall`. Within this element are various others that define the method name and parameters for the call, as shown here:

```
<?xml version="1.0"?>
<methodCall>
    <methodName>examples.getStateName</methodName>
    <params>
        <param>
            <value><i4>41</i4></value>
        </param>
    </params>
</methodCall>
```

As you can see, this is similar to the approach we took in defining the payloads for our Web services in Chapters 6 and 7. XML-RPC provides a standard structure for defining each process call that ideally should allow you to have a generic listener that can take a request for a consumer and proxy that call to the service logic, returning the result set. A response to an XML-RPC request will then be structured similarly with a root node of methodResponse, as shown here:

```
<?xml version="1.0"?>
<methodResponse>
    <params>
        <param>
            <value><string>South Dakota</string></value>
        </param>
    </params>
</methodResponse>
```

You might have noticed a lack of attributes in these tags. This is by design, not coincidence. The original authors believed that attributes were a redundant element in XML and unnecessary. We saw earlier in Chapter 3 how the same data can be presented in elements versus attributes, which would certainly support the redundancy opinion. XML-RPC takes a strict "all-element" approach to defining a service's interface.

XML-RPC includes support for various arrays and other user-defined structures that give the format quite a bit of extensibility. It also has a defined structure for the provider to communicate errors that occur in the process to consumers.

Although it isn't specified, XML-RPC calls and requests can be defined through DTD or XML Schemas, just as we did with the Web services we built in Chapters 6 and 7. Because these definition files have no special considerations, the use of these techniques will be unique per implementation and/or solution.

Using XML-RPC primarily has two perceived benefits: it provides a consistent format for exposing a service's functionality, and it allows generic functions for consumers and listeners to handle the XML-RPC calls and responses. Once a developer is familiar with the structure of XML-RPC calls, he or she should be able to analyze the entire service fairly quickly. However, the benefits from the latter decrease with the complexity of the Web service and the development of more-advanced parsers.

First, the standard structure of XML-RPC used "as is" comes with some inherent limitations (as any standard structure ultimately would.) For instance, every single value in an XML-RPC call must be a parameter in the method call or response. This means that any session or presentation data in the parameters is stored under the methodCall and methodResponse nodes, which results in a very flat structure that doesn't discern the nature of the data or its purpose. Although alternatives are available, using custom data types means that you lose much of the benefit from the standard structure because the generic listeners will need the logic necessary to interpret that data. Basically, if you have to build unique structures for defining your Web services interface, you have to start questioning the value in conforming to the XML-RPC specification.

Secondly, today's parsers are far more advanced than the parsers were in 1998, when parsing XML data was more problematic because the parsers did not contain the ability to validate XML data. This standard format provided a simple way of programmatically validating at least the top-level nodes within a call and response. Today, we have more options that allow us to validate directly against a DTD or XML Schema, which means much less work on our part to establish a trust in the data.

Also, the strides made by parsers in making XML data easier to manipulate makes any XML document much easier to work with. It can be argued that the difference between working with an XML-RPC call and a similarly structured but nonstandard document is minimal, especially if the XML-RPC call contains many new structures.

Regardless of whether XML-RPC is used, a service provider can still benefit from defining consistent interface documents, much as we did for the hotel reservation Web service. There we defined a single format that could contain any of the five requests or five responses, yet had a consistent root node, service variables, and payload defined.

We didn't concern ourselves then with making our interfaces standard between the calls and the workflow because they were very different processes with very different objectives. Making the weather checker and the hotel reservation Web services consistent with each other would have provided little benefit, and likely more overhead for each, because additional nodes would need to be added to encapsulate both processes in a consistent container.

Our reusability also didn't suffer as much from not using a consistent format across all services because we separated the listener and responder. We had one process working to receive and route the Web service call while the responder handled the parsing of the request and building of the response. This allowed us the flexibility of defining the most efficient and sensible XML document for our interface and yet gave us some reusability from service to service. If we added the logic to the listener for handling the various requests, it could easily be reused for other Web services.

Overall, the XML-RPC has some appealing features that make it a viable format for your Web services, especially Web services without workflow. Supporting the necessary processes for integrating a workflow will likely require more customization to the format than it may be worth.

Perhaps the biggest question with XML-RPC is its shelf life. As much as the industry tries to push technologies to the limits, a frozen specification is sooner or later going to get left behind. I suspect at some point that either the author will decide to revise the specification, or it will become obsolete. Dave Winer also contributed to the original SOAP specification (which we will look at shortly), and, although he says the two standards can coexist, he knows that there can be, by definition, only one de facto standard. In fact, he has started a grass-roots developer effort to bring SOAP back to a simpler standard through the Busy Developer's Guide (http://www.soapware.org/bdg), which is an attempt to repackage XML-RPC inside a SOAP envelope.

The community site for XML-RPC can be found at http://www.xmlrpc.com. There you will find the specification along with implementations for nearly every platform and environment. Also of interest is a book on XML-RPC by Simon St.Laurent, Joe Johnston, and Edd Dumbill titled *Programming Web Services with XML-RPC* (O'Reilly Internet Series).

SOAP (Simple Object Access Protocol)

SOAP was actually started back in 1998 by Don Box of DevelopMentor, Dave Winer of Userland, and Microsoft's COM/MTS team. Unfortunately, politics kept it from being publicly introduced until 1999. It's reemergence coincided with the release of Don Box's now infamous article "Lessons from the Component Wars: An XML Manifesto" (http://msdn.microsoft.com/workshop/xml/articles/xmlmanifesto.asp). In it, Don identified the issues inherent in communicating between different middleware technologies and identified XML as a potential solution.

After the release of SOAP 1.0 in 1999 by the original authors, IBM entered the picture and assisted with the fairly minor changes that were made prior to the 1.1 release in 2000. Although the objective was to maintain the simplicity of XML-RPC, they wanted something that could be more extensible. To accomplish this objective, the concept of a request and response model was exchanged for a more general envelope model with a header and body. The envelope and body are mandatory, and the header is optional. The code that follows is a sample SOAP request from the specification:

```
<SOAP-ENV:Envelope
   xmlns:SOAP-ENV="http://schemas.xmlsoap.org/soap/envelope/"
   SOAP-ENV:encodingStyle="http://schemas.xmlsoap.org/soap/encoding/">
   <SOAP-ENV:Body>
      <m:GetLastTradePrice xmlns:m="Some-URI">
         <symbol>DIS</symbol>
      </m:GetLastTradePrice>
   </SOAP-ENV:Body>
</SOAP-ENV:Envelope>
```

SOAP and XML-RPC

One of its distinctions with XML-RPC is SOAP's inclusion of additional TCP/IP header information. Whereas XML-RPC does specify values like Content-Type and User-Agent, it does not add attributes. SOAP adds the SOAPAction attribute, which is meant to communicate the intent of the request. This is intended as a hint to the HTTP server on the type of request being made. SOAPAction could allow for more efficient routing of the request without opening the entire message. Although this attribute inclusion is required for all requests according to the SOAP specification, the specification does not place a requirement on providers to utilize or resolve SOAPAction. The following example is of a valid TCP/IP header for a SOAP request:

```
POST /StockQuote HTTP/1.1
Host: www.stockquoteserver.com
Content-Type: text/xml;
charset="utf-8"
Content-Length: nnnn
SOAPAction: "myAppRequest"
```

Another distinction with XML-RPC is its support for all Internet protocols, not just HTTP. As such, SOAP is not intended exclusively as a request-response mechanism so that it can utilize asynchronous protocols such as SMTP or UDP. However, HTTP is still likely to be the most common transport protocol for SOAP. For those cases in which HTTP or another round-trip protocol is utilized, a SOAP response will be contained in the same envelope structure. A sample SOAP response is shown here:

```
<SOAP-ENV:Envelope
   xmlns:SOAP-ENV="http://schemas.xmlsoap.org/soap/envelope/"/>
   <SOAP-ENV:Body>
       <m:GetLastTradePriceResponse xmlns:m="Some-URI">
           <Price>34.5</Price>
       </m:GetLastTradePriceResponse>
   </SOAP-ENV:Body>
</SOAP-ENV:Envelope>
```

As you can see through both of these examples, namespaces is a major component of SOAP. Although this does add to the complexity of SOAP, it does help to ensure the integrity of the message for consumers and providers.

The SOAP Approach

The authors of SOAP were trying to make it a very extensible format, but this intent might be the specification's biggest drawback. Its many defined tags and values may be pure overhead for a simple Web service. Although they were designed with the best of intentions, without widespread support and adoption you may have to support SOAP specifications that you or your consumers never use. A good example of this is the `SOAPAction` TCP/IP header attribute that we discussed earlier. The usefulness of such a loosely defined attribute (and whether it should be included at all) has been the subject of some debate. Yet, even with this ambiguity, the attribute is a required component of a SOAP request.

Another example of ambiguous overhead is the global `mustUnderstand` attribute, which is required of all SOAP Web service providers to support. If the provider intends to ignore this piece of information, which could be any piece of data, the request should not be processed. Although there is definite value in a consumer needing to ensure that a Web services interface doesn't change on them, communicating a change or lack of support through the failure of a request seems a bit too late in the process to guarantee the integrity of the application consuming the service. This is like putting in the middle of a bridge a sign saying it isn't connected on the other side. Wouldn't you like to know the bridge isn't complete before you start to cross?

As explained by the authors of SOAP, the `mustUnderstand` attribute is also intended as a negotiation mechanism for the kind of features that the consumer would like the Web service to support. This seems a rather inefficient means for negotiating a partnership, but it probably looks good on paper.

The Status of SOAP

The current SOAP 1.1 specification was published in April 2000. In March 2001, SOAP was submitted to the W3C and became a component of the XML Protocol (XMLP) Working Group:

> *The goal of XML Protocol is to develop technologies which allow two or more peers to communicate in a distributed environment, using XML as its encapsulation language. Solutions developed by this activity allow a layered architecture on top of an extensible and simple messaging format, which provides robustness, simplicity, reusability and interoperability.*
> —XML Protocol Working Group (`http://www.w3.org/Architecture/`)

Along with SOAP, other initiatives in XMLP include data serialization and defining a more structured mechanism for the transport of data over HTTP.

It is not clear yet what effect these efforts will have, but a final recommendation is targeted for the end of 2001, with the group dissolving in April of 2002.

The XML Protocol Working Group published the first working draft for version 1.2 in July 2001. As such, aside from some unnecessary overhead, the biggest obstacle to the successful widespread adoption of SOAP is its "moving target" status: not only is another revision in the works, but also a new process and new contributors are involved now that it has fallen under the W3C. Unlike revising a server, tool, or even a programming language, modifying a standardized communication vehicle for interoperability will keep widespread adoption from becoming a reality. At the very least, we will get little benefit from the common tools envisioned by the standardized protocol until some foundation is finalized.

These two shortcomings are also where XML-RPC, the main alternative standard, draws its strength: it is frozen and has a simpler structure that presents constraints instead of overhead. Although neither is an ideal situation for developers, the benefits of a standard are realized only with consistency in the industry. For that reason, I am still a strong believer in building a Web services infrastructure around TCP/IP and XML until these other technologies mature. Anything more will either limit you or beg for modifications due to continuing revisions; anything less is not warranted because all Web services standards and initiatives are based on these two core technologies. This approach will neither limit your ability to use these emerging standards nor send you down a potential dead end.

One thing SOAP does have right now is incredible momentum. The industry's largest players all recognize it as a suitable standard, which makes it a very powerful player in the future of Web services. Vendors have almost had to join in support of SOAP for the same reasons that they have supported XML rank and file. Namely, if you don't support it, your competitors could hold a significant advantage over you. However, I do believe that the true success of SOAP has, and will continue to have, more to do with the concepts behind it than the specification's details.

You can find more information on the SOAP specification as well as some implementations on DevelopMentor's site (`http://www.developmentor.com/soap/`). You can get more information on the XMLP activity at the W3C site (`http://www.w3.org/2000/xp/Activity`).

WSDL (Web Services Definition Language)

WSDL is the culmination of several independent efforts to provide a standard format for defining the interfaces of Web services. By the summer of 2000, IBM had developed the Network Accessible Service Specification Language (NASSL) and the Interface Definition Language for SOAP-RPC (XIDL), and Microsoft had developed the Services Definition Language (SDL) and the SOAP Contract Language (SCL). Realizing that the success of Web services depended upon one consistent format for defining Web services, these longtime rivals collaborated to standardize on the Web Services Definition Language.

A standard definition method for Web services is perhaps even more important than standardizing on the communication mechanism itself. After all, if you speak the same language (XML) and have a dictionary (WSDL), you can develop an understanding of any terms you might come across (such as methodRequest, methodCall, procedureCall, and so on). However, if you did not have a dictionary, saying the same word over and over will not aid in your understanding of what it represents. With a standard dictionary format, we can reach an understanding of the information that a Web service wants submitted and the information it will return, regardless of the semantic terms used to describe it.

Keeping with this same analogy, once a Web service and all of its data elements are defined, if it isn't expected to change, you no longer need the WSDL. However, some think that the consumption of Web services could be, or even should be, dynamic. In that case, the application would utilize the WSDL each time to build the request for the Web service. Although the practicality of this is limited due to HTTP latency and the logic necessary to make truly dynamic Web services calls, some developers are working on the standard with that nirvana in mind.

If you discount the need for dynamic calls, you leave the door open for what is actually necessary as an IDL for Web services. Is it a programmatically accessible set of data, or could it be a human-readable document with a consistent structure? Many people in the industry are pondering this thought, and a consensus will not likely be reached anytime soon.

Although WSDL is designed to be protocol independent, most implementation efforts have been invested in SOAP bindings. This is due to the simple fact that the technology drivers of WSDL are also the drivers behind SOAP. Bindings are also available for HTTP and MIME.

WSDL itself is composed of a structured XML document that effectively wraps the XML Schema documents defining the payloads for your Web service. The root node is a definitions element with child elements consisting of types, message, portType, binding, and service. Listing 9-1 is an example of what the WSDL for a stock quote service might look like, courtesy of the specification.

Listing 9-1. The WSDL file for a stock quote Web service

```
<?xml version="1.0"?>
<definitions name="StockQuote"
targetNamespace="http://example.com/stockquote.wsdl"
    xmlns:tns="http://example.com/stockquote.wsdl"
    xmlns:xsd="http://www.w3.org/2000/10/XMLSchema"
    xmlns:xsd1="http://example.com/stockquote/schema"
    xmlns:soap="http://schemas.xmlsoap.org/wsdl/soap/"
    xmlns:soapenc="http://schemas.xmlsoap.org/soap/encoding/"
    xmlns="http://schemas.xmlsoap.org/wsdl/">
```

```
<types>
    <schema targetNamespace="http://example.com/stockquote/schema"
      xmlns="http://www.w3.org/2000/10/XMLSchema">
        <complexType name="TimePeriod">
            <all>
                <element name="startTime" type="xsd:timeInstant"/>
                <element name="endTime" type="xsd:timeInstant"/>
            </all>
        </complexType>
        <complexType name="ArrayOfFloat">
            <complexContent>
                <restriction base="soapenc:Array">
                    <attribute ref="soapenc:arrayType" wsdl:arrayType=
                        "xsd:float[]"/>
                </restriction>
            </complexContent>
        </complexType>
    </schema>
</types>

<message name="GetTradePricesInput">
    <part name="tickerSymbol" element="xsd:string"/>
    <part name="timePeriod" element="xsd1:TimePeriod"/>
</message>

<message name="GetTradePricesOutput">
    <part name="result" type="xsd1:ArrayOfFloat"/>
    <part name="frequency" type="xsd:float"/>
</message>

<portType name="StockQuotePortType">
    <operation name="GetLastTradePrice" parameterOrder="tickerSymbol
      timePeriod frequency">
        <input message="tns:GetTradePricesInput"/>
        <output message="tns:GetTradePricesOutput"/>
    </operation>
</portType>

<binding name="StockQuoteSoapBinding" type="tns:StockQuotePortType">
    <soap:binding style="rpc" transport="http://schemas.xmlsoap.org/
      soap/http"/>
        <operation name="GetTradePrices">
            <soap:operation soapAction="http://example.com/
```

```
                           GetTradePrices"/>
            <input>
                <soap:body use="encoded" namespace="http://example.com/
                    stockquote" encodingStyle="http://schemas.xmlsoap.org/
                    soap/encoding/"/>
            </input>
            <output>
                <soap:body use="encoded" namespace="http://example.com/
                    stockquote" encodingStyle="http://schemas.xmlsoap.org/
                    soap/encoding/"/>
            </output>
        </operation>
    </binding>

    <service name="StockQuoteService">
        <documentation>My first service</documentation>
        <port name="StockQuotePort" binding="tns:StockQuoteBinding">
            <soap:address location="http://example.com/stockquote"/>
        </port>
    </service>
</definitions>
```

In March 2001, WSDL version 1.1 was submitted to the W3C, where it awaits a working group to start working on the first W3C recommendation. This is an example of vendors developing a standard and handing it off to a standards group for acceptance. This specification is a long way from being finalized as a standard, but many are pressing on, believing that it is inherently tied to SOAP and its success.

You can find the current WSDL specification on the W3C site (http://www.w3.org/TR/wsdl).

UDDI (Universal Description, Discovery, and Integration)

To be able to consume a Web service, you have to know that it exists. UDDI is a consortium effort started by Ariba, IBM, and Microsoft to establish the next generation of yellow pages for the Internet. In technical terms, UDDI roughly acts as a DNS for Web services.

UDDI consists of two main components: the UDDI syntax, which specifies business and technical criteria, and the business registry, which contains the data in this syntax. The syntax is XML based and defines information about organizations and their services. The registry actually consists of three different components, which are identified as white pages, yellow pages (my earlier comment referring to the yellow pages was actually less of an analogy than you might have thought!), and green pages.

The white pages consist of company identification and contact information. The yellow pages categorize organizations based on a standard taxonomy, with geographic locations, product and service areas, and industry codes. The green pages expose technical information about the services provide by a company, such as WSDL and service guidelines. The UDDI business registry allows users to look up organizations, products, and services either through a browser at `http://www.uddi.org/find.html` (see Figure 9-1) or through tools that can programmatically interpret the UDDI syntax.

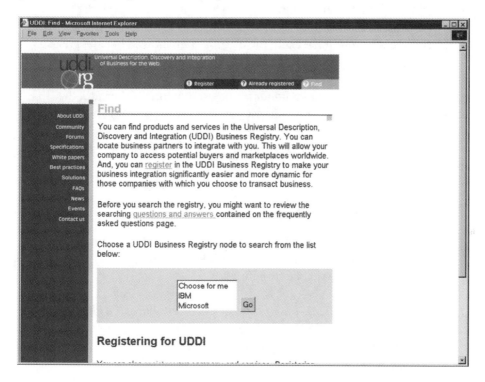

Figure 9-1. The UDDI business registry

There is currently no charge to either use this directory or list your organization on it. It is understood that this may change over time, however. It will be up to the operators of the different registry instances. Currently, the only two operators of UDDI registries are IBM and Microsoft. Theoretically, anyone can host a public or private registry.

The UDDI business registry specification also includes the logic for replicating information between various registries. This is important for maintaining failsafe registries with consistent information.

Although the momentum for UDDI has not been as high among the developer community, the business community can appreciate and understand the concepts and benefits behind UDDI better than it can WSDL's and SOAP's, which require more technical knowledge and understanding. In fact, large companies that look to UDDI to solve internal challenges have generated the most interest.

Many companies are so large that they have a variety of systems built on different technologies exposing different processes. UDDI is a potential solution for exposing these interfaces and their details across departmental boundaries. Through the business registry, they could expose the interfaces and contact information for systems across their entire organization. This feature may be the biggest selling point for such a directory concept: the time a developer has to spend on either understanding an interface or rewriting an existing, unknown interface should be minimized with the use of a standardized business registry.

The open draft for UDDI version 2.0 was released in June 2001, and the timeline calls for a version 3.0 by the end of the year. Eventually, the consortium intends to hand over UDDI to a standards board (potentially the W3C, the IETF, or both). At that point, IBM and Microsoft may also turn over the registries that they are currently hosting.

For information on the UDDI specification and the business registry, visit the community Web site (`http://www.uddi.org`).

ebXML (eBusiness XML)

ebXML is a collaboration of UN/CEFACT (United Nations Centre for Trade Facilitation and Electronic Business) and OASIS to define a globally standard XML format. Its mission is explicitly defined:

> *To provide an open XML-based infrastructure enabling the global use of electronic business information in an interoperable, secure and consistent manner by all parties.*
> —ebXML Mission (`http://www.ebxml.org/geninfo.htm`)

The 18-month effort resulted in the first specification being approved in May 2001, but future revisions are already being discussed. This very broad and ambitious standard includes specifications for defining company profiles and processes, and discovering them through an ebXML repository. It attempts to be an end-to-end standard for an electronic marketplace, defined through multiple initiatives:

- Collaboration Protocol Profile and Agreement (CPPA)

- Implementation, Interoperability, and Conformance

- Messaging Services

- Registry/Repository

ebXML CPPA defined the Collaboration Protocol Profile (CPP) and the Collaboration Protocol Agreement (CPA) for documenting a company's capabilities and willingness to collaborate with partners electronically. The first version of this specification has been completed, but another version is likely forthcoming.

The Implementation, Interoperability, and Conformance initiative of ebXML facilitates the interoperability of infrastructures and applications that follow the ebXML specification. Its goal is to create a conformance plan, reference implementation guidelines, and baseline interoperability tests.

ebXML Messaging Services hold the most value to developers working with Web services. Although this started out as an independent initiative, ebXML incorporated the SOAP specification into its messaging services in the March 2001 specification. What this means is that the message format for ebXML transactions are SOAP compliant. This was somewhat of a coup for SOAP because ebXML was distancing itself from unrelated initiatives. It demonstrates how much support SOAP has managed to generate.

> **NOTE** *Although the specification does not address Web services explicitly, ebXML's view of business services can easily be carried over to Web services.*

This group's approach to specifying standard business processes was to take advantage of the lessons learned through nearly 25 years of experience with EDI and define an EDI-like standard based on XML. Although EDI is used today for transferring data documents between partners, ebXML takes the concept further by defining some transaction-level details that could be utilized for Web services.

Much like EDI, ebXML has a very rigid format and tag-naming convention that can make the building and parsing of data complicated if done manually. However, this standardization would make it very easy for vendors to provide very reusable solutions that can work with ebXML. Here, in Listing 9-2, we see a sample transaction for creating an order:

Listing 9-2. An ebXML order transaction

```
<?xml version="1.0" encoding="UTF-8"?>
<SOAP-ENV:Envelope  xmlns:SOAP-ENV=
  'http://schemas.xmlsoap.org/soap/envelope/'
  xmlns:eb='http://www.ebxml.org/namespaces/messageHeader'>
    <SOAP-ENV:Header>
        <eb:MessageHeader SOAP-ENV:mustUnderstand="1" eb:version="1.0">
            <eb:From>
```

```
                        <eb:PartyId>urn:duns:123456789</eb:PartyId>
                </eb:From>
                <eb:To>
                        <eb:PartyId>urn:duns:912345678</eb:PartyId>
                </eb:To>
                <eb:CPAId>20001209-133003-28572</eb:CPAId>
                <eb:ConversationId>20001209-133003-28572</eb:ConversationId>
                <eb:Service>urn:services:SupplierOrderProcessing</eb:Service>
                <eb:Action>NewOrder</eb:Action>
                <eb:MessageData>
                        <eb:MessageId>20001209-133003-28572@example.com
                        </eb:MessageId>
                        <eb:Timestamp>2001-02-15T11:12:12Z</eb:Timestamp>
                </eb:MessageData>
                <eb:QualityOfServiceInfo eb:deliverySemantics="BestEffort"/>
        </eb:MessageHeader>
    </SOAP-ENV:Header>
    <SOAP-ENV:Body>
        <eb:Manifest SOAP-ENV:mustUnderstand="1" eb:version="1.0">
                <eb:Reference xlink:href="cid:ebxmlpayload111@example.com"
                   xlink:role="XLinkRole" xlink:type="simple">
                        <eb:Description xml:lang="en-us">Purchase Order 1
                        </eb:Description>
                </eb:Reference>
        </eb:Manifest>
    </SOAP-ENV:Body>
</SOAP-ENV:Envelope>
```

This standardized structure would obviously prevent you from building
custom interfaces for Web services, but, if you wanted to provide a Web service
based on one of the defined business processes, ebXML might be a good
solution for you. After all, many companies will want to be able to accept orders
through a Web service, and the functionality that's standardized through ebXML
might make it easier for consumers to use your service if they are following the
same process and payload definition for other partners. Although ebXML will
provide a lot of capabilities right out of the box, don't expect to tailor it for more
specific needs.

ebXML's registry and repository initiative will develop and recommend the
discovery and retrieval of business services utilizing the standard Registry
Information Model (RIM). This follows the common approach of exposing information and metadata on products and services through a globally accessible
directory. Through this directory, trading partners can access an assortment of
data on companies, their processes, and the definition of their data elements

through various libraries. Because the specification designates no hosting community or organization for these registries, it is assumed that any organization could host their own ebXML repository.

If ebXML catches on, it could potentially define many of the components necessary for the lifecycle of standard, business-related Web services: discovery, definition, and implementation. However, the main force working against it is vendor support. Although many vendors assisted with the specification, they did not have the participation level of many of the other standards efforts, and some have come right out to criticize the ebXML specification.

One of the main reasons used to justify the lack of vendor participation was the projected 18-month turnaround on the first specification (which it did take). This timeframe was perceived to be too long for vendors to wait on it to develop their strategies and solutions. Although it might seem ideal that vendors could have been provided an extended amount of time to develop their offerings in the Web services space, the reality is that vendors are much too concerned with gaining or losing a competitive edge over each other to take a patient approach to a new market. And, although waiting on ebXML might have slowed some development efforts, it could also be argued that vendors are not as far along with their Web services solutions as they would have anticipated at this point.

You can find out more about ebXML and its many components at the official Web site (`http://www.ebxml.org`).

XLANG

XLANG is a scheduling language created by Microsoft for the orchestration component of its BizTalk Server product. *XLANG* doesn't seem to stand for anything, but rather seems to just be the name given this language. The XML-based language is not a standard at this point, but Microsoft did release the XLANG specification for public comment in June of 2001.

XLANG is now being extended as a language to automate business processes between Web services. Although the process can be transactional, the transaction that is supported is decoupled, meaning it supports any action having an equally opposed action to reverse the step. (This is similar to the undo feature of, say, a word processing application.)

XLANG's biggest advantage is the working example of its capabilities within BizTalk Server. Nothing is more effective when selling technology than seeing it in action; most people agree it works well. The XLANG specification can be found at `http://www.gotdotnet.com/team/xml_wsspecs/xlang-c`.

XAML (Transaction Authority Markup Language)

XAML—developed by a consortium comprising Hewlett-Packard, Bowstreet, IBM, Oracle, and Sun—is a vendor-neutral standard to support transactions between Web services. This includes the traditional two-phase commit transaction as well as the compensatory action approach found in the XLANG specification.

XAML is obviously a competitive alternative to XLANG, at least on some levels, but there may be room for both to coexist primarily because XAML is focused on transactions and XLANG does stretch across the broader automation process category. XAML also hasn't produced a lot since its announcement in October 2000, whereas XLANG is used today within BizTalk's orchestration feature.

You can find out more about XAML at its community site (http://www.xaml.org/).

XKMS (XML Key Management Specification)

XKMS was established by VeriSign, Microsoft, and webMethods in November 2000 as a protocol for registering and distributing private keys using the XML standard. The specification was then submitted to the W3C in March 2001 and became part of the very broad XML Protocol Activity.

The specification comes in two different components: XML Key Information Service Specification (X-KISS) and XML Key Registration Service Specification (X-KRSS). X-KISS defines the protocol for trust services, and X-KRSS defines how Web services can accept public key information. With both implemented, a Web service will be able to integrate authentication, digital signature, and encryption services into their own processes and potentially the applications that consume them.

For more information on XKMS, you can get the specification at http://www.w3.org/TR/xkms/. You can get more information on the concepts behind XKMS from VeriSign's site (http://www.verisign.com/developer/xml/xkms.html).

SAML (Security Assertion Markup Language)

SAML is an effort by OASIS to provide a framework for exchanging authentication and authorization information via XML. SAML is actually the collaboration of the previously distinct but similar efforts behind S2ML (http://www.s2ml.org) and AuthXML (http://www.authxml.org). In early 2001, both organizations agreed to submit their specifications to OASIS to reduce duplicate efforts.

SAML would likely be an alternative to the XKMS standard in development at the W3C. OASIS's goal is to produce a specification for a vote by its membership in September 2001. You can check its status and get

more information on the specification at the OASIS Web site
(http://www.oasis-open.org/committees/security).

XML-SIG (XML Signature Syntax and Processing)

The purpose of XML-SIG is to develop a standard for digitally signing applications and documents via XML. This W3C-led effort could have the potential to
serve as a security mechanism for trusting transmissions between Web services
and their consumers.

XML-SIG was started in 1999 and reached candidate recommendation status
at the W3C in April 2001. You can check its status and view the specification on
the W3C XML-SIG site (http://www.w3.org/TR/xmldsig-core).

Vendor Strategies

Vendors have great influence on the success and failure of technologies in our
industry. They have the research and development resources that can devise
tools and solutions, and they have the marketing engines that can make these
products successful. No standards body can compete with that.

But, with that in mind, vendors can also tend to get ahead of themselves.
Trying to run before you walk can be a dangerous thing when working with technology. In the ongoing battle to be first to market, companies sometimes jump
the gun on technology before it's truly tested and ready. This is as true with Web
services as it was with Web browsers.

Many tools and services are both available and in development for building
and supporting Web services. Some of these use current standards or standards
efforts, and some are standalone solutions. As Web services continue to reveal
themselves as solutions for an integration need, it is important to keep an eye on
the vendor strategies.

In the next sections, we'll take a look at where many of the leading vendors in
Web services are and which direction they are heading. We'll see what role Web
services actually play in their strategy and which ones seem to be more marketing
than substance. Equally important are which strategies seem to be in cooperation
with other efforts and which ones are taking on the area with their own approach.

Ariba

Ariba is an industry leader in developing business-to-business (B2B) commerce
marketplaces. Although it's not a direct player in the Web services market as of
right now, I mention the company because of its involvement in developing
some of the emerging standards related to Web services. In reality, its strategy is
more focused on data integration than application integration.

As we discussed in Chapter 1, there is a big difference in focus between integrating data and integrating processes, and Ariba is definitely focused on the former. Instead of assisting developers in building applications (like IBM or Microsoft), the company is focused on delivering a platform of applications that helps companies exchange data with their partners. Ariba's core offering is a Value Chain Management (VCM) platform called the Ariba Commerce Services Network.

Ariba is one of the three key founders of the UDDI standard. (The other two are IBM and Microsoft.) Its interest in the UDDI effort is much more in the area of e-commerce than Web services. If UDDI does succeed in becoming the *Yellow Pages* of the Internet, Ariba wants to make sure that it and its marketplaces are involved. The company certainly knows the value in such a concept, and it is clearly a big driver and supporter of the standard.

Ariba was also involved in the first announcement of the WSDL standard, although its involvement has been less than it has been with UDDI. In both cases, Ariba has not trumpeted its involvement in those standards to the extent that IBM and Microsoft have.

You can find out more about Ariba and the company's products at `http://www.ariba.com`.

BEA

Creator of the popular Java application server WebLogic, BEA has been involved in many of the emerging standards around Web services. That involvement, however, has not led to a strong presence among the active Web services players in the industry. In fact, BEA's 6.0 release of WebLogic in June 2001 did not have any Web services-specific features or functionality.

One of WebLogic's main competitors is IBM's WebSphere Application server, and IBM has done a much better job of both producing tools focused on Web services and in capturing the Web services buzz. And, even though BEA has been involved in some standards efforts, those efforts pale when compared with IBM's or Microsoft's.

That said, BEA has made great strides through the summer of 2001 to catch up with the competition. First, it released a series of white papers on Web services architecture and adopting Web services with the BEA WebLogic E-Business Platform (`http://www.bea.com/products/weblogic/server/paper_webservices.shtml`). It followed that up with the release of WebLogic 6.1 in July 2001, which was self-described as the Web services release of WebLogic. Then, later that month, BEA acquired Microsoft rival Crossgain, presumably for its Web services expertise.

Although it seemingly got off to a late start, it looks as if BEA will be a big player in the near future, and its platform deserves some consideration if you plan to build Web services on the Java platform.

You can get more information on BEA and its products at `http://www.bea.com`.

Bowstreet

Bowstreet can easily be considered the earliest corporate proponent of Web services, or at least the concept because the name *Web services* came after its entry in the market.

> *Bowstreet was founded in January 1998 on the idea that companies will compete on the services they provide, not on the products they sell.*
> —Bowstreet Web site (`http://www.bowstreet.com/aboutus/ corporatehistory.html`)

Bowstreet has focused on the integration of Web services into what the company literature calls *business webs* through tools that it provides. Although business webs are treated as a community of customers using Web services, it might be more appropriate, technically, to think of it as the integration of one or more Web services into an application.

Bowstreet's strategy has been fairly consistent since its inception: to minimize the bottlenecks that occur from the technical effort necessary to implement Web services. Their belief is that a company's IT department won't be able to keep up with the demands of business to utilize Web services. Although we certainly aren't there yet, once Web services do take off, we'll most likely see that Bowstreet has a valid point on where our limitations may lie in the adoption of Web services.

To address what Bowstreet believes is a fundamental limitation on the industry's ability to utilize Web services, it has developed a parametric approach to building applications utilizing Web services. This approach, brought to Bowstreet by Chief Technology Officer Andy Roberts, has been used in manufacturing for years to gain efficiencies by modeling products out of intersecting parts that allow designers to treat them as modular entities that are then interchangeable. Bowstreet has utilized this same approach in creating a software infrastructure, allowing companies and their partners to treat Web services as parts, plugging them into applications as needed.

To help customers build applications with Web services, Bowstreet offers three products, which consist of their overall solution: its Web services directory, the Business Web Factory, and the Business Web Portal.

Web Services Directory

Bowstreet's Web services directory was one of the first attempts at cataloging Web services that are available from companies and organizations. The directory can be accessed through its Web Factory and Web Portal product or through a browser at `http://www.bowstreet.com/webservicesdirectory/webservices`. Bowstreet's objective is to get providers to list its Web services on this directory so that Business Web Factory users can discover and implement them more easily. (See Figure 9-2.)

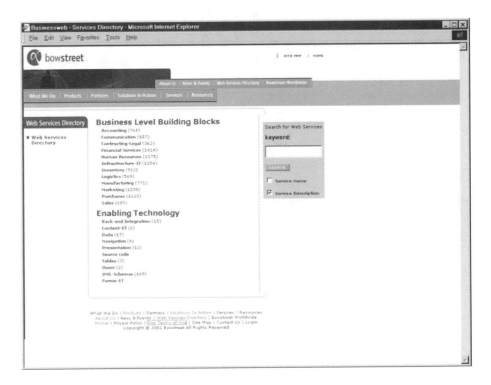

Figure 9-2. Bowstreet's Web services directory

Bowstreet developed an ontology that organizes the services across industries, companies, and functionality to help service seekers find the available services. The directory contains more than 10,000 services, and, even with the ontology, it can be time consuming to look through, especially if you are looking for something specific. It well illustrates the need for a good standard to organize and display available Web services.

The directory is split into two different categories at the highest level: Business Level Building Blocks and Enabling Technology. Unfortunately, the services referenced in the directory probably distort most people's definition of what Web services are. The Building Blocks category consists of several stand-alone applications, Web-based interfaces, and even document schemas for integration systems that could hardly be called Web services as we have come to understand them in this book. The Enabling Technology category consists of more presentation-centric services that are specific to Bowstreet's Business Web Factory. Looking through this portion of the directory might remind you of looking through online catalogs of VB controls or Enterprise Java Beans (EJBs).

Business Web Factory

The Business Web Factory is the core of Bowstreet's solution set for companies implementing Web services. It is an application server that is specifically catered to Web services-based applications and consists of two components: Designer and Customizer. Designer is the interface that allows the owner to add services to their collection of offerings available to their customers and partners. The Customizer then allows those customers and partners to generate a custom application catered to their needs.

To illustrate this relationship, think of AAA Conferences as the Business Web Factory owner. It would consume the hotel reservation system functionality through the factory, allowing users to check hotel availability, retrieve hotel content, and make a reservation. Through the software, AAA Conferences could customize the process for each event, if necessary. It could even provide different content for multiple devices, such as WAP, handhelds, and Web browsers. If these customizations were not necessary, it might be difficult to justify using the Business Web Factory. Because it is designed for "massively customized" service offerings, if your services are not either massive or customized, the value may not be realized from the infrastructure that Bowstreet provides.

The other caveat for benefiting from Bowstreet's Business Web Factory is that you are the owner of the application. If you are not the first link in the chain (as we discussed in Chapter 2) and do not host the user interface, you will not be able to take advantage of the benefits from using the factory. The Customizer does not allow partners "as is" to specify profiles for services that have no user interface. In fact, Bowstreet's current offerings do not provide a lot of assistance to pure Web services providers. If they were to take this same approach to provide a more back-end-centric solution, it would definitely be a product worth considering for managing the consumer profiles and dynamic interfaces that we first discussed in Chapter 5.

If you do plan on providing multiple services through your own interface to multiple customers or even multiple devices, the Business Web Factory is well worth considering. Between its process logic for capturing profiles for multiple partners and the easy user interface that those partners can use for creating a profile, the Business Web Factory will not only help relieve the burden on your IT department, but will also speed the adoption of your services.

Business Web Portal

The Business Web Portal is the latest offering from Bowstreet that capitalizes on the success of Business Web Factory by generating customized enterprise portals for an organization. Just as partners can take advantage of the Business Web Factory to build custom applications, internal staff can utilize the Business Web Portal to aggregate internal services (ranging from email to ERP systems to CRM solutions) into a single portal interface for business users.

For the same reasons you would consider the Business Web Factory, you would consider the Business Web Portal. If you want to deliver massively customized enterprise applications using Web services, there is currently no better solution that Bowstreet's offering.

You can get more information on Bowstreet, the Business Web Factory, and its other offerings at `http://www.bowstreet.com`.

Hewlett-Packard

Hewlett-Packard's offering in the Web services space is E-speak, an open services platform. As you might imagine from the name, E-speak has a broader scope than just Web services, including any method for collaborating over the Internet. This includes shared data as much as shared processes.

Although HP has been involved in some of the major standards initiatives for Web services, the company has remained fairly steadfast in its own platform since unveiling it in 1999. They even refer to Web services as e-services, seemingly rejecting the name that the rest of the industry has accepted.

Although most of their focus seems to be on competing with data-exchange platforms like RosettaNet and BizTalk, HP does provide a solution that supports Web services in concept, if not in name. In fact, HP's biggest contribution to Web services may have been its architecture, which was the first service-oriented architecture released by a major vendor.

> A *service-oriented architecture* (SRO) is a conceptual architecture that defines a loosely coupled system, allowing processes to interact without breaking when a change or error occurs.

Unfortunately, the proprietary underpinnings of E-speak likely kept it from taking off as hoped. E-speak itself actually consists of two components: E-speak Service Framework Specification and Netaction (formerly the E-speak Service Engine.)

E-speak Service Framework Specification

HP's Service Framework Specification (SFS) is a set of standards that will allow e-services to interact. SFS is touted as a complete end-to-end solution that incorporates the discovery and integration of e-services. Through an asynchronous messaging framework based on XML, it can even allow the negotiation and agreement of terms to aid in building the business relationship between partners.

Although it is a proprietary (but open source) specification, it does support many of the emerging standards for Web services such as SOAP and UDDI. The specification is also designed to be platform and language neutral. The only implementation available based on the E-speak specification is HP's own Netaction.

Netaction Software Suite

Netaction is the latest release of what was previously called the E-speak Service Engine. This incarnation utilizes the J2EE application server that HP acquired when it purchased Bluestone Software in January 2001. Netaction is intended to target enterprises that want to develop, integrate, and deploy e-services. Netaction also signaled a change in HP's strategy by utilizing some standards (like SOAP) within E-speak, but it still contains proprietary components.

The initial industry feedback after the first release of this suite has been mediocre. Most of the criticism has been related to a lack of integration and some of the deficiencies with the E-speak specification. But, although E-speak is standing in defiance of the current standards efforts, the neutral approach to platforms could make Netaction a powerful solution for bridging the gap between the Microsoft and Java platforms. With future releases, it will surely be looking to compete with the more seasoned IBM's WebSphere and Microsoft's .NET platform. Netaction is currently available on any platform supporting JDK 1.2.2 and higher.

You can get more information on E-speak from HP's Web site (http://www.hp.com/e-speak) and the E-speak community site (http://www.e-speak.net).

IBM

IBM is another company that is well positioned to be the bridge between the Microsoft and Java worlds with its aggressive work in deploying tools and solutions for Web services. IBM is the only vendor that can hope to compete with Microsoft's developer following, and the company has only increased that strength with its involvement in open source and Linux specifically.

IBM has worked side by side with Microsoft on several of the emerging standards for Web services including SOAP, WSDL, and UDDI. Web services truly caught the industry's attention when these two rivals started cooperating to define standards to support them.

WebSphere Application Server

IBM's core offering for exposing Web services is its popular WebSphere Application Server. With version 4.0, this server—which supports the latest versions of SOAP, WSDL, and UDDI—claims to be the most complete application server for Web services available on the market.

The engine itself is a Java 2 Enterprise Edition platform with full certification; it is available on more than 35 platforms. As we saw in Chapter 6, it is not an overly intuitive application server, so don't expect to pick it up overnight. If you go with a complete IBM development environment (IBM HTTP Server and Visual Age), you will maximize the benefits of WebSphere and its interaction with those products. Deviating from that combination will require even more time for setup and troubleshooting development issues.

Web Services Toolkit

For those who don't want to use IBM WebSphere for their application platform, there are also a host of other Java libraries and toolkits that are freely available for download from the alphaworks site (`http://alphaworks.ibm.com`). Chief among those offerings is the Web Services Toolkit (WST).

IBM's Java-based WST provides a runtime environment for developing Web services utilizing SOAP, WSDL, and UDDI. It also includes several samples for developers to work with and learn from for both the Windows and Linux platforms. This toolkit has also been regularly updated to incorporate the latest releases of standards.

For more information on the Web Services Toolkit, refer to the Alphaworks WST download page at `http://alphaworks.ibm.com/tech/webservicestoolkit`.

Web Services Test Area

The Web Services Test Area is actually IBM's UDDI browser, giving users visibility into some of the Web services hosted in the test area (`http://demo.alphaworks.ibm.com/browser`). With it, you can browse Web services that are listed, finding information on any one of them. (See Figure 9-3.)

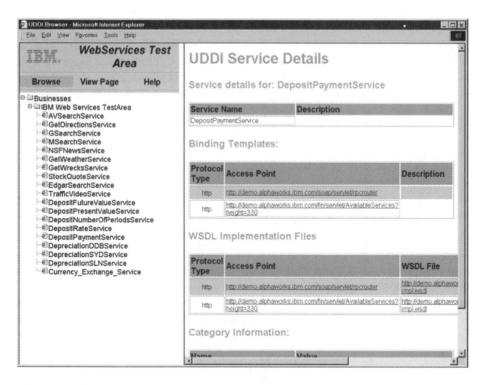

Figure 9-3. IBM UDDI browser

For more information on IBM and its products, visit their corporate site (`http://www.ibm.com`).

Microsoft

Microsoft has been very involved in helping to develop the emerging standards for Web services. However, Microsoft has also been very deliberate in demonstrating a lack of support for standards—such as ebXML and XAML—with which it does not agree either politically or technically. In the standards that Microsoft does intend to support, the company almost always takes a leadership role in helping to drive its direction.

Regardless of your feelings about Microsoft's products or approach to business, you have to recognize it has learned its lesson from getting a late jump on the Internet in 1995. In fact, Microsoft CEO Steve Ballmer was one of the first to publicly use the phrase *Web services* in September 1999. Ever since, the company has been very aggressive in trying to capitalize on the potential of Web services, which led to a fundamental shift in corporate strategy in June 2000.

.NET

Microsoft's corporate-wide focus is the .NET platform. Although it has at times been somewhat of a confusing marketing message, fundamentally, the idea behind .NET is "software as a service" (in other words, Web services). Microsoft has long focused on software, and particularly the operating system as the core of its strategy. This shift from software to services is a significant undertaking that will ultimately change Microsoft's business model.

Although the .NET platform includes a host of products (which are categorized as tools, servers, XML Web services, clients, and .NET experiences), at the core is the .NET framework. With a Common-Language Runtime (CLR), this framework allows all of Microsoft's languages (Visual C++, Visual Basic, JScript, and the new C#) to take advantage of a common set of functionality. In fact, Microsoft has exposed .NET to allow other vendors or organizations to enable other languages through this CLR. Fujitsu took advantage of this opportunity to provide COBOL. NET, enabling COBOL developers to build applications on the .NET platform.

Another potential advantage facilitated by this CLR is inherent interoperability among the supported languages. Previously, the Microsoft platform facilitated interaction among different languages through the COM/DCOM layer. Whereas applications had to enable this layer to take advantage of this interoperability, .NET makes it more seamless. This means that VB developers will be able to take advantage of the functionality in C# as easily as functionality in VB code.

Similar to the approach that Java takes by having a portable virtual machine, the CLR also gives the potential for Microsoft or others to create a portable runtime environment. Efforts are already underway by Corel to provide a CLR implementation on the freeBSD platform, and other vendors have announced similar plans for other platforms. The first operating system that will come with the .NET framework built-in will be the upcoming "Whistler" release from Microsoft currently scheduled for 2002.

The .NET platform consists of the following five areas:

Tools—IDE for developers to design, build, and deploy Web services

Servers—The enterprise servers that will support .NET Web services and applications (such as SQL and BizTalk)

Services—Building block services that will serve as the core to many other services and applications

Clients—Devices and systems that will consume .NET processes and applications

Experiences—Access to information in an integrated fashion

Visual Studio .NET

Visual Studio .NET is the tool that Microsoft has created for helping developers to build the next generation of applications for the .NET platform. With Visual Studio .NET, building both thick- and thin-client applications will be made much easier by the tighter integration possible through the CLR.

Building a Web interface is now as simple as building form interfaces with Web Forms. This drag-and-drop interface will allow developers to treat Web elements as controls to create their Web applications. Form interfaces are also getting revamped with the Windows Forms package. With this new package, interface designers can utilize visual inheritance for control reusability, greater precision in element sizing and placement, and more-powerful graphics that will allow designers to break out of the typical gray boxes.

Another version of Visual Studio, called Visual Studio .NET Enterprise Architect, also provides more functionality in the areas of software modeling, database modeling, and development frameworks and templates. This release will work with VS .NET to provide architecture guidance to developers as they work.

For more information on the .NET platform and Visual Studio .NET, check out the book *C# and the .Net Platform* by Andrew Troelsen (Apress). You can also get more information at Microsoft's .NET site (`http://www.microsoft.com/net`).

Hailstorm

The single biggest challenge for .NET adoption is the pricing model. However, this same challenge applies to all Web services. Web services could be priced by use, subscription, or through indirect pricing like advertising and value-added services. To test the waters in this area, Microsoft has created Hailstorm.

Hailstorm is a suite of Web services provided by Microsoft on a subscription basis. With beta releases due towards the end of 2001 and a full release in 2002, Hailstorm will be based on Microsoft's Passport service. This will be an avenue for users to store and access personal information such as calendars, address books, and payment preferences through a variety of devices. Hailstorm will utilize the SOAP standard, making it available to any development platform, but it will no doubt integrate best through the Visual Studio .NET IDE.

Although the final implementation of Hailstorm is not known at this time, the services that Microsoft is promising will actually be a blending of Web services and Peer2Peer services as we discussed in Chapter 5. Through this service, users will be able to connect directly with Hailstorm to enter information, authorize access, and set preferences. Applications will then be able to request that information to provide users with a more streamlined and personalized service.

The biggest obstacle to Hailstorm will likely not be technical, but political. This service will require users to place a great deal of trust in Microsoft and its service, and some privacy advocacy groups are likely to get involved in this area. Although Microsoft may take some abuse by being the first one to take this step, the company will clearly have the advantage in consumer Web services if it can clear this privacy hurdle.

MSXML Parser

Prior to the .NET platform and tools shipping, Microsoft has led the way in providing XML parsers. First previewed in March 2000 and currently on version 4.0, the parser has been updated constantly to keep up with the revised specifications of XML Schema, SAX, and DOM. As we saw in Chapters 6 through 8, Microsoft has added some great features to allow developers to utilize the MSXML parser as their one-stop shop for building and consuming Web services.

SOAP Toolkit

For those who don't make the immediate jump to Visual Studio .NET, Microsoft has a SOAP toolkit that helps developers expose their COM objects as Web services through Visual Studio 6. Similar to IBM's Web Services Toolkit, this kit comes with plenty of samples and utilities that allow developers to build and deploy Web services fairly quickly utilizing SOAP, WSDL, and UDDI. It is available for free on Microsoft's Web services site (http://msdn.microsoft.com/webservices).

Sun

Sun's party line is that, while other vendors are jumping on the Web services bandwagon, Sun was doing it all along; they just called it something different. Because Sun has been involved in XML since its inception and has been developing remote processes through RMI and CORBA, the company believes that experience is on its side. If you believe that solutions are defined entirely by their underlining technology, you might buy into this reasoning.

Because Web services are old news to them, Sun has taken the concept one step further by promoting "smart services." These are services that would dynamically connect based on a scenario, negotiating the connection and communication in real time, and consuming each other. Sun refers to this as *spontaneous federation*, and it takes the concept of Web services and merges it with smart devices or agents. As I have said before, although the vision is feasible, we need to make sure that we learn to build and deploy these simple "static" Web services before we get too far ahead of ourselves.

Although Sun has eventually supported the major Web services standards being developed, it is clearly more interested in the potential of ebXML. In fact, Sun is the biggest company to fully embrace ebXML. Of course, this means that, even though Sun supports the non-ebXML flavor of Web services standards (SOAP, WSDL, UDDI), it has plenty of opinions on its shortcomings. Most of them revolve around its eagerness to push Web services into real-time connectivity, which those standards have some support for, but have not been targeted for.

Sun ONE

Sun announced its Web services strategy in February 2001 and unveiled Sun ONE (Open Net Environment). ONE is a solution consisting of Sun's Java 2 enterprise platform, Forte development tools, and iPlanet software.

Philosophically, Sun is using ONE to promote its belief in using open standards to develop applications that are interoperable. If thinking of the Internet as a series of interconnected nodes, the company believes that the adoption of Web services will be hindered if every node on the Internet does not look very similar. It proposes that Java be the language that runs on every node because Java is so portable. Of course, this theory makes more sense if you believe that every node will be using services in the same way for the same purposes. Whenever customization is introduced into these nodes, the argument for deploying duplicate logic throughout tends to provide far less benefit. Unfortunately, very few organizations have similar back end systems, which means that they all need different middleware to either expose them as Web services or incorporate Web services into their processes.

Logically, ONE is defined by Sun as consisting of seven components:

Platform—Operating system, virtual machine, and device

Service Creation and Assembly—Development environments

Identity and Policy—Security and profile management

Service Container—Technologies for deploying Web services to end users

Service Delivery—Technologies for delivering content and information

Service Integration—Technologies that can bridge systems or platforms

Applications and Web Services—Technologies that can deliver services components and applications

Technically, ONE consists of an architecture based on Java and XML. More specifically, a series of Java APIs are available that will provide all the necessary functionality for building and consuming Web services within a Java application:

Java API for XML Processing (JAXP)—Provides support for the DOM, SAX, and XSLT standards

Java API for XML Data Binding (JAXB)—Allows developers to bind XML Schemas to Java objects

Java API for XML Messaging (JAXM)—Provides support for asynchronous XML messaging systems

Java APIs for XML-based RPC (JAX/RPC)—Allows remote procedure calls via SOAP

Java API for WSDL (JWSDL)—Provides support for WSDL

Java API for XML Registries (JAXR)—An interface into Web services directories and repositories like the UDDI Business Registry and the ebXML registry

These six APIs were established by the Java Community Process (JCP). You can find more information on JCP at its Web site (`http://jcp.org`). Aside from these APIs, the value proposition of Sun ONE is the J2EE platform itself with its iPlanet server product. Developers who are familiar with it will no doubt feel comfortable building Web services using this platform, but IBM and BEA both offer viable alternatives to Java developers building and deploying Web services.

WebTop

The first initiative specific to the Sun ONE platform is WebTop. This is described as "a development tool for providers to deliver productivity tools in a hosted environment." The goal is for WebTop to provide consistent access to applications across a variety of devices, allowing users to distance themselves from their desktop and yet remain productive. This "true smart Web service" was in beta testing as of July 2001.

You can get more information on Sun ONE and WebTop at Sun's site (`http://www.sun.com/software/sunone`).

Summary

The success of Web services is a story that has yet to be written. I personally believe that Web services have the potential to be the solution to long-standing issues in supporting partnerships and cooperation between organizations. Potential does not always manifest itself in reality, though, and we will have to see where we end up. At one point, "push technology" was going to be the next big thing, so just calling something a great solution and making it so are two different things.

What I have done in this chapter is identified the areas and activities that we need to keep an eye on if we want to find out where the industry will try to take Web services. There are gaps in our current capabilities, and there are potential solutions being discussed and developed. Standards need to be watched for and tools anticipated. Vendors are trying to contribute to the ideals of Web services, and some haven't yet communicated what their objectives are.

No matter which standards are adopted, no matter which vendors lead the market, and no matter which technology your company adopts, meaningful Web services can be developed only with careful thought and planning put into their architecture and model. This book emphasized that thought and provided you with some real-life solutions with which to model, design, and build your Web services.

Index

Apress Titles

ISBN	LIST PRICE	AUTHOR	TITLE
1-893115-01-1	$39.95	Appleman	Appleman's Win32 API Puzzle Book and Tutorial for Visual Basic Programmers
1-893115-23-2	$29.95	Appleman	How Computer Programming Works
1-893115-97-6	$39.95	Appleman	Moving to VB.NET: Strategies, Concepts, and Code
1-893115-09-7	$29.95	Baum	Dave Baum's Definitive Guide to LEGO MINDSTORMS
1-893115-84-4	$29.95	Baum, Gasperi, Hempel, and Villa	Extreme MINDSTORMS
1-893115-82-8	$59.95	Ben-Gan/Moreau	Advanced Transact-SQL for SQL Server 2000
1-893115-90-9	$44.95	Finsel	The Handbook for Reluctant Database Administrators
1-893115-85-2	$34.95	Gilmore	A Programmer's Introduction to PHP 4.0
1-893115-17-8	$59.95	Gross	A Programmer's Introduction to Windows DNA
1-893115-62-3	$39.95	Gunnerson	A Programmer's Introduction to C#, Second Edition
1-893115-10-0	$34.95	Holub	Taming Java Threads
1-893115-04-6	$34.95	Hyman/Vaddadi	Mike and Phani's Essential C++ Techniques
1-893115-50-X	$34.95	Knudsen	Wireless Java: Developing with Java 2, Micro Edition
1-893115-79-8	$49.95	Kofler	Definitive Guide to Excel VBA
1-893115-56-9	$39.95	Kofler	MySQL
1-893115-87-9	$39.95	Kurata	Doing Web Development: Client-Side Techniques
1-893115-75-5	$44.95	Kurniawan	Internet Programming with VB
1-893115-19-4	$49.95	Macdonald	Serious ADO: Universal Data Access with Visual Basic
1-893115-06-2	$39.95	Marquis/Smith	A Visual Basic 6.0 Programmer's Toolkit

ISBN	LIST PRICE	AUTHOR	TITLE
1-893115-22-4	$27.95	McCarter	David McCarter's VB Tips and Techniques
1-893115-76-3	$49.95	Morrison	C++ For VB Programmers
1-893115-80-1	$39.95	Newmarch	A Programmer's Guide to Jini Technology
1-893115-81-X	$39.95	Pike	SQL Server: Common Problems, Tested Solutions
1-893115-20-8	$34.95	Rischpater	Wireless Web Development
1-893115-93-3	$34.95	Rischpater	Wireless Web Development with PHP and WAP
1-893115-24-0	$49.95	Sinclair	From Access to SQL Server
1-893115-94-1	$29.95	Spolsky	User Interface Design for Programmers
1-893115-53-4	$39.95	Sweeney	Visual Basic for Testers
1-893115-29-1	$44.95	Thomsen	Database Programming with Visual Basic .NET
1-893115-65-8	$39.95	Tiffany	Pocket PC Database Development with eMbedded Visual Basic
1-893115-59-3	$59.95	Troelsen	C# and the .NET Platform
1-893115-54-2	$49.95	Trueblood/Lovett	Data Mining and Statistical Analysis Using SQL
1-893115-16-X	$49.95	Vaughn	ADO Examples and Best Practices
1-893115-83-6	$44.95	Wells	Code Centric: T-SQL Programming with Stored Procedures and Triggers
1-893115-95-X	$49.95	Welschenbach	Cryptography in C and C++
1-893115-05-4	$39.95	Williamson	Writing Cross-Browser Dynamic HTML
1-893115-78-X	$49.95	Zukowski	Definitive Guide to Swing for Java 2, Second Edition
1-893115-92-5	$49.95	Zukowski	Java Collections

Available at bookstores nationwide or from Springer Verlag New York, Inc. at 1-800-777-4643; fax 1-212-533-3503. Contact us for more information at sales@apress.com.

Apress Titles Publishing SOON!

ISBN	AUTHOR	TITLE
1-893115-73-9	Abbott	Voice Enabling Web Applications: VoiceXML and Beyond
1-893115-45-3	Anderson	Beginning Web Services for .NET
1-893115-37-2	Bock/Singer	.NET Security
1-893115-39-9	Chand/Gold	A Programmer's Guide to ADO .NET in C#
1-893115-99-2	Cornell/Morrison	Programming VB .NET: A Guide for Experienced Programmers
1-893115-72-0	Curtin	Building Trust: Online Security for Developers
1-893115-71-2	Ferguson	Mobile .NET
1-893115-42-9	Foo/Lee	XML Programming Using the Microsoft XML Parser
1-893115-55-0	Frenz	Visual Basic for Scientists
1-893115-36-4	Goodwill	Apache Jakarta-Tomcat
1-893115-96-8	Jorelid	J2EE FrontEnd Technologies: A Programmer's Guide to Servlets, JavaServer Pages, and Enterprise JavaBeans
1-893115-49-6	Kilburn	Palm Programming in Basic
1-893115-38-0	Lafler	Power AOL: A Survival Guide
1-893115-58-5	Oellermann	Architecting Web Services
1-893115-89-5	Shemitz	Kylix: The Professional Developer's Guide and Reference
1-893115-40-2	Sill	An Introduction to qmail
1-893115-26-7	Troelsen	Visual Basic .NET and the .NET Platform
1-893115-68-2	Vaughn	ADO Examples and Best Practices, Second Edition

Available at bookstores nationwide or from Springer Verlag New York, Inc. at 1-800-777-4643; fax 1-212-533-3503. Contact us for more information at sales@apress.com.

apress™

books for profess·

DATE DUE

DEMCO, INC. 38-2931

About .

Apress, located in Berkeley, CA, is an innovative pu.
needs of existing and potential programming profes:
stands for the "Author's Press™." Apress' unique autho.
from conversations between Dan Appleman and Gary C
regarded computer books. In 1998, they set out to create a
emphasized quality above all else, a company with books th
in their market. Dan and Gary's vision has resulted in over 30
of the industry's leading software professionals.

Do You Have What It Take
to Write for Apress?

Apress is rapidly expanding its publishing program. If you can write and re
compromise on the quality of your work, if you believe in doing more then 1
documentation, and if you're looking for opportunities and rewards that go fa.
offered by traditional publishing houses, we want to hear from you!

Consider these innovations that we offer all of our authors:

Top royalties with *no* hidden switch statements
Authors typically only receive half of their normal royalty rate on foreign sales. In contrast,
Apress' royalty rate remains the same for both foreign and domestic sales.

- **A mechanism for authors to obtain equity in Apress**
Unlike the software industry, where stock options are essential to motivate and retain
software professionals, the publishing industry has adhered to an outdated compensation
model based on royalties alone. In the spirit of most software companies, Apress reserves a
significant portion of its equity for authors.

- **Serious treatment of the technical review process**
Each Apress book has a technical reviewing team whose remuneration depends in part on
the success of the book since they too receive royalties.

Moreover, through a partnership with Springer-Verlag, one of the world's major publishing
houses, Apress has significant venture capital behind it. Thus, we have the resources to
produce the highest quality books *and* market them aggressively.

If you fit the model of the Apress author who can write a book that gives the "professional
what he or she needs to know™," then please contact one of our Editorial Directors, Gary
Cornell (gary_cornell@apress.com), Dan Appleman (dan_appleman@apress.com), Karen
Watterson (karen_watterson@apress.com) or Jason Gilmore (jason_gilmore@apress.com) for
more information.